POWER, PRIVILEGE, AND THE *POST*

POWER
Privilege
AND
THE *POST*

The Katharine Graham Story

CAROL FELSENTHAL

G. P. PUTNAM'S SONS   NEW YORK

Published by G. P. Putnam's Sons,
200 Madison Avenue, New York, NY 10016.
Published simultaneously in Canada

The author gratefully acknowledges permission to reprint material from the
following:
Howard Bray, *The Pillars of the Post: The Making of a News Empire in
Washington* (New York: Norton, 1980).
Felix Frankfurter Papers, Harvard Law School Library, Cambridge, MA.
Katharine Graham, "Learning by Doing," *Bulletin,* American Academy of
Arts and Sciences, vol. 42, no. 8 (May 1989).
David Halberstam, *The Powers That Be* (New York: Knopf, 1979).
Merlo J. Pusey, *Eugene Meyer* (New York: Knopf, 1974).
Chalmers M. Roberts, *In the Shadow of Power: The Story of The Washing-
ton Post* (Cabin John, MD: Seven Locks, 1989).
Lynn Rosellini, "The Katharine Graham Story," *Washington Star,* Novem-
ber 13–17, 1978 (five-part series).
Larry van Dyne, "The Bottom Line on Katharine Graham: The Woman,
the Newspaper, the Empire," *Washingtonian,* December 1985.

Library of Congress Cataloging-in-Publication Data

Felsenthal, Carol.
Power, privilege, and the Post : the Katharine Graham story /
Carol Felsenthal.
p.   cm.
Includes bibliographical references and index.
ISBN 0-399-13732-7
1. Graham, Katharine, 1917– .   2. Newspaper publishing—
Washington (D.C.)—History—20th century.   3. Newspaper publishing—
Political aspects—United States.   4. Publishers and publishing—
United States—Biography.   5. Washington Post.   I. Title.
Z473.G7F45   1992   92-31600 CIP
070.5′092—dc20
[B]

Designed by MaryJane DiMassi
The text of this book is set in Times Roman.

Printed in the United States of America
1   2   3   4   5   6   7   8   9   10

This book is printed on acid-free paper.
∞

ACKNOWLEDGMENTS

Writing a book about a Washingtonian while living in Chicago is not easy. A good husband helps a lot, and I thank Steve for keeping this book on top of our family's agenda, and for his unfailingly sound judgment. I also thank our children for, among many things, helping me put work in perspective—our daughters, Rebecca and Julia, for their independence, humor, and generosity; our new son, Daniel, for his boundless curiosity and sweetness. My mother, Ruth, was there when I needed her, as was often the case; in-laws Eve and Jerry did everything from testing the children on their spelling words to driving them to lessons; Aunts Jean, Esther, and Bette gave unstintingly of their time and love. I thank also my friends Harriet and Rick Meyer, who greeted each of my accomplishments and failures as if they were their own.

My agent, Philippa "Flip" Brophy, of Sterling Lord Literistic, is not only smart, persistent, straightforward, and unflappable; she is also a friend. I have, for this and my previous book, benefited immeasurably from the wisdom of my editor, Faith Sale, who has the deserved reputation of being one of the best in the business. She is wonderfully assisted by Sara Brock, a model of organization and helpfulness. When my manuscript arrived on Faith's desk it was longer by a third than expected. She and the talented editor Laura Yorke worked long and hard, and displayed a sense of how this book should flow that sometimes eluded me. It is often said that line editing has gone the way of the manual typewriter. Not at Putnam, where, after Faith and Laura had their go, copy editor Anna Jardine—meticulous and intelligent—had hers. She didn't miss a thing, so whatever inconsistencies, irrelevancies, irrationalities remain are mine.

I thank also Roxanna Deane, chief of the Washingtoniana division at the D.C. Public Library. I first came to rely on her when I was writing about Alice Roosevelt Longworth, and she was equally helpful this time around.

A biography of a contemporary figure depends on interviews. Without the scores of people who opened their homes and memories to me, I could not have written this book. Having been warned by many that persuading people to talk about a woman as prominent and powerful as Katharine Graham would be next to impossible—especially for a midwesterner who is decidedly not a part of her world—I am here to report that they were wrong.

For my mother, Ruth Greenberg,
and in memory of my father, Louis H. Greenberg

CONTENTS

CONTENTS

POWER, PRIVILEGE,
AND THE *POST*

Chapter 1

FROM A LONG LINE OF RABBIS AND MINISTERS

Some children are born to parents who struggle so that their sons and daughters may do better in life than they did. Other children are born to parents who are themselves so brilliant, so extraordinarily talented, that no matter how good the parents' intentions, the children are doomed to come in second.

Katharine Meyer, now known to the world as Katharine Graham, was born into the latter sort of family. Her mother, Agnes Ernst Meyer, was a woman of stupendous drive, competence, creativity, guts, and soaring self-confidence. Many found her insufferable and even ridiculous, while others looked beyond the bombast to recognize her genuine gifts; her friend Thomas Mann wrote in 1943 to thank her for extricating him from a passport snafu: "The impression grows *that you are running the country.*"[1]

Katharine's father, Eugene Meyer, was a man whose long life encompassed several distinguished careers, any one of which—even part of one—would have satisfied the most ambitious of men. Had Eugene not been born a Jew in an age when Jews who were too powerful were suspect, his name would be known today to every schoolchild. As it was, he made millions on Wall Street before he turned forty, and served seven presidents, in positions that he sometimes invented but that he nearly always carried out with intelligence so stunning as to render himself irreplaceable. In 1933, fifty-seven years old and exhausted, Eugene planned to retire. Instead, he bought at a bankruptcy sale *The Washington Post*—a newspaper that had sunk to the level of joke. He then laid the foundations from which grew the paper that today is one of the world's most respected, influential, and profitable.

In 1859, Eugene's father, Marc Eugene Meyer, left his home in Strasbourg, the capital of Alsace, France, in search of a better life in California. It has been said that he was fleeing anti-Semitism,[2] but probably more pressing were the greatly reduced prospects for making his fortune in France after the death of his father. He was seventeen when he reached San Francisco.

He has been described as a "penniless orphan,"[3] and while it is true that Eugene, as he was called, had no money and no father, he did have a mother, Sephora Loeb Meyer, who let him go to California despite fears that he would contract yellow fever, gold fever, and bad habits. And he had something more valuable: illustrious forebears who had lived in Alsace for generations. His father had been a rabbi and a member of Strasbourg's civil governing body; his grandfather, also a rabbi, had been appointed by Napoleon Bonaparte to the Congress of Jewish Notables charged with determining the legal status of French Jews.[4]

Eugene carried a letter of introduction from Alexandre Lazard in Paris to a Meyer cousin in San Francisco, Alexandre Weill, a representative for Lazard Frères, the investment banking firm that had helped finance the Revolutionary War and the French and Indian War and that would do likewise in the Civil War.[5] Simon Lazard, a businessman from the banking family, put the young man to work as a stockboy in a dry goods store, and Eugene soon acquired a safe and the trust of miners who deposited their gold; the store became a sort of frontier bank, and its clerk a rudimentary banker.[6]

A year later, in 1860, Eugene left for Los Angeles, this time carrying a letter of introduction to Simon Lazard's cousin Solomon Lazard, who gave Eugene a job as a clerk/bookkeeper in the S. & A. Lazard general store on Alameda Street. Eugene lived in the back room, although he often slept on the counter, gun in hand, ready to protect the merchandise. He learned Spanish so that he could talk to the Basque sheepmen who left their money with him, secure in the knowledge that it was stashed in a safe in his room and would be protected by the double-barreled shotgun that hung on his wall.[7]

Eugene and Solomon Lazard soon formed a partnership—Lazard providing most of the money, and Eugene the sweat and savvy—to operate a department store, which they called The City of Paris.[8]

In 1864, at twenty-two, Eugene Meyer joined Lazard Frères; in 1867 he married Solomon Lazard's sixteen-year-old sister-in-law, Harriet Newmark,[9] who came from a pioneering clan of great vigor and enterprise.

Since leaving Germany in 1824, Harriet's father, Rabbi Joseph Newmark, had stopped in several American cities, founding synagogues as he went, including the Elm Street Synagogue in New York,[10] and eventually settled in Los Angeles. "Wherever you went in California during the gold rush days," says one writer who has studied Joseph Newmark's family, "anyplace you found ten Jews, he had a burial society, some sort of charitable society."[11] Rabbi Newmark became a pillar of southern California Jewry, establishing, among other institutions, the synagogue that exists today as the Wilshire Boulevard Temple.[12]

When his youngest daughter married Eugene, Rabbi Newmark and his wife were delighted with the match: here was a young man obviously on his way up.[13] (A year later, Eugene became a partner in Lazard.)

By the mid-1870s, Eugene bought out Solomon Lazard to take control of The City of Paris, which would grow to be the largest and most elaborate department store in the Southwest. Eugene had a large home, commensurate with his status in the Jewish community, and three daughters, and wanted for only one thing more—a son, an heir to his accomplishments and dreams. On October 31, 1875, to the joy and relief of his parents, Eugene Isaac Meyer was born. Although two more sons and two more daughters followed, Eugene remained his father's most honored and favored child.

When Alexandre Weill decided to return to Paris in 1884, Eugene sold the department store and moved back to San Francisco, which he much preferred to the "one-mule town" of Los Angeles,[14] to take Weill's place at Lazard Frères. Eugene became president of a local bank,[15] and began grooming nine-year-old Eugene Jr. to inherit his station. He hired a German drillmaster to tutor the boy in the classics and in foreign languages.[16] When classmates called him "sheeny" and followed with their fists, Eugene Sr. hired James J. ("Gentleman Jim") Corbett, later heavyweight champion of the world, to teach Eugene Jr. how to box. After a couple of lessons he "kicked the hell out of the kids" who had insulted him.[17]

For the Meyers, who were Reform Jews, life was comfortable and quite secular. In the style of German Jews, Eugene studied for confirmation rather than for bar mitzvah. On confirmation day he played hookey because—as he explained to his father, who respected the boy for his decision—he was unwilling to go to the altar and lie that he had "perfect faith" in each tenet.[18]

For the academic year 1892–1893, Eugene Jr. enrolled at the University of California at Berkeley, where he was unchallenged but happy. He became, to his father's dismay, a crack poker player. Although distressed that he could not join a fraternity—they did not admit Jews—Eugene Jr. would gladly have whiled away his undergraduate years there,[19] but the idyll ended with his father's announcement that the family was moving to New York. The news provided Eugene Jr. with that year's most valuable lesson: his father, for all his success, was still beholden for his job to the Lazard brothers in Paris, who had "asked" him to take over the New York operation; he was, the son recognized, a self-made man but not his own man.

Eugene Sr. seriously considered refusing the move because the uprooting would be painful to Harriet, whose health suffered from her having given birth to eight children without medical care.[20] She developed diabetes and for years had not played an active role in family life. The maternal role had fallen to the Meyers' oldest child, Rosalie, who had married Sigmund Stern, heir to the Levi Strauss fortune, and who would remain in San Francisco. (The Meyers' second-born, Elise, married Sigmund's brother Abraham Stern.) In the end, Eugene Sr. took the Lazards' offer; he saw that it would translate into a more lucrative position to hand over to his first son.

On arriving in New York, Eugene Jr. was put to work in the Lazard office as a $12-a-week messenger. In the fall of 1893, he enrolled at Yale, where the anti-Semitism was deeper and more inconvenient than at Berkeley. Jews were not welcome, even in the official university residences, so Eugene Jr. shared a room in a rooming house with another Lazard Frères employee's son.[21]

In the spring of 1895, Eugene graduated with a Phi Beta Kappa key and an interest in psychology, which he would have made his profession; but his father chose for him to work in Lazard's New York offices. He was granted two years in Europe, officially to study languages and foreign banking.[22] He was drawn frequently to Paris and to an uncle, Zadoc Kahn, grand rabbi of France, who was then working with Émile Zola in a passionate defense of Alfred Dreyfus. Eugene would never forget sitting in Kahn's apartment and listening to the mob on the street below scream: *"À mort les Juifs!"* (Kill the

Jews!)[23] But he was more impressed by his uncle's connections—to the Rothschilds, especially, whose box at the opera Kahn always shared.[24]

Alexandre Weill, then manager of Lazard in Paris, promised Eugene that if he went to the firm's London office he would eventually become its head—if, it was understood, he married a Lazard,[25] as his own father had done. Eugene would have refused the offer anyway, but that stipulation made it impossible even to consider. In addition to resenting the French Lazards' high-handed treatment of his father, he considered them not very smart or forward-looking.[26]

Eugene came home to his apprenticeship at Lazard's New York office, but he did not stay long. Restless, and frustrated that his suggestions for new lines of financial services went unheeded by the firm's management, he resigned; the decision profoundly hurt his father.[27] In 1901, at age twenty-five, he took his $50,000 savings (accumulated by investing the $600 his father had given him for not smoking before his twenty-first birthday) and a $200 Lazard Christmas bonus, bought a seat on the New York Stock Exchange, and opened his own investment house, Eugene Meyer, Jr.,[28] and Company. "I worked all my life to make you a place in the company," was his father's shocked rebuke.

The son's mind could not be changed, and the power in the relationship shifted to the younger man. Eugene Sr. left Lazard soon thereafter, and his son then managed his affairs.[29] The poker-playing Berkeley freshman seemed gone forever. Eugene appeared older, more sagacious and reliable than his years. That, combined with his confidence, boldness, and combativeness, served him well in the unregulated financial markets.

As head of a radically different kind of investment company, he was able to give free rein to the ideas that Lazard had stifled. He created the first statistical office of any New York investment house. He put engineers and scientists on staff to allow him to make decisions based on knowledge of economic conditions and demographics.[30] He employed fact-finding techniques that spawned a "clinical analysis" of U.S. Steel; this set a precedent in the industry, and led him to become one of the company's bigger stockholders. He hired analysts whose detailed reports invariably made him better briefed than competitors, better able to predict crises and plot risks.[31]

Eugene invested with great profit in copper, steel, motorcars, and chemicals. His first year out, it was said, he made half a million dollars.[32] J. P. Morgan would later warn an associate, "Watch out for that fellow Meyer, because if you don't, he'll end up having all the money on Wall Street."[33]

By 1904, Eugene Meyer could begin to indulge his inclination for philanthropy and public affairs. He gave regular gifts to Yale, specifying that the money be used to train young men for public service careers.[34] He also began to consider his personal life.

When he wasn't multiplying his fortune, he liked to spend time with Irene Untermeyer, the daughter of an attorney who was battling for government control of the stock market and who charged the banking industry with profiting from slum housing built for Jewish immigrants. The Untermeyers introduced Eugene to the Henry Street Settlement, where he spent many evenings mixing with left-wing activists.[35]

Eugene resisted allowing his relationship with Irene to turn serious. His early bouts with anti-Semitism had left him determined to avoid that scourge rather than fight it, and marrying a Jewish woman would not advance that goal. Had he married a Jew, says Sidney Hyman, a writer who interviewed Eugene extensively, she would have to have been one of the *"Our Crowd* types" (i.e., of pure German Jewish stock—a Straus, a Schiff, a Morgenthau); at one point, indeed, it looked as if Eugene might marry a Morgenthau. Another member of the Meyer family was interested in a man of Polish Jewish extraction, and according to Hyman, "that would have been worse than miscegenation."[36] Writer June Rossbach Bingham came from that stratum of Jewry: *"Our Crowd* starts with my great-aunt Hattie Lehman Goodhart saying, 'There are people we visit and people we wouldn't visit.' "[37]

Although Eugene had been appalled by the stipulation that he marry a Lazard to advance his prospects in the firm, he was searching for a beautiful Wasp who could move confidently in the intellectual and social circles that he intended to make his own. And he found her on Lincoln's Birthday, 1908, as he and a friend browsed in a Manhattan art gallery. Studying the Japanese prints was a slender, golden-haired, blue-eyed beauty, almost twelve years younger than he and several inches taller, wearing a gray tweed suit and a gray squirrel hat topped by an eagle feather. "That's the girl I'm going to marry," Eugene vowed.

*

Agnes Elizabeth Ernst was born in New York City on January 2, 1887, and grew up in then rural Pelham Heights and later in the Bronx. Her parents were both immigrants from northern Germany: her father, Frederick Ernst, came from Hannover and a line of Lutheran clergymen that stretched back to the Reformation; her mother, Lucy Schmidt Ernst, was from a family that had lived for more than three hundred years in the same village near Bremen.[38]

Frederick Ernst, a lawyer, worshipped Luther, Wagner, and harsh discipline—which included subjecting his children to cold baths every morning, whatever the season. Agnes's oldest brother, Carl, disappeared during adolescence to escape the family's rigid piety.[39]

But Agnes adored her father, who would awaken her to watch the sunrise. She admitted to having developed a "father fixation,"[40] which would soon turn to what she described as "hate" and "exaggerated burning shame,"[41] as her father had an affair with a client, neglected his law practice in favor of writing embarrassingly amateurish books and plays, and informed his daughter that, instead of going to Barnard College, which had admitted her on scholarship, she would go to secretarial school and help support the family. After his irresponsibility had left the family in such terrible debt and humiliation, that seemed to Agnes a terrible injustice and she simply refused. She would have been considered a strikingly strong-willed young woman in any era, but in that one, she was extraordinary.

She entered Barnard in the fall of 1903, when she was just sixteen, studying mathematics, philosophy, and literature, and feeling, she said, "as if I were going to heaven." After her freshman year she lost her scholarship because of a "poor attitude toward the professors" and "insolence," as one professor complained; she supported herself by tutoring, working other part-time jobs, and one year, serving as the principal of a Baptist summer school in a Hell's Kitchen settlement house, where she was reputed to have made peace between rival gangs. (One Barnard professor, John Dewey, appreciated and encouraged her self-assertiveness, and a friendship between the two lasted until the end of his life.)[42]

Upon graduation in 1907, Agnes asked the editor of New York's *Morning Sun,* one of the era's more literate dailies, for a job. "We don't employ women on the *Sun,*" he barked. "That's why I want to work for you," she replied. He hired her; never before, she later bragged, "had a woman set foot in the city room."[43]

Her mother wept, and her father wailed, "I would rather see you dead."[44] Still, he was happy to accept the part of her meager wages—some weeks as little as five dollars—that she sent home.[45]

The editor would not actually assign her any stories, but ordered her to find them on her own. And she did, "braving snake charmers in apartments crawling with reptiles or tracking down stories at the insane asylum on Ward's Island. Nothing daunted me, if only it promised additional income."[46]

Occasionally her interests and her impecuniousness jibed. She pursued the then unknown Alfred Stieglitz and Edward Steichen at 291 Fifth Avenue, where, as the mainstays of the Photo-Secession gallery, or "291," the first in New York to show photography and modern art, they propounded the radical notion that photography was art. She quickly recognized their talent, spent hours interviewing them, and wrote an enthusiastic page-one story for the *Sun*.[47]

When she met Eugene Meyer she was both attracted and repelled. She would later write that she "was always unconsciously looking for a father substitute," and she found him in the millionaire bachelor, who couldn't have been more different from her father. (He was so dependable that, barely out of his teens, he had mapped out his life—the first twenty years would be devoted to getting an education, the next twenty to becoming very rich, and the third twenty to public service.) "There is a strength in Eugene that compels all his sisters and brothers to turn to him in times of indecision or trouble," his sister Rosalie wrote to Agnes, "and he has never failed us."*[48]

The problem was that Agnes, who was bursting with platonic passion for scores of men and ideas and causes, could not work up much for this short, Semitic-looking man of business. He would invite her to lunch, and she would bring along one of her poor male artist friends.[50] She went to Paris for a year's study at the Sorbonne,[51] over Eugene's protests, and then gave him a play-by-play of her infatuations and near misses at the hands of the day's most brilliant artists—her lunch with Matisse; her heroic efforts to resist the advances of Rodin ("Nothing I could say ever explained to him . . . why I was unwilling to pose nude on horseback with javelin in hand for a statute of Boadicea"). While accepting Eugene's money to pay her bills, she boasted of her flirtations in her letters and filled them with

*In 1906, when Eugene heard about the earthquake and fire in San Francisco, where Rosalie lived with her family, he grabbed his moneybelt and a gun and rushed out on railroad magnate E. H. Harriman's own train from New York. "I knew you would get here, Eugene," his sister said in greeting.[49]

the names of the famous people she met—Marie Curie, with whom she took fencing lessons; Gustav Mahler; art critic Leo Stein and his sister Gertrude, whom she found ugly and masculine: "I have always distrusted masculine women, and found their self-assertion distasteful."[52]

Eugene remained determined to win this thoughtless, pompous young woman, believing that marriage and motherhood would tame her. He appreciated her intelligence, her voracious curiosity, the energy and aggressiveness and self-confidence that rivaled his own. "She was brilliant and outspoken, and Eugene liked people who were brilliant and outspoken," observes June Bingham, whose parents were friends of the Meyers'.[53] Joanna Steichen, Edward's second wife, heard much from her husband about the young Agnes: "It's easy to think of Agnes as this foolish, romantic narcissist, and she was, but she was a woman with brains and guts and talent and ambition."[54]

When nearly two years had passed since Eugene first saw Agnes, he began to wonder if he shouldn't cut his losses and find another woman suitable to be his wife. At the first sign that Eugene might be tiring of the chase, and inclined to withdraw himself and his fortune, Agnes decided to marry him.

Over lunch at the Waldorf-Astoria in late January 1910, she told him she planned to return to Paris to "straighten out [her] inner confusion."

"I have decided to get away for a bit myself," he replied. "I'm going to take a trip around the world, starting next month."

"Why, how long are you going to be away?"

"Oh, at least six months."

As Agnes later recalled, "The thought that he was about to disappear for such a long time made me feel as if the ground were caving in beneath my feet. For several minutes I was silent. Then I heard what seemed to be my voice saying very quietly: 'I'm going with you.' "

"Yes, I know that," Eugene said. "I have your tickets."[55]

She excused herself to find a telephone to cancel an appointment, a date with another man.[56] She suggested they marry soon, on Lincoln's Birthday, the second anniversary of Eugene's initial glimpse of her.[57]

The conclusion that Agnes married Eugene for his money is inescapable; it would have been impossible for her, she said, "to marry anyone who was not well-to-do. For the only dowry I had to bring a husband were my father's debts and my own. . . . Henceforth I would be free of the crushing burden of debt."[58] And Eugene harbored no illusions that she was marrying him for love.[59]

They were married at the Ernst home in the Bronx, with guests limited to the two families. The ceremony was conducted by the pastor of Trinity Lutheran Church, and the groom's Judaism was invisible, except in the faces of the Meyer family. Agnes's mother, Eugene later told a friend, "was very shocked that she should have chosen a heathen."[60] But like Eugene's parents, the Ernsts had little leverage to complain. In his father-in-law's eyes, Eugene was less a Jew than a source of financial salvation. The newlyweds had not yet embarked on their around-the-world honeymoon when Eugene paid off all of Frederick Ernst's debts.[61]

They spent a week at Seven Springs Farm, Eugene's newly acquired house in Mount Kisco, Westchester County, on rolling and wooded terrain above Byram Lake. From there they went to Washington, D.C., and a ball given by Mrs. Herbert Wadsworth and attended by Cabinet members, Supreme Court justices, and Washington high society. Eugene realized that he was the only Jew in the ballroom, but rather than feel saddened by the anti-Semitism that produced such a scene, he was cheered and heartened about his choice of Agnes, as he watched her move among the guests with "assurance and grace. Though only twenty-three, she was a wife who could be relied upon to do her part well in any social setting."[62]

On the honeymoon, Agnes quickly shed her premarriage bohemian airs and acted as if she were to the manner born, traveling with a maid, compliments of her husband, who also brought his valet. Agnes, who had been accustomed to third-class travel through Europe, was now ensconced in a private railroad car, wearing a $60,000 string of matched pearls from Tiffany. When she pronounced her maid unsuitable, her sister-in-law Rosalie arranged for a substitute, Margaret Powell, a trained nurse, who accompanied the newlyweds on the rest of the honeymoon and returned with them to New York.

The honeymoon lost its glitter when they reached Korea and found a letter to Eugene from a brother-in-law with the news that Agnes's father had approached him for a loan.[63] That left Agnes in bitter tears, and her mood was not lifted by the nausea and weariness that accompanied the early weeks of pregnancy. Nor was it helped by what she perceived as Eugene's fading solicitousness, as he became preoccupied with a dispute in the U.S. copper industry that, because he owned so much copper stock, might have left him in ruins. (Eventually he took temporary leave from the honeymoon to tackle the seemingly impossible task of bringing the two sides together. While he was at it, he bought a substantial share in a mineral flotation company.)

In Paris, their last stop, they began to buy the impressionist art that would line the walls of their city and country homes. They made their choices with the help of Agnes's friend Edward Steichen, who had become a scout of modern art, suggesting to Stieglitz that the works of Picasso, Matisse, and Cézanne be exhibited at "291." The Meyers bought four Cézanne paintings for some $10,000 each,[64] as well as several Picassos. Eugene had the confidence to ignore cabled warnings from leading American collectors that wasting money on such "junk" would make him look foolish.

Back in New York in August 1910, the Meyers moved to a home on Fifty-first Street, directly opposite St. Patrick's Cathedral. Agnes, two months pregnant, nonetheless returned to her premarriage haunts, especially "291," where she joined Steichen and Stieglitz in their crusade to interest New Yorkers in modern French art. The gallery became a magnet for the likes of IWW leader Big Bill Haywood, Emma Goldman, Max Weber, Mabel Dodge, and Carl Sandburg, who had recently married Steichen's sister.[65]

The contempt that Agnes felt for domestic routine—she threw in the wastebasket the calling cards left at her home during her frequent absences[66]—extended to the expectation that women occupy themselves with bearing and rearing children. Agnes was singularly unsuited to motherhood. She greeted Florence, the baby conceived on the honeymoon, with the exclamation, "What a horror!" and described her daughter as a "wretched-looking object, made even more hideous by the abrasions [left] on her poor little temples [from] the forceps." To Agnes's dismay and apparent surprise, the baby wanted to eat: "This limp object attacked my . . . nipples and caused more excruciating pain which never abated." After "weeks of horror," her only compensation was "to look at myself in the mirror and realize . . . that the slender figure to which I was accustomed had returned. . . . I became a conscientious but scarcely a loving mother."[67]

Not even conscientious. Agnes cheerfully admitted, in fact

bragged, that she would forget to go home to nurse the baby "if I happened to get too deeply involved in one or the other of my extramural activities." The baby was left with Margaret Powell, known in the family as "Powelly," who stayed sixteen years beyond the honeymoon to rear Florence and the children who followed. "Reminded by my over-flowing breasts that I was neglecting my infant, I would rush back . . . to find the nurse walking the floor to comfort a baby screaming with hunger."[68]

A year after Florence's birth, in 1912, Agnes served on a committee that funded maternity centers in New York City[69]—the first of the good works that would occupy the rest of her life. If she saw any irony in her concern for the babies of the masses and her lack of concern for her own, she never let on.

That year was a tough one for Eugene. His brother Walter, a Harvard lawyer practicing in New York, would have died from typhoid had Eugene not ordered his doctors to use a highly experimental method of blood transfusion. But not even Eugene could save the youngest of the Meyer children, twenty-eight-year-old Edgar, who was aboard the *Titanic* and who, as his brother feared, was so unselfish that he stayed to help launch the last lifeboat.[70]

The loss of Edgar was one of the hardest losses of Eugene's life. Edgar had been his business partner and his favorite brother, the one who, it was planned, would take over when Eugene left business for public service at age forty.[71]

Soon after Edgar's death, Agnes became pregnant again. Eugene hoped that his second child would be a son—a way to salve the hurt over Edgar. Elizabeth Meyer, known in the family as "Bis," was born in February 1913.

Eugene, a staunch Republican, had already been made gloomy by the election of Woodrow Wilson, a Democrat; to Eugene's mind, this was bad for business. What happened next was near personal financial collapse: with the stock market down, Eugene was caught with overextended holdings, and unless he could borrow money to carry him through the crisis, he would have to sell a large amount of stock.

Although he did not quite go broke, he came close, and immediately had to reduce expenses. The family had been living in a townhouse at Seventieth Street and Park Avenue, which they had furnished by going to London and buying three vanloads' worth of old English furniture; Steichen had painted murals for the spiral staircase. Eugene sold the house and moved his family to the St. Regis Hotel.

Another death occurred that year—Frederick Ernst's. "I could not mourn him," Agnes later wrote.[72] Nor could Eugene, who, finally, was relieved of having to send his father-in-law money.

Death and financial troubles notwithstanding, Agnes continued blithely along on her latest pastime—acquiring men, searching for what Joanna Steichen calls "passionate love." Steichen, a psychotherapist, explains that Agnes "always longed to be courted and admired and loved. She was trying to re-create what she had with her father as a child, when Daddy seemed like his own kind of genius. [But then he] left her."[73]

Having a newborn at home again proved no impediment to Agnes. She became outrageously flirtatious, so long as the men—preferably writers, philosophers, artists (or at least collectors)—were successful, renowned, and willing to pursue strictly platonic flirtations. The more famous, the more brilliant, the older the men, the better. She wanted the outside world to believe she was engaged in great sexual passions, although, as one observer remarked, she was nothing more than "one of the great teases of the Edwardian age." There was something about Agnes that gave away the ruse. "I've always had the feeling," Joanna Steichen says, "that Agnes was terribly interested in romance and not terribly interested in sex." One of her daughters insists: "She didn't have sex with them, period."[74]

Among Agnes's early conquests was philanthropist and art patron Charles Freer, who had made his millions manufacturing railroad cars. She met him in 1913 (she was twenty-six, he fifty-seven) at an exhibition of Oriental painting.[75] He would send his agents deep into China to buy paintings and jades, and then he and Agnes would select those worth including in the gallery he planned to build.

Although Freer had a sexual interest in women—he and architect Stanford White once "hired young Italian girls to swim nude before them while they dined in a grotto at Capri"[76]—he is said to have had congenital syphilis and so to have been celibate in his later years. To Agnes he was "an aesthete in every phase of life—in his home, in his appreciation of good food and good wines, above all in his love of beautiful women."[77]

Eugene, so preoccupied that year, seemed willing to let Agnes pursue Freer, whom he trusted enough to take later as a business associate. Eugene may have recognized that he could not restrain

Agnes, and so better to indulge her than to guarantee an ugly show-down. Still, Eugene insisted, Agnes later wrote, "that I invite a friend to accompany me into the dangerous lair of Prince Charming"[78]—not surprising, when one considers that Agnes bombarded Eugene with the most intimate details of her "affair." She would later visit Freer and artist Katharine Rhoades, who had become his secretary. In a letter to "Dear Old Euge," she confessed, "Freer and I get so sweetly intimate even before [Katharine] that I sometimes have a desire to have him all to myself."[79]

Agnes's appearance was not what it was during her Barnard years. Despite her assertion to the contrary, she never regained her pre-childbirth slimness, and left the impression of being large-boned; she was increasingly described as a "Valkyrie, a Wagnerian heroine."[80] She compensated by presenting herself as intellectually eons beyond any other woman then alive—garnering the lifelong dislike of some of her gender.

Her ludicrously pompous pronouncement after her first trip abroad—"I lived totally in a world of ideas"—was the prelude to a continuing issuance of such nonsense. "Who has not seen the Russian ballet between 1909 and 1912 has no concept of what ballet can be," she announced gravely.[81]

In 1914, the mother of two girls aged three and one felt especially restless, and "rebellious over what I interpreted as the crushing of my personality."[82] She sailed alone, in May, for Europe. Eugene, who would not have accompanied her even if he had felt like it, because he "smelled" the coming of war and radically changing business conditions in America, was furious. As her ship approached South-ampton, Agnes, who never failed to retreat when she feared she had pushed Eugene too far, wrote him, "I have already decided that I shall never again go away without you."[83]

She also never failed to put Eugene's concerns out of mind the moment she felt she had adequately addressed them. She wrote him of every man whose heart, she claimed, still leaped at the sight of her. From Berlin she described how Alfred Walter von Heymel, an aristo-cratic playboy and publisher from Leipzig who had designed the hat she wore when Eugene first saw her, "took me to his charming apartment for tea. Don't be shocked. It was full of domestics and as proper as any ménage."[84]

From Vienna she wrote Eugene of a reunion with Dr. Julius Tandler, a professor and socialist leader with whom she had gone mountain climbing in Austria the year before her marriage: "My old feeling for him reestablished itself immediately," while "tears came into his eyes." His wife, whom Agnes dismissed as "this hellhound . . . fatter and coarser than ever," was outraged.[85] Agnes made a special trip to Fontainebleau to see her old friend Rodin, whose lechery she had so often and so graphically described to her husband.[86]

He was in no mood to hear of her flirtations. Stuck at home with children, servants, his view that the world was poised on the brink of disaster, and a business outlook that was equally grim, he complained to a friend that Agnes had "deserted" him for "a little vacation, rest and pleasure. . . . Alas, this is a world of woe! Only when I retire to Seven Springs Farm and take a walk in my nice, old hemlock wood . . . do I begin to believe that there is some consolation somehow—somewhere."[87]

Agnes soon had a letter from Eugene, who was willing to overlook certain of her escapades but was furious about von Heymel: "I was distinctly annoyed to learn that you had gone to von Heymel's apartment alone." His anger had not cooled when he wrote the next day: "I am asking myself what I have done to deserve this sort of treatment."[88]

The unforgiving tone of this letter sent Agnes into full retreat: "Last night as I lay in bed I had only one feeling, 'How did I ever get anybody to marry me, anyway—most of all you.' I have a big picture of Florence in my room . . . that comforts me a lot. At least my babies are sweet, aren't they, honey?" In a subsequent letter she told him she wanted another baby.[89]

She ended her stay in the French countryside at Steichen's house in Voulangis (he then commuted between New York and France), a region that, within a few weeks, was overrun by the Germans.* On July 31, she sailed home, to an irate Eugene, the world war erupting while she was crossing the Atlantic. She later admitted that she worried much more about facing him than she did about the war. "Know that I will work for you always—in any and every way," she wrote Eugene. "This is a sweet expression," he acidly replied, "and I am sure you would do so—if you happened to think of it."[90]

---

*Steichen cabled Eugene for advice. "Suggest immediate orderly retreat," he counseled. Steichen and his family retreated to the Meyer farm in Mount Kisco, where they spent the rest of the summer.

Agnes described to Eugene a nightmare she had had while sailing home. She was watching a glorious sunrise with her father, when it faded and all that remained was his face, "with an expression of sadistic triumph" that seemed to say: "I've got you. You are just another me. And you are doomed to go the way I did." "I could not help but realize," Agnes admitted, "that in escaping from home responsibilities I was repeating the self-centered, irresponsible conduct of my father which had cost his wife, his children, and especially his only daughter, such bitter humiliation."[91]

Once in New York, Agnes lapsed into habits as selfish as ever.

Preoccupied with the business opportunities spawned by the war, Eugene had no time to notice. He had seen and studied the gaps in American industry—copper and chemicals chief among them—and moved to fill them. He helped create Anaconda Copper, which supplied the Allies with wire for their communications network, helped establish dye-manufacturing facilities that would later become National Aniline & Chemical, and formed a company to supply the U.S. Navy with blue dye for its uniforms. While he passed up the chance to become one of the two largest shareholders in General Motors—the head of GM had offered him forty-nine percent; he insisted on fifty-one—he made millions on Fisher Body.[92]

In 1915, at forty, Eugene was worth nearly $60 million and was, by every account, a businessman of rare brilliance. Although Bernard Baruch was better known to the public, Eugene was smarter, bolder, and cooler. "Baruch really did lean very heavily on Eugene," says Harvey Segal, an economist who wrote Baruch's obituary for *The Washington Post*. "When Eugene said, 'Barney, don't do something,' he didn't."[93] Eugene enjoyed telling how in their early days of investment banking he and Baruch had underwritten a securities issue, which, on the morning it was offered, appeared to be failing miserably, with bidding for the shares far below the asking price. By eleven that morning Baruch was in Meyer's office, "shaking and wringing his hands." "Have someone . . . announce from the steps of the sub-Treasury in Wall Street that the offering price will go up by two points at twelve noon," he advised Baruch. The announcement was made, and the issue quickly sold out.[94]

Eugene was well aware of his gifts. He told one man who worked for him that "there were not more than twelve men in the world who fully understood how money was created, and he was one of them."[95] He had much to teach, and finally, in June 1915, he received his student, a son—the only male born to the Meyers. The birth of Eugene III, known in the family as "Bill," prompted from Agnes the first and last expression of joy at the arrival of a Meyer child. "With surprise and a feeling of guilt toward the older girls, . . . I now felt a ridiculous sense of achievement."[96]

Eugene's business was booming, and he moved his family from the St. Regis to 820 Fifth Avenue: he had bought the building, and the Meyers would live in the entire top floor and half of the floor below.[97]

Eugene also began planning for an estate at Mount Kisco. Rather than expand the 150-year-old farmhouse, he decided to have a house built on his property's highest hill, also the highest point in Westchester County.[98] The Meyers rejected Edward Steichen's advice that they hire Frank Lloyd Wright as their architect.[99] Instead, at Charles Freer's suggestion, they chose Charles Platt, who was then drawing plans for the Freer Gallery of Art in Washington, D.C.

If Eugene had not yet learned the lesson, he now had proof that marriage to a Wasp would not shield him from anti-Semitism. As his Mount Kisco neighbors were letting him know that if he planned to be there for long stretches, or permanently, the family would be "snubbed socially," Eugene was buying additional land, including the lake at the foot of his property, to ensure his privacy from them.[100]

In October 1916, Eugene recognized that the United States might soon be drawn into the European war against Germany and Austria. It was time, and right on schedule, for him to embark on the third phase of his life plan—twenty years of public service. He began to liquidate his firm so that he could volunteer for war service; but to his chagrin, he was barred from training because of his color-blindness.[101] Realizing that there were other ways to serve his country, he took himself to the nation's capital—a move that would have a profound and not always happy effect on his growing family.

Chapter 2

ROUGH BEGINNINGS: MR.—AND MRS.—MEYER GO TO WASHINGTON

Katharine, the fourth Meyer child, was born on June 16, 1917, in New York City, just as her father moved to Washington. Kay, as she was called in the family, lived her first three years with next to no contact with her father and almost as little with her mother, who, after spending that summer in Mount Kisco, followed her husband.

Public service was not much on Agnes's mind, and she certainly had no intention of performing the typical woman's work of rolling bandages for the Red Cross. What drew her to the capital was the opportunity to launch a salon to attract the important men assembled in wartime Washington. Her home, she knew, would quickly develop a reputation as a place where great minds discussed great issues over—and this was no small item—the finest food and wine. It would be said routinely that Agnes Meyer had the best chef in Washington.

The infant Katharine and her siblings, the oldest of whom was six, were left in the New York apartment with Powelly and various servants, including a German cook who rolled out apple strudel on a massive stainless-steel table. "The doorman would put our roller skates [on us]," Bis recalls, "and we grew up in Central Park and the zoo, [with] that wonderful smell of peanuts." Presiding at the entrance to their apartment were two "lady Buddhas," now in the Freer Gallery, at whose feet the children sat to pull their boots on and off.[1]

Grandparents on both sides visited. Granny and Grandpa Meyer, who lived nearby in an apartment on Central Park West, were "omnipresent." Agnes's mother, "Grossmutter," worried endlessly that the half-Jewish children would go to hell because they had not yet been christened.[2]

Meanwhile, in Washington, Eugene had rented a large house on K Street, and Agnes was on her way. Her slightly exotic looks—by Washington standards, at least—made an instant impression. One prominent Washington attorney described her in 1917: "She wore a close-fitted gown of white panne velvet. Around her golden hair she wore a white band. . . . I said to my companion: 'Did you ever see anything like that? Don't you think she would be a perfect type for one of the Grail Bearers that Sir Edwin Abbey has been painting?' "[3]

Eugene's first attempts at public service made him wonder what he was letting himself in for. He asked his friend Supreme Court justice Louis Brandeis to help him find a way "to give my time and work to the service of the country." While Brandeis wrote letters on his behalf, Eugene wrote directly to President Wilson and, when there was no response, to Bernard Baruch, then in charge of raw materials for the Advisory Commission to the Council of National Defense. Baruch also failed to answer Eugene's letters, although he would later claim that it was he who brought Eugene Meyer to Washington. The dollar-a-year appointment that Brandeis was finally able to secure for his friend was humiliatingly trivial: advisor to the Army on the purchase of shoes and cotton duck. Eugene accepted; after all, it was a way to get started, and he did not want to insult Brandeis.[4]

When the president finally responded with something more substantial—service on a commission being sent to Russia to establish relations with the provisional government of Alexander Kerensky, which had taken power after the February 1917 revolution—Eugene was delighted. He prepared himself assiduously, wrote letters to such experts as Felix Frankfurter, then in the War Department, and recruited and pledged to cover the expenses of two physicians who would instruct the Russians in the use of a new typhus vaccine.

Then Eugene was summoned to the State Department and, without apology or explanation, told by Secretary of State Robert Lansing, "We have some cables that make us think that you'd better not go on the Russian mission."[5] In less delicate terms, Kerensky, himself a Jew, objected to the presence of Eugene Meyer; Jewish financiers were, in Kerensky's estimation, "the world's archetypal oppressive capitalists."[6]

At first deflated and embarrassed—the appointment had been

announced in the newspapers—Eugene recovered quickly, vowing not to let his religion hamper him, and to stick to what he knew best: preparation of the U.S. industrial base for war. He resigned his advisory post with the Army and went to Bernard Baruch's office, understanding that his disorganized friend had ignored his letters because he knew that Eugene would outwork, outorganize, and outshine him. Uninvited, Eugene began to organize Baruch's office: he ordered furniture, answered unopened mail, acted as liaison for various foreign missions, assembled a technical staff, and defined policies. He also bombarded President Wilson with ideas on how to pursue the industrial side of the war more effectively. Wilson incorporated many of these into White House policy.[7]

Eugene soon had his own section to head—the nonferrous-metals division of the War Industries Board—and then, leapfrogging Baruch, the staunch Republican Eugene Meyer was named by the staunch Democratic president to be the dollar-a-year director of the War Finance Corporation, Eugene's own precedent-setting brainstorm to provide government loans to industries necessary to the conduct of the war.[8] He contributed $70,000 of his own money and, at an additional personal cost of $100,000, brought to Washington businessmen who could not afford to serve without a stipend.

For his trouble, Eugene was summoned before congressional committees, accused of making money off the government—of using "Jewish power" to run the government—and denounced by a congressman who asked on the House floor: "[Is it] not true in the United States today that the Gentiles have the slips of paper while the Jews have the lawful money?"[9]

Eugene certainly would have preferred not to be lambasted in the House of Representatives in such obviously anti-Semitic terms—especially when he was trying to conduct his life so that his Jewishness would be as near to invisible as possible—but he cared little about public praise. When Agnes scolded him for not distributing enough copies of a speech he was about to deliver—"The trouble with you, Euge, is that you don't have any ego"—he replied, "That's all right, Ag, because you have enough for both of us." Eugene was the sort of public servant who stayed focused on the unglamorous work needed to shove the bureaucracy behind his agency's goals.

When Eugene turned his attention to personal matters, it went not to his children, who remained with Powelly in Manhattan, but to the Westchester County estate, which, by mid-1919, was near completion. His neighbors seethed with anger, jealousy, and fulfilled expectations. One described the place as "the most impressive house Mount Kisco residents had ever seen," with "a water tower which would be seen above the trees for miles. . . . The Meyer family immediately became enemy aliens, flaunting their wealth and spoiling the view."[10]

The three-story house, which looked like a French château—certainly not what Frank Lloyd Wright would have designed—was, as one frequent visitor puts it, "monumental"[11] and lavish. Built of stone from a quarry Eugene had opened on his property, and topped by a heavy slate roof, it was said to have cost—in 1919 dollars—more than $2 million.[12]

The house had "kitchen facilities suitable for a royal household,"[13] a Turkish bath, a bowling alley, an organ that piped music throughout, an outdoor swimming pool, and an indoor one of Olympic dimensions, built from white marble installed by stonemasons imported from Italy and, during construction, housed in tents on the grounds.[14] There were studies and sleeping rooms galore, one of the latter overlooking the lake and named the "Freer Room," in hopes that the Meyers' friend would visit Mount Kisco often, but he died in September 1919.*

The grounds, about 750 acres, were equally luxurious, featuring sunken gardens, greenhouses in which orchids grew, lily ponds, an orangery, complete with a mural by Steichen,[17] tennis courts, stables, and trails leading to several hundred acres of open fields and woods. A railroad spur provided easy access to New York City, and in a pasture cattle grazed, awaiting slaughter by the family butcher.[18]

In 1920, Eugene Meyer found himself in disagreement with the secretary of the treasury, David Houston, who argued that the need for a government-backed mechanism to finance exports had ended. Eugene warned that Europe was far from recovered and that if such a policy were implemented, the American economy would be crippled by severe deflation. The new treasury secretary prevailed. Eugene resigned, and activities of the War Finance Corporation were

---

*The Freer Gallery of Art, home to his collection of Chinese and Japanese art, opened in 1923. In his will, Freer named Eugene, Agnes, and Katharine Rhoades as the gallery's lifetime trustees, with veto power over all purchased additions to the collection.[15] Freer also specified that Agnes was the only person who could give any of her own pieces to the gallery. "He knew that if Mother esteemed it, it was going to be worthy of the Freer," Bis says.[16]

suspended. A year later, when his prediction of a business collapse came true—the economy went into the sharpest decline in American history—President Harding recalled him to revive the WFC and serve again as its managing director.[19]

During his brief hiatus from government, Eugene went to New York and merged National Aniline & Chemical with three other firms to create the Allied Chemical Corporation.[20] He also listened to an offer from Adolph Ochs, publisher of *The New York Times,* to join the paper on the business side. Eugene refused, partly because he realized, somewhat to his own surprise, that he preferred the editorial side. But the meeting with Ochs planted a seed in his mind that "publishing a good daily paper could be another form of public service."[21]

When Eugene answered President Harding's call and returned to Washington, it apparently occurred to him and Agnes, even in those years when upper-class parents typically did not pay close attention to their children, that the distance separating them from their off-spring was excessive. Eugene moved the children and the family's servants to Washington.

He bought a huge, dark place, complete with towers and a coach house, on Connecticut Avenue. "When I was a little girl," recalls Jean Ulman Friendly, who played with the Meyer children, "that whole area where that huge apartment is [2101 Connecticut Avenue] was just their house."[22] They used the coach house as a playroom[23] and the expanse of land in back for baseball games that drew children from throughout the neighborhood.[24]

Katharine was sent to nursery and kindergarten at one of the country's earliest Montessori schools, on 35th and Volta. When she was six, in 1923, she moved to the Potomac School, just off Connecticut Avenue and a short walk from home.

Eugene remained managing director of the War Finance Corporation through the presidency of Warren Harding and into that of Calvin Coolidge, who disbanded it in 1925. Out of government, Eugene again toyed with the notion of channeling his zest for public service into publishing a newspaper. He made a bid for one of the capital's morning dailies, the *Herald,* which, like the afternoon *Times,* was owned by William Randolph Hearst. The *Herald* was rumored to be losing a million and a half dollars a year. Still, Hearst was not interested, and he dismissed Eugene with, "I always buy newspapers, never sell them."[25]

By May 1927, Eugene was back in government, appointed by Coolidge to clean up, reorganize, and serve as commissioner of the Farm Loan Board. Two years earlier, Eugene had repeatedly warned the secretary of the treasury, Andrew Mellon, that "rampant malpractices were imperiling the integrity of the . . . Federal Farm Loan System's banks"; he believed that when several of the system's largest banks were thrown into receivership, some of the officers should be criminally prosecuted. As commissioner, he was immediately attacked by various congressmen, some of whom may have been involved in the corruption and known that Eugene knew they were; yet without regard for "political sensitivities" in either party, he persisted in the cleanup.[26]

While Eugene was in the hot seat, Agnes was casting herself as a genuine doorbell-ringing, get-out-the-vote cog in Boss Ward's machine. She had to admit, of course, that Ward was the Republican boss of Westchester County, site of the Meyers' country estate, and that, as head of the Westchester County Recreation Committee, she was promoting music festivals rather than swapping garbage pick-up for votes. Agnes credited Ward with "driv[ing] me out of being a no good intellectual and into becoming a practicing American citizen. He turned my eyes away from myself"—a feat, in fact, that no one else in her long life would ever accomplish.[27]

Agnes's children quickly saw the irony in their mother's working to improve recreation in the county when recreation in her own home ranked dead last on her list of priorities. Seven Springs Farm should have been a child's delight, but neither Agnes nor Eugene had seen to it that the children knew how to take advantage of it. The story has often been told of ten-year-old Kay waiting for a friend to arrive and "innocently ask[ing] her mother what they would do when the friend got there. Her mother flew into a rage. How dare she ask that when there were horses to ride and a swimming pool and all these wonderful things? And Kay remembers saying yes, but she did not know how to do any of those things."

Agnes loved to expound on the challenge of bringing up children while pursuing work outside the home: "It takes health, careful planning and often grim determination if married women are to carry two jobs at once, responsibility to husband, home, children and to public service. No matter how proud the family members may be of Mother's outside activities, she must be prepared to accept their fierce and natural jealousy of all energies not devoted to them."[28]

That the children and their parents then lived in the same house was largely irrelevant, because the children's needs continued to be met by the cook, by Powelly, and by Alfred M. Phillips, known in the family by his last name, the chauffeur who drove them to school. Jean Friendly cannot recall ever seeing Agnes when she played at the Meyer house: "She was not the type of lady who would be down in the kitchen making fudge."[29] Kay would later tell a friend that she felt like an orphan while growing up.[30]

Bis remembers that Agnes, who had a secretary living in the house, was often incommunicado in her "Chinese Room," working with a "Chinaman" on her book *Chinese Painting As Reflected in the Thought and Art of Li Lung-Mien 1070–1106*. Affection, says Bis, was afforded by Powelly, who would take the children into the woods and "with an open fire and a fry pan make the most marvelous chicken with all the gravy mixed up in it."[31]

So erratic was Agnes's schedule that Bis finally suggested hanging a blackboard at the front door, "like the one at school where notices are posted. Then when we go out, we could see whether you are going to be home when we come back from school—or in Texas."[32] The proposal was "a sort of protest"—Bis's way of telling her mother, "I get embarrassed when I'm asked where you are and I don't have any idea."[33]

Although Agnes liked to berate her gender for not accepting its natural role as nurturer and its capacity for "warm, understanding" relationships—she presented Ilse Koch, "Beast of Buchenwald," as an example of "what happens to the female when she forgets her role as the guardian of . . . human compassion"[34]—she had no capacity whatsoever for nurturing or understanding children. Katharine, the child who correctly perceived herself as the one her mother liked least, suffered most. With good reason, she could imagine that every time her mother deigned to cast her glance upon her, what she saw was not an earnest little girl trying so very hard to please, but a girl who was unworthy of her namesake, Katharine Rhoades, the artist whom Agnes described as one of the "most beautiful young women that ever walked this earth."[35]

Agnes routinely showed off her first- and second-born daughters, Florence and Bis, as the family beauties. The last of the Meyer children, Ruth, born in 1922, "blonde and ethereal,"[36] was the creative one. Bill was special merely by virtue of being a male. Agnes casually volunteered, "As a mother I preferred boys."[37]

"I thought I was the peasant walking around brilliant people," Kay later remembered. She was indeed isolated. While Florence, Bis, and Bill formed a trio, Bis explains, "Kay got to be grouped with Ruthie. Kay was downgraded to the nurse's care, while we had Mademoiselle," the governess who taught them French and other subjects.[38]

Florence would never be close to Kay. Libby Rowe, Jean Friendly's sister, recalls Florence "acting a role. She was the literary member of the family. She wasn't that much older, but she pretended to be. She put on airs. She read everything and told us about it, but she was rather aloof, floating off on her own. She had a dreamy quality."[39]

Bis "was very bright and very lively," in Rowe's memory, with "much more self-confidence than Kay in every situation." Bis, with her natural grace, charm, style, adventurousness, and mischievousness, contrasted with the ever practical, plodding, and retiring Kay. "Bis outgrew the governess early," Rowe says, "and so the chauffeur was her governess. When we were in school he would drive us around and see that we didn't get into any trouble. Bis was always the one who said, 'We haven't lived if we haven't been to a wrestling match. We haven't lived unless we've been to a burlesque show.' Phillips was our chaperon. He saw we didn't get into the burlesque show. He sat with us during the wrestling match. He was Bis's governess, but not Kay's."[40]

Kay's natural ally in the family should have been Bill—the sibling closest in age—but he had eyes only for his older sister Bis, who, in turn, extravagantly admired Florence. And while Ruth was definitely just the baby sister, tagging along and as shy as could be, Kay was not given much thought by anyone.[41] "She wasn't included in an awful lot of things," Bis admits.[42]

Her isolation, coupled with her need to please her mother, made her the butt of sibling teasing and sometimes cruelty. When Kay was four, her brother and sisters, angry with her for telling Agnes about some mischief or other, dragged her into the bathroom and taped her mouth shut. "The three oldest of us considered her a tattletale of a high degree," Bis says. "I remember large tears rolling down her cheeks, it was really sad."[43]

Florence and Bis, at least in their younger years, seem to have developed a healthier relationship with their mother than Kay ever would. Having stronger self-images, they were better able to put

Agnes in perspective, even to appreciate her intellect and energy, and consequently suffered less from her indifference and malice. When Kay was ten she told her mother that she had just finished reading *The Three Musketeers.* "Undoubtedly a waste of time," Agnes replied, "unless you read it in the original French"[44]—which, she added, she had, and at an earlier age. Agnes was about to leave for Europe when Kay asked permission to have her hair bobbed. Agnes said no. Kay had it bobbed anyway and feared a scene when her mother returned, but Agnes didn't even notice.

Eventually Kay developed an armor, albeit wobbly, to protect herself from Agnes. But it took years, and she was far beyond childhood when she told a reporter, "I came from this incredibly high-powered family. My mother was sort of a Viking. Very bright, and utterly contemptuous of everyone else."[45]

A close friend who calls Kay's upbringing a nightmare describes an incident that "epitomizes the Meyer household": Agnes looked at Kay one morning, noticed that her daughter was maturing physically, and began to lecture her on menstruation. "Oh, Mother," Kay interrupted, "that happened to me a year ago."[46]

Eugene was certainly not cruel, and not exactly indifferent, but he was preoccupied. Libby Rowe recalls him as "a much warmer, easier person to talk to [than Mrs. Meyer]. We had a good time with him. We used to tease him. He wore high-button shoes. We were always telling him how unfashionable he was. He was very genial when I was with him."

The Meyer children found him easier to talk to, not quite so intimidating—less the important personage than Agnes. Rowe remembers that "when Agnes came into a room, the children would stand up."[47] As Eugene got older he was sometimes described as kindly. No matter how old Agnes got, nobody ever used that word to describe her.

Still, if the subject was not a public or political one, Eugene made little effort to find out what his children were thinking. The study of psychology that had so fascinated him as a youth was lost; even his only son got short shrift. That distinguished Eugene from his own father, who involved himself closely in every step of his son's development.

When Eugene did turn his attention to his children, instead of being advisor, teacher, counselor, companion, he became a goader, never letting them forget that he expected them to be the most brilliant in academics, sports, and dinner-table conversation. Agnes might have let the children drift while she tended to her own affairs, but Eugene wanted to be sure that when he worked, the children did likewise. The result was excessive scheduling, even during summers in Mount Kisco. "I don't think we ever had something called a rest in our lives," Bis observes. After making their own beds, they reported, on time, to the dining room for breakfast with Eugene (Agnes always had hers in bed). There they apprised their father of their progress in academics and athletics. "Dad would field questions," Bis recounts, "testing us." Next they called on Agnes on her sleeping porch, where they recited Molière and La Fontaine in French. "I used to get in a swivet if I broke down and got stuck," says Bis. "It was tragedy."[48] Then on to lessons from nine until noon. The Swiss governess, Mademoiselle Otth, taught them arithmetic and French; Mademoiselle Meyer, imported from France (and no relation), drilled them in history, literature, and more French.[49] Swimming, tennis, and riding lessons—they were eventually taught these sports—came next. Nowhere on the agenda was there time for fun for fun's sake or for accommodating the emotional side of growing up.

Katharine's oldest son would later say about his grandmother: "Her children felt they were neglected or squashed or held up to some unattainable standard. They were expected to be beautiful and glamorous and perfect. And they were taught that they were failures if they weren't."[50] Even Eugene's authorized biographer, while painting a most flattering portrait of him and a mostly flattering one of Agnes, could not condone their approach to child-rearing: "Neither parent took time to teach the children the routine mechanics of living, and Father's goading in the direction of success was often undercut by Mother's penchant for criticism and belittlement of what they did."[51]

Bis says that the children accustomed themselves to receiving no praise. "My father simply passed on what had happened to him as a young man. He told the story of his reporting proudly that he had come in second in his class on some test and his father said, 'Why not first?'" Decades after Eugene's death, Bis saw a letter he had written to his sister Rosalie. "To my astonishment, Dad said, 'Bis graduated from Potomac first in her class, and it was one of the proudest days of my life.'"[52] He never said it to her.

Still, as the spunkiest of the children, Bis has warm memories of life with Father during summers at Mount Kisco. The children would follow him to his study, where they would watch as he called his office in Manhattan before commuting there. He would light a cigar and flick the ashes into a straw wastebasket, which they expected would go up in flames. "Our life while he was there was right on his tail, whatever he was doing. We used to watch him shave."[53]

Bis also remembers fondly summer camping trips that Agnes organized around archaeological themes. Eugene normally pleaded the urgency of work and stayed home, while Agnes departed with a contingent of archaeologists and servants and children over age nine. The first trip was to New Mexico, where the group "pack tripped" into a remote area to see Native American dances. Sometime later a delegation of Native Americans, including several who had served as guides, came to Washington to testify before Congress. Bis recalls their trooping up to the Connecticut Avenue house to dance for the Meyers and their guests.[54]

Often there were guests at lunch and dinner—eighteen was not an unusual number—and the children, if invited, were expected to contribute intelligently. The identity of the guests changed as administrations came and went, and as the targets of Agnes's affections and enthusiasms shifted, but the caliber was consistent—Supreme Court justices, senators, presidential candidates, college presidents, and the best-known theologians, philosophers, musicians, and writers.

When Bill invited a friend to spend the weekend at Seven Springs Farm, the young man asked, "Any *interesting* people going to be there?" Joanna Steichen, whose husband was a frequent guest, wonders, "How much of this pressure [could] a person take, of this competitive intellectual brilliance? A lot of the daily human affectionate things that one likes to think of as going on between parents and [children] didn't go on."[55]

Agnes and Eugene preferred the idea of family to the reality. Each year, Edward Steichen was summoned to Mount Kisco to photograph all the Meyers standing on the edge of the lily pond—each year in the same position, and with the same unmet emotional needs that were only sometimes visible to the camera.

Eugene would later have regrets about his relationship with Bill, but Agnes had none about her relationship with any of her children. Her blather on the subject of child-rearing increased alarmingly in volume, misogyny, and sheer hypocrisy: "In my opinion, humility is the greatest possible asset in any human being, particularly in women." She attacked American women as "more cruel, more selfish and more materialistic"[56] than their husbands, and decried "the egoistic desires of women," which prevent them from accepting "the discipline of marriage, the subordination of self that it entails. . . . Infantilism . . . the desire for a false self-expression, and a consequent desiccation of instinct lead all too many women to despise the role of housewife, to reject their children and resent the father."[57]

The Meyer children had no religious structure on which to lean. Eventually, to calm Grossmutter's fears about the hereafter, Bis says, "we all got christened at home on Connecticut Avenue by a friend, Dr. Johnson of the Episcopal church opposite the White House [St. John's on Lafayette Square]. That was the extent of religion in our youth."[58] They did occasionally go to the very tony church, but that fell more in the category of social than spiritual.

Agnes had no political ambitions for herself, only for Eugene, whose appointments opened doors for her. She was delighted when the taciturn Calvin Coolidge announced that he did not "choose" to run for reelection in 1928. She was rooting for Herbert Hoover, a sometime visitor to the Meyer home, who, she hoped, would name Eugene secretary of the treasury. Although Eugene did not much like Hoover,[59] he helped swing the New York delegation behind him, contributed $25,000 to his campaign,[60] and would happily have accepted the treasury position.

No offer was forthcoming, and it was felt in the family that if Eugene had been christened an Episcopalian, Hoover would have made the appointment. After Hoover's first few months in office, Eugene resigned as commissioner of the Farm Loan Board because he did not like the agricultural policy of the new administration. His departure was not mourned by Senator Smith Brookhart, Republican of Iowa, who blasted him as a "Judas Iscariot to the cooperative movement" and added that his departure indicated "the end of . . . traitors working in the interests of the financiers."[61] Brookhart aside, Eugene was so widely praised by farmers and editors of farm journals that he was often mentioned—but not by the new president—as a good choice for secretary of agriculture.

Eugene claimed not to be interested in any position, Cabinet or otherwise. "I have given some of the best years of my life to public service,"[62] the fifty-three-year-old said; a long vacation at his farm was his only ambition.

*

But Eugene Meyer had something more on his mind than lazy afternoons. As was becoming a habit during his stints away from government, he tried to buy a newspaper—this time *The Washington Post,* which had flourished under the ownership of John McLean but was floundering under the hand of his alcoholic playboy son, Edward, who suffered a nervous breakdown in 1929. In May, Eugene offered $5 million for the enfeebled *Post,* assuming that offer was far too generous for Ned McLean, no matter how drunkenly irrational he had become, to refuse. What Eugene had not counted on was Ned's wife, the socially ambitious Evalyn Walsh McLean, who persuaded her husband to retain the paper and its power, dwindling though it was.[63]

Out of government and twice rebuffed in his attempts to buy Washington newspapers, Eugene might well have decided to move his family back to New York. But he had the public service bug and preferred Washington. So did Agnes, who could be a bigger fish in a pond admittedly more parochial but stocked with important dinner guests. A grander house was needed, and the Meyers moved to a stone mansion at 1624 Crescent Place, perched atop a rise off 16th Street, complete with columns, a circular drive, a front-yard fountain, and statues of Roman senators, on whose heads Bis's boyfriends deposited their hats.* The Meyers added a staff of twelve servants, including footmen,[65] and a priceless art collection, including bird sculptures by the Romanian Constantin Brancusi, whose genius Agnes was early in recognizing.

Eugene's supposed long rest on his farm started with a trip to Paris in the early summer of 1929. Agnes was to have a portrait bust sculpted by Charles Despiau, a pupil of Rodin's and a fierce competitor of Brancusi's; Despiau and Brancusi represented opposing schools of sculpture. According to Agnes, one evening, when Brancusi heard that Agnes had allowed Despiau to sculpt her, he "looked at me as if I had driven a dagger into his heart; he fell into an oppressive silence which ruined the remainder of the evening." When she said good night, Brancusi looked at her defiantly and vowed, "I'll show you what a portrait of you is really like." The artists' feud

---

*Its original owner was diplomat Henry White, husband of Margaret, one of the Rutherfurd girls on whom Edith Wharton modeled her characters.[64]

eventually "produced another masterpiece," a black marble head of Agnes that Brancusi called "La Reine pas Dédaigneuse" (The Not Disdainful Queen) and her children called "Agnes's Knee."[66]

That fall, a restless Eugene went to Wyoming, near Jackson Hole, where he bought what he described as "a small ranch" on which he "could run a few cattle." The Red Rock Ranch covered 600 acres.[67]

When President Hoover offered a string of what Eugene considered inconsequential jobs, he found it easy to say no. He also declined a plea from Louis Brandeis, who "put heavy pressure" on him to lead a delegation to study the possibilities for industrial and economic development in Palestine, map out a program, and raise $25 million to finance it.[68] The argument turned hot, but the friendship survived—even in the face of Eugene's unconvincing protestation that, after twelve years of government service, he had earned the right to spend time with his wife and children.

Eugene had much more on his mind during those latter months of 1929. He had been watching the stock market and growing increasingly alarmed at the "crazy" speculation and "dizzying heights" to which stock prices were climbing, and at the Federal Reserve Board's disinclination to do anything to stem the "gusher." He suggested to Hoover that the Federal Reserve and the Treasury Department encourage people to buy bonds. He warned his friends, many of whom later credited him with saving them from ruin, that a collapse was imminent.[69] His own wealth was secure in the debt-free Allied Chemical Corporation.[70]

Eugene was at his ranch in Wyoming on October 29, 1929, when the market crashed. The president immediately sought his advice, although it was not until September 1930, almost a year later, that Hoover informed him, "I'm going to appoint you a member of the [Federal Reserve] board and then governor. . . . I won't take no for an answer." Eugene had no intention of saying no. He felt he was the right man for the job.

Some U.S. senators did not agree, and Eugene had to endure an acrimonious confirmation hearing, during which he was accused of being a professional public office seeker.[71]

The same month her father was appointed to the Federal Reserve Board, Katharine, following in the footsteps of Florence and Bis, started secondary school at Madeira, which was then in its original building on 19th Street near Dupont Circle. Bis describes the setting as something of a slum and recalls traveling through cobblestone alleys to reach the school's five or six buildings.[72]

The sisters were fortunate that their father, not their mother, made the schooling decisions. Even though Agnes had had an unconventionally good education, which she cited, ad nauseam, as the reason for her many contributions to society, she did not take the time to seek out a similar experience for her daughters. Determined that his daughters be educated, not merely "finished" but prepared for college, Eugene chose Lucy Madeira Wing—who in 1906 had founded the all-girls preparatory school—to do the job. Libby Rowe, who also attended Madeira, explains that at the time "it wasn't fashionable to be educated, so the fashionable schools in town looked down on Madeira, and we at Madeira thought that we were the tops because we were learning something and these [other] girls weren't."[73]

When Lucy Madeira Wing decided to move her school out of the District of Columbia and build a campus, with dormitories, along the Potomac in Greenway, Virginia, Eugene first tested her commitment by challenging her to sell $212,000 in bonds, then personally loaned her, without collateral, $300,000. (The Virginia campus opened in 1931, Kay's sophomore year.) He also gave the school $25,000 worth of bonds, the interest on which was to be used for scholarships for daughters of public servants living in the District—a variation on the contributions earmarked for public service–spirited students that he had been giving to Yale.

Allegra Maynard, later Madeira's headmistress, recalled, "I didn't know [Kay's] mother and really never needed to, but I was, as all of us who are interested in the school were, very much interested in her father and *his* interest in the school. Indeed Kay's father was the person who made 'the new school' possible."[74]

Kay excelled at Madeira—athletically, academically, and extracurricularly, serving as class president, head of the student body, and editor of the school paper, *The Tatler*.[75] But despite Lucy Madeira Wing's rough-scrabble background, noble sentiments about democracy, and distaste for elitism, at Madeira Kay went about her business of studying, and playing field hockey and lacrosse, in a privileged and isolated environment. Nobody at that time was more immersed in trying to pull the country back on course than her own father, yet she was oblivious to the Depression.

*

In late 1931, Eugene tried to persuade President Hoover that the United States should lend money to help stimulate the world economy, that it should take the lead in cutting war debts and reparations. Without such action, he argued, the European economy could collapse, and aggravate the American collapse. When the president dismissed his concerns, Eugene took matters into his own hands, warning fellow Federal Reserve Board members that action was desperately needed. After the European banking structure fell and the American depression intensified, he proposed the Reconstruction Finance Corporation as a device to steady the economy. Having shepherded the measure through Congress—Hoover signed it into law in January 1932—Eugene then served as the head, simultaneously, of the RFC and the Federal Reserve. (The Democratic leader of the Senate said that his party would support the bill creating the RFC only if Meyer ran the agency.) The RFC loaned up to $2 billion to banks, insurance companies, and other financial institutions, mostly in rural areas and small cities, eventually making loans at the rate of a hundred a day to accomplish what Eugene had intended—sharply reducing the number of bank failures.[76]

In this dual role, Eugene Meyer was, many believed, the most powerful man in the financial sphere since Alexander Hamilton. He knew he had more power than any one man should have, and worried about it, but he couldn't seem to extricate himself.

Six days a week Eugene worked mornings at the Federal Reserve and afternoons at the RFC; he divided his nights (until the early-morning hours) and his Sundays between the two. "I was in the room [once] when he walked into the wall," Bis recalls, "missing the door. He was just so exhausted he couldn't see where he was going."[77]

Without telling Eugene, Agnes went to see President Hoover, whom she fancied her confidant, to warn him that if her husband did not ease up, he would die on the job.[78] Later in the year, a series of conferences left Eugene so spent that Agnes called Treasury Secretary Ogden Mills and told him that unless Eugene was removed at once from the RFC it would have no chairman and the Federal Reserve Board no governor, "as Eugene would not last a month."[79]

With the presidential election coming up, Eugene could see that politics would diminish the RFC's ability to perform. Some suspected that the Democrats, with nominee Franklin Roosevelt poised to take the White House, recognized that a continued depression was the best insurance of getting there. Hoover's supporters, especially

Eugene, were disillusioned with him. Even Agnes, with all her vaunted insider ties to the White House, could see that Hoover was a lost cause. "Eugene is trying to save the country," she wrote in her diary, "and the President is trying to save Hoover."[80]

In July 1932, a profoundly fatigued Eugene decided to give up the RFC—believing, apparently, that he had laid a strong foundation for others to build on. He turned his attention to the Federal Reserve Board, where he felt increasingly frustrated and alone as he watched members pursue "such idiot" policies as tightening money and raising interest rates—policies that were dooming the economy and the administration. Eugene, explained economics reporter Bernard Nossiter, "understood that in a depression what mattered was the stimulation of the output by every available means. The means available to the central bank is to supply more money and lower interest rates. [Other board members] confounded the old man at every turn. The old man fought them valiantly and lost."[81]

On March 4, 1933, Franklin Roosevelt's inauguration day, Agnes and Eugene, who was still governor of the Federal Reserve, were invited to a reception at the White House. Agnes was horrified by the new First Lady, and deemed the reception "undignified and shabby" and Eleanor's announcement at its end, "Now your party is over," contemptible.

Eugene returned to the White House on March 24 to meet with the president and his wife over a "tray luncheon," and to tender his resignation. Roosevelt asked him to stay on until a successor was chosen.

It remains unclear whether Eugene jumped or was pushed. Sidney Hyman says unequivocally that "Roosevelt asked him to stay on."[82] More likely, Eugene knew he had no choice but to resign. Roosevelt was determined to sweep out the old crowd. And for all of Eugene's bucking of the status quo, he was a conservative who was shocked by Roosevelt's disregard of the gold standard. "Roosevelt didn't want conservatives," says economist Robert Nathan. "Eugene Meyer was not a liberal. He was not a government activist."[83] (Interestingly, James Byrnes, FDR's head of the War Mobilization Board and Truman's secretary of state, would later pay tribute to Eugene for organizing the RFC and thus taking the government into banking; he was, in effect, "one of the earliest New Dealers."[84])

For his part, Eugene later declared that the new president "didn't know anything about finance, economics or law."[85]

Although Eugene won much editorial praise (the *New York Herald Tribune* opined that as Federal Reserve governor he had done "more than any one man, with the single exception of the President, to turn the tide of the depression"), he considered himself a failure.[86] So dispirited was he that, uncharacteristically, he took to blaming Agnes. According to Hyman, he always said, "Agnes didn't want me to [quit], because she liked dealing with Herbert Hoover." Eugene could not let go of the notion: "I should have quit and led the fight from the outside when I saw where it was going, but you see, Agnes imagined that she was being the honest broker between me and Hoover."[87]

Eugene seemed, this time, genuinely on the brink of retiring. He told some friends that he was mulling over an offer from Boss Ward to run Westchester County—which would be the equivalent of a powerful U.S. senator's going to run a city ward. He told others that he and Agnes intended to retire to Mount Kisco and grow apples for applesauce.[88] Agnes did not see applesauce in her future any more than Eugene saw Wall Street in his. He had been turning down proposals from various businesses whose principals promised to "boost his fortune into the billions."

Agnes had described Eugene as being at "death's door" when he resigned, but two weeks of rest turned him feisty, restless, and underfoot. She later quipped that she had married him for better or for worse but not for lunch.[89] She could not bear having him around, especially because, on the very day that Eugene submitted his resignation to FDR, Agnes fell in love, again—this time with Ignacy Jan Paderewski, the Polish pianist and statesman, who had played in one of Agnes's Westchester County music festivals. She hosted a dinner for him afterward, and when their eyes met over the entrée, Agnes, in her words, "let him have my soul entire." She confessed to her diary, "I do not care that he is one of the greatest living statesmen. I do not care that he is the world's greatest living artist. I am captured and held by the greatness of his soul and its indescribable beauty. Is it of any significance that on the 24th a great meteor fell from the heavens? What a day. A great star falls from the heavens. Eugene resigns from the political firmament and I fall in love with Paderewski."[90]

One morning when Eugene had been particularly grouchy, Agnes urged him to take a walk. As he was descending the grand staircase, he ran his hand along the banister, then held up his palm, glared at the dust there, and scolded Agnes, "This house is not properly run."

"You'd better go buy *The Washington Post*," she snapped.[91]

And so he did.

Chapter 3

EUGENE—
AND HIS DESCENDANTS
—GET A NEWSPAPER

Before leaving the Federal Reserve Board, Eugene had learned that *The Washington Post,* which had disintegrated apace since his look at it four years earlier, was about to be forced into a sale. One person wanted it at least as much as Eugene did. Granddaughter of Joseph Medill and first cousin of Colonel Robert McCormick, both publishers of the *Chicago Tribune,* and sister of Joseph Patterson, publisher of the New York *Daily News,* Eleanor Medill "Cissy" Patterson was a friend of Eugene's and a friend and sometime rival of Agnes's.

Three years earlier, in 1930, Cissy Patterson, then forty-nine and lacking any newspaper experience, decided she wanted to run a newspaper. She approached William Randolph Hearst, as Eugene Meyer had done earlier, with a bid to buy *The Washington Herald.* Hearst could not dismiss Cissy, a friend of his and of his mistress, former showgirl Marion Davies, as easily as he had Eugene, and eventually he agreed to hire her as *Herald* executive editor. It was a monumental leap of faith on Hearst's part, for not only had Cissy never run anything more complex than a large staff of servants, but a woman had never before been editor of an American metropolitan daily. Hearst had dispatched his general manager, Frank Knox, to Washington to introduce Cissy to the horrified nearly all-male staff: "She won't last six months," he assured them.[1]

Cissy had befriended the Meyers in 1917, just after her noisy and shocking divorce from an abusive, alcoholic Polish nobleman who had once kidnapped their baby. (The child's return was secured through the intercession of President William Howard Taft and Czar

Nicholas II.)[2] Agnes counted Cissy among those who had been warmest to her when she arrived as a stranger in the snobbish capital. She found Cissy witty and charming but also extremely feline, and resolved to "see to it that I do not get scratched."[3]

It was not long, however, before Agnes found Cissy—who was her equal in intelligence and, although more than five years older, much more than her equal in sensual appeal—disturbing and distracting. If Agnes was a phony free spirit, Cissy was a genuine one; while Agnes engaged in her tortured affairs of the heart, Cissy's sexual escapades titillated official Washington.

Although Eugene often whispered to Agnes that he thought Cissy was having an affair with this man or that, and although he was well aware that Cissy's family harbored several serious anti-Semites, the two got along well. But when the news hit Washington that Ned McLean had finally driven the *Post* into bankruptcy, Cissy's goodwill toward Eugene cooled. The paper was in receivership, unable to pay its newsprint bill, and a D.C. federal court had ordered it put up for auction so that $700,000 worth of debts would be paid. Its circulation, bled by Cissy's unforeseen success with the *Herald,* then stood at barely 50,000. Ned had been ousted as publisher by the paper's trustee and had been committed to a mental institution by his wife.

Cissy feared that no matter how ruined the paper's condition, Eugene would want it. She knew that a man like Eugene, who had so eagerly taken on a bankrupt national economy, would not be daunted by a bankrupt newspaper.

She called Hearst and pleaded with him to buy the *Post,* alone or with her. Next she called Eugene and asked if she could dine with him and Agnes that evening. She cornered him after dinner, Eugene remembered, on whether he intended to buy the *Post.* He told her he had no such intention, "no feeling about it at all"; later he would claim that Cissy's question had planted an idea in his mind that had not been there before.[4] An entry in Agnes's diary predating not only that dinner but also Eugene's resignation from the Federal Reserve, shows just how disingenuous Eugene's account was: "If he succeeds [in acquiring the *Post*], it will be a sensation and we shall have a reputation for Machiavellian behavior"[5]—referring to their having informed friends that they were retiring to Westchester County.

The auction was set for June 1, 1933, on the steps of the old *Post* building on E Street. Eugene had heard that Ned McLean's wife,

Evalyn, determined to have the paper for her sons, was trying to raise money by pawning her most famous possession, the 44.5-carat Hope diamond. Eugene was certain that Cissy would persuade Hearst to bid. Rather than bid for himself and by his very presence goad Cissy into cajoling Hearst to raise the ante, Eugene retained a young lawyer, George Hamilton, Jr., to bid for him.

Hamilton advised Eugene that the *Post*'s assets, which consisted mainly of its Associated Press franchise and its name (John Philip Sousa had immortalized it in his 1889 "Washington Post March"), were worth about $100,000. Its building and presses were so antiquated as to be barely functioning. Still, Eugene instructed the lawyer that he was willing to pay up to $2 million.[6]

The crowd gathered that evening included some of Washington's most prominent citizens: Cissy, of course, accompanied by a Hearst lawyer who would bid on behalf of the newspaper magnate; Evalyn McLean, dressed in black, with the colossal stone that she had been unable to sell or pawn fastened to her chest; Mary Harriman Rumsey, as agent for her brother, W. Averell Harriman, and for Vincent Astor; and Alice Roosevelt Longworth, there just for the fun of it. Bascom Timmons, a Washington correspondent from Texas, was there acting for publishers Amon Carter and Marshall Field III and for Jesse Jones, who had followed Eugene as RFC chairman,[7] and George Hamilton was representing an unidentified client.

Timmons opened the bidding at $250,000 and dropped out soon after. At $600,000, Mrs. McLean dropped out. The lawyer for Hearst bid $800,000. Hamilton went to $825,000. Cissy wanted Hearst's lawyer to raise him and begged the auctioneer to delay knocking down to Hamilton until she could telephone Hearst for permission. Three times the auctioneer was about to declare the property sold, and he delayed three times, until Hamilton threatened to withdraw his top bid.[8] Acknowledging that Hearst would go no higher—he had been hurt in the 1929 crash and the cracks in his empire were just becoming visible—a dejected Cissy finally admitted, "I have nothing further to bid." The paper went to Hamilton; on whose behalf he was bidding no one was certain—except Cissy.

She had quickly deduced that Hamilton was Eugene's shill and that Eugene had acquired the potentially valuable property—for which, four years earlier, he had offered $5 million—for a mere $825,000. Cissy was furious. She could easily have raised that amount on her own had she not been Hearst's employee and thus not allowed to bid against him. "Sorry we did not get the *Post*," Hearst wired, "but experience and evidence of our friendship and coopera- tion means [*sic*] more to me. I hope you are not disappointed."[9] She was exceedingly disappointed, and even as the gavel hit the auction table, Cissy was plotting her revenge.

The rest of Washington was slower in guessing the new owner, who had agreed to delay announcing his identity for the ten days it would take the bankruptcy court to issue final approval of the sale. That was plenty of time for rumors to multiply. The most persistent had Eugene Meyer as the new owner, but serving as a tool for a Republican faction that sought to harass FDR. Another had Eugene buying the paper to turn it into the booster for the 1936 Republican presidential nomination of Ogden Mills, who would finally appoint Eugene to the position he so wanted, secretary of the treasury.[10]

With the sale ruled legal and conclusive, Eugene went public on June 12. The next day the *Post*'s masthead carried his name as president and publisher, along with a statement: "I acted entirely on my own behalf, without suggestion from or discussion with any person, group or organization."[11] He assured readers that the news- paper's duty was to "the public . . . and not to the private interests of its owner," and that opinions would be confined to the editorial page—a dig at Hearst, Colonel McCormick, and the Chandlers of the *Los Angeles Times,* none of whom observed such niceties.

High-minded statements aside, the *Post* was thoroughly disreputa- ble, the poorest of the capital's five dailies.* It was diminished to twelve-page editions, and pathetic when compared with Washing- ton's top paper, the *Evening Star,* which was fat with advertisements. The *Post* had so little advertising that rates for the big department stores had slid to six cents a line.[12]

Born in 1877, two years after Eugene Meyer, in the red-light district at the foot of Capitol Hill, the *Post* had been owned since 1905 by the hugely wealthy McLean family, publisher of *The Cincin- nati Enquirer.* John McLean also owned the District's gas company, its street railway system, and one of its leading banks. His wife was a Beale, a member of the highest stratum of Washington society, dubbed by Henry Adams as Washington's "reigning empress."[13] For all that, McLean's paper was down and dirty. He cared most about

---

*The others were the *Evening Star,* the *Herald,* the *Times,* and the *Daily News,* an afternoon tabloid published by Scripps Howard.

reporting crime, scandal, "happy news," and sports. *Post* reporters were dispatched across the nation to cover baseball, but no one was sent to the 1908 presidential nominating conventions. In 1912, a front-page story about the theft of the Mona Lisa was illustrated with the wrong picture.[14]

In 1916, an income of half a million dollars a year and a relatively robust *Washington Post* passed into the inept hands of McLean's son. Like his father, Ned McLean declined to assign a reporter to the presidential campaigns or the world war but sent writers all over the country in search of baseball stories. Reporters working on breaking news were required to stop by the city desk, where they were issued streetcar tokens: taxis were out of the question, and so were long-distance telephone calls.[15]

In July 1919, Ned did find it within his resources to escalate a race riot. After two days of violence in Washington, then seventy-five percent white, the uproar appeared to be cooling; miraculously, there had been no fatalities. The *Post* returned things to the boiling point with a front-page story detailing where and when white vigilantes, incensed over "recent attacks on women by Negroes," would confront blacks. Under the headline "Mobilization for Tonight," the paper issued a call for whites to attack blacks: "The hour of assembly is 9 o'clock and the purpose is a 'clean-up' that will cause the events of the last two evenings to pale into insignificance." Nearly forty deaths resulted.[16]

Ned and Evalyn—daughter of an Irishman who had "struck it rich" in the Colorado goldfields—lived a life of depravity, squandering their fortune on alcohol, drugs, and dinners for two hundred, which often featured prostitutes standing nude on pedestals in the garden. Warren Harding, Ned's drinking, poker, and golf buddy, was invariably in attendance.

Ned often became so rum-soaked that to hoist his drinking hand to his mouth, he was forced to fashion a bar towel into a wrist-neck pulley.[17] Evalyn would later charge that Ned brought his mistress to editorial conferences and made the *Post* building the scene of all-night debaucheries.

Ned and Evalyn were regulars at the White House (which Alice Longworth referred to as a "saloon" and a "brothel" in those years—during Prohibition, Harding openly served liquor upstairs, and he entertained his girlfriends in a White House closet while the First Lady pounded on the door[18]). Flo Harding did object when

Ned, urinating into the East Room fireplace, misaimed and soaked the leg of the Belgian ambassador.[19] But she did not object too loudly, because she wanted her husband to be reelected, and the *Post* was his shameless mouthpiece.

Ned McLean's hiring practices were, at best, unconventional. John Riseling, for example, a German-Irish Catholic from Philadelphia, who went to *The Philadelphia Inquirer* straight out of high school and was "loaded with . . . 'street smarts,' " walked into the front office one day in 1923, just as the Sunday editor "was being poured into an ambulance with an aggravated case of the d.t.'s." Riseling immediately became Sunday editor—at the top of a one-man staff—and eventually city editor. He replaced the often absent police reporter Joe Grant—who was actually a D.C. police detective whom Ned had met in a saloon brawl and to whom he had offered a job[20]—with Shirley Povich, who had also joined the paper in 1923. Povich was then only eighteen (and his only connection to newspapering was that he had been Ned's golf caddy), but Ned started him at the top, as sports editor at the enormous salary of $50 a week.

Ned was headed for disaster. His friend Warren Harding died on the return from an official trip to Alaska, some claimed by his own hand. The *Post* was hemorrhaging money and readers, helped along by Ned's most eccentric hiring decision: in 1923 he named as editor another Harding pal, Colonel George Harvey, a vicious anti-Catholic, anti-Semite, and racist. It was in Colonel Harvey's smoke-filled hotel room that Harding had won the Republican presidential nomination in 1920; Harvey also had coined Calvin Coolidge's campaign slogan, "Coolidge or Chaos," and he lived in the White House, writing *Post* editorials and Coolidge's campaign speeches with barely a pause in between.[21]

Through it all, Ned was carrying on an outrageously expensive affair with Rose Davies, sister of Hearst's mistress Marion; the two publishers were thus out-of-wedlock brothers-in-law. According to Frank Waldrop, later *Washington Times-Herald* editor, "Ned McLean was drunk all the time. Nobody was running the *Post*. I used to know a fellow who was in the business department down there. He said, 'Hell, Ned McLean came in there when he needed some money and just scooped everything out of the cash drawer. He took $90,000 in cash right out of the till in one year.' "[22]

Eugene Meyer approached the running of *The Washington Post* with real joy. One reporter observed that "the *Post* is for him—in a luxury sense—what steam yachts and strings of race horses may be for some other wealthy men."[23] The day Eugene took possession, he stopped at the paper's "miserable" cafeteria for a cup of tea and discovered he had left his wallet elsewhere. He explained to the cashier that he could not pay: "I haven't a dime to my name. I just bought a newspaper."[24] On that same day, recalled Shirley Povich, "we had a party at the Willard Hotel, we invited him, and inevitably the crap game started. . . . [He] had the dice at this point. And here is Mr. Meyer . . . famous banker, with all of his lofty associations in world affairs, but he was street smart, too. . . . When he held the dice and [took] his first roll, he [said], 'Come on, seven. I gotta meet the payroll.' "[25]

When the first flush of excitement faded, Eugene began to see just what a herculean task lay before him. He was fifty-seven, an age when men of his stature were lazily dictating their memoirs, but he was faced with reviving a paper that he himself called "mentally, morally, physically and in every other way bankrupt"[26]—and at a time of momentous change, when every day brought big news. A week of Eugene's tenure had not passed before FDR signed legislation giving the government control over industry in an effort to bring the nation out of the Depression. Five weeks had not passed before Hitler pronounced the Nazi Party Germany's only political party and threatened to punish parents who opposed him, by taking away their children.

Eugene's confidence was not much boosted when he realized that the dregs of writers and editors who had stuck to the disintegrating *Post*—Ned McLean had slashed salaries and, during bankruptcy, the receiver had cut wages an additional ten percent—could not even spell the new publisher's name correctly.[27] Although Rhodes scholars and Ivy League graduates were not much in evidence on any newspaper of that era, the derelicts Eugene had inherited showed little sign of having attended grade school. They were most proficient at lighting matches under cockroaches[28] and spearing rats with letter openers.

Still, several promising people had survived the McLean era. City editor John Riseling stayed on, and so did Shirley Povich. Merlo Pusey, a Mormon from Utah, joined the *Post* in 1928, became a distinguished editorial writer, a poet, and eventually the biographer of Charles Evans Hughes and Eugene Meyer; and Edward Folliard, a *Post* reporter in the McLean years who had left for the *Herald,* returned to the *Post* in 1934.

The paper's Gothic-Romanesque building, an ornate, six-story cut-stone edifice at 1337 E Street NW, on the same block as the National Theater and across the street from the District Building, was variously described as antiquated, reminiscent of castles along the Rhine, and "uncomfortable, crowded, a very difficult place to work." Kay would later characterize it as "a ramshackle, creaking structure that rattled violently when the presses rolled."[29] The two dilapidated presses broke down so often that an electrician was permanently on duty.[30] A fireman should have been also, because the pressroom—in the basement of the building, whose all-wood interior included a center staircase that went up the six floors to an attic—regularly caught fire. "In the summer the heat would rise out of the pressroom,"[31] recalls Elsie Carper, who went to the *Post* in 1939 to file clippings and stayed fifty years. For the bedraggled staff in this building without air-conditioning, things were hellish. That the cage elevator broke down regularly or, when it did run, ran so slowly that going up the stairs in hundred-plus heat seemed preferable did not help morale.

Harry Gladstein, the *Post*'s circulation manager, termed the paper "a daily miracle." When copies came off the rickety presses they were "tied into bundles and placed on the old conveyor belt which led literally to a hole in the wall at the rear of the building. . . . If no one was readily available in the alley to take the bundles, they just fell to the ground."[32]

Eugene often said that he considered his purchase of the *Post* a gift from him to the people of Washington.[33] He let the equipment and the building rot and put his money into the editorial page, setting out to hire some good men, columnists especially. Fellow publishers were flabbergasted at the salaries he offered: as much as $25,000—and this in the midst of the Depression.[34]

He did not bother much with upgrading local, national, and international reporting. He knew that competing against *The New York Times* for international news and the *Evening Star* for local would take decades and even more millions than he was willing to spend. On the national side, one man continued to cover the State Department and the White House. On the international side, editorial-page writers pontificated on the state of the world from their desks on E Street. Coverage came from the wire services, or from *Post* editors regurgitating State Department press releases, or from an occasional reporter dispatched via streetcar to cover a diplomatic reception. A

Post reporter once remarked that the paper "will cover any international conference there is, as long as it is in the first taxi zone."[35]

Eugene had wanted to own a newspaper because he cared about influencing policymakers—as British press magnate Lord Northcliffe put it, "Of all the American newspapers, I would prefer to own the Washington *Post* because it reaches the breakfast tables of the members of Congress."[36] So what Eugene needed most were editors and writers who could marshal the facts and persuade.

That first year, Eugene hired as editorial-page editor thirty-nine-year-old Felix Morley. A Rhodes scholar, son of an eminent mathematician at Haverford College, brother of novelist Christopher Morley, and a Quaker, Morley had been director of the Geneva office of the League of Nations and was a veteran of *The Baltimore Sun* and beats in the United States, the Far East, and Europe. "If the rest of the *Post* was held in generally poor esteem for years to come," wrote Hedley Donovan, soon to be a *Post* reporter and later editor in chief at Time Inc., "Morley's editorial page would quickly be read and respected."[37]

Having led his life on a plateau so far above general humanity, Eugene had a basic ignorance of why people read a newspaper. "Meyer spent a lot of money, and he got the carriage trade such as it was, which is only a handful among the policymakers in the government," explains Frank Waldrop. "But he didn't have a readership that had to look at [the paper] every day to see what the hell was happening next. Meyer thought that having a serious attitude was what publishing was all about."[38]

Eugene knew nothing about sports. Strolling through the sports department one day in 1934, he noted general gloom—the previous year the Washington Senators had won the American League pennant; the next year the team was in seventh place. "What's wrong with the Senators?" he asked Shirley Povich. "It's their pitching," Povich explained. "Can we buy a pitcher?" Eugene asked. "How much do they cost?"[39]

Comics were even more of a mystery to him—a detail not lost on Cissy Patterson, who, when the *Post* was in bankruptcy, had taken over its contract for several New York *Daily News–Chicago Tribune* syndicated strips (the syndicate was owned by the Patterson-McCormick family). These were not just any comics; their characters were better known than the president: Dick Tracy, Andy Gump, Skeezix, and Winnie Winkle. Cissy argued that the comics were hers to keep, that the sale of the *Post* had voided its five-year contract. Eugene responded to Cissy's potentially fatal maneuver by asking, "Are comics important?" Yes, his horrified business manager told him,[40] and he advised him that if he let Cissy take them, the *Post* was doomed—no matter how many summa cum laude Harvard graduates wrote for the editorial page.

Cissy pulled out all the stops. While the comics were still running in the *Post,* she also ran them, bannering her triumph—a judge had dissolved the restraining order *Post* lawyers sought forbidding Cissy to run them—and urging *Post* readers to switch to the *Herald,* sure to be the exclusive outlet for the comics.[41] Eugene's lawyers sued the *Herald* for "illegal use," claiming Meyer had bought the *Post* as well as its comics. Cissy called Eugene to remind him that her brother Joe had helped create *Dick Tracy* and *Gasoline Alley* and had named Winnie Winkle and Andy Gump. The comics, she added, were a "family affair." Meyer replied that family ties were irrelevant: he owned the rights to the cartoons in Washington, and that was that.[42]

For nearly two years, the case climbed from court to higher court, as each ruled in Eugene's favor. Finally Cissy petitioned the U.S. Supreme Court, which refused, giving Eugene his victory. He celebrated by bannering a six-column cartoon of a Supreme Court justice pointing to the front page of the *Post* and ordering Dick Tracy, Skeezix, and the others, "To your Post!"

Cissy asked Eugene for permission to distribute the following Sunday's color comics, which had already been printed. He agreed but rubbed her nose in her defeat, asking her "to acknowledge the courtesy in a box on the front page of the news section" and instructing her how to word her acknowledgment: "The comics [are] appearing by the courtesy of Eugene Meyer, who, in the future, will have the sole right to publish them in Washington." Just to make sure, the *Post* carried its own note on Saturday.

This was all too much for Cissy, who at great expense scrapped the comics, and left the *Post* to bestow empty credit on itself.[43] She sent her chauffeur to Crescent Place with a package, beautifully wrapped with flowers. "How nice of Cissy," Agnes said as Eugene peeled away the ribbons and orchids, freesia and sweet pea, and forget-me-nots. But inside the box was a pound of raw hamburger meat with a card that read: "So as not to disappoint you—take your pound of flesh." His moment of puzzlement was interrupted by Agnes's groan: "It must be a pound of flesh for a dirty Jewish Shylock."[44]

"I think she was always ashamed of having done it," says Frank Waldrop, but "she was goddamned mad and wanted to hit him in the balls."[45] Hope Ridings Miller, who joined the women's section of the *Post* that year (she eventually became its society editor), says without hesitation that Cissy was anti-Semitic.[46] So does Luvie Pearson, wife of columnist Drew Pearson and a film critic for Cissy's paper. "She was anti-Semitic, no doubt about that."*[47]

Although Eugene's commitment to a first-class editorial page would never weaken, he did learn something from his fight with Cissy: that the mass audience newspapers need if they are to attract the advertising that will make them profitable cannot be found among devotees of distinguished commentary.† He came to understand also that his fellow publishers, instead of thinking him a shrewd operator and feeling threatened by the caliber of men he was hiring, were having a hearty laugh at his expense. According to Hedley Donovan, "He came to realize that he was making a fool of himself in front of other publishers who thought this was a rich man being taken for a ride."[50] As he watched the *Post* lose money at an alarming pace, Eugene reached a pivotal conclusion: "In the long run, if you're going to have a free newspaper, it has to make money. It should not rest upon a family fortune."[51] After making "every mistake in the book," he determined that he would stick to his goal of upgrading the credentials of his employees but would cease the indulgence of outlandish salaries.[52]

When Hedley Donovan, a Rhodes scholar, was hired in 1937, he was paid $25 a week, half of what eighteen-year-old Shirley Povich had fetched from Ned McLean fourteen years earlier.[53] Eugene invited Donovan and another new reporter, John Oakes, whose credentials were even more impressive than Donovan's—Rhodes scholar, magna cum laude graduate of Princeton, nephew of Adolph

---

*Eventually Cissy and Eugene made up. He had no desire to publicize her anti-Semitic stunt by allowing the grudge to fester into Washington legend. Eugene did not put anti-Semitism at the top of his list of objectionable behavior, and he seemed willing to forget and forgive. When the wife of Assistant Secretary of State Sumner Welles mistakenly invited the two to the same dinner party, Cissy rushed to embrace Eugene and "they talked the whole evening."[48] But a reconciliation between Cissy and Agnes was more problematic—as Hope Miller says, it became "a Mexican standoff."[49]

†Numbers at the *Post* were improving, but only relative to the depths to which they had plunged. In the first year of his ownership, Eugene boosted readership by 25,000 and advertising by fifty percent, but annual losses remained heavy.

Ochs of *The New York Times*—to "his grand embassy-style residence" for dinner. The two elaborately qualified and underpaid young men were, Donovan recounted, fed "very well in a dining room decorated by Rodin and Cézanne." Then Eugene "broke out the brandy, pushed back his chair, and said expansively, 'Well, when do you young men think you will be worth your salaries?' . . . I mustered enough audacity to say, 'It would be hard not to be.' "[54]

Robert Estabrook, later editor of the *Post*'s editorial page, was reluctant to take a job at the paper because he had been offered ten dollars more at a paper in Schenectady.[55] Frank Dennis liked to tell the story of "the guy [who] put a want-ad in the paper for a lost dog. He offered $100 for the return of the dog, and after a week nobody had shown up or given any information about the dog, so he went down to the paper. There was only one person there: the receptionist. And he said, 'Where is everybody?' The receptionist said, 'They're all out looking for the dog.' "[56]

Every couple of months Eugene would cut the number of copyboys, leaving their duties to top editors. He did his part too, stopping at the *Post* after dinner. "He'd walk around with his big cigar," Hedley Donovan recalled, "still in black tie, asking $25-a-week reporters . . . what they were working on . . . who they had interviewed, had they gotten anything the other papers didn't have."[57] He would return to Crescent Place in a taxi, having let his driver, Phillips, retire for the night. He did not get out of the taxi without asking the driver whether he took the *Post,* if not why not, and would he let Meyer arrange for home delivery to start immediately. Later, in a speech, Kay recounted that her father "badgered all his friends for ads" and that she was once "taken to buy a dress—the only time such a thing occurred—from an advertiser whose shop was on the second floor of a building on unfashionable G Street."[58]

Shirley Povich was in Eugene's office "just after he'd dictated a letter to some New York bank president. Charlie Paradise, his secretary, was taking the dictation and Mr. Meyer's last words were, 'Charlie, send that air mail.' About four minutes later, he bethought himself, he called Charlie Paradise back and [said], 'Charlie, this is Friday, the bank won't be open Saturday, send that regular mail.' I knew then that we were in good hands."[59] Another *Post* staffer was charged with delivering multiple copies of each edition of the city's afternoon papers to the newsroom. "One day I was coming up on the elevator . . . with about seven copies of the *Times,* the [*Evening*] *Star,* and the [*Daily*] *News.* And Eugene Meyer got on the elevator. He

stared at me and the papers for the estimated twenty minutes or so
. . . that it took to go from the first to the second floor. And finally,
just before the door opened on the second floor, he [said], 'Tell me,
are we paying retail for those papers?' "[60]

Eugene also came to realize that the prestige of covering Washington in the New Deal days, when all eyes were fixed on the capital,
went a long way toward compensating for paltry wages. Men like
Hedley Donovan and John Oakes knew that the thinner the ranks,
the faster they could move up. It would take Donovan only two years
to move to the national desk; at age twenty-seven he was covering the
White House—at *The New York Times* he would have toiled until
age forty or even fifty before reaching that level.[61] Oakes had barely
gotten to know the desk sergeant's name when he moved from the
police beat to covering Congress. Because Donovan had been to
Oxford, he was invited to write for the brains section of the Sunday
paper, and became its authority on British politics.[62]

In 1935, with parsimony in mind, Eugene hired a new managing
editor, Alexander "Casey" Jones, a tightfisted, hard-boiled, hot-
tempered conservative, former city editor of *The Milwaukee Journal.*
In his history of *The Washington Post,* Chalmers Roberts, himself a
Post reporter, described Casey Jones as "a gravel-voiced conservative of Welsh descent . . . [with] the instincts of the 'Front Page'
school of journalism."[63] Frank Dennis, who was hired by Jones,
recalls that "every once in a while Casey would get some kind of
tantrum which would cause him to write an editorial which we would
print on the front page at his dictation. It wouldn't be labeled 'Editorial,' but it would be boxed."[64] He liked hard news, hated "interpre-
tive writing," and ordered his reporters simply to "write what the
man said."[65] He was studiously anti-intellectual, to the point of being
lowbrow. Dennis remembers Jones giving him "a little briefing about
what the *Post* was all about. He told me what a wonderful staff he
had. He told me about Shirley Povich, he told me about the editor,
Felix Morley, and he told me about the society editor, Hope Miller.
He said, 'She's the best society editor in town. . . . She's the only one
who's invited to the embassies of the European community. . . . All
the other society editors in town are invited to the nigger embassies.
But . . . Hope is the only one who can get into the real embassies.' "[66]

The Washington Post continued to lose money and gain respect.
The paper made news when FDR praised one of its editorials as an
honest and clear reflection of his foreign policy views. "*The Washing-*

ton Post has been raised from collapse to an honored place in the first row of American journals," a reporter for *The Christian Science Monitor* wrote, noting the presidential tribute.[67]

FDR was much less enamored of Eugene Meyer when he helped to smash the president's court-packing plan. Roosevelt claimed that he wanted to add justices to the Supreme Court because the "nine old men" already on it could not keep up with the work load. Eugene was not alone in understanding that what really concerned FDR was that the justices had declared unconstitutional several pieces of key New Deal legislation, but unlike others, Eugene was in a position to do something about it. When Chief Justice Charles Evans Hughes assured his friend Eugene Meyer that the justices were not behind in their work, Eugene dispatched his paper's Capitol Hill reporter to interview Hughes. The reporter humored Eugene but had no intention of contacting Hughes; reporters simply did not interview Supreme Court justices. A few days later, Meyer asked the reporter if he had seen the chief justice yet. When he explained that he had not and why, Meyer insisted that he go immediately. Instead of scolding him, as the reporter expected, Chief Justice Hughes fed him facts that proved FDR's argument spurious. The resulting story—backed up with editorials—more than any other ensured the death of the court-packing plan.[68]

The auction of the *Post* was big news in the late spring of 1933. Even the girls at Madeira, busy with exams, had wondered who the buyer might be. Nancy White, who roomed next to her and whose father was a top executive at Hearst, joined in the speculation with Kay Meyer. "It never occurred to me," Kay said later, "that the buyer . . . could have been my father."[69]

Nearly two weeks later, in Mount Kisco, Kay heard her mother ask her father, "What's next? Now that you have it, what do you plan to do with the *Post*?" Agnes answered Kay's puzzled look, " 'Oh, didn't we tell you? We forgot to tell you. We bought the *Post*.' . . . The family was not even aware that I didn't know."[70]

She went about her business, still largely undirected, unconsidered by her parents, ready, the next year, to enter Vassar College, not because it was necessarily the right school for her, but because Bis had gone there for a while, and so had Miss Madeira.

Chapter 4

KATHARINE STARTS HER EDUCATION

Vassar was so much the school of choice for Madeira graduates that they went there as naturally as they had coming-out parties. Kay did precisely what was expected of her, enrolling at the all-girls college in Poughkeepsie, New York, in the fall of 1934.

Florence had chosen Bryn Mawr, which, with its aura of being the brainiest of the Seven Sisters, appealed to her; but she soon transferred to Radcliffe. Bis had gone to Vassar—where she was a classmate of Mary McCarthy's and an inspiration for a character in *The Group*—but she got no "sparks" there and left after two years to spend her junior year in Munich, and then went to Barnard and Columbia.

In those years, Vassar was still considered a premarital perch for nice girls from good Republican families. Kay would later recall herself then as "an unquestioning Republican" who, like her parents, supported Herbert Hoover over Franklin Roosevelt.[1] But by the time Kay arrived at Vassar, only the most unreflective debutante could escape the world crisis. "You can't forget that this was the [time of the] Depression and the rise of Mussolini and Hitler," observes Connie Dimock Ellis, Kay's best friend at Vassar. "You couldn't just sit back. There was loud discussion going on."[2] Economics overtook English as the most heavily subscribed major.[3]

The distinguished and liberal faculty—which in a 1932 straw vote went as predictably for FDR as the students went for Hoover[4]—began to exert more influence. It became fashionable for girls with the most knee-jerk Republican notions suddenly to question their world of privilege as they confronted, at least in the classroom, some harsh realities. There was, says Vivian Leibman Cadden, who was among a new breed of Vassar student—Russian Jewish, left-wing activist, from New York City, on scholarship—"a wonderful excitement that pervaded that campus."[5]

Jane Whitbread Beyer, a junior when Katharine was a freshman, remembers "picketing at strikes in the Hudson Valley, and marching on Main Street in a peace demonstration, and going by the busload to Albany to protest loyalty oaths for teachers and students."[6] Kay Meyer was among the eighty Vassar students at that Albany demonstration. Participating took no special pluck. Elizabeth Welt Frank, also two years ahead of Kay, recalls that Dean C. Mildred Thompson paid the bus fare for a couple of the girls to go to Albany. She reportedly assured the students that "we had a right to do whatever we wanted as long as we didn't use the college name in what we were doing."[7] In fact, Vassar president Henry Noble MacCracken, a liberal, albeit a mild one, led the delegation.

The faculty put on a play in 1936 to raise money for the Republican side in the Spanish Civil War and, in a straw vote that year, went for socialist Norman Thomas. "In some ways," says Vivian Cadden, "I would have thought that it might take courage not to be a liberal."[8] Betty Frank recalls that "Vassar had a reputation for being a hotbed of radicalism where rich girls were sent and turned into communists."*[9]

Still, Vassar in the mid-1930s remained a ladylike sanctum with the most conventional notions of decorum. Betty Frank, news editor of the college paper in 1935, describes the aftermath of an interview she conducted with journalist Max Lerner on a train to New York City. She was to ride only as far as necessary to get the story, but they were talking so intently about Thorstein Veblen that she ended up accompanying Lerner all the way to Manhattan. "I got called into the president's office the next day. I didn't look like a Vassar girl. I had dirty white saddle shoes on. I don't think he was concerned about the possible immorality of my going to New York with a guy

---

*Even a decade before Kay's time, parents complained that their daughters had been "ruined" by the college. William Van Duzer Lawrence, the founder of Sarah Lawrence, sent his daughters to Vassar in the 1920s; when Vassar president MacCracken solicited him for a donation, according to Harold Taylor, later president of Sarah Lawrence, "Mr. Lawrence said he wouldn't give a nickel to Vassar. He sent his girls there and they came back argumentative and man-hating. If he had a college, he'd want one where they were taught to be womanly. That's how [Sarah Lawrence] got started."[10]

who had quite a reputation as a ladies' man, but he didn't like me not to be very well dressed."*[11]

Still, in the midst of some outmoded rules and quaint concerns presided a predominantly female faculty that was truly distinguished and made Vassar, among the Seven Sisters, second only to Bryn Mawr as a school for girls who were serious about academics. "The women teachers were singular in their intellectual stature," says Jane Beyer, "and their support of the idea that you could be what you wanted to be."[13]

Perhaps the most respected and influential was Helen Lockwood, "a left-wing English teacher" and "a great force," in the words of Betty Frank. In the economics department reigned Mabel Newcomb, the only woman invited to the Bretton Woods Conference, at which plans for the International Monetary Fund and the World Bank were established. Hallie Flanagan, who ran the experimental theater, directed plays that drew New York City critics to Poughkeepsie. Another leading light was Winnifred Smith, who taught modern European drama and who, according to Vivian Cadden, "knew Shaw and Ibsen and Pirandello. She was [one of those] great spinster schoolteachers who had devoted their lives to scholarship."[14]

Eugene noted Kay's interest in journalism at Madeira, and he recognized that she was different from her sisters. While Florence floated from passion to passion, eventually proclaiming that she would dance professionally or die, and Bis, who had so many talents—for the violin, for athletics, for theater and film—seemed to have no clear idea how to channel them, Kay was eager to work. Eugene had noted approvingly that, unlike Bis, who had spent most of her days at Vassar riding horses, "Kay plans to be a student, not an athlete."[15]

Kay lost no time in joining the campus paper, the *Miscellany News,* and in shedding her parents' Republican conservatism. The two decisions were related. It was the paper's editors, rather than the leaders of various campus groups, who organized protest activities, including the Albany demonstration. Connie Ellis describes the *Miscellany News* staff as "outspokenly to the left"; Betty Frank says the paper was a "hotbed of college radicalism."[16]

As left-wing students of that era went, Kay was moderate. "She

---

*Bryn Mawr girls affected what Bis terms "a false skein of sophistication which in dress consisted of being dirty." She recalls that once when Florence and the daughter of *New York Herald Tribune* columnist Mark Sullivan took the Paoli local to Bryn Mawr, another passenger dropped a dollar in each of their laps as he walked by them.[12]

wasn't a Red or anything like that," says Jane Beyer.[17] She lobbied against the loyalty oath, helped found the Liberal Club, and pushed for passage of the American Youth Act "proclaiming solidarity between students and workers."

Kay qualified for the twice-weekly paper in the usual way—by trying out for a spot as an "apprentice editor," that is, a reporter. She was sent on assignment, had to write a story, and then was to await the decision of the paper's staff. Jane Beyer, who became editor in chief, admits that "we chose the people whose reporting was considered the best and, I suppose unconsciously, the people we liked the best."[18]

Kay remained shy, humble, self-effacing—never mentioning, during her tryout or after, that she was the daughter of the publisher of *The Washington Post.* When Kay was chosen as a freshman reporter, Beyer claims, she wasn't even aware Kay's family owned the paper. "She was not an aggressive person at all," says Beyer.[19] Betty Frank recalls her as "quite retiring" and "self-apologetic." She was not the kind of girl who would become the protégée of a brilliant professor like Helen Lockwood or who would, after hours—*Miscellany News* girls had no curfew—go out drinking with a professor, as Betty Frank did with Alan Porter, "a brilliant man, crazy, a communist." Kay lacked the verve of Betty and Jane, who went to Val-Kill—the cottage-of-her-own that Eleanor Roosevelt kept at Hyde Park—to interview the First Lady, while her friend Nancy Cook lounged on a nearby couch, a "fuzzy, fleecy blanket over her tummy" and a "forbidding look" on her face.[20]

Kay was tall and pretty—with dimples, bright eyes, black curly hair[21]—and, once she got comfortable, even outgoing. She looked up to the older and more journalistically accomplished Jane Beyer, who responded. She found Kay "very attractive to be with. She was very interested in being on a newspaper and very interested in hearing what you had to say and [in] being exposed to a [leftist] point of view."[22]

Kay certainly did not flaunt her wealth or her family position. If there had been any of that, says Vivian Cadden, "I certainly would have been sensitive to it, because I was probably the poorest of any of them."[23] Her friends recall Kay dressing just like everyone else—in worn-out, dirty saddle oxfords, tweed skirts, and Brooks Brothers sweaters.[24]

Had Agnes paid attention, she would have found Kay's dress

unfashionable and masculine, but of course Agnes did not pay attention. Kay's letters home were routinely answered by her mother's secretary with the opening, "Your mother says . . ."[25]

Jane Beyer remembers going with Kay one weekend to Mount Kisco, where she was impressed with "the sort of feudal character of the mansion," and another weekend to Washington, where the front doors were "at least [nine feet] high. I had a hard time finding the bell." (In its central city location, Crescent Place was so outsize that it was sometimes mistaken for the Library of Congress.) She noted how quickly Kay clammed up in the company of her mother. The guest at lunch was the head of the Liberty League, a "very reactionary lady. I remember arguing with everyone just the way I would anywhere about politics and so forth." Jane had the impression that "Agnes and Eugene were exhibiting me to this woman as a brilliant radical." Kay seemed rather embarrassed by this and, in her mother's presence, said "even less than usual."[26]

Kay straddled the traditional and the new at Vassar. She was elected to Daisy Chain—the sophomores judged to be the prettiest,* who carried the braid of daisies through which seniors marched at commencement. But she also traveled to Ohio State University for the founding convention of the American Student Union, an organization often, and justifiably, charged with being "dominated" by communists.[28]

Kay was accustomed to the *Miscellany News* girls and their charmingly naive "we couldn't care less" attitude about her father's position. The American Student Union activists were much more sophisticated, and Kay Meyer, hardly a leading journalist or activist, was one of only five people elected to the ASU executive committee.† "They knew by that time who she was," explains Betty Frank; she has no doubt that that was why the ASU wanted Kay on its board.[29] "Perhaps they saw her as a malleable political innocent, or had an eye on her bankroll, or her potential publicity value."[30]

Kay mixed daily with Jewish students—in the ASU and at the *Miscellany News,* where, according to Vivian Cadden, there was

---

*According to Jane Beyer, a committee of girls who had been among the chosen in past years went around to the various dining halls every night and "sat and eyed everyone and decided who they thought were the likeliest prospects."[27]

†Members of that charter ASU executive committee included Molly Yard, later head of the National Organization for Women; James Wechsler, later the crusading liberal editor of the *New York Post;* and George Edwards, later a judge on the Sixth Circuit Court of Appeals.

"probably a higher proportion than in the college itself."[31] Still, Jews were scarce at Vassar, probably because of a quota.[32] In later years, Kay said that she did not realize she had any Jewish blood until somebody at Vassar asked her how it felt to be Jewish,[33] but there is no evidence that she was moved to consider her paternal heritage. "I don't think anyone had any sense of her being Jewish any more than she had a sense herself," says Vivian Cadden.[34]

In 1936, Andrew Mellon, former secretary of the treasury and former U.S. ambassador to Great Britain, called on Eugene Meyer with an offer: to pay Meyer all that he had put into the *Post*—which was plenty, as the paper was then losing in excess of a million dollars a year—and a million dollars on top of that. "I realize, Mr. Mellon," Eugene replied, "that in facing you, I face resources of at least $300 million, but without being discourteous, I must tell you right now that you haven't enough money to buy the independent sort of newspaper I am trying to build."[35]

Determined not to sell, Eugene knew he had to ready a successor. Although he had bought the *Post* to influence government rather than to create a family institution, he felt he had a responsibility to keep the paper in the family and out of the hands of the likes of a Cissy Patterson. But who could succeed him? Agnes, he knew, would have no compunction about using the paper to promote whatever person or cause happened to catch her fancy that week. And in Bill and his two older daughters he saw no interest or aptitude.

But in Kay he recognized a seriousness of purpose absent in his other children. According to Bis, Eugene had come to see Kay as being most like himself. He paid her the compliment of comparing her to a Chinese doll: "If somebody knocked her over she'd just pop up again." "Watch my Kay, she's the one," he told Alice Roosevelt Longworth. "She's got a hard mind. She'd make a great business-man."[36] She was also obviously interested in a particular business. She had been editor of the Madeira *Tatler* and had then devoted much time to the Vassar paper. The summer after Eugene bought the *Post,* while Agnes and the rest of the family went to Mount Kisco, Kay worked at the paper as a copygirl. The next summer she worked for the Mount Vernon, New York, *Argus.*

Still, it was difficult for a man of Eugene's background to imagine a woman—a mere girl at that point—as a worthy successor. "I worked on the paper when I was young," Kay later explained, "but there was never any idea of my going on it permanently."[37]

Bill would have been the natural successor, but Eugene knew that his son did not have what it took. "Bill wasn't anything like his father," says Roswell Gilpatric, later the family lawyer and a member of the *Post* board.[38] By temperament, says June Bingham, he was "a sweet man, really sweet, a gentle soul, which would have been hard work in that household. And hard to be the only boy—two older sisters and two younger sisters, powerful mother and very powerful father, and expectations that were probably just beyond his powers and his desires."[39]

Bill had gone to Yale, as his father had expected him to, but he lacked diligence and purpose. His passions were not for journalism and certainly not for banking, but for radical politics and for flying and diving. Bill once informed his father he wanted to abandon his studies and train as a night flier. Rather than talk to his son himself, Eugene summoned his friend Captain Edward Rickenbacker to Mount Kisco to dissuade him.

But Eugene could not dissuade Bill from following another, in Eugene's eyes even more precarious, course. While at Yale, Bill tried to learn more about his Jewish heritage, and he was troubled by the stringent quota at the school.[40] He befriended Edgar Siskin, a graduate student in anthropology, son and grandson of rabbis, and himself the rabbi of a local congregation, Temple Mishkin Israel. Bill soon became the president of the Jewish student organization, and on more than one Friday evening, he conducted the service and gave the sermon from the pulpit of the temple. "He was very much interested in Judaism," says Rabbi Siskin. "He had read a good deal about it and, I think, had more or less made up his mind to identify [himself] as a Jew. . . . He told me about his struggle with his Jewishness, the fact that he had not been raised as a Jew."[41]

Eugene feared that his son was doing everything he could to alienate himself from the establishment at Yale. He marched much further to the left than Kay and her friends at Vassar, and he would later date Vivian Cadden, whom Betty Frank describes as "a Russian Jewish poor girl, who was born with a copy of Lenin in each hand."[42] Eugene often said being left-wing in one's youth was just fine because there would be plenty of time later to "hobnob with conservatives."[43] But Bill was carrying youthful indiscretion too far. One *Post* employee invited to the Meyer mansion paused in the drawing room before a portrait of a young man. "That's my son Bill," said Eugene. "He's a radical."[44]

Bill ranked ninth nationwide in the collegiate diving league, and as his grades suffered, Eugene and Agnes worried that he was "water-logged." They arranged for him to study at the London School of Economics under Harold Laski, a British political scientist and family friend. Bill and Bis, who had gone to work for director Alexander Korda, shared a flat in London.[45] As a result of his studies with Laski, a Labourite who verged toward Marxism—he believed in the inevitability of revolution in Britain and abroad—Bill went to do research in the Soviet Union. While there he received an invitation from the Russians to stay and teach diving.

Bill reluctantly went back to Yale but reported to his father that the Soviets were developing "a really constructive society." He became so preoccupied with the Spanish Civil War that Eugene feared he would go off to fight for the Loyalists. In a letter to his father Bill admitted he would go to Spain if he thought he could help fight fascism. Later, he was falsely accused of recruiting for the Loyalists.[46]

If Bill was not the successor Eugene wanted, neither was Florence or Bis. After studying ballet in the Soviet Union and France, Florence was about to make her New York debut as a "featured dancer" in *The Eternal Road,* a Max Reinhardt spectacle with music by Kurt Weill.[47] Bis, who had studied violin at Columbia and played with the Columbia and Juilliard orchestras, went off to London to work for Korda and then to Hollywood to be a scriptwriter for Selznick International.[48]

Although Ruth was only a teenager in 1936, it was already clear that she had only modest intellectual ambitions. Gentle and good-natured, she was, according to one friend, "pretty much off in the corner. People were saying, 'Poor Ruthie.' "[49] Sidney Hyman recalls her as "a sweet, loving person" who didn't quite fit in.[50] Another family friend describes her as "sort of left over, pretty much neglected by her parents, an underachiever." According to Harold Taylor, "She wasn't as smart and as strong-minded as the others [in the family]."[51]

It was Agnes who most wanted to run the *Post,* for a number of reasons—all of them the wrong ones. For openers, she could not bear it that Cissy Patterson had made a big splash at the *Herald;* the paper was taken seriously and read, as one of her biographers wrote, "in the big homes and embassies on Massachusetts Avenue." Then there were the stories of Cissy's sexual magnetism, of her turning up at night in the grimy city room, wearing Oriental brocaded pajamas, and having such presence that "all eyes riveted on her when she made an entrance."[52] (Sidney Epstein, then a sixteen-year-old copyboy at the *Herald*, recalls Cissy in her crimson silk pajamas, the pants "billowing" as she entered the newsroom flanked by two gigantic dogs that "petrified" the reporters.[53])

Agnes comforted herself that at least Cissy did not own the *Herald*; she was, at the end of the day, merely an employee. But even that changed—and at Eugene's expense. Hearst found himself millions in debt, unable to meet his payroll and lurching toward bankruptcy. Cissy borrowed money against her *Chicago Tribune* stock and raised $1 million to help Hearst stave off the inevitable.[54]

Faced with the need to liquidate and consolidate immediately, Hearst was about to accept Eugene Meyer's offer of $650,000 for the *Herald*—until Cissy found out about the impending deal from Hearst's general manager, who was also her lover. She knew that Eugene had reached the same conclusion she had—that Washington could support only one morning paper.[55]

"I called Mr. Hearst at three in the morning," Cissy later recalled, "and commenced to cry on the phone. . . . And he said, 'Well, Cissy, you tell me what you want [me] to do and I will tell my folks to do it.'" Although she really wanted only the *Herald*, she told him, she would take the *Times* as well, and suggested that he lease them to her with an option to buy, which option she quickly exercised.[56] Cissy was delighted; Agnes was envious.

And then there was syndicated columnist Dorothy Thompson, whose outsize success made Agnes all the more eager to get her hands on the *Post*. Confidante of Sigmund Freud and Franklin Roosevelt, intensely sensual and attractive to men, Thompson had almost single-handedly created the persona of intrepid girl reporter who somehow became, as Agnes longed to, the star of every story. Thompson had not let marriage to Sinclair Lewis or motherhood slow her down, and she spent much of the early 1930s reporting from Europe. Her expulsion from Nazi Germany on Hitler's orders brought her worldwide acclaim. Her column, "On the Record," ran in some two hundred newspapers—including *The Washington Post*.[57] In 1939, *Time*, which rarely gave such treatment to women, put Thompson on its cover and paid tribute to her in words that Agnes coveted: "She can do more for a cause than any private citizen in the United States."[58]

Agnes's role at the *Post* was negligible. Her favorite causes and

institutions—the Freer Gallery, for example—got a bit more attention, but, said Hedley Donovan, "as far as the policy positions the
paper took . . . or [decisions on] who got promoted," she had no
power. Donovan had been on the job about six weeks when he had
his first brush with Agnes: "I was sent to the Meyers' house to cover
a national convention of social workers. She was entertaining at a
tea; a hundred, a hundred fifty women were there. I made a few
jottings of things that were said, and was visualizing a tiny story, and
when I was leaving, she handed me a list of [the names of] all the
women present and said it would be wonderful if the *Post* could print
the list. I said, 'Well, I doubt if we could print all these names,' and
she seemed extremely disappointed. I said, 'Well, maybe we could do
it in six-point type'—which is about as small as it gets."[59]

Agnes, who did not need to be told that getting her list published
did not exactly rival clashing with Hitler or consulting with Roosevelt, was angry and disappointed. But her husband had no choice,
says Roswell Gilpatric; he knew that "if she got into the act on
editorial policy and personnel, she'd just dominate the scene." Many
times, Gilpatric recalls, he heard Agnes express "frustration about
what was going on at the *Post*. If she had [had] some voice in it, she
[would have done] things differently."[60] That, precisely, was what
Eugene feared. Hardly a week passed that Agnes did not provide him
with another reason why she was not suited to run the paper.

Eugene's biographer later suggested that Agnes's discouragement
at not having a bigger role at the *Post* made her turn to drink.[61]
Eugene's response was to lock up the liquor, but that was not always
possible. In the summer of 1936, after Kay's sophomore year at
Vassar, the Meyers gathered at their ranch in Jackson Hole for a
pack trip in the mountains. After Agnes's horse ran away with
her—she was rescued by Ruth and a cowboy—she began drinking to
calm her nerves. She was soon plastered, and a disgusted Eugene
refused to speak to her. Enraged at Eugene's reaction, Agnes fled the
ranch for a camp high in the mountains. After several days, her
children climbed the mountain and persuaded her to come down.[62]

In her memoirs, Agnes offers a typically revisionist account:
"When Eugene and the children decided to return to the ranch [from
a family hike] . . . I remained at our last camp, an idyllic spot at an
elevation of 9000 feet, for the enjoyment of complete solitude, which
is essential every now and then to my well-being." Her daily activities, as she described them, included "long solitary climbing expedi-

tions. Every morning I lay in a shaded spot beneath giant trees next to a meandering trout stream and read Mann's *The Magic Mountain* and *Joseph in Egypt* in German, while squirrels, mink and various birds circled around me, curious as to why I lay so still hour after hour. As when I first beheld Chinese painting, I fell in love—passionately in love—with Thomas Mann's style."[63] And with Thomas Mann.

Eugene, realizing that she alone in the family had the aptitude, decided to encourage Katharine's journalistic tendencies. Perhaps he hoped she would choose a similarly inclined husband, who could then be counted on to run things—it was not unknown in newspaper dynasties (at *The New York Times,* for example) to turn things over to sons-in-law, regardless of the daughters' qualifications. Eugene had allowed his older daughters to wander through their educations, but he took hold of Kay's and concluded she had had enough of Vassar. The school was not rigorous, not demanding enough; it was a contradiction in terms to think she could get a first-rate education at an all-female college: males were needed to raise the level and volume of debate. He chose the coeducational, and serious, University of Chicago. In a letter to fellow Yale graduate Robert Maynard Hutchins, Chicago's innovative, brilliant young president, Eugene explained that his daughter had it in mind "to become a professional journalist."[64]

Chapter 5

KATHARINE PREPARES FOR THE *POST*

Hutchins had become president of the University of Chicago in 1929, at age thirty, and would forever after be known as the "boy wonder." His notion was to reorganize American higher education, scrapping grades, focusing on ideas rather than facts, having students concentrate on primary sources—the "Great Books"—rather than memorize and regurgitate from the reams of documents written about them.

Eugene saw Hutchins's brainchild as an extension of the classical curriculum he had followed at Yale, but a vast improvement, because his studies had demanded rote learning and memorization. A program like Hutchins's could teach Kay to think, reason, argue, and write, and those were skills that would serve her well if she, one day, ran the *Post*.

Kay too felt that she had outgrown Vassar. Her friends say that she wanted "more of a melting pot of ideas,"[1] more independence, exposure to students from other classes and countries. She wanted a school at which "they took ideas seriously," says Harold Taylor, "where they were concerned with social issues. There was much more intellectual ferment [at the University of Chicago] than at Vassar, a lustier educational program." Kay also wanted to be out on her own more, Taylor says; when she was in the East, with her parents relatively nearby, she could never have the sense of freedom a young woman needed.[2]

The explanation advanced by one of Kay's *Miscellany News* colleagues that Eugene pulled Kay out of Vassar because he felt it was too radical[3] is farfetched. Aside from City College of New York, few schools were more radical than Chicago, which in 1935 had suffered bad publicity when drugstore magnate Charles Walgreen withdrew his niece from the university, explaining that he was "unwilling to have her exposed to the Communist influences."*[4] Partly as a result, the Illinois legislature threatened to revoke the school's tax-exempt status.

Another of Kay's *Miscellany News* workers speculates that Kay feared she would not be asked to join the editorial board of the Vassar paper. (In fact, she was asked later in her sophomore year, after she had made the decision to transfer to Chicago.) "I don't think Kay was a very gung-ho, creative reporter," says Betty Frank. "She was terribly shy. I don't know whether she would have actually gotten to the top slot on that editorial board. She was withdrawn. She was just a rich girl who didn't quite know where she belonged," a follower not a leader.[6]

On arriving in September 1936, Kay did not attempt to join the University of Chicago newspaper, but her father encouraged her interest in the family paper by having the *Post* mailed to her daily. She occasionally wrote him with criticisms, one of which—expressing disgust that the editors had extended the just reelected FDR a front-page welcome when they had opposed him editorially during the campaign—prompted Eugene to reply: "I do not agree with you. . . . I'm afraid that your Chicago atmosphere and remoteness prevent your exercising the good, keen, journalistic understanding in this matter which I know you would have been capable of had you been here on the spot."[7]

The "Chicago atmosphere" to which Eugene referred was International House, far and away the most cosmopolitan of the university residences, with its mix of students—American and foreign, undergraduate and graduate, male and female (the men's floors alternating with the women's). In the dining room, debate seldom stopped. Among the regular diners—they did not live there—were Thomas

---

*His niece was taking Social Science I, for which students were required to read *The Communist Manifesto* but also Herbert Hoover's *American Individualism.* After class one day, the niece approached the professor, Frederick Schuman, and asked him if he believed in free love. "Only for myself," he quipped, and the girl, not realizing he was being facetious, duly reported to her uncle that the professor was propounding free love and that the class was being taught communism. After learning the facts, Walgreen changed his mind and became a generous benefactor.[5]

Mann's daughter Elisabeth and her husband, antifascist professor Giuseppe Borgese. In residence were some young Germans who had been sent over by the Nazis, including one who was "an absolute, thoroughgoing Nazi," according to I-House resident Sidney Hyman, whose long relationship with the Meyer family started when he met Kay that year. German Jewish refugees lived at I-House too, and "the encounters between them [and the Nazis] were really something." There were students from Holland, France, Britain, Japan, and everyone "would be at each other's throats."[8]

The discussions at I-House were often poignant, given the life experiences of its residents. But George Reedy, then head of the university's Socialist Club (and later Lyndon Johnson's press secretary), recalls another side of Chicago in those years: "You could walk [in] any dormitory and hear heated arguments between exponents of Thomas Aquinas and exponents of Marxism. Students would sit up very late at night yelling and screaming at each other. The big thing that really divided the campus was Neo-Thomism versus Marxism."

While Vassar had only the occasional student from a lower-middle-class family, Chicago had many. Reedy worked his way through school washing dishes and playing the trombone. "Most of the students were broke," he says. "We were getting through by the skin of our teeth. There was a relatively small group [of] those fairly comfortable financially, and there was a kind of gulf. It was almost being out of the swim to be comfortable financially during those days."[9]

Kay did not want to stand out as a rich girl, yet with her roommate, Taylor Hannacord Churchill—a left-leaning Lake Forest heiress who had transferred from Sarah Lawrence—Kay shared a "bath suite": two bedrooms and a private bath at twice the regular room rate.[10] Still, Kay took care not to flaunt her wealth. She drove a beat-up Buick—but a convertible[11]—and wore the uniform then in vogue for female students, which Reedy describes: "a sweater, a little bit too big, relatively long dresses, down to mid-shin, bobby socks, saddle shoes. Almost everybody looked fairly much alike."

During her two happy years at Chicago, with hundreds of miles between her and Agnes, challenged by her studies and her political activism, Kay showed more self-confidence than before. "I don't remember if I ever even spoke to her," says George Reedy. "She was rather striking. She had a dark, vivid complexion, dark hair. I noticed her, and I think most people did notice her as she walked by."[12]

Sidney Hyman insists that his relationship with Kay was an "au-thentic platonic friendship"—for a time, he dated her roommate—but he recalls Kay with the words of a man more than half in love: "Her very physical stride was like [that of] the captain of a trium-phant hockey team going to receive the prize. Emerson said first be a good animal, and there was this animal vitality in Kay, exuberance, a belly laugh, a bright, hell's-bells air. I have to say quite frankly that I was in love with this woman, not in an erotic sense, but personally. She was the most remarkable woman I'd ever encountered. We were very, very intimate friends, [but there was] nothing of the romantic nature." Hyman, who is short and slight, speculates that perhaps it was their "physical mismatch" that kept their friendship from blos-soming into romance.[13]

Hyman had earned his undergraduate degree at Chicago in 1936 and was back as a graduate student; he was an ASU executive board member and editor of the left-wing magazine *Phoenix*. Born in Ben-ton Harbor, Michigan, he was the son of a rabbi. That he was a Jew of Eastern European extraction seems to have made no difference to Kay, and he became her frequent escort.

After her first year at Chicago, and with some hesitation—she feared that her new friends would be intimidated by her family's wealth—Kay invited Hyman and another friend to drive to the "farm" at Mount Kisco. Hyman's mouth was agape as they pro-ceeded up the winding drive to the house, past greenhouses, formal gardens decorated with Brancusis, and a grand sweep of lawn. Hyman, who had never been beyond eighty miles of Chicago, recalls that "the foyer alone was practically as big as a basketball court."[14]

In internal ASU politics—characterized by Hyman as "a fierce struggle between those of us who would become liberal Democrats and the Stalinist/Trotskyite crowd from New York"[15]—Kay stuck with the moderate camp, never moving to the left of the New Deal. In George Reedy's memory she attracted notice because virtually everybody else was some sort of radical. "In those days, being a radical meant you were a communist, a socialist, or an anarchist. She probably would be regarded as radical by a moderate Republican."[16]

Kay was a true believer in the right of workers to organize, and she and Taylor Churchill leafletted against sweatshops with members of the International Ladies Garment Workers Union. On Memorial Day, 1937, the roommates passed out coffee to strikers at Republic

Steel's South Chicago Works, offered to baby-sit, and stood vigil at the gate, where earlier a confrontation with company police had left ten dead and ninety wounded.[17]

Kay chose Hutchins's Great Books program, which attracted, says Sidney Hyman, a handpicked group of no more than eighteen students. It was a "highly elitist group, elitist in the sense that you nominated yourself, you applied. And relatively few people did apply, because they knew that it was rough"—so rough that some students had nervous breakdowns. Hyman credits the Great Books as "the decisive experience in my education. You met Tuesday night from seven to nine. You spent a whole week preparing for those two hours. It was like boot camp, a very rough intellectual experience." Not only were students subjected to Hutchins and philosopher Mortimer Adler, who had persuaded Hutchins to bring the course to Chicago, but "now and then other eminent professors would sit in, and they would taunt you as well." Hyman turned in what he thought was a brilliant essay about the tenth *Federalist* paper by James Madison. "This [is] much too long," Hutchins told him. "You can throw half of it away, and it doesn't matter which half."[18]

Although Hyman says that the Great Books had "a tremendous impact on Kay," she would remember Chicago with less enthusiasm. She found more intellectual fulfillment there than at Vassar, yet "still not enough. But that was my fault more than anyone else's. I think I knew what I wanted, but I didn't know how to go about getting it. I had a certain lack of direction."[19]

Kay was happy to be away from Agnes, but she was hurt by her mother's lack of interest. Sidney Hyman noticed, and was furious on his friend's behalf: "She was a lousy mother. I don't think she had the faintest idea about what was going on in the minds of her kids, what their experiences were, she was so preoccupied with herself."[20] June Bingham agrees: "Agnes had no idea what her children were thinking. If they hadn't written a book, it wasn't worth her while to find out."[21]

Hyman recalls two occasions when Agnes did visit—she stopped at the university when she was in Chicago for other reasons—and stayed for dinner at I-House. The conversation was always about Thomas Mann, "because that's what she was interested in." Kay sat in silence. She wasn't given an opportunity to say anything, Hyman explains; "Agnes absorbed all attention to herself."[22]

Unfortunately, neither Agnes nor Eugene had a reason to be in Chicago on the day in June 1938 that Kay graduated. A congratulatory note arrived, though, signed by her mother's secretary and with Katharine's first name misspelled. Friends, who saw her burst into tears, threw her a party.[23]

In the months before Kay's graduation, Eugene urged her to start her career at *The Washington Post.* "You ought to be in on the job of putting it to the top," he wrote her. "It is much better sport fighting to get there than trying to stay there after you have gotten there." But Katharine said no to returning to Washington and living in her parents' house. Her professor of economics, Paul Douglas, later a U.S. senator from Illinois, used his influence to get her a job on the *Times* in Chicago.[24]

First, however, she took a train trip with Eugene to San Francisco. As she would later recall, "I fell in love with that city. I chucked my pride and asked my father to help me get a job there. The San Francisco *News* [a Scripps Howard afternoon paper] said they would take me for two months." Her reporter's salary was $21 a week; she promptly joined the Newspaper Guild.

For Kay, a major attraction of San Francisco was the chance to live with her warm and abundantly sympathetic Aunt Rosalie and Uncle Sigmund Stern, pillars of Jewish high society.

Eugene kept abreast of every detail of his daughter's work, and when, after the first week, she told him that she wanted to quit because she found the job and the city strange, he coaxed her to stay for the experience.[25] The advice was exactly right. She arrived in San Francisco in the midst of a violent dockworkers' strike. An editor later remembered assigning her "to a routine employer-labor meeting, and she phoned in such an excellent account that she promptly was sent on more and more important stories. . . . Miss Meyer showed a remarkable grasp of the issues and events. Soon she was our chief outside reporter on the strike. Seldom have we seen anyone take hold of a tough assignment as she did."[26] She became the "hot car girl," riding the trains and reporting on whether or not the longshoremen would unload them.[27]

She spent hours every day at the Pacific Coast Labor Bureau at the foot of Market Street. Sam Kagel, who ran the office, remembered her as "a very objective reporter, a digger. When she would cover the union side in our office, she always made it a thing to check out the employers who were involved. She certainly wasn't shy when she wanted to find out about a story."[28]

The same quality that at Vassar found Kay both protesting loyalty oaths and picking daisies was evident in San Francisco. She proudly proclaimed her membership in the Guild and didn't hide her fascination for the Marxist Harry Bridges, who was leading the longshoremen in striking the waterfront. She drank twenty-five-cent boilermakers with union leaders at a longshoremen's bar,[29] and at night donned an evening gown for the opening of the opera and dinner at Del Monte's Bali Room.

Eugene followed her every move, noting that her comings and goings made the society pages. "I want to advise not going out every night," he wrote her, "for the work you have to do in the day, late hours every night on social jaunts will wreck your otherwise good health."[30] He asked her to send him copies of her stories and assured her that her waterfront beat was a good one because "that is where the hot news is."[31]

Meanwhile, Cissy Patterson was more and more successful. In January 1939, she merged her papers into *The Washington Times-Herald*—ten daily editions carrying constantly updated news—and moved up to first place in circulation, pushing the *Post* back to third and attracting advertisers by offering the same rates for a bigger circulation.[32] "The *Times-Herald* [is] first in circulation," Eugene joked glumly, "the *Star* first in advertising, and the *Post* first in operating expenses."[33] While Eugene's deficit remained stubbornly high, Cissy's, that first year, came down by nearly $300,000.

This made Eugene's courting of Kay all the more ardent. She had been in San Francisco for seven and a half months when she bowed to Eugene's pleas to come home and work for the *Post*. He offered her a $4-a-week raise to learn every aspect of the paper's operation. *Time* magazine duly reported: "To Washington, D.C., went comely, twenty-one-year-old Katherine [*sic*] Meyer, daughter of Publisher Eugene Meyer, to handle . . . the 'Letters to the Editor' department of her father's *Post*. Said Father Meyer: 'If it doesn't work, we'll get rid of her.' " Accompanying the item was a photograph of Kay in a gold lamé evening gown.[34]

Returning to Washington was difficult. "What I am most interested in doing," Kay had written Bis, "is labor reporting, possibly working up to political reporting later. As you can see, that is no help to Dad. He wants and needs someone who is willing to go through the whole mill, from reporting, to circulation management, to editorial writing, and eventually to be his assistant. This presents the payoff in problems. I detest beyond description advertising and circulation, and that is what a newspaper executive spends most of his time worrying about. . . . I doubt my ability to carry a load like the Washington *Post* and . . . damn well think it would be a first-class dog's life."[35] But even worse than working in dreaded circulation and advertising was giving up Aunt Ro and putting herself at the mercy of her mother.

Going home meant having to witness the squabbles between her parents. Agnes's irrepressible passion for Thomas Mann seems finally to have exasperated Eugene, who through most of their marriage had been content so long as he did not have to watch Agnes make a fool of herself. Some years earlier, on arriving home, he had dispatched Florence to the drawing room; there, behind the closed door, her mother was entertaining a new amour, Indian diplomat Shrinvasi Sastri, with whom, Agnes wrote, she had "journeyed through leagues of emotions." Florence handed her mother a note: "Daddy wants you to know that he is at home."[36]

While Kay was still in San Francisco, Agnes had written to her about Thomas Mann in terms that must have made her daughter blush. "I adore him openly and he returns it diffidently. I have the feeling I am one of the few people and one of the very few women he has ever liked." She insisted that Mann visit her often, which was a burden on the nervous, hypochondriacal insomniac who hated having his routine interrupted. After one visit, she wrote that she felt she had descended "from the top of Mt. Everest to its base"; the two "god-seekers" had gone "their way together, for a little while."[37]

Sidney Hyman had seen the two at Mount Kisco: "Mann himself was an old stultz, never looked at you directly. And Agnes would just be flipping all over, pushing her face into his with this intensity."[38]

During the latter part of his life, Mann did write to Agnes more than to anyone else.[39] Perhaps he felt that if he failed to meet her standards of solicitousness she would withdraw her patronage. In 1938, after Mann and his wife, Katia, decided to make the United States their home, it was Agnes who arranged for them to reenter from Canada as official immigrants;[40] Agnes who eased the way for Mann's appointment as a lecturer at Princeton, with a $6,000 salary chiefly from the Rockefeller Foundation, whose trustees, Agnes informed him, are "all friends of mine"; Agnes who later arranged a consultantship in Germanic literature at the Library of Congress, with an annual salary of $4,800.[41]

Kay told John Oakes, whom she started to date soon after arriving at the *Post,* that her father entered her mother's bedroom one day, saw on her bed the latest Mann novel, picked it up, threw it down, and exclaimed, "That man in the house again!"[42] Eugene would later complain to Sidney Hyman that "there was always a stranger in the house."[43]

What irritated Eugene most, one relative says, was that "he was forced to entertain the wives of the men in her life."[44] Katia Mann was the biggest trial: she disliked visiting the Meyers but knew that it was in her family's interest that the visits continue—thanks to Agnes, Mann had noted in his diary, "I scarcely have any financial problems in America."[45] As Bis puts it, "After all, Mother really worked hard at selling Thomas Mann to America. She wrote the first reviews about him and familiarized large audiences with his work."[46]

Sometimes, as with Paul Claudel, poet and former French ambassador to the United States, the visits would last for weeks on end. He wrote poetry and religious tracts for Agnes and, she said, "put my soul on the rack and stretch[ed] it to the limit of its capacities."[47] (Claudel, she explained, was trying to save her soul by begging her to convert to Catholicism.)

As she aged, each new platonic passion seemed to consume Agnes more than the last. Her big-boned frame was in perpetual readiness to pounce on any man who met her standards for physical and intellectual beauty. At dinner parties she would position herself at the door, ready to snatch the best pick as the men returned from their cigars and brandy.

Agnes prepared for her increasingly elaborate soirées as a great conductor prepares for the performance of his life. Before one dinner she grew furious when her maid was late to help her dress, and when the woman's distraught son rushed in to report that his mother had died en route, she showed only irritation.

By immersing herself in her work, Kay kept out of Agnes's way. Besides choosing and editing letters, Kay's duties included writing headlines, helping to lay out the op-ed page—deciding which of the syndicated columns to use—and writing editorials. She worked in a cubbyhole on the third floor, over the pressroom. "I want to tell you it was hot!" she said later. "But no one seemed to mind. Everyone cared enormously about what they were doing."[48]

The letters column presented a problem to both Kay and June Bingham, who later held that job. "There were so few in those days," Bingham recounts, "that I used to call up my friends and say, 'Hey, could you write a letter? I need to drum up some trade.' "[49]

There were few women at the *Post* in 1939—only one on the news staff—and thus the "striking brunette," as one old-timer remembered Kay,[50] stood out. So rare were female bylines outside the women's pages that in 1938, when Hope Miller finally persuaded the ever frugal Casey Jones to send her to cover the wedding of President Roosevelt's son John in Nahant, Massachusetts, and her story ran on the front page, somebody tampered with her byline to make it read: "Hope Ridings Miller, Post Racing Editor."[51]

John Oakes, four years Kay's senior, was a nice, serious, smart boy from the German Jewish aristocracy. He had not met Kay before, although, as he puts it, "some of my family knew her family." John's father, George Washington Ochs-Oakes, was the younger brother of Adolph Ochs, who had bought *The New York Times* in 1896 and had once offered Eugene a job. There were snickers around the newsroom that Johnny Oakes saw a path straight to the top by marrying the boss's daughter, but Kay knew that with his family ties to the *Times* he did not need the *Post*. (He would eventually become editorial-page editor at the *Times*.)

Agnes and Eugene Meyer didn't much like him. Perhaps because he was Jewish, perhaps because he was not in direct line to the top of the *Times*. (His father had been given a lesser Ochs paper in Philadelphia to run.) Perhaps Eugene, whom Oakes found "terribly pompous," recognized that the young man did not completely approve of him. "I felt that Eugene was too interested in making the paper pay. He was so rich it wouldn't have made any difference. He was willing to lower the *Post*'s standards in order to get some of the sensational readership away from the *Times-Herald*."

If Eugene retained doubts whether Kay could run a major newspaper, and perhaps in the back of his mind hoped that she would marry someone who could, this highly principled, somber young man who cared most for the quality of the news and commentary columns and scarcely for the financial side that made high standards possible was probably not the man. Agnes found Oakes, not the sort to flatter or feign interest in her, to be a stuffed shirt. For his part, Oakes recalls that "Kay was intimidated totally by her mother," and admits that Agnes, "a Brünnhilde type," scared him a little.[52]

Although many of their friends expected them to marry, Kay did not date Oakes exclusively. She also went out with Drexel Sprecher, a Wisconsin native and a lawyer for the National Labor Relations Board. They often double-dated with Theodore Kheel, also an NLRB lawyer, and his wife. All four were avid New Dealers. Kheel describes Kay as charming but shy. "She certainly wasn't aggressive or bold. You would not [feel] that she was thinking, 'Oh, my father owns *The Washington Post* and I'm somebody special for that reason.' "[53]

Florence was the first of the Meyer children to marry. She was "given to crushes on theatrical figures," Bis explains,[54] and in the summer of 1939 she married Oscar Homolka, a Viennese character actor. He was also a member of the Progressive Citizens of America, which would run Henry Wallace's presidential campaign in 1948 and be accused of being a communist front. That Agnes and Eugene did not have high hopes for this union did not much matter to Florence. For years Agnes had broken up one romance of hers after another;[55] an attempt to elope when she was sixteen was foiled by Phillips, the chauffeur. Despite her passion for dancing—"I couldn't live without it," she told an Associated Press reporter[56]—her career never went anywhere and she soon gave it up.

Bis, twenty-five in 1938, also had had her romantic problems. Eugene's biographer described her as the "most out-in-the-open rebel in the family . . . [who] challenged her father's rules of social and moral conduct." She was constantly defying her parents, yet part of her wanted to satisfy them; "she tried by becoming engaged to a relative of one of their friends, but [then] wisely broke it off."[57]

As for Kay, Eugene was delighted with her dedication to the paper, her long hours, her habit of returning to the *Post* after dinner. He felt sure that ultimately she would marry somebody more hardheaded than Oakes, but if her romance with him turned more serious, well, the family could accept him. He was, after all, part of the great *New York Times* clan, and was of German Jewish origin and so, almost by definition, not showy about religion. He was conscientious, if humorless, and smart in a bookish way, and he could grow into a role at the *Post*. If Kay did not marry for a while, that was fine with Eugene too—more time for her to devote herself to the paper.

Then she met Phil Graham.

Chapter 6

THE MOST
OUTSTANDING MAN
OF HIS GENERATION

A group of the capital's most eligible bachelors, including John Oakes and a contingent of top graduates of Harvard Law School, shared Hockley Hall, an Arlington, Virginia, mansion on a wooded height overlooking the Potomac. During Christmas week 1939, Oakes took Kay to a party there. As soon as she was introduced to Phil Graham, Harvard Law graduate, clerk to a justice of the U.S. Supreme Court, Oakes was smart enough to make a speedy and graceful exit.[1]

On their first date, Phil told Kay that she would marry him. By their third, they were engaged and Phil had informed her that he would take no money from her father, that she would have only two dresses, and that when his clerkship ended, they would move to his home state of Florida, where he would enter politics. People who knew him understood why Kay could do nothing but nod yes.

Phil Graham was routinely described as the most magnetic young man in a city packed with the finest of them, all there, in one way or another, to help FDR change the course of history. "Of all the young men of my generation," says Sidney Hyman, "he had the most energy, dash, imagination, charm, wit, capacity, looks."[2] Marietta Tree described Phil as "knockout attractive."[3] But more than that, people thought he would become at least a Supreme Court justice or, more probably, president of the United States.

His early years would not seem to have destined him for such accolades. Philip Leslie Graham was born on July 18, 1915, in the

Black Hills of South Dakota, in a mining town called Terry that is no longer on the map—its sole claim to fame being that it was near the site where Calamity Jane died.[4] Light-years separated the Graham family and its hardscrabble life from the Meyers, who that year moved into their Fifth Avenue apartment with their two daughters, newborn son, and retinue of servants. Eugene's wealth was then estimated at nearly $60 million.

Phil's father, Ernest, was of Scottish ancestry, born and reared on a farm in Croswell, Michigan. He was a 1907 mine engineering graduate of the Michigan School of Mines, ten years Eugene Meyer's junior, and his luck was as bad as Eugene's was good. After graduation he had drifted to Montana, where he operated a gold mine,[5] then, around 1910, to western South Dakota, where he operated a small mine near Deadwood.

He found Florence Morris teaching school in the Black Hills and married her that same year—also the year Eugene and Agnes married. It would be easy to say that there the resemblance ended, except that Florence Morris Graham, educated only roughly by comparison, was every bit Agnes's intellectual equal. Within a few years the Grahams' first child, Mary, was born, and two years later, Phil.

Ernest Graham did not strike it rich as a miner. With the outbreak of the world war, he enlisted as a private. He rose to the rank of captain in the Army Corps of Engineers, and forever after called himself "Cap."

Upon his discharge, he returned to Croswell with his wife and children, to manage his family's down-at-the-heels general store and dairy herd. Through some side work he did for the beet-sugar mill in Croswell, he met the general manager of the Pennsylvania Sugar Company, or Pennsuco, who offered him the management of an experiment with growing and refining sugarcane on about 70,000 acres of Florida Everglades muck land—about half of it under water at least some of the time. Pennsuco already held contracts to process the sugar from the largest mills in Cuba, but company officials worried about Cuba's political instability and wagered that the Everglades could become the new sugar bowl for the United States and even the world.[6]

So in 1921, Cap Graham grabbed the opportunity to become the resident manager of the Pennsuco sugarcane plantation, lodging his family on a houseboat in the Miami Canal, where the Grahams' third child, William, was born. The area was then a mosquito-infested wilderness, some twenty miles from downtown Miami in the northwest reaches of Dade County. "A godforsaken place out in the woods," says John Stembler, a boyhood friend of Phil's,[7] but a place where six-year-old Phil found some new playmates, Miccosukee Indians, one of whom, Charlie Tiger Tail, taught him to wrestle alligators for sport as well as to hunt and fish.

Meanwhile, Cap Graham was discovering that the cultivation of this swamp was a difficult matter, as he wrestled with hurricanes, frost, muck fires, mosquitoes, malaria, floods. In 1922, he supervised the planting of 1,500 acres of cane, but a flood prevented the harvesting and destroyed most of the crop. Three years later, another flood destroyed all the cane and led the company to the inevitable conclusion: Some crop other than cane must be grown. As if to confirm Pennsuco's decision, a hurricane struck in 1926, and Ernest Graham was told to transform the operation to truck farming—beans, potatoes, cabbage. By 1931, the Depression deepening, prices of farm products having plunged, Pennsuco withdrew completely from the Everglades,[8] offering its manager as much of the land as he could pay taxes on, which turned out to be 7,000 acres.

By 1932, Ernest had converted the land to still another use—one that he had experience with from his years in Michigan, dairy farming. Finally he was in the right place at the right time. There was a big demand for dairy products: because of the boom in Miami land values in the early 1920s, land once used for dairy farming had been converted for more lucrative purposes. He later added Angus cattle, and could eventually boast 2,500 head of dairy and beef cattle.[9]

Graham's Dairy stood on the edge of a city that had no way to grow but bigger, and recognizing that, Ernest began to buy real estate. "He started a dairy farm out in Dade County," explains Frank Waldrop, "and the goddamn city came and ran over it and made him rich against all reason."[10]

After four years on the houseboat, Ernest moved his family into the modest two-story, coral rock house that had been built for the Pennsuco head man. He would live there until two months before he died, some forty years later, working just as hard, living just as frugally, and expecting the same of his children.

There wasn't much tolerance for any activity but work in Cap Graham's house. He "worked like a dog all his life," says John Stembler, and "had the self-discipline to develop a business empire. He was a little gruff, but very bright, very forceful, very honest, not very complicated."[11] His only vacations were visits to his mother back in Croswell.[12]

Ernest would never forget where he came from—or let his son forget. George Smathers, a high school friend of Phil's, then his college roommate, and later a U.S. senator from Florida, describes Ernest Graham as "rough-hewn," a tough disciplinarian and taskmaster who "wasn't given to a lot of small talk. He used to work Phil very hard, and Phil had a lot to do with actually running the dairy."[13]

Phil's mother had other things on her mind. She was gentle and, especially compared with Ernest, genteel, but there was nothing easygoing about her. She was as determined as her husband, if not more so, but her goals were different. Florence considered the time her son labored in the fields to be wasted; likewise the time he and George Smathers spent duck-shooting or doing most anything but reading. Since Phil was a boy, no matter how tough the times, Florence subscribed in his name to *The New Yorker;* she wanted him to appreciate good writing, to know what was playing on Broadway, to understand that there was a fascinating world outside the swamp.[14] She was, Smathers says, relentless, always teaching. "Every time we went down there she had something along the intellectual side. She wanted you to stop what you were doing. 'Take this home, George, read this.' Might be an article on the Supreme Court. She would talk to you about the things you ought to be reading, [would tell you not to] waste your time too much on sports."[15]

Phil skipped grades in elementary and junior high school. In 1927, at age twelve, he went on to Miami Senior High,[16] the only white high school in the county (there was a separate high school for blacks). While friends such as George Smathers went out for sports, Phil— who, Smathers recalls, "couldn't have weighed 120 pounds soaking wet"—went out for the debating team. Smathers says Phil was "the first intellectual I ever really knew. He had a tremendously bright mind and could assimilate anything, understand anything." In addition, "everyone liked him. I don't think Phil ever had an enemy when he was growing up."[17] He was president of his class and, on graduation in 1931, he was voted the wittiest.[18]

Florence would have liked for Phil to go to one of the schools mentioned regularly in her *New Yorker*—Harvard or Yale or Princeton; Ernest thought a public education was good enough, and the recently opened University of Miami would allow him to live at home and help on the dairy farm. Florence won, sort of, by getting her husband to agree to send Phil to the more established state university in Gainesville.

In those days the University of Florida was all male, with a student body of about 3,200 mostly middle-class boys from the middle, northern, and northwestern parts of the state. It was a conservative school and, although public, had a religious orientation and a very large contingent of Baptists.[19]

Still, there was plenty of freedom for good-old-boy hell-raising. Phil, who had grown to six-foot-two and been nicknamed "Musclebound," was not, John Stembler says, particularly handsome. He had not dated in high school but was "a would-be ladies' man. He was insecure, younger than the rest of us."[20]

He joined the Sigma Alpha Epsilon fraternity, where he became friendly with another smart fellow, who, according to Smathers, drank too much whiskey. Phil, unfortunately, did not handle whiskey well, but he could still raise hell, "because he didn't have to study. He was the smartest guy I have ever known in my life. And he succeeded in [making] a lot of guys at Florida [flunk out], because they would try to do what Phil would do. They would fail and Phil would be getting A's."

Ernest Graham, whose dairy farming had not quite caught on and whose wife was growing more ill each day with what turned out to be cancer, made an unannounced weekend visit to the Gainesville campus. "Phil was already dissolute," Smathers remembers, "having a wonderful time. There was this contest [to see] who could step over this fence. Everybody was staggering so bad you couldn't get over the damn fence, [falling] down laughing. Lo and behold, here's Mr. Graham. He jerked [Phil] out of school, gave him a milk route starting at four a.m."[21]

That is how Phil spent what would have been his junior year. He would later describe how he had taken a year off from college to help his father at a time when bankruptcy threatened. He never talked about how, during that year at home, he watched his mother die; about how disappointing it must have been for her to know that her son was delivering milk when he should have been devouring the liberal arts; about how powerless she must have felt in her illness to change her strong-willed husband's mind or to steer her beloved son in the right path. Before her death, Florence extracted a promise from her husband: He would see to it that Phil went to Harvard Law School, which the Miami lawyer who had lent Ernest the money to get his dairy farm going had assured her was the best.

Phil returned to Gainesville as a junior in the fall of 1934. His classmates noticed no big change in his behavior; he continued to spend more time carousing than working. He had always been high-strung; now that tendency was a bit more pronounced. "He was very emotional," says one college friend. "He was moody and sometimes sort of a loner," but nobody considered his behavior in any way abnormal. (One man who knew him much later recalls hearing that one night when Phil was in college he "ran nude through the town for no particular reason. He seemed very disoriented when they picked him up.")[22]

In Phil's senior year, 1935, Ernest came to Gainesville again. "You've got to stay here," John Stembler recalls Phil telling him. "Dad's bringing somebody over he wants to marry and wants me to meet." According to Stembler, Phil and his sister, Mary, "were less than enthusiastic."

Hilda Simmons, who grew up in a small west Florida community where her father was the town doctor, was, in Stembler's memory, like a rural schoolteacher. To college boys Stembler and Phil, "she seemed like an old maid, but she was only twenty-eight or twenty-nine." Ernest had met her on a bus ride between Tallahassee and Jacksonville. Phil eventually got along well with her, but, says Stembler, "Mary and Hilda were never close."[23] Perhaps Mary took offense that Hilda settled into the old stone house in such a thoroughgoing fashion that Florence seemed to have all but disappeared, seldom to be mentioned again.

A year later, his dairy farm now successful, Ernest made the first of several runs for political office, this time for a seat in the state senate. The family was described in newspaper articles as if Hilda were the natural mother of the three Graham children, although she and Mary were less than a decade apart in age. (When Ernest died, in 1964, his obituaries failed to mention that a first wife had preceded Hilda.)

In June 1936, Phil graduated from the University of Florida with a major in economics. He had applied to Harvard Law, but his grades were not consistent and he had done poorly on an entrance examination; he was denied admission.[24]

Ernest had mixed feelings about sending Phil to Harvard, or any law school for that matter. He believed his son had had enough education and that any more would simply reduce the chances of his ever returning home to join his father's business. If Phil had to go to law school, then the University of Florida, where both Stembler and

Smathers were headed, was good enough for a Florida boy. But Ernest felt duty-bound to make at least one attempt. Back then, the admissions process at Harvard Law was looser. Cap Graham, on his way to becoming a major landowner and a politician of some clout— the state senate district for which he was running extended from just south of Fort Lauderdale in the north almost to Key West in the south; no bill involving that district, which included all of Miami, could pass without that state senator's approval—knew he could open the door for his son.[25] Ernest called Claude Pepper, an Alabama sharecropper's son who had made good, a 1924 graduate of Harvard Law, and like Cap Graham, that year a candidate for public office. He had lost his race for U.S. senator from Florida in 1934 but was running again (and would win this time). "His father assured me that Phil had a fine mind and would do well if admitted," Pepper recalled. "I called James Landis [who had been Pepper's classmate at Harvard], by then the dean, and on my say-so he agreed to give young Graham a chance."[*26]

Phil happily left for Cambridge, determined to work hard and make his own life. With a new mother installed in the Graham house and even a new sibling on the way, Phil felt as if he had no place in that family. His half brother, Robert, was born that November, the same week Cap Graham won his seat in the state senate.

Harvard Law was like no school Phil had ever seen. As his classmate Philip Elman puts it, "They let the maximum number in and then they busted you out." The competition was fierce. "In my time they flunked out one-third," Elman recalls. "I was scared to death my first year. I developed a duodenal ulcer because of the stress."[27]

It was in many ways the perfect environment for Phil Graham. That he had not gone to prep school or an Ivy League college, that his father was a dirt-under-the-fingernails farmer did not mean a thing. It was, as Professor Felix Frankfurter described it, "the most democratic place in the world—a strict meritocracy, where family connections, Ivy League ties didn't count."[28] Phil Elman agrees:

---

*Pepper would later feel that Phil had not repaid his debt properly. In 1950, George Smathers, then a U.S. congressman, challenged Pepper for his Senate seat. Phil supported Smathers, who ran a campaign that even today is considered one of the most vicious in U.S. history, with Smathers accusing Pepper of being "the leader of the radicals" and an advocate of treason. Smathers won the election, and Pepper was out of the Senate for good; he would later win a House seat and serve until his death.

Pepper mentioned Landis as dean already in 1936; he actually became dean in 1937.

"Law school grades may not have been a very good, reliable measure of merit. Yet your whole career depended on how you made out on five examinations in your first year. If you did very well and you were one of the top men in the class, everybody looked up to you. It didn't make any difference that you were Jewish or poor or crippled. People were described in terms of what their grades were."[29]

Phil Graham's grades were very good indeed. In his second year, as one of the top fifteen in the class, he took a place on the editorial board of the *Harvard Law Review*—the premier publication of its kind. One could do no better than to become an editor of the law review, except to become an officer or, even better, to become president, "the most coveted honor obtainable at the Harvard Law School," in Professor Felix Frankfurter's words.[30]

Phil desperately wanted the presidency, in part, explains Nathan Halpern, a University of Southern California graduate who went to Harvard Law on scholarship, because he felt like an outsider. Unlike Halpern, who liked to talk about how he had come from the "Wild West," Phil took no pride in his outsider status. But Phil was determined to become not just any insider but the consummate insider. To campaign for the presidency was verboten, not to mention bad form. Halpern had become a *Law Review* editor with Phil and thus was eligible to vote for the president. Phil asked him to lunch shortly before the election and "tried to persuade me that he would make a better president than anybody. I was a little taken aback because I didn't think you ever politicked for any of these offices. I said nothing and was noncommittal."

Phil was working hard to establish a bond between them—Halpern the Jewish scholarship student from California, and Phil the Florida cracker. "Phil always denigrated himself and his family. Since he knew I was poor, he always put himself down at that level, [said] that he came from poor stock, southern stock. It took me a long time to find out that he came from what in those days was a fairly prosperous family in the dairy business." At a dinner for *Law Review* editors, Phil brought over "an attractive girl" and introduced her to Halpern as "my shiksa"—a condescending and offensive way, Halpern thought, of showing that Phil, a Protestant, could speak the Jew's language.[31]

In June 1938, Phil Graham of the Florida Everglades was voted president of the *Harvard Law Review* by his fellow editors. Tenth in the class and a graduate of a state university, Phil bested Theodore

Tannenwald, Jr., first in the class and a summa cum laude graduate of Brown.

Some members of the class—although not Tannenwald, who says that Phil "was a much more mature person than I was"[32]—saw anti-Semitism lurking, because, customarily, the victor was the man with the highest grades. Nate Halpern calls Phil's election "peculiar"; there was an undertone of anti-Semitism in speeches made on Phil's behalf.[33]

Felix Frankfurter made the point years later: "That Phil should have been chosen president not only by his equals but by some who probably were his intellectual superiors is striking evidence of how his peers and contemporaries felt about him."[34] Another law professor at Harvard, Henry Hart, Jr., said that Phil was ready not only to be editor of the *Law Review* but also, even as a student, to be dean of the law school.[35]

Naturally, Phil came to the attention of Felix Frankfurter, whom FDR would name to the Supreme Court the next year. No one at the law school was more important to know: Frankfurter served as a kind of talent scout for Supreme Court and appellate court judges, and would recommend, almost always from *Harvard Law Review* ranks, whom these judges should choose for clerkships, which were passports to the most lucrative and prestigious jobs. Judges would often hire Frankfurter's recommendations sight unseen.*

Phil met Frankfurter through the good offices of Edward Prichard, Jr., familiarly known as "Prich," a brilliant and obese law student from Kentucky, a graduate of Princeton, who was a year ahead of Phil. What brought them together was their intellect, wit, and interest in public life. "Prich was reputed to have run away from kindergarten to go to the courthouse," recalls his widow, Lucy, and like Phil, he had been a great high school debater. His family had had money, owned racehorses, but had gone broke during the Depression, so Prich went to both Princeton and Harvard Law on scholarship.[37]

---

*Frankfurter chose the clerks for Judges A. N. and Learned Hand in New York. "The Hands never interviewed any law clerk," says Phil's classmate Bennett Boskey. "They took whomever Felix sent them. He sent me to Learned Hand. I never saw [him] until the day I showed up on the job." After Boskey's year with Hand was over, Frankfurter sent him to the Supreme Court—to clerk for Justice Stanley Reed and then Chief Justice Harlan F. Stone. Boskey explains that judges—Supreme Court and otherwise—simply had confidence in Frankfurter's decisions. "He had selected [Oliver Wendell] Holmes's law clerks, he had selected [Louis] Brandeis's law clerks. Felix spent a great deal of his time trying to spot what he thought were promising young lawyers and sending them where he thought they belonged."[36]

"Prichard was the young genius," recalls Ted Tannenwald. "We all bet that [he] would be governor of Kentucky ten years after we were all out of law school."[38] *Life* magazine once ran a photograph of Prich at Harvard above the caption "The Future Governor of Kentucky."[39]

In a sense Prich and Phil brought out the worst in each other. As Lucy Prichard reflects, "Some of these people who are meteors when they're young have this reputation to uphold. They want to be smart. It can get rough. Both of them would say the thing that everybody else was thinking and wouldn't dare to say. And they knew they were supposed to keep up their reputation for brilliance and fun. That's a little burden to bear."[40]

Prich was already well entrenched with "FF," as only he and FDR called the distinguished professor. Frankfurter would later remember that Prich brought Phil, newly elected president of the *Law Review,* around to meet him: "One day there stood in my doorway this mountain of a man and a slender, laughing youth who danced into my room rather than walked into it, and then with a twinkle in his eye and a gay wisdom he worked his way into my heart and never left it again. There was a sort of instinctive friendship between Phil and me and it deepened and grew more important to us with the passage of years. . . . The three of us went to lunch and we became the close friends that we always were, from first to last."[41]

The relationship with Frankfurter bred a certain contempt. Phil "knew whom he should get close to, and he did," says Nate Halpern.[42] "Felix liked his court jesters," Ted Tannenwald comments, including in this group Phil Graham and Phil Elman as well as Prich. "They all played up to him, even though they might disagree with him, and I just wouldn't do that."[43] But Tannenwald chose to go into private practice after graduation, and so had no particular need to cultivate Frankfurter.

Phil worked hard as *Law Review* president; he smoked heavily, and was emaciated, in need of sleep, and often nervous. Tannenwald describes him as "very intense, volatile. I saw him fly off the handle. He could browbeat people if he had to and wanted to, and he did, but he set very high standards for himself and expected people around him to live up to the same standards."[44] One *Law Review* editor characterized Phil as a playboy, who "went out with women, screwed around, drank a lot."[45] Other editors say that Phil did drink, but not excessively; they have no memory of his being a playboy.

Elman recalls the *Law Review* as "a twenty-four-hour-a-day job,

seven days a week." Most of the editors—not Tannenwald, however—skipped class just about entirely, in favor of staying up all
night and sleeping during the day. Once on the *Review* they were
granted enormous leeway by the faculty and administration, which
expected only that they maintain at least a B-minus average.

When Phil graduated, in June 1939, he went to Washington to
clerk for Supreme Court Justice Stanley Reed—on the recommendation of Justice Frankfurter. For a short time he moved into 1913 S
Street, a house that John Oakes, Hedley Donovan, and others had
moved into the year before. Also in residence were Ed Prichard,
whom Frankfurter had chosen as his clerk; Edwin Huddleson, Phil
Graham's predecessor as president of the *Law Review,* clerk then to
Judge A. N. Hand and later to Justice Frank Murphy, and eventually a cofounder of the Rand Corporation; and Allison Dunham,
clerk to Chief Justice Harlan Stone and later a law professor at the
University of Chicago.

So many of the Harvard Law class of '39 wanted to live at S Street
that some of its residents grabbed an offer from a Navy admiral who
had recently received orders for Hawaii, to rent Hockley, his large,
white-columned house in Arlington, Virginia, at a very small sum.
John Oakes, Prichard, and Phil were among those who made the
move to Hockley, along with Edwin McElwain, who had been Chief
Justice Charles Evans Hughes's clerk; Adrian "Butch" Fisher, who
became a legal advisor to the State Department and head of the
Disarmament Agency; W. Graham Claytor, Jr., clerk to Judge
Learned Hand and Justice Louis Brandeis, and later secretary of the
Navy and head of Amtrak; and William Cary, future head of the
Securities and Exchange Commission.

Felix Frankfurter was delighted to see his favorite, Phil Graham,
living with such splendid housemates. He and Chief Justice Stone
had frequently been dinner guests at S Street, and they continued the
tradition at Hockley.

Frankfurter liked to think of Hockley as a second-generation
"House of Truth."* It was not exactly that. Sometimes it seemed

---

*During World War I, Frankfurter, along with Walter Meyer (Eugene's brother), Walter
Lippmann, Philip Kerr (later Lord Lothian, and Britain's envoy to the United States), and
others, had lived together on 19th Street in Washington. It was, as a biographer of Lippmann's
wrote, "a kind of commune for young men in the government. The half-dozen resident
bachelors . . . invited everyone who was famous, important or interesting. They argued about
politics, and took themselves so seriously that Justice Holmes, a frequent visitor, dubbed the

more like a southern plantation, complete with lawn parties for a hundred, and black waiters serving mint juleps to such guests as Dean Acheson, later Harry Truman's secretary of state, for whose powerful law firm several of the Hockley boys worked, and Justices Hugo Black, Stanley Reed, Frank Murphy, as well as Frankfurter and Stone. Presiding over all was a white-coated butler named James, inherited from Acheson when, it was said, Mrs. Acheson dismissed him after he was discovered in a compromising position with a maid.[47]

John Oakes says that there was nothing even vaguely decadent about the goings-on at Hockley. "These fellows were all very hard-working, and there was absolutely no sign of free and easy sex."[48]

But there was political passion in abundance. Oakes, then on *The Washington Post*'s Supreme Court beat (that he often dined with the very justices he reported on seems not to have been an issue), had covered Frankfurter's Senate confirmation hearings, including the accusations that he was a communist and Colonel Robert McCormick's condemnation of him; he had covered also the appointment of Hugo Black and the uproar over his previous membership in the Ku Klux Klan. One Sunday morning, Oakes recalls, "Prichard came down in his dressing gown with the *Post* in his hand, and he stood there denouncing me because I had a story about Justice [James] McReynolds, who was known as one of the most reactionary members of the Supreme Court; none of our group would be a law clerk to McReynolds, of course. Prichard was so furious at me for writing a piece about McReynolds that didn't denounce him, didn't say what a reactionary SOB he was. And this [was] the atmosphere—highly contentious."[49]

To Oakes, Phil Graham was furthest left of all; "a Stalinist, really a communist fellow traveler," is how another Hockley resident described the Phil Graham of these years.[50] Oakes remembers "bitter arguments between Phil and Adrian Fisher over the question of whether we should be supportive of the Finns in the Russian invasion of Finland, [which] was considered an absolute moral outrage to everybody, liberals and everybody else, even those who were basically sympathetic to the Soviet Union. Phil was arguing very

place the 'House of Truth.'" Other visitors included Herbert Hoover and Eugene Meyer, who would joke that he was "condescendingly" invited to some of the "highbrow" debates "as a . . . Philistine observer and recipient of their superior thinking."[46]

strongly that the Russians had a right to do this. If you could defend the Russian invasion of Finland, you had to be pretty damned far left."[51] Prichard would later say that he and Phil were "sort of half-assed apologists" for the Soviet Union.[52]

One evening, Phil told Oakes "that he wanted me to know he and Kay had gotten engaged. I was very surprised. I had no idea anything that serious had been going on, but I said, 'Congratulations, I think you would fit each other very well.' And I thought that too."*[53]

Kay wanted her father to see just how extraordinary Phil was, but she feared that the two strong-minded men, poles apart ideologically, would clash. She had not known Phil long, but knew him enough to agree with her former suitor Oakes that he was prone to "talk more left than he really was, just for an argument."[54]

When she heard her father express his confidence in the younger generation, Kay grabbed the opportunity to bring them together. As Eugene's biographer later wrote, Kay informed her father that "the greatest of the upcoming young men was Phil Graham." "I'd like to meet him," Eugene responded, and Kay arranged a dinner, inviting two other young men, "so that it would not be too obvious that the host was looking over a prospective son-in-law."[55]

Kay worried when the after-dinner conversation turned to FDR's failed attempt to pack the Supreme Court. Eugene, more than anyone else in the country, was responsible for derailing the plan, and Phil, like the president, was extremely impatient with some of the old conservatives on the court. Eugene then pulled out a caricature of Justice Black in a KKK robe. Predictably, Phil defended the by then liberal justice in a spirited but good-humored argument.

Certainly Phil would have come with the highest recommendation from Felix Frankfurter, whom Eugene had first met, introduced through his brother Walter, during the 1912 presidential campaign. Even though Meyer and Frankfurter would often disagree about FDR, they would remain friends for life.[56]

As for Agnes, she could not have been happier about Kay's choice. She found Phil extremely attractive, and the prospect of making him her own loomed pleasantly.

On June 5, 1940, less than six months after their first meeting, Phil and Kay were married—like her parents, in a Lutheran ceremony,

---

*Oakes soon left the *Post* for the military. After the war, he went to work for *The New York Times*.

with the reception at Mount Kisco. Phil's father was there, but he was not happy about the match. Not only did he realize he likely would never reclaim his son, but he would not have known what to do with him if he could. Running that year for another term in the Florida senate, Cap Graham was an arch–southern conservative who thought of FDR and his big government as evil and un-American, and of Phil as an otherwise good boy corrupted by the ways of Washington.

And another thing, the older Graham did not much like or trust Jews. He blamed the Jew Felix Frankfurter for turning Phil to the left. And the Jew Eugene Meyer was the very embodiment of all Cap Graham distrusted—Wall Street, great concentrations of Eastern wealth.[57] (During the 1920s, Cap had bought some stock and lost some hard-earned money. As one of his sons recalled, "He vowed that in the future the only stock he would buy would have . . . four legs and a tail."[58]) To have his son marry the daughter of a powerful Jew, no matter how Lutheran the ceremony, was painful—and to celebrate at Seven Springs Farm, that monument to ill-gotten wealth filled with its unfathomable art, seemed somehow to be mocking Cap Graham and his traditions. That Eugene Meyer was not an FDR backer was a small matter, because his paper certainly was.

One friend of the family reports that Graham was heard to "cuss out the kikes." But another friend explains that the general attitude in Miami was that there were "a lot of Jewish people of the more objectionable type. I don't think that Ernest Graham was the most enlightened person in the world."[59]

Hope Miller remembers Kay Meyer "coming in with a half-page of notes about the wedding. She told me, 'My father thinks this should run. Could you please play it down a little?' " She was, according to Miller, very timid.[60]

"We all thought this was the man of our generation most destined, most qualified to be president of the United States," Sidney Hyman says, "and it would be the good fortune of the United States if he [became] president. He was an incredibly charismatic figure."[61] Alan Finberg, later a lawyer for the Washington Post Company, observes, "Phil was a much better catch for [Kay] than she was for Phil. He was a blazing star."[62]

It would not be an easy marriage.

Chapter 7

KAY TAKES VERY EARLY RETIREMENT

When Kay Meyer arrived at the *Post,* editor Felix Morley noted in his diary that she was "a well-poised and intelligent girl who evidently was to be groomed as the eventual owner-publisher."[1]

With her marriage, Kay's ambitions died. Perhaps it was her assumption that her father no longer took her seriously as his successor and was passing the mantle to the son-in-law whose potential, like his own, knew no bounds. Nothing was said, but as Eugene's biographer later wrote, "If Graham would interest himself in the paper, with Kay at his side, that might well be the ideal solution."[2] Fascinated as he was with public affairs, Phil could not help but take an interest in the *Post.* As for Kay, her belief that this man was destined for greatness was so overpowering that it was a privilege to do anything to ease his way.

Even Agnes, who would have been inconsolable had Kay been handed the power, could step aside for a man—particularly one so dynamic and charismatic, and so gifted he would surely recognize Agnes's own gifts. Phil alone seemed almost able to tame her: a word or a glance from him could even neutralize a dispute between her and her husband. Agnes clearly preferred Phil to Kay, who found this not only understandable but advantageous—if Agnes had eyes only for Phil, then Kay was less likely to be the target of her withering assessments.

In the meantime, another Supreme Court clerkship—one that he knew would prove all-consuming—awaited Phil. Having placed him with Stanley Reed for the 1939–1940 session, Felix Frankfurter took Phil for himself for the following year.

The newlyweds, still clinging to the idea of remaining independent of the Meyer millions, set up housekeeping in the decidedly downscale neighborhood of Burleith, just outside Georgetown, in a $75-a-month two-story rowhouse on 37th and R.

Wanting to be the conventional helpmeet, and as different as possible from Agnes, Kay suggested that she quit her job and learn to cook—this from a woman who was said to have rarely even seen the kitchen in the houses she grew up in. (Bis recalls her own first attempt to boil an egg: "I had never had it presented except out of the shell, so I cracked the shell and put the egg in the water and expected to have a boiled egg. Imagine my astonishment."[3]) "My God," Phil told Kay. "I don't think I could stand having you wait around with a pie for me to come home from the Court. You continue to work and we'll pay a maid with what you make."[4] So Kay worked, but without the commitment she had had before. She moved to the Sunday department to write fluff about such events as the Cherry Blossom Festival; she also, however, wrote for the "brains" section—including a review of a book by two of Thomas Mann's children.[5]

Phil would arrive home late, often with a fellow clerk or two in tow, after hours of arguing, cajoling, and socializing with Frankfurter and his former clerks—among them Joseph Rauh, Jr.,* Adrian Fisher, and Edward Prichard. "There were four of us," recalled Joe Rauh, "who had been Felix's students and law clerks [whom] he kept very close relations with. He had no children, we were the children."[6] Phil Elman, whose clerkship for Frankfurter followed Phil Graham's, was the last of this elite group.

Frankfurter was closest to and most demanding of Phil Graham. "They were both great gossips," recalls Elman. "They loved to talk about people in Washington, deflate the stuffed shirts."[7] And Mrs. Frankfurter, a difficult and depressed woman, a Wasp who had married a Jew, saw something in the intense, preternaturally energetic Phil that landed him the premier spot in her affections. At one dinner for her husband and his clerks, Marion Frankfurter gave a speech in which she referred to Phil, Prich, Fisher, and Rauh as "the

---

*In 1947, Rauh, Frankfurter's first clerk, founded Americans for Democratic Action with Eleanor Roosevelt and others.

four barbarians," because, in Rauh's words, "we would scream at him. And he'd scream at us."[8]

After his year with Frankfurter, Phil moved to a job that was at . least as taxing and that placed him at the front line of the war preparedness movement—attorney for the Office for Emergency Management, under Wayne Coy, and for the Lend-Lease Administration, under Oscar Cox, general counsel for both that agency and the OEM. An expediter par excellence who refused to take no for an answer, Phil arranged for $8 billion in V-loans to defense plants,[9] and hatched the idea of encouraging wartime conversion with government loans to industry; he drafted the bill for the latter himself, finessed it through Congress, and personally secured the signature of every Cabinet member.[10] He also played a major role in boosting the output of high-octane gasoline.

He was a charter member of what came to be known as "the goon squad," a group of young New Dealers who, in the days before Pearl Harbor, met on Monday evenings in the apartment of economist Robert Nathan, who by day was in charge of developing military requirements to help the nation mobilize for war. In addition to Phil, Rauh, and Prich, the group included Isaiah Berlin, diplomat, Oxford don, philosopher, and great friend of Felix Frankfurter, and Lauchlin Currie, the first professional economist to work in the White House. The company was all male; wives were not welcome.

Phil played a starring role. To some he seemed a brash upstart, but others recognized that he was the son-in-law of the publisher of *The Washington Post,* and the *Post* was leading the way in pushing for American involvement in the war. In August 1940, Meyer fired his editor, the Quaker isolationist Felix Morley,* and replaced him with the interventionist Herbert Elliston. Financial editor and columnist for *The Christian Science Monitor* and earlier its correspondent in China, he had refused to become a Christian Scientist, thereby, in effect, refusing the editorship of the *Monitor.*[12] Within a week of arriving at the *Post,* Elliston called for "speed, and more speed" in entering the war; "every minute," he said, "the heat of the European blaze is hotter and closer!"[13]

The goon squad was known for leaking and feeding information

---

*After the fall of France, Morley had written that Britain "knows . . . it has the full sympathy of the American people. . . . The British must not be misled, however, into assuming from this that the United States is likely to enter the war."[11] Morley went on to become president of his alma mater, Haverford College.

to selected reporters and columnists, and Phil had an inside line to journalists who were squarely in the interventionist camp. The preferred newsmen included Alfred Friendly, a favorite of Eugene Meyer's who had moved to the *Post* in 1939 from the *Washington Daily News;* and Drew Pearson and his partner, Robert Allen, who since 1932 had been writing the syndicated column "Washington Merry-Go-Round," an offshoot of their shocking and best-selling books that exposed the political, social, business, and sexual secrets of Washington's most powerful; the column, then in Cissy Patterson's *Times-Herald,* would soon move to the *Post.* *

Through Felix Frankfurter, who was said to talk to FDR nearly every day, Phil, Rauh, and Prich also had a line to the president. Although Frankfurter never attended a goon squad meeting—that would have been below his dignity, explains Bob Nathan—he was thoroughly involved. He "had his fingers in the pie, all over the place," and he "loved to deal with Roosevelt. Felix was a real maneuverer, had almost a mischievous love of manipulation and maneuver."[15] He advised "Frank," as he called FDR, that the British had been too slow to mobilize; according to James Simon, who has written extensively about the Supreme Court and its justices, Frankfurter served the president as "administrative consultant, military strategist, legal counselor and cheerleader . . . [using] his former law clerks . . . Rauh, Prichard, and Graham as couriers to do his work and bidding in the middle echelons of the government wartime bureaucracy."[16]

For the goon squad, the work was mesmerizing, all-involving, satisfying in a way that nothing could possibly be. They were making a difference, and seeing the results. In August 1941, FDR was talking about "clouds of planes" that the United States was supposedly producing. "Phil and I were going through the top-secret documents on production," Joe Rauh recalled, "and we find there's only one four-engine bomber that had been delivered to the Air Force [the

---

*Sparks had been flying between Cissy and Pearson, who, on top of being her ex-son-in-law, was much too interventionist for her tastes. Staunchly isolationist, Cissy spouted the line that U.S. entry into the war might be in the best interest of Britain or the "international bankers" (i.e., the Eugene Meyers of the world) but not in America's. She hinted that the accounts of Nazi slayings of Jews had been exaggerated by Jewish executives in the communications industry. On the floor of the House of Representatives, a Pennsylvania Democrat attacked Cissy, her brother Joe, and their cousin Robert McCormick for "hating Roosevelt more than they hate Hitler."[14]

month before, in July]. So [we] wrote a memo from Wayne Coy to [top FDR aide] Harry Hopkins saying, 'There's something wrong here. One plane delivered, a four-engine bomber to England to the air corps. Here's the president talking about "clouds of planes," he probably ought to know about this.' So Coy signs the memo, sends it over to the White House. Three or four hours later he gets a hot memo back from Hopkins saying, 'I don't know where you get your information, but it's absolutely wrong.' God. Phil and I were scared to death. We'd done something terrible. We went to see the guy who made up the charts and tables, Robert Nathan, and he gets out a whole batch of yellow sheets. We're dying and sweating. He says, 'I made a mistake.' Phil and I almost died. 'There weren't *any* four-engine planes delivered.' So we rushed back to Coy, and he sent another memo over to Hopkins: 'There weren't any delivered in July.' Coy had absolute faith in Phil and me. And he sent [the first memo just] on our say-so."

Nobody was in the preparedness movement with more heart, soul, and sweat than Phil Graham. "All we wanted to do was get into the war and stop Hitler," said Rauh. "You might have thought Phil was Jewish like some of us who wanted to stop Hitler so badly."[17]

On December 7, 1941, Phil, Rauh, and another colleague were working, as they often did on Sundays, writing the ninety-day report for the Lend-Lease Administration, due in Congress the next day. "We were having a bite of lunch in some dump near the office," Rauh recounted, "and when we came out of the restaurant, I heard a voice holler at me—it was [James] Lawrence Fly, the chairman of the Federal Communications Commission. [He] said, 'Don't you know they bombed Pearl Harbor?' He gave us whatever little he knew. He was on his way to the office because he was head of war communications and there were lots of things to be done. I said, 'Thank God,' and Phil said, half agreeing, of course, 'We shouldn't be talking that way.' What he meant was, [people] were going to say enough that the Jews had gotten us into the war without somebody proclaiming it."

Whatever social life went on was merely an extension of the preparedness effort—the Sunday baseball game, for example. "All of us, the young and the not so young New Deal people, came," remembers Nancy Wechsler, who was in Washington in 1941 with her husband, James, of American Student Union fame. The men played; the women, for the most part, watched. To Nancy, Kay Graham seemed "very shy, very withdrawn. And Phil was ebullient and very attractive and full of ideas. I never heard her assert herself in that period."[18] Libby Rowe, whose husband, James, was FDR's secretary, recalls Phil as "a dominating presence" and "such a great talker there wasn't time to get into the conversation. Kay didn't sit in a corner or anything like that, but he was the dominating member of the family, brilliant, entertaining, she the appreciator of his wit."[19]

Unlike Agnes—again, surely deliberately unlike Agnes—Kay wanted to have children, and to devote herself to them, at least when she wasn't devoting herself to Phil. But having children was not as easy for her as it had been for her mother. Kay's first pregnancy continued to term, but the baby was born dead, strangled by the umbilical cord.[20] Kay, being Kay, believed this was somehow her failure, especially as her friends delivered healthy babies. The tragedy was redoubled in this family so consumed by the idea of primogeniture, because the dead baby was a boy and Kay felt that she had somehow deprived her perfect husband of his first son. "Kay went through hell," says Libby Rowe.[21] Two miscarriages[22] followed before she finally gave birth to Elizabeth, called "Lally," in 1944.

Kay told no one that her husband, who always appeared so perfect to the outside world, had periods of despair. Although it was not clear why, and the episodes passed quickly, Kay blamed herself; she focused on the death of the baby boy and the suffocating wealth and stature of her family.

The plunges in Phil's otherwise relentlessly high spirits may indeed have been triggered by his sensitivity to being the poor son-in-law. The audacity and arrogance behind his ability to get things done were also bound to breed resentment, and thus came whispers that Phil, the redneck southerner, had married Kay for her father's money, power, and position and the instant legitimacy they bestowed upon him. Phil wrote an article for *The Atlantic Monthly* under the byline of his boss, Wayne Coy, who gave him half the $800 fee. His colleagues describe his waving the four one-hundred-dollar bills about with a giddy exultation, as if to say, "Look at me, I can make money too."[23]

On weekend visits to Mount Kisco, Phil appeared both to enjoy the farm and to sneer at its overstated opulence. Betty Frank and her new husband visited Kay and Phil there: "We'd come up with dirty socks and pajamas thrown into an old suitcase, and the butler would unpack for [us]. There would be a Brancusi in the middle of the floor." She recalls Kay and Phil "standing under the old man's window and singing the 'Internationale' to needle him." The impulse, she says, was surely Phil's.[24]

Phil Graham had an advantage over his father-in-law. He was a Scottish Methodist in a city that was as deeply anti-Semitic as any in the country. In some ways, Washington made an exception for Eugene Meyer. "He was like [Bernard] Baruch," explains Newbold Noyes, once editor of the *Star*, and a member of the clan that, with the Kauffmann family, owned the *Star*. "He was somebody people, even anti-Semites, would recognize as a superior guy." Noyes says that his grandfather, Frank Noyes, president of both the Associated Press and the *Star*, was an anti-Semite but still played bridge almost every afternoon with Eugene.[25]

They played at the Metropolitan Club, which allowed a few Jews, but as few as possible.* Other clubs, the Chevy Chase for example, strictly barred Jews. Luvie Pearson, Drew's widow, recounted: "I went to a party at the Chevy Chase Club, in a private dining room, on the part of somebody whose father was a big publisher friend of Drew's, and she had [invited] Morris and Gwendolyn Cafritz. [He was Jewish, and an extremely successful real estate developer; she was not Jewish, and second only to Perle Mesta as a Washington hostess.] The morning after the party, [the hostess] called me up and said, 'You know, Luvie, you won't believe it, but I've already gotten a hand-delivered notice from the Chevy Chase that one more offense and I'm out.' And I said, 'Well, what was your offense, darling? That was the most well-behaved party I've ever attended in my whole life.' She said, 'I had the Cafritzes. You're not allowed to have any Jewish people.'" When Pearson mentioned this to the father of a friend of hers, who was "a big scene at the Chevy Chase," and asked whether the story could be true, he answered, 'Of course it's true. I'm the head of the board, and that's what we do. We cannot let anyone break down our standards.'"[26]

The fears of their Mount Kisco neighbors that the Meyers would ruin the neighborhood had obviously proved wrong. Still, Eugene

---

*According to Luvie Pearson, the Metropolitan Club took *New York Times* Washington bureau chief Arthur Krock as its "club Jew. The point about taking Arthur was that he would keep all the others out."

and Agnes would never have close friends among the locals. Only when John Henry Hammond, Jr.,* the liberal son of a neighbor, pushed his father to lobby on Eugene's behalf was he asked to join the Mount Kisco Golf and Tennis Club.[27]

In his memoirs, Hammond, a great-grandson of Cornelius Vanderbilt, wrote that "Father reminded the directors of the club that funds were low and suggested that it was wrong to bar such wealthy and distinguished neighbors simply because they were Jewish. The club . . . should invite Mr. Meyer and Mr. Straus [Jesse Isidor Straus, president of R. H. Macy & Co. and former U.S. ambassador to France] and their families to join." The directors' ingenious solution to this problem, Hammond explained, was to allow the Meyers and the Strauses to join, but only as honorary members, "which meant that they could not bring their friends to the club." Both Meyer and Straus declined the invitation.[28] But Bis recalls occasionally playing tennis at the club after Eugene answered the directors' plea to help them sort out finances and stave off bankruptcy.[29]

Eugene strove not to draw attention to his Jewishness. He was exceedingly careful that his paper's editorial position show him to be, before all else, a patriotic American. For that reason he would forever resist the entreaties of Zionist friends such as Louis Brandeis and Felix Frankfurter to take up the cause, at least financially, of a homeland for the Jewish people.

Many of those close to him, including Agnes, were distressed when Eugene's paper seemed to view the lack of an armed Austrian resistance to German annexation as proof that the Europeans accepted Hitler as a political leader. The *Post* ran a long analysis of the attraction of Nazism that sounded, Agnes said, as if the paper were offering its "approval of Fascism as a program."[30]

Although Eugene helped several of the Dreyfuses escape the Nazis, for the most part he kept his distance from pleas that he use the *Post*'s power to get close relatives out of Europe. Deborah Davis wrote that Eugene was "strangely cold" in his response and that Meyer relations were sent to the gas chambers at Auschwitz.[31] He did help refugees, though not specifically Jewish refugees, by leasing Clovercroft, a 200-acre estate in Fauquier County, Virginia, to house

---

*Hammond, a jazz critic, producer, and discoverer of Billie Holiday, Count Basie, Sarah Vaughan, Bob Dylan, and Bruce Springsteen, became vice-president of jazz recording at Columbia.

and educate sixteen British children, sons and daughters of officials sent to dangerous zones.

And he offered unsolicited investment help to his Wasp friends who would have done fine without him. Joanna Steichen says that while it is unlikely he "sat down and tallied up the benefits, it did help [Eugene and Agnes] in establishing and maintaining a position they might not otherwise have had." Eugene helped Edward Steichen manage his money, and did likewise for psychiatrist Marion Kenworthy. Esmond Romilly, a nephew of Winston Churchill, and his wife, Jessica Mitford, were also beneficiaries of Eugene's largesse.[32]

Once the United States had entered the war, Phil Graham was eager to go where the action was. In December 1941, Felix Frankfurter wrote a letter of recommendation to the commanding general of the Third Corps Area on behalf of Phil's application to join the Army Air Corps. Frankfurter praised his student and clerk for his "zeal, intrepidity, complete devotion to the task at hand, . . . capacity to arouse confidence in other men, and that sparkling humor that makes the wheels go 'round."[33] The next spring, Phil joined the Air Corps as a private, having turned down a commission so that he could see combat.

In 1941, Bill Meyer graduated from medical school at Johns Hopkins, ready to begin his career in the Public Health Service at Walter Reed hospital in Washington. But after Pearl Harbor, he immediately volunteered for service, and became a medical officer with the Sixty-fourth Fighter Wing, which would see action in North Africa and Italy.[34]

Eugene continued to struggle with the question of succession— "I've got to know what will happen to this paper when I'm no longer around," he confided to a friend in 1942.[35] If Phil pursued his plan to return to Florida and practice law as a prelude to a career in politics, he would develop ties and commitments that had nothing to do with Washington or the *Post,* and Eugene might lose him for good.

He recognized that if anyone—anyone other than himself, that is—could put *The Washington Post* on top, it was Phil. That Phil had no background in journalism was irrelevant: he knew more by instinct than other men knew by training. "If he believed in something, no effort was spared," says Sir Isaiah Berlin. "Phil really was a man of action and, above all, not a loser. He was a winner by nature."[36]

Politically, and to some degree temperamentally, Phil had much in common with Eugene. Yes, Eugene remained a Republican, but nobody was more supportive of FDR on foreign affairs; nobody had a better or earlier record of bringing the government to bear on problems in the nation's economy; nobody was a stronger proponent of the idea that government had a role to play in the lives of the citizenry.

As for his son, Eugene didn't feel he had what it took to manage the *Post* or, for that matter, his own affairs. Unlike his parents, Bill Meyer longed to live a middle-class life, but he hadn't the vaguest idea what constituted such a life. He thought a family ought to be on a budget, but he had to ask his father, "How do you put all this stuff together?" Eugene replied testily, "Would you ask Heifetz how to play the violin?"[37]

There were two unanswered questions, then: Did Phil want the paper? What to do about Bill?

There was no need to ask, What about Kay? Her father knew that she, who was going through a series of fruitless pregnancies, would be delighted to stand behind Phil while he ran her father's paper. And she would be able to stay in Washington, away from Phil's alarming family and the dreadful prospect of having to perform as a candidate's wife.

Eugene made up his mind to approach Phil at once. But before he set out for Harrisburg, Pennsylvania, where Phil was in intelligence school, he had to reach an understanding with his son.

The atmosphere was hardly one of frank and easy exchange when Eugene summoned Bill to Crescent Place to ask if he would be interested in "the job at the *Post.*" Bill was smart and sensitive enough to realize he could not compete with Phil in Eugene's estimation; the meeting with his father was merely a formality. "You could sense that the old man saw in Phil the son he wished he had," recalled Bernard Nossiter, later a reporter at the *Post.* "The sun shone around Phil's head."[38] Bill asked for three days to think it over. In a surprisingly candid moment in Meyer's authorized biography, Merlo Pusey wrote: "It is indicative of their relationship that Meyer sent Wayne Coy . . . to discuss the big decision with his son. . . . In the end [Bill] decided to stay in medicine because he was already in it and because he feared, without saying so, that he might not get along with his father in a business relationship."[39]

The choice of Wayne Coy as go-between is striking. Although then the assistant director of the Budget Bureau, Coy had been Phil Graham's boss, mentor, and fan. If, even before Phil joined the family, Bill felt he could never live up to his father's level of competence, how painful it must have been for him that just as his father was losing the commanding edge by virtue of age, just as he might feel it was safe to emerge, he now had to contend with a brother-in-law who was so frustratingly and obviously his superior in the ways men measure men. Virtually the only thing Bill did that pleased his father was to wed Mary Adelaide Bradley, a graduate of Vassar now studying bacteriology at Johns Hopkins, and the daughter of the Reverend Charles Bradley of Boston.

"I'm sixty-seven," Eugene told Phil. "I've got to know if you are interested in coming to the paper."

He stressed that he was asking Phil to commit to a newspaper that was bleeding $1 million a year. It was, Kay Graham would say in a speech years later, "the one paper in town that everyone just assumed would go out of business."[40] The *Post*'s pathetic national staff had not improved much since Eugene took over—one man covering the House, one the Senate, one the White House, with the State Department thrown in for good measure.[41] (Three years would pass before Eugene would send reporters to cover World War II, Edward Folliard in Europe and sports editor Shirley Povich in the Pacific.[42]) On Friday afternoons, when Frank Dennis had to decide, almost entirely on the basis of advertising volume, how big the Saturday edition was going to be, sometimes the choice was only between eight and twelve pages.[43]

Still, the *Post* was winning kudos for its editorials—and that, for Phil, was everything. While he was away at war, the national press took note of the *Post* in a way that confirmed for him the effect he could have at the helm of this paper. In 1943, *Time* called it "one of the world's ten greatest newspapers."[44] In 1944, a writer for *Fortune* said that the *Post* "ranked among the first half-dozen newspapers in the U.S."[45]

It was, however, not an easy decision for Phil, who "had some apprehension about the son-in-law situation," according to Hedley Donovan.[46] "Phil was a little bit of a Hamlet at that time," Joe Rauh recalled, "about whether he should do [it]. He didn't just say, 'Yes, I'm coming. Boy, what an opportunity!' "[47] But he did give Eugene enough encouragement to assume that he would cast his lot at the *Post*. Eugene did all he could to prepare the way for Phil's arrival—

both by accomplishing some of the unpleasant belt-tightening himself and by asking Wayne Coy, early in 1944, to join the company as assistant to the publisher "in order to make the position that Phil would occupy more comfortable for him."[48] The year before, Eugene had hired an editorial writer, Alan Barth, who had played in those Sunday baseball games and whose enthusiasm for the New Deal, Phil knew, matched his own.

Meanwhile, Kay continued to work at the *Post,* in editorial and then, when she seemed eager to diminish her role, in the circulation department. "I was pregnant and Philip was away and I was just looking for a mindless job to make the time go faster," she later explained. It did not occur to her that she could use this experience to prepare for a management position at the *Post;* back then, she "was honestly convinced that women were inferior to men."[49] She later reflected further: "I didn't really want deadlines and editorial work. I wanted something mechanical and eight hours a day. So I went to work, thinking it was easy—ha, ha—on the complaint desk at the circulation department. I remember all the complaints unattended to and the frustration of trying to pacify enraged subscribers. . . . I also remember the man who called in . . . claiming to be a friend of Eugene Meyer and by God, if we didn't get him his paper he'd go straight to Meyer. I said, 'Okay, we'll do our best but I am his daughter and I don't remember your name.' "[50]

In 1942, Agnes Meyer resigned as chairman of the Westchester County Recreation Committee—a position in which she showed what she could do when she aimed the full force of her competence at a project. Having started in 1923 with a few playlots, she had brought to the county a cultural center, music festivals, athletic events, summer camps for children, and an arts-and-crafts program.

Agnes seems then to have decided to devote herself to Thomas Mann. Planning a visit to his home in Pacific Palisades, an oceanfront district in west Los Angeles, Agnes fired off a letter expressing her seething offense that during her last visit, Mann's wife and children had intruded too much on their time together—time which, in Agnes's mind, was somehow sacred and beyond domestic routine. "We devoted two whole mornings to one another," Mann wrote back in exasperation, "were undisturbed and alone for hours both days, talked, had a reading and a walk on the beach, and then I believe you once gave us the pleasure of coming to lunch with me *en famille,* in the sphere in which my life is lived. But the idea that you saw me only *en famille* is an illusion of memory."[51] Agnes dismissed the Mann children as draft dodgers and shirkers; she implied that somehow they would be to blame if Bill or Phil—both of whom, she underscored, had *volunteered* for service—were harmed. Mann did not attempt to mask his annoyance, although he certainly could not afford to lose her financial patronage. Both his sons had been trying to enlist, he wrote her, and one had even gone to France "in order to fight. He was thanked for that by being clapped into a concentration camp for three months."[52]

Sometime later, Mann really let loose: "I have suffered bitterly and long from your having nothing but feelings of scorn and rejection for my children." After vehemently defending them, Mann captured Agnes as well as anyone when he said of their friendship: "I served it faithfully and with care. Serving is the very word. For years I have devoted to it more thought, nervous energy, work at the desk, than to any other relationship in the world. I have let you participate as well as I know how in my inner and outer life. On your visits I have read aloud to you for hours from new work no one else has seen. I have shown the most sincere admiration for your patriotic and social activities. But nothing was right, nothing enough. . . . You always wanted me different from the way I am. You did not have the humor, or the respect, or the discretion, to take me as I am. You wanted to educate, dominate, improve, redeem me. In vain, I warned you, with all kindness and delicacy, that this sort of thing was an attempt on an unsuitable object, that at the age of nearly seventy my life was too thoroughly formed and fixed." And then to the delicate subject of Agnes's patronage: "We can hardly forget what we owe to one another. I say to one another for I was able to accept without loss of dignity and kindness and support, the easing of life that you offered, since you led me to believe that they were not unreciprocated benefits."[53]

Florence Meyer was also living in Pacific Palisades, with her two young sons and an unraveling marriage to Oscar Homolka, which, recalls June Bingham, was "just a nightmare. He was sadistic, I've been told. He always acted the villainous part in the movies. He didn't have to act. That was his character."[54] (They would eventually divorce, in 1946.) Agnes told Florence that if she wanted to see her, she should travel to San Francisco; it would be more convenient for Agnes, after she saw Mann.[55]

Florence, who had deliberately distanced herself from her parents, had become obese. She bore little resemblance to the dancer once described as "tall, lithe-limbed . . . with a sleek, dark, shingled head." She had taken up photography, mostly portraits, but since most of her subjects were friends of her parents', she knew she was not really independent. Her photographs of Mann, Aldous Huxley, Charles Laughton, and Charlie Chaplin (when making movies he often asked her to stay on the set and photograph the actors) appeared in various art journals.[56]

Mann was offended by Agnes's lack of priorities—Florence being a case in point. His problems with Agnes were predictable, because she took pleasure not in the intellectual rewards of the relationship but in showing it off. When Mann visited Mount Kisco, Agnes made certain that everyone knew. As he noted in his diary in 1938, before the relationship soured: "Countless number of people for lunch . . . More company at tea."[57] June Bingham recalls her mother's observation that "Agnes tended to talk about her deep friendship with Thomas Mann, when you wanted to report on your tennis game."

Bingham found Agnes at this time to be given to "pronouncing on high, a little like Jehovah. She just blew her trumpet wherever she happened to be."[58] Agnes had long before garnered the contempt of Alice Roosevelt Longworth, who described her as "an aggressive Teutonic type, frightfully solemn. I preferred Eugene."[59] That women were more critical of Agnes than men is not surprising: "she preferred men, period," says Roswell Gilpatric; "she preferred the company of men and the ideas of men."[60]

Agnes was drinking too much, and the more she drank, the more exaggerated her airs. Eugene kept the liquor locked up, but Agnes managed to drink anyway. "Part of the problem in that relationship," says Joanna Steichen, "was that these people did not know how to speak directly about emotional and personal things, certainly not to each other."[61] Harold Taylor says simply that "they led separate lives."[62]

Eugene really had no choice. He was as strong a personality as Agnes, and autocratic to boot, but he was not a braggart or a blowhard. She could be overpowering, both emotionally and physically. As June Bingham recalls them, he was "short, rather squat, much smaller than Agnes. She came on as a Valkyrie, and he came on as a dapper little man, bald and cheery."[63]

Eugene learned to tune Agnes out, escaping into bridge—and increasingly, into the *Post*. At the office he became a popular and ubiquitous figure, shuttling between departments, asking questions, and in the manner of a kindly uncle, showing remarkable sensitivity to the well-being of his employees.

One reporter remembers Eugene, on his rounds, stopping at his desk and asking him why he looked so glum. "I had just bought a little house and the furnace had exploded. [I] had put all the re-sources [I] had into that house. And I told him that. I was trying to figure out how to replace it. He said, 'How much does it cost?' 'Eight hundred dollars.' He wrote me a check right there. He said, 'This is a gift. You don't have to report it as income.' I may have asked him why he was doing this for me, and he said, 'Well, you're a good person, and I want you to be productive.' He got a lot more than eight hundred dollars' worth of loyalty and affection over the years."[64]

Frank Dennis, the assistant managing editor, who was in charge of the paper from four p.m. until midnight, recalls that Eugene phoned him every night "to find out what was going on, and how was I playing the news. He didn't dictate. It was as if he owned a grocery store and called up to find out how much business we had that day." When he didn't phone he would stop by, sometimes in evening dress, sometimes, probably deliberately, at precisely the time Dennis went to dinner. He might suggest that they go together— always to the Willard Hotel or the Hay-Adams, where they would talk about the newspaper business or national affairs. Eugene would expound that the *Post*'s best bet for climbing out of the red was to increase advertising, and circulation would follow (the opposite of the conventional wisdom); or that the defense establishment should be coordinated into one department—but he would never touch on personal matters.[65] As Al Friendly put it, "To be sure, he was out-going and easy in casual dealings with the staff, [and] his demeanor invited friendly relationship. But there was also a line, invisible but nonetheless clear, against undue intimacy (even when he once briefly joined an after-hours crap game with the printers)."[66]

Generous though he might have been about helping an employee with a financial problem, Eugene had next to no concern about how the rest of humanity lived. "A crew of people showed up one day," Frank Dennis recalls, "and worked all week, and the word got out that the [*Post*] building was being air-conditioned. All of us working stiffs were grateful for that—you know how Washington is in the summer. Lo and behold, they air-conditioned Mr. Meyer's office. It's funny . . . the only guy in the building who didn't really have to have air-conditioning. It never would have occurred to him."[67]

A few years earlier, when the Newspaper Guild threatened to strike if its demands were not met, Eugene tried to placate the staff by describing his own sacrifices on the path to success. These, he assured his employees, included giving up his yearly trips to Europe and his acquisition of Old Masters. The speech backfired, and people who had disdained the Guild rushed to sign on.[68]

Perhaps nothing showed the gulf separating Eugene Meyer from working reporters better than what the press dubbed an "elegant brawl" between him and Jesse Jones. Jones, a Democrat from Texas and one of the bidders for the *Post* in 1933, served on the board of the Reconstruction Finance Corporation when Meyer was chairman, before becoming chairman himself. In 1942, Jones, who owned banks, real estate, and a Houston newspaper,[69] was serving simultaneously as chairman of the RFC, head of the Federal Loan Agency, and secretary of commerce; he was perhaps the most powerful financial figure in America.

For whatever reason—Eugene may have been jealous—*Post* editorial writers were highly critical of Jones, accusing him of procrastination in expanding stockpiles of aluminum and magnesium and in managing the nation's rubber shortage.[70] One day Eugene was checking proofs of the next day's editorials, when he came across one titled "Mr. Jones's Excuses." He asked its author to add a sentence: "The chief reason for [Jones's] failure is a boundless ambition for power that has led to his taking on more jobs than he can successfully manage."

At an Alfalfa Club dinner the next day, Jones approached Eugene, mumbling threats and profanity, seized him by the shoulders, and shook him so hard that his pince-nez fell to the floor and shattered. Eugene, some seventy-five pounds lighter and several inches shorter, was about to attempt a right to Jones's jaw when friends stepped between them. When Eugene was leaving, Jones, accompanied by former New York congressman John J. O'Connor, approached him—to apologize, Eugene thought.[71] Instead, Jones grabbed him by the lapels and started to shake him again. O'Connor, who blamed the *Post* for his defeat four years earlier, joined the fray, screaming, "Let me get at the son of a bitch." A guest sprinted to the piano and let loose with a passionate rendition of "The Star-Spangled Banner," and at once everybody stood at attention.[72] Eugene got the last word, sending a message to FDR that the president had just missed being rid of one of his "fastest-growing liabilities." The *Post* continued to criticize Jones.

It was a great story, covered by every major paper in the country—except *The Washington Post*. Meyer explained that he felt it improper to comment on something that had occurred in a private club. To compound the injury, he confessed to an *Evening Star* reporter that he had taken boxing lessons from Gentleman Jim Corbett.

Phil Graham received the highest grade in his class at officers' candidate school and won a commission to first lieutenant.[73] By 1943, he was back in Washington at the Pentagon, helping unravel Japanese military codes. He relished his important work, but in a letter to Felix Frankfurter he admitted, "It is hard for me to regard myself as any kind of a 'soldier,' " and mentioned several men of their acquaintance who had died in the war, including a Harvard Law graduate and Hockley resident. "And it isn't fair or right that they should do all the fighting," he went on, "while some of us keep on living back here in the same comfort and luxury."[74]

Indeed, there were social functions galore for Phil and Kay, including the June wedding, in the garden at Mount Kisco, of Bis Meyer, then living in New York and on the staff of *Reader's Digest,* to Major Pare Lorentz of the Army Air Corps, whom she had met when working in Hollywood as a scriptwriter for Selznick. Both Agnes and Eugene disapproved of the match. Lorentz, divorced and the father of two, was born and reared in West Virginia; he moved to New York to review film for newspapers and magazines, including *Vanity Fair* and *Town & Country*. By the time Bis met him, Lorentz was known for writing, directing, and producing New Deal–sponsored documentaries; two of them, *The Plow That Broke the Plains* (1936) and *The River* (1937), both with scores by Virgil Thomson, became classics of their kind. Among Lorentz's fans were FDR, who named him head of the United States Film Service, and James Joyce, who called the script for *The River* "the most beautiful I have heard in ten years." When Congress refused to appropriate funds for the Film Service, Lorentz went to RKO as a director and producer,[75] but his tenure was brief and unsuccessful.

After marrying into the Meyer millions, Lorentz worked on a few documentaries, but as Harold Taylor says, "He really didn't do an awful lot after that."[76] Although Bis remained active in her community, and in matters such as education and social welfare, she faded from public view after her marriage. Joanna Steichen calls her "probably the most talented member of that generation in that family, [who] unfortunately got boxed into the conventional female thing of [marrying]." She was a very talented artist, who after marrying "never produced another anything."[77]

Sidney Hyman remembers the Bis Lorentz of those years as "electric, very thin, very chic, very much of the world of theater and film. Everything she did, whether it was playing tennis or playing the violin, had panache." She was also very intimidating: "Every time I saw her," Hyman says, "I felt on guard, I didn't want to appear foolish. I felt she would be very quick to snap me, almost like a matchstick." And it was likewise for Kay, whose life then consisted of waiting—for Phil to be sent overseas, for a pregnancy to yield a baby. Hyman had "the sense that [Bis] almost cowed Kay."[78]

In mid-1944, Phil left for the southwest Pacific and became an intelligence officer on the staff of Far Eastern air commander General George Kenney in the Philippine bombing campaigns. Phil performed with his usual knack for slicing through red tape, setting up shortcuts for Kenney to receive information that General Douglas MacArthur's staff was withholding from him, as well as arranging a meeting with Roosevelt that the Pentagon had barred.[79]

In the fall of 1945, Phil Graham, recipient of the Legion of Merit, was discharged from the Army as a major. He had, presumably, every reason to feel happily expectant. The Grahams' daughter was joined in 1945 by a son, Donald. "Kay and I grow happier every day about his being a boy," Agnes wrote to Eugene.[80] (Two more sons, William and Stephen, followed in 1948 and 1953, respectively.) Phil was returning home to a wife who worshipped him, in-laws who adored him, and a clear route to the top of *The Washington Post*. Yet he still suffered from periods of dejection. "Yesterday I was saturated with gloom and had been for some days and could see nothing bright at all presently or for some time to come," he wrote home the month after Donald's birth. But he could bounce just as quickly into high spirits: "Today for no good reason I feel quite jubilant, life seems better and easier; and all in all I feel that it is my oyster."[81]

In January 1946, Phil assumed his $30,000-a-year position as associate publisher of the *Post*—presiding over Herbert Elliston, who ran the editorial page; Casey Jones, the newsroom; and Ben Gilbert, a favorite of Meyer's who had joined the paper in 1941, the city desk.

Kay retired from the circulation department. Perhaps she sensed that her presence would broadcast the fact that Phil had the second most powerful job on the paper because he was the owner's son-in-law. Or perhaps she was merely following the droves of women leaving newspapers to make room for returning veterans. "A fortress of glorious male isolationism"[82] was how Chalmers Roberts, who wrote the official history of the *Post,* described the paper's newsroom at the outbreak of the war. Jean Reiff Hailey, for example, got her chance to cover the police beat only because the regular reporter, Al Lewis, was in the Marines. "At the end of the war," Hailey recalled, "when the fellas started coming back . . . the *Post* started firing women from the newsroom like crazy. . . . They didn't fire me because by then I knew every cop in town."[83]

Retirement was not easy for Kay, especially when it was coupled with having Phil back. She had grown accustomed to her freedom, and now she was under his disapproving gaze. June Bingham and her husband, Jonathan, who had both grown close to Kay while Phil was in the Pacific, saw a disturbing change. "She was very different when Phil [came back]," June recalls. "We had gotten to know her when he wasn't [around], and she was outgoing, fun, and bright, and had convictions. It was a pleasure to be with her. And then when he was around, she was a mouse." The Binghams did not like the way Phil treated "Kate," as he then called her: "There was a little too much of the taming of the shrew, except she didn't need to be tamed."[84]

One friend speculates that Kay allowed herself to be squashed "because she did not want to be anything like her mother."[85] "In a funny way," says June Bingham, "[Phil] was Agnes Meyer in male clothes." Although "he was bright, sharp, [and] could charm the birds off the trees, he was potentially cruel, somebody I would never drop my guard with. He was self-centered, self-important, arrogant. You had a feeling when you were with him that you had to be witty or otherwise hold your peace, and Kay, I think, held her peace pretty much."[86]

When Kay retired, she really retired. *Post* employees of those years do not recollect seeing her in the building.[87] She would later remember having to advertise for a laundress a year or two after Phil became associate publisher: "I was so dense and remote from Phil's struggles . . . that I put the ad in the *Star*. Somehow Phil discovered this ghastly fact and it's truly lucky that the marriage survived that event."[88]

Phil had been at the *Post* for less than six months when Secretary of State James F. Byrnes approached Eugene about becoming the first head of the World Bank. Byrnes assured him that he was being asked only to launch the bank, to put it on sound footing; someone younger would then take over. Next Harry Truman made his pitch, the first president to confront a truly reluctant Eugene Meyer. He knew this was a tough job that several qualified candidates had already turned down, and he had no desire to leave the *Post*. "I don't want to be president of the World Bank," he told Kay and Phil. "I want to run the *Post* and fight for what I think is right."[89] But Eugene knew that he could not, in good conscience, turn it down. He had been a participant at the Bretton Woods Conference in 1944, at which the principle for such an institution had been approved, and he knew that it had not moved beyond that laudable principle, mainly for lack of a leader. He knew that the World Bank, in which an initial twenty-eight nations would participate, and which would lend money for the public good instead of for profit, could make a real difference and that he, if anyone, could make it work.

Eugene told Phil that banking is "my first love and I'm interested," but "if you don't want me to, I won't go." "You must go," Phil replied.[90] With those words, Phil, age thirty, moved to the top as acting publisher. In one sense, Phil, as impatient a man as ever, was relieved. He would have the chance to run things as he saw fit, without the supervision of his patron in the adjoining office.

Phil hosted a farewell party, a lively and affectionate affair at which the *Post*'s talented young cartoonist Herbert Block (Herblock) presented Eugene with a cartoon of him counting out a $2 billion loan to a foreign plenipotentiary, whom he then asked, "And how about a subscription to *The Washington Post*?"[91] Phil might have been excused for believing that Eugene would never return to the paper—but that was not to be the case.

Eugene had not been at the World Bank a week when he clashed with its directors, who had been in their jobs for almost a year before his arrival and some of whom felt they should run the bank. Some were determined to restrict American influence by limiting Eugene's role and keeping control in the hands of the directors. The American director seemed to view the bank as an adjunct to the State Department, where he had previously worked, and impeded Eugene at every turn.[92]

He was miserable, especially when he thought of what he had given up. Rather than advise Phil on handling *The Washington Post,* he found himself asking his son-in-law's advice on handling the directors of the World Bank.[93] In a letter to a fellow publisher, Eugene lamented, "We both were in the newspaper business, but you have had sense enough to stick to it."[94] And he told his secretary, "I could stay and fight these bastards and probably win in the end, but I'm too old for that."[95]

He decided to quit, less than six months into his tenure and with only two weeks' notice, justifying his haste on the grounds that he had done what Truman and Byrnes had asked, and that the ten-year plans he was then formulating would be better executed by a younger man. Merlo Pusey contended that Eugene's explanation was subterfuge, that he was uncharacteristically more concerned with his own interests than the bank's. "His abrupt departure," Pusey wrote, "left the bank in turmoil that could have been avoided if he had remained until his successor could take over."[96] More likely, Eugene realized that the *Post* had supplanted banking as his passion, and he wanted back in. He had served six presidents in major roles and now pronounced the public service phase of his career over.

The *Post* reported that Eugene would keep an office at the paper but would not "return to its active administration in his former role of editor and publisher."[97] Although Phil was somewhat soothed by being allowed to hang on to the title of publisher, friends suggest that he was not happy about his father-in-law's taking back the title of chairman of the board and the role of active participant. Phil and other members of the Meyer family had encouraged Eugene to stay on at the World Bank.

Phil knew that despite his fancy title he was still his father-in-law's salaried employee, and the fact was driven home when, later in 1946, Phil tried to hire John Sweeterman, vice-president and general manager of the *Journal-Herald* in Dayton, Ohio. Phil offered Sweeterman an annual salary of $30,000—the same as his own—but had to increase the offer to $35,000.[98] Sweeterman had a reputation for controlling costs, and Phil wanted him because he knew Eugene had just hired management consultant Richard Paget with the instruction: "Young man, this company is losing a million a year, and I want you to undertake a study and give me some recommendations so I'm losing only half a million a year."[99] As long as Eugene subsidized the paper, he would exert control unacceptable to Phil—control that carried over to his private life.

Kay was accustomed to living in something grander than the rowhouse on 37th Street. She had heard about a place that seemed more suitable for the publisher of *The Washington Post*—an eight-bedroom brick mansion on 31st and R, one of the most valuable houses in Georgetown, complete with columns, a circular driveway, expanses of lawn, and a view over Georgetown from the rear and Oak Hill Cemetery from the front.* It was not affordable on Phil's $30,000 a year, so Kay went to Eugene for the down payment.[101]

Friends say that Phil could never shake the idea that the *Post* had been a dowry of sorts for marrying Kay. But if it was a dowry, it was an unsatisfying one: while Eugene let Phil keep the title of publisher, he made no move to transfer ownership to him or even to him and Kay. Consequently, Phil was torn between loving his new career and feeling cornered and used—the kept son-in-law—when he might have been practicing law and starting a political career. He watched with envy as some new and old Washington friends and peers, such as John Kennedy, Lyndon Johnson, and George Smathers, were elected to Congress—making policy, not merely reporting it. He despaired that he had made a terrible mistake.

Phil turned his anger toward Eugene Meyer because, Bernard Nossiter explained, "Phil was not a self-made man. Phil was a man made by the old man. My guess is that when Phil married this ugly duckling, which she was, insecure, nervous, bright perhaps, but much too timid, he must have heard an awful lot of talk, joshing, but [also] serious talk about, 'Oh boy, I can see why you married her.' Who knows? Phil was an ambitious man. Perhaps that was a motive, to promote himself, get himself a rich father-in-law and a standing high jump into the upper reaches of Washington. Yep, a man on the make Phil certainly was."[102]

Luvie Pearson recalled a comment Phil always injected into conversations: "The only smart thing to do is to marry the boss's daughter. That's what I did. I wouldn't be anyplace." Phil was "obviously very competent and very bright, but he also realized that he couldn't possibly be where he was without the Meyers. That ate him up. He had to keep proving himself and proving himself."[103]

*

---

*The owner immediately preceding the Grahams was William ("Wild Bill") Donovan, head of the OSS; the mother of Watergate burglar G. Gordon Liddy had grown up there.[100]

Al Friendly would later praise Eugene for not reclaiming the role of publisher. "He returned . . . as chairman of the board, where his financial advice and prowess proved indispensable, but he left to Phil Graham all the decisions proper to a publisher, without kibitzing or second-guessing him. Meyer was no Indian giver."[104]

Others say that the division of labor between the two was neither so clear nor so amiable. Eugene presented himself as "just the old man called chairman of the board," who was ready to counsel Phil when asked. But Phil rarely asked, preferring advice from John Sweeterman. Deborah Davis claimed in her biography of Katharine Graham that when Eugene "did interject himself, Phil called him 'an irascible old man' and said he would run the newspaper his way or return to the practice of law."[105]

The result was that Eugene, for the first time in his life, did not have much to do. "I'd see Eugene come in in a tuxedo on a Saturday night, with the secretary of the Navy or defense or some big Cabinet officer or Supreme Court justice," recalls Morris Siegel, who arrived at the *Post* in 1946.[106] Eugene enjoyed playing tour guide, but there was no longer much point to it. It was difficult for this man who placed such a high value on time to face, suddenly, so few urgent demands on his time. Reporter Murrey Marder, who also began at the *Post* in 1946, recounts a story frequently told about Eugene in his heyday, when he could turn an hour into a new government program or a change in the direction of the stock market: "He came into the sports department one day and there was a lot of excitement, so he asked someone what was happening." Shirley Povich told him that distance runner Paavo Nurmi had just broken a world record by 20.5 seconds. Eugene looked at Povich and asked, "Is that important?" "Oh, yes," Povich answered. "That's a new world record." Eugene, the banker, said, "Twenty point five seconds. I wonder what he'll do with that time."[107]

Albert Manola, another who joined the *Post* in 1946, has memories of Eugene that are touching, but sad too: "He'd come up on Sunday afternoon, Agnes would apparently lose track of him. The chauffeur deposited him in front of the *Post* building, and he would wander around and ask the pressmen to make him a hat and things like that. He'd have a cigar in his pocket. He would offer to trade cigars with me." (Manola, who smoked five-cent cigars, was surprised that the cigars Meyer traded cost only a dime. He expected more from a man of Meyer's wealth. One Sunday morning Manola went to the Statler Hotel and bought a fifty-cent cigar. "When Meyer came in that Sunday afternoon, he was really surprised that I had gotten him the kind of cigar Winston Churchill used to send him, made in Cuba. He didn't say anything, just took it. The next time he came in he brought me a twenty-five-cent cigar.")[108]

As Phil's hand grew stronger, Eugene took to riding the cage elevator and calling out the floors, striking up conversations with people who interested him. One day he greeted an Army captain, still in uniform, who recognized him and said he had come by to see if there might be an opening on the editorial page. "See Herb Elliston and tell him I sent you," Eugene said. Thus Robert Estabrook, a midwesterner who before serving in the Army had been editor of the *Gazette* in Cedar Rapids, Iowa, was hired as the $70-a-week junior editorial writer and editor of the letters column.[109] He would later become editorial-page editor.

But at the end of the day it was Phil making the important decisions. Eugene Meyer and Kay, the daughter he had once considered his heir, were lost in the shadows of a man who was becoming increasingly powerful—and unpredictable.

Chapter 8

PHIL AND AGNES
JOCKEY FOR POSITION

The one member of the Meyer family unwilling to be lost in Phil's shadow was Agnes, who knew that his ascension would deprive her of any real power at the *Post*. So she shifted her ambition to becoming what Hope Ridings Miller calls a "star writer."[1]

Agnes would later credit her son and son-in-law with launching her writing career. In 1942, as Bill Meyer and Phil Graham were about to go off to war, they pleaded with her to drop her plans to write about Mann and Tolstoy, and instead to write about problems on the homefront.[2] More likely, Agnes took up writing because of the notices garnered by her rivals: Cissy Patterson—"the most powerful woman in America," according to *Collier's*—and Dorothy Thompson, who had, Winston Churchill said, "shown what one valiant woman can do with the power of a pen."[3]

Agnes saw the *Post* as her vehicle, and she circumvented Eugene's ban on publishing anything by a family member (namely, Agnes) with a series of articles for the Associated Press describing how the average English family coped during the blitz. Next, after touring war production centers in the United States, she described in another series the horrid living conditions of war workers.[4] (Weary of the arguments, and recognizing Agnes's determination, Eugene quietly allowed her pieces to appear in the *Post*.)

Although Agnes still could not stomach Eleanor Roosevelt—one reporter described the First Lady as Agnes's "pet aversion," speculating that among their differences might have been that "Mrs. Roosevelt goes about with women; Mrs. Meyer likes the company of men"[5]—she set herself up as Eleanor's Republican counterpart, sticking her nose into American institutions and communities that had gone largely uncovered and in the process becoming a scold to her detractors and a thorough and persistent reporter to her fans. Harry Truman later remarked, "There isn't a day that goes by without my getting a letter from that Meyer woman or Eleanor Roosevelt, telling me how to do this job."[6]

In her popular and long-running syndicated column, "My Day," Eleanor Roosevelt had a strict limit of five hundred words. Agnes would have abided by no such restriction and undoubtedly would have been amazed that anyone would want to put a cap on her opinion. Her series, which typically ran on the news pages for days at a time, were a burden on *Post* managing editor Casey Jones, who hadn't assigned the pieces in the first place. He "dreaded her appearance in the newsroom," recalls Ben Gilbert, "because she frequently would drop an article on his desk and he knew he was expected to run it."[7] One reporter remembers Jones's confession that "he didn't know what he'd do if she turned in one more piece. Her pieces went on forever and he didn't dare cut them."[8] It fell to Elsie Carper to negotiate every cut with Agnes, and Agnes "fought for every syllable," Ben Gilbert says. "Elsie could be in the diplomatic corps without going through the foreign service."[9]

Agnes's attention to public education was sparked by her brother, Frederick, who had started as a classroom teacher in the Bronx and worked his way up to superintendent of New York City's high schools. "She became interested in public schools," says Elsie Carper, "because she was a product of the public schools. She could see that they were not nearly as good as they were in her day."[10] Agnes testified before Congress in support of a bill to provide federal aid to public schools, and so impressed at least one congressman that he voiced his regret that state superintendents and boards of education could not read her reporting and hear her testimony.[11]

She was ahead of *Brown v. Board of Education* in criticizing segregated schools. After visiting such D.C. black schools as Shaw, Hine, and Terrell—she was among the very few whites ever to set foot in them—she coined the epithets "Shameful Shaw," "Horrible Hine," and "Terrible Terrell." When Agnes arrived at a school by chauffeured car, wearing an enormous hat atop her big-boned frame, speaking with her commanding voice—"Brünnhilde with a typewriter," one of her friends described her—the staff practically stood at attention.[12]

She took on other dicey subjects as well, such as the corrupt

Edward Crump political machine in Memphis, problems of migrant workers,[13] and conditions in the coal mines of eastern Kentucky— her articles being used in a congressional hearing on the welfare fund demanded by John L. Lewis and his United Mine Workers.[14] Lewis, who won his battle with the operators, told Agnes that she was the "make-weight in a delicate situation."[15] She also wrote about riots in Columbia, Tennessee, during which twenty-three blacks were arrested; her articles were introduced at trial and were considered instrumental in freeing all but two.[16]

Elsie Carper, among others, says that the *Post* was lucky to have Agnes Meyer; her stories gave stature to the paper.[17] Her pieces on the war production centers were described by *Saturday Review of Literature* as "the best, most nearly comprehensive report on social conditions in wartime America."[18] Her articles on education had such an impact—"distinguished journalism," says Ben Gilbert, that made "many whites aware of appalling conditions in the city's black schools"—that the D.C. board of education later waived a rule against honoring living people and voted to name an elementary school for the Meyers.[19]

For all that, Eugene would have preferred that Agnes keep away from the newspaper. He would never cease to be amazed at how self-deluding she could be, how she would forget that she was writing for the *Post* for one reason only, because her husband owned it. As she became overblown about her accomplishments—"I broke the back of the Crump machine," she boasted—she concluded that the nation deserved more of her copy. Eugene was alarmed at the sheer volume of it. Agnes frequently quoted him as saying that while she was often a headache she was never a bore.[20] After a pile of her copy landed on his desk, he confided to a reporter, "You know, she's beginning to be a bore."[21]

Agnes's crusade against federal funds for parochial schools began with her passion for a man—two men, actually. Early in 1945, Sidney Hyman introduced Agnes to Saul Alinsky, a Jew from Chicago's Maxwell Street ghetto, a University of Chicago graduate, a community organizer and self-styled agitator for a "democratic revolution." In 1939, Alinsky had organized Chicago's Back of the Yards neighborhood, made infamous in Upton Sinclair's *The Jungle*.

Agnes's series for the *Post* describing Alinsky's "We the People" campaign was more a love letter to her latest soulmate than an objective analysis. Sanford Horwitt, Alinsky's biographer, described its "tone of near euphoria"; Agnes wrote, for instance, that his movement represented well over a million people; even Alinsky, a formidable self-promoter, claimed only a quarter that many.[22]

Befriending Alinsky took no special nerve. He had many prominent friends, among them Marshall Field III, who reprinted Agnes's series in his Chicago *Sun.* Agnes made a hefty contribution to Alinsky's campaign and promoted *Reveille for Radicals,* his appeal for what Agnes called an "orderly revolution."[23]

Alinsky was just her kind of radical—a man who could be streetwise and gratuitously crude, particularly when in the company of limousine liberals, but who preferred to hold forth on the nation's impoverished while drinking fine wines, smoking Dunhills, and enjoying the comforts of plush hotels or the Meyers' homes, which he visited often.[24]

Alinsky, who called himself an agnostic, introduced Agnes to Auxiliary Bishop Bernard Sheil, a Chicago liberal and pro-labor founder of the Catholic Youth Organization. He had helped Alinsky in the Back of the Yards battle, and he soon replaced him in Agnes's affections. They met at Mario's, an Italian restaurant under the CYO office: "Bishop Sheil entered with the light step of an athlete in perfect training." He was, she gushed, "an old friend whom I was meeting for the first time. Was the Bishop right when he said weeks later that we were at home with each other because we both love God above everything else?" In an article that resulted, Agnes idolized Sheil as "a robust saint. . . . His spirituality represents no barriers to a non-Catholic. . . . Like that of a great poet, it has been forged by the role of mediator between heaven and earth."[25]

Nicholas von Hoffman, who before becoming a journalist was an Alinsky disciple, said that Agnes could not have more thoroughly misjudged Sheil. "He was a man who was, in my opinion, quite corrupt. He lived in a style that was so far beyond anything that you can justify for a clergyman. He had a string of polo ponies."[26]

Having been relieved of Agnes's ardor, Alinsky was, according to von Hoffman, "pressed into service" as a go-between, often accompanying the bishop on stays at Mount Kisco. Whether this was a sexual affair or, more likely, still another platonic passion, von Hoffman doesn't know. But he does know that Agnes had an exact replica of Sheil's episcopal robes made for her. "They would sometimes have their, the newspaper word is 'trysts,' at Mount Kisco, and

Saul described to me this memorable moment of the two bishops, one girl bishop, one boy bishop, wandering through the gardens of Mount Kisco holding hands."[27]

Agnes's desire to improve public schools was confused with both her desire for Sheil and her anger at the Church for not bowing to her lobbying to have him appointed archbishop and eventually cardinal.[28] Her campaign to prohibit federal aid to parochial schools came off sounding anti-Catholic. She once made a speech saying no American mother would want her daughter to become a nun.[29] She also charged that the "Catholic hierarchy" was out to destroy the First Amendment.[30]

Agnes found herself fighting alongside a strange ally—Eleanor Roosevelt. They plotted strategy together when, in 1949, New York's very conservative Francis Cardinal Spellman wrote an open letter accusing the former First Lady of "anti-Catholicism . . . unworthy of an American mother!" Bishop Sheil was one of the few members of the Catholic hierarchy to come to her defense.[31]

With the help of her friend Harold Taylor, Agnes organized the National Committee in Support of the Public Schools,* and served as its chairman. Its goal was to increase government financial support for public education and to deny federal aid to parochial schools.

In September 1948, the Meyers were invited to dinner with H. L. Mencken at the home of his publisher, Alfred Knopf. "Mrs. Meyer inclines toward uplifting," Mencken wrote in his diary, "and is somewhat alarming. She is now carrying on a campaign against what she describes as a Catholic plot to seize the public schools. I argued with her that if it succeeded the schools would be greatly improved but, like all uplifters, she has no sense of humor. She dragged me into a side room to belabor me. Also, she invited me to dinner in Washington. I simply can't imagine going."[32]

When Agnes's writing took on its anti-Catholic tone and Catholic readers of the *Post* threatened a boycott, Phil restrained his mother-in-law. He also decided to get rid of managing editor Casey Jones, described by one reporter as "a very primitive conservative type"[33] who had little regard for the complex, issue-oriented stories that appealed to Phil.

---

*Its successor is the National Committee for Citizens in Education.

Jones's replacement was forty-three-year-old James Russell Wiggins, a self-taught man from a poor family, with a ravenous appetite for books, an unshakable belief in "the people's right to know," expertise in constitutional law, and unbending integrity. Over twenty-five years, he had worked his way up to editor of the *Dispatch–Pioneer Press* in St. Paul, but was fired for being too interventionist.[34] After a short stint at *The New York Times,* he went to the *Post* in 1947.

Late that year, Phil launched "The Magazine Rack," a Sunday column to review current periodicals, and asked Kay to write it. She agreed, but without much enthusiasm.

It was harder for Phil to find a job for Eugene, who, out of the line of authority and fire, seemed to be aging quickly. He spent much of his time now playing bridge at Crescent Place with two new and favorite partners, Jean Friendly and Luvie Pearson, and at the Metropolitan Club with Frank Noyes. Phil realized that Eugene needed something more, and in 1947, when the *Post* still had no correspondents overseas, he asked Al Friendly to accompany Eugene to Europe.

The highlight of the trip was lunch with Winston Churchill at Chequers. Eugene had brought the former prime minister two large boxes of Havana cigars, which gradually improved his dour mood, even though he was not allowed to smoke at the time and resorted to holding them against a candle flame and sniffing them. "As the meal went on," Friendly later told his wife, "there was a lot of wine and then there were brandies, and [Churchill] got more and more expansive. It was like talking history." An audience with the pope came later.[35] That trip proved a tonic for Eugene, who then wrote an eloquent argument for the Marshall Plan.

Along the way, he grew close to the thirty-five-year-old Friendly, son of Edward Rosenbaum (Friendly used his mother's maiden name to avoid anti-Semitism) and husband of the Meyer children's playmate Jean Ulman, a Gentile and a third-generation Washingtonian.

While Kay receded ever further into the background and Eugene struggled to find his foothold, Phil was becoming the dominant presence on the paper. With his charm, his easy way with profanity, his first-name familiarity, he was developing a cadre of loyalists.

A constant flow of notes from Phil to his reporters commenting on stories let them know that the publisher read the newspaper and appreciated good work. Sportswriter Morrie Siegel recalls Phil's frequent visits to the sports department: "To have the publisher come back to bullshit was better than a five-dollar-a-week raise. I didn't know many big shots then, and he was maybe the best."[36]

Elsie Carper remembers Phil's "open door" and his persuading her to give up her reporting job, set up a personnel department, and become its manager. She knew nothing about personnel, but he convinced her that it was crucial to have someone who knew about newspapers running the department. "Because I had that position I knew all of the things that he did for employees at the paper."[37]

For all the good cheer and good reviews, Eugene sensed how uncomfortable his son-in-law was in the role of employee. On July 23, 1948, Eugene gave Phil $75,000 as an outright gift. With that money, supposedly to be paid back later, Phil bought seventy percent of the voting stock (3,500 shares) from Agnes and Eugene; Katharine bought thirty percent (1,500 shares).[38] Eugene explained that the discrepancy in stock holdings was intentional: "A man should never feel that he is working for his wife."

There was, realistically, no fear on anyone's part that Kay would suddenly become feisty and seek to gain control. Kay herself dismissed as utterly ridiculous the notion that Eugene had handed control to Phil but really retained it through her: "[Phil] thinks I'm an idiot. Honestly, I have no influence."[39]

Eugene gave his other children no ownership in the *Post,* in accordance with his belief that in a family-owned business only one person could run things.[40] Roswell Gilpatric, the Cravath, Swaine & Moore lawyer who handled many of the family's legal matters, explains that had Eugene given the *Post* to all of his children, "you would have had what you have in the Bingham family, where second and third generations don't get along."[*] There was no detectable bitterness among his other children that the family jewel was handed to Kay and even more so to an outsider, because Eugene "equalized his bounty among his children by giving the other three other parts of his fortune."[41] To give the paper to Phil and Kay seemed the obvious solution, says Bis, although she adds that Florence "questioned whether her sons would have access to jobs on the *Post.*"[42]

---

[*]In the Bingham family of Louisville, fighting between siblings led to the sale of the *Courier-Journal and Times* to Gannett in 1986.

What Eugene did was truly extraordinary. "The way in which he ceded control of the paper to Phil," remarked Bernard Nossiter, "turned over control in his own lifetime, that's pretty rare."[43] For all his mixed feelings, Phil also recognized his father-in-law's rare generosity.

The day after Eugene gave Phil the *Post,* Cissy Patterson stole the stage again—by dying, in bed, allegedly of an inadvertent mix of sleeping pills and liquor. She had remarked, in the presence of her chauffeur, "They'll have a damned good fight when I'm gone. I've fixed that!"[44] And so she had, via her complicated and peculiar will and her estrangement from her only child, Felicia, the ex-wife of Drew Pearson. Her estate turned out to be worth more than $16 million. Cissy left Felicia a tax-free annual sum of $25,000 and gave the *Times-Herald,* then Washington's most widely circulated paper, to Frank Waldrop and six other executives, who were dubbed first "overnight millionaires" and next, and more permanently, the "Seven Dwarfs."[45]

When he heard of Cissy's death, Phil rushed from Mount Kisco to Washington to inform one of the Dwarfs that the *Post* planned to make a bid for the *Times-Herald.*[46] But Felicia filed a formal notice of contest, claiming title to the entire estate on the grounds that when the last will was executed, Cissy was of "unsound mind," that she had been the victim of "undue influence," and that, in any case, the will favoring the Seven Dwarfs was not Cissy's last. A rash of break-ins and suicides—including the apparent suicides of Cissy's former treasurer and her former social secretary—seemed to support Felicia's claim, and sparked rumors that one or more of the Dwarfs had poisoned Cissy, afraid that she was about to alter her will. On the night she died she had talked to dinner guests about "great changes" in her will.[47]

After five months of squabbling, Felicia settled out of court, and Phil Graham immediately resumed his efforts to buy the *Times-Herald.* The *Post* continued to lose money, and Phil knew that his only hope for profit lay in buying the competitor, merging parts of the paper into his own, and then promptly closing it.

The seven owners, all in their fifties and sixties and contemplating retirement, seemed happy to sell. They needed money for inheritance taxes, mechanical improvements, and working capital, and were horrified when they had to borrow money to meet the payroll. Almost exactly a year after Cissy's death, Phil offered $4.5 million of Eugene's money for the paper, including its building. Although neither he nor his father-in-law cared about Cissy's *Chicago Tribune* stock, Phil proposed buying her two-hundred-plus nonvoting shares. He thought this beefed-up offer would clinch the deal, but instead it doomed it. The prospect of having Eugene Meyer and Phil Graham hold shares of the McCormick–Patterson trust alarmed Colonel Robert McCormick, who, as soon as he heard the news, set out to block the sale. He did not mind if the family lost the *Times-Herald;* in fact, Cissy had left the paper to the Seven Dwarfs in part to keep it out of the Colonel's hands, as she knew he had no special feeling for her paper or for her (he was heard loudly singing after being informed of her death). But McCormick did not, under any circumstances, want the *Tribune* stock to be spread.[48]

McCormick offered to match Phil's bid for the *Times-Herald.* Phil was distraught. McCormick had previously shown no interest, and Phil thought he would be up against only Hearst, Samuel Newhouse, and Scripps Howard—any of whom Eugene could outbid.[49]

Phil raced back to Washington from a family vacation in Narragansett, Rhode Island, to put together another deal. He and Eugene worked all night on an offer containing more money for the paper, and much more for Cissy's units of the McCormick–Patterson trust. If more money was needed, Agnes offered to contribute her assets, including the Crescent Place house. But the seven *Times-Herald* owners never even considered this proposal; they happily accepted McCormick's, which yielded each around $650,000, far less than Phil's last offer would have. They were as confident that McCormick would keep the paper open as they were that Phil would fold it.

According to Eugene's biographer, when Kay heard that the *Post*'s chances were dead, she wept and left the children in Narragansett to join Phil, who had told her that if he didn't get the *Times-Herald* he would "just die for a week." His spirits lifted after he read a book on the ups and downs in the careers of Colonel McCormick and Joe Patterson. "I do think we are going to make it," Phil told Kay.[50]

Almost immediately McCormick made his first mistake. Instead of letting Cissy's seasoned editor, Frank Waldrop, run the paper, McCormick appointed his niece Ruth Elizabeth "Bazy" Tankersley, a Tribune Company director, to run it. With no direct male heirs and a desire to keep the paper in the family, McCormick was using the

Times-Herald slot as a tryout for the *Tribune.* Tankersley, Waldrop explains, was the "lineal inheritor of the torch," McCormick's insurance that the paper he really cared for would remain in the family.*[51]

But the Colonel's biggest mistake, Waldrop says, was buying the paper for the wrong reason—"to show Washington he thought it contemptible." He despised FDR and wanted to turn the *Times-Herald* into a Washington outlet of his prized *Chicago Tribune.* He ignored the warning that what worked in one city would not necessarily work in another. He made the paper stodgy, eliminating Cissy's "rape and murder page" and ignoring her most important constituency—the "government girl."[52] He poured money into the *Times-Herald,* but his *Tribune* clone was at best a third-rate imitation, and boring to boot. Cissy's money-maker was soon losing between half a million and a million dollars a year. Eugene made another pass at buying the paper, and McCormick declined; Eugene knew, although he could still not convince Phil, that it was just a matter of time.

After quarreling with Tankersley, a well-meaning but naive woman, McCormick was forced to take over personally. "McCormick wasn't interested," according to Waldrop. "He was an old man, he was sick, he was bored, he was worried that he was going to die. He didn't know who was going to run the Tribune Company. He put [Tankersley] in here to try to do it, and she flunked. After that he just wanted out."[53]

If Phil could not own the *Times-Herald,* he wanted at least a fair chance at competing with it, which he felt was impossible so long as the *Post* remained in its E Street antique. So Eugene put up $6 million to build a new *Post* building at 1515 L Street NW, complete with color presses and air-conditioning.[54] At its opening in 1950, Eugene wore a pressman's cap and clutched a certificate declaring him an honorary member of the union. General George Marshall, then secretary of defense, dedicated the new building. Phil stood by happily but restlessly.

That same year, again with Eugene as his money man, Phil bought

---

*Tankersley's parents were Medill McCormick, a U.S. senator from Illinois, and Ruth Hanna McCormick, daughter of Ohio political boss Mark Hanna and, briefly, a member of Congress. Tankersley's husband, Garvin, had been a city editor of the *Times-Herald.*

a Washington radio station. Also in 1950, influenced by his new friend CBS president William Paley, he bought the Washington CBS affiliate, WTOP-TV; three years later came the purchase of WMBR-TV in Jacksonville, Florida. Phil considered the television stations money-makers that would cover the *Post*'s continuing annual losses. Eugene did not see the future of the infant television industry and thought Phil would be wiser to stick to print, but he went along— anything to lift Phil's spirits and keep them up. The total cost of the stations was $7.8 million;[55] in hindsight they were a spectacularly good buy.

These deals could not relieve Phil's sadness that his closest friend, Ed Prichard, disbarred and disgraced, was going to prison. Prich had returned to Kentucky after the war to practice law and enter politics. He had been the right-hand man to Secretary of State James Byrnes and had grown close to two Kentuckians, Chief Justice Fred Vinson and Vice-President Alben Barkley. His prospects were exceeded only by his arrogance and braggadocio. In the fall of 1948, Prich was charged with stuffing a ballot box for the U.S. Senate election in Kentucky. It was done, apparently, as a prank. "There was no need to stuff that box," says Ben Gilbert, "because his candidate was going to win anyway. It was just a matter of Prich's trying to demonstrate that he was one of the boys"[56]—that he was not some Washington elitist. Prich panicked and asked a state judge for advice. According to Joe Rauh, the judge "ratted on him, told the U.S. attorney."[57] Somebody was out to get Prich, there being no shortage of people who found his brilliance insufferable.

Phil Graham and Rauh wanted to appeal the conviction to the Supreme Court, but could not: four justices, including Felix Frankfurter and the chief justice, felt so close to Prich that they refused to hear his appeal. In July 1950, his options exhausted, Prich entered the Federal Correctional Institution at Ashland, Kentucky.

Almost immediately, Phil and Rauh began to lobby President Truman to pardon their friend. The president issued a pardon, and by Christmas of that year, Prich was home. But his prospects and career were shattered. Eventually he was readmitted to the bar and became a respected figure in Kentucky, but always behind the scenes.*

---

*Prich spent the last years of his life navigating around the country in a wheelchair giving speeches.[58] He was nearly blind and required daily dialysis. When he died in 1984, four state governors attended his funeral.[59]

*

Kay had completely accepted the female role of making certain that everybody else was happy and satisfied. It was an exhausting responsibility because she, more than anyone else, was captive to Phil's moods. A few hours of sleep were enough to keep him flying for days at a time, conquering this and that with stunning energy and creativity. Kay, with just one outside duty—writing "The Magazine Rack"—seemed chronically overwhelmed and fatigued, both physically and emotionally. At dinner parties, while Phil dazzled the guests with his wit, she fell asleep in her chair; one friend describes her as seriously exhausted. Rather than loosen the domestic ties, she decided to give up the column, her last direct link to the *Post* and her premarriage ambitions. "After a while I got too busy with the family to keep it up, but I didn't dare tell Phil I was going to stop," she later explained. "I just stopped one day without telling him about it."[60]

Domestic life was becoming more complicated. Phil, gregarious to start, now had professional as well as personal reasons for entertaining. Kay was like the shoemaker's ill-shod child: her mother was one of the great hostesses of Washington, but she herself had barely a clue how to entertain graciously and was terrified at the prospect of failing, of proving unworthy of Phil.

Before she mastered the art of properly running one house, the Grahams had two. In January 1951, Phil and Kay bought Glen Welby, a historic Fauquier County estate on 348 acres of bluegrass in Marshall, Virginia, near the very wealthy community of Middleburg.[61] They staffed it with a maid and a cook.

Well before his introduction into the ranks of the landed gentry, Phil took a turn, gently to the right—away from the ideological politics of his New Deal days to the practical politics of what was soon to be the age of Ike. His politics, says Jean Friendly, became "the art of the possible. Phil was a pragmatist, completely." Compromise, he knew, was the way you got things done.[62]

In 1947, he and Saul Alinsky had exchanged angry letters over a *Post* story that repeated charges that a union leader was a communist collaborator. Phil charged Alinsky with playing into the hands of "the Party boys. . . . I simply can't believe that it's 'progressive' to agree with every act . . . committed by the Soviet Union."[63] In 1950, Felix Frankfurter, who had himself made a rightward shift, worried that Phil had gone too far in that direction; he lectured Phil that he had lately had to defend him "vigorously . . . against the charge of responsibility for editorial views that . . . aroused criticism on the part of friends" of Phil's.[64] Frankfurter next took Phil to task for allowing his editorial-page editor to call for Secretary of State Dean Acheson's resignation—a demand also being made by Senator Joseph McCarthy, albeit for different reasons.[65]

Sir Isaiah Berlin claims that Phil "was shocked by the behavior of the Russians, and that moved him to the right."[66] Cynics charged that Phil's shift had more to do with wanting to make himself palatable to Colonel McCormick in hopes of improving his chances to buy the *Times-Herald.*

On February 12, 1951, McCormick's *Chicago Tribune* ran a story that opened: "Sometimes called 'the *Washington Pravda*' after the Communist party newspaper in Moscow, *The Washington Post* is chalking up a telling record for defending Reds and pinkos . . . and violent attacks on pro-American members of Congress."[67]

Perhaps with that story in mind, Phil told Murrey Marder, then covering the "Red beat," that he had heard that an officer of the United Electrical Workers was a communist agent. "I want you to run this down. It will be a hell of a story if it's true." Marder showed little enthusiasm, but he knew what Phil was thinking: "It was important to him because the *Post* was under tremendous attack." After a few days Marder reported back to Phil what the House Un-American Activities Committee and the International Security Subcommittee were saying. Phil, according to Marder, said, " 'Well, that's all very interesting, isn't it?' and I said, 'No, Phil, these people think he's a communist agent and maybe he is, but they can't prove it,' and he said, 'But you told me a lot of interesting things here.' I said, 'Yeah, there are always a lot of interesting things around any kind of accusation.' He said, 'Well, let's write it,' and I said, 'Write what?' 'What you just told me.' I said, 'Phil, that's not a story.' " They argued further, until, in exasperation, Marder blurted, "You mean you want a [Robert] McCormick job done on him." Phil "almost went through the ceiling in a cloud of steam and smoke." Marder stalked out of Phil's office, suspecting that he had just lost his job, but Phil calmed down and nothing was ever said.[68]

Phil was trying to reform not only the paper's image but his own as well. In addition to serving as a trustee of George Washington University and the University of Chicago, he became active in the Advertising Council and was the guiding spirit on the board of the Committee for Economic Development—founded after the war by the CEOs of leading corporations as an alternative to the hidebound chamber of commerce, as an organization for men of moderation.[69]

Some people suspected that a statement of Phil's in July 1951—"I am becoming a strong Ike man"[70]—was also part of the campaign to rehabilitate himself and his paper. In explaining his move to the Republican side, Phil joined his father-in-law in citing disgust with corruption in the Truman administration and also the belief that Eisenhower was the best man to prevent Robert Taft from securing the 1952 Republican nomination and shifting the party from an internationalist to an isolationist stance; Eisenhower was also the best man to curb Joseph McCarthy's witch-hunting excesses.

Earlier Eugene had directly urged Eisenhower to run for president, even breaching journalistic ethics by airmailing to him advance copies of the results of Gallup polls (he was able to obtain them as a special favor from George Gallup) that showed he was the one man who could beat both Taft and the Democrats.[71] But Phil played an even more important role. For the first time since Eugene had bought the paper, the *Post* endorsed a presidential candidate—in an editorial written by Phil himself that called this "declaration of preference" an "exercise of our independence, not an abandonment of it."[72] Herbert Brownell, Jr., a strategist for Eisenhower and later his attorney general, said the *Post*'s endorsement was the most effective Eisenhower would ever receive. The same week the *Post* ran excerpts from his campaign biography, *The Man from Abilene.*[73]

When Phil went out of his way to embrace not only Eisenhower but also his running mate, Richard Nixon, his critics were convinced that it was Colonel McCormick, not the Republican ticket, that was uppermost in Phil's mind. It could be argued that Eisenhower was not all that appealing to McCormick, especially after he took the nomination away from Taft, but Nixon was just McCormick's kind of guy. Phil spent an afternoon with "Dick" at the Burning Tree Golf Club in Bethesda, Maryland, and reported to friends that he was a better man than met the eye.[74]

Phil vetoed publication of a Herblock cartoon of a stolid-faced Ike saying, "Naughty, naughty," to McCarthy and Nixon, who were drawn as "smear artists with buckets and dripping brushes."[75] As Herblock's Nixon began regularly to feature the sinister five-o'clock shadow, Phil ordered the cartoonist to "shave Nixon." Herblock complied, although he got the last laugh by drawing Nixon clean-shaven but with a set of strings at the back of his head to indicate that he was wearing a clean-shaven mask.[76] During the last two weeks of the campaign, Phil ordered Herblock to take his anti-Ike, rabidly anti-Nixon cartoons on vacation.[77]

Herblock was not the only *Post* contributor whom Phil censored during this campaign. A few days before the start of the Republican National Convention, Agnes Meyer gave a speech in Detroit in which she railed against public support for Catholic school education. Concerned that Catholics who supported McCarthy would view this as a further attack by the *Post* and that her opinions would draw Catholics away from Eisenhower (whom Truman was busy denouncing as the "captive candidate" of anti-Semites and anti-Catholics,[78] Phil took strong action. He ordered that a disclaimer, ostensibly by Agnes, but actually written by Phil, run beneath the text of the speech when it appeared in the *Post:* "The views expressed in my Detroit speech are my own and do not reflect the opinions of *The Washington Post.* . . . I do not participate in the formation of editorial policies."[79]

Phil's doubts about his candidate's willingness to fight McCarthy started during the campaign when Eisenhower refused to denounce the senator publicly and cut from a speech praise for General George Marshall, then one of McCarthy's targets. Things did not improve after Eisenhower's victory. Phil drafted a statement for him to issue: "I feel impelled to make clear that the tactics of Senator McCarthy are in direct opposition to my fundamental beliefs," but the president ignored him. McCarthy slandered Eisenhower's appointees as recklessly as he had Truman's, and regularly referred to the *Post* as the "Washington *Daily Worker.*"

Phil was depressed by how little difference he made. That feeling, combined with exhaustion from his work on Eisenhower's behalf, resulted in the first of what appeared to be physical collapses. He spent three months in bed, then came back with a vengeance, disgusted with Eisenhower and unwilling to stay silent while McCarthy ruined reputations. Next time he backed a presidential candidate, he would make certain he had influence not only during the campaign but also after the victory. Meanwhile, *The Washington Post* would become the strongest anti-McCarthy paper in the country.

Bob Estabrook recalls that Phil's suggestions for anti-McCarthy editorials included one, which won a Sigma Delta Chi Award, that warned Eisenhower against justifying his submission to McCarthy by hiding behind Churchill's statement that "in times of great danger it is permissible to walk with the devil until you have crossed the bridge."[80] In May 1953, when McCarthy was at the height of his influence, Phil told a group from the National Council of Jewish Women that McCarthy's "big lie" technique made Nazi propaganda chief Joseph Goebbels "look like an amateur."[81] McCarthy in turn demanded that the post office investigate how much it cost to "subsidize the distribution," via second-class mailing privileges, of the communist *Daily Worker* and the *Post,* "a paper typical of those that feel freedom of the press means freedom to deliberately lie and to twist and distort facts." Phil countered that McCarthy "has given no evidence that he is qualified to become chief censor of what news may be sent through the mails. . . . If Senator McCarthy would close his mouth long enough to read a little American history, he might discover that he is ignorant about the meaning of freedom of the press."[82]

When Agnes entered the fray, Phil at first made no attempt to squelch her. In one speech, she charged that McCarthy "stirred up hatred and used every device to destroy the confidence of Americans in each other. . . . [He is] our modern Grand Inquisitor . . . a dangerous, clever and ruthless demagogue . . . another Huey Long." She individually assailed congressmen who were in McCarthy's corner, including Harold Himmel Velde of Illinois. McCarthy answered by saying he would "waste no time reading speeches by the management of the Washington *Daily Worker,* much less answer them."[83] Velde, who was fed information by a HUAC investigator, charged that in 1946, Agnes had written to the English-language propaganda magazine *Soviet Russia Today,* lamenting: "It simply makes you sick at heart when you hear many radio commentators speaking so unjustly and disdainfully of the Russians." Agnes immediately denied having written such a letter; it turned out that the writer was a Mrs. G. S. Mayer of Port Clements, British Columbia.

Again Agnes became a lightning rod for the right wing, and again Phil began to worry. "She was a burning woman of principle," explains *Post* and *New York Times* editorial writer Karl Meyer, "but as with many burning people of principle, her intolerance and arrogance were almost an adjunct."[84] As Murrey Marder observes, "There was a general feeling that the *Post* was already in such an embattled position that it didn't need anybody else setting off skyrockets inside the building."[85]

The paper's powerful stand on McCarthy was causing it to lose advertisers. Joe Rauh recalled Phil's anxiety over being "a trustee of this very valuable property, in charge of it. But at the same time it wasn't his money. It was the Meyer family's money, and he was up against this tyrant, and advertisers were being ugly."[86]

Phil turned his energies toward controlling editorial writer Alan Barth, an unbending civil libertarian and Bill of Rights advocate who, Phil felt, almost went out of his way to offend advertisers. When Barth wrote an editorial questioning the FBI's vacuum-cleaner approach to gathering information on government employees, Phil refused to publish it, as the business community was sympathetic to the FBI. Barth expanded it into an article for *Harper's,* defying Phil's specific request not to.[87]

It was widely held that thanks to Herblock and Barth, *The Washington Post,* a third-rate paper in many respects, had "the most distinguished editorial page in the country."[88] The two men were, says former *Post* reporter and editor Erwin Knoll, the conscience of the paper.[89]

Phil was often on the verge of firing Barth and was just as often talked out of it by Barth's original sponsor, Felix Frankfurter, or by Russ Wiggins. Phil derisively referred to Barth and some of his colleagues as "fifth-floor liberals,"[90] but mostly he let things ride, not willing to risk a break, or his reputation among people whose respect he craved. "I was in the middle on these things," recalls Bob Estabrook. "Phil would give me hell because of something Alan had written, and I would try to tone it down without destroying the point, and it didn't please anybody."[91]

The two coexisted in an angry standoff, Barth holding his ground and Phil being forced to back down. Still, explains Erwin Knoll, "while Alan had occasional problems [with Phil] that deeply aggrieved him, he also felt that he would have had much greater problems most anywhere else."[92]

Trying to appease those whose opinions he respected and the advertisers whose dollars he needed, Phil turned his attention to less controversial topics that allowed him more control over the public agenda.

One was a clean-election bill that Phil basically drafted and lobbied through Congress as "the most important political reform of the century." It outlawed individual campaign contributions and provided for financing through bipartisan mass money-raising, and thus removed the need for candidates to seek funds from the underworld, special interest groups, and people coveting high public appointments. A correspondent for *Time* wrote that the *Post* "helps make the news it reports."[93] Phil took that as a compliment.

Earlier he had led the paper on a crusade against gangsters in U.S. politics, which allowed him to fine-tune his kingmaking skills. *Time* reported that he "conceived a congressional investigation and began scanning the U.S. Senate to cast a likely Senator in the top role. Graham hit on the virtually unknown junior senator from Tennessee. But [Democrat] Estes Kefauver was reluctant. Graham gave him a long pep talk, finally exploding: 'Damn it, Estes, don't you want to be Vice President?' That was the speech that launched Kefauver into his celebrated investigation" (and his unsuccessful run for vice-president in 1956).[94]

Phil was also intrigued by local issues and by the prospect of loosening the *Star*'s grip on them. Ben Gilbert, then city editor of the *Post,* explains that the *Star* was "part of the Board of Trade, maybe the principal decision-maker on the Board of Trade. When big decisions were made, they were always made by the *Star,* and the *Star* got the lion's share of the local news that the District commissioners had controlled, such as the budget. All the good stories went to the *Star* and all the housekeeping stories went to the *Post* and the *Times-Herald.*"[95] The causes Phil took as his and the *Post*'s own were the related ones of home rule for the District, integration, and a revitalized downtown. He broke every canon of journalistic ethics by lobbying hard for these, not only on the editorial page but also in the news columns, claiming that racism was behind the reluctance of Congress to grant home rule and that "not even the forms of self-government allowed to the conquered Germans and Japanese are granted to the residents of Washington." He created the Federal City Council, charged with replacing areas of black-occupied tenements in southwest Washington with high-rises and townhouses. (Meanwhile, the *Post*'s record on race was poor. When, in 1952, it hired Simeon Booker, its first black reporter, he was made to use a specially designated washroom. When he wrote an article pointing out that Phil's grand vision was displacing thousands of poor blacks, with no plan to relocate them, it was buried in the back of the paper.[96])

Ben Gilbert made the perfect lieutenant. "Phil Graham gave me an assignment," he recalled. "I was to watch the city. When something was happening that needed his attention . . . I was to see him." Phil's dictum was simple: Stories that reflected badly on integration or home rule must never see print. Gilbert agreed completely that the *Post*'s business was not so much reporting the news as it was pushing the community to be a better place to live—for all, including the poor and black. As one *Post* reporter put it, "Ben cared for the city and the paper—in that order." The paper, Gilbert said, must be "a vehicle for positive change."[97]

Gilbert was born in New York City and was a graduate of City College. He changed his name (from Goldberg) to land his first newspaper job, and had come to the *Post* from the *Star-Times* in St. Louis when he was twenty-three; four years later he was city editor. He relentlessly drove himself and his reporters, expecting them to share his dedication and stamina—as a reporter, he often wrote two or three front-page stories a day.[98] He had learned at the St. Louis paper "that a few dedicated reporters could frequently run circles around more affluent, more leisurely newspapers,"[99] and at the *Post* he quickly developed the reputation for being a tyrant. He did not talk to his reporters; he shouted at them.

Clashes between Gilbert and others, such as Ben Bradlee, who believed in more straightforward reporting, were waiting to happen. Bradlee's background could not have been more different. From a New England pedigreed family, Bradlee had the confidence and casualness bred of wealth and connections that went beyond Gilbert's imagination. Bradlee had meant to get a job at *The Baltimore Sun* in 1948, but it was raining hard when the train pulled into Baltimore, so he rode on to Washington. A letter from Christian Herter, a future governor of Massachusetts and U.S. secretary of state, and a recommendation from Walter Lippmann, an old family friend, helped him land an $80-a-week police-reporting job at the *Post*.[100]

In 1949, officials at the Interior Department ordered the desegregation of one of the swimming pools it ran in the District of Columbia. Gilbert assigned Bradlee and another reporter, John London, to cover what was expected to be a rocky transition, and then went home for the evening. The two brought their story at nine p.m. to John Riseling, the night city editor. Riseling had been a newspaperman during the 1919 riots and was wary of the *Post*'s again aggravating a racial flareup into a riot. "So when Bradlee and London reported their story to [Riseling]," Gilbert recalls, "he thought it was worth three paragraphs on the local page." And that is where it ran. Bradlee, who considered it front-page, headline news, was outraged. The *Post* was describing as an "incident" what to him was a full-fledged riot—two hundred whites battling two hundred blacks in a daylong engagement. Bradlee later remembered shouting at Gilbert, "This great fucking liberal newspaper can't even say what happened."[101] Gilbert insists that Bradlee's target was really Riseling, who called Gilbert at home to report that Bradlee "was doing a rain dance in the middle of the city room."[102]

In the midst of that, Bradlee felt a finger on his back and heard, "That's enough, buster." There was Phil Graham, ordering Bradlee upstairs, where the secretary of the interior, his undersecretary, and Clark Clifford, then special counsel to President Truman, were gathered. Graham told Bradlee to describe the riot, and then informed the president's men that the *Post* would keep the story buried if all the District's pools, not just the one designated by Interior, were immediately closed for the summer and opened, integrated, the next summer. They agreed.[103] (Gilbert disputes this version of events: "Phil did nothing to [squelch] the strong follow-up story I put in the paper the next day. I never got any directions from Phil not to run the story. I have no doubt that he was pressing for the full integration of the pools, but it took some time for that to occur."[104])

Bradlee did not see much of a future for himself at the *Post*. He wanted to be a foreign correspondent, or at least on the national desk, and he believed, correctly, that Gilbert would block him. Gilbert had once told a local reporter, "Do you know there are people who've been working here for thirty years and they don't cover the federal government?"[105] Bradlee asked Phil to send him overseas as a correspondent. Phil said no. How about a recommendation for a Nieman fellowship, Bradlee persisted. "Fuck you, Bradlee, you've been to Harvard."[106] In 1951, Bradlee quit the *Post* and went to Paris, where he worked as a press attaché at the American embassy. Two years later he tried to return to the *Post* but couldn't obtain an acceptable salary, so he joined *Newsweek*—then controlled by Vincent Astor—in its Paris bureau. Arnaud de Borchgrave, whom he replaced at the magazine, remembered the young Bradlee as "devastatingly handsome. . . . I used to joke that women lined up in front of his apartment for fifteen minutes of his time."[107]

Phil Graham next turned his attention to Robert Barrett, whose promotion from chief of detectives to superintendent of police in Washington he intended to stop. The *Star* (and the *Times-Herald*)

and the members of the District Committee in Congress all supported Barrett; Phil considered him a racist—burglaries in white
neighborhoods, for instance, reportedly were higher-priority than
homicides in black ones. When the *Post* failed to prevent Barrett's
appointment, Phil and Ben Gilbert, who choreographed the *Post*'s
crusade, allegedly ordered reporters to write "at least one anti-police
story a day." Phil even personally asked President Truman to have
Barrett removed. When Truman refused, Phil arranged for a Senate
subcommittee on crime to investigate the police superintendent; the
result was Barrett's retirement, with pension, and the suicide of a
police captain found guilty of pocketing part of a $300 donation for
a precinct Christmas party.[108] But Barrett managed to get the last
slap, disclosing that Gilbert had been a member of the Young Communist League at City College. Phil wrote an editorial defending his
city editor, which Gilbert calls "a cherished possession, a remarkable
endorsement for a young editor."[109] Still, some thought the revelation stalled Gilbert's advancement at the *Post,* where he spent nineteen years as city editor.*

Bob Estabrook remembers an editorial he wrote, as acting editor
of the editorial page, calling Senator Owen Brewster of Maine "an
errand boy for Pan Am, which in fact he was. He was on their
payroll, we found out later." The airline's PR man threatened to pull
its advertising if the *Post* didn't kill the editorial. Estabrook and
assistant managing editor Frank Dennis refused, and Pan Am made
good on its threat, withdrawing $125,000 of advertising. "Phil never
mentioned the issue to me, never," says Estabrook. "And the *Post*
was losing money at the time."[110]

The man Phil really wanted as editor of the editorial page was
James "Scotty" Reston of *The New York Times,* but Reston, who
would figure notably in the *Post*'s later history, declined.[111] In 1953,
with Herb Elliston frequently ill and away from the paper, Phil gave
the job to Estabrook.

In October 1953, Agnes Meyer published her memoirs, *Out of
These Roots: The Autobiography of an American Woman.* It was
prominently and positively reviewed in the Sunday *Washington Post*
with a line that must have made Katharine flinch: "She [Agnes] has

*Still sensitive on the subject, Gilbert insists, "I was in the YCL for only nine months, a naive
recruit who quit in disgust on discovering that it was just a [Communist Party] front."

been, as I happen to know, a solicitous mother and a devoted wife."[112]

The one person in the family whose career deserved formal memoirs had done nothing about writing them. Some years earlier, when Bis had wanted to write her father's biography, he told her he was not ready.[113] Kay decided it was time to engage a professional. Another, much sadder motive was that the family needed someone to pay attention to an increasingly unhappy and grumpy Eugene. No one had the time or inclination to listen to his war stories, which, as his business responsibilities faded, he told and retold more often. Rosalie Stern, Eugene's beloved older sister, would gladly have listened, but she lived across the country and was well into her eighties. One friend recalls "sitting next to him when he called [her] in California to wish her a happy birthday. His eyes filled up with tears. I had a general sense that if Rosalie [had] said, 'Gene, jump off the Empire State Building because it's going to be good for you,' he would have."[114]

In 1954, Kay asked her friend Sidney Hyman to write her father's authorized biography. Hyman had remained very close to Kay and grown close to Phil, whom he continued to admire extravagantly. He would baby-sit for the Graham children when Kay and Phil traveled abroad, calling himself the "resident Dutch uncle." And he had a résumé since leaving Chicago that both Eugene and Phil could appreciate: He had worked for Senators Paul Douglas, J. William Fulbright, and Hubert Humphrey. He had written speeches for Adlai Stevenson and done research for Dean Acheson. He had written about Marriner Eccles and his term at the Federal Reserve Board, and his recent book *The American President* had been well received.

His task was larger and more difficult than that of a conventional biographer. "Agnes became enraged with me," he recalls, "because, while up in Mount Kisco, I took an afternoon off to go to New York [City]. I had to get away. She was enraged because she was left with her husband. She just didn't want to be with him." Even Hyman could understand why. "She was always the foil of his barbs. He was a very witty person. She would throw her head down roaring with laughter, and you would wonder how often shafts went through without touching any bone. Some of the things that were said in great glee I winced [at] because they hit too close. [One evening] she burst into tears, saying, 'This is too much.' I never heard her give him back what he gave her. Agnes Meyer was not a witty person. She was a person of great enthusiasms."[115]

Hyman agreed to have a draft ready for Eugene's approval in a year and a half[116]—which turned out to be much easier promised than accomplished. Eugene had no real desire to see the project finished, Hyman claims, and would release information in agonizingly slow installments. "Being with him was like [watching] a strip-tease dance." Eugene omitted almost all personal material, telling Hyman, for example, "Well, I was born in 1875, and one day in 1914, I was walking down Fifth Avenue and I ran into Bernie Baruch and Bernie Baruch said, 'Gene, what do you think the price of copper should be?' . . . I said, 'Wait a minute, what happened?' He said, 'That's not important.' " He never mentioned his Jewish roots in Los Angeles, and never discussed the *Post* period. He would repeat the same stories time and again. "I was a companion to him," Hyman says. He never wanted the biography completed, as it "would be his tombstone inscription."

Hyman remembers Phil and Kay saying they didn't care whether the book was actually finished or not; Agnes "never wanted it finished, because as long as I was there, she didn't have to be." Free from her husband's disapproving stares, she drank and agonized over her writing. "I don't know about the birth pangs of an elephant, but I sympathized," Hyman says. "The speeches and articles would take weeks and weeks of moaning and groaning." She would ask Hyman for help and then forget the source of some of her best lines. "She'd start quoting back to me things I'd given her two days before, completely [overlooking] where they came from."[117]

One night Phil took Hyman aside and said, "Your book has got to be impossible to write. This family needs a novel."[118]

Chapter 9

ELATION AND DECLINE

Robert McCormick, ill and fearing death, was at his home in Florida in January 1954 when he called Kent Cooper, an old friend of his and Eugene's, and the former general manager of the Associated Press. "Get hold of Meyer and see if he wants to buy the *Times-Herald*," McCormick told him.[1] "I am wondering," Cooper wrote Meyer, "whether you expect to be in Palm Beach any time soon for I would like very much to talk to you about a business matter of importance to you."

Instantly guessing that the Colonel was ready to sell, Meyer replied that he planned to be in Florida within the next few days. Accompanied by Phil and *Post* business manager John Sweeterman, Eugene met Cooper, who warned them that McCormick would insist on recovering his purchase price of $4.5 million, plus the $4 million he had spent on new presses and on an addition to the building. "That's all right with me," Meyer responded. "It's a deal," the Colonel said on hearing Meyer's answer.[2] McCormick had carried a debt of gratitude to Meyer since 1942, when Meyer stood with him during his battle with the AP—a fact that explains in part why the Colonel would sell to a man whose worldview differed so much from his own. "McCormick [was] the kind of man who [paid] his bills," says Frank Waldrop, "and he never [forgot]."[3]

McCormick, a longtime director of the AP, got himself into trouble by ordering that AP dispatches on New Deal subjects be edited to suit his slant and by publishing secret war plans in the *Chicago Tribune* three days before Pearl Harbor. Members of FDR's Cabinet suggested that McCormick be arrested for treason. His fellow AP directors were also furious with him, not because of any damage he might have done to the country's war effort but because they knew that FDR was angry enough to pursue the AP for antitrust violations. (The AP then excluded publishers in cities where rival papers subscribed to the service.) Such a move by the Justice Department had been under consideration since 1939, when Cissy Patterson's *Times-Herald* was denied the AP service because the *Post* carried it. Any publisher who considered an applicant a direct competitor could cast a veto, and Eugene Meyer readily did so.

In Chicago, McCormick was about to do the same to Marshall Field III, who, in 1941, had launched the liberal *Sun*. McCormick had no intention of letting Field in, ever. But his fellow AP directors wanted him to relent, hoping that would pacify the Justice Department; only McCormick would suffer, and they could keep the monopoly everywhere else.

McCormick not only refused to bend but, according to Waldrop, told publishers that "he would start newspapers in competition with them if they did not join him against Field." The only person who spoke up for the beleaguered McCormick was Eugene Meyer, who took the floor at the AP's annual meeting and carried the day.[4] McCormick won that battle, and he knew that he could not have without Eugene Meyer.*

While McCormick felt uncomfortable with Phil Graham, he felt completely at ease with Eugene, a contemporary and a fellow Yale man. Eugene had demonstrated that he was worthy of McCormick's respect, asserts Frank Waldrop. "He had been a tough competitor, he had learned while doing, and shown himself under stress to be a gentleman. So why not?"[6]

When Eugene suggested their lawyers be summoned to Palm Beach to draw up an agreement, the Colonel said Eugene's word was enough. Eugene and Phil were told that one of McCormick's associates would be in touch with them in March. In the meantime, Eugene asked a lawyer at Cravath, Swaine & Moore, Frederick "Fritz" Beebe, who had been handling the Meyer family estate planning, to counsel them on the sale.

For Phil the wait was unbearable. He had convinced himself, and

---

*He lost the war, however, when the Supreme Court invalidated the exclusionary rule that permitted existing members to blackball competitors.[5]

not irrationally, that his very future hung on acquiring the *Times-Herald*. That year the *Post* would lose about a quarter of a million dollars;[7] its advertising manager told his counterpart at the *Times-Herald* that the paper was " 'on the ropes' and about to fold."[8] It got to the point, says George Reedy, "where both the *Post* and the *Times-Herald* were slicing up the market [the *Times-Herald* had 250,000 readers, the *Post* 204,000] in such a way that neither of them could really make it. One of them had to go."[9]

February and nearly half of March passed without word from McCormick. Phil's mood grew bleak.

Then, on March 13, Kent Cooper called Phil to inform him that a *Chicago Tribune* representative would soon contact him. Phil wired his father-in-law in Jamaica.[10] As Eugene flew home that evening, a *Tribune* vice-president called Phil and set a meeting for the following day. *Post* executives were summoned and warned not to tell anyone, even their wives, about the impending purchase. McCormick feared an antitrust action by the Justice Department.

The next day, McCormick called a *Times-Herald* board meeting and asked each director, "Should I sell to Eugene Meyer?" All assented, except Bazy Tankersley, the paper's former editor; "a little to the right of Attila the Hun," according to one Washington insider,[11] she was appalled at the prospect of handing a morning monopoly to, in her eyes, the liberal Eugene Meyer and his left-wing son-in-law.[12] McCormick agreed to give his niece forty-eight hours to raise the money to buy the paper herself, but he warned her not to tell anyone of Eugene's offer.[13]

Under those terms, it was impossible for her to succeed, and she came up $6 million short. Among those who turned Tankersley down was Jesse Jones, who later told her that had he known she was trying to buy the *Post* out from under Eugene Meyer, he would happily have given her the money.[14] The bloated, self-satisfied *Star* had not even considered buying the *Times-Herald;* that mistake would prove its undoing.

In a state of elation, Phil dispatched John Hayes, a *Post* executive vice-president, and Stanley Temko, an associate at the *Post*'s Washington law firm, Covington & Burling, to Chicago to complete details of the sale. When Hayes said he would call for airline reservations, Graham pounced: "The hell you will. You'll go by train. . . . I don't want to hear that a plane had crashed carrying a . . . *Post* [down payment] check for $1.5 million."[15] Phil was

bursting to tell someone. Shirley Povich, then covering spring training in Florida, was one of the few people he could trust to keep a
secret. "Hold your breath for twenty-four hours. I think we finally
have it."[16]

On Wednesday, March 17, St. Patrick's Day, Hayes and Temko
were in McCormick's Chicago office, where Phil had arranged for a
private telephone line so that the sale could be reported immediately.
Nerve-wracking impediments still loomed. Bazy Tankersley was begging for more time. Clarence Manion, a former dean of the Notre
Dame law school and a disillusioned FDR supporter turned extreme
right-winger, dashed in and out of the Colonel's office in a last-ditch
effort to stop the sale. Phil ordered Hayes to pay whatever it took to
close the deal.

At noon, Hayes called Phil: "Okay. You've got it." Phil was
overjoyed. Kay "screamed in ecstasy."[17] Eugene had a more reflec-
tive response: "This," he told Sidney Hyman, "makes the *Post* safe
for Donny," referring to Kay and Phil's oldest son, then eight years
old.

That afternoon, Washington's *Daily News* announced the sale.
The McCormick family motto—"Death Rather Than Desert the
Faith,"[18] printed that morning on the *Times-Herald*'s front page—
assumed a tragic irony for employees who knew they had been sold
out. (The *Times-Herald* building was soon converted into a *Post*
warehouse.)

The paper was a gift from a rich man to the son-in-law he often
called "the greatest godsend I ever had."[19] It was one expensive gift.
The final price, paid with alacrity by Eugene, was $8.5 million for the
Times-Herald, plus $1.8 million for severance pay and incidentals—a
total of $10.3 million.[20]

It is doubtful Eugene would have bought the *Times-Herald* without Phil's prodding, yet that was the most important decision in
company history. Bernard Nossiter said that "Eugene's greatest contribution as a publisher was to accede to Phil's plea to acquire the
Times-Herald." Ownership gave the *Post* a monopoly—oddly, because, as Hedley Donovan pointed out, Phil was "a very vigorous
anti-trust type," at least during his Supreme Court clerkship days,
and here was the *Post* laying the foundation for its future dominance
"by raw capitalistic muscle."[21]

Eugene's wisdom in limiting family ownership to Phil and Kay
was then evident. "We had a very different kind of ownership," says

Newbold Noyes, later the *Star*'s executive editor. "Our ownership was split up among scores of maiden aunts who were entirely dependent on the dividends that were coming in. It wasn't a very good situation in which to take a flyer on something." Noyes appreciates the fact that the supposed newspaper pros at the *Star* missed the opportunity while the outsiders grabbed it. "The funny thing about it is that my family had never done anything except work on newspapers."[22]

Florence Meyer Homolka, who was bringing up her two sons on her own, felt as if she had been cheated out of the *Post*. When she heard of Eugene's remark about the paper's now being "safe" for Donny, she fired off an angry letter to her father demanding a "full explanation" of how he planned to provide for *her* sons. Eugene explained, in a letter drafted by Phil, that they did not want the *Post* to have "fractionated management," which inevitably led to a policy of "not antagonizing people"; he felt she was "insuring their future in the best way that you can, namely to bring them up as intelligent, decent, interested, and kindly people."[23] Florence was hardly placated.

Eugene Meyer, wearing a pressman's paper hat, pushed the button that started the presses for the first edition of what would, for a short time, be called *The Washington Post and Times-Herald.* Although the *Post* basically swallowed Cissy Patterson's pride and joy, it did retain some of her more popular features—mostly at the insistence of John Sweeterman, who saw that the paper had to expand beyond its intellectual, elite readership to capture the middle class.

Phil Graham agreed completely with Sweeterman. He issued an order that no feature of the *Times-Herald* could be cut without his permission. Bernard Nossiter recalled asking Al Friendly why the paper bothered keeping conservative columnist George Sokolsky and Walter Winchell?* "And the answer was: 'Phil now feels very strongly that since we are a monopoly morning paper we owe an

---

*The *Post* soon stopped running Winchell's gossip column, although it continued to buy it in order to keep it out of the *Star*. Winchell, who was then enormously popular—his column boasted 50 million readers and his Sunday-night radio broadcasts attracted ninety percent of all radio listeners—was furious not only that the *Post* was not running his column but that it was preventing the *Star* from doing so. "Mr. Meyer," Winchell once asked Eugene, "how much does it take to buy this newspaper?" "I can tell you this, Mr. Winchell," came the answer. "The last man who asked me that question was sitting in that same chair where you sit now, and he couldn't buy this newspaper, and his name was Andrew Mellon."[24]

obligation to present all points of view and not just ours.' "[25] (Phil did ax Westbrook Pegler, a viciously anti–New Deal and antilabor columnist.) Unlike Eugene, Phil knew just how important comics were, and he kept all the *Times-Herald* strips.

In 1955, to mark his eightieth birthday, Eugene divested himself and Agnes of about a half-million dollars of their nonvoting stock. The beneficiaries, 711 veteran *Post* employees and circulation contractors, were allowed to hold the stock only while they were employed; when they left they had to sell their shares. Those who bought up stock from other employees who left the paper or preferred the cash would end up making, in some cases, many millions of dollars.*

The divestiture was part of Eugene's preparation for death—a preparation that began with the decline and death, early the next year, of his eighty-six-year-old sister, Rosalie Stern. Eugene lost the person he cared for most, and he would never recover. So beloved a figure was she in San Francisco that the city's flags flew at half-mast after she died.†

Phil Graham was thinking more about his father lately, his nostalgia mixed with guilt for having abandoned him and the business he built by nerve and the sweat of his brow in favor of the business of a megamillionaire whose position was handed him at birth. Ernest Graham was rising in Phil's estimation as Eugene was falling. The elder Graham, as state senator, had made a name for himself crusading against alleged mob influence on Florida horse and dog tracks. In 1944, while his son was in the Pacific, Cap Graham had run a credible, lively campaign for the Democratic gubernatorial nomination on a platform of more funds for education and jobs for veterans.[27] (Ernest finished third in a field of six, a casualty of geography.

---

*When Elsie Carper retired in 1989, she was said to be worth $15 million. She had hung on to her stock and bought that of others whenever she could.

†Rosalie was president of the city's Recreation and Park Commission, having served on it from 1919 until two weeks before her death. She gave the city Sigmund Stern Recreation Grove, helped finance public concerts held there, and contributed generously to the symphony, the opera, and chamber music groups. She was a major benefactor of the University of California, but even though it was the family school, she gave more to Stanford. She never forgot how helpful the Stanford boys were in 1906 after the earthquake and fire, when they supplied the Stern family with milk.[26] Among the speakers at her funeral, conducted by a rabbi, was Admiral Chester Nimitz.

Nobody from south Florida would win statewide office until 1950, when George Smathers was elected to the U.S. Senate.)

Ernest Graham had become nearly as rich as Eugene—his cattle farm alone covered 7,000 acres, and his holdings had become so valuable that some 162 acres he had given to Phil went on the market a couple of years later for $486,000.[28] Nevertheless, Phil idealized his father as a simple, gruff, direct man, quintessentially American, a self-made, Horatio Alger figure. He especially enjoyed Shirley Povich's story about the man who looked like a farmer who stopped him at Hialeah racetrack one day and said, "You're Shirley Povich of *The Washington Post.* I live here in Miami, but I subscribe to the *Post,* and I recognize you from your picture on the column, and besides, I've got a son who works for the *Post.*" "Who's that?" Povich asked. "Phil Graham,"[29] the man answered.

Phil even became attracted to his father's primitive politics—"All I've raised is a bunch of Communists," Ernest liked to lament to his friends[30]—and to his anti-Semitism. Phil's feelings of being the "kept son-in-law" of a Jew also intensified. He began to affect the attitudes of a poor country boy and to enjoy caricaturing Eugene as grotesque, bloated, gauche—Jewish. Among his favorite anecdotes was the one about Eugene's complaining to Agnes that when she went to Mount Kisco for the summer, leaving him in Washington, she took too many of the servants with her. "I've left you the butler, the cook, and a housemaid," Agnes protested. "But you know that I can't stand camping out," Eugene replied.[31]

Eugene had taken an interest in the development of the banking system in Israel,[32] and this fact irritated Phil—for no rational reason, because Phil had, according to Bob Estabrook, an emotional commitment to the country and "certainly supported Zionism."[33] Sir Isaiah Berlin recalls his discomfort at being a target of Phil's anti-Semitic outbursts. "I went to lunch [at the Grahams'] once, and he was either drunk or in some kind of neurotic state. And he began to mock me, my attachment to Zionism and to [Israeli president Chaim] Weizmann. He was a bit rough."[34]

Phil had spells of despising his father-in-law; he would call him a "kike" to his face, and threaten that if Eugene tried to intrude into the paper's management he would take up the practice of law. Phil insisted that, without Eugene's money and power, "I would have made it on my own," and that had he not acceded to Eugene's demand to take over the *Post,* and instead returned to Florida to practice law, "I might be in the Senate now."[35] In a display of disturbing projection, he accused Eugene of being an anti-Semite, claiming that he never hired Jews at Allied Chemical.[36] Frank Waldrop recalls Phil's assurances "that he knew how to deal with Jews because as a kid he drove a milk truck in Miami and used to deliver cottage cheese" to them.[37]

As "kike" was sprinkled more regularly into Phil's conversation, some of his friends began to question his mental health; a few even spotted classic symptoms of manic-depression. Phil Elman remembers that Felix Frankfurter was "sad, sad about Phil's being ill. Phil was doing and saying some terrible things. He was a sick man."[38] But George Smathers, among others, saw nothing odd about Phil's behavior: "I never heard [Phil] say anything that would indicate to me that he was the least bit anti-Semitic, not the least." Smathers adds, however, that "if Phil was angry and trying to hurt somebody, he might say, 'Well, that's a kike for you.' But I don't think [he] had any basic dislike of all the Jewish people. I knew a lot of Jewish boys [he] was very friendly with."*[39]

To the outside world, this state of affairs would have been considered amazing. During Phil's energized, up cycles, no one was more dazzling. "Phil Graham walked into a room and took it over," David Halberstam wrote, "charming and seducing whomever he wished, men and women alike. No one in Washington could match him at it, not even, in the days before he became President, John F. Kennedy. He was handsome and slim and when he smiled . . . everything stopped. He was the Sun King."[41] Jean Friendly remembers that he "could get on the tennis court without a racquet in his hand and defeat you. You cannot imagine what an influence he was on everybody around."[42]

Phil's craggily handsome face adorned the cover of *Time* for April 16, 1956, under the headline "A Montage of the American Dream," and it seemed only natural that he should be gazing out from one of the world's best-known magazines. Even the conservatively slanted weekly fawned over him, "an energetic charmer" with "a Lincolnesque look." As for his paper, *Time* claimed: "Across the presidential

*CBS head William Paley, for example. In fact, it was Phil who seconded Paley for membership in Washington's Metropolitan Club and was, according to Paley's biographer, "dismayed to learn that the club had requested that Paley's name be withdrawn because he was Jewish."[40]

breakfast tray and over the coverlets and coffee cups of the most influential people in the world's most influential city looms the capital's most influential paper. . . . From Foggy Bottom to the fog on the Hill, Washington reaches for the *Post* as Broadway reaches for *Variety* or bankers for the *Wall Street Journal.*"[43]

Some months before Phil was chosen as a cover subject, his friend Richard Clurman, *Time*'s press editor, had arranged for him to have lunch with Henry Luce. Luce was impressed, but his editors had come not to praise Phil but to pan him and his newspaper. The *Time* writer assigned this cover story, Lester Bernstein, explains that "*Time* was then being edited by politically conservative types—the executive editor later became Richard Nixon's chief speechwriter— who looked at this as an opportunity to stick it to liberal journalists in general and *The Washington Post* in particular."[44]

Bernstein struggled to keep the story fair, and Phil basked in its glory.[45] Although written by Bernstein, the article was reported by a Washington bureau correspondent for *Time* named James Truitt. So pleased was Phil with the result that he would later hire both Bernstein and Truitt.

There was one dig, though, that certainly did bother Phil—the observation that he had "started at the top ten years ago without ever having covered a news story, written an editorial or sold an ad. . . . He became a newspaper publisher by marrying the boss's daughter."[46] Kay paid dearly for that comment.

Overweight, pale, dowdy, and thin-haired, Kay was Phil's most convenient target. His magnificent verbal agility, when aimed at a person who had sparked his anger, contempt, or self-loathing, was truly terrible. "What he did to Kay to destroy her was awful," recalls Jean Friendly. "He was so clever, he was like a dentist's drill, [knowing] just where to hit the nerve."[47] The nerve, according to Bernard Nossiter, Harvey Segal, and others, was Kay's Jewish blood. "He played the Horst Wessel song* to her," said Nossiter, "he called her a dirty Jew. He found the nerve that would vibrate the house. I think this was Phil also pouring shit on himself. This comes under the heading of psychopathology and not politics."[49]

Nossiter insisted that Phil was not expressing anti-Semitism so

---

*Horst Wessel was a young Nazi murdered by communists; Nazi storm troopers sang the song, which he had composed, in his memory as they celebrated Hitler's rise to chancellor. It became the official song of the Nazi Party and later the second official national anthem, after "Deutschland über Alles," of the Third Reich.[48]

much as he was digging at what he knew most bothered Kay about herself—her Jewishness and her plain looks. Phil used anti-Semitic slurs "in the most barbarous fashion to cause her the maximum pain. If she had been a devotee of the single tax, he would have found something in Henry George to beat her over the head with."[50] "It was awful," Libby Rowe remembers. "He called Kay a Jewish cow."[51]

Phil had no compunction about letting everybody know he found Kay distasteful. Jean Friendly says he disparaged Kay in front of everybody and, most wicked, in front of their children.[52] At dinner parties, he would ask the guests, "Do you know the first thing Kay does every morning? She looks in the mirror and says how lucky she is to be married to me." No matter who was at dinner—a Supreme Court justice, a university president, Phil's new friend Lyndon Johnson and his wife, Lady Bird—Kay was invariably the butt of her husband's jokes. Nothing was off-limits, not her medical problems, her weight, her clothes, her intellect. (He would tell twelve-year-old Lally, for example, that her mother was uncultured and that she should try to be "better."[53]) Kay herself told Chalmers Roberts: "I was always the butt of family jokes. You know, good old mom, plodding along. And I accepted it. That's the way I viewed myself."[54]

When Phil was cruel, recalls Jean Friendly, Kay shrank. "It was tragedy, utter tragedy."[55] She became like the abused child who lurks in the shadows for fear of getting hit. "She was always two paces behind," friends say.[56] A longtime Washington reporter describes Kay then as "terribly thwarted and restricted through her mother and her marriage." She was "an unbelievable mouselike woman who didn't move a muscle, who followed behind [Phil]."[57] She allowed herself to be completely controlled by his moods, his whims, his opinions. The Kay Meyer who once expressed herself forcefully, who strode across campus "like the captain of a triumphant hockey team," was gone. If she was inclined to express an opinion or tell a story, even at a family dinner, she would censor herself, anticipating Phil's debilitating disapproval. Her stories were always deemed too long, too boring, too banal.[58]

So emotionally battered was Kay that she laughed at the jokes made at her expense, no matter how personal. Marietta Tree felt that Kay simply did not seem to mind; she "laughed hysterically at everything [Phil] said. She adored him."[59] When he joked that he had married her for her father's money, "Kay was just marvelous about it," said Luvie Pearson. "She just laughed. Anything he did was right."[60]

Kay would remember of those years that, besides devoting time to assorted good works, tennis, and bridge, she did all the "scut work: paid the bills, ran the house, drove the children."[61] "I was the kind of wife that women liberationists talk about," she would admit. "I was a second-class citizen and my role was to keep Phil happy, peaceful, calm and functioning, and the children the same. I guess because I'd been brought up by nurses and governesses and never saw my parents, I compensated by spending as much time as I could with my children."[62] And to her, Phil "was so glamorous that I was perfectly happy just to clean up after him."[63] Yet Kay appreciated her plight in a way that made it more poignant. Before she gave up the "Magazine Rack" column, she wrote a caption for a photograph of herself and Phil to appear in the *Post:* "Philip Graham of this paper rather hogs the camera while his wife . . . lurks in the background." She was always "lurking in the background," she later recalled, playing "idiot" so that Phil could "run around Washington being brilliant."[64]

Kay was at her worst in those years; Phil, at least to the outside world, was at his best. One friend observed that they were less like husband and wife than like "prince and attendant."[65] Bernard Nossiter remembered the annual party that Phil gave at Glen Welby for *Post* reporters, editors, and executives. "Kay would be so nervous and tight and clenched that she could barely shake anyone's hand or squeeze out a word, and Phil, of course, [would be] beaming and making verbal love to all the wives."[66]

Erwin Knoll also recounts Kay's behavior at these annual events: "She went around apologizing for his language, which was incorrigible. He was profane at all times. In front of [everybody]. I don't think he knew how to talk any other way. He was charming, but he had this macho compulsion to talk in obscenities."[67]

Despite her background, Kay seemed ill at ease at Glen Welby. Her home, her dinners, her clothes all lacked elegance and style. She knew it, of course, and neither her mother nor her husband would ever let her forget it. Sidney Hyman describes Agnes as "impatient with Kay's taste. Because Kay had no taste. She had no style. Agnes disparaged her for that."[68] Kay would say of her exaggeratedly unstylish appearance, "Nobody had ever taught me how to do it."[69]

Phil particularly abhorred Kay's lack of style because she was, in his mind, a reflection on him. If she was so plain and shy, then perhaps he had married her for her money. Before an important party, he would call an editor at *Harper's Bazaar* and ask her to find something suitable for Kay to wear.[70] But Kay needed more intensive care, and Phil would also come to depend on Shirley Clurman, Richard Clurman's wife, to keep Kay from being too much of an embarrassment.[71] As *Time*'s director of public relations, Shirley knew Phil; she had never met Kay. He arranged a lunch for them to meet. After a long and friendly meal, Kay told Shirley, "I'm so glad to meet you. I always thought my husband was having an affair with you, but now I can see that he wasn't. You're a nice girl."[72]

Kay started out relying for fashion advice on Washington cave-dweller friends, with whom she felt more comfortable, but not even Lorraine Cooper, the very stylish wife of Senator John Sherman Cooper, or Evangeline Bruce, wife of Ambassador David Bruce, known throughout the world for her elegance and taste, could pull Kay together.[73] Kay would later turn to Babe Paley; William Paley's wife, Kay said, "really knew how to do it." At a lunch with her, Kay met Truman Capote, who was unimpressed: "She was extraordinarily shy, a person who really didn't express her opinion. Not well-dressed, seeming not to have any interest in that at all. She was a person who just didn't care."[74]

In many ways, Phil damaged Kay's confidence more than Agnes ever did. He could be meaner and more cruel than Agnes, who would not have bothered to waste her animus on so unworthy a target as Kay. Agnes was often absent, while Phil was virtually inescapable, his unforgiving eye trained on his nervous wife. Agnes would become so caught up in herself that she hardly noticed her children. Her selfishness rendered her barbs less targeted, relevant, and hurtful. Phil was so attuned to his wife that his arrows always pierced.

Once Kay married, Agnes's attentions turned to Phil; for her, Kay might as well have been a girl hired to bear his children and run his house. This does not mean that Agnes never hurt Kay. An oft-told story has Kay, children in tow, approaching her husband and her mother as they talked in a hallway at Mount Kisco. "Pardon us, dear," Agnes said, "we're having an *intellectual* conversation."[75]

Of Phil and Kay's children, Lally especially grew to have a certain contempt for her mother. She worshipped her father, the parent with the interesting life and magnificent connections. When she needed information on the English Inns of Court for a history paper, she wrote to Felix Frankfurter: "Daddy suggests that you might be able to help me." Dutifully the Supreme Court justice chose some books from the court's library and had them sent to Lally. She became so familiar with Frankfurter that she would soon call him "the little judge."[76] Kay, on the other hand, "was terrified of Lally," recalls Joanna Steichen, "terrified in the sense that she indulged her in everything she wanted."[77]

Agnes didn't help; she encouraged her grandchildren to denigrate their mother. She maintained that the reason grandchildren and grandparents got along so well was that they had a "common enemy."[78] Lally was Agnes's favorite, and Agnes volunteered that as far as her grandchildren went, she preferred the girls. "As a mother, I preferred boys, but the sex has revenged itself on grandma. I adore my granddaughters."[79]

Phil had become obsessed with the nitty-gritty of politics. Inevitably, he was intrigued by the notion of president-making, an itch that had started with his prompting Estes Kefauver. Although Phil would have liked to be president himself, he recognized that his career had prepared him to be the grand manipulator, the real power. Disgusted and ignored by Eisenhower, he was back in the Democratic fold, initially supporting Adlai Stevenson in 1956. He was soon entranced by Lyndon Johnson, however, and pushed him as a much better candidate than Stevenson (although he quickly realized that Johnson would have to wait until 1960).

Agnes got into the act as well. In 1956, she voted Democratic for the first time, backing Stevenson to the hilt. Her work for him would again bring her close to Eleanor Roosevelt, who also avidly supported Stevenson.

Speaking out against McCarthy had made her appear more liberal, but, says Jean Friendly, it was Phil who turned Agnes from Republican to Democrat. In fact, something much more important, and typical of Agnes, was operating here: she was in love again.

She wrote Stevenson passionate letters, which she then insisted on reading aloud to an embarrassed Sidney Hyman, who had been Stevenson's speechwriter in 1952. She described the friendship as "very personal . . . a beautiful and incredible friendship . . . harder than a love affair."[80] Stevenson used to read the letters to his very close friend Marietta Tree, who recalled their content. "She'd say to him, 'I just want you to know a little bit about my past. I was very much in love with . . .'" And then she would mention Claudel, Mann, and others. She seemed to want to tell him, "Now you are the lucky recipient of my love."[81]

Hyman viewed this relationship as genuinely pathetic: Stevenson's interest, he claims, did not extend beyond Agnes's pocketbook and the influence he naively believed she had at the *Post*. Stevenson knew that approaching Phil Graham would be a waste of time. Later he claimed he had tried to approach Eugene, but when Agnes was present—and she always was—he could not get a word in. When Agnes was hospitalized with some routine but major surgery in 1956 (Hyman recalls it as a hysterectomy), she wrote out a check to Stevenson for $25,000 from her hospital bed. (One man who knew Stevenson well quipped that "Adlai had a great succession of older women who adored him, and they had the common situation of all being very rich.")[82]

Stevenson was no different from any of Agnes's other amours, in that he could never satisfy her. Marietta Tree recalled that "Agnes used to shower him with gifts, mainly [from] the Far East—jade, bowls, beautiful objects—which I'm sure he never appreciated at all or had time to look at." Agnes wrote him long letters every day, which even he, "the master of the small note," could not keep up with. "She was," Tree said, "obviously insatiable."[83]

Phil had his own sort of love affair with Lyndon Johnson, because, says Karl Meyer, who joined the *Post* in 1956, he was "in many ways what Phil in his own fantasy life wanted to be."[84] Bob Estabrook remembers Phil "playing the role of Tommy Corcoran.* Phil was a fixer par excellence."[85] And Johnson, unlike Kefauver and some of the other weaklings whom Phil had attempted to turn into big men, was at least worthy of being manipulated. Phil "enjoyed being around Johnson," explains George Reedy, "because Johnson was the epitome of the politician." Phil "looked upon Johnson somewhat the same way a moth looks upon a candle."[86] Phil admired what Bob Estabrook calls Johnson's "raw skill in manipulating the Senate."[87] Both men saw politics as the implementation of power, and anyone who did not as hopelessly idealistic, not deserving of the game. "Johnson was blunt and candid about the use of power," says Erwin Knoll, and Phil "was enamored of that kind of macho politics."[88]

---

*Corcoran, a brash aide to FDR, knew better than just about anyone how to finesse and finagle the president's programs through Congress and the bureaucracy.

Arnaud de Borchgrave agrees that Johnson and Phil were "very similar, very crude, very bottom-line."[89]

The two were inseparable, linked by their love for strategizing and scheming. Both were branded as southerners, although neither was really—not Phil, the native South Dakotan, and not Lyndon, the Hill Country Texan. Both felt like outsiders who had bent the bastions of eastern intellectual elitism—Harvard Law School and *The Washington Post* in Phil's case, the U.S. Senate in Johnson's—to their will. LBJ, George Smathers points out, was "a little bit like Phil's father: not too well educated, a little rough-hewn, blunt. Johnson would say vulgar things and get away with [them]"—and so, of course, would Phil.[90]

On the other hand, both were attractive and bursting with charisma. Libby Rowe recalls introducing Agnes to Lyndon Johnson for the first time. "Oh, he's just like Phil," she responded instantly. "They were both larger than life," Rowe explains, "going great guns. Some people have that extra electricity, vitality, about them. Come into a room and the decibels would rise, everybody would be more alive. That was the way with Johnson: he'd come into a room and everybody was galvanized."[91]

There was another reason for the bond between Graham and Johnson: both suffered from undiagnosed, untreated manic-depression.* The illness, with its violent ups and downs, allowed the two to interact spectacularly. When their manic peaks coincided, no pair had more energy, more confidence, more fabulous goals in mind. Hell-bent as each was on dominating the conversation—their impa-

---

*George Reedy is "absolutely positive" that Johnson was manic-depressive. He recalls accompanying Johnson, then vice-president, to UN secretary general Dag Hammarskjöld's funeral in Sweden in 1961. "Johnson hated funerals. He didn't go to a funeral unless he absolutely, positively had to." But as the U.S. representative he had no choice. "He rigged up a meeting in Paris with the general who was in charge of NATO, to get away early from the funeral reception. Once he got in the air, his spirits soared. He told me to set up dinner for the whole party at the best restaurant in Paris. So we set it up at La Tour d'Argent, and by the time we got [there], the manic phase had passed and the depressive phase had set in. That was one of the worst dinners of my life. He wanted to get the hell out of there, and he'd ask, 'How do you say "quick" in French?' I'd say, 'Try *"vitement,"* ' and that wouldn't work. I'd say, 'Try *"tout de suite."* ' Well, he *tout de suite*-ed all over the place. The waiter got flustered. You don't eat that way in a French restaurant. And finally we got to the end. He said, 'Well, what do I have for dessert?' I said, 'Try the profiterole.' Now, ordering a profiterole at La Tour d'Argent is like ordering an ice cream cone at Le Grenadier. But I knew he could get it quick, and I knew he'd like it. So we got him back to the hotel, and I thought I had him tucked safely in bed. Thank God. I went to get a drink, and when I walked back in, damned if he wasn't sitting there with a couple of secretaries. He was in a manic mood again."[92]

tience when anyone tried to get a word in edgewise was legendary—
they nevertheless managed to communicate. An observation made
by one historian after interviewing Johnson might just as well have
described Graham: "He held a conviction of his own centrality in the
universe, bordering on egomania."[93] Coinciding depressive spells
were not as frequent between the pair. When depression hit Phil, he
retreated to his farm and drew the curtains. Both men had underlings
who understood how to handle them, cover for them, and prepare
for the inevitable return of hyperactivity and hyperexpectations.

Phil persuaded Johnson that if he hoped ever to be president, he
needed a program. It was Phil who pulled out his yellow legal pad
and drafted a plan for social change that would become known as the
Great Society. Johnson himself would later credit Phil with writing
"the whole Great Society."[94]

Once Stevenson had again lost the White House for the Democrats
in 1956, Phil focused on making sure that Johnson would be the
party's candidate four years later. And with that goal in mind he
pushed Johnson to make the Civil Rights Act of 1957 his cause. The
bill had been passed by the House, and Phil advised Johnson that if
he wanted the presidency he had to shed his segregationist image by
piloting it through the Senate, where he was the majority leader.
Johnson was in a tough position—squiring the bill would hurt him
in Texas; killing it would hurt his national ambitions. So, following
his political instincts and the advice of Phil Graham—who bolstered
his advice with some very helpful editorials in *The Washington
Post*—Johnson decided to weaken the bill, but just enough to save
his Texas constituency without fatally disillusioning his hoped-for
national one. It was a brilliant piece of work. The version of the bill
that Johnson pushed through the Senate had everything cut out of
it except voting rights, and even there the enforcement provisions
were enfeebled.

Joe Rauh, along with Clarence Mitchell of the NAACP, was the
top lobbyist for the bill, and he was determined that it be passed in
its undiluted form. Phil knew that Rauh was the man whose mind he
had to change, so in the spring of 1957 he invited Rauh and his wife
to spend a Saturday at Glen Welby. "Oh, by the way, I've invited
Felix [Frankfurter] too," Phil mentioned offhandedly. "Will you
stop by and pick him up?"

Rauh soon realized that Phil had enlisted the Supreme Court

justice in his campaign to soften Rauh's resolve. "On the way out, all Felix does is tell me that the only thing that matters is voting rights. I made it clear I didn't agree with him. I was too naive to see the plot yet.

"So we got out to Phil's place. We went out in a rowboat on the pond, and then went to start drinking and have dinner, and Phil started on me: 'Everything is voting.' I started to get a little bit of the flavor of this—Frankfurter, Graham, and Johnson were a cabal, [trying] to end the opposition to what Johnson was doing, because we were screaming that Johnson was wrecking civil rights. So they pounded on me. I was slow on the pick-up, but even I saw it by dinnertime: Phil and Felix had it all lined up.

"They reported to Johnson that I was fairly adamant, not easy to handle. Johnson did go ahead and emasculate the bill, and then the civil rights leaders had the choice of that bill or nothing. I argued for taking the bill, on the grounds that you had to show you could do something in civil rights." Rauh's argument won over most of his colleagues. "That son-of-a-bitch friend of yours certainly helped us put this bill through," Johnson told Phil. He called Rauh one morning at six to report, "Lyndon says you saved the bill."

Rauh would remain somewhat uncomfortable about Frankfurter's role. "Felix was so close to Phil in 1957. He and [Phil] were working together with Johnson on a bill that you might think a Supreme Court justice shouldn't be working on."[95]

With Phil believing that he could accomplish almost anything, early that September came the Little Rock school integration crisis. Here Phil had to lobby the president, seeming to forget that while Senator Johnson had requested his help, President Eisenhower had not.

Arkansas governor Orval Faubus defied federal law by ordering the Arkansas National Guard to keep blacks from entering a white high school. Unasked, Phil spent sleepless nights formulating an integration plan for Ike to follow. He worked the phones sixteen hours a day. He talked to Governor Faubus on one side and NAACP executive secretary Roy Wilkins on the other. He called Joe Rauh at three in the morning to ask how to contact NAACP chief counsel Thurgood Marshall, and to declare, "This is what we've got to do."[96]

Phil publicly suggested that he and the president accompany a black student to Central High School in Little Rock, the president holding one of the student's hands, Phil Graham the other. Eisenhower, not surprisingly, ignored Phil and his proposal, although he did return to Washington from a Newport golf vacation and order that federal troops be sent to Arkansas.[97]

For all Phil's public posturing on the Little Rock crisis, his private views toward blacks were complex. According to James Reston, Phil believed it was his " 'Christian duty' to support the blacks, and that the United States would lose the Cold War if it continued its racial prejudices."[98] But Bob Estabrook says that three years earlier, when the U.S. Supreme Court, in *Brown v. Board of Education,* found the principle of separate but equal schools unconstitutional, "Phil wasn't as gung-ho as some of the rest of us were. I had the feeling he thought we were moving too fast at some times."[99] In one instance when Phil nearly fired Alan Barth, the trigger was Barth's insistence on pushing integration harder than Phil wanted it pushed.[100] Not long before the Little Rock crisis he vetoed one of Agnes's stories because its attack on segregation was too strident.[101]

These positions might be explained by Phil's upbringing and the fact that he could not afford to alienate advertisers. Less understandable were Phil's occasional outbursts. "We would have a black guest at lunch," Estabrook recalls, "and Phil would go out of his way to be racially insulting, seemingly as a way of showing that he was one of the boys. 'You niggers think this or that' [he would say], obviously trying to get a rise out of the person. He knew [the person] wouldn't think he really meant it; still, it was a technique that I found offensive. He would talk like a redneck just to be provocative."*[102]

Even people who were around Phil only in a casual way could see that he was "off his center." Newbold Noyes recalls going sailing on Chesapeake Bay a few times with Phil and Kay. "I never felt as comfortable with him as I did with Kay. Kay had a direct, sweet quality. I had a nervous feeling about Phil always. I may have sensed that there was something wrong with him, that beneath all this intelligence, he laughed a little too loud. He just didn't quite come across to me as a balanced person."[103] Nathan Halpern, who lived in New York, hadn't seen much of Phil since law school. He was shocked to get a firsthand report from his friend Edward R. Murrow—"the first inkling I had that something was the matter with

---

*On the other hand, *The Washington Post* was out in front on pushing for desegregation of the schools, and to segregationists it was among the most hated of newspapers.

Phil"—after Murrow saw Phil during a weekend visit with Agnes. "When he came back he told me, '[Phil's] in a very bad way. . . . Mentally, he's not focusing. Something's the matter with him.' "[104]

George Reedy began to pick up similar signals. "Phil did become a little eccentric in his thinking as time went on. One had the feeling that he wasn't tracking. He would say things that were not very logical. He seemed to think things were happening that weren't, that he should have known weren't happening."[105]

By the end of October 1957, Phil had sunk into a full-fledged depression and, with Kay, retreated to the farm in Virginia. His doctors ordered rest. He told three of his aides that he had had a nervous breakdown and was going to Glen Welby to recuperate.[106] He and Kay stayed there for a full six months, Phil spending his days and nights in bed, curtains drawn, or fishing on Lake Katharine.[107] The burden on Kay was terrible—to pull him out of a despondency that seemed to have no bottom. She would sometimes talk to him for eight hours at a time, trying fruitlessly to lift his spirits.[108]

The *Post* executives and editors who covered for him—he designated John Sweeterman and Russ Wiggins to run the paper—referred to Phil's mental illness as "Problem A." Bob Estabrook recalls: "Russ, Al Friendly, and I were quite frank in our discussions about what to do about Problem A, Phil's excesses."[109] They did not share with Phil's employees the nature of his problems. "They always had some kind of excuse," says Erwin Knoll; "that he had hepatitis, some kind of lingering illness."[110]

A manic state followed, and Phil went back to Washington in preparation for returning to the *Post;* but his friends knew that he had not recovered. Kay called Joe Rauh: "Phil's ready to go out. Can he, I, and Prich come over for the evening?" Rauh saw immediately that Phil was sick; his talk was a stream of profanities. "Our son and his fiancée were here. Phil wouldn't talk that way in front of a young lady. It was sad. We acted as if nothing had happened." Kay did also. "I never saw her shout or correct," said Rauh. "She'd just take it."[111]

Newbold Noyes remembers Phil's profanity—in front of women too—as extreme; it might have been comical had it not been so pathetic. "He got to a stage where he couldn't hold a conversation with anyone without absolute gutter language streaming out, for no reason at all. He wasn't angry, but every other word was a four-letter word, and talking with a woman [was] no different."[112] An old-time

Post editor said he could not bear to be in Phil's company: "Obscenity in mixed company is out of my line."[113] Another editor was "astonished" by Phil: "Was there ever a sentence that didn't have the word 'fuck' in it, or 'fucking'?"[114]

There is a genetic, physiological predisposition to manic-depression, and many of Phil's friends believe the profession he chose exacerbated it. He was enormously frustrated, Karl Meyer contends, to realize that publishers did not have the kind of power they were purported to have. Publishers' power is "hostage to the organization they're part of, and that is different from running a corporation. Newspapers can do many things, they can make issues, they can publicize people, but when it comes to the great decisions of war and peace, press power is marginal."[115]

If his editorial writers promoted one of Phil's favorite people or causes, they did so, says Murrey Marder, because they too supported that cause or person. "Sure, he could have come back and said, 'This is the way it's going to be, and I don't care what the hell any of the reporters say—it's my newspaper.' If he had done that he would have had a different kind of newspaper, and he knew that."[116] Phil was an "energetic lobbyist" for his views, explains Karl Meyer, but he could not "impose" them on everything the paper did.*

Meyer insists that Phil Graham was simply unsuited for the role of publisher. "Part of Phil's mental problem was that he was a ferociously ambitious fellow who really wanted to be president of the United States, or at least a figure of political consequence, but he was running an institution with a very tricky form of power. It's not a coincidence that so many great publishers have gone mad or otherwise have been mentally unhinged—[Lord] Northcliffe, or Hearst. Megalomania is a common problem."[117]

---

*Meyer recalls, for example, going to his first dinner party at the Grahams' and telling Russ Wiggins that he loved writing editorials but did not agree with the *Post*'s editorials on foreign policy and agriculture, then written by Merlo Pusey, a coreligionist of Secretary of Agriculture Ezra Taft Benson. "So in addition to the natural affinity in conservatism between Pusey and Benson, there was a certain religious resonance: Benson was not only Mormon but an elder of the church." Wiggins's response to the young editorial writer's complaint was a roar of laughter. "He waved his hand and said, 'Phil, come over here. Repeat to Phil what you just said.' I repeated as tactfully as I could my demur on the agriculture thing, and Phil laughed and said, 'Join the club. We don't agree with him either.' That was the first inkling I got of one of the realities of newspaper work. If you have any kind of serious newspaper with serious and qualified people, there are limitations in the power of the publisher and editor. You hire people, you give them their head, and they say and do things you don't agree with, and you have to swallow it."

Phil was not a journalist by instinct or by inclination. Milton Viorst, a reporter for the *Post* in the late fifties, explains, "Phil did have an agenda. Phil was not a journalist. Phil was a politician disguised as a journalist. He used the power of the paper for his own personal political objectives."[118] Frank Waldrop believes that Phil had a destructive need to be "loved, admired, asked, consulted." He was caught in the terrible vise of feeling he needed to be charming all the time. "There's a point at which being charming, witty, and all the rest is really not necessary," says Waldrop. "Phil couldn't not do it, couldn't not turn it on."[119] And because Phil was a man who wished to persuade people, not merely inform or entertain them, he took scant pleasure in running the *Post*.

The *Post* was, especially when compared with leading papers such as *The New York Times,* still pretty thin stuff. The national staff numbered seven, and the international staff was virtually non-existent—a few stringers and reporter Ferdinand Kuhn, who wrote from Washington and paid his own expenses on occasional trips abroad.*[120]

But then the *Post* started to make money. In 1954, it had lost $238,000. Between 1955 and 1957, profits exceeded $2 million a year.[122] *Star* executives had guessed wrongly that the *Post* would hold at most a fifth of the *Times-Herald*'s quarter-million readers; in fact, it held on to 180,000 and expanded to a circulation of nearly 400,000, to become the nation's ninth largest paper,[123] and the fifth in total advertising linage. Much sooner than anyone expected, the *Post* switched from plugging its Pulitzer Prize winners to plugging its circulation lead; the *Star* did the opposite.

It was about that time, in 1957, that Phil decided to open foreign bureaus. John Sweeterman, who liked things as they were, had to figure out how to accomplish Phil's desire while spending the least amount of money possible. (The *Post* still acted like the impoverished daily it had once been. When Erwin Knoll arrived in 1957,

---

*The *Post* was so short-staffed that when Bob Estabrook offered Karl Meyer, fresh out of Princeton with a Ph.D. in government, a job as an editorial writer, he warned him that his responsibilities would also include choosing letters to the editor, editing the columns that ran on the editorial page, and writing about Latin America.[121] In 1960, when Fidel Castro became newsworthy, the *Post* still had no correspondent posted to Latin America, so it sent Tom Wolfe, a Yale Ph.D. in American studies, then covering government in Prince Georges County. He had no experience in international affairs, but someone noticed in his records that he had had four years of Spanish.

carbon paper was still issued by the sheet, "when you could prove that the last one was all used up."[124]) Murrey Marder, who with his posting to London became the paper's first foreign correspondent, recalls: "Originally [Chalmers] Roberts was going to be the correspondent. Then the question came of who would pay for the school for his children, and that's why he was not the first foreign correspondent. My wife and I didn't have children." To cut the cost to the bone, an exchange was effected: *The Guardian*'s Washington correspondent moved into the *Post* and Marder moved into *The Guardian*. No money changed hands.[125]

Phil came up with another way to reduce costs—requiring a very reluctant Marder to file nightly reports from London with WTOP, the *Post*'s Washington radio station. Marder balked and Phil pleaded: "We could then split the cost of this operation between the *Post* and WTOP."[126]

Marder had been in London for about a year and a half when Sweeterman dropped by to inspect his operation. He "looked around, looked around, said nothing, and we went to lunch. I finally said, 'You're worried about the cost.' 'Yeah.' 'How can you be worried about the cost? You're paying my salary and that's about it. You're not paying rent.' 'Tell me, what do you think of Walter Lippmann?' 'What do you mean, what do I think of him?' 'Well, do you think he does a good job?' 'Yeah, I think he does a very good job, the best job of anybody in the world in journalism. What's your point?' 'If you think he does such a good job, he does it in Washington. Why do you have to be over here?' "[127]

By the late 1950s, Eugene Meyer was going downhill fast. He was a beloved figure at the *Post,* where he still made regular appearances. "He would come around the newsroom maybe three or four times a month," recalls Milton Viorst, "and the new reporters would introduce themselves to him. It was more of a formality. A very old doddering man who had long since lost that edge that made him the brilliant businessman he was many years before."[128] Many of his cronies had died (his only surviving brother, Walter, died in January 1957*), and the younger men who had not known him in his decades

---

*The two had never been close. A lifelong bachelor, Walter was quirky, peculiar. He devoted nearly his entire career to fighting one lawsuit to save the Cottonbelt Railroad. He won in the end and left his relatives large chunks of suddenly valuable stock. He lived in the Yale Club in New York City and also kept a house in Westchester County where the Meyer children were frequently sent for lunch. Bis recalls that her uncle Walter was "always talking about potable

of power did not seek him out. Nobody knew better than Eugene that his history-making days were over. Although President Eisenhower still asked after him, it was to appoint him a member of the Committee on Purchases of Blind-Made Products, not the Federal Reserve or the World Bank.

Eugene's mind frequently drifted to the glories of the past. Sidney Hyman was there when Bernard Baruch came to visit. "They embraced, tears in their eyes, two elderly gentlemen. Gene said, 'Bernie, why don't we go back to Wall Street and make those characters walk the plank?' "[130]

Al Friendly continued to be solicitous of Eugene. Bernard Nossiter, then the *Post*'s young economics reporter, was dispatched by Friendly to Crescent Place to visit with Eugene. The old man, he was told, was "feeling lonely and out of it. I was sent to cheer him up, and instead he cheered me up. We were mired in the second Eisenhower recession at that point, and he already had seen the signs that pointed to an upturn, and he was right." He had "all his wits. He was speaking somewhat slower and in a halting tone, but [was] remarkable, no question about that."[131]

Eugene was not so much appreciated by his family. "Awareness of his shrunken role came as a shock to Meyer one night," his biographer wrote, "as he prepared to dress and go downstairs for a party Agnes was giving. One of his daughters asked why he wanted to make the effort in his weakened condition. 'You're ashamed of me,' he said accusingly, but accepted the hint and kept out of the hubbub below."[132]

As the deterioration of his body far outpaced that of his mind, Eugene felt enormous anger. He sometimes took it out on Agnes, who, typically, was concerned most with her own well-being. In August 1957, she wrote to Kay that Eugene was in a mood "of deep dissatisfaction with everything" and that she was "the target of his inner turmoil. . . . I actually get frightened about the future. When he was strong, I could fight back. That is out of the question now. He conquers through weakness and I am helpless. The only people who can help me, therefore, are you and let's admit it, especially Phil who can say anything because he is the one person who can do no wrong."[133]

Eugene seemed, incredibly, not to notice Phil's hostility toward

water." He would occasionally be asked to come to dinner at Mount Kisco, but "if you asked him [to come] for dinner on Thursday he might turn up on Tuesday or Friday."[129]

him and toward Kay. Shielded by his daughter, he was also largely unaware of Phil's mental problems. As a man of action, Eugene would have found it hard, in any case, to reconcile himself to the fact that Phil's problems were emotional. It was Phil's physical health not his mental health that concerned Eugene. "Phil is too skinny and too high-powered,"[134] he would say. Sidney Hyman explains that "Eugene could construe it as a case of terrible overwork because Phil was spreading himself in a thousand different directions."[135]

Eugene never did realize the severity of his son-in-law's problems. Suffering from both cancer and heart disease, Eugene was in and out of the hospital, where a kind of death watch hovered, with visitors Edward Steichen at one end of the corridor and Alfred Phillips, the Meyers' chauffeur, at the other. Steichen's brother-in-law Carl Sandburg, a Meyer family friend who used to stay at the Washington house and read stories to the children, was also there.[136] The watch ended on Friday afternoon, July 17, 1959, when eighty-three-year-old Eugene choked on orange juice, fell into a coma, and died.

Deborah Davis reported that Eugene had told Felix Frankfurter, who in turn told some of his clerks, that he wished to be buried in Israel. But those who knew him well—Sir Isaiah Berlin, Sidney Hyman, Ben Gilbert—insist that it is beyond the realm of possibility that Meyer would have made such a request. Bis calls the story "wrong, totally" and points to the care her father had taken in building a mausoleum, which contained the remains of his parents and a marker for his brother Edgar, in Kensico Cemetery near Mount Kisco.[137]

A private funeral service for the immediate family was held at Crescent Place. The memorial service was held the next Tuesday, and the only thing Jewish about it was the lying in state. The body was later cremated. The *Washington Post* obituary offered a bit of family history, without once mentioning Eugene's Jewish roots or prominently Jewish forebears.

The service at the All Souls Unitarian Church was conducted by the Reverend Dr. Duncan Howlett, the church's minister. Before her husband's death, Agnes had written to the Reverend Howlett explaining that Eugene "never had any official connection with the Jewish religion as neither one of us . . . [has] any feeling for orthodoxy; as far as Eugene is concerned I am reminded of something John Dewey said when accused of 'Godlessness.' 'I am as good a Christian as any of them.' "[138]

Certainly Agnes had mixed feelings about her husband's religion.

Sidney Hyman says she thought she would have been a happier person with Eugene if he had been everything he was—except Jewish. But Hyman qualifies this: "Normally the burial would have been on a Saturday, [but] she had enough sensibilities about it to say that it would be against the Jewish custom to bury him on Saturday. It took me by surprise that she had that kind of delicacy about her."[139] Agnes received many awards from Jewish groups, and a year after Eugene's death she went to Israel to study Histadrut, the Israeli labor movement.[140] Five years later, the Meyer family endowed a medical research center at Hebrew University in Jerusalem in memory of Eugene.[141]

Still, an ugly streak of anti-Semitism emerged. Agnes regretted that her children and their children would never escape their Jewish blood. When she was drinking, says Joanna Steichen, she did not hide these regrets. Agnes once recounted the frightening experience of one of her daughters, who was traveling in Europe during the Hitler era. After some German officers had looked at her passport, they called her a little Jewish girl. "The sad thing was," Steichen says, "after telling that story Agnes turned to us and said, 'She didn't really look Jewish, did she?' "[142]

Agnes was not happy when her youngest daughter, Ruth, married a Jew, and the wrong kind of Jew at that. "She married a very ordinary obstetrician/gynecologist," Steichen explains, "a nice man. When he wasn't around, Agnes was always a little bit scornful of him."

Eugene's memorial, which Karl Meyer terms "a bloodless affair,"[143] attracted eight hundred of Washington's most powerful. Agnes had asked Chief Justice Earl Warren to deliver the eulogy, which was actually drafted by Sidney Hyman.* Among the notables present were Secretary of the Treasury Robert Anderson, chairman of the board of governors of the Federal Reserve William McChesney Martin, Jr., Lyndon Johnson, Senator J. William Fulbright, Felix Frankfurter, Drew Pearson, political columnist Joseph Alsop, and George Gallup. Representing the household staff was Phillips, Eugene's faithful chauffeur.

Phil declared the service sterile and meaningless, and hissed that

---

*Warren "was involved up to his neck in court work," Hyman recalls, "and Phil asked me to prepare the draft. It never in a thousand years occurred to Agnes Meyer that Earl Warren would not have the time, that somebody [else] might have drafted it." When Agnes remarked to Hyman on the beauty of Warren's eulogy, he had to bite his tongue to keep from claiming authorship. "I never told her. Kay knew and Phil knew, and that's all that was necessary."[144]

Kay and her dead father were nothing but kikes. At the same time, he reviled them for trying to pass as Wasps.[145]

Nevertheless, Eugene's death left Phil with a horrible sense of loss and emptiness. "Phil never quite believed in his own success," said Bernard Nossiter, "and when the old man died, there must have been a connection between the two. Phil was determined to do himself in to prove that he wasn't entitled to what he got."[146]

Adding to Phil's despair were the severe psychological problems of one of his closest friends, Frank Wisner, Jr. Southern-born, a veteran of the OSS under "Wild Bill" Donovan, Wisner had become a partner in an old-line Wall Street law firm; but law bored him, and he went to work for the CIA, running a secret war against the Soviets. According to one writer on U.S. intelligence, he became the "impresario of Cold War clandestine operations" for the CIA.[147]

Wisner's depression became pronounced around the same time as Phil's.* He began to act erratically, to drink heavily, to require hospitalization for nervous exhaustion. On one occasion he had to be carried out of CIA headquarters by hospital attendants. He too was a manic-depressive.

The year of Eugene's death and Wisner's decline, Phil started treatment for manic-depression with psychiatrist/psychoanalyst Leslie Farber, chairman of the faculty of the Washington School of Psychiatry. Not surprisingly, Farber's plan was to treat Phil with analysis, period. Analysis was then widely deemed an effective therapy against a disease today considered the result of physiological chemical imbalance.

Farber was himself an analysand of psychiatrist Harry Stack Sullivan, who had headed the Washington School of Psychiatry in the 1930s and 1940s. Farber had written extensively about Sullivan, and those who knew Farber well agree that writing, especially literary criticism, was his real interest. According to Frank Waldrop, Farber "wasn't satisfied with practicing psychiatry. He had considerable literary taste."[148]

Farber was probably the wrong doctor for Phil, who needed intensive psychiatric treatment, not allusions to literature. A close profes-

---

*In Hungary in 1956, Wisner had encouraged the freedom fighters to believe that the American military would help them in their revolt against the communists. Wisner pleaded with the U.S. government to send help but was ignored, and later was ordered home.

sional and personal friend of Phil's told Harvey Segal, a neighbor of Farber's, that while he was treating Phil, Farber "was borrowing large sums of money from him" and "was always very anxious to give up his practice and write."[149] Phil, presumably, was going to make this happen for him.

Farber became the kind of intellectual heavy-hitter in Washington who would have appealed to Phil Graham—he made it seem less that he was seeing a psychiatrist, and more as if he were seeking the company of one of the capital's most provocative thinkers or writers. It was Farber, for instance, who persuaded philosopher Martin Buber to come from Israel to lecture in Washington. Phil developed an intense interest in Buber and asked Karl Meyer to cover the lecture for the *Post*.

In December 1959, Phil outlined the strategy that he believed would result in Lyndon Johnson's nomination for president in 1960. He predicted that Kennedy and Johnson would be the only candidates who would come to the Democratic National Convention with sizable blocs of delegates. Kennedy would not quite make it, and the convention would settle on Stevenson as the northern candidate— thus creating a nomination fight between Stevenson and Johnson. Johnson could not help but win, Phil conjectured; Harry Truman, Richard Daley, Carmine De Sapio, and other political pros would throw their support behind Johnson because they had never liked the effete Stevenson and, more important, they figured he could not win.[150]

And so for Phil Graham it was off to the convention and a chance to be a kingmaker. For Kay Graham, the most painful three years of her life were ahead.

Chapter 10

THE KENNEDY YEARS

Declaring that Eisenhower had provided "eight years of the dreariest and phoniest mediocrity," Phil arrived in Los Angeles for the Democratic National Convention in 1960 in a mood of sheer mania, determined to make LBJ president. Kay was with him, as was his much younger half brother, Bob, whom Phil had urged to go to law school—Bob had recently finished his first year at Harvard Law—and then set up as a delegate organizer and floor manager for Johnson. It seemed to Ernest that another son was getting away.[1]

In Adlai Stevenson's corner was the irrepressible Agnes, who that year publicly renounced her membership in the Republican Party as she denounced Richard Nixon. According to Marietta Tree, "Agnes was responsible for getting up the movement and the money" for the Democrats to draft Stevenson in 1960.[2] Eleanor Roosevelt was also ardently working for Stevenson and intensely debating strategy with Agnes.*

Phil did not take these rich ladies and their candidate seriously. According to Bob Estabrook, his attitude was: "This [is] just one of her operations, and poor old Aggie, we'll let her have her fling."[3] But Phil did attend the party Agnes gave for Stevenson, hoping to shove him onto Johnson's bandwagon. Could he have breakfast with Johnson the following Sunday, Phil asked the still hopeful but twice defeated candidate.[4]

---

*Agnes would later work for Kennedy, as a national vice-chair of his campaign committee. She and Eleanor would be furious with him when, after his election, he failed to appoint Stevenson secretary of state.

As soon as Phil realized that Johnson was not going to make it, he hatched the plan for Kennedy to select Johnson as his running mate. Johnson himself would later credit Phil with pushing Kennedy to choose him. He told biographer Doris Kearns Goodwin that Phil "told Kennedy to make me Vice President."[5]

Phil was renowned for his powers of persuasion, but putting this team together would take a wizard. First of all, neither man liked or trusted the other, and between Johnson and Robert Kennedy there was genuine loathing. Persuading Johnson, who still hoped to be president in 1960, to play number two to a rich man's kid would be at least as difficult as persuading Kennedy to take him.

On Tuesday, the day before Kennedy won the nomination, Phil had lunch with Johnson and was startled by his unrealistic desire to continue fighting for the top spot. Johnson had his people spreading rumors that Kennedy's father had been pro-Nazi and that Kennedy suffered from the potentially fatal Addison's disease. Phil recognized that Johnson was exhausted and irrational, and wisely decided not to broach the subject of the vice-presidency just then. "A Negro couple from his ranch were in the room throughout our lunch," Phil later wrote, "and the three of us converged upon him, disrobed him, pajamaed him and got him in bed." While Johnson napped, Phil "scribbled some thoughts (and clichés) about the world situation" for LBJ to use in a speech that afternoon.[6]

Once Kennedy clinched the nomination, Phil and Joseph Alsop hurried to his suite at the Biltmore and explained the virtues of Johnson as running mate. Phil argued that without Johnson, Kennedy would lose Texas and thus the election. "Your problem is simple," he told Kennedy. "You pick Johnson for vice president, take Texas, and win. Or you don't take Johnson, and you lose."[7]

Next Phil had to persuade Johnson to accept the number-two spot. Speaker of the House Sam Rayburn, a fellow Texan who had enormous influence with Johnson—"he thought that Rayburn was his daddy"[8]—was allegedly urging him not to accept. A good argument could be made, and Rayburn was making it, that Johnson would be crazy to give up the enormous power of Senate majority leader for the ignobility of the vice-presidency. Johnson called another Texan for advice—John Nance Garner, who had gone from a leadership position in the House to two unhappy terms as vice-president under FDR. Garner, best remembered for saying that the vice-presidency "isn't worth a pitcher of warm piss," told Johnson to stay put. Phil countered that while the relatively detached style of

Eisenhower allowed Speaker of the House Rayburn and Senate majority leader Johnson to be almost coequal partners with the president, in an activist, same-party administration, Johnson's power would be much diminished.

Johnson correctly suspected that the Kennedys would so insult him that he would have to decline the offer. That would leave Kennedy free to claim credit for having made the offer with older voters, Texans, and southerners, who liked Johnson and distrusted Kennedy.

Kennedy did apparently dispatch his brother, armed with evidence of strong opposition in the North, to urge Johnson to turn down the offer. But on arriving at Johnson's suite that Thursday, Bobby Kennedy was granted an audience with Sam Rayburn, while Phil, arriving at the same time, rushed to meet Lyndon and Lady Bird in another room. Phil called Kennedy from there to argue that "southern gains would more than offset liberal losses." Having gone more than a week with next to no sleep, Phil said he was "as calm as Chileans on top of an earthquake." At his urging, Kennedy called Johnson and formally and directly made him the offer, which Johnson accepted.

Bobby Kennedy, who had left the suite angry that Johnson had foisted him off on Rayburn, was distraught. The offer, he insisted, was pro forma and not meant to be accepted. He went back to Johnson's suite. This time he spoke directly to Johnson, urged him to turn down the offer and instead become chairman of the Democratic National Committee. Although Bobby was, in fact, relaying his brother's wishes (as well as his own), Johnson thought he was acting independently, and never forgave him. From then on, Johnson referred to Bobby as "that little shit-ass."[9]

In a state of near nervous collapse, Johnson called for Phil, who again got "Jack" on the telephone. Kennedy assured Phil that the position was Johnson's for the taking. Phil urged Kennedy to tell Johnson himself, and he did. Lyndon and Lady Bird stood in the entrance of their suite, Phil said, "looking as though they had just survived an airplane crash," Johnson holding his typed acceptance statement. "I was just going to read this on TV when Bobby came in, and now I don't know what I ought to do," he said to Phil. "Of course you know what you're going to do," Graham told him. "Throw your shoulders back and your chin out and go out and make that announcement. And then go on and win. Everything's wonderful." And so he did. Phil described himself as feeling "wildly elated."[10]

Another daunting task awaited Phil: persuading liberals, blacks, and labor to go along with Johnson as vice-president. Rebellions were breaking out all over. The Liberal Party in New York, for example, so opposed Johnson that it was threatening to refuse to list Kennedy on the ballot.[11] Joe Rauh and other D.C. delegates—especially blacks—were enraged because Kennedy had assured them he would choose Hubert Humphrey or "another Midwestern liberal."[12] "Kennedy made me a promise it wouldn't be Johnson," Rauh recalled, and "the black delegates were wild at the idea of Johnson."[13] Robert Nathan, also a D.C. delegate, recounts that after word hit that Kennedy had picked Johnson, Rauh was interviewed on television, saying, "Jack, if you can hear me, don't do this."[14]

Phil threw himself into his task with a vengeance—lobbying, cajoling, making promises and threats, working at a manic pace without sleep or food or perspective, a cigarette dangling from lips that seemed never still. He put his newspaper to use, flying the *Post* to Los Angeles and into the hands of delegates every morning. "He kept the Johnson flame alive," Rauh said.[15]

Some people who were close to the action believe that Phil exaggerated his role—that no one had to persuade Kennedy to take Johnson, because he was the first to realize that without Johnson he would lose. Others claim that it was Joseph Kennedy who ordered his son to give the second spot to Johnson. As for persuading Johnson to say yes, some credit Sam Rayburn, who, much as he disliked Kennedy, despised Nixon and knew that he would win if Johnson were not on the ticket. And others, including Rayburn, said that Lady Bird feared her husband would work himself to death if he stayed in the Senate, and threatened him with divorce unless he accepted the nomination.

Still others argue that Johnson coveted the vice-presidency. According to Hope Ridings Miller, Rayburn told her "he didn't think anybody could have kept LBJ from taking it."[16] Johnson reportedly told Clare Boothe Luce, "I looked it up: One out of every four Presidents has died in office. I'm a gamblin' man, darlin', and this is the only chance I got."[17]

Although Phil lobbied other newspaper publishers to endorse Kennedy, the *Post* endorsed neither candidate. Phil explained that because of its unique position in the capital, the paper should maintain an independent, nonpartisan attitude.[18] Yet no one doubted for a second where Phil stood. Knowing that he would have a place in the inner circle, Phil desperately wanted Kennedy to win.

Phil was particularly captivating that year. "I could feel patronizing toward a Kennedy who was running for the presidency," says Sidney Hyman, but "to feel patronizing toward Phil Graham, I'd [think] the Lord God Jehovah would strike me dead with a lightning bolt, that this would be the ultimate heresy. [Phil] was an outsize figure."[19]

Phil harbored a similar view of himself. A crack heard often in Washington, and attributed to Phil, went: "I'm better-looking than Jack Kennedy, I'm more successful with girls, I'm a lot smarter. Why is he president?"[20]

Phil got good and drunk at the inaugural balls.

Some two months later, Phil was in a state of euphoria reminiscent of his mood upon purchasing the *Times-Herald.* This time he was transported by the possibility of buying *Newsweek.*

The weekly magazine was then a distant, blander second to *Time,* with a circulation of only 1.4 million. The controlling-interest stockholder—fifty-nine percent—was philanthropist Vincent Astor, who had died in 1959, his holdings reverting to a foundation named for him. (Astor, in league with W. Averell Harriman, had been one of the unsuccessful bidders for *The Washington Post* in 1933.) The board of the foundation wanted to sell, and so did Astor's widow, Brooke.

Among the many who wanted to buy were Doubleday, Samuel Newhouse, John Hay Whitney, and Norton Simon. Also in the running were Malcolm Muir, *Newsweek*'s seventy-five-year-old chairman of the board, who had started *Business Week* for McGraw-Hill and who for years had run *Newsweek* for Astor, accumulating thirteen percent of its stock; and Osborn Elliott, then *Newsweek*'s managing editor, who was scrambling, with senior editor James Cannon, to raise money.

It was Oz Elliott, realizing that his efforts were futile, who brought Ben Bradlee, then a member of *Newsweek*'s Washington bureau, into the race. From his short stint at the *Post,* Bradlee knew Phil Graham, and it was his idea to approach him. "Ozzie baby," Bradlee assured Elliott, "I know where the smart money is. It's in Phil Graham's pocket."[21] Bradlee confided in *Post* reporter Morrie Siegel about

Muir: "This jerk is running [*Newsweek*] right into the ground. And I'm going to try to get Phil to buy it."[22] Bradlee, it is said, was even more appalled at the prospect of Newhouse's acquiring *Newsweek*.[23]

Bradlee arranged to meet Phil at his home. The two talked until three in the morning and Bradlee spent the rest of the night meeting Phil's nine a.m. deadline for a memo explaining why he should buy the magazine.

Once Phil decided to proceed, he set his sights on charming the members of the Vincent Astor Foundation board into submission. He dispatched Bradlee, whose parents had been friends of the Astors', to make the initial approach to Brooke Astor, and then followed with a personal visit. She would later tell friends that Phil Graham was the most charming man she had met in years.[24]

Phil next sent Al Friendly to Rome to meet with Averell Harriman, then U.S. roving ambassador, to convince him to sell Phil the twelve percent of *Newsweek* stock that he owned. Friendly, who had worked for Harriman as a speechwriter, arrived at his hotel at eight in the morning. "What the hell are you doing here?" Harriman asked. "I'm here to offer you two million dollars for your *Newsweek* stock." Not only did Harriman accept the offer, he cabled the Astor Foundation trustees to recommend the sale to the *Post*.[25]

Phil was never better at the big gesture, the crisp decision, than he was that year. When he heard that Muir's best offer was $45 a share, he offered $50, which was about twenty-four times the magazine's earnings per share. "I thought to myself, 'Oh, nuts, don't drag along,'" Phil recalled.[26] He moved to New York for the duration, taking a suite at the Carlyle; there he installed a special phone line to the office of Allan Betts, the banker who ran the Astor Foundation for Brooke. He wrote Betts a down-payment check for $2 million—crossing off his own name on the personal check and writing in the *Post*'s—with the nonchalance of someone paying a telephone bill.[27] "I didn't know how the hell to add zeroes after the two million," he later recounted, "so I just wrote 'Two million dollars' and went squiggle-squiggle with the pen."[28]

It came down to the Washington Post Company against Doubleday. Both were offering the same deal—$15 million for the magazine, for forty-five percent of a television station, for two radio stations, and for $3 million in *Newsweek*'s cashbox. But the *Post* had Phil Graham—as Allan Betts said, "I've never been so impressed by a man in my life"[29]—and Fritz Beebe, the Cravath, Swaine lawyer who had counseled Eugene and Phil on the *Times-Herald* acquisition and who now arranged for Phil to best Doubleday by offering cash, one-third of it borrowed from the Prudential life insurance company.

Phil's charm could take him only so far. It was Beebe who did the hard negotiating that made possible the purchase first of the *Times-Herald* and then of *Newsweek*. Beebe was seven months older, light-years more mature, infinitely more steady and patient than Phil.[30] Kermit Lansner, a *Newsweek* senior editor who would become executive editor in the Phil Graham regime, recalls Beebe as "a man of enormous probity and a good deal of judgment."[31] He became the quiet, steady presence in Phil's manic life.

The deal was brilliant—for a net cost of just over $9 million, Phil got what David Halberstam would call "one of the great steals of contemporary journalism."[32] Yes, the selling price was $15 million, but offsetting that were the $3 million in *Newsweek*'s till and the TV station, which was promptly sold for $2.5 million.[33]

Phil was ecstatic. En route to celebrating at '21' with the Elliotts, the Bradlees, and the Beebes, he "jump[ed] up and down so energetically in the taxi that his gray fedora was squashed down on his head. 'We bought it! We bought it!' he cried."[34]

Nearly everyone was on a high that evening. Elliott, whom Phil named editor of the magazine, would have a salary twice that he had earned before. Bradlee, whom Phil named Washington bureau chief, would receive a finder's fee of Washington Post Company stock options later worth some $3 million.

Oz Elliott had met Kay only briefly before. He described her as "quiet and shy."[35] She was also sick with tuberculosis. That morning her doctor had told her she had a spot on one lung, but she waited until the next morning to tell Phil, not wanting to dampen his excitement.[36] She waited another month before taking to bed for three months.

To Phil, Kay was, as usual, a drain, certainly not someone to impress his new friends. Like Bradlee, Oz Elliott was a pedigreed Wasp Ivy Leaguer—a New Yorker rather than a Boston Brahmin—with an edge: smart-talking, appealing, impassioned about the issues of the day.

The other wives seemed daunting to Kay. Fritz Beebe's German-born wife, Liane, was charming and witty, "a European beauty . . . whose family background was so complicated that she insisted the only way it could be explained was that her grandfathers were sisters."[37] Bradlee had divorced Jean Saltonstall and married, in 1956, the very blonde and beautiful Antoinette "Tony" Pinchot, an accomplished artist, who was close to Jacqueline Kennedy; the latter would remind her husband, "You know you always say that Tony is your ideal."*[38]

For Kay, this evening was a taste of things to come—the Kennedy years, when everybody, it appeared, was so bright, so witty, so attractive. Yet here she was, so clumsy, with looks that merited not a second glance and conversation that was stunted into near muteness, so fearful was she of saying something that would reflect badly on Phil.

The day after he bought *Newsweek,* an article in *The New York Times* characterized Phil as "the embodiment of every young newspaperman's dream of glory. At the age of forty-five, he presides over one of the nation's most flourishing publishing enterprises and knows with certainty that his newspaper . . . is required reading for some of the most influential men in the country. He is a friend, adviser, confidant and goad to a dazzling spectrum of Washington society, including the President, the Vice President, influential Senators, Congressmen, ambassadors, and such lesser arbiters of capital living as columnists, reporters and aspiring hostesses." The article mentioned Kay once, her full first name misspelled.[39]

Phil had acquired a magazine of not only national but international reach, something the *Post,* for all its influence in the capital, could never have. He had a fresh constituency to wow, and did he ever. At *Newsweek,* Phil was not thought of as Eugene Meyer's son-in-law. He was the knight who would rescue the magazine from mediocrity. Things had become so bad at "Boozeweek," as the magazine was called in recognition of its heavy-drinking ad salesmen and editors,[40] that rather than try to compete with *Time,* the staff kept its eye on third-string *U.S. News & World Report.*

At a get-acquainted meeting with his new editors, Phil coined a line so stirring that it is used even today. Composing his thoughts literally on the back of an envelope, he told his new employees that the journalist's responsibility is to set down the "first rough draft of history."[41] According to Thelma McMahon, a secretary in the Wash-

---

*She was the daughter of Amos Pinchot, a renowned Bull Mooser who had helped Teddy Roosevelt build his Progressive Party in 1912, and a niece of Gifford Pinchot, a conservationist and two-term governor of Pennsylvania.

ington bureau since 1950, with Phil's arrival, "all of a sudden every-thing was energized."[42]

Phil's predecessor, unaffectionately known as "Old Man Muir," was a tiny man, recalls McMahon, who "struck fear in [people's] hearts when he came around. Old Man Muir ruled it with an iron fist. He wasn't of this generation's thinking. Things were very straitlaced. I'm sure Muir was horrified by Phil Graham. It was two generations clashing."[43] What Muir thought of the new chief of the Washington bureau, Ben Bradlee—who was nearly as gratuitously profane as Phil Graham—is not hard to imagine.

Phil quickly rid *Newsweek* of both Muir and his son, once the heir apparent. He made Malcolm Sr. chairman of the executive commit-tee of the board and invited Malcolm Jr., the magazine's executive editor and, in Thelma McMahon's words, "not as capable as Mr. Muir [Sr.] hoped he was,"[44] to move to Washington for an unspeci-fied executive position on the *Post*.

The *Post* people, of course, resented having to welcome the son who was not nearly as competent as the father who himself had been put out to pasture. There was a more generalized discontent as well. Ben Gilbert recalls Russ Wiggins's displeasure at the new acquisi-tion; if you were running a newspaper, Wiggins felt, you shouldn't be in any other business. "He was not thrilled at acquiring the television [stations], and that was his attitude about *Newsweek*. It [was] going to be a dilution of attention."[45] Wiggins also had seen a Phil Graham very different from the one who was then spellbinding New Yorkers. With only one print property to worry about, Phil's concentration was already scattered. That Phil had not bothered to give his own paper advance word of the *Newsweek* purchase, forcing it to rely on wire copy, was to Wiggins a bad omen. Then there was the contempt that newspapermen felt for newsmagazine editors and their rewrites of the news that the "real" reporters had already printed.

Post staffers were also bothered by Phil's spending so much money on *Newsweek* while the *Post* struggled under carbon-paper rules and strangulation budgets for domestic and foreign coverage. That same year, for example, when the science correspondent asked if he could rent a car to cover a space launch, he was told it would cost too much.[46] Meanwhile, in Manhattan, "Phil did wonders for us," Ker-mit Lansner recalls. "He opened the checkbook. We wanted a bu-reau here, so he said, 'Okay, have a bureau here.' He raised everybody's salary right away, not quite to *Time* levels. We all felt rich for the first time, we were making $30,000 a year."[47]

Phil wanted *Newsweek*'s foreign editor, Arnaud de Borchgrave, to return to New York to become managing editor for the international editions. De Borchgrave, who preferred living abroad, was reluctant. "Phil wrote me a letter and said not only was I getting a stock option and a big raise but he was giving me a free apartment in New York, a penthouse on the corner of Forty-eighth and Second. And he sweetened the pot to the degree that I just couldn't refuse anymore."[48]

There was a darker side to Phil's largesse. There were more generous salaries and editorial budgets, but there were also limousines, flunkies, and assorted hangers-on. First among them was James Truitt, the man who had reported the *Time* cover story on Phil in 1956. Truitt has been described variously as Phil's "speechwriter," "gofer," "procurer," "confidant," "man Friday."[49] But he was also smart, creative, and deft at spotting cultural trends. His friend Cord Meyer, a CIA man and later a newspaper columnist, says that at *Time,* Truitt was "the first person to describe the Beat generation. He made a hero of Jack Kerouac."[50]

While he was in Phil's employ, Truitt's role changed. Harvey Segal had the impression "that Truitt was a procurer of women for Phil. Phil's adventures were legendary. I'd meet a lady and be told she was one of Phil's many mistresses." According to Thelma McMahon, it was rumored Truitt was the person "who planned all those rendezvous" with a woman who became seriously involved with Phil. To Jean Friendly, Truitt was "another nut, for a while part of the whoring group."[51]

Although there had been gossip earlier in Washington about Phil's flings, it was when he started spending time in New York, living at the Carlyle, that the rumors began in earnest. Added to these were stories about his overindulgence in liquor and prescription drugs. He carried with him a bottle of Miltown.[52] (He was also a two-pack-a-day Parliament smoker.[53])

Then, just as New Yorkers were getting used to his whirlwind ways, he descended into another depression, and dropped from sight.

Back in Washington, Ben Gilbert busied himself carrying out Phil's program. When Phil did return, the causes he pushed seemed more quixotic, eccentric. He tried to put the *Post* behind the building of a national aquarium at Haines Point. Unable to persuade his editorial writers—"Those dummies on the editorial page, they don't understand why this aquarium is important"—he ordered Gilbert to buy a small aquarium and have it installed outside the editorial writers' offices. That didn't work either.[54]

Then there were other, less benign projects that Phil used his paper, both news and editorial columns, to champion—such as an urban renewal plan that gerrymandered out property in the District owned by Agnes Meyer, and a freeway system that included a loop around the central city that would have destroyed whole neighborhoods.[55]

In general, though, Phil was not paying much mind to the *Post* or to *Newsweek*. In 1961, he gave up the office of *Post* publisher to John Sweeterman, retaining for himself the titles of president and chief executive officer. That same year, he persuaded a reluctant Fritz Beebe to give up his law partnership to become chairman of the board of the Washington Post Company. Beebe, who loved being a lawyer,[56] had his office in New York in the *Newsweek* building, and spent much of his time overseeing the magazine.

At this time, say men who were then close to Phil professionally, it would have made sense for him to bring his increasingly withdrawn and unhappy wife into the company. Given the intensely chauvinistic tenor of the period, and his need to distance himself from anyone tied to the Meyer fortune, perhaps Phil simply couldn't. Roswell Gilpatric recalls that Phil studiously avoided introducing Kay "into the counsels of the company. She was very much on the outside"[57]—so much so that Harvey Segal cannot remember having ever seen Kay at the *Post* from 1961 to late 1963.

"Now I am completely free of duties!" Phil exulted.[58] Possibly even too free for his own good. With Sweeterman and Beebe running things for him, he was free to poke his nose into the Kennedys' business. According to Pierre Salinger, John Kennedy's press secretary, Phil was one of the elite group of journalists—others were Ben Bradlee, Joe Alsop, Walter Lippmann—who could simply pick up the telephone and call the president.[59]

One call that Phil made was to urge Kennedy to choose David Bruce as secretary of state. The job went instead to Dean Rusk, but Phil got the consolation prize when Kennedy fed him the exclusive about the appointment. So close were the two that the president seemed sometimes to forget that his friend owned *The Washington Post* and *Newsweek*. As Salinger recalls, "When the *Post* published a story saying that Dean Rusk was going to be secretary of state, we hadn't announced it yet. Kennedy called me in and said, 'There's just too much leaking going on. I've got to find out who leaked this story.' And so I did an investigation and came back to him four hours later and said, 'I know who leaked the story.' He said, 'Oh, great, who?' I said, 'You. You told Phil Graham.' "[60]

It was Phil, with help from Joe Alsop, who convinced Kennedy to appoint C. Douglas Dillon secretary of the treasury. Dillon, a Republican millionaire investment banker, who had served in Eisenhower's administration, first as ambassador to France and then as undersecretary of state, was a very tough sell to make to Kennedy, who had vowed to get rid of all of his predecessor's men. Beyond that, Dillon and his wife had contributed more than $26,000 to Nixon in 1960; it was known that had Nixon been elected, Dillon would have been his choice for secretary of state or treasury.[61] The latter was a key Cabinet post, because the issues of balance of payments and the flight of gold from the country loomed so large.[62] Arguing against Dillon, Democratic senators told Kennedy that his administration's success would ride on his choice for secretary of the treasury.

Members of JFK's Cambridge contingent, including Arthur Schlesinger, Jr., John Kenneth Galbraith, and Paul Samuelson, were horrified at the prospect of Dillon, whom, Schlesinger said later, "we mistrusted . . . on principle, as a presumed exponent of Republican economic policies. . . . I could recall no precedent for giving a vital cabinet post to a sub-cabinet official of a defeated administration, especially . . . an official who had contributed to Nixon's campaign and might well have been Nixon's nominee for the same job." Schlesinger and Galbraith rushed to Washington to review the slate with Kennedy's brother-in-law Sargent Shriver. When they dined one evening with Phil Graham, they were "distressed by his impassioned insistence that Douglas Dillon should—and would—be made Secretary of the Treasury."[63]

Kennedy made the appointment, and Dillon became one of the most effective and influential members of his Cabinet. Dillon remembers that Phil called to inform him that he was lobbying Kennedy to make the appointment—a notion the lifelong Republican found "crazy." "Think about it," Phil said, and the next thing Dillon knew, the young president was knocking at his door, confessing that he was "terribly upset" at the rate at which gold was flowing out of the country and that "frankly, he didn't think there were any Democrats available who would satisfy the international financial community."[64]

After that Phil thought he could do anything. He quickly cultivated Robert Kennedy, assuring him that he would do just fine as attorney general, a position for which he was ill prepared. Phil read his former law school classmate Phil Elman a letter he had written to John Kennedy promoting Elman as assistant attorney general for legal counsel (that is, White House lawyer). Elman recalls Phil looking "like hell, like a man who had been under great pressure. He had written [the letter] in longhand, on a yellow legal pad, many pages, and he read me the paragraph relating to me. He wanted to be sure that what he was representing would be something I would back him up on, [and] that I would have an absolute, undivided loyalty to Bob Kennedy. Phil described [him] in words that were a revelation to me—how sensitive Bob was, and insecure, how he needed help, and that he was a tender person, compassionate. It was almost as if he loved Bobby Kennedy."

Elman, who styles himself a political "independent, not a political person," did not get the job.[65] In her biography of Kay Graham, Deborah Davis claims that the turndown showed Phil's lack of clout with the president.[66] Elman says this conclusion is nonsense. "He had enormous influence. I didn't get that job because they gave it to [Nicholas] Katzenbach, a much better choice than I was. They made me a commissioner of the Federal Trade Commission, which was all right with me."

Phil Graham served Robert Kennedy faithfully, even turning his editors and reporters into researchers for the new administration. Seated next to Phil at a White House correspondents' dinner, Kennedy told him that he feared Washington was on the brink of a racial explosion. Phil assigned Ben Gilbert and Eve Edstrom, the *Post*'s "social problems" reporter, to write a memo outlining the issues and proposing solutions. They concluded that it was time for home rule and predicted major riots. "I suggested a White House assistant on District affairs," recalls Ben Gilbert, "who would harness the federal government on the District's behalf."[67] Phil shared the report with Kennedy, who appointed him head of a task force to tackle the problems enumerated in the memo.

Inevitably, Phil crossed the line between acceptable and unacceptable interference in his paper's editorials. "Phil made the paper a defender of JFK and the Bay of Pigs [invasion]," says Karl Meyer.[68] It has been charged, and persuasively, that Graham and other *Post* higher-ups had advance knowledge of several Kennedy administration covert operations, including the Bay of Pigs fiasco,* which they chose to keep from their readers.

Joe Rauh was in Phil's office the day after the bungled operation: "Phil was just completing a memo to Jack about 'Chin up,' bucking him up. 'It's not going to determine anything. You're going to be a great president.' Phil showed it to me. I remember thinking at the time, Boy, you've got to be close to the president to write him something like this."[69]

Phil did more than write a "chin up" letter. He made sure that neither *Newsweek* nor the *Post* chastised the administration too harshly over the Bay of Pigs.[70] "The Kennedy administration was exploiting the *Post*," says Bob Estabrook, "and probably had been exploiting Phil too." That Estabrook reached this conclusion is no surprise. Phil killed an editorial in which Estabrook was critical of U.S. performance. Estabrook recalls that as "the beginning of my own downfall. I had tried to consult with Phil but Phil was here, there, and noplace—you couldn't get in touch with him. So I wrote what I thought about the thing, and the next morning I found that the editorial had been pulled and something else had been put in its place. I had to believe that Phil knew more about [the operation] than I did, because he was in daily touch with these people and he was particularly close to the intelligence community."[71]

In the summer of 1961, *Post* editor Russ Wiggins asked Estabrook, "How would you like to be London correspondent?" Estabrook knew he was being kicked upstairs, and agreed because he had no choice. So began a *Post* tradition—exiling to London top editors no longer wanted in Washington. Estabrook immediately called the man he would replace as London correspondent, Robert E. Lee Baker, to ask for help in finding an apartment. Baker "didn't even know anything about it," Estabrook recalls. "It was a brutal way to do this, and of course I had no way of knowing that they hadn't told him."[72] Phil let Estabrook retain the title of editor of the editorial page, while he put Wiggins in charge of both the editorial page and the paper as a whole.

In 1962, during the Cuban missile crisis,† Phil again placed himself

---

*On April 17, 1961, some 1,500 Cuban exiles, CIA-trained and American-armed, intent on ousting the communist government of Fidel Castro, arrived in Cuba's Bay of Pigs. The Cuban army captured or killed most of them.
†In the wake of the Bay of Pigs, the USSR secretly built missile-launching sites in Cuba. When U.S. reconnaissance planes detected the construction, President Kennedy demanded removal

188   POWER, PRIVILEGE, AND THE *POST*

at the service of the Kennedy administration. Pierre Salinger says, "It became clear to me that both *The New York Times* and *The Washington Post* knew the direction we were moving in. I went to see [Kennedy] and said, 'If they publish this tomorrow, before everything has been planned, and before you go on the air and announce what you're going to do, it will help the Soviets, it will give them a twenty-four- or thirty-six-hour advantage you don't want to give them.' I know he called Phil Graham to get the *Post* not to publish it, and somebody at the *Times*. They both held back."[73]

There were other instances in which Kennedy used Phil and his publications as if they were house organs. After the Kennedy–Khrushchev summit in Vienna in June 1961, Phil turned Kennedy's grim warning of impending nuclear war—75 million Americans could die, he told Phil—into news and editorial coverage. And on another occasion, the *Post* suppressed a story about a woman who was suing Kennedy for breach of contract, claiming to be his first wife. (The *Post* was not nearly so helpful as *Newsweek*. Pierre Salinger says that Ben Bradlee was "in effect recruited" to dispel the "growing rumor that Jackie was [Kennedy's] second wife."[74]

The closer friendship, in fact, was not between the Grahams and the Kennedys but between the Bradlees and the Kennedys. Ben and Jack had known each other well since 1957, when Bradlee left *Newsweek*'s Paris bureau for its bureau in Washington and young Senator Kennedy bought the house next to his on P Street in Georgetown.[75] On election night, 1960, Ben and Tony Bradlee celebrated with Jack and Jackie at Hyannis Port.[76] The two couples would often have late dinners at the White House, just the four of them, after the riffraff politicians had been shown the door.[77] Once, one writer reported, "they gathered in Jackie's bedroom to watch an NBC special on the Kremlin, while Jack wandered around in his underdrawers."[78]

Much as Kennedy admired Tony, he was in love with Mary, her sister. Kennedy had known Mary Pinchot Meyer—considered the most beautiful girl in the Vassar class of '42—since his days at Choate and had met her often at Joe Alsop's, but their affair did not start until January 1962. It blossomed during meetings in her studio—the Ben Bradlees' carriage house—and in the White House,

of the missiles and imposed a naval blockade on the island. A potentially deadly showdown between the United States and the Soviet Union seemed inevitable until the Russians suddenly backed down, agreeing to dismantle the missile sites.

where she was said to visit often when Jackie was away. Kennedy could rest completely assured that not even the vaguest hint of this affair would ever find its way into the pages of *Newsweek;* Bradlee, Pierre Salinger says, was fastidious about not publishing anything he obtained through his social tie to the president. He would go with an item "only if he was sure it would not get him into hot water with Kennedy."[79] Yet Bradlee was too good and too curious a newsman not to keep notes of his time with the president. The ground rules, however, were clear. Nothing was to be used while Kennedy was in office. Thelma McMahon recalls that Bradlee frequently had dinner at the White House, and "with Kennedy's permission, he dictated to me his recollection of the previous evening. He said, 'Thelma, some-day, after Kennedy is out of office, I'm gonna put together a book.' "*[80]

Many at the *Post* were troubled—and made jealous too—by the cozy tie between the president and *Newsweek*'s Washington bureau chief. Karl Meyer says that Bradlee "would be the first one to admit that he really compromised his role as a journalist during the Kennedy years, to the extent of showing Kennedy advance things from *Newsweek,* [and] really being promoter and publicist for the Kennedys."[82]

Newsweek employees are defensive on this point. "Sure, we were had, but then everybody was had somewhere along the line," says Kermit Lansner. "There were certain things we did that were useful. Don't forget, the great fear in the newsmagazine business is that you have a wrong story sitting there. Sometimes Ben would get a hint [from Kennedy] as to where we might be wrong, and that would be useful."[83] Jim Cannon says simply, "Obviously Ben liked Kennedy better than Nixon, that wasn't a mystery to anybody. So did ninety percent of the other reporters around the country. What he got for that friendship is one hell of a lot of information other people didn't get."[84] Years later, Bradlee would tell a reporter for *The New York*

---

*Bradlee did write that book, a sycophantic, but between-the-lines fascinating, account called *Conversations with Kennedy*. It was crucified by some reviewers, including Garry Wills, who said that the relationship was part chitchat, often about women's breasts, but that it was clear "Kennedy got more than the latest jokes from his sessions with Bradlee. . . . The President called Bradlee on Saturday morning to find out what *Newsweek* would be running in its 'Periscope' feature next week and . . . to inform Bradlee what *Time* would be carrying on its cover. Bradlee cleared stories with Kennedy [for instance, a feature on the family] and warned him of breaking features."[81]

Times that he had no apologies for his relationship with John Kennedy. "I mean here is a United States Senator who moved in next door to me whose wife must have been impregnated the same day as mine, and so he becomes the President and [I] say, 'Oh, sorry, I can't talk to you'?"[85]

Phil Graham got as much as he gave in his relationship with JFK. Kennedy appointed him chairman of the board of incorporators for the Communications Satellite Corporation (COMSAT), whose purpose was to establish an American space communications system. Partly government-owned and partly to be sold to private investors, COMSAT was a tricky proposition, and Nicholas Katzenbach, who lobbied the bill establishing the corporation through Congress, specifically recalls Kennedy telling him he wanted Phil Graham as chairman—"somebody with a lot of ability to make it work, and with all the right connections to make it work."[86]

With the high intensity that marked him at his most effective, Phil threw himself into the task. "Phil Graham came to New York with a list of people to call and talk to," Jim Cannon says, "and in an afternoon, he put that whole thing together, whom he wanted on the board, what they would do, who would be chairman . . . a masterful piece of work in an afternoon on the telephone."[87]

But the assignment was important to Phil for a more troubling reason. He had a constant craving for excitement, which, for a time, COMSAT satisfied. "After the acquisition of *Newsweek* and the *Times-Herald* and the various stations," Roswell Gilpatric explains, "he needed some adrenaline in his system. At that time the *Post*'s financial resources weren't such that he could go out and keep on making these major moves."[88]

After Eugene's death, when Agnes no longer had to face his disapproval and the locked liquor cabinet, "she became," Sidney Hyman claims, "gross-looking from drink. I used to see her on some mornings when she had fallen down the steps, black eye, scarred face." The family called her "Thimble Belly," but it is not clear whether because she had a very low tolerance for liquor or because she drank a lot. Whenever she encountered Hyman, still wading through Eugene's papers trying to finish the biography, she attempted to cover her face, "wishing that I didn't see her."[89] Says Harold Taylor of this period, "She was plastered most of the time."[90]

It was obvious to Agnes that Hyman neither liked nor respected her, even intellectually. So when he told her that Eugene's extreme reticence had slowed his writing and the manuscript would be further delayed, Agnes reportedly ordered her lawyer to pay him off with $50 and have him sign a release on what he had written.[91] Hyman, who by then had a wife and children, jumped at the chance to extricate himself. Agnes gave his work to Merlo Pusey and commissioned him to finish the project, an authorized one over which the Meyer family had control.*

Friends noticed that Agnes, now speaking almost reverently of Eugene, seemed to like him better in death than in life. Hyman certainly saw this: "She discovered how central he was to her life. People in general came to their home because of him, not because of her."[92]

But Agnes continued to entertain lavishly, even more lavishly than she had during Eugene's life, and the powerful, rich, and famous continued to come. Not only did she have what Arthur Schlesinger, Jr., has called "the best cook in Washington,"[93] but during summers she chartered a boat and invited friends to join her—perhaps her way of commandeering a captive audience. On one of these cruises, she hired the flagship of the Norwegian coast guard and invited, among others, Harold Taylor and Clayton Fritchey, a syndicated columnist who was then special assistant to U.S. ambassador to the UN Adlai Stevenson.[94]

Taylor, a frequent guest at Mount Kisco, recalls with pleasure the lunches with luminaries—Stevenson, Chief Justice Warren, Edward Steichen, Robert Oppenheimer. But eventually the easygoing Taylor found that he could not both satisfy Agnes's need for attention and lead his own life. She couched this need mostly by pressuring him to stay involved in the National Committee in Support of the Public Schools. "She wanted me to come to Washington much more than I could go, because the committee work was one of a number of things I was doing." When he told her that he had to cut back, she started to sob. "Agnes could see at that point that we weren't going to be as close as we had been. It's as if I had passed my boyhood and gone out the other side and become an adult."[95]

Busy with his projects and plans for the Kennedys, and his acquisi-

---

*The book, *Eugene Meyer*, was published in 1974 by Knopf. Pusey had won both a Pulitzer and a Bancroft for his two-volume biography of Chief Justice Charles Evans Hughes, published in 1952. This bland work, however, was no prizewinner.

tions, Phil also paid less attention to Agnes. He sometimes took her to *Newsweek* luncheons, but to the young, fast-talking editors there she was a curiosity. If they treated her with condescension, she returned the favor. "She used to break wind very loudly," recalls Arnaud de Borchgrave. "We didn't laugh. We looked at each other and were on the verge of splitting our sides."[96]

Around this time, now in her mid-seventies, Agnes finally began to reach out to women, not her daughters—those relationships would never be good—but to other women. "She was wonderful to me," says Joanna Steichen, "always kind and thoughtful." She sums up Agnes's late-in-life attitude toward women: "Agnes was a lousy mother but she was a very good friend. I credit her with my social education. I came from a timid little nuclear family, [and] I learned a lot from Agnes, from being in her house and talking to her and observing her and how things worked."

Steichen remembers going to Washington for one of Agnes's birthday parties—as usual, black tie—which was being hosted by Phil and Kay. Besides Steichen, staying with Agnes were a professor of English from Cornell and his wife. "That was in the early 1960s, when long dresses were not popular for middle-class social functions. I packed this wonderful [short] brown dress and apparently the [professor's wife] also packed a dressy short dress. In Agnes's house the maid unpacked for the ladies, so if she needed to, [Agnes] knew what everybody brought. We dressed for dinner, assembled in the downstairs hall. Agnes had a little tiara on [and] a chartreuse short evening dress. We got to Kay's house, and Kay and Bis were greeting people, and the first words out of their mouths were, 'Oh, Ma, you're wearing a short dress,' and I suddenly realized what she had done. She was so thoughtful to her guests, not wanting to embarrass these two middle-class ladies who didn't know how the aristocracy did things."

The younger Agnes probably could not have befriended someone who was young, vibrant, and beautiful. "But when I knew her she was in her seventies," Steichen says, "and probably [she took] a certain narcissistic pleasure in the fact that young and beautiful women wanted to be her friends. She needed admirers, she needed people to care about her, and she could be very charming and seductive and get [people] to care about her."[97]

Luvie Pearson, whose tie to the Meyer family had been mainly to Eugene and their bridge game, recalled that Kay pleaded with her to help with her mother. "I'd take her out to the farm, we'd go swimming, and she'd help me with a grandchild of mine I was then teaching to speak [who] was deaf. I came home one day, and she was on the floor [with him]. She'd gotten him these blocks and things to teach him how to speak and put two and two together. She was marvelous. We had a good time. We laughed." Agnes, Luvie explained, "was doing it out of the kindness of her heart, because I was a friend. I was trying to help her a little, after she needed to adjust to being a widow, and she was helping me."[98]

Agnes's favorite grandchild, Kay and Phil's oldest, Lally, went to Radcliffe in September 1961. Events at home would make her grow up faster, on the one hand, and keep her from ever really growing up, on the other. Lally would find herself entangled in what would become the great love affair of her father's life and the great humiliation of her mother's.

Chapter 11

BREAKUP AND
BREAKDOWN

Phil started 1962 on a high note—hiring Walter Lippmann to write a column for *Newsweek* and winning the right to distribute his newspaper column nationwide. Lippmann, the man whom Teddy Roosevelt had called the most brilliant of his generation and whom Woodrow Wilson had employed to draft the Fourteen Points, would add immediate prestige to the magazine. Phil was willing to pay whatever it took to get him, and it took a lot—$75,000 a year plus ninety percent of syndication fees, a generous annual stipend to his wife after his death, a New York apartment, two secretaries, a research assistant, an AP news ticker, office and travel expenses, and a limousine.[1]

Jim Cannon recalls that Phil amused himself by turning the contract-signing into a kind of cloak-and-dagger operation. Phil dispatched Cannon to La Guardia Airport to pick up the contract from a *Washington Post* secretary and carry it directly to a Wall Street law office where Lippmann would be waiting; once Cannon saw Lippmann's signature on the dotted line, he was to call Phil with a one-word code, whereupon Phil would break the good news to Osborn Elliott and other top editors.

For his next conquest, Phil dispatched Elliott on an eight-city tour and, in his absence, hired Emmet John Hughes to alternate with Lippmann. The *Newsweek* editors, Cannon says, "were not very enthusiastic."[2] Elliott would later write, "I was hurt and angry and embarrassed that Graham had not consulted me before taking Hughes on."[3]

Emmet Hughes was a man who appealed to Phil on a personal, emotional, and intellectual level much more than did the haughty Lippmann. Hughes had been Henry Luce's closest aide, and then Nelson Rockefeller's, and would become Phil's. Richard Clurman, who knew him well both personally and professionally, describes him as "an extraordinary fellow, very lazy, the kind [who] never cracked a book but always got an A on the final exams. So he could have inherited [*Time*], could have inherited *The Washington Post*. He was very unusual when he applied himself."[4] Around the office he was called "Eminent John Hughes," as he agonized constantly over his Catholicism or lapses therein, marrying and remarrying. He wrote brilliantly when he felt like it, which was rare, and drank way too much when he felt like it, which was often.

It was inevitable, perhaps, that Phil's next major acquisition would be female.

In Paris on COMSAT business, Phil ordered Larry Collins, then head of *Newsweek*'s Paris bureau, to find him a secretary who could take dictation in English. Collins asked Robin Webb, an Australian who was his girlfriend's "best pal" and who had been working in the bureau as a secretary and stringer. "She did take very good shorthand," Collins remembers.[5]

Phil summoned Robin to his hotel for some dictation, then asked her to hand-deliver a highly confidential COMSAT-related letter to Bill Paley at CBS in New York. Collins had no choice but to let her go. Robin did not have an American visa, and it was after embassy hours. Phil told Collins, "I'll get Chip [Charles Bohlen, the U.S. ambassador] to open his fucking embassy. I'll tell him to get his ass into gear and over to his frigging consulate. Open it up and give the girl a visa."[6] At dawn the next day Robin had her visa, and Phil instructed her: "You are only to give this letter to Bill Paley personally, not to his secretary." He drove her to the airport and accompanied her as far as he could before security guards stopped him. When she turned to say good-bye—according to Arnaud de Borchgrave, who heard the details later from her—"he grabbed her in his arms and kissed her passionately."[7]

At the airport in New York, a limousine awaited her with flowers and a note directing her to proceed to the Carlyle and, except to deliver the letter to Paley, not to leave the hotel room until Phil arrived, as he did three days later. "She called me right away," de

Borchgrave recounts, "and said, 'Incidentally, what am I supposed to do? Larry wants me back immediately. It's all very embarrassing.' And I said, 'Phil being our boss, you'd better carry out his orders. Stay until he gets back. Call Larry and tell him what you're doing.' "[8]

Robin Webb, the daughter of an Australian public official, had been a journalist in Australia. When she turned up in Paris, Collins, in the style of the times, hired her to replace his vacationing secretary. "Because my number-two spot in the bureau was vacant, I kept her on afterward as a stringer. She did some very good pieces for me."[9] She was an attractive blonde but, according to de Borchgrave, "not a big bombshell or anything like that."[10] Collins describes her as "very much an Australian girl, kind of matey."[11] Jim Cannon puzzles over why Phil was so attracted to her: "If she had been a willowy beauty or [an Italian] princess, you would have understood better, but she was unimpressive physically, socially, in terms of beauty, in terms of intellect." He adds that "she had the vilest mouth of any woman I had ever met up to that point, and maybe still." Phil, he concedes, was profane, but he "could also be literary. He knew when [and when not] to talk dirty. She didn't."[12]

In some accounts, Robin is portrayed as the manipulative slut—a woman who saw Phil Graham as a ticket to wealth, position, and power. To Larry Collins that is "absolutely incorrect. The last thing in the world that Robin was was manipulative. She was very—as the Australians tend to be—almost bluntly straightforward."[13] De Borchgrave calls her "rather proper, no easy lay."[14]

She simply fell passionately in love with Phil, as was no surprise to anyone who knew him. When in a manic phase, Phil was irresistible. At first, Robin was alarmed by Phil's intensity, the relentlessness of his pursuit, his extreme generosity,[15] but she quickly accustomed herself to the attention and the perks. Phil put his employees at her disposal, and this, inevitably, bruised some feelings. "I was working one Saturday," Mel Elfin remembers, "and the chief of photography came in. He said, 'Mr. Graham just called me. He said Robin wants to learn how to take pictures. I want you to send the best photographer to the best store in New York, buy the best equipment, spend the weekend instructing Robin how to shoot pictures.' " When Robin asked Elfin, then education editor, to do a story on the American Junior College in Paris, he "checked into it because she was walking around the office in New York like queen of the plantation." (Elfin adds that when he got to know Robin, he found her not imperious but "nice.")[16]

After less than a week in Phil's company, Robin understood he had no interest whatsoever in concealing the affair from friends, colleagues, family, casual acquaintances, even the president of the United States. "I was with President Kennedy," relates a man who was close to both Kennedy and Graham, "[when] Phil called the president. I watched the president's face: first he turned red, then he turned angry, then he hung up. Phil was in bed with Robin Webb, screwing her, and he was introducing her to the president over the phone. Kennedy told me. That was the first inkling I had that Phil was really off his rocker."[17]

Both Robin and the president quickly accustomed themselves to the affair. "She used to tell me about how exciting it was to live with Phil," de Borchgrave says. "Once she was at the Carlyle and Kennedy was on a higher floor. He called down. Phil and Robin were in bed at four in the afternoon. 'I'm on my way down to discuss de Gaulle,' the president informed Phil. He came with all sorts of secret CIA files. She leaped out of bed and put on her peignoir and her robe, and said, 'Should I stay in the bathroom?' 'No, don't worry,' Phil said. He was in his shorts and sat on the edge of the bed with Kennedy, and Kennedy was going through all these confidential things in front of Robin."[18]

Arthur Schlesinger, Jr., reads Kennedy's attitude toward Phil's behavior quite differently: "Kennedy was very much embarrassed when Phil took off with Robin Webb, [embarrassed] by his efforts to get Kennedy to confer a sort of spurious legality on it. Kennedy certainly didn't want to appear to be siding with Phil on this matter against Kay. He recognized that Phil wasn't himself."[19]

People who knew both the president and Phil say that de Borchgrave is probably right—that while Kennedy may have been insulted by Phil's treating him as just one of the guys, Kennedy's own philandering was so flagrant that he would not have judged Phil. "At one point I got Arthur Schlesinger on the phone," recalls Jean Friendly, "and I said, 'You have got to get these men under control. It's a scandal.' " She claims that "in some ways Phil was dominating Kennedy. And the pair of them were sleeping around with the same people."[20]

There was also the matter of the president's affair with Mary Meyer, Ben Bradlee's sister-in-law. Kennedy knew that Phil was aware of the intimate details of the affair, including that the president and Mary had used drugs in a White House bedroom shortly before he convened a White House conference on narcotics.* Kennedy, horrified at how recklessly Phil conducted his own affair, saw that he could no longer trust him to keep any information confidential.

Phil launched into another streak of acquisitions, which Jim Cannon, who was summoned to hear his plans in early 1962, describes as using "*Newsweek* as the basis for creating the largest communications empire in the world." Phil made Cannon a vice-president of the magazine, put his office between his own and Fritz Beebe's, and charged him with carrying out the vision.[25]

First Phil tried to buy the *New York Post,* using President Kennedy's brother-in-law Stephen Smith as his intermediary.[26] Veteran *Post* editor James Wechsler was an old friend of Phil's, and when the paper's owner, Dorothy Schiff, moved Wechsler from editor to editorial-page editor—an apparent switch from crusading liberalism to gossip, celebrities, and human interest—Phil decided to buy the paper and put Wechsler back where he belonged. He failed, as Dorothy Schiff had many millions of dollars' worth of shutdown liabilities that made the paper very difficult to sell,[27] but not for lack of trying. Wechsler's widow, Nancy, remembers, "Phil would call him and say, Meet me at the corner of such and such streets. He'd be in a limousine and [they] would have an intense talk. He was really flying very high."[28]

Phil wanted to buy other papers as well, including the one in Sioux

---

*In July 1962, they allegedly smoked marijuana that Meyer supplied, Kennedy supposedly advising her that cocaine was better and promising to obtain some for her.[21] On this occasion Kennedy reportedly said, "My God, what if the Russians come now?"[22]

Mary Meyer was murdered in October 1964, eleven months after JFK's assassination, while walking on the towpath along the old Chesapeake & Ohio barge canal in Georgetown. A black man was tried for the crime but acquitted and released, and the murder remains unsolved. Meyer was known to have kept a diary of her affair with the president and is said to have extracted a promise from two close friends, Jim Truitt and his wife, Ann, that in the event of her death they would preserve the diary and show it to her son when he became twenty-one. It has been widely reported that Meyer's sister, Tony Bradlee, tore apart her house after the murder in a fruitless search for the diary. She later found it in her sister's studio and turned it over to James Angleton, CIA counterintelligence chief, who allegedly told Ben Bradlee that he was going to burn it.[23] Suggestions have been made periodically that Mary Meyer's death was spearheaded by the CIA, which wanted to keep the diary from falling into the wrong hands. Meyer's husband, Cord, a former CIA agent, calls the conspiracy notion "absolutely crazy. Jim [Angleton was a] very close friend of ours, and he successfully dealt with a diary that might have been very embarrassing, assured that it didn't come out. That was not done to protect state secrets or anything like that. It was done to protect a friend."[24]

Falls, to honor his South Dakota birth. And he wanted three more television stations to bring him up to the legal limit.[29] Phil's assistant Jim Truitt persuaded him to buy *ARTnews*. Kermit Lansner, who had been an associate editor of that magazine before he joined *Newsweek,* recounts, "I was in Paris when I got this call one night—typical Phil, middle of the night. It was Phil asking my advice."[30] On the other end of the scale, Phil acquired a twenty-percent stake in the new Washington Senators, an expansion baseball team that lasted about a decade in the capital.

Then Phil turned his attention to *The Washington Post.* He wanted much wider national and international reach, but he lacked the money to make it possible, especially while juggling so many other acquisitions. Meanwhile, he had his eye on Otis Chandler in Los Angeles and the improvements the young publisher was making on the *Los Angeles Times,* a right-wing paper even more provincial than the *Post* but vastly more prosperous. Phil's brainstorm was for the two papers to split the cost of foreign, national, and regional coverage by pooling their resources in a joint news service. David Halberstam quotes Phil as telling John Sweeterman, "They've always been financially successful and editorially weak, and we've always been editorially successful and financially weak. So we're at about the same place."[31] More important, Phil and Chandler were at about the same place in their careers. Erwin Knoll, who would become the service's first editor, on the Washington end, observes: "They were both relatively young publishers who had just inherited their newspapers and were eager to make their mark." They were "jealous of the prestige and the unique position of *The New York Times,* and were looking for a way to push their papers into that league."[32]

The negotiations were difficult. Phil left the lawyers out, and took Al Friendly and Erwin Knoll with him to Los Angeles. He brought the deal off brilliantly, understanding that he had to satisfy the newsmen in Los Angeles that the Washington hotshots would not step all over their turf, or turn them into the money men behind an essentially East Coast operation.

On the plane to California, Phil asked Knoll for a sheet of paper. "A couple of minutes later he handed me this list: 'Rome, London, New Delhi, Hong Kong . . .' A list of eight or ten world capitals. And he said, 'These are the places I'm thinking of staffing, when we set up the news service.'" Phil asked Knoll if they could be filled within two or, at the outside, three months. "I was just staggered. I had looked at that list and thought, Okay, this is a five-year program, a ten-year program." Knoll could conclude only that Phil "was manifesting a kind of grandiosity that was not too closely in touch with reality."[33]

Next, Phil decided that George Gallup had dominated the polling business for too long. Louis Harris, who had done some of Kennedy's polling in 1960, was a relative unknown. "Phil came into the office in New York one morning," recalls Jim Cannon, "and said, 'You and Bradlee get your friend Harris in here. I want to set him up in business.' "[34]

Yet Phil's vision of a communications empire was stymied. As Cannon notes sadly, "Phil's mental health did not permit [it], and we never did it."[35]

Clark Clifford, President Kennedy's personal lawyer and an advisor to Democratic presidents since Harry Truman, had warned Kennedy of Phil's "instability." Kennedy had earlier asked Clifford to be "his eyes and ears on COMSAT." So the president heard about it when, during a COMSAT board meeting, Phil got into a fistfight with a lawyer.[36] Increasingly, he conducted his business, personal and otherwise, from his office couch, drinking, crying, throwing books and water glasses, and working the telephone. He would sometimes call Lyndon Johnson, just to taunt him: "You'll never be president, Lyndon. This is the end of the line. Just vice-president."[37]

He also took to calling the president, until Kennedy asked Kay to do what she could to stop him. According to Hedley Donovan, "He several times called up the White House in the middle of the night to tell this or that to Kennedy. Kennedy finally had to [instruct] the White House switchboard not to put Mr. Graham through after nine p.m."[38] Once when Phil got angry at *Post* editor Russ Wiggins, he called Kennedy and asked him to fire Wiggins.[39]

On another occasion, when Phil began to "berate" Kennedy over the phone, and Kennedy tried to quiet him, Phil shouted, "Do you know who you're talking to?" According to David Halberstam, Kennedy replied, "I know it isn't the Phil Graham that I love and respect."[40]

Bob Estabrook recounts the time Phil "was in seeing Kennedy, and he grabbed the red phone, literally lifted the receiver, and said, 'Scramble the planes,' and Kennedy had to come on, 'This is the president. Cancel the order.' "[41] Another time, according to Karl Meyer, Phil "got by the guards at the White House and walked right into the Oval Office to see Kennedy and started haranguing [him].

Kennedy called Russ Wiggins and said, 'Mr. Wiggins, Phil Graham is in my office, could you send somebody to help get him out?' "[42] It was on that occasion that Phil told Kennedy he was going to divorce Kay and marry Robin Webb.[43] Around the same period, Phil called Secretary of Defense Robert McNamara, who was then feuding with some top military men, and announced that he was phoning for two reasons—first, he was going to marry Robin, and second, McNamara's feuds were hurting the nation and he, Phil, intended to mediate. "Phil, I've got a wonderful wedding present for you," McNamara replied. "I won't edit *The Washington Post* for you anymore if you'll give me back the Department of Defense."[44]

Disenchanted with the president, Phil did what he could to irritate him. One means was Harvey Segal, who left his professorship at New York University's business school to work as a temporary editorial writer on economics for *The Washington Post*. "In May of 1962," Segal recounts, "Kennedy tried to roll back steel prices, and there was a terrible break in the stock market. Everybody was very nervous about the economy. I was very much for cutting taxes and getting the newspaper to endorse a tax cut. Now that blended in beautifully with Phil. He was very unhappy over the Kennedy administration. He began writing memos to Kennedy, copies of which he sent to me. I hardly recognized my sort of sober-economist ideas. He put in one that the future of Western civilization hung on cutting taxes." Segal's phone once rang at three a.m.: "Phil went to see Kennedy on the [presidential yacht] *Honey Fitz* with a lot of stuff I had initially prepared and then he had hyped up. He had come off the *Honey Fitz* in the middle of the night and [then] called me."[45]

The business of the *Post* had to continue, of course, and Phil dipped in and out of it. Walter Lippmann was promoting *Wall Street Journal* writer Philip Geyelin for the *Post*'s editorial page, and Phil, casually mixing newspaper and magazine people, dispatched Bradlee to offer Geyelin the job of writing editorials on foreign affairs. "If you take this job, you'll be the next editor of *The Washington Post*," Bradlee promised Geyelin; this pointed again to trouble in store for Russ Wiggins, not to mention Bob Estabrook, who, although he was in London for the *Post,* continued to be listed on the masthead as editor of the editorial page. Geyelin declined, figuring that the job "was a real nutcracker. I'd be working for Wiggins, whom I was supposed to subvert," and understanding that he would be expected to serve as Phil's mouthpiece.[46]

In the meantime, Estabrook was trying to get Phil to clarify his status; in desperation, he phoned Phil at home. "I remember getting Kay out of bed. She called Phil, and he couldn't have been more distant about it. I then got a letter saying, 'You have been selected for a very great honor. You are now chief foreign correspondent. You have the same status as Cy Sulzberger,* but you couldn't write like him, "Go, go, go." ' It hit me right in the solar plexus, because then it became perfectly clear that although Phil never did answer my question about [the job as] editor of the editorial page, I was being in effect fired and this was a created position. It was Phil's way of not meeting a problem."[47]

Phil's top people, Russ Wiggins, Al Friendly, and John Sweeterman, began to fear that he was irretrievably lost. No one, except perhaps Jim Truitt, could continue to describe his behavior as brilliantly eccentric. He had taken to bringing Robin Webb to the newsroom and introducing her as "the next Mrs. Graham" or simply "Mrs. Graham" and then loudly joking about how they planned to spend the afternoon.[48] Anyone who knew the ignominious history of *The Washington Post* could not help but think that Phil was following in the fatal footsteps of Ned McLean, who used to bring his mistress to editorial conferences.[49]

People "had to distance themselves from Phil," recalls Sir Isaiah Berlin. "When he went off the edge he became more and more abnormal, more and more violent."[50] Al Friendly, who genuinely loved Phil, watched in despair and began to catalogue Phil's increasingly bizarre orders and the action, if any, taken in response.[51] Phil even tried to enforce a one-jump rule for the front page—all stories but one were to be completed on that page.[52]

John Sweeterman would call Kay to tell her what outlandish order Phil had just issued and ask her what to do. It was not that he valued Kay's advice, but, explains Alan Finberg, later general counsel of the *Post* and *Newsweek,* "Sweeterman knew that if something happened to Phil"—and it was only a matter of time—"Kay would hold the A stock."[53]

---

*Cyrus Sulzberger, nephew of *New York Times* publisher Arthur Hays Sulzberger, was the paper's chief European correspondent. He enjoyed carte blanche to travel anywhere in Europe, cover any story he wanted, and supervise all of the paper's European correspondents.

Karl Meyer says that Russ Wiggins "knew how to handle Phil, and he was the one who took the heat when Phil was off the rocker."[54] Erwin Knoll remembers "one night when Phil Graham called the paper and demanded that Wiggins's name be removed from the masthead between editions. He wanted him fired immediately, God damn it."[55]

Bob Estabrook, on the other hand, says that it was Al Friendly who "could work with Phil in a way others couldn't. Al was independently wealthy, so he could stand up and tell Phil off when he needed to."[56]

But even his position could not last. Jean Friendly remembers that Phil called after she and Al had gone to bed: "Come up and see me," he demanded of them. "He was in his pajamas. Kay was dressed. We had the most strained kind of conversation. And then we came home, and the next thing I knew the phone rang again and it was Phil. 'I didn't want a circus. I want you to come up here.' " Jean did, alone this time, and he asked her to drive around and then accompany him to his office. "He talked and talked and told me all about falling in love with Robin, and I just listened." The next day, Phil called Al and, referring to the paper's glass-fronted offices, said, "You live in that fishbowl down there. Turn your back to where the glass is, so people can't see your face." He informed Al he was going to marry Robin, and told him to tell Jean.[57]

Phil bought Robin a house on exclusive Foxhall Road. When he moved out of the R Street house—Arnaud de Borchgrave says that the story has been told a hundred times—"Kay ran out on the sidewalk in her nightie in the very early morning, begging him not to leave."[58]

With Robin, he hosted dinner parties to which he invited his and Kay's friends. A few were outraged and declined his invitation, but many, for professional reasons, could not. Says Kermit Lansner, "Phil would call us from an airplane, speaking from on high," as if commanding his troops' presence at some social event or the other.[59]

Many couples were split on how they dealt with invitations from Phil. Al Friendly "went out to the house a lot when they lived on Foxhall," recalls Jean, "but that was because he was Phil's managing editor." She adds that of course her husband's allegiance "had to be to Phil." But hers did not. "I didn't receive Robin here, and I never went to Phil's place when he was living with Robin. I just couldn't do it. Phil did call me, and I would say, 'Phil, I'm at home to you.

You may come anytime you want, but I can't receive Robin.' He didn't come."[60]

One Friday, Arnaud de Borchgrave received a call from Phil: " 'You're going to have dinner with me tonight at the Carlyle, in my suite, with Robin and Lally, and they are meeting for the first time, [it's a] very important occasion. Teddy White and twelve other people will be there.' I said, 'I'm very sorry, Phil, I can't. Not on Friday night.' " Friday night—the night before the magazine closed—was the busiest time at *Newsweek,* and editors routinely worked until two or three in the morning. But Phil insisted, and called Oz Elliott to be sure that de Borchgrave met no resistance on that end. De Borchgrave remembers eighteen-year-old Lally as hurt and angered, and after the dinner, Robin remarked to him, "My gosh, she really hates me, doesn't she?" Later, Phil showed de Borchgrave a letter Lally had written him expressing hatred for de Borchgrave. Phil could not understand her feelings; it was obvious to de Borchgrave that "she could see how well Robin and I knew each other from *Newsweek* days. Lally must have said, 'Aha! He's part of all this.' "[61]

Jean Friendly says that Phil destroyed Lally.[62] Yet she needed to blame someone other than her father, given the strong bond that she and her brothers, but she especially, had with him. Their mother, who was trying to shield them from his illness, seemed depressed; their father was unpredictable, yes, but also inspiring.

If Phil could not be the great father to Lally—and if she could not love him and approve of him unreservedly—he would force himself on his employees and others who, in one way or another, depended on him. To some of his targets it seemed as if he wanted to do what he felt the Meyers had done to him—sapped him of independence, smothered him with favors, made him heel.

Kermit Lansner was then buying an apartment in New York City. "I needed *Newsweek* to say that I was good for a loan of $10,000 to buy it. I had a mortgage, but I needed the $10,000. It came to Phil's attention. He said, 'Where's the house?' I said, 'It's on West Eightieth Street.' He said, 'You don't want to live there.' Then he began getting on my case in a very abrasive, difficult way. He said, 'We'll lend you the money to buy a house on the East Side, which is really where you want to live.' I remember saying, 'Leave me alone, do me a favor and just sign this thing saying my salary's enough to cover this [loan].' We had this very intense debate and it was rather poignant. Finally he said whatever blasphemy he was using then and, 'You think you can be independent.' "[63]

Phil was more successful with Lyndon Johnson, who, although terribly uncomfortable with Phil's illness, was still tangled in his web. Phil chose and helped pay for a house that he felt better reflected the vice-president's status. The Elms, on Foxhall Road, had been occupied by assorted celebrities. Johnson had no desire to move from his suite in the Wardman Park Hotel, but seemed unable to resist Phil.[64]

Erwin Knoll recalls that Phil insisted he see Phil's doctor for a complete physical. Knoll protested that he felt fine, but was persuaded by Al Friendly, who said, "Let's do this just to please Phil."[65]

When Arnaud de Borchgrave, in a job dispute with Oz Elliott, threatened to quit, Phil stepped in. He "called me at eleven at night and said, 'I'm picking you up tomorrow, and bring Eileen [de Borchgrave's wife]. You're going to spend the weekend in the country with us.' I said, 'Phil, there's no way you can talk me out of this.' " Phil sent his plane for them, and then "spent the whole bloody night sitting on our bed—we were desperate for sleep—telling us one story after another, all night, nonstop. [At four or five in the morning] Eileen was sound asleep next to me and I was still struggling to stay awake. Phil yanked me and said, 'And you're not quitting.' I said, 'Yes, Phil, I am quitting, don't worry about it.' 'You're not quitting. That's an order. I'm telling Oz. I'm getting you a $10,000 raise and another stock option.' I think we slept one hour." Phil got his way.[66]

Much more menacing was the looming, ugly divorce that Phil wanted desperately and Kay, despite the pain and humiliation, did not.[67] The top editors at *Newsweek,* according to one of them, discussed endlessly what they would do if asked to testify in court, getting down to such specifics as whether to say, "We perceived him as disturbed," or "He was just an eccentric publisher, which is common enough in publishing history."[68]

Kermit Lansner found a college psychology textbook and looked up manic-depression. "I remember calling Oz and saying, 'Let me read you this page: "heightened eroticism, foul language, acquisition mania, feelings of omnipotence, a tendency to disrobe in public." ' "[69]

Fritz Beebe seemed struck nearly mute by the conflict between Phil and Kay, because of his "deep loyalty to the Meyer family. On the other hand, he had deep loyalty to Phil personally. Here was this tremendous turmoil going on around him, and Fritz is sitting in the middle and not talking. Ludicrous. Fritz was the only one who knew everything. He was really trapped."[70]

Others, among them Arnaud de Borchgrave, moved without hesitation into Phil's camp. "They bet on him," Lansner explains. "They bet that he would walk away with the marbles." De Borchgrave maintains that his decision had nothing to do with office politics, but that he found Phil "mesmerizing. Very few people have had that power over me in my life. Kind of guy who could get you to volunteer for a suicide mission."[71]

Another *Newsweek* editor, Ben Bradlee, was solidly in Phil's camp. Bradlee, it was reported to Kay, was dining out on the line, "There's nothing wrong with Phil that a good divorce wouldn't cure."[72]

Kay put up a remarkably brave front, giving parties on her own and inviting those who had remained allied with her—and she never forgot or forgave those who turned down her invitations. A *Washington Star* profile later described her at this time as sitting through her dinners with eyes "filled with tears." A guest at one party later reported that "she had to hold her head back to keep the tears from falling. She was grief-stricken. Why she gave those parties, I don't know. She never seemed to enjoy them."[73] But Marietta Tree, for one, remembered a dignified Kay Graham, who "tried to behave as if everything was perfectly all right," and "wouldn't mention a thing."[74] June Bingham agrees: "She never complained about him. She was loyal, long-suffering."[75]

And she remained so, even when Phil told anyone and everyone the unthinkable—that he planned to cut Kay out of the *Post* and hand it over to Robin. He changed his will to leave a third of his estate to Robin and the remainder to his children. Then he changed it again, cutting the children's share to one-third and increasing Robin's to two-thirds. He hired Edward Bennett Williams to handle the divorce. Realizing that Phil was not of "sound mind," Williams apparently tried to placate him without taking any specific action.[76]

When Phil threatened to hand the *Post* to Robin, Kay started to worry. Her father had given the paper to Phil, but with the expectation that Phil would turn it over to Donny. That fall, Donny would enter Harvard, and it would not be long before he was ready for the *Post*.

Before Phil had added this latest piece of nastiness to the breakup, Agnes was merely irritated with him for, in Joanna Steichen's words, "making a public spectacle" of himself. "I don't think she would have cared if he had quietly had affairs. That's what people do." But a married man did not, in Agnes's world, marry his girlfriend. Agnes took to referring to Robin as "that awful girl,"[77] and the idea that Phil planned to snatch the family jewel from her grandchildren enraged her.[78] To Marietta Tree, Agnes was a "tower of strength," much more eager to fight Phil than Kay was.[79]

Agnes gave a cocktail party, a formal affair, on the grounds of Crescent Place; she stood with Kay in a receiving line. Joe Rauh and others recognized it as a virtual coming-out party for Kay—a signal that she would not be beaten by Phil, that she would gather herself for a fresh start. "It was quite wonderful," said Rauh, "really very touching. Everybody came and buoyed [Kay] up at a very critical time."[80]

The party also signaled a change in Agnes's treatment of her daughter. Kay would later relate that around the same period, "I was giving a party for my eighteen-year-old daughter [Lally]. As we were doing the preparations, my mother said, 'Darling, you're so good at lists!' I swear [that was] the first compliment she ever paid me."[81]

Phil soon sank back into depression, confiding to Edward Bennett Williams, "You know, my biggest trouble is how to get out of bed in the morning . . . how to get up and face life."[82] Phil joined Kermit Lansner and two or three other editors for lunch at the Plaza Hotel in New York, and "it was infinitely sad. He was in total self-deprecation," as if to say, "There's a world out there and I'm nothing."[83]

Away from the paper for long stretches, Phil would send Jim Truitt, then a vice-president of the *Post,* as his emissary to editorial meetings. Harvey Segal, who at the behest of Russ Wiggins had resigned his academic appointment to go permanently to the *Post,* recalls that Truitt, like Phil, was drinking heavily. "I always remember him coming to the eleven-o'clock meetings bleary-eyed and obviously hung over. We [felt] that he was a spy to represent Phil's point of view."[84]

On November 27, 1962, Kay's sister Florence, fifty-one and very overweight, died of atherosclerosis (there were also rumors of a fatal mix of alcohol and drugs). Bis shared a room with her mother in Florence's house in Pacific Palisades, where the funeral was held. "I remember her saying to herself, 'Everything is going to be all right.' "[85] Agnes chanted it, as if repetition would make it so, even though she knew that everything would not be all right. How could it be, when the son-in-law she loved more than she did her own children was so obviously, so flagrantly, not all right?

Chapter 12

PHIL FALLS

Phil resigned from COMSAT "for reasons of health" in January 1963. (According to Clark Clifford, he finessed Phil's resignation on orders of the president.)[1] Later that winter he was committed voluntarily to Chestnut Lodge, a private psychiatric hospital in Rockville, Maryland, recommended by his psychiatrist, Leslie Farber. Known to cognoscenti as "the Lodge," it had a reputation for treating the rich and famous, and resembled more the summer resort it had once been than a hospital. Although Farber was not formally affiliated with Chestnut Lodge, he continued to treat Phil with psychotherapy, as was consistent with the hospital's policy of avoiding drugs whenever possible.

After persuading his doctors to discharge him, Phil, with Robin, headed for New York, determined to arbitrate a bitter printers' strike that had started the previous December and resulted in the closing of the city's major dailies. President Kennedy had urged that an independent third party be brought in, but presumably he did not have in mind Phil Graham, who owned a major newspaper and could never be considered independent.

Phil, however, did not see it that way. First, he arranged to meet Bertram Powers, the charismatic and highly principled forty-year-old president of Local 6 of the International Typographical Union. Powers, married to a Ph.D. and not the stereotypical union chief, made national news when the president charged that he had led a strike that had "long since passed the point of public toleration."*[2] Stunned by the attack from his hero,[4] Powers kept silent.

Phil had heard that *Time* was planning a cover story on Powers, and wanted to find out if *Newsweek* should follow suit. He approached one of the picketers outside the *New York Times* building with a message for Powers to meet him at the Carlyle. Powers met not only Phil but also "the beautiful blonde from Australia." Powers recalls that Phil patted Robin on her belly and said, "That's my baby"; Robin, he explained proudly, was pregnant with his child.[5] (Others who were close to the couple say that Phil, severely alcoholic, was engaging in wishful thinking.[6])

The two men talked for six hours, Phil covering his yellow pads with notes. Phil asked Powers what he was looking for. "Naturally I couldn't tell him what I would settle for, but I could give him a feel for what the ballpark was."[7] According to Theodore Kheel, the labor lawyer whom Mayor Robert Wagner had assigned to bring the two sides together, Powers's demands were "outrageous. They would have destroyed the newspapers, and Phil went over each item and said, 'Well, that's reasonable. I think you ought to get that. That's okay. We got that in Washington'—which he didn't."[8] Powers remembers that Phil assured him: "You're not asking for anything you're not entitled to."[9]

Within minutes of meeting Powers, Phil concluded that Kennedy had made a mistake in denouncing him; and with Powers at his side, Phil called the president at his vacation home in Palm Beach. According to Powers, Phil told Kennedy "how correct the union's position was," and said that "everybody had it all wrong, that the publishers were the people who were the bad guys in this dispute. And then the tone of the conversation changed, and I could tell without hearing that the president asked [whether I was] present while this call was going on. Graham answered yes. Whereupon apparently Kennedy gave him a dressing-down for allowing a conversation to be overheard by a third party, because suddenly Graham began to say, 'Yes sir, yes sir, yes sir, you're right, sir, yes sir.' "[10]

As angry as Kennedy was with Phil, he also worried that Phil might be right, in the sense that by denouncing Powers the president

---

*It was said that Phil's friend Scotty Reston, then chief Washington correspondent for *The New York Times,* had urged Kennedy to make the attack. "The idea that a workingman, this grease monkey, could stop the great *New York Times* from being published was offensive to [Reston]," Theodore Kheel observes.[3]

had cast him as the underdog.[11] For advice, Kennedy called Supreme Court justice Arthur Goldberg, a labor lawyer who had served as Kennedy's secretary of labor before Kennedy appointed him to the Court. Goldberg told Kennedy to call Theodore Kheel and have him call Phil.[12]

"Why don't you come over?" Phil suggested. Kheel agreed, and when he arrived at the hotel suite, Phil "came to the door in a bathrobe. He said, 'Hi, I'm Phil Graham and this is my fiancée, Robin Webb. We're going to get married as soon as I get a divorce from Kay Graham. Come on in.' Those were his opening words." (Kheel did not mention that in 1939, when Kay Meyer was dating NLRB lawyer Drexel Sprecher, they often double-dated with Kheel and his wife.)

Phil asked Kheel whether he wanted to settle the dispute. "I said, 'Of course.' I'd only been working on it for ninety days without success. 'You get the mayor to name me to head a board of arbitrators and we'll make a decision' [Phil said]. Powers had taken the position that he would not agree to arbitration. I said that to Phil, and he said, 'The hell he won't.' "

Kheel describes Phil as "performing in his best manic manner. He was obviously putting on a show for Robin, what a big shot he was." He called Bertram Powers from his bedroom. "I'm trying to get Ted Kheel to arrange for me to be the arbitrator," Phil told Powers, "and this is the decision that I will make: I'll give you the thirty-five-hour week, I'll give you this, I'll give you that." Powers said he would not accept arbitration, even though Phil was giving him virtually everything he wanted. "Powers said no," Kheel explains, "because he, believe it or not, is a man of principle."

Meanwhile, in the living room of the suite, Kheel asked Robin whether she had ever met Kay Graham. "No, I never met Kay, but we talked once on the telephone when Phil and I were drunk and we got her on the phone. I have nothing against Kay Graham. She can have the children, obviously, and she can have the house. But if she thinks she's going to get *The Washington Post,* she's mighty much mistaken." Her answer, Kheel says, "absolutely floored me."

Phil returned to inform Kheel that Powers would not agree to arbitration, but would accept mediation if Phil were named mediator. Kheel was stunned: *he* was the mayor-appointed mediator. "I can't tell you that I can do that," Kheel replied. "I have to talk to Bob Wagner." Phil switched gears: "Aren't you supposed to call the president back? Why don't we get him now?" The next thing Kheel knew, Phil was on the phone with Kennedy. "I'm with Ted Kheel here, and he's having trouble with these goddamned publishers. They won't go along." Phil made no mention of Powers's intransigence. "Here he is. I'll put him on." The president first asked Kheel, "Can you talk now?" Kheel, understanding that Kennedy didn't want Phil in the room, answered no, and they agreed to speak later. Saddled with the new problem of how to get rid of Phil Graham, Kheel phoned his former law school classmate William P. Rogers, who, as a partner in a powerful New York/Washington law firm, counted *The Washington Post* among his clients. To Kheel's plea for advice, Rogers answered, "Thanks very much. Keep me posted."

Kheel next called the publishers of the New York dailies, who were appalled by Phil's actions. The gist of their reactions, Kheel says, was: "If you bring that bastard in, we're leaving." Finding himself in the ridiculous spot of mediating between the publishers and Phil Graham instead of the publishers and the unions, Kheel then went back to Phil and explained, "Somehow or other, the publishers have gotten word, and they've threatened to walk out if we bring you into it." "Those bastards," Phil answered. "I'm not surprised, but I suppose you fellows have to live with them." He accepted Kheel's explanation, but asked for one favor: to meet with the mayor. Kheel called Mayor Wagner and told him, "I've arranged to get rid of Phil Graham, and all we have to do is have breakfast with him." Wagner agreed: "Fine, bring him around."

The breakfast at Gracie Mansion immediately preceded a meeting at City Hall between the publishers and the union leaders. Kheel remembers that "Robin was in attendance" and that Phil was "constantly showing off for her benefit. He said to the mayor, 'You bring me down to City Hall this morning and I'll get this thing settled for you.' So the mayor looks at me. I had gotten him into this, and now Phil was insisting that he come down, so I interrupted and [told the mayor], 'Well, Bob, I think it would be very helpful if we got Phil, but there's no way the publishers will allow it. They'll walk out. We can't possibly have him down.' "[13]

Phil had no choice but to accept that verdict, but he was still owner of *The Washington Post* and *Newsweek,* and he would damn well exert his editorial clout. He had *Newsweek* publish a pro-union story and summoned Al Friendly to write a sympathetic profile of Bertram Powers. Phil himself wrote an editorial on the strike that was so one-sided Wiggins said he would quit before he ran it.

While Phil was promoting Powers, his *Post* editors were writing a lead Sunday editorial headlined "A Threat to a Free Press," denouncing the unions.[14] The editorial infuriated Phil, who responded by writing a letter to the editor, which he had Robin type and Powers sign, as if Powers had written it himself. The letter, disputing the editorial point by point, ran across four columns.[15] Phil was angry enough with Wiggins over the editorial that he ordered Friendly to take over Wiggins's job, but Friendly refused. "If you [make me] do it, I go," Friendly warned him,[16] and Phil backed down.

The strike dragged on through the winter and early spring. New York finally had its newspapers again on the morning of April 1, 1963.

Ironically, Phil might have had what it took to settle the strike. Lester Bernstein, then *Newsweek*'s national affairs editor, observes, "It was staggering to know how many different considerations there were. And [Phil] had devised a sort of calculus of how you could trade off one for the other and arrive at a solution that in his view wouldn't cost the publishers more than they could bear, and would satisfy the union. It presupposed not only a thoroughgoing knowledge of this highly complex subject matter, but an ability to manipulate it like a chess master. I had no idea then that this guy was mentally ill. I thought, Here's a genius. It was a tour de force."[17]

Phil was nursing a curious and contradictory disdain for his fellow publishers that made him feel all the closer to Powers. "I can do— any publisher can do—whatever he wants to do, and it won't be reported," Phil told the union leader. "I can go out to Times Square right now and shit, and you wouldn't read a word about it in any paper."[18]

That spring, Phil and Robin went to Europe, his first stop a London hospital where Sir Isaiah Berlin was recovering from surgery. Out of respect for Berlin, who was close to Kay, Phil did not bring Robin. "I had a long talk [with] him about life," Sir Isaiah recalls. "I expected him to be much more abnormal, from what people said. He told me in a very amusing way what it was like going into the hospital the first time. He was asked by somebody what he did, and he said he owned *The Washington Post*. He might as well have said that he was the Chinese emperor. People thought he was quite mad."[19]

Next, Phil called Bob Estabrook at his Hampstead home to inform him that he and Robin would be by that afternoon for tea. "It was a very pained affair," Estabrook recounts. Phil expected him and Eldon Griffiths, *Newsweek*'s London bureau chief, to reserve the Connaught Hotel for "a party for royalty." Griffiths, a British subject, was able, by "pulling a lot of strings," to reserve the Connaught for dinner. "We had no royalty or nobility," Estabrook says, "but we did get a number of sirs and ladies, among them the publisher of the *Telegraph*.* After the first or second course, in a loud voice from the head table, Phil said [to Robin], 'Come on, dear, let's go up to bed.' And Eldon and I were left during that loud hush to try to put things back together and keep the evening going. He left and nobody saw him again."[20]

Another gathering at the Connaught was arranged by Arnaud de Borchgrave, who had been ordered by Phil, on the spur of the moment, to gather all *Newsweek*'s foreign correspondents, and some from the *Post,* for a dinner. Larry Collins, present as the magazine's Paris bureau chief, relates that the purpose of the meeting was two-fold: First, having just come out of the "nuthouse," Phil saw it as an opportunity to "reassert his authority over the editorial direction of the magazine." That he did, in a speech that still leaves *Newsweek* people marveling. It was "a brilliant, almost off-the-cuff talk to us on what a journalist's job was. It was the best description that I've ever heard of what a newspaperman should be."[21] And Phil's second purpose was "to introduce Robin in her new capacity as the woman who was going to become his wife."[22] He presented her to the assembled as "the next Mrs. Graham."[23]

Also at this dinner, in enumerating his planned improvements for the *Post,* Phil announced that he was bringing in Robert Manning. He did not say in what capacity, but one *Post* correspondent assumed Phil meant as managing editor to replace Al Friendly. An old journalism hand, Manning was then assistant secretary of state for public affairs in the Kennedy administration. Phil may have had it in mind to push Friendly into Russ Wiggins's job and to push Wiggins upstairs into oblivion. But Manning had had only one "very brief" conversation with Phil, who had asked him what he planned to do on leaving the government. "I replied only that I intended to return

*Michael Berry, whose wife, Pamela, was one of Kay's closest friends, owned the London *Daily Telegraph.*

to journalism in one way or another." The next thing Manning knew, "I got a note of congratulations from one of the correspondents who had been at that dinner. That surprised the devil out of me. I didn't know what she was talking about."[24]

Phil and Robin proceeded to Rome, where they vacationed for four or five days with Curtis G. "Bill" Pepper, then *Newsweek*'s Rome bureau chief, and his wife, Beverly, a prominent sculptor.

Phil still had it in him to make a good business decision. For $8.4 million he bought a forty-nine-percent interest in Bowater Mersey Paper, a Nova Scotia company that supplied most of the *Post*'s newsprint,[25] and he bought it at a time when paper costs were rising.[26]

But in many respects, Phil was deteriorating so fast that his friends could only cast their eyes down in shame. Oz Elliott recalled that at lunch with *Newsweek* editors, Phil joked about his own daughter: "Pretty bright for a little Jew girl."[27] It became routine for him to refer to his own children as "kikes" or "little yids,"[28] and he would telephone one of his oldest and most loyal friends, Joe Rauh, and make anti-Semitic slurs.

Rauh and other friends and employees insisted that this was nothing more than a symptom of his illness. "The suggestion that there was any anti-Semitism there before the illness, I just would reject and resent," Rauh said.[29] "There's absolutely no doubt in my mind that this anti-Semitism bit was pure madness," agrees Newbold Noyes. "It was just so totally unlike him that it was unbelievable."[30]

At the same time, Phil told friends that he was searching for religion to bring some shape and rootedness to his life—real religion, he would specify, not that sapless Unitarianism so popular in Georgetown and so gratingly on display at his father-in-law's funeral. He first called on Scotty Reston, a devout Protestant with Scottish ancestry like his own. "I'm afraid my faith was not strong enough to help," Reston recalled.[31]

Phil was increasingly drawn to Catholicism, particularly the brooding and, to Phil's eye, serious variety practiced by his friend Emmet Hughes. He recruited the much-divorced Hughes as his spiritual guide, and "on occasion Hughes would come to Graham's room in the Carlyle to find him disheveled, unshaven, but walking around reading a Bible aloud."[32]

Richard Clurman got a call from Hughes one night warning him not to let Phil in if he showed up at Clurman's house: Phil might have a gun and might be dangerous. Clurman's wife and their two-year-old son were alone at home, "and sure enough [Phil] came. It was beyond her capacity not to let him in. He went into my son's room and took him up in his arms and sat with him, and just babbled for about an hour or so, and pecked her on the cheek and left."[33]

Marietta Tree called what happened next "a horror opera."[34] Phil and Robin went to Phoenix for a meeting that annually drew the nation's most powerful newspaper owners and editors. Jean Friendly felt that if Phil made that trip it might be his last. "I tried so hard to stop [him from going]. Kay was here sitting with me in my bedroom, and I got the doctor [Leslie Farber] on the phone and said, 'You've got to stop him, he's crazy.' And he said, 'You're right, but I can't do it by myself.' And I said, 'Get somebody else to help you.' And of course he was overwhelmed by Phil. Everybody was overwhelmed by Phil."

Al Friendly remained in Washington to help get the paper out, and Jean waited by the telephone for the bad news she knew would come. What she did not expect was that it would come from Robin Webb, who said she "needed help, she was desperate, he was beating her up."[35] Others reported that Phil had been drinking with abandon and, between bouts of violence, announced that he was going to marry Robin, perhaps right there in Phoenix. (That he was still married to Kay seems not to have occurred to him.)

Phil arranged a dinner, which he billed as "the Last Supper." With twelve "disciples" present, he went around the table assigning a role to each. When he came to Emmet Hughes, Phil, no longer trusting him, said, "And you're Judas."[36]

At the main banquet, Phil's dinner partner was Maggie Savoy, women's editor of *The Arizona Republic*. She found Phil "so fascinating, but just so crazy, haywire, bonkers"—and very drunk.[37]

Phil interrupted a banquet speech by Benjamin McKelway, editor of the *Washington Star* and a member of the AP board of directors, and seized the lectern to tell his peers that they were fat, stupid cowards who wouldn't know the truth if they sat on it. And, he said, "he wouldn't wipe his ass with their papers."[38] The thunderstruck audience stared in disbelief, but Phil was just warming up. He singled out various publishers and began to revile them. Newsmen who had stayed behind in New York and Washington were soon abuzz with vivid descriptions of Phil's "around the bend" but "brilliant" performance. "He went through everybody," recalls Arnaud de Borchgrave, "including Otis Chandler of the *Los Angeles Times,* berated every one of them for their lack of balls. Nobody knew how to stop him." He was "devastating and brilliant and accurate, [and] did beautiful caricatures of each of the big shots present."[39]

Phil announced that he was going to tell them who in Washington was sleeping with whom, and that he might as well start at the top with John Kennedy, who was sleeping, in the White House, with Mary Meyer. While his audience waited for the next name to drop, he declared, "I don't know what you other sons of bitches are going to do, but I'm going to go home now and screw my girl."[40]

As he left, he began stripping off his clothes, and some in the immobilized audience of supposed movers and shakers feared that they would soon face a naked as well as an irreparably damaged owner of *The Washington Post*. Ben McKelway's wife, Margaret, whom Newbold Noyes describes as "a withdrawn, quiet, Helen Hokinson* type of woman, without being funny," walked out on the stage, took him by the hand, and said quietly, "Phil, come with me. You're going to go back and sit down."[41] Phil offered no resistance as she put him in his seat.

In the meantime, a newsman in the audience had phoned the president, who immediately called Kay to say that he was ordering a military jet to transport Leslie Farber to Phoenix.[42] Phil, together with his entourage of psychiatrists and attendants and Emmet Hughes, would be flown back to Chestnut Lodge in a chartered plane; they would stop in Chicago to be met by Lally and the Friendlys' son Al, Jr.[43]

At the Phoenix airport, after punching an airport detective, Phil had been wrestled to the ground, forced into a straitjacket, and injected with sedatives. That was how Lally saw her father.[44]

Left behind in Phoenix, Robin, in tears, called de Borchgrave in New York. She told him that *Post* executive vice-president John Hayes had handed her a check for a thousand dollars, hoping, apparently, to buy her permanent silence. "I tore it up and threw it in his face," she said sobbing.[45] De Borchgrave arranged to buy a ticket for her to New York and told her to take a taxi from the airport to his apartment, where he would meet her and pay the fare.

---

*Hokinson's satiric drawings of middle-aged society matrons, habitués of garden clubs and matinees, appeared in *The New Yorker*.

"I brought her upstairs when she arrived," de Borchgrave says. She was "still sobbing, in a state of shock, couldn't get over what had happened. My wife, having the flu, couldn't go out, couldn't fix dinner, so I decided to take Robin out to La Maisonette at the St. Regis, which was a great 'in' place to dine. [I was] thinking that I'd cheer her up. I noticed Emmet Hughes on the dance floor."[46]

Because Hayes had failed in his clumsy attempt to make Robin go away, Kay was forced to huddle with other members of the family—especially Phil's brother Bill[47]—and with the upper echelon of *Post* people to figure out what to do about Robin. They were prepared, says one *Newsweek* editor, "to buy her off." When they asked her what she wanted, reportedly in a manner less insulting than Hayes's, they were surprised when she answered that all she wanted was a one-way ticket to Australia.[48]

"I think [she] behaved really well," says Jean Friendly, "and Kay does too." She adds that Robin never tried to capitalize on the relationship and always refused to discuss it with writers and reporters.[49] Kay recently told Oz Elliott, "I've come to believe Robin is a very nice person. She's never given a press conference or interview, or embarrassed us."*[50]

When Phil assured Bertram Powers that he could defecate in Times Square and no newspaper would report it, he knew what he was talking about. It was almost as if he wanted to prove his point, his self-hatred feeding the disdain he felt for his colleagues. He had undoubtedly chosen to have his ugly breakdown practically in their laps. With the exception of Sarah McClendon at her small Texas news service, no one in the country printed a word of it.

In a deep depression, Phil asked Kay to take him back. She agreed, so long as he sought help in a serious way.

On June 20, 1963, Phil was admitted again to Chestnut Lodge. This time he seemed resigned to the fact that his affair with Robin was finished, and determined to regain his mental health and make things work with Kay. She visited him daily, bringing lunch and staying for tennis. According to Luvie Pearson, despite what Kay

---

*Robin's journalism career came to an abrupt end. She went to work for the Australian delegation to UNESCO,[51] later married Alan Edwards, a member of the Australian foreign service who would reach the rank of ambassador, and had a son. She remained friendly with Larry Collins and was seen by some *Newsweek* people in Vietnam, where her husband was posted, but she largely dropped from sight. She now lives with her husband in Canberra.[52]

had been through, she still loved Phil "absolutely. Kay always did everything to try to bring Phil to his senses and keep the marriage together. That was her objective. She thought when he agreed to go to Chestnut Lodge that that was it, that everything would be hunky-dory."[53]

Others visited him as well, including Oz Elliott, who arrived full of dispatches from *Newsweek,* in which Phil seemed vitally interested. "When I first came in here," Phil told him, "the thing that scared me most was that I might sink to [his] level"—he pointed at a fellow patient shouting obscenities. "But now, while I can't yet *see* the shore on the other side, I know it's there."[54] Phil did not ask to see Jean Friendly, but Al visited and so did the Friendlys' youngest child, Nicholas, who, Jean says, "just thought Phil was God."[55]

Phil had been at the hospital for six weeks, when, on Saturday morning, August 3, he persuaded his doctors to let him check out, with Katharine, for a day at Glen Welby. None of his friends was surprised that he was able to swing a pass. "He could convince anybody of anything," says Jean Friendly.[56]

That morning Kay called Joe Rauh, and "in a voice sounding so much better than it had been for a while, totally renewed and refreshed, [said] 'We're going to the farm today. Phil's much better and he'd like to see you. Could you go out there [Chestnut Lodge] on Tuesday?' And so I was all set to go."[57]

Kay and Phil "had a happy morning together," recounts Jean Friendly. "They played some tennis."[58] Then, in the early afternoon, Phil announced that he was going bird-hunting, the sport his mother had tried to talk him out of in favor of reading. Just after one p.m. Kay went to her second-floor bedroom for a nap.

Phil went to a first-floor bathroom, sat on the side of the bathtub, propped a .28-gauge sportsman's shotgun against his head, and pulled the trigger. Kay and Phil had been alone in the house except for the servants, two of whom, trailed by Kay, rushed to the grisly scene.[59] The Fauquier County deputy sheriff, who conducted an inquiry into Phil's death, reported that a single shell had blasted through his right temple; he had toppled, instantly dead, into the tub, and no note had been found.[60]

None of his friends doubted that Phil Graham, age forty-eight, had planned to commit suicide. The invitation to visit the following Tuesday, said Joe Rauh, "was obviously part of Phil's genius in talking his way out of Chestnut Lodge, obviously a dodge to get to the place where he knew the gun was."[61]

"I never could understand why they'd leave this guy in a house alone with a rifle," Morrie Siegel says. He remembers when he met Phil, Robin, and Edward Bennett Williams in a restaurant and Williams asked Siegel to stay with Phil while Williams got his car—so unwilling was he to leave Phil alone for only a few minutes, and even in the company of Robin.[62]

Bill Meyer, who, says his sister Bis, "worked his head off to help Phil," was devastated. "In a way he blamed himself for one of the doctors involved." She will say no more, but she obviously means Leslie Farber.[63] Other family members blamed Farber and the hospital for making what they considered a serious medical error by allowing Phil to leave. June Bingham, who has written two books on psychiatry, says, "They certainly let him out at a time when his manic-depression was lifting, which is the time that is most dangerous. It's not when they're depressed, it's when they're beginning to come up that they commit suicide."[64] (Chestnut Lodge now has a policy that any patient allowed home on a pass must be accompanied by a staff member who stays with the patient at all times.[65])

Phil's course of treatment immediately became the subject of agonized speculation. At Chestnut Lodge, during Phil's day, the preferred method of treating manic-depression was psychoanalysis. Some of those close to Phil argue that such treatment constituted a kind of malpractice.

But that was thirty years ago, when much less was understood about manic-depression, now also called bipolar affective disorder and known to involve a chemical imbalance and to have a genetic component. Lithium, the drug of choice, estimated to help seventy percent of manic-depressives, was not approved for use in the United States until 1969. Other drugs were being tried before then, but not at Chestnut Lodge.

Apparently Leslie Farber needed no one to accuse him of providing Phil with less than ideal treatment. Frank Waldrop claims that after Phil's suicide, Farber "left town, because he was so humiliated that a patient had outsmarted him. Phil seduced him."[66] Judging Farber (or any psychiatrist involved with Phil Graham) too severely, contends June Bingham, would be unfair: "To find a psychiatrist who would be bright enough for Phil would be very hard. If the doctor is giving you an enema, that's all right, but if he's trying to engage your psyche and you're smarter than he is, it isn't going to work."[67]

Scotty Reston, Oz Elliott, and others stress that no doctor could have prevented Phil from committing suicide. "When Phil killed himself," says Dick Clurman, "he did the right thing. He'd have [had] no credibility for the rest of his life."[68] He made the supremely rational decision that, while he might appear better from time to time, he would never really get better. "Phil was not going to live any longer as a flawed person," says Jean Friendly.[69]

Phil's last concern was not that Kay and the children be taken care of after his death, not that the newspaper be in good hands, but that the public learn the inside scoop on a story Phil felt no one, including his friend Teddy White in his *Making of the President, 1960,* had gotten quite right. No one had given Phil enough credit for persuading JFK to choose LBJ as a running mate. Phil sent a long memo to White on the subject, which White appended, almost verbatim, to his *Making of the President, 1964.* *

Now Phil Graham's whole troubled enterprise was thrown into the lap of his wife—a woman who could not have been more ill prepared, or more terrified at the prospect of becoming the next Phil Graham.

---

*White stated that Phil's account was "probably as close as we shall ever get to the truth of how the present President of the United States [Johnson] was introduced to the succession."[70]

Chapter 13

KAY RISES

Jean and Al Friendly were among the first to get word of Phil's suicide. On their way to Glen Welby, they picked up eighteen-year-old Donny, then between his freshman and sophomore years at Harvard and working in the Washington bureau of *The New York Times*. On the return trip, Jean drove with Donny beside her in the front seat, Kay and Al in the back. "Kay, you've got to take over the paper and you've got to run it, and you can do it," Al was telling her, again and again, as if by repetition he could make her believe something she deemed impossible. "I can't, you know I can't," she repeated just as often.[1]

But by evening, when Joe Rauh and his wife dropped by her house in Georgetown, Kay was directing her attention to a matter she had not considered for well over twenty years—how to play a story.[2] And what a story it was: a front-page obituary/tribute, complete with the news that Phil's death was a suicide. Until that day, not even the most oblique mention of Phil's breakdowns and hospitalizations had ever seen print in Washington.

Agnes Meyer, with Lally in tow, was then on another of her star-studded cruises. The day before Phil's suicide, her private yacht, carrying, among others, the Drew Pearsons and the Earl Warrens, had sailed from Athens en route to Istanbul. When the yacht arrived in Istanbul harbor, Luvie Pearson recalled, the American embassy woke the Warrens with the news of Phil's suicide. Luvie brought Lally back to Washington for the funeral. Bill, fifteen, and Stephen, eleven, were summoned home from summer camps in Vermont and

Colorado, respectively.[3] Agnes did not return for the funeral, partly because her worsening arthritis made travel difficult and partly because she did not wish to face the horror of what had happened.

Russ Wiggins was at his home in Maine and Al Friendly was making his unplanned trip to Glen Welby, leaving Karl Meyer on weekend duty at the *Post* that Saturday. Phil's assistant Joseph Paull came running to him: " 'Karl, the publisher has just shot himself and you've got to write the editorial.' Here I was, a young kid having to write an editorial about a publisher whose mental condition had been [kept] secret from readers of the paper."[4] His moving editorial appeared the day after Phil's suicide, accompanying a front-page obituary: "There was no detail of journalism he regarded as too trifling to engage his sympathetic attention," Meyer wrote, "and no person beyond reach of his concern. His rangy figure and quicksilver wit were as familiar a part of our enterprise as the fonts of type in our composing room." Meyer put a pleasant spin on Phil's fatal illness: "Mr. Graham invested the full capacity of his mind and heart in anything that deeply moved and interested him. He was not a person given to qualified commitments to his country, his enterprise or his friends. It was this quality that precipitated the illness that led to his death."[5]

Felix Frankfurter eulogized Phil in a letter to the editor of the *Post*.*[6] Herblock drew a cartoon, titled, simply, "Legacy," showing Phil's empty office and a handwritten note atop his desk describing the *Post* as an "independent newspaper . . . capable of indignation over injustice."[8] *Newsweek* weighed in with descriptions of Phil's ability to "dissolve pomposity" and "lighten tedium," his sympathy for "the great and . . . weak alike," his "electric" personality.[9] *Time* devoted a full page to an evaluation of Phil's derailed promise, a more honest evaluation than appeared in other publications, but devoid of any mention that Phil had been *Time*'s cover boy just seven years before.[10] The most moving eulogy ran in the *Washington Daily News*, which merely reprinted the Edwin Arlington Robinson poem about the "imperially slim" Richard Cory, who "glittered when he walked," who was "schooled in every grace," who, "one calm summer night, went home and put a bullet through his head."[11] At the

---

*Harvey Segal recalls that when the long letter arrived, Al Friendly edited it, excising the justice's observation—considered disrespectful—that "only a Sigmund Freud could figure out what Phil's troubles were." The *Post* printed the letter a week later, robbed of its poignancy.[7]

Post, as Harvey Segal explains, people were relieved "because it was so damned uncertain, working under a capricious madman."[12]

The eulogies poured in, most of them notable for their dishonesty. John Kennedy praised Phil's "quiet and effective leadership"; Lyndon Johnson's tribute noted his family, "in whom he had great pride"; Treasury Secretary C. Douglas Dillon paid tribute to Phil's belief that "responsibility and objectivity go hand in hand with journalistic enterprise."[13]

But Joe Rauh's comment on the death of Phil Graham was perhaps the most poignant. He pinpointed the enormous waste: "If you'd have said in 1940 or 1941 who were the people in this town most likely to succeed, most likely to carry out the important things, you'd have said Phil and [Edward Prichard]. They both destroyed themselves by their own hands. One takes his own life and one takes his own life in a way, with a stupid prank in the ballot box. It always made me so unhappy that people of such talent and ability, character, everything, destroyed themselves."[14]

Those few who could be clear-eyed about Phil saw how pathetic he had become: it was his self-absorption, not his passion for justice and all the rest, that knew no bounds. As William F. Buckley, Jr., put it, in a column published a week after the suicide, Phil was an example of a "man profoundly and primarily in love with himself."[15]

One person who most likely did not read the Buckley column, which ran in *The Miami Herald* and prominently mentioned the "other woman," was Ernest Graham. Since 1960, when he suffered the first in a series of strokes, he had been so ill that he had not been told of his first son's hospitalizations for severe depression; and he was not told now of his suicide.[16]

For the family there was a private funeral service on Monday, August 5; for the public, a memorial service on Tuesday at Washington's National Cathedral, which drew a thousand people, among them the capital's most prominent. John Kennedy slipped in a side door and took a front-row seat. Also in attendance were Attorney General Robert Kennedy, Treasury Secretary Dillon, former secretary of state Dean Acheson, former CIA director Allen Dulles, Supreme Court justice Arthur Goldberg, and retired justice Felix Frankfurter, who arrived in a wheelchair. Robert McNamara was there, and McGeorge Bundy, Theodore Sorensen, Pierre Salinger, Alice Roosevelt Longworth, John Sherman Cooper, Stuart Symington. "Anyone who was anyone was there," Arnaud de Borchgrave recalls[17]—with the conspicuous exception of Lyndon Johnson, who still could not bear to go to funerals, or think about death.[18]

Although many were there mainly to be seen, there was no shortage of deeply aggrieved mourners. Joe Rauh described Edward Prichard looking "like the wrath of God."[19] Karl Meyer recalls the Graham children "shaken, stunned, as if the world had collapsed around them."[20] The children had chosen the Easter hymn ("The strife is o'er, the battle done") and Isaac Watts's "O God, Our Help in Ages Past."

If Phil found Eugene's service to be rootless, one wonders what he would have thought of his own, this most high-church affair officiated by the Right Reverend Angus Dun, retired Episcopal bishop of Washington, who flew in from his summer home in Massachusetts.[21] The Reverend Dun eulogized Phil "for his high intelligence and his restless and creative energy of mind and spirit, for his openness to the hurts and sorrows of his fellows, his hatred of injustice," and read from Paul's Epistle to the Romans: "As many as are led by the spirit of God, they are the sons of God."

Phil's body was cremated, and the remains placed in the historic Oak Hill Cemetery in Georgetown, directly across the street from the R Street house. Kay can look out her window and see the tombstone, just a few feet within the iron gate, a plain marble tablet that carries only the inscription "Philip Leslie Graham 1915–1963."

The will that was probated was the one filed in 1957. Fifty-five percent of the voting control in the Washington Post Company went to Kay. In the split second that it took Phil to blow out his brains, Kay was transformed from emotionally abused helpmeet to financial titan—or so it said on paper.

On the morning of Phil's funeral, Katharine Graham rehearsed, over and again, the remarks that Scotty Reston had helped her compose. Later that day she would deliver them before the board of directors of the company. She was terrified of these men who had heard or watched Phil belittle her, who knew the degrading details of his affair with Robin. They felt sorry for her, she knew, but they could barely hide their contempt for the very idea of this shrinking, fragile woman running a multimillion-dollar corporation.

A *Washingtonian* magazine writer later described Kay's anxiety about this meeting and her approach to the car that would take her to the *Post* building: "Lally followed along trying to calm her. The moment was so confused that Lally hopped in the back seat and rode along, though she was still in her nightgown."[22] En route, Kay continued to rehearse her lines.

Those who knew Kay well at the time stress that her total lack of preparation and confidence cannot be overstated: "Kay really knew nothing when Phil killed himself," says Richard Clurman. "She knew nothing about anything. She wasn't even a Washington socialite. She seemed a pleasant woman whom you sympathized with [for] being married to this electrifying, kinetic figure. Kay was a big brown wren in every department."[23] Howard Simons, who had joined the *Post* in 1961 as a science writer, said that Kay reminded him of "a shaky little doe, coming on wobbly legs out of the forest."[24]

What Kay did not realize is that the men who ran the *Post* and *Newsweek* were nearly as nervous as she. A *Time* writer suggested that Kay most likely would serve as the titular head, but he implied that of course a woman—especially a woman with no experience—could never actually run the place. He speculated that Al Friendly would assume that role.[25] Most of the top editors would have been delighted with that transition, rather than have operating power vested in John Sweeterman, a ruthless cost-cutter.[26] Also, as contemptuous as they were of Kay, they feared the consequences of an outside takeover and wanted the paper kept in the Graham family. Ben Gilbert explains, "I think the attitude of everybody was that she should [take over, and things] would be structured to give her all the support that she needed."[27] According to Bis, "The people working on the *Post* demanded that she take over."[28]

Media moguls such as Otis Chandler and Samuel Newhouse ("vultures," Kay later called them[29]) had begun circling the wounded *Post* even before Phil's death, and not surprisingly, since some of them had witnessed Phil's performance in Phoenix. Once described as "a graveyard superintendent [who] goes around picking up bones, preying on widows and split families,"[30] Newhouse—whose son now runs the empire—had tried to buy the *Times-Herald* in 1949 and *Newsweek* in 1961. This time he was determined to succeed. Such was the upheaval at the *Post* that even the phlegmatic *Star* was said to have expressed interest.[31]

Staffers at *Newsweek* were even more worried. They understood Kay might harbor what they considered an irrational hatred for the magazine because of Robin's affiliation with it. They feared she might blame the *Newsweek* fraternity—Arnaud de Borchgrave, Oz

Elliott, Larry Collins, Ben Bradlee—for promoting the affair and contributing to her awful humiliation.

They also knew that it was the Post Company people in Washington, not those in New York, who had her ear, and that some on the newspaper were uncomfortable with the acquisition of the newsmagazine from the start. "She was advised by a lot of people," says Richard Clurman, "to get rid of *Newsweek,* because Phil had owned it for such a short period of time."[32] Then the word spread that a Newhouse or a Newhouse representative had called Fritz Beebe just after Phil's death and offered $100 million for *Newsweek*[33]—more than ten times what Phil had paid two years earlier.

Oz Elliott described Kay entering the meeting looking "ashen, dressed in black, her eyes downcast."[34] She later said that the ordeal was "agony"; as she made her way into the room she could not stop thinking of a scene from *The Vagabond King*: "the moment when the suddenly enthroned vagabond—for the first time dressed in royal robes—descends the great stairs, slowly and anxiously, tensely eyeing on either side the rows of archers with their drawn bows and inscrutable faces."[35] She assured the men that she had no intention of selling anything, not the *Post,* not *Newsweek.* Her only desire, she explained, was that the paper be safe until Donny was old enough to take over. In the meantime, she said in her quivering voice, she would go to work.

"But I didn't go in intending to take over," she later insisted. "I thought I'd just be a family coordinating hand for a while."[36] Eugene's remark on buying the *Times-Herald* in 1954—"This makes the *Post* safe for Donny"—seemed to be coming to fruition.

Kay required large doses of bucking up. Agnes did most of that. "Kay Graham didn't have a better booster in the world than her mother," marvels Jean Friendly.[37] And Agnes had a captive audience for a month: at Lally's insistence, Kay returned with her and Luvie Pearson to the Aegean and Black Sea cruise that had been interrupted by Phil's death. Agnes lectured Kay on Eugene's fervent desire that the *Post* remain in the family. She reminded her daughter that for more than two red-ink decades Eugene had poured his own money into the paper. Columnist Clayton Fritchey later observed, "It was widely assumed [that Kay] would sell the paper, or turn it over to someone like Scotty Reston. . . . I think it was ultimately because of her mother that Kay had the gumption to take it on."[38]

The cruise was the perfect tonic for Kay. For Agnes, turning her attention to her daughter in a way she had never done took her mind off Phil, whom she could not forgive for killing himself. "She felt terribly betrayed by his suicide," according to Joanna Steichen. "She used to say [that she told Phil], 'You and I are alike, we bend, everybody else snaps and we bend. Everybody else breaks.' Then he betrayed her. He broke."[39]

Back home and faced with her responsibilities, Kay was petrified. Anything seemed easier than actually going to work. "She never thought she would pull it off," says Sir Isaiah Berlin. All of Agnes's reassurances began to seem preposterous. While visiting C. Douglas Dillon and his wife in Florida, Kay walked on the beach with the vacationing secretary of the treasury and admitted she "didn't know anything" about the paper. Should she sell it, she asked him, look for someone to run it for her, or try to run it herself? He urged her to do the last. Likewise, Kay called on George Ball, who had been a colleague of Phil's at the Lend-Lease Administration and was then undersecretary of state. She told him that after Phil died, "I was all rusted up inside. I have to face the problem of taking on the paper and I don't know anything about the paper. If you have any ideas I'd like to have them. I need help."[40]

Kay assumed the presidency in September (she would add the title publisher in 1969 and chairman of the board in 1973), moved into Phil's office, acquired his secretary, Elizabeth Hylton, and tried to learn the job.

Not only was she saddled with her ignorance of both the editorial and the business sides of the paper, she was burdened equally by Phil's outsize reputation. And she did not have it in her to lighten the load. Fortunately for her, Fritz Beebe, chairman of the board, was ready to help. He had, with his top executives, been running the company as Phil slid toward suicide, and he now saved Katharine from the strong urge to retreat into obscure widowhood. As Roswell Gilpatric says, Beebe was at her "right hand." He was barely three years Kay's senior, but she thought of him as "an older brother, an elder statesman to lean on, an éminence grise." Because of him, "Kay had time to gain altitude and speed in her job while she had a legal advisor plus a board chairman with whom she could work out her decisions."[41] Karl Meyer says that "Fritz was an extraordinarily important business figure for the *Post,* giving confidence in its creditworthiness. [He was] a shrewd hand who knew his way around New York—banks, Wall Street, that was Fritz's role."[42]

The *Post* of that period desperately needed that strong hand.

"Raggedy," Frank Waldrop called it; "rickety," said Kermit Lansner.[43] The company had serious cash-flow problems, because Phil had given away stock options to his employees as if they were Monopoly deeds. Some of those plans were then maturing and ready to be cashed in.

Beebe, it is widely agreed, knew how to guide Kay. The businessmen, says Philip Geyelin, were given to patting Kay on the head and saying, "Don't you worry." But Beebe did not do so—he was "too sensitive, too much of a friend."[44] He was not power-hungry; he wanted only to train her and perhaps return to his real love—the law.

Kay viewed herself, it must be remembered, as an interim person. "I started out with the idea," she observed in a speech years later, "that I should learn enough to be knowledgeable and intelligent, should I ultimately have to make any important decisions. It never occurred to me that I would manage anything. . . . I assumed everything would go on much as before, with the men already running things continuing to do what they were doing."[45]

But she soon saw that the only business plan she had—to cling to the sidelines and delegate—was not viable. "I quickly learned my first lesson," she said in the same speech: "Nothing stands still."[46] She began groping toward a more hands-on approach.

Some of the men around Kay vastly preferred the figurehead role for her, and when they saw the first faint signs of her becoming more serious, they resisted, forgetting—to their everlasting regret—that she owned the company. "What she needs is a good f———," was an expression that some of these men, unwilling to take orders from a woman, liked to use.[47] Others called her "Mama," although not to her face.[48]

Outside the *Post*, she was similarly dismissed by her publishing peers. At one meeting a prominent publisher polled other publishers—all male but Graham—for their opinions. "I was thinking all the way around the table what I was going to say," Kay recalled, "and then he skipped me! He ended at my right."[49]

That she was treated in this manner was not surprising, if one considers both the era and the image Kay projected. She suffered from a kind of catatonia, interrupted by outbursts, apologies, and recriminations. Instructing a secretary, making a comment at a meeting were excruciatingly difficult for her, and giving a speech was out of the question.[50] She admitted that a story that sounded outlandish enough to be apocryphal was true: Before the *Post* Christmas party in 1963, at which she was expected to offer some innocuous remarks,

"I was walking up and down at home saying 'Merry Christmas' to everybody. The children were convulsed by that. They'd say, 'Really, Ma, do you have to practice "Merry Christmas"?' "[51]

She summoned Karl Meyer and several others to help her write her first public speech as company head. "She had never given a public speech," Meyer recalls. "She was afraid of making a fool of herself. She appealed to all our sympathy and help and support, and we all felt an enormous sense of concern."[52]

Even in a purely social setting, Kay felt she did not know how to talk to sophisticated columnists and opinion makers and presidential speechwriters, for whom easy conversation and camaraderie seemed to come so naturally. When Phil was alive, she saw that he was the best of all at it, and as his wife, she kept her mouth shut or talked quietly to other wives about children, schools, and the help. Shortly after Phil Graham's death, the Phil Geyelins invited Kay to their house for Geyelin's fortieth-birthday party. "She was really wound up tight," he says. "She felt embarrassed. [Syndicated columnist Rowland] Evans, who was a dear old friend, had some gags, other people brought presents, and she felt uncomfortable."[53]

Kay was subject to relentless self-laceration, so much that a seemingly casual comment to John Sweeterman or another executive or editor would return at three or four in the morning to haunt her. Lying awake in a panic, she would replay the remark, certain of its inanity and ignorance. She was sure to say something equally banal the next day, and so the whole distressing process would repeat itself.

Staying in the arena took enormous courage. She could easily have withdrawn and allowed Beebe to carry on until Donny was ready, but something—pride, a sense that it was in her blood to run the company—kept her from walking away. She would tour the *Post* building with Sweeterman, trying to understand the mechanics of typesetting, printing, and distributing a newspaper. She was, at age forty-six, in the equivalent of nursery school. What was the difference between hot and cold type? What was an agate line? Why independent rather than Teamster distribution? New presses? Color presses? She took courses, read textbooks.[54]

And she knew enough to know that she still did not really understand. She did not have that natural aptitude and ability that made these things seem second nature to Phil. As she told her sister Bis, "There are things I'll never catch up with, the kind of training and experience that most people in this kind of job have had."[55]

Some executives—Sweeterman is usually mentioned first—took

advantage of her yawning lack of confidence. One oft-told story has her dissolving into tears when he criticized her for using company funds to buy a pin for a retiring switchboard operator.[56] Alan Finberg contends that Sweeterman thought he was acting for the good of the company: "He's from another generation. So it's certainly nothing personal against Kay. He probably felt the same about all women."[57] Frank Waldrop explains that Sweeterman, "a perfectly honest and perfectly good man, didn't stop to study the problem of whom he was dealing with. Trouble with Sweeterman and all those fellows is that they didn't know much about women at all—okay, you marry one, you hop into bed with her, have some kids, then you get on with your work."[58]

Kay would later tell friends that Sweeterman had deliberately kept her from learning about the business side of the company.[59] "There were some empires within the company that were not anxious to help me learn," she said. "They didn't take to a woman."[60]

She rented an apartment in New York on the twenty-first floor of the UN Plaza, with neighbors who included Robert Kennedy and Truman Capote. She spent two days a week at Beebe's side at the corporate offices in the *Newsweek* building, seeing to the affairs of the company and learning about the magazine.

At the *Post* she attended the Tuesday editorial meetings for senior editors. At *Newsweek* she attended cover conferences. But she was "very hesitant to speak," recalls Mel Elfin. "She would sit on the couch, and sometimes she would even whisper in the ear of the editor sitting next to her."[61] According to Jim Cannon, "If someone said, 'Well, what do you think, Kay?' she would say, 'Well, I'm depending on you guys to make it a better magazine.' "[62] De Borchgrave recalls that as "unsure of herself" as she was, "every once in a while she'd say, The French ambassador told me such-and-such last night at dinner and I think we should do a story on so-and-so. Everybody would sort of nod approvingly, which meant that we'd go ahead and ignore it. She never insisted, never pushed."[63]

Kay was not only uncomfortable with *Newsweek,* but disdainful, showing a tendency to belittle the magazine at dinner parties and not hiding a desire to see it fail. Her feelings were not surprising. Some years later, Karl Meyer became the *Post*'s New York correspondent and, like his predecessors, was given a standing invitation to attend the magazine's weekly news conferences. "What a difference there was [between the] meetings where Kay was present and the ones where she wasn't." When she was absent, the meetings had "a locker-room atmosphere. It was all male. The minute she was in the room, the whole tenor of the meeting would change. And I think that [sexism] might explain a lot of her resentment."[64]

One *Newsweek* president described Osborn Elliott as making the mistake of not deeming Kay relevant. "Kay, I'll explain it to you when I get more time," was Elliott's method of dealing with her.[65] She tolerated that sort of treatment, she later claimed, because she was too overwhelmed to notice. "I didn't think, 'Oh, he's condescending because I'm a woman.' I thought, 'He's condescending because I don't know anything.' "[66]

But she devised her own way of paying these men back—by seeking the counsel of outsiders, the higher wisdom of influential male friends who were only too happy to court her. First she turned to Defense Secretary Robert McNamara, a former president of Ford Motor Company and, says Phil Geyelin, "always a great source of support and comfort and encouragement."[67] Polly Kraft, an artist who was married to political columnist Joseph Kraft, recalls how "Kay really counted on [McNamara's] business sense. She adored [him] and really listened to him, and [he] helped her have self-confidence about what she was doing. He was very gentle with her."[68] Arthur Schlesinger, Jr., a Harvard professor who had become special assistant to JFK, and John Kenneth Galbraith, then a professor at Harvard and an unofficial advisor to the president, were two others who counseled Kay, mainly in the editorial sphere. Whether or not it was Kay's intention, by calling on them for advice she signaled her contempt for the professional journalists, insinuating that they lacked the depth of her new set of brilliant men.

On Friday, November 22, 1963, Kay flew to New York on the company plane for lunch with the editors of her magazine and two guests—Schlesinger, whom she brought with her from Washington, and Galbraith, who had come from Cambridge for the meeting. As Oz Elliott would recall with some irritation, "Kay had invited the New Frontiersmen in to talk about *Newsweek,* particularly about how its 'back of the book' sections might be improved. I wasn't looking forward to the session; after all, who were these people to tell us how to run a magazine?"[69]

Kay showed her ignorance of weekly newsmagazines; she had chosen the worst day of the week for her get-together—Friday, the day before the issue closed. Having to chat up the owner and her friends while a magazine waited to be put out resulted in an under-tone of anxiety among the staffers. Kermit Lansner recalls that he and other editors "had been spelling each other, sitting with our guests, while the other guy[s] ran back and did something else." He was surprised when the door opened and he saw the red hair of a copy editor, who whispered his apologies and said, "There's a report on the wire that the president has been shot."[70]

Schlesinger ran off to make a phone call in search of more infor-mation; the rest went to Oz Elliott's office, where there was a televi-sion set. Schlesinger would later describe them as "huddled desperately around the nearest television. . . . In a few moments, Galbraith and I were on Katharine Graham's plane bound for Washington. It was the saddest journey of [my] life."[71]

Feeling the first twinges of power, Kay issued what was probably her first order—for Elliott to fire de Borchgrave, whom she blamed, as one *Newsweek* editor says, "for having thrown Robin in Phil's way."[72] Her evidence would not have held up in a court of law, but it was enough for her. "It was planted in Kay's mind," de Borch-grave says (he thinks by Emmet Hughes, who saw Robin Webb and him at La Maisonette after Phil's breakdown in Phoenix), "that somehow I had plotted the whole thing to get Robin into Phil's bed to feather my own nest for my career."[73]

But Kay did not have the confidence to push Elliott to do some-thing he refused to do, and he refused to fire de Borchgrave. "The compromise," says de Borchgrave, "was that I was to go abroad and get lost"; a "magnificent job" as chief foreign correspondent was created for him.[74]

De Borchgrave was not the only *Newsweek* man Kay resented. Other resentments would fester over time and grow more lethal, but she would let them go until she felt more secure.

When Phil's father died, on March 14, 1964, at age seventy-nine, Kay went to Miami for the funeral[75]—an event that must have been filled with poignancy, for she must have wondered what would have become of Phil had he returned to build his father's business. The line from Phil's front-page *Miami Herald* obituary probably haunted her: "The publisher once said that he never intended to spend his adult life in Washington."[76]

In the hands of Phil's brother Bill and half brother Bob, who had returned to Florida after graduating from Harvard Law in 1962, the Graham empire flourished.* As time went on, Kay could not help but see the striking parallels in the lives of Phil and Bob, and the striking difference: Bob would do with his life what Phil had only dreamed about. Bob dipped into the family business, made his fortune, then parlayed his Florida roots and relationships into a seat in the state legislature, turned that into the Florida governorship in 1978—the first Miamian in the state's history to accomplish that— and a U.S. Senate seat in 1986. George Smathers describes Bob Graham in terms once used for Phil: "the best political animal that I have seen come along since I don't know who . . . better than Kennedy, better than [Johnson], better than Truman, better than Nixon."[78]

Even when nearly a year had passed since Phil's death, his two younger sons seemed unable to grasp the frightfulness of it. Donny responded by becoming ever more disciplined and studiously sane, but Lally expressed her emotions otherwise, occasionally erupting in anger that her father would leave the family with such hideous permanence. She drew closer to her mother, who appreciated the companionship.

In July 1964, Kay and Lally went to the Republican National Convention in San Francisco and watched Barry Goldwater win the nomination. Kay did not have to be reminded that Phil would have been cruising the back rooms in pursuit of the real story. Her editors and top reporters did not brief her much because she did not seem all that hungry for information. "She was not uninterested," Ben Gilbert explains, "but it was not that kind of vacuum-cleaner approach to everything that Phil had."[79]

Gilbert also recalls how shaken she was by the hostility toward the press that pervaded the convention. Former president Eisenhower attacked "sensation-seeking columnists and commentators,"[80] and Richard Nixon joined him; Goldwater blasted the Newspaper Guild for being, like all unions, communist. Gilbert, sensing the concern of

---

*The Graham Company was devoted to cattle ranching and a dairy business. SENGRA was the land development and management company named to honor Bill and Bob's father, state senator Graham; its centerpiece, Miami Lakes, an innovative, self-contained community, remains a model of advanced city planning. By 1972, the Graham family would own 19,000 acres in Florida and Georgia; George Smathers would later estimate the family's wealth at well over $200 million.[77]

the new publisher, plotted an escape route through which he would lead the *Post* group should the crowd's anger overcome its reason. His fear seemed real, if exaggerated.[81]

In August 1964, again accompanied by Lally, Kay went to Atlantic City for the Democratic National Convention. Although she felt more at ease with the Democrats, the inevitable comparisons with Phil and his insider's role at the 1960 convention pointed up her inadequacies, she thought, and by convention's end she wanted nothing more than to return to Glen Welby for a rest. (It had not taken her long to start using the Virginia farm as a retreat, despite its association with Phil's suicide.)

Kay was at the airport, ready to leave in the company plane, but the takeoff was delayed: LBJ was arriving via helicopter to board *Air Force One,* and her plane could not take off before the president's. So there she waited, no stockings, her dirty, matted hair unattractively wrapped in a bandanna.[82] She did not want to see anyone, least of all the president of the United States, but there came Lyndon, lumbering over, commanding her to come along for the weekend to his Texas ranch with him and Lady Bird, and his running mate, Senator Hubert Humphrey, and his wife.

That April, President Johnson had invited Kay, Fritz Beebe, and other *Post* business and editorial higher-ups to lunch in the White House family dining room[83] so he could solicit the paper's support for his planned expansion of the American role in Vietnam. He was pleased but not surprised when the *Post* endorsed his escalation after the alleged attack on two American destroyers by North Vietnamese gunboats in the Gulf of Tonkin.*[84]

While he was delighted with the paper's editorials, Johnson became uneasy with its news coverage: the dispatch of a *Post* reporter to Saigon, and the resulting decrease in reliance on wire-service copy, had made it increasingly in-depth and critical.

The president did not say so to Kay, of course, but he wanted to be sure that the *Post*'s editorial columns did not go the way of its news columns; he wished to stem this creeping criticism. So he virtually scooped Kay onto *Air Force One,* sending his Secret Service agents to find her luggage. Lally returned home.[85]

Kay was flattered and admitted to being "goggle-eyed."[86] Had this trip been planned, she would have worked herself into a state of high

---

*The Tonkin Gulf Resolution, enthusiastically passed by Congress, authorized Johnson to retaliate and provided a mandate for future military action.

intimidation, but there was no time for that. She felt awkward around the president, and she sensed that he felt awkward around her; but he devoted himself to her that weekend, personally squiring her through waterskiing, picnics, and a visit to his elderly aunt. Kay recognized that he was currying favor with her, just as he did with important male publishers, and she appreciated it.

He talked movingly about how much he missed Phil, volunteering that he owed him his vice-presidential nomination. By weekend's close, Kay felt so emotionally bonded that she asked for some time alone with him. He motioned her to his bedroom, then sprawled on the bed while directing her to a chair. According to Deborah Davis, Kay told him "that in general she thought the two of them were in agreement politically, [and] that as much as she had admired President Kennedy, Phil had gotten along with him better [than] she had. She told Johnson that she respected the legislation he had gotten passed. She was for him, and she wanted to make sure he knew it. She said that her mother wanted to contribute to his campaign and wondered if there was any particular direction in which he would like it to go."[87] Johnson again gave her the administration line on Vietnam; she gave him a hug and a kiss.

He had her where he wanted her. In her note thanking him for the weekend, she wrote, "I feel exactly as though I were the heroine of one's childhood fairy tales, put on a magic carpet and carried in three swift hours into Never Never Land." She signed it "devotedly" and could not have been more complimentary, obsequious even. She also praised his choice of Hubert Humphrey as running mate, observing, "I felt that unlike Phil—*I* should not offer you political advice."[88]

That summer of 1964, Johnson had vowed repeatedly: "We are not about to send American boys nine to ten thousand miles to do what Asian boys ought to be doing for themselves."[89] Kay believed that promise and the rest of the administration's position on Vietnam, but she did not defy her editors' decision that the *Post* would continue its only-once-broken tradition of making no endorsement in a presidential race. That fall, in the presence of Russ Wiggins, she told the president so. When tears came to LBJ's eyes, reportedly, she added, "Oh, we're for you a hundred percent." Wiggins, much as he admired Johnson's Vietnam policy, was horrified.

Frank Waldrop was disappointed when Kay, in an interview with *Women's Wear Daily,* volunteered that any man could do a better job than she.[90] "She's smarter and tougher and colder than [Phil will] ever be," Waldrop had once told neighbors of Kay's. "She has guts."[91] Then, in the spring of 1964, she compounded her blunder in an interview with the industry trade magazine *Editor & Publisher,* saying she did not find it difficult to be a woman executive in a man's business because "after a while, people forget you're a woman."[92]

"Don't ever say that," Waldrop wrote her. "Keep them scared of you. If they don't do what you tell them, bust them. They should be proud to be working for you."[93]

When Elsie Carper saw the *Women's Wear Daily* piece, she was appalled. "I remember reading [it] and slamming the newspaper down on the desk and going up to see her and saying, 'Mrs. Graham, if you feel that way, then I ought to quit and every woman on this newspaper ought to quit.' " Carper's complaint, Kay would later recall, "made a deep impression on me."[94]

Some would say that Kay Graham never really changed her opinion of the capabilities of women. But little by little, this woman who believed in the innate superiority of men, who believed, at some level, that women who were aggressive and dominant would turn into monsters like her mother, began to catch on.

The boost in Kay's confidence in the year after Phil's death was striking. Joanna Steichen remembers lunch at Mount Kisco: "Kay was called to the phone and went two or three rooms away—they were long, long rooms, the doors were open—and you could hear this great booming voice and great booming laugh and a very authoritarian person, really utterly, fully in charge."[95] At a time when even professional women used their husbands' last and first names, Kay started to sign "Katharine Graham" instead of "Mrs. Philip L. Graham." She redecorated the bedroom she and Phil had shared. She began to see Phil in a colder, more objective light. And she stopped wishing aloud that Donny would hurry through Harvard and take over the paper. Any thoughts of selling the paper had vanished. When Samuel Newhouse, who still wanted the *Post,* asked Clark Clifford to sound Kay Graham out, Clifford was struck by her response: "She said flatly that she wanted to keep it, that it wasn't for sale to anyone, at any price."[96]

In late 1965, Polly Wisner's manic-depressive husband killed himself—in a manner eerily similar to that of Phil's suicide, delivering a shotgun blast to his head in the bathroom of his Maryland farm. Kay and Polly had been good friends, but this drew them even closer.[97] Kay's advice to Polly showed how far she had come: "We are not going to give up and do nothing except go to Europe and go out to lunch, and live like Washington widows."[98]

Harvey Segal, who headed a committee to persuade *Post* staffers to pledge to the United Fund, saw a striking new side of Kay, who, as Phil had in the past, was heading the Fund for the entire Washington area. At the time, representatives of the Red Cross threatened to run a drive separate from the Fund, their money source. "Katharine came in there and said, No way. She was great, she stiffened all of these spines. She said, 'Look, we're not going to be blackmailed,' and by God, the Red Cross didn't get one dime more than she wanted to give them. I suddenly realized that this lady knew how to use power."[99]

Jim Cannon was also impressed by Kay's take-charge style. After Phil's death, a friend who was deputy secretary of defense asked Cannon to come to work in government. Kay heard about it, called him in, and told him, "You don't want to do that. Those people over there, I know them all, and they will ruin you as they've ruined everybody else they've needed to use. You don't want them to use you, and I don't want them to use you. I don't want you to leave *Newsweek*." She offered him a job that existed at *Time* but not yet at *Newsweek*—chief of correspondents. "She showed confidence, concern, and professional consideration," Cannon said.[100]

Some recall that Kay had learned to use her vulnerability—"like a honeypot," as Karl Meyer put it.[101] Others called it the "poor little widow" act.[102]

But she was still insecure at heart, and physically weak. "She wasn't well," Jean Friendly says. "She had TB, another bout."[103] Stories of her fainting on the St. Albans tennis courts made the rounds, as did reports of her frequent lapses into apparent sound sleep at press dinners, testimonials, private dinner parties.[104] Although friends speculated about a medical cause for this behavior, her problem may have been nothing more serious than sleep deprivation—her habit of awakening before dawn to, as she put it, "redo my mistakes, play them over, let what I've done wrong gnaw at me. A lot of erosion takes place. I die a thousand deaths, especially after a public appearance."[105] She went to outlandish, time-consuming lengths to prevent mistakes from occurring. One *Post* staffer recalled going over a speech with her forty times before a company meeting.[106] She had a morbid fear of appearing uninformed, of being unable to anticipate questions.

*

On November 28, 1964, Lally, a senior at Radcliffe, married Yann Ralph Weymouth, Harvard '63, then an architecture student at MIT. Agnes considered Yann an almost perfect match for Lally. He was a distant cousin of George Weymouth, the realist artist, and moreover, son of Ralph Weymouth, a retired rear admiral.*

He did have one drawback—he was Catholic. While that was not as disturbing as bringing a Jew into the family, Agnes would have much preferred a Wasp. Weymouth reassured Agnes that he was not obnoxiously devout.

The ceremony was at the U.S. Naval Chapel in Washington, with the Reverend Virgil Timmermeyer, chaplain, officiating. Lally wore a white brocaded satin gown with a court train; the late-afternoon reception was at Kay's R Street house.

There was no shortage of celebrities at the pre-wedding luncheons and the ceremony—among them Adlai Stevenson, Hubert Humphrey, and Felix Frankfurter, who three weeks earlier had handwritten a touching note to Lally: "As your daddy's closest friend . . . I could not possibly feel deeper sorrow that he is not here to launch you on life's most potentially happiest adventure, but also its most exacting. . . . I know how much he loved you, how deeply he hoped that you would know happinesss and fulfillment, and how grateful he was for his delight in you and the happiness you gave him. For all these reasons I do not think I am deceiving myself when I say that he would have liked to have me lead you down the aisle . . . and nothing would have given me more pleasure." Were he not "disabled," Frankfurter added, "I would actually dare to invite you to put your arm through mine and walk you through the aisle."[107]

On the outside, at least, Lally was a conventional young woman. She had made her debut three years earlier at the Washington Debutante Ball given by her grandmother. She was marrying a Harvard man who had been a member of the Porcellian Club. They would be setting up housekeeping in Cambridge. Yet Kay had a sinking feeling as she sent her firstborn off with a set of disposable fry pans and a sweet-tempered husband who bore a striking physical resemblance to Phil. Kay told friends that she feared that Lally, whose strong personality recalled Phil's, would chew Yann up and spit him out for breakfast.[108]

*

*Yann's sister is Tina Weymouth, bass player for the Talking Heads.

Earlier that month, November 1964, Lyndon Johnson had invited Kay to the White House for a dinner celebrating his and Lady Bird's wedding anniversary. As Kay described the scene, "After dinner he was very preoccupied, and [at] about eleven or twelve, he left and went to bed, which meant that everyone could leave. I was saying good night to Mrs. Johnson. His bedroom was next to the Oval Room and he opened the door and said, 'Come here.' . . . I thought he was talking to someone behind me and I said, 'Who, me?' and he said, 'Yes, you.' Abe Fortas [a presidential advisor, soon to be appointed by LBJ to the Supreme Court] was standing on the other side of the room and he said to him, 'You too.'

"He got us both in the bedroom and the *Post* was lying on the bed. It had a big headline about [Walter] Tobriner [president of the D.C. board of commissioners] appointing a new police chief for Washington. The President had told Tobriner to tell him before he appointed anyone because he wanted to appoint some kind of superchief . . . to clean up crime. For some reason Tobriner, incredibly, had failed to tell him. He was furious. [The *Post*] had supported Tobriner's appointment, so somehow it was my fault.

"He just started dressing us down in the famous Johnson way, yelling at me and saying it was [the *Post*'s] idea to appoint this man who had done such a stupid thing. As he was doing that I . . . realized he'd started taking off his coat and shirt and tie, throwing them on the bed and talking all the time.

"I was pretty new at this sort of thing, and I could not believe that I was there in the bedroom, being dressed down by the President as he was getting undressed. I thought, When is he going to stop? He suddenly got down to the nitty-gritty and said, 'Turn around.' . . .

"When he had his pajamas on he got in bed and finished telling me off. Finally he said good night and Abe and I left."[109]

If Johnson was distressed about local coverage, he could not have asked for better editorial support on Vietnam. As David Halberstam observed about Kay, "She liked being respectable, and was very uneasy about being different from the norm. In the highest circles of Washington in 1965, those who dissented on Vietnam were different, were not quite with it."[110]

Kay was close to three of the capital's most committed hawks—Robert McNamara, McGeorge Bundy, and Joseph Alsop—all of them mentors. When the president had McNamara or Bundy call Kay with a "clarification" or a new angle, those points often found their way into the editorials. (Not because Kay demanded it, but because Johnson's men were also calling Russ Wiggins.) A writer for *Time* commented that "*Post* editorialists have often done a better job of explaining President Johnson's . . . policies than [has] the president himself."[111] Johnson exulted that "the *Post*'s editorials were worth fifty divisions."

One person close to Kay during this period says she became very susceptible to flattery, as was not surprising; the rarity of a woman in such a high position led inevitably to media celebration, to overblown praise. Henry Brandon, the London *Times*' man in Washington, was first in what became a long line to dub Kay the most powerful woman since Queen Victoria.[112]

McGeorge Bundy—"Mac" to friends—was, according to Harvey Segal, particularly shameless in his flattery (he too made the Queen Victoria comparison). As a member of the *Post*'s editorial board, Segal attended luncheons in Kay's private dining room at which key members of the administration or outside policymakers would address editorial writers, reporters, and editors. "Bundy used to, in effect, come over to keep the *Post* in line and keep it from being critical on Vietnam. It was embarrassing. He would obviously flatter her and at the same time turn on anybody who [disagreed]. One of the big things during the Vietnam period was the validity of the so-called body counts that McNamara was putting out. [Bundy] would try to crush [those who questioned or disputed the counts], destroy them, and then he would turn—I thought in a revolting way—and say something nice about her." Segal recalls Kay acting "deferential" toward Bundy. "I don't even know if she noticed what was going on."[113]

Karl Meyer, who had been writing *Post* editorials since 1956, thought that relations between the paper and the administration were too incestuous, and he pleaded with Kay in 1965 to send him to London. "Kay had at her dinner table, continually, the senior people in the government. All the senior editors at the *Post* were socially friendly with the secretaries of state, assistant secretaries of this, that, and the other." Meyer later left the *Post* for *The New York Times*, where he was able to "deal at more arm's-length distance with the people in power."[114]

In February 1965, Kay and Oz Elliott took a trip around the world, stopping in Japan and, for a few days, in the war zone in South Vietnam. They had been personally briefed by the commander in chief himself, who arranged for them to meet with General William Westmoreland, Ambassador Maxwell Taylor, McGeorge Bundy, then in Saigon on an official visit, and assorted top South Vietnamese officials. Kay and Elliott were helicoptered to a Green Beret outpost, toured strategic hamlets, secured areas, and delta villages surrounded by Vietcong.[115]

Just as Johnson had expected, the pair returned more gung-ho than ever. "Once you were there," Kay explained, "you had to do what was necessary to hang in."[116] According to David Halberstam, "She came home and talked with members of the editorial board, and some of them were dismayed by her tone. It was as if she had made a USO tour out there, it was all so wonderful."[117] Later, at a lunch in the *Post* dining room, Kay put the question of U.S. withdrawal from Vietnam to the assembled editors. City editor Stephen Isaacs was the only one who voted yes. "You're so stupid," she admonished him. "You're not thinking."[118]

Still, some of her people continued their critical reporting. Murrey Marder reported on the civil war in the Dominican Republic in 1965, in which the United States sent troops to bolster a military junta against communist rebels. Johnson was furious with the reporting by both the *Post* and *The New York Times,* and when Marder returned from vacation Al Friendly told him, "We're [going to] completely redo the Dominican crisis. The administration is screaming bloody murder." In hopes that he would see the light, Marder was given free access to State Department documents and spent days poring over papers, in the process discovering a cable that showed that the U.S. government had coached the right wing—first to request American troops, and second to request them as a means of saving American lives, rather than as a means of preventing a communist takeover of the country, the terms in which the junta's first request had been couched. "Al was astounded," Marder recalls, "because he [had] really believed what the State Department people told him."

Marder wrote his story, then even less along the lines the administration wanted, filling all but a quarter-page of the Sunday "Outlook" section.[119] Johnson was not amused. He could see that it was beyond Kay's power to control the news columns.

The president was, however, pleased with Agnes, whose reputation as a whirlwind of good works continued, and the plaques and testimonials to her accumulated. After he signed the Education Act of 1964, the landmark bill for federal aid to education, Johnson credited Agnes with persuading him of the need for federal funds in this area.[120] She also led the drive to establish a Cabinet-level Health, Education and Welfare Department. When presenting Agnes with an award in 1963, the superintendent of the District of Columbia's public schools revealed how she had anonymously "sponsored many programs that have helped the hungry and the unprotected in our schools."[121] Her friendship with Walter Washington, then executive director of the National Capital Housing Authority, resulted in quiet contributions to housing developments for the poor and the elderly.[122]

Agnes was the do-gooder liberal, so sympathetic and generous to large groups, yet so cruel and selfish to individuals, including her own children. While she was especially caustic about her youngest, Ruth, the Scarsdale housewife and mother (she called Ruth's friends "nobodies from nowhere"[123]), her disapproval of her son was equally snobbish. "Oh, I wish Bill would get a better house. He makes it such a point to live like everybody else, such an ordinary life," Joanna Steichen remembers Agnes complaining, although only in Agnes's estimation could Bill have been considered middle-class. One of his daughters said of their house on Cape Ann, in Massachusetts, "People used to mistake it for the yacht club."[124]

As for Kay, even her newfound prestige couldn't protect her. At a lunch she had arranged with architect I. M. Pei, Phil's friend and later hers, Kay responded to something Pei said: "I didn't know that." Agnes, who wanted to meet and cultivate Pei, shot back, "What's surprising about that? You've never known anything."[125]

Mel Elfin, *Newsweek*'s education editor, moved to Washington in 1965 as bureau chief, arriving just after John Gardner became secretary of HEW. When Agnes's National Committee in Support of the Public Schools met in Washington that year, she invited Gardner to be the convention speaker and asked Kay to introduce him. Giving a speech was hard enough for Kay, but the prospect of having Agnes in the audience, watching her every misstep, filled Kay with panic. She asked Elfin to write the introduction. "I put together two pages. The audience laughed and applauded. Kay comes off the stage and Agnes says to her, 'That was pretty good, Kay.' Kay beamed. I thought to myself, Is this the first time she ever said anything that nice to her daughter?"[126]

Even more daunting to Kay was the hobnobbing with world leaders that came so easily to Agnes and to Phil. Kay recognized that she would not always have the president and his men arranging her itinerary; that in every world capital she would need someone who knew the turf and the players.

Karl Meyer, who had been sent to London with Kay's intercession, was ambitious and sophisticated enough to be her entrée, and he quickly realized that the toughest part of his assignment was not covering London but satisfying Kay. He had some stiff competition from Pamela Berry, wife of the owner of *The Daily Telegraph,* who was, Meyer says, "an extremely well-informed political figure, an unrivaled source of accurate political gossip. [She] knew everything that was going on in London." Meyer would plan a dinner for Kay, who "expected Cabinet-level people," but it was Berry, with whom he was in a tug-of-war over Kay, who was getting them. He came to dread Kay's one or two annual visits. The pressure was such that Meyer would reproach himself for years for mistakes he made in lining up luminaries.[127]

In some respects, Kay remained a matron of exasperating narrowness, as if she were finally claiming one of the privileges of her birth—the right to behave like a spoiled brat, a right that had been largely denied her by Agnes and Phil, with their insistence that she constantly prove herself worthy of them. She once broke an appointment that Meyer had worked diligently to arrange, because it conflicted with her appointment with her hairdresser.

But there was about Kay such a hesitancy and honesty that Meyer could not stay angry long. He and the other men around her knew, after all, that it was only two years earlier that Phil had gone his messy way through London with Robin, making an ass of himself at every stop. That Kay could carry on under the burden of such memories was admirable.

"Kay once confided to me," Meyer recalls, "that she felt helpless socially. She said, 'You know, the only way I can visit foreign countries is if there is someone there who can hold my hand and take care of everything.' She was worried that people were scrutinizing her relentlessly."[128]

They were.

Chapter *14*

KAY AND BEN

Katharine Graham would soon give those who were watching her something to talk about. As long as Phil's people ran it, the *Post* would never be hers, so she set out to put in place men who owed their loyalty, their advancement, to her. Feeling more comfortable on the editorial than the business side, she started in the newsroom.

In the summer of 1964, just a year after Phil's death, she made her first stab at change, pleading with James Reston, the most take-charge man she could think of, to oversee the editorial side of both the *Post* and *Newsweek*.[1] She knew that Reston was dissatisfied at the *Times*. With the death of his friend and patron the publisher Orvil Dryfoos, and his replacement with Arthur Ochs "Punch" Sulzberger, Reston felt pushed out of the inner circle. The feeling was confirmed when Sulzberger named Turner Catledge executive editor. Reston reportedly didn't want the job, but he would have liked being asked.[2]

Probably at Kay's request, Walter Lippmann lobbied Reston to make the move. The *Times* was already the "foremost newspaper of the nation," Reston recalled Lippmann telling him, "and there was little I could do there except carry on the tradition, whereas the *Post* was just on its way to becoming a great newspaper and I could make a larger contribution."[3]

He could also make a lot more money. When Phil tried to hire Reston for the *Post* in 1953, he "got out a big yellow pad and jotted down a long catalogue of figures, doubling my salary, and adding offers of stock, family insurance, and other inducements. . . . 'Add them up, you dumb Scotchman,' he said."[4] Kay's offer was much more subtle: He could continue to write his syndicated column, and she would give him so much salary and stock that he would never have to worry about money again. But the answer was still no: "Your offer has touched all kinds of human feelings . . . but I just can't do it." He remained at the *Times,* where he felt he had more influence on policymakers.[5]

Apparently at Reston's suggestion, Kay next invited Robert Manning, who was still working for the State Department, to lunch. She planned not only to persuade him to join the *Post* but to have him enumerate the paper's deficiencies. Just the thought of taking a man to lunch made Kay anxious, so she asked managing editor Al Friendly to join them.*

As Manning recalls, the lunch started with Kay's "curious [questions] about what my plans were once my government service ended." Al Friendly "sort of turned it into an interview, as if I had applied for a job, addressing me as if I were a neophyte, [with] an insulting line of questioning. By that time I'd had a lot of experience in journalism, and I felt as if I were being addressed by someone who was considering hiring me as a copyboy." (Manning had worked for the United Press and *Time,* and as *New York Herald Tribune* Sunday editor.) Both he and Kay found themselves uncomfortable. It was obvious to him that Kay was too weak to control the tenor of the lunch and that Friendly was "feeling very threatened."[6]

Nothing came of the meeting, except that Friendly found out he had cause to worry and Kay learned not to invite the incumbent the next time she interviewed a prospective managing editor. The experience also gave Kay the opportunity to reflect on her vague discontent with the quality of the *Post*—and with Friendly. But she did not trust herself, and fell back to her habit of soliciting the opinions of the men she respected: What did they think of the *Post*?

Richard Clurman says he knows of at least three people—Reston, Lippmann, and himself—who told Kay "straight out that while her late husband was a great guy, he was a terrible newspaperman," and that "despite the loveliness of Al Friendly, and the goodness of Russ Wiggins, [the *Post*] was a crummy newspaper." Further, he recalls

---

*That was a perfect example of the colossal insensitivity for which Kay would become infamous. Whether she was aware of Phil's announcement in Europe that he was bringing Manning in as a potential managing editor—Friendly's replacement—is not known, however.

telling her, "Kay, don't confuse the paper with the radiance of Phil. The *Post* is not a good paper."[7]

That was hardly a novel opinion. "Rudderless, uninspired, unimaginative, with a demoralized staff and a lackluster performance," says Erwin Knoll, looking back at the *Post* in those years.[8] Bernard Nossiter was then making the rounds with a quip he admitted he stole from de Gaulle: "*The Washington Post* is like Brazil. It has a great future—and always will have."[9] I. F. Stone was then being widely quoted as saying the *Post* was an interesting paper, "because you never know on what page you'll find the front page." Indeed, the *Post*'s page one, with its lead story from a wire service and a handful of short reports not jumped inside, did not look very different from the front page of a small-town daily.[10]

Lippmann was troubled by the *Post*'s continuing editorial support of U.S. policy in Vietnam. "I think [he] felt we were pretty slavish in carrying out the administration's wishes," says Bob Estabrook, "as I, in retrospect, think we were."[11] Bob Manning felt that even "less adventurous" papers had begun to question the war. Wiggins and Friendly, Manning says, were "not riding the wave of the future."[12]

Kay needed a more concrete reason to get rid of Friendly, and she found it in his penchant for long vacations, a month in the spring and a month in the fall, at a house Jean Friendly had acquired on the south coast of Turkey. (Friends say he would have cut back had Kay expressed concern.)

"What plans have you for a successor?" Kay finally asked her old friend. According to Nossiter, Al mumbled something about the assistant managing editor: "Oh, I don't know. Jim Clayton [looks] like an interesting chap, but I haven't really thought it through."[13]

Kay was enraged. Her friends warned that if she did not do something fast she would end up owning a second-rate paper of negligible influence and murky future. Although she knew that the paper's deficiencies were not of her making, she also knew it would be her fault if things were allowed to slide further. She understood too that as long as the *Post* was in the hip pocket of people like McNamara and Bundy—the very people from whom she sought approval—it would never be a great newspaper.

Lippmann, as well as Edward Bennett Williams, had been telling her that Ben Bradlee, Washington bureau chief of *Newsweek,* had the energy, the charisma, and the ruthlessness to lead the *Post* from mediocrity to greatness.

Benjamin Crowninshield Bradlee, a Boston Brahmin by birth and a buccaneer by bearing, appealed to Kay almost in spite of herself. Witty, gravel-voiced, blasphemous, with the irreverence bred of high birth—descended from Salem, Massachusetts, shippers; educated at Dexter, St. Mark's, and Harvard, the fourth generation of his family to go there—Bradlee had the self-confidence (one critic called it a "preppy, tweedier-than-thou arrogance") to be a fascinating mass of contradictions. She decided to talk to him. It would not be easy to sit across the table from this man who knew more of the gruesome details of her husband's philandering than she did and whose cruel one-liner—"There's nothing wrong with Phil that a good divorce wouldn't cure"—had hurt so much, but she planned lunch with him anyway, at the private F Street Club.

"What do you want to do next?" she asked Bradlee at this meeting that was so awkward for her she vowed afterward never again to take a man to a business lunch. "Do you want to run *Newsweek*?" she ventured, more as a conversation starter, but also perhaps as a sign of early doubts about Oz Elliott. Bradlee looked her in the eye and said he was not interested in running *Newsweek,* but "I'd give my left one to be managing editor of the *Post*."[14]

Then, as Kay later recounted, he started to lobby her for the position, pestering her to make a decision: "And I kept saying, 'Ben, for God's sake, cool it.' And he'd say, 'Why? I'm ready.' And I said, 'Give me a little time.' And I thought, Well, is he being too pushy? And then I thought, Well, that's a sign of what we need."[15]

She offered Bradlee the chance to join the *Post* as deputy managing editor for foreign and national news—coequal with his former boss Ben Gilbert, who was deputy managing editor for local news—with the understanding that within six months he would replace Friendly as managing editor.

Many were scratching their heads: How in the world could Kay hire this man? Not only was he her nemesis, but he was casual in his approach to work. To Richard Clurman, he was a "playboy journalist, a gadabout semi-socialite."[16] At the same time, Bradlee was extracting from Kay the pledge that she was fully committed to making the *Post* a great national newspaper; that she would support him—and make money available—so he could hire good young reporters and open new bureaus; that she would freeze all vacancies until he arrived.

The fact Kay was willing to oust Al Friendly—hired by her father, and managing editor since 1955—showed that she meant it: the quality of the paper would come before comfort, friendship, and old family ties. And she demoted Friendly in a way that Jean—Kay's childhood playmate, one of Eugene's favorite bridge partners— would never forgive. Rather than tell him herself, Kay had Lippmann, Bradlee's biggest backer, take Al to the Metropolitan Club for lunch to break the news. "I would rather have heard it from you," he said to Kay afterward.

"Kay fired me," he told his wife, who described him as looking "pea-green and ice-cold. His life was over, because basically *The Washington Post* was more important to him even than his family. He just loved it so."[17] He was slated to head the American Society of Newspaper Editors[18] and asked Kay if he could stay on in some editorial capacity, because the ASNE president had to be currently employed as an editor. Bradlee said absolutely not, and Kay went along with him.[19]

Bradlee did not so much want Friendly out of the *Post* as he wanted him out of Washington, and so, in the tradition of Bob Estabrook, he was sent to London. He showed his mettle when, from his perch there, he set out to report on world events anywhere the *Post* did not have a correspondent. He won the Pulitzer Prize for his coverage of the Six Day War in the Mideast and was in Czechoslovakia the day Soviet troops crushed the Prague Spring.[20] But he would never really recover from being shunted aside. "He felt muscled out by Bradlee," says Estabrook.[21] "Bradlee couldn't wait," Jean comments, still bitter; it was "over Bradlee's dead body" that her husband's stories were given good play. She denounces Bradlee as "an opportunist, buttering up whoever needed buttering up at the time."[22]

If anyone snickered at the fact that he now doted on rather than ridiculed Kay, Bradlee had neither the inclination nor the time to care. He arrived at work early and, more often than not, stayed until the early hours of the next morning.

He took hold immediately. Some months before Kay deposed him, Friendly had offered Estabrook the job of chief of correspondents, domestic and foreign. Returning to Washington to assume his new post, Estabrook found Bradlee in charge and his own expectations dashed. "Russ Wiggins came to me and said, 'You never wanted to be chief of correspondents, did you? I want you to be my deputy.' I found out later that he did not mean deputy editor of the paper, he meant deputy editor of the editorial page, of which I had been editor. I spent a rather fitful year as deputy editor [of the editorial page]." Later, Estabrook recalls, "Bradlee remarked to me in passing, 'I queered that deal.' "[23]

Bradlee was building his own team of hard-nosed reporters and editors. He appointed Howard Simons to be his assistant managing editor, but for the most part hired from outside—such stars as David Broder from *The New York Times;* Stanley Karnow, who had been a foreign correspondent for *Time* and *The Saturday Evening Post* and a special correspondent for the London *Observer;* Richard Harwood from the *Louisville Courier-Journal and Times;* Ward Just from *Newsweek;* and Nicholas von Hoffman from the *Chicago Daily News.* The size of the newsroom staff doubled.

He quickly stamped the paper with his strong personality and preferences, haranguing reporters to look for what he called "holy shit" stories as opposed to "four-bowlers"—stories so boring that readers' heads were falling into their oatmeal at breakfast tables all over Washington. The first to smell a dull story, Bradlee once showed up at an editors' meeting with a toy siren, which he switched on whenever an editor proposed a story that was too dense or murky.[24]

Bradlee's stance was then studiously apolitical (he would not even reveal his position on the war in Vietnam), and his fawning relationship with Jack Kennedy behind him, he pushed his belief that boosterism, or "spin," had no place in the news columns. Ben Gilbert would later say that he did not know what Bradlee really believed in, outside of the Washington Redskins.[25]

Bradlee traded freely on his upper-crust connections,* sharing with Kay a penchant for snobbery, for judging employees by where they went to school. "I once heard him say he felt the social context of reporters was important," recalled Richard Harwood.[29]

Kay was privately and good-naturedly mocked for her "old-

---

*His father, Frederick "Beebo" Bradlee, was an All-American football player at Harvard and, in his son's words, "sort of a golden boy" (the model, it was said, for one of J. P. Marquand's proper Bostonians in *The Late George Apley*).[26] His mother was Josephine de Gersdorff, whose grandfather had been a founding partner of what was then known as Cravath, de Gersdorff, Swaine & Wood, the white-shoe Manhattan law firm that would later handle personal and corporate matters for the Meyers and the Grahams. His great-uncle Frank Crowninshield, an editor at *Vanity Fair*[27] in the 1920s, once said that he wanted the magazine to be read by "the people you meet at lunches and dinners."[28]

money lockjaw" speech, for her use of words like "divine" and "ghastly," for her limited knowledge of how ordinary people worked for a living. Writer Jane Howard described Kay asking a European correspondent, "Oh dear, you don't have to *live* on your *salary,* do you?"[30]

The other side of her snobbery was not amusingly anachronistic, but it helped explain her attraction to the Waspy Bradlee: she had no tolerance for people who were "too Jewish." German Jews with their origins so distant as to be invisible were one thing, but Jews who carried the mannerisms and accents suggesting pushcarts and Brooklyn and City College of New York were another. Once, while watching an interview with a *Post* editor on television, Kay turned from the set with an expression of revulsion on her face and said to those gathered in her office, "He's sure a schlump. He's so *Jewish.*"*[31]

Mel Elfin recalls a dinner Kay hosted for some visiting relatives of her father's, Alsatian Jews. In an apparent effort to make her guests feel comfortable, she invited Jewish editors—but then she served pork.[33] Some might see anti-Semitism in such behavior, but others, including one former top executive, see simply "upper-class snobbery." A Jew who looked right, talked right, acted right—who was, in other words, "presentable"—would be perfectly acceptable to her. For her employees to be "presentable," the executive adds, was "very important to her."[34] Mark Edmiston, later president of *Newsweek,* agrees more or less: "She would prefer someone who was tall, Christian, and well-dressed."[35] Someone like Ben Bradlee.

Bradlee looked dashing in white tie, but he was even more appealing growling at reporters, a leg rakishly atop his desk, sleeves rolled to his elbows. He swore like the sailor he once was, but also spoke exquisite French. When he was immortalized later in the film *All the President's Men,* he was the only person who was more attractive than the actor (Jason Robards) who played him.

Bradlee would develop a cult-hero status. "In the way that airline pilots have for years mimicked Chuck Yeager's assured West Virginia drawl," observed one writer, "so too have the young bulls at the *Post* attempted to make themselves over in Ben Bradlee's profane club-man image. Thus the archetypal male *Post* reporter or editor is lanky and tall [and] swears like a longshoreman. The more aggressive

*The man in question was said to be Howard Simons, the son of Polish immigrants, who would be more responsible than anyone for bringing her paper its Watergate fame.[32]

careerists . . . wear broadly striped Turnbull & Asser shirts. Just like Ben."[36]

Lawrence Kramer, a *Post* reporter and editor who became executive editor of the *San Francisco Examiner,* is not alone in attributing to Bradlee almost mythic qualities. "He can say more with an action, without saying anything, than anybody I know. Just the way he walks around a room. You just felt it. Everything he did had something to it."[37]

Lally had chosen as her husband a man who resembled Phil physically; Kay, who, friends explain, had decided to marry herself to *The Washington Post,* chose for it a man who resembled Phil in personality. The man who ran the paper—not only pushing Al Friendly out of the managing editor's slot but also replacing Russ Wiggins as executive editor—would become a sort of nominative husband.

"Ben surely reminds Kay of Phil," said Bernard Nossiter.[38] "Kay liked volcanic men who, by God, set out and took what they wanted," says Eugene Patterson,[39] who was soon to become the *Post*'s managing editor. Bradlee also shared with Phil the ability to make Kay laugh—and Phil *could* make Kay laugh when he was not making her cry.

But Bradlee could not play by Phil's rules, and he was smart enough to know that. Kay no longer had to abide a man who did not respect her. Peter Derow, a *Newsweek* executive, and for a time chairman, says that Kay "respects brashness" but the brash person must be "someone who respects her, never puts her in a compromised position."[40] Mark Edmiston agrees: Bradlee was constantly in the limelight, but not at Kay's expense.[41] In fact, totally dependent on her for his job, he would now take Kay's side over all others. Edward Kosner, who would become editor of *Newsweek,* says Kay knew that Bradlee "would lay down his life, that Ben was fiercely loyal to her, to the *Post,* and that he would sacrifice himself for the good of the *Post.*"[42]

Bradlee knew precisely how to work his charm on Kay. "Like Phil," says Karl Meyer, "[he] exudes an irrepressible charm, saying all the things you might say about what he's just done and then winning your sympathy and then seducing you."[43] "I know I'm a shit," Bradlee would comment when he did something that angered Kay. She could not help but smile.

Others quickly recognized that he could get most anything he wanted from her. "The Kay card" became newsroom shorthand for that ability.[44] Ben Gilbert tells of the time that Bradlee decided to have the metropolitan editor and the foreign editor switch jobs. "[He] had not told her of his plan, but Kay heard about it the next morning (it had been announced in the newsroom) and came steaming toward Bradlee's office. She told him: 'It's the silliest thing I ever heard [assigning the two men to desks that they knew little about].' Bradlee put his arm on her shoulder, led her into his office, and closed the door. After thirty minutes, she emerged and said: 'Maybe you are right. It may work.' "[45]

Bradlee would spend many evenings at Kay's Georgetown house discussing ideas, building her confidence, hiding his natural impatience when she did not get things fast enough. He told her that she was the one with the power, that she could become more powerful than the president of the United States. In the end, like the rest, he became a flatterer, but he did it with style and humor. "When she was being pompous," wrote David Halberstam, "Ben Bradlee would tell her that only the most powerful woman in the world could say something that arrogant."[46]

Anybody who was near them much noticed the obvious sexual pull—studied on his part, genuine on hers. "When she was around, he seemed to strut just a little bit more," Halberstam observed. "His voice became . . . rougher and a little raspier. She . . . seemed almost schoolgirlish."[47] According to former *Post* reporter and editor William Greider, "Her relationship with Bradlee has sort of an animal energy to it on both sides, which is not quite the same as sex and love."[48] Former city editor Stephen Isaacs told a *Vanity Fair* writer about a meeting in Kay's office to which Bradlee was late—and, Isaacs said, on purpose. "We're sitting in there and you could hear Ben coming. It was almost like an animal growl. . . . He entered the room, and he had rolled up his sleeves—and I know he had rolled up his sleeves [for effect] because I had seen him in the newsroom not long before and his sleeves had not been rolled up. . . . He has extremely muscular forearms—and he had done it to reveal this muscle to Kay. . . . The sexual energy of him, and her titillation [were] about as obvious as my stomach. . . . I once asked her about it and she acted like a little girl . . . denying it, but in fact it was very clear: she was very much, and I don't mean this in a carnal way, she was very much in love with Ben."[49]

It was no surprise that Tony Bradlee—artistic, spiritual, determined to have a close family life*—and Kay did not like each other. A close friend of Tony's, Polly Kraft, insists that Tony and Kay did not dislike one another. "They just had nothing in common. They weren't really interested in each other. Kay and Ben had a common interest in the *Post,* and Tony was not interested in the *Post* or politics."[50] Much as he would have liked to be at Kay's A-list parties, "Ben simply didn't go," says Phil Geyelin. "And the main reason he didn't go, I think, was that they bored the hell out of Tony."[51]

Kay was coming out of her shell, but not fast enough for her UN Plaza neighbor and newfound confidant, Truman Capote, who decided to throw the Black and White Ball at New York's Plaza Hotel in November 1966 to introduce Kay to the people who really mattered. "It was the first big party ever given in her honor," says Richard Clurman.[52] Capote saw that Kay needed to be brought out, and the notion that this was a middle-aged coming-out ball gained currency. (Kay herself later described it as "an odd, overaged and gray coming-out party."[53]) Capote told a *Washington Star* reporter that Kay had been so "beaten down" by her mother and husband that "she hadn't built up an identity. She's a person who's only twelve years old. . . . People kept saying, 'Who is this Mrs. Graham that Truman is giving a party for?' They didn't have the faintest idea."[54]

Capote was determined to make the powerful, rich, and glamorous notice the dowdy Mrs. Graham, who just happened to own one of the potentially most profitable media properties in the world.†

"It was a big event," says Richard Clurman. "People were flying to Europe so they didn't have to say they weren't [invited to] the party." What Capote had billed as "The Ball of the Decade" soon became "The Party of the Century." Polly Kraft remembers it as "the most glamorous party I had ever been to."[56] The designer Halston remarked: "I've never seen women putting so much serious effort into what they're going to wear."[57]

Capote made up the guest list, allowing Kay only five invitations.

*She had four children from her first marriage and two with Bradlee.
†As the *New York Herald Tribune* neared death, the *Post* in 1966 acquired part-ownership of its Paris edition, renamed the *International Herald Tribune* after the parent paper folded. The acquisition brought, as *Post* historian Chalmers Roberts wrote, "a major new source of prestige for the *Post*. . . . For the first time many important . . . people discovered that there was another must-read American paper besides the *Times,*"[55] which later became another owner of the paper. The *Trib* was composed largely of stories from the *Post* and the *Times*.

Among the names on his list were Giovanni Agnelli, the president of Fiat, and his wife, Marella; William and Babe Paley, Norman Mailer, Frank Sinatra, Rose Kennedy, Lee Radziwill, Lauren Bacall, Philip Roth, Walter Lippmann, Lillian Hellman, Samuel Newhouse, Cristina Ford, William F. Buckley, Jr., Marianne Moore, Claudette Colbert, Pamela Hayward, Charlotte Ford, Tallulah Bankhead, Cecil Beaton, Harry Belafonte, Candice Bergen, Irving Berlin, Leonard Bernstein, Richard Burton, Bennett Cerf, John Kenneth Galbraith, Shirley MacLaine, Alice Roosevelt Longworth, Marisa Berenson. Greta Garbo was one of the few no-shows.

Clurman recalls Kay as "nervous"; others say she was very excited. Kraft likens her to "a little girl who had been given a great big all-day sucker. 'You mean, for me? For me?' "[58] That afternoon at Kenneth's, the exclusive Manhattan hairdressing salon, Kay headed to the second floor, where the unimportant customers went, rather than to the third, where the renowned gathered. A hairdresser told Kay in passing that the salon was overwhelmed by the Black and White Ball; had she heard about it? "You won't believe it, but I'm the guest of honor," she replied. She was sent straight up to Kenneth, although, she noted, she "had to wait while Marisa Berenson had curls placed all over her head."[59]

Karl Meyer says the ball was a milestone in Kay's transition from shy widow—she described herself at the time as living like a monk—to international powerhouse.[60] That *Vogue* magazine chose to run a gushing profile of her by her friend Arthur Schlesinger, Jr., in its January 1967 issue was, undoubtedly, a direct result of the ball.

Capote and Kay became so close that they cruised the Aegean together, and Kay gave a party in Washington in honor of the publication of *In Cold Blood.* Then, as he did with other women friends, he violated the trust of discretion by exposing her private life to reporters. (He told *Star* reporter Lynn Rosellini, for example, that Kay's mother "never had a nice thing to say about Kay in her life. And then Kay married that bad number. . . . There was something about his total non-Jewishness that appealed to her."[61])

To some at the *Post* who were keeping their noses to the grindstone, the Capote extravaganza was troubling. Harvey Segal remembers Alan Barth, the unshakably liberal editorial writer hired by Kay's father, as "privately horrified by that ball. He expected more from Kay, more social consciousness." One wit quipped that the guest roster read like "an international list for the guillotine."[62]

*

The preeminent topic for the *Post* in 1966 was the war in Vietnam, and how the paper should cover it. For Kay, the matter was complicated by the situation of her own son and heir, Donny, who graduated from Harvard in June and could have started the climb to the top of the *Post*. Instead he decided to enlist in the military, and he could not be dissuaded. Although Kay, just starting her own climb at the paper, was no longer impatient for him to take over and sympathized with his desire for real-life experience, she was not happy with his decision. Donny, in keeping with the *Post*'s line on Vietnam, was opposed to unilateral withdrawal—at *The Harvard Crimson* he had been so prowar that he was once presented with a live hawk—but he could not accept the inequities of the selective service system. Lally later explained that he went because "he thought it unfair that rich kids could get out of the draft."[63]

Two months after graduation, Donny received his orders. He spent a year in Vietnam, in the public information office of the First Cavalry Division, working mostly as a photographer on the division's magazine and newspaper. Writer Barbara Matusow reported that although he tried earnestly to remain anonymous, Senator Edward Kennedy arrived in Vietnam requesting a meeting with PFC Graham. "From then on, the major in charge of Graham's unit tried to prevent him from going into combat situations. The major figured he would be finished if anything happened to his very important charge."[64] Donny had been in Vietnam barely a week when he decided the United States should get out.

Despite Donny's doubts and Kay's growing independence, the *Post* remained squarely in President Johnson's corner. And it did so long after other papers, such as the once hawkish *New York Times,* began to waver. On Christmas Day, 1966, Harrison Salisbury reported on the *Times'* front page that U.S. bombing of Hanoi had resulted in residential and civilian casualties—contradicting official statements that no U.S. bombs were being dropped on the city. Meanwhile, *The Washington Post* editorialized that the attacks were "the most restrained bombing of modern war," and on New Year's Day, the *Post*'s George Wilson scolded Salisbury for citing casualty figures "identical to those in a communist propaganda leaflet."

Four months later, after Dr. Martin Luther King, Jr., preached from the pulpit of Riverside Church on Manhattan's Upper West Side on April 4, 1967—"I could never again raise my voice against the violence of the oppressed in the ghettos without having first spoken clearly to the greatest purveyor of violence in the world today, my own government. . . . I speak for the poor of America, who are paying the double price of smashed hopes at home and death and corruption in Vietnam"—the *Post*'s lead editorial warned: "Many who have listened to [Dr. King] with respect will never again accord him the same confidence." That, like many of the paper's pro–Vietnam war editorials, was written by executive editor Russ Wiggins, an unreconstructed hawk. His rule that "no one ever had to write an editorial contrary to his own beliefs" meant that his staff, all of whom opposed the war, were silenced.[65]

The *Post* stood fast in Johnson's corner in May 1967, when the *Washington Star* appealed for a bombing halt, as had other mainstream publications, including *Life,* the *Los Angeles Times, The Miami Herald,* the *Richmond Times-Dispatch.*[66] People whom Kay trusted and respected, Walter Lippmann among them, told her that the *Post* must change its position. LBJ was incensed at Lippmann, the man he had once called "the greatest journalist in the world" and of whom he had boasted, "He is a friend of mine." According to Karl Meyer, Johnson had "his staff comb through old columns in quest of Lippmann blunders. . . . These were then maliciously read aloud at White House dinner parties." The two stopped speaking, high administration officials boycotted social events that Lippmann might attend, and he soon wrote his farewell column and left Washington, which, he explained, he no longer found hospitable.[67]

Kay was relieved that Wiggins was scheduled to retire in December 1968. In the meantime, she and Bradlee, with advice from Lippmann, had been lining up their new players. Both Bradlee and Lippmann were pushing hard for Philip Geyelin, forty-four, then *The Wall Street Journal*'s chief diplomatic correspondent.

The campaign to hire Geyelin, whom Phil Graham had tried to hire twice, had resumed in 1966, when, on orders from Kay and Bradlee, Russ Wiggins again called in Bob Estabrook: "How would you like to be the new UN bureau chief?" Wiggins asked him. Although it meant a thirty-percent cut in salary, Estabrook says, he saw no alternative, "so I started a new bureau. This was Kay's way of getting me out of the way."*[68]

---

*Later, in 1971, when Estabrook told Kay that he was quitting as UN correspondent, her response to the twenty-five-year *Post* veteran was, "Oh, good, we can close the UN bureau." According to Karl Meyer, who as the *Post*'s New York correspondent shared offices with Estabrook, "Bob was crushed. It was the only time I ever heard him utter a bitter remark about that family."[69]

Geyelin signed on as an editorial writer in 1967 and became editor of the page in 1968. As deputy editor he chose Meg Greenfield, a Washington editor for the liberal *Reporter* magazine, who had developed a reputation as a writer of great force and originality.

Before he accepted the job, Geyelin spent a weekend with Kay discussing "whether she and I were ideologically compatible on a whole range of questions. She was uncomfortable with the *Post*'s position on Vietnam. And she really did want to turn us around, but she did not want to go to the mat right away." They agreed that Geyelin would slowly move the editorial page off its pro–Vietnam war course, because, as Geyelin explains, "if you changed the position of a newspaper 180 degrees just overnight, it's very unsettling to readers."[70]

But in the months before Wiggins left and Geyelin took the top spot, even his mild questioning of the war sparked shouting matches. Frank Waldrop sneers that "Russ Wiggins was running the *Post* editorial page as an alibi for Lyndon Johnson."[71] Geyelin recalls that at editorial meetings in 1967, "[Wiggins] would say 'I'm told . . .' and I would know that [Secretary of State Dean] Rusk or Johnson had called him. He had a sense of being pretty well wired in and was talking at a higher level than I was."[72]

Johnson was good and angry at the *Post,* but he did not necessarily blame Kay, who he believed was being used by the likes of Lippmann, Geyelin, and especially that haughty favorite of John Kennedy's, Bradlee—"the Georgetown set."[73] As late as December 8, 1967, Kay was still sending the president self-effacing notes of sympathy: "These times are so difficult that my heart bleeds for you. . . . It seems that the burdens you bear . . . are almost too much for one human being. The only thanks you ever seem to receive is a deafening chorus of carping criticism. Unlike Phil, I find it hard to express emotion. I can't write in the eloquent words he used. But I want you to know I am among the many people in this country who believe in you and are behind you with trust and devotion."[74]

This was an expression partly of her natural subservience to powerful men, and partly of her fear that Johnson would withdraw the access to the White House that she had come to enjoy; but it was also an expression, insists Geyelin, of Kay's conflict over Donny's service in Vietnam. "She would have found it very difficult to be presiding over a newspaper opposing the war that her son was fighting."[75]

*

Other clashes were occurring between the old-timers, such as Ben Gilbert, and Ben Bradlee and the clique of reporters in whom he had already inspired fanatical loyalty. Robert Kaiser, for example, with degrees from Yale and the London School of Economics, was covering the District of Columbia just as it was making the transition from being governed by the U.S. Congress to home rule. So intensely did Gilbert want home rule to succeed that he had no compunction about censoring stories that might impede it—including a piece Kaiser wrote about a black teenager being accosted by the police. Kaiser asked Bradlee to step in, and after a loud exchange, the piece ran.[76]

The irrevocable break occurred in 1967, just before the final step toward home rule, when President Johnson decided to appoint Walter Washington as the District's first mayor-commissioner. This was a victory for Gilbert, who had been grooming his friend Washington for the job.

Kay Graham also had been grooming Washington. (Her and Bradlee's first choice was Edward Bennett Williams, but Johnson felt he needed a black.) According to Gilbert, *Post* executive vice-president John Hayes was pushing for John Duncan, who had been the commissioner since 1961. "The White House wanted a recommendation, and so Kay had a meeting—John Hayes, Ben Bradlee [and me]—and we debated the merits of these two people. Kay sent word that she preferred Walter Washington." Gilbert calls Kay's decision "noteworthy," because kingmaking on the local level had historically been the exclusive province of the Kauffmanns and Noyeses of the *Star*.[77] Unlike Phil Graham, Kay and Bradlee would not let their preference stand in the way of a scoop. When the president made his decision to appoint Washington, Gilbert was tipped off, perhaps by Washington himself, but he was warned that the tip was strictly off the record. Gilbert told Bradlee "in confidence." Bradlee ordered city editor Stephen Isaacs to get the story, and he assigned several reporters, including Elsie Carper, who confirmed the lead by verifying that the FBI was completing a background check on Washington.

Gilbert recalls that LBJ's special assistant Joseph Califano "called [Bradlee] to ask him not to use the story because of his fear that LBJ would change his mind"—no one doubted that Johnson was capable of wrecking Washington's chances just to punish Ben Bradlee and his boss. "There was no better way to get Ben to run a story than to pressure him not to," Gilbert continues.[78] Califano, reportedly at

Gilbert's behest—although Gilbert denies this—called Kay to appeal
to her known preference for Washington and to warn her of the
consequences. This was not the Kay Graham to whom Johnson and
his men had grown accustomed: she backed Bradlee, coolly informing Califano that it was not the *Post*'s business to make Walter
Washington mayor.[79]

No one told Gilbert. As Isaacs would later recall, he and Bradlee
"dummied a phony story on page one so that Gilbert wouldn't know
we'd gotten the story." That evening, Bradlee and Isaacs went to a
party at Gilbert's home and did everything possible to keep the news
from him—blocking calls and intercepting the driver who delivered
the first edition of the *Post* to senior editors' homes each night.[80]

When he found out, Gilbert was livid. He charged Bradlee with
showing a lack of confidence in him. In his rage, he may have missed
the dual message: From then on the *Post* would act as reporter, not
player. With Kay's blessing, Gilbert had been stripped of his power
and Bradlee now controlled the newsroom.[81]

LBJ, predictably irate, waited several months before announcing
the appointment.[82] In the meantime, whenever a *Post* story or editorial or reporter displeased him, he ordered his assistant Jack Valenti
to "call Kay Graham and ask her how that stupid SOB could write
that." Valenti told Lynn Rosellini that during the first calls Kay
reacted with "anxiety and timidity," but gradually developed a kind
of amused and ironic detachment.[83]

Later in 1967, recognizing that bold action was needed—perhaps
in one of his manic states when he believed that control was just a
phone call away—the president of the United States telephoned the
president of *The Washington Post*: "I was with her in her house in
Washington," Roswell Gilpatric recounts, "when a call came
through from President Johnson and he asked Kay if she would meet
with Clark Clifford. Johnson was trying to engineer a transfer of
control of ownership of the *Post* into other hands. I thought she
handled it very properly: deferential to the president, but just as firm
as she could be—the *Post* was not for sale and not even the president
of the United States was going to change her mind. I think [Johnson]
thought he would bowl over Kay, the widow who didn't know what
it was all about."*[84]

---

*Clifford says he has "no recollection" of Johnson's ever asking him to take on such a task,
although it is possible that the president made the approach first and planned to bring Clifford

With her refusal, the gloves came off. "[Johnson] stopped speaking to me, literally, for a while," Kay recalled. "Even if I saw him in a big group he would not speak to me. I mean he wouldn't say hello. I didn't even get asked to tea for two thousand at the White House."[88] If the president answered her overtures at all, it was with an icy note.[89]

Things cooled on her side too when she began to reflect on how Johnson had, in late fall 1967, in effect pulled out of the Cabinet her friend Bob McNamara, who seemed to Johnson to be turning alarmingly dovish. She called LBJ's treatment of McNamara "really terrible."[90] (Clark Clifford, who had opposed the war early on, but who publicly stood behind Johnson and every escalation, replaced McNamara.)

Yet for all her anger, Kay did not want to see Johnson go. He had become the adversary, but at least he was a familiar one. She watched in dismay as antiwar candidate Senator Eugene McCarthy made a spectacular showing against him in the New Hampshire primary on March 12, 1968. And on March 31, when Johnson made the incredible announcement, "I shall not seek, and I will not accept, the nomination of my party as your president," it is said that Kay Graham wept.[91]

The now lame-duck president told her, with enormous sadness, "If Phil were running the paper it would have been a different presidency for me."[92]

When George Ball* resigned as ambassador to the UN so that he could openly support Hubert Humphrey in the presidential campaign, LBJ asked Russ Wiggins to replace him. Kay was happy to see him go, three months ahead of schedule, in September 1968, and his departure severed the few remaining threads of civility between the *Post* and the White House.

---

in later. George Reedy calls the notion of Johnson's engineering a takeover of the *Post* "implausible." But like others, he says it is possible that Johnson was putting out feelers, that had he sensed the slightest receptivity or wavering in Kay, he would have pounced and put others (Clifford, perhaps) to work to ease the *Post* into friendlier hands.[85] "Johnson was testing something," speculates Frank Waldrop. "She might have been scared and yellow and wanted to run for the money, and if he heard the right sort of echo, he'd say, 'All right, let's get to work and get the money.' "[86] William Greider, who, like Waldrop and Reedy, had not heard of the approach, conjectures that Johnson was "just putting the squeeze on her. That's the sort of mind game these folks play with each other: You're not in the club anymore. We want to buy your newspaper."[87]

*As LBJ's undersecretary of state, Ball had been a quiet critic of the administration's Vietnam policy—and a source for Phil Geyelin.

Finally, Ben Bradlee became executive editor with responsibility for the news side, reporting to Kay. Phil Geyelin, who had responsibility for the editorial page and also reported to Kay, recalls that he and Bradlee "made a pact early on: I would never set foot in a story conference and he would never set foot in an editorial conference."[93]

Bradlee's job as managing editor was now open. It should have gone to deputy managing editor Ben Gilbert, and when Kay and Ben Bradlee decided on an outsider, Eugene Patterson, Gilbert knew his days were numbered.

Patterson, a war hero, a member of LBJ's civil rights commission, a recipient of an honorary degree from Harvard, and a Pulitzer Prize winner for his editorials on race relations while he was editor of *The Atlanta Constitution,* arrived at the *Post* just one day after Wiggins left to become UN ambassador. "Ben understood that vacuums need to be filled instantly," Patterson says. "Well, he filled Russ's vacuum by moving right into his office and becoming executive editor. Then he knew that there would be a tremendous power struggle within the existing cadre of editors for the managing editor's job, and so he [had to] fill that in a hurry, and he picked me from the outside. That's not a very comfortable way to be installed. It was very hurried and the knives were out."[94]

One of the people who were upset was Howard Simons. Kay confided to Patterson that "she had Howard out to the farm one weekend to put him back together. Simons suggested to her that my coming would indicate to him that she was ashamed of her Jewishness."[95]

Patterson's first personnel move was to strip Ben Gilbert of most of his power. When he was managing editor, Bradlee, who was bored by local news, let Gilbert keep the metropolitan side answering to him. To Patterson, that made "second-class citizens out of all the metro reporters. They should report to the managing editor, just as the national side does. I told Gilbert I was going to make that change and announce it at a staff meeting, and that I didn't want this to look like a demotion for him. I gave him a lot of other duties that he had not [previously] carried, but it clipped [his] wings."[96]

Some months earlier, after the assassination of Martin Luther King, Jr., Gilbert had undergone a graver humiliation when one of Bradlee's new hires, Nicholas von Hoffman, was given the plum assignment of writing the lead story on King's funeral. Von Hoffman, a writer of dramatic and provocative style, told Bradlee and national editor Larry Stern, "Look, every step of this is going to be covered by television, so if we do the standard news thing, we're going to be telling our readers what they already know because they will have seen it with their own little eyeballs." Bradlee and Stern agreed. "The Rev. Dr. Martin Luther King Jr. led his last march today. He was in a cherrywood coffin, carried in an old farm wagon hitched to a pair of downhome mules," began the story, which is now included in many journalism textbooks.

"Ben Gilbert had a fit," according to von Hoffman, "and said, 'There's no way that you're going to lead *The Washington Post* with this piece of garbage. This is nothing but a very bad, very long sidebar.'" Stern disagreed and called Bradlee, who was out of town, to settle the dispute.[97]

Gilbert still sounds angry when he remembers the incident: "It was not a lead-the-paper story. It was a feature. Also, it endeavored to put down the whole affair and denigrated Dr. King. [Von Hoffman] called it a cherrywood casket when everybody else called it mahogany. I told Larry Stern the story had to be modified or we had to use something else as the lead."[98] Small changes were made as a compromise. But the future, obviously, belonged to Ben Bradlee and his stable of stars.

Gilbert was vilified. "No man was more hated in my time on that newspaper," says Nicholas von Hoffman.[99] Kay joined in by blaming Gilbert for, among other things, the defection of Tom Wolfe, in 1962, to the *New York Herald Tribune*. "Kay [felt] that I allowed this brilliant 'journalist' to leave the *Post*." Gilbert had assigned him to write about the Prince Georges County government. Wolfe described it as the "sewer beat."[100]

Not surprisingly, Gilbert developed an ulcer. Bradlee is said to have phoned Gilbert's wife to ask about his health, and when she told him that her husband was about to undergo a blood transfusion, Bradlee quipped, "Blue, I hope."[101]

Before long, Gilbert came to Patterson and told him, "Look, I don't have a place in this newsroom anymore. My wife said to me the other night, 'Your telephone doesn't ring anymore.'" After an unhappy stint as an editorial writer on metropolitan affairs, he left the *Post* in 1970.[102]

Kay decided to take a much more active role in the 1968 political conventions. She accepted an invitation to be on the *Meet the Press* panel questioning New York governor Nelson Rockefeller the day before the opening of the Republican National Convention in Miami Beach, although she was almost immobilized at the prospect of looking foolish beside fellow panelists Otis Chandler, publisher of the *Los Angeles Times*; John Knight, publisher of *The Miami Herald*; Vermont Royster, editor of *The Wall Street Journal*; and Ralph McGill, publisher of *The Atlanta Constitution*.[103] According to Mel Elfin, she recruited him, David Broder, and Chalmers Roberts to prepare her. First they wrote questions, and then, as she delivered them, they played the role of the candidate, even staging a dress rehearsal at the WTOP studios in Washington. "She barely opened her mouth," Elfin recalls of the real event.[104] She would later describe it as "a disaster."[105]

Now that Johnson had withdrawn his candidacy, and with the upheaval in the country over the war, and the riots after King's death, Kay was moving toward supporting the same Richard Nixon whom Phil had embraced in 1952 and then harshly rejected. In July 1968, she invited Nixon to lunch at the *Post* with her editors. He was suspicious and unreceptive. Still, when he won the nomination, she suggested an editorial that praised his "commendable comprehension of some aspects of the nation's social ills." Nixon, seasoned and experienced, the editorial claimed, was the right man to lead the country through this turmoil.[106]

At home, meanwhile, Kay was contending with Agnes, who continued drinking uninhibitedly. Joanna Steichen, who vacationed with her in Barbados, remembers that the butler had to help his fat and disheveled employer down to the beach. "The last winter there was terrible. She was drunk most of the time, falling down, bad enough that Kay had the *Washington Post* plane meet our plane at Kennedy."[107] Harvey Segal recalls once seeing Agnes when she was "just sort of numb with alcohol."[108]

Agnes was so unmanageable that her children intervened, and she improved. "She had made [a] really monumental effort to stop drinking," explains Joanna Steichen. "She did it in a very comfortable way. The head of psychiatry at the George Washington University Medical Center would come by her house for a session every morning. Of course, the family had donated a whole wing to the hospital, and he wouldn't charge her. In those last couple of years, she was apparently managing to limit her drinking, at least much of the time when people were around, so that she was pretty lucid."[109]

Her drinking may have been tamed, but not her ego, which then verged on the preposterous. When Agnes invited Paul Ignatius (who had gone from being secretary of the Navy to being president of the *Post*), his wife, and several others to lunch, she "dominated the entire conversation. Nobody got a word in edgewise." When Nancy Ignatius expressed an interest in China, Agnes "clapped her hands, one of these Victorian maids came into the room, and she sent her up to the attic [to get] a piece of Chang bronze. Whereupon [Agnes] had a new platform on which to talk, mainly on how really she was more responsible than Mr. Freer for collecting the great Chinese works of art—and we were off again."[110]

Agnes also took to bragging that she, not Eugene, was responsible for building the family's fortune. Ignatius says Kay told him of Agnes's claim that while her husband was investing in copper mines in Chile she was buying Cézannes.[111] Agnes complained, "I never received any credit for making good investments on my own. I bought those paintings after I was married and had some money. The most I ever paid for one was $10,000. Now they are worth millions."[112] Eugene, in fact, paid for everything—her past debts, her future debts, her father's debts, and the paintings.

And then there was Donny. Home on leave in January 1967, he married Mary Linda Wissler, a 1966 graduate of Radcliffe who had been a fellow *Harvard Crimson* reporter, and daughter of the chairman of the department of pathology at the University of Chicago School of Medicine. Mary, who went to Radcliffe on a scholarship, was nearly as sobersided and unassuming as her husband. While Donny was in Vietnam, she went to law school at New York University.

Kay hoped that Donny would go to law school or business school before joining the *Post*,[113] but he announced that he intended to put in a few years as a policeman. "He feels that to be a good publisher you should really know the town you live in,"[114] Lally said of her brother, who joined the Washington Metropolitan Police Department in January 1968.

"On hearing the news," wrote Lynn Rosellini, "Al Lewis, the *Post*'s veteran police reporter,* hurried to Mrs. Graham's office. 'I

*Lewis was so comfortable with the cops he covered that he was said to "pad around [police] headquarters wearing slippers and a badge."[115]

can stop it!' Mrs. Graham recalls him saying. Mrs. Graham, who didn't like the idea of her son joining the police, nonetheless rejected Lewis's plan." For eighteen months, Donny walked a beat, partly on Capitol Hill and partly in adjacent slums.[116]

"I always admired him for his willingness to go to Vietnam and his willingness when he came back not to be a little rich boy but to join the police force," says Eugene Patterson. He remembers running into the police chief and asking him about Donny. "Is he a good cop?" The chief's response: "He's a fine cop. But I'm worried he's going to get himself killed. He's such a believer in people that he can go into the toughest part of town and get a call to break up a domestic fight and he'll go into that house without even a gun drawn."[117]

In his new role, Donny was at odds with his generation, especially during the 1969 antiwar demonstrations. His wife would later observe: "We lived in a row house on Capitol Hill. I was working for a very liberal circuit court judge while I was in law school, but Don would leave in the morning in his police uniform and go to protect the White House from the demonstrators. Meanwhile, all our friends, who had come to join in the demonstrations and were camping out at our house, would roll up their sleeping bags and go out and demonstrate. Then we'd meet in the evening and compare notes."[118]

Kay worried about Donny and about her own performance. And soon she had something new to worry about—"Style."

Chapter 15

THE *POST* GETS "STYLE"

In 1968, with the "new journalism' in full anti-establishment flower, executive editor Ben Bradlee decided that the *Post*'s daily women's section, "For and About Women," had to go. "Traditional women's news bored the ass off all of us. One more picture of Mrs. Dean Rusk attending the national day of some embassy . . . and we'd all cut our throats."[1]

Bradlee was determined, says Eugene Patterson, to launch the "age of realism in women's pages, the clear, cold-eyed approach, [the] news behind the potted palms." And although he "couldn't quite articulate what he was trying to do," Bradlee had a grand plan "to cover the private lives of our readers."[2]

As was typical of Bradlee, he had the concept and the guts to initiate the change, but not the patience to implement it. "Style," as it was called, was actually put together by David Laventhol—a "typographical wizard," says Patterson—who would become its first editor. Still, Patterson admits, "we were inventing as we went along, day by day. And we weren't at all sure where we were going."[3]

That worried Kay Graham. It would never have occurred to her to dump the women's pages. She, after all, had been one of those society matrons who were being told that they and their good works and assorted afternoon activities were no longer legitimate subjects for news coverage. Bradlee would later tell an interviewer that the birth of "Style" was "the only time in our long association . . . [when] we really disagreed on something. She wanted to nibble at it, do it gradually."[4]

So Kay bit her lip, questioned Bradlee constantly, and complained. And he did exactly what he wanted to do, which was to produce a section that would be so revolutionary yet so right for the times that it would be copied by nearly every major paper and many minor papers across the country.

"Style" debuted on January 6, 1969, with a lead story on Ruth Eisemann-Schier, who was on the FBI's most-wanted list—about as far from standard women's-page fare as one could imagine.[5] Readers were shocked, but none more than Kay Graham. She worried about losing the fashion advertising (including that of department stores) and the respect of her friends who were accustomed to polite coverage of their teas, not stories about abortion, homosexuality, extramarital sex—all of which were soon fare for "Style."

Bradlee gave a soapbox on "Style" to Nicholas von Hoffman, whose column resembled nothing that had run on any women's page before. He glamorized the young and the hip and trivialized the rest, on one occasion ridiculing the hairdos of wives of Vietnam POWs and on another suggesting that prisons be abolished. "On a good day," Bradlee would later comment, "Nick could cancel 200 to 300 subscriptions."[6]

On the third day of "Style"—when the lead story was about a train—Kay Graham exploded. "You men have gotten hold of my women's section," von Hoffman remembers her screaming, "and there's no food, no fashion, no parties, nothing but this goddamn train!" Dave Laventhol went to calm her and, according to von Hoffman, returned "limping, covered with scratches and cuts. Then Bradlee came back, looking very grim, and came over and told me, '*You* go up there and talk to her!' So I went up there, and she was in a fury: 'You bastards, what the hell do you think you're doing? So, what do you have to say for yourself, you son of a bitch?' 'Toot, toot,' I said. She looked up at me and kind of smiled, and said, 'Get the hell out of here.' "[7]

Bradlee won that battle and most that followed. "I can't edit with your fucking finger in my eye," he would shout at her, and she would back down.[8]

Kay even kept quiet when Bradlee hired Sally Quinn to cover parties—the way a national reporter would cover a political campaign.[9] Dubbed "Poison Quinn" by Norman Mailer, and soon presiding over a trio of acid "antisociety" reporters known as "Murderers' Row," Quinn set Washington society on its ear. As one writer chronicling the evolution of "Style" put it, she "had a knack for approaching people, putting them at ease and getting them to hang themselves with their own quotes."[10]

She was the daughter of Army general William "Buffalo Bill" Quinn, one of Barry Goldwater's best friends. She had been to Smith College and before that had attended finishing school in Switzerland, but was, she liked to say, "expelled . . . for chasing after the goatherder."[11]

Quinn had been doing some odd jobs for *The Washington Post Magazine* when Phil Geyelin interviewed her to be his secretary. "I instantly realized she was overqualified," he recalls, although until then her journalism experience was limited to dating the *New York Post*'s Washington correspondent Warren Hoge. A picture of her— young, blonde, and sexy—had run in *The Washington Post Magazine,* and Geyelin showed it to Bradlee. "She'll never fly at home," Bradlee said. "Your first secretary probably should be a little bit more mature." Soon after, when Bradlee mentioned that he was looking for someone to cover parties, Geyelin suggested Quinn: " 'She's sophisticated, she's smart, she knows her way around town, and she will walk up to anybody and ask anything.' And he said, 'Can she write?' And I said, 'Nobody's perfect.' "[12] Sally got the job.

Ben Bradlee is often depicted as having bamboozled Kay Graham to get his way. What is missed is Kay's cleverness—she saw that Bradlee could make her mediocre paper great, and if he used her, then she used him too. Hiring him and giving him carte blanche were the two best decisions of her career.

He operated under one rule, which was that he was the exception to all rules. His counterparts elsewhere in the company might become nervous Nellies waiting for the ax to fall, but he would not be among them. The more independent, the more cavalier he seemed—while always taking into account Kay's feelings—the more she would respect him. She admired this outlaw side of him, this arrogance, he knew, and he would only gain in stature.

Bradlee, almost alone among the top people at the *Post,* understood how to treat Kay. "He got on her wavelength right away because he treated her like one of the boys," says Arnaud de Borchgrave. "[He] used four-letter words all the time, and she loved it. We were being very deferential, calling her 'Mrs. Graham,' Ben was saying, 'Why don't you fuck off?' Ben understood that she wanted to be part of this hard-bitten, hard-living newspaper circle." (A former *Washington Post Magazine* editor recalls Kay at a dinner party describing Bradlee's response to a reader who had written with a complaint about the *Post.* "Dear Asshole," Ben wrote back. She thought it very charming, and told the assembled, "At that point we decided not to let Ben answer letters anymore.")[13]

The woman who had had to rehearse saying "Merry Christmas" began peppering her conversation with more expletives than even Ben Bradlee could manage. The older men could never get used to it. "She talked like a truck driver," says Joseph Laitin, a veteran news and PR man, and later the paper's ombudsman. "I was taken aback."[14]

Nicholas von Hoffman once wrote a story about Kay's hairdresser, Kenneth. I found him very charming, I did this light piece. Kay stopped me in the corridor and said, 'I saw the piece you did on [Kenneth], and I liked it.' Then she looked at me and said, 'If you'd dumped on him, I would have cut your nuts off.' There was a glint in her eye." On another occasion, von Hoffman recalls, "I'd done something that she highly disapproved of. It might have cost her advertising. She came into the newsroom and saw me, and she remembered the sin I'd committed. She shouted at me, 'Von Hoffman, you son of a bitch,' took off her shoe, and fired it across the newsroom at me, hit an ashtray that went splatter all over the place. Then she said, 'You son of a bitch, give me my shoe back.' "[15]

Harvey Segal was making up the editorial page one day, trying to fit a column from Vietnam in which Joseph Alsop "was going on in a very obvious way about the gleaming, rippling triceps of the airmen as he watched them in the sun." He saw Kay out of the corner of his eye, called her over, and showed her the passage. "Oh my God," she told Segal, "that's Joe being faggy. Of course, cut it."[16]

A *Post* writer, accustomed to Kay's new manner, was reportedly "unperturbed" when, breezing through the newsroom, she stopped long enough to tell him, "Your column this morning was a piece of shit." He replied, "Kay, don't hold back. Tell me how you really feel."[17]

Employees of Stanton Cook, former publisher of the *Chicago Tribune,* claimed that they could always tell when Kay had been in to see him, because afterward he would start "talking dirty." He was otherwise, says Frank Waldrop, "a rather prudish sort of guy."[18]

*

Bradlee managed to cater to Kay's needs while refusing to compromise the newspaper, at least beyond a certain point. At her request, but reluctantly, he gave a perch on "Style" to Jim Truitt, who was believed by many to be severely impaired by his drinking and carousing with Phil. (Bradlee understood that he was being told, not asked.) "Truitt never recovered from Phil's death," says Mel Elfin. Kay kept him around, one *Newsweek* editor surmises, because he "was essentially Phil's creation, and why should he be suddenly thrown out to the wolves because Phil committed suicide."[19]

Kay's motives, however, were not completely altruistic. As Nicholas von Hoffman evaluates it, Truitt "did the family enormous service, [showed] enormous loyalty. He was kind of the chief of the family retainers, he knew everything, absolutely everything."[20] Harvey Segal characterizes Truitt's knowledge of the family as "a subtle blackmail."[21] The last thing Kay wanted was for Truitt to write his memoirs or to give an interview.

Soon after Phil's suicide, Kay had sent Truitt to *Newsweek*'s Tokyo bureau, where he eventually became bureau chief. The posting was a payback for his loyalty and, more important, a means of keeping him quiet. At first, according to Kermit Lansner, he was "drinking a tremendous amount, but then he pulled himself together and did quite a reputable job."[22] Eventually he relapsed, and Mel Elfin remembers "always getting calls: 'Your correspondent is dead drunk in an army hospital in Korea.' "[23]

Truitt was soon called home to *Newsweek*'s Washington bureau, where he had his good moments and, Elfin says, "terrific sources. I remember his telling me even before they surfaced that there was going to be a group called the Black Panthers."[24] But in Thelma McMahon's opinion, he did not contribute much. "The man was erratic, destructive, some days he would come to work, some days not." When Truitt left *Newsweek* to return to the *Post,* McMahon cleaned out his office and found evidence that "he was obsessed with pornography."[25]

When he landed at "Style," in 1968, "he had gotten to the point where he'd send us memos written in three different-color inks," says Nick von Hoffman. "He was a profoundly disturbed man."[26]

Eventually Bradlee had to take a stand, and he ordered Patterson to fire Truitt. "Fritz Beebe himself got into the act," Patterson remembers. "He called me one day and suggested that we lay some rather serious money on Truitt, because we didn't want him to leave unhappy."[27]

Truitt, hospitalized with a nervous breakdown, was furious with Kay and even more so with Bradlee, whom he suspected, rightly, of being the impetus behind his firing. He divorced his wife, moved to Mexico, and plotted his revenge. Five years later, he was virtually the sole source for a *National Enquirer* story exposing JFK's romance with Mary Meyer, their use of drugs in a White House bedroom, and the role allegedly played by Ben Bradlee in covering it up.*[28]

Kay was moving on to other difficult relationships with other difficult men—one of the most problematic being Richard Nixon, whose nomination and election she supported in 1968. (Her newspaper remained neutral.) She wanted to befriend Nixon, as she had Lyndon Johnson; but as in the past her newspaper stood in her way, and to her credit, she let it.

Even when the *Post*'s positions were, in Nixon's opinion, right, Kay and Bradlee and Geyelin, those Georgetown snobs, seemed to be saying, "Just kidding." For one, they refused to restrain Herblock, whose cartoons indelibly etched on the public's mind the president's sinister five-o'clock shadow and, as David Halberstam wrote, "stamped him and defined him as no Democratic politician could."[29] In 1969, for example, while the *Post* editorially supported Nixon's nomination of Clement Haynsworth, Jr., to the U.S. Supreme Court, Herblock drew viciously anti-Haynsworth cartoons that some commentators thought contributed to the Senate's rejection of the nomination—the first time since 1930 that a nominee had been so spurned.†

"I never knew Kay to get upset with Herb," says Eugene Patterson. "Sometimes Phil Geyelin would shake his head and say, 'You would never know that this cartoon goes with our editorial position,' but nobody ever really crossed Herblock because he was pretty much king of the mountain. Herb would not take any direction." Nixon

---

*Truitt committed suicide in Mexico.

†Opponents charged Haynsworth, chief judge of the U.S. Court of Appeals for the Fourth Circuit and a man whose credentials were first-rate, with having opposed civil rights and labor causes and having failed to separate his business and judicial roles. He looked good compared with Nixon's next nominee, Judge G. Harrold Carswell of the Florida Court of Appeals, one of whose backers had said publicly that the judge was mediocre. Carswell was also rejected. Judge Harry Blackmun was eventually confirmed.

made one attempt to thaw the relationship. Patterson remembers a phone call from Herbert Klein, the president's director of communications: "The boss was really intrigued with that cartoon this morning." (It was "brutal," Patterson says.) "My God, you mean he liked that?" he asked. "Yeah," Klein said, "he got a real chuckle out of that. He would like the original if Herb would give it to him." Patterson went to the cartoonist's cubbyhole to deliver the request. "His face turned bright red: 'I'll never give him an original of anything. And you can tell Herb Klein that.' "[30]

Then there was Nick von Hoffman, who, in Nixon's opinion, was given ridiculously free rein. The Nixon tapes would later reveal the president referring to von Hoffman as a "nut" in a conversation with his top aide Robert Haldeman, and wondering, "Jesus Christ, why do they carry that son of a bitch?"[31]

On a personal level, Kay continued to court Nixon, and he continued to reject her. Kennedy and Johnson had both dined at her house, Nixon pointedly refused. Kay had been invited to the White House during Nixon's first year in office but never after.[32] "There was no relationship," says Patterson. "Nixon might as well have been in Seattle." He adds that Attorney General John Mitchell went to the *Post* for lunch, as did John Ehrlichman, assistant to the president for domestic affairs. But Haldeman could not be brought around. Patterson, whose daughter was dating Haldeman's son, saw him at a St. Albans School reception and said, "Bob, I hope I can call you and get you to come over to Kay's dining room and sit down with us and talk." Haldeman's response: "We don't accept lunches at *The Washington Post*."[33] Nixon had ordered members of his staff to refuse invitations to Kay's dinner parties.

The president's mouthpiece, Spiro Agnew, continued to attack the *Post*. He had been quoted as saying that *Newsweek* was fit only to line the bottoms of bird cages, and had let it be known that he did not read the copy of *Newsweek* delivered to his home on Sunday night—before it was available to the public[34]—so Mel Elfin was surprised when, at Christmastime 1969, the vice-president accepted an invitation to dinner at Elfin's house with Kay Graham and a group of *Newsweek* and *Post* editors.

Elfin then lived in a townhouse on 29th Street, near the Sheraton Park Hotel, where the Agnews lived. "This is a nice house, Mel," the vice-president said as Elfin opened the door. "Judy [Mrs. Agnew] and I pass it all the time when we take walks. Tell me, how much did you pay for it?"

In Washington, Elfin explains, it is customary for the guest of honor to leave at eleven. "The Secret Service is downstairs in my recreation room waiting for him. And about ten minutes after eleven, Spiro, who's sitting next to Mrs. Graham on my couch, says, 'Mrs. Graham, there's something I wanted to tell you. On the day after Richard Nixon chose me as his nominee for vice-president, the most important and greatest day of my life, your newspaper [editorialized] that Nixon's choice of [me] as his vice-presidential candidate [was] the worst choice since Caligula picked his horse to be consul. I bid you good night.' Then he got up, walked across the room, out the door. I barely recovered in time to escort him to the door. The Secret Service followed. We were all sitting there with our mouths agape. He had been waiting for this moment to hit her with this. He accepted [the invitation] just to tell her off. We were all dumbfounded."[35]

The next May, in a speech before the American Jewish Congress, Kay accused the Nixon administration of creating an atmosphere more repressive than that caused by McCarthy's witch-hunt.[36]

Nixon struck back. Reporters for the *Post* later obtained a secret memorandum of May 1970 from presidential aide Jeb Stuart Magruder to Haldeman: "1—we have a team of letter-writers who are pestering *The Washington Post*. . . . 2—I have asked [deputy assistant to the president for congressional liaison] Lyn Nofziger to work up the House roundrobin letter to the *Post*." Further, Magruder suggested putting "someone on *The Washington Post* to needle Katharine Graham."[37]

What bothered Nixon was that Kay Graham did not attempt to dictate what her reporters covered or how. To a remarkable degree, she lived up to her pledge to keep her nose and her opinions out of the news columns. "I don't tell people what to do all the time. I'm interested in finding people, developing them, giving them leeway and backing them up," she told a reporter for *Time*. She was not the creative one, the one with the ideas, but she had a quality characteristic of the best newspaper publishers and owners: the ability to recognize talent, hire it, let it express itself, accept change.

Some argue that if Kay had had more nerve, more experience, been less dependent on Ben Bradlee, she would have been bolder in trying to shape the paper. But whether her reticence resulted from timidity or principle—it was probably a combination of both—she did not meddle in news coverage.

When a particular story angered her, she would chew out the reporter—and do it in front of others, with, one could persuasively argue, a chilling effect on bystanders—but that would generally be that. There would be no repercussions on the reporter's rise through the ranks.

Bill Greider was at his desk in the newsroom when he found himself Kay's target. "It was a wonderful moment because [some] other reporters were standing around and they started backing away like there [was] a grenade at my feet. They're seeing this immolation in the newsroom. And she was really pissed. On the other hand—and this is what people leave out—she said it and she got it out of her system. That was the end of it." Greider had other experiences with Kay that confirmed his opinion that she was determined not to run the sort of paper her husband had run. After the election of Jimmy Carter, Greider wrote a piece for the "Outlook" section pointing out that although Carter ran as a Washington outsider, his Cabinet was loaded with "retreads from the Great Society, all deeply implicated in the war in Vietnam." Carter had run "with a good deal of man-of-peace rhetoric" but was choosing Cyrus Vance, Joseph Califano, Jr., Harold Brown, Zbigniew Brzezinski,* all of them with "blood on their hands. I went back to the library and got the rhetoric [they] had used in their bloodthirsty days. I ran it all. It was an uncompromising piece. Most of these people were [Kay's] good friends and [it] was a direct attack on that sort of liberal establishment of which she is a member. She came up to me in the newsroom [the next week] and said, 'Well, I didn't like your piece Sunday, but I suppose we should have run it because a lot of people feel that way.' You don't get publishers much better than that."

When Kay's close friend Richard Helms—head of the CIA in the Johnson and Nixon administrations and, says Greider, "a member of that dinner-party world"—was indicted,† hostess Joan Braden and her husband, Thomas, himself a former CIA man, threw a dinner party for Helms to boost his spirits. "All of these characters

---

*Vance, Carter's secretary of state, was deputy secretary of defense in the Johnson administration; Califano, secretary of HEW, served in the Johnson administration as special assistant to the secretary of defense, as deputy secretary of defense, and as special assistant to the president; Brown, secretary of defense, served as secretary of the Air Force during the Johnson years; Brzezinski, who became Carter's national security advisor, was a member of the policy planning council of the State Department during the Johnson administration.

†Helms was convicted of failing to testify "fully and accurately" before a Senate committee about covert CIA operations in Chile. In 1977, he received a two-year suspended sentence and a $2,000 fine.

showed up," recounts Greider, "to toast Helms—McNamara, Kissinger, the whole bunch. And we got word of it. I wrote again a fairly nasty piece: How wonderful it is that the establishment is circling around poor Helms, who's under indictment for lying to the Congress. I described the menu and the toasts, and a good deal of the detail came from Joan Braden, who couldn't resist the idea of being written about in *The Washington Post*. In the course of this I discovered that Mrs. Graham had been invited to this dinner and for one reason or another didn't attend. I literally didn't think about it, [that] of course this [was] going to piss her off. In the atmosphere of that newsroom, that was not a problem. She came up afterward and said, 'Bob [McNamara] was very unhappy with your piece, [and] he says you got the toast wrong. What he said was . . .' That was her only comment. And then she told me, 'Thank God I didn't go to that party.' "[38]

She said all the right things about keeping her friendships separate from her newspaper, and for the most part, she meant it. She told one journalist: "The danger when you get to know government figures is that you begin to see things from their point of view and to sympathize with their problems, which is really not the job of the press. The job of the press is to stay distant. . . . Whoever is my friend . . . has to understand that the paper is independent."[39]

One night Truman Capote had dinner with Kay and another newspaper publisher. "He was furious about something the *Post* had printed about him," Capote later told Lynn Rosellini. "He went after her like a tiger. She said, 'I can't be totally in charge. I don't run the news department.' He said: 'If it had been me and they wrote anything like that about you, I would have killed the story.' She said: 'Well . . . that's the difference between you and me.' "[40]

Eugene Patterson describes Kay's role as that of critic. "She would call me up, say, on a Sunday morning and ask me a lot of questions that I had to go back to the drawing board on and reconsider. She was a very good newspaper reader and a very ruthless questioner, but she never called and said, 'My God, I don't want any more of this printed.' "[41]

At *Newsweek,* Arnaud de Borchgrave says, she "never once interfered editorially. She would make a suggestion, but if it wasn't carried out she didn't get upset."[42] Kermit Lansner agrees: "We had more editorial independence than probably any other journal in the United States at the time. We had a terrific run."[43]

When her editors at *Newsweek* rejected her cover suggestions, and the marketplace proved them right, they did not hesitate to remind her how wrong she was. "Every once in a while," Lester Bernstein recalls, "I taxed her for expressing surprise and implicit disapproval [about] putting something on the cover which turned out to be one of the best covers we ever did—John Lennon's murder." When he later reminded her that she had opposed the Lennon cover—she argued that by the time the magazine got to readers the murder would be "ancient news"—she said, "Well, I'm not an editor."[44]

When Kay pushed a cover subject hard enough, her editors took note, sometimes. She would tell a reporter for *Washingtonian* magazine of her repeated suggestions to devote a cover to the third world; that issue, she admitted, turned out to be one of the year's worst newsstand sellers. "Everybody [at *Newsweek*] was very pleased at that," she added with a little laugh.[45]

Kay's major editorial contribution was her skill at using her social contacts to feed tips, leads, and gossip to her reporters. Edward Kosner calls her "a genuine inside-dopester. She knew a lot more of what was going on than the *Newsweek* correspondents did. You'd be a fool not to listen to what she had to say."[46]

While press critics expect owner-publishers to keep their opinions out of the news columns, few expect such niceties to extend to the editorial page. Even the most ardent advocate of the separation of church and state would agree that, in broad terms, it's acceptable for the page to reflect the owner's politics. So would most savvy editorial-page editors. Phil Geyelin certainly did.

Like Patterson, Geyelin found Kay to be a keen questioner at editorial conferences. "She challenged whatever was said. She'd ask the sharpest questions." Even if the questions were not all that informed, they showed that she wanted to know more: "she's got an enormous interest, intellectual curiosity."[47]

Although Ben Gilbert recalls that during his final year at the *Post,* when he worked as an editorial writer, "she was very circumspect about giving the editorial people any orders, you could figure out from what she was saying where she would prefer you to come down."[48] When her feelings were strong, she expressed them forcefully. Harvey Segal remembers her attending an editorial meeting to make sure that the writers would "thunder" against a proposal in Virginia to sterilize the state's unmarried mothers.[49]

While Phil Graham's practice had been to demand proofs of the next day's editorials by six p.m., Kay was considerably looser. Phil Geyelin did brief her, but only when an editorial was unusually controversial. She never asked him to change or kill an editorial, "never laid down a doctrine. It was the perfect relationship between editorial-page editor and owner."[50]

What made this laissez-faire approach possible was a bottom line that Geyelin understood and accepted: the "no-surprise rule," which to Geyelin meant that "if we were going to write anything that departed in any substantial way, or even appeared to, from the things we'd said in the past, I would talk to her about it." Further, "if over a long period of time the paper was taking positions [such] that Katharine would wake up in the morning and discover she didn't approve, and [if] that was happening a lot of the time on a lot of things, somebody would have to go, and it wouldn't be the owner."[51]

It wasn't until he was on the job that Geyelin discovered what her staff referred to as "Kay's sacred cows": Robert McNamara was certainly one and, increasingly, so was Henry Kissinger.

Six years younger than Kay, divorced in 1964, Kissinger was an occasional escort, especially before his remarriage in 1974. In return, he felt free to phone her directly with complaints. "Henry called, and are you sure we're right about Turkey?" Geyelin remembers her asking. "Why don't you just call him and discuss it with him?" And so Geyelin would. "Every time I [did], he said, 'Oh, I didn't mean to get you involved.' I'd say, 'Henry, when you call my publisher do you really think you're not getting me involved?' He would argue his side and I'd tell him how we felt." And that, Geyelin says, was that. There was never any attempt to argue him into changing the paper's position. "It was very smooth."

That Kay's second-guessing continued and widened along with her circle of acquaintance and influence neither upset nor surprised Geyelin. At a typical Washington dinner, he explains, the male publisher "sat between two women, [for example] the wife of the secretary of state [and] the wife of the chief justice. Of course in Katharine's case, she might be sitting next to the [men] with the clout. And so she got an earful every time she went out."

Kay would call *Post* editors to ask whether they were sure of their ground. Whether they were or not, Geyelin says, she would ask them to hear out whoever the offended party might be. "It wasn't, Talk to Henry and change our position. It was, Talk to Henry and satisfy yourself that you've heard his side of the argument."[52]

Kay would patiently listen to friends who felt they had been maligned by her paper, and she learned that if she listened long enough, they might hang themselves with their own words. Mel Elfin recalls having lunch with Kay in her dining room at the *Post* one Monday just as *Newsweek* went on sale with a story about alleged ethical breaches by staff members and friends of Vice-President Hubert Humphrey: "[We'd] tried to call Humphrey and he wouldn't talk to us. Liz [Hylton, Kay's secretary] pokes her head in and says, 'The vice-president's on the phone.' Hubert was in a rampage about the story, yelling and carrying on." He complained to his friend Kay that her reporters were "slandering wonderful young people," and that they had not bothered to call him before going with the story. Then, with Kay on one extension and Elfin on another, "Hubert finally says, 'And that's the reason, Kay, why I didn't talk to your people when they called me on Saturday.' Suddenly he realizes he's admitted that we called him. He bursts out laughing and says, 'Okay, you win.' She could be very supportive in cases like that."[53]

Kay tried to bridge the gap between government officials who were involved in one way or another with the escalation of the war in Vietnam, most of them middle-aged or beyond, and her young and almost exclusively antiwar editors and reporters. She invited both sides to dinner parties, perhaps believing, naively, that if only they would get to know one another, understanding and respect would follow. Bill Greider recalls several such invitations, "clearly 'Let's let the young people meet the old people and see if they can talk to each other.' [There was] a really heavyweight list of people, sprinkled with a few reporters and a few editors. On the whole [the gatherings] never worked. If that's what she wanted, we didn't get engaged in anything resembling serious conversations."[54]

In the end, however, Kay was probably not a woman of enough backbone and confidence to resist the entreaties of new and powerful friends. More than likely she would have slipped into running the sort of paper her husband ran—not because, like Phil, she wanted to manipulate world events, but because she so longed to please. What stopped her from falling into this trap, and from presiding over a mediocre paper, was Ben Bradlee.

"Bradlee was a great shield," says Greider.[55] He would listen respectfully to the complaints Kay passed on from her friends, and not let them go any further. She remembered one instance in which she "got down on bended knee" to Bradlee and begged him not to run a story by gossip columnist Maxine Cheshire about a date Kissinger had had in Hollywood with two women who, apparently unbeknownst to him, were strippers who had costarred in a porno movie, and one of whom was famous for balancing full glasses of champagne on her breasts. Kay told Kissinger's latest biographer, Walter Isaacson, that when the article did appear, "Henry was so furious that when he called I had to hold the phone away from my ear." He later told Kay, "Maxine makes me want to commit murder. Sally [Quinn] makes me want to commit suicide."[56]

At a Pentagon briefing during Robert McNamara's final days as defense chief, Harvey Segal remembers, reporter George Wilson asked, "Mr. Secretary, how do you feel when you go to bed every night knowing that by the next morning there'll be x number of thousands of war casualties in Vietnam?" According to Segal, "McNamara turned white, walked off the platform. I heard that Katharine personally reamed George Wilson out, I gather really threatened him."[57]

Wilson, who still writes for the *Post,* says that his relations with McNamara were "indeed strained," but that Kay never chewed him out, never complained directly to him. "I do know," he adds, "McNamara's deputies complained about me to *Washington Post* executives. But Ben Bradlee served as a firewall for us on the staff."[58]

There are many stories about Bradlee's going up against a politician or business leader in defense of a reporter, even when he was not completely confident that the reporter knew what he or she was doing. *Post* ombudsman Richard Harwood recalls that when Senator John McClellan of Arkansas complained to Bradlee about a story Harwood was writing, Bradlee responded that the senator could go fuck himself.[59] When reporter Leonard Downie was working on a series exposing the shenanigans of speculators who, in league with savings and loan officials, targeted the inner city, a delegation of S&L executives marched into Bradlee's office threatening to withdraw their institutions' advertising. "I threw them out," Bradlee reportedly told Downie. "Now can you tell me what you're doing?" To Downie's explanation, Bradlee responded, "Just make sure it's right!" The paper lost hundreds of thousands of dollars in ads after the series ran—a fact, Stephen Isaacs says, that Bradlee never burdened him with.[60]

Paul Ignatius, who became *Post* president in 1969, recalls hearing Kay talk "disparagingly about lady publishers,"[61] meaning women who owned newspapers, usually through the death of a father or husband, but who confined their role (or had their role confined for them by the strong men in their employ) to essentially that of hostess. She realized to her dismay that she was becoming one of them. She knew she had to give the editorial side independence, but the business side was another matter altogether.

Chapter 16

FREE AT LAST

In 1969, Oz Elliott asked to be relieved as editor of *Newsweek*; he had held the position since 1961, when Phil acquired the magazine. Elliott had done his share of condescending to Kay, and he certainly was closely identified in her mind with Phil, but it was he, not Kay, who made the move. Explaining that he wanted some business-side exposure, he took the title editor in chief, vice-chairman. His replacement was Kermit Lansner.

Elliott was not alone in wanting to learn more about the business side. Since she had taken over, Kay had focused on editorial. With two very strong men—Fritz Beebe and John Sweeterman—running business for her, Kay did not have much to do. As Mark Meagher, later a Post Company president, puts it, "It isn't that she was indecisive. She never had anything to decide. It was all being done for her. Virtually nothing was done [by Kay] between 1963 and 1970 except caretake. The only thing [she did] that had enormous significance was [develop] the relationship with Bradlee."[1]

But Kay had no intention of becoming irrelevant, a fate she saw awaiting her if she left editorial duties to Bradlee and didn't engage in business affairs. While she had initially feared taking them on, now she was ready to grasp a foothold—before she became a footnote.

Friends and colleagues noticed that she started talking about wanting to win a Pulitzer Prize for management. While retaining her faint disdain for the businessmen who ran the *Post*, she developed a crush on business wizards, the men who made big deals, who ran Fortune 500 companies, who seemed so glamorous and shrewd.

Polly Kraft recalls her surprise at the obvious change in Kay's priorities. She seemed fascinated by "business and money and how it's made. She suddenly got really interested in CEOs."[2] Her social circle widened to include such financial titans as investment banker Felix Rohatyn, a senior partner at her grandfather's firm, Lazard Frères.* Phil Geyelin says the change was so pronounced that Ben Bradlee and he would joke about it[3]—not in front of her, of course.

Kay began to ask more questions and, as one executive terms it, to "buzz around" with John Sweeterman, who by all accounts would have preferred that she confine her buzzing to Ben Bradlee. A man of the old school who believed that women had their place, and it was not in the printing plant or, for that matter, the boardroom, Sweeterman never learned how not to patronize Kay Graham. It was he who suffered most directly from her change in attitude and direction.

"John was a guy Katharine had to get rid of," says Mark Meagher, "so she could exercise some muscle."[4] Furthermore, Sweeterman was Phil's man. Just as she had taken control of editorial by putting her own man in, so she planned to take control of business. But Sweeterman was daunting and competent; many would credit him with capturing the market and making the paper's later monopoly status possible.[5] Kay did not have the confidence to fire him: she would humiliate Sweeterman until there was nothing left for him to do but quit. Bradlee would show her how.

At a meeting to allocate the next year's newsroom budget, Kay watched as Bradlee humbled Sweeterman by winning several million more than Sweeterman wanted to give him for hiring big-name reporters, opening new bureaus, increasing editorial salaries.[6] Anyone who understood the politics of the *Post* recognized that Sweeterman might as well have tendered his resignation then and there.

The casualty of the battle was a building for the *Post* designed by I. M. Pei, envisioned as a breathtaking addition to the District's downtown. The paper had run out of space in the L Street headquarters, opened in 1950, and in the mid-1960s, Katharine had decided to commission a building that would make a statement.

So she went to the most renowned, hiring I. M. Pei, whose dramatic preliminary plan garnered the enthusiasm of nearly everyone, including Beebe and the cheapskate Sweeterman.[7] Then Ben Bradlee

---

*Rohatyn, a takeover specialist and advisor to politicians, was architect of the plan to stave off New York City's financial collapse in the mid-seventies.

got involved. Estimates showed that the building would cost approximately $50 million, some $20 million over budget. Bradlee warned Kay that the cost would eviscerate the newsroom budget and put the company in dangerous debt. Ben Gilbert, who sat on the building committee, understood that it was not the plans for the building that Bradlee wanted to destroy, it was Sweeterman.[8]

One *Post* higher-up who followed very closely the discussion and termination of the plan calls Bradlee's concerns phony. "It was a power play, nothing more. It had nothing to do with the architecture. I think he liked the architecture. Kay was siding with Bradlee after Sweeterman had mobilized the entire paper to plan this great new building. Every significant executive on the paper had been involved in that planning process for several years. That was going to be thrown away." In his opinion, had Sweeterman opposed the Pei plan, Bradlee would have been all for it, and damn the cost.[9]

Officially Sweeterman retired,* but actually he was forced into early retirement. First his role was curtailed, and then he was moved into a small office in an annex on 16th Street.[10]

Faced with hiring a man to lead the business side, Kay asked Robert McNamara, whose newspaper experience consisted of being interviewed and, increasingly, lambasted by the press. She did not want another member of the old-boy newspaper network, one of the types she had grown accustomed to seeing at publishers' meetings, the retreads who went from one paper to another, who knew Phil, who knew her history, who could not quite bring themselves to take her seriously. That they also knew the increasingly complicated business of putting out a newspaper profitably she considered beside the point.

McNamara strongly recommended Paul Ignatius, who was about to leave the Pentagon. A Harvard MBA, three years Kay's junior, Ignatius had no newspaper background whatsoever; he had been assistant secretary of the Army under Kennedy, and undersecretary and then assistant secretary of defense and secretary of the Navy under Johnson. John Prescott, then a top executive at Knight Newspapers, speculates that McNamara advised Kay: "Sure, he doesn't have any newspaper experience, but he has been in business and he was able to get supplies in and out of Vietnam. So I think he could run a two-thousand-employee newspaper."[11]

Typically, the person who runs the business end of a newspaper is

---

*He remained a director of the Post Company long after his departure.

called publisher—the title that was also Phil's until he gave it to Sweeterman in 1961. Having by then decided to free himself of day-to-day business affairs, Phil had retained the titles of president and chief executive officer. Kay, who had held the more modest title of president, decided—as a sign that she was ready to lead the *Post*—to call herself publisher; Ignatius was given the title of president.

His first assignment was to review the building fiasco. A month later he reported to Kay and Beebe that the Pei plan was impractical.

Pei was paid $2 million for his plans, thanked for his time and attention, and dismissed. Ignatius, with his Pentagon skills, "set up a structure to get that new thing built in absolute record time."[12] He brought in a largely unknown industrial architect from Detroit, Albert Kahn, who had designed the L Street building[13] and now produced "a box," in Kermit Lansner's opinion.[14]

"The result," Ignatius agrees, "isn't the most beautiful building in the world, and we knew we were going to lose that, but it was an adequate building."[15] Strictly adequate. It was a compromise that became a permanent irritant to Kay, who knew that Phil would somehow have made the Pei plan work. "With more experience I think I would have studied it more carefully and not been so hasty," Kay told a reporter years later. Mournfully she added, "We set out to give the town a distinguished building, and look what we got."[16] She would—unfairly, given his late arrival on the project—blame Ignatius. Bradlee, as always, escaped any blame.

By 1969, the *Post* had reporters and editors who had never met, much less been charmed by, Phil Graham. It had women who thought of Kay Graham as the most powerful woman in publishing, as a role model rather than some cast-off casualty of a husband's philandering. This gave Kay a new and inspiring feeling.

Yet Fritz Beebe continued to be Kay's mentor and guide, to set direction and make the hard decisions. Once the inexperienced Ignatius took over for the seasoned Sweeterman, Beebe became more involved than ever. "When I took the job," Ignatius recalls, "Fritz Beebe was more than just involved. Fritz was really running the company."[17] It was Beebe who negotiated and signed off that year on the purchase of the Post Company's third television station—joining the two acquired by Phil in the early 1950s. The Miami station was given the call letters WPLG, in honor of Phil Graham.[18]

When the decision was made to scrap Pei's plans, it was Beebe who fired the architect. People on the *Post* became accustomed to having

Beebe in on even routine meetings. Bob Estabrook recalls that when he met with Kay shortly before he left the *Post,* she had summoned Beebe from New York to attend the meeting. According to Estabrook, she was concerned that he might ask for a raise, and did not know how to deal with the request. Ignatius, although in Washington, was not asked to participate.[19]

In early 1970, former president Johnson accepted Kay's invitation to lunch at her dining room at the *Post* with her and her top editors, including the despised Ben Bradlee and Phil Geyelin. Depressed and bored in an unlikely retirement at his ranch, Johnson had jumped at the opportunity to explain himself to his erstwhile critics.[20] The tables had turned: Kay Graham, the timid widow, was now on the ascendant, the potential powerhouse.

"It was really a fascinating sidelight on history to sit and listen to this bird," says Eugene Patterson. "He had grown his hair kind of long, like the Vietnam demonstrators, and he showed his age, but he did love to talk." He was accompanied by his assistant, Tom Johnson, a White House fellow and deputy press secretary who had followed his boss to Texas.

Tom Johnson's function was to supply the backup data, the documents LBJ needed to vindicate himself. Patterson recalls that he "brought a whole file drawer full of paper, so [LBJ] would simply hold his hand out over his shoulder and Tom would whisk out a paper." The former president was "mellow and philosophical, and he wasn't whining or denouncing or thundering or anything. He just came to talk to the boys at the *Post* after all the years of combat. He was trying to get his spin on history before we got around to writing it."[21] With his long arms flailing, jerking backward for the document that proved his point, it appeared that Johnson would take off Ben Bradlee's head. "We were laughing about whether or not Johnson would actually hit [him]," Phil Geyelin says, "as he reached for a letter from Abe Fortas."[22]

The lunch, which Geyelin terms "epic, riveting," started at noon, and four hours later the ex-president was still holding forth. "About five, people were looking around and saying, 'Are we going to get a paper out or not?' " Finally Lady Bird called and ordered him across the street to the Madison Hotel, where they were staying: "Come home for your nap, Lyndon, because we've got to go out for dinner." He stayed at the *Post* another half-hour.[23]

Before he reluctantly left, Johnson said, "I don't care what the

Post ever says about me. I'll never forget that Phil Graham went down to his farm one weekend and wrote the whole Great Society."[24] It was a finale worthy of LBJ, for its passion and for its reminder that Kay Graham, well into middle age, might be moving toward power, but Phil Graham was already a giant at barely past forty.

Kay did not pay much attention to the emerging women's movement until March 1970, when *Newsweek*'s editorial women filed a federal sex discrimination complaint with the Equal Employment Opportunity Commission, charging that the magazine had long discriminated against women. Their lawyer, in this first such suit against a media organization, was Eleanor Holmes Norton, later EEOC chairman.

Kay was in Barbados when Fritz Beebe called and told her the suit had been filed. "Well, which side am I supposed to be on?" she asked. "It's not funny," he replied.[25]

It was a suit that Kay should have seen coming. When, that same month, *Newsweek* ran a cover story on the women's liberation movement, the editors commissioned an outsider to write it because, Oz Elliott claimed, there were no qualified females on staff to do the job.[26] On the Monday when the issue hit the stands, a letter from her incensed female employees hit Kay Graham's desk: "Women have rarely been hired as, or promoted to, the positions of reporter, writer, or editor; they are systematically by-passed in the selection of bureau correspondents and are routinely given lower titles and pay. . . . Incredibly, *Newsweek* was unwilling to work with any woman on staff on writing this week's cover story. . . . In addition to the day-to-day atmosphere that discourages women as professional journalists, women are pointedly excluded from public functions which represent *Newsweek*."[27]

In an interview with a *Miami Herald* reporter that ran that March, Kay contended that the Post Company did not "deliberately discriminate against women." She raised the possibility of "grounds for misunderstanding" and said that she was sure *Newsweek* editors, meeting with the women that very day, "can iron out the misunderstanding."[28] They could not. The suit went forward, and was eventually settled without a hearing.*

---

*Two years later, charging that *Newsweek* editors had not kept their promises, the women filed another EEOC complaint, this time winning specific commitments, including promises for hiring quotas. In 1980, a similar suit was brought at the *Post* and settled.

There was nothing hidden or subtle about sex discrimination at newsmagazines. Writer Elizabeth Drew would recall being told by a bureau chief in the early 1960s, when she was a writer-editor for *Congressional Quarterly*: "We don't hire women."[29] In his memoirs, Oz Elliott admitted that *Newsweek,* like *Time,* put its women in the role of researchers and kept them there—the irrational but intractable law being: "Once a researcher, always a researcher."[30]

"No doubt we were sexist," Kermit Lansner admits. "We had what we called 'Elliott girls,' on this terrible shift on Friday night, till three in the morning, when our regular secretaries would go home. There was a lot of copy-delivering. The young women who sat on that shift wanted to be researchers. We had Nora Ephron, Susan Brownmiller." Given their later success, Lansner shakes his head in amazement as he says, "They were gofers."[31] Eugene Patterson claims that Kay was aware of the problem and complained aloud at the *Post* in the late 1960s that she "couldn't get 'those goddamned people at *Newsweek*' to hire some women. You couldn't tell her that women weren't equipped to do more than be just researchers."[32]

But as the women's movement took hold and became more mainstream, many of Kay's employees found her insufficiently enthusiastic. Despite the poignancy of her life's experiences, she did not particularly identify with her "sisters" and their struggles. She described herself as "middle of the road" as far as the feminist movement was concerned. One old friend recalls that when advocates of the Equal Rights Amendment were trying to get her support for the cause, "she said no. She didn't see the need. People just emerged or they didn't." What eventually persuaded her to back the ERA was hearing that Mary McCarthy had asked her husband, Edmund Wilson, to take out the garbage and he refused.[33]

The women who worked for Kay did not understand that her goal was to be accepted and respected in a man's world, not some feminized version. Kay had assured an interviewer in 1970 that a woman could rise to the top of any of her enterprises.[34] But more than one high executive of the *Post* has remarked on Kay's obvious preference for men. Not only is she said to have more confidence in their business and editorial sense, but as did her mother, she plain likes them better. As Mark Edmiston puts it, "She was pressured to put a woman on the board—highest-ranking woman CEO in the world, and for years she never had a woman on the board. She's not fond of women. She's not comfortable with women."[35]

Some women blamed Ben Bradlee for the paucity of females at the

Post, but had Kay wanted Bradlee to run a different sort of paper, he would have.* Caught between two worlds, she found it hard to relate to the wives of her top executives—women whose position was not unlike that she had once occupied. Lester Bernstein describes her as "dismissive of wives, dutifully polite but nothing more."[37] Even when Mark Edmiston was president of *Newsweek,* Kay confused his wife with his secretary, both of whom are Italian-American and wore their dark hair long. "The wives [to her] are just not terribly relevant."[38]

At the same time, Kay's rarefied background made it difficult for her to relate to working women and especially to mothers who left their children with baby-sitters—both because they needed the money and because they liked the work. "Style" reporter Myra MacPherson recalls that Kay asked her, " 'Are you still working part-time?' and I said, 'I never worked part-time.' And she said, 'But you have the children.' "[39]

Still, she made many of the politically correct moves, which left her with the largely undeserved reputation for being a feminist. In 1971, having met Gloria Steinem, through friends, she invested $20,000 to help launch *Ms.* magazine.[40] And with assistance from Meg Greenfield, she retired the old Washington custom of separating men and women after dinner. One evening at Joe Alsop's, when the men went to the host's study for brandy, cigars, and serious conversation and the women went to a bedroom to powder their noses and chat about children and servants, Kay and Meg simply went home, not to return at ten forty-five, when the men, by custom, "rescued" the ladies upstairs.[41]

Likewise, but almost inadvertently, Kay helped liberate the Gridiron Club—which refused to admit women to its ranks of prominent newsmen. In 1972, for the first time in its eighty-seven-year history, the Gridiron asked women, Kay Graham among the chosen fifteen, to come as guests to its annual dinner. Kay was delighted, as she told a *Washingtonian* reporter. She was unaware that the organization Journalists for Professional Equality had picketed the Gridiron dinner the previous two years, charging sex discrimination. Members of that organization, labeling the invitations tokenism, urged her not to

---

*As late as the mid-1980s, the dearth of women in important positions—with the exception of Meg Greenfield—was glaring. On Joe Laitin's first day as ombudsman in 1986 he attended an editorial conference. "Two things impressed me: there were no black editors, and women played a very unimportant role."[36]

Kay Graham jubilantly leaving U.S. District Court with Ben Bradlee in 1971, after a victory in their fight to publish the Pentagon Papers, the classified history of the Vietnam war. Kay's decision to proceed, despite frightening pressure from the Nixon administration, was the most important of her career, and it boosted *The Washington Post* into the big leagues. *(AP/Wide World Photos)*

Eugene Meyer, who made millions on Wall Street before devoting himself to public service, testifying before Congress in 1932. As head of both the Reconstruction Finance Corporation and the Federal Reserve Board, he was the most powerful man in the nation's financial sphere since Alexander Hamilton. *(UPI/Bettmann)*

Agnes Meyer entering the White House in 1946 to advise President Truman on handling veterans' problems. Truman would later say, "There isn't a day that goes by without my getting a letter from that Meyer woman or Eleanor Roosevelt, telling me how to do this job." *(AP/Wide World Photos)*

Florence, the oldest Meyer child, with her husband, Viennese actor Oscar Homolka, just after their marriage in 1939.
(UPI/Bettmann)

Bill Meyer on his wedding day in 1940. As a student at Yale he explored his paternal Jewish heritage, but he later married the daughter of a prominent Christian clergyman—a decision that pleased his parents, who did their best to "pass" in Washington's upper circles of influence.
(AP/Wide World Photos)

Ernest Graham on his
Florida dairy farm.
*(Historical Association of
Southern Florida)*

Phil Graham in 1947.
Brilliant and charming, he
dominated the *Post* and Kay.
(AP/Wide World Photos)

Agnes and Eugene in 1953,
at a dinner honoring Bishop
Bernard Sheil, one of the many
men with whom Agnes conducted
intense but platonic affairs.
(AP/Wide World Photos)

Closing the deal: Eugene Meyer (fifth from left), flanked by Fritz Beebe and John Sweeterman, as the *Post* acquires the *Washington Times-Herald* in 1954. This was a man's game, but Kay and her mother were invited to witness the final transaction. Phil is at far right, on the phone. *(UPI/Bettmann)*

When an unprepared Kay took over in 1963, she was so nervous and shy that she had to rehearse a "Merry Christmas" greeting to her employees. *(AP/Wide World Photos)*

Kay with Truman Capote in 1966 at the Black and White Ball he gave to introduce her to society. Kay would later describe it as "an odd, over-aged and gray coming-out party." *(UPI/Bettmann)*

Stephen Graham and Lally Weymouth, Kay's youngest and oldest children, in 1980, before the New York opening of a play he produced. *(UPI/Bettmann)*

Kay at a press conference in London in 1979 with former British prime minister Edward Heath and former West German chancellor Willy Brandt. *(AP/Wide World Photos)*

Kay chatting with old friends Nancy Reagan and Henry Kissinger at *Newsweek*'s fiftieth-anniversary party. *(AP/Wide World Photos)*

May 1991: Newly appointed CEO Donny Graham; his mother, who retained the title of chairman; and Ben Bradlee, who would announce his retirement the next month. *(AP/Wide World Photos)*

attend. "Then I got a letter signed by a great many of the women at the paper, saying, Please don't go, because we're not allowed to be members. I didn't understand what they were getting at. I thought that [the invitation] was a sign of progress. I invited them to come have dinner with me at the house, and they absolutely convinced me they were right." (Women were admitted as members of the Gridiron in 1975, the first year that Kay accepted the club's invitation.)[42]

With time, she became more feisty on the subject of women's rights, although her commitment did not extend much beyond the verbal. Robert Manning recalls chatting with her in her office about getting together at Martha's Vineyard. As he was leaving, he said, "Well, I'm not sure when our dates are, but I'll call your girl and let her know." Kay responded: "Not 'girl,' sonny. We don't use that term around here."[43]

Polly Kraft asserts that "as each year has gone [by], one has seen in Kay more and more real interest in women, in women's causes. When she likes women, she really likes them."[44] But the women she likes are sometimes not quite what the more feminist of her employees have in mind. Nancy Reagan, for example, whom she got to know, according to Hedley Donovan, through her father's old California contacts. "While Reagan was governor and was coming to Washington, bringing Nancy with him, Kay had a phone call from some mutual friend in San Francisco that Nancy was coming and didn't know anybody in Washington and was awfully shy, so Kay organized a little ladies' lunch for her, and they hit it off very well."[45]

Before another Reagan trip to Washington, around 1970, Kay called Nancy and asked, "Would you and the governor come to dinner?" Nancy, Kay recounted, "said, 'No, we can't because Ronnie's giving a speech [he was going to the Alfalfa Club dinner, which then didn't allow women] that night.' And I said, 'Oh well, that's too bad. Would you like to come anyway, and I'll have some people for you?' And she, being in this old-fashioned mold, somebody's wife, thinks you never want to see *her*, said, 'Oh no, let's not do that—you don't want me.' And I just laughed and said, 'Nancy, we're supposed to get over that. Now of course I want you. You come to dinner, and then if Ronnie wants to come after the speech, fine. It doesn't matter.' And so she came and I gave a dinner for her."[46]

When Governor Reagan was in Washington in 1971 to speak to the National Press Club, Kay threw a dinner party for the couple. Nancy nearly pulled him off the podium during the question-and-answer period after his speech so they would not be late for the dinner. Reagan explained with a grin, "Yes, we are dining with the liberal press."[47] The news may have left some reporters puzzled, since Reagan had just called Vice-President Agnew "a fine, gentle, sensitive man . . . an asset to the presidential ticket and an asset to the country." Agnew, Reagan said, was a "serious thinker," as young people might realize if they didn't attend "[so] many social science courses."

While Agnes Meyer would have found Nancy and Ronald Reagan dull company and the governor's opinion of Agnew and his critics preposterous, the three probably would have been more or less in sync in their opinion of the women's movement. Until the end of her life, Agnes maintained a fervent belief in the general superiority of men, the sole exception being herself. Eugene Patterson recalls that Kay "rolled her eyes to the ceiling" when her mother asked what she thought about the women's movement. "Kay, of course, somewhat lamely said it was a movement whose time had come. Old Mrs. Meyer dismissed it witheringly. 'It's nothing but penis envy.' That wiped out the women's movement."[48]

On the other hand, Agnes continued to take strong stands on women's issues, and she did so long before those views were fashionable. As early as 1956, she had decried the burgeoning rate of illegal and sometimes deadly abortion, stopping just short of calling for legalization. She lobbied for a nationwide contraceptive program, saying that same year: "Contraceptive knowledge should assuredly be in the possession of every adult, if women as well as men are to function as truly free human beings."[49]

During the middle and late 1960s, Agnes continued to talk about her pride at Kay's taking over at the *Post,* but the old feelings of contempt remained. What was really bothering her, said Roswell Gilpatric, was that she "wished she were Ben Bradlee's boss."[50]

Kay remained the dutiful daughter, visiting Agnes regularly, and usually with an escort—sometimes Nicholas von Hoffman, sometimes Mel Elfin, sometimes Eugene Patterson—a man who freed her from having to impress her mother and kept Agnes's temper in check by making her feel as if she were still in the swing of things. When Kay gave a dinner party that included Agnes, Mel Elfin, who knew the ins and outs of education issues as well as anyone, was usually invited and "always would be seated next to Mama. I enjoyed her.

She could be funny, she was knowledgeable, she was tough, and as dinner companions go in Washington, she wasn't bad. I attribute whatever success I had in Washington to the fact that I could speak the same language as Agnes Meyer."[51]

In 1970, Agnes, for much of her life a chain-smoker and scotch guzzler,[52] was eighty-three years old and looked every year of it. Not even she, with her enormous capacity for self-delusion, could fool herself into thinking she was attractive. "She had a few strands of hair that she pulled back," recalled Marietta Tree, and "she looked awful, much too overweight."[53] Increasingly hobbled by arthritis, since 1967 she had been confined to a wheelchair, and the lack of physical activity exacerbated her corpulence and grumpiness. But "her will and her strength of mind prevailed over her physical resources,"[54] says Roswell Gilpatric.

She continued to try to influence the *Post*'s editorial stands and to write for the paper. Kay was embarrassed, but rather than confront her mother directly, she told her editors not to be bullied. Unbelievable as it was to Kay, they found the older Agnes amusing and informed. Phil Geyelin recalls that when she phoned "to discuss her views about education, I enjoyed talking to her. I mentioned it in passing to Kay. Her reaction was irritation. 'You don't have to listen to my mother at all.' Made it perfectly clear that she was not to have a voice on the editorial page. I said I wasn't cowed."[55]

Eugene Patterson remembers that Katharine came in one morning "looking very, very chagrined. She put a manuscript on my desk and very apologetically asked if I would read [it], and be absolutely ruthless and critical as to whether it was publishable or not. 'It was written by my mother,' she said. Sure enough, Agnes had written a piece on the Freer [Gallery] and its genesis and its life and times, and it was really a very good piece." Patterson was happy to publish it, although Kay suspected his sincerity.[56]

In the summer of 1970, Agnes was struggling to write another volume of her memoirs and continuing to promote the cause of public education as chairman of the National Committee in Support of the Public Schools. In August, she called D.C. mayor Walter Washington to tell him that she wished she could "get about a little better so that she could join [him] on the firing line to make this a model city."[57]

Agnes died at Mount Kisco on Tuesday, September 1, 1970. Kay happened to be visiting at the time.[58]

Agnes's Lutheran roots were as well hidden in her memorial service at the high Episcopal Washington Cathedral as Eugene's Jewish roots had been at the All Souls Unitarian Church. The service was conducted by the Right Reverend William Creighton, bishop of Washington, and the Reverend Canon Charles Martin, headmaster of the very Episcopal St. Albans School.

The eulogy was delivered, at Katharine's request, by former chief justice Earl Warren. It was heavy on quotations from Agnes's autobiography, all taken at face value. One can only imagine what went through Katharine's mind as Warren said, "She understood that love without criticism is corrosive and that criticism without love is destructive."

Agnes would have been delighted by the quantity—350 relatives and friends attended—but more by the quality of the turnout: Clark Clifford, Edward Bennett Williams, Senator George McGovern, New Dealers Tom Corcoran and Ben Cohen, Joseph and Stewart Alsop, Mayor Walter Washington, British ambassador to the U.S. John Freeman. LBJ sent a written tribute—"I have known few champions of liberty that were her equal and fewer who stirred the conscience of the nation as effectively"—as did President Richard Nixon, who praised Agnes as a woman of "great strength and great spirit." Testimonials also arrived from Yitzhak Rabin, Averell Harriman, Walter Lippmann, Arthur Ochs Sulzberger, Eric Sevareid, Dorothy Schiff, John Hay Whitney, Kingman Brewster, David Rockefeller, C. Dillon Ripley, Omar Bradley, and George Meany.[59]

Not long after Agnes's death, Kay gave a small dinner at Crescent Place for her sisters and brother and a few higher-ups from the *Post.* As Eugene Patterson recalls, "They had met to go over the estate and divide up the paintings and things. We had dinner out in that great vestibule, paintings still on the walls. I mean, we're talking Rembrandts and the like."[60] Nick von Hoffman, who had escorted Kay to a few of Agnes's dinners, remembers once asking Kay, "You mean you grew up in this place?" It was, he says, "so huge and overwhelming and gray, although just dripping with art treasures."[61] In the library was a Cézanne, in the vestibule a huge stone Buddha, here and there Brancusis, a Monet, and upstairs in one of the bedrooms a Renoir.

"It has to be an institution," says June Bingham. "I can't imagine any individual living in it."[62] (The short-lived Antioch Law School used the house for a while; next it became part of the Meridian International Center, a nonprofit education organization.)

Agnes's children gave away her art, mostly to the Freer and the National Gallery. They gave the estate at Mount Kisco to Yale, but later Yale gave it back, unable, according to Roswell Gilpatric, who handled the transaction, to "make sufficient use of it."[63] Ownership later passed to the Agnes and Eugene Meyer Foundation, for use as an independent study/conference center.

Agnes's death seemed to release Kay to become more fashionable. At Babe Paley's suggestion, she started wearing Halston, for a while exclusively, until he stopped designing for private customers. Then she moved to the collections of Oscar de la Renta, Yves Saint Laurent, and Hubert de Givenchy.[64] Long gone from Kenneth's B list, she now focused excessively on her hair. In 1973, Washington's *Star-News* reported that the "powerful publisher of *The Washington Post* . . . pays Kenneth's hairdressing salon in New York $500 once a week to have one of his famous minions fly down to [do her hair in] Washington where a car, hotel room and expenses are provided for him."[65]

Kay Graham's image would match what would soon become an almost ubiquitous way of describing her—"the most powerful woman in the world." Events of the early and late 1970s would make that billing only a bit of an exaggeration.

Chapter 17

KAY PASSES THE TEST

After not quite seven years of marriage, Lally divorced her architect husband, Yann Weymouth, in 1971. Getting married, Lally would later say, was "horribly rash."[1] Whether she meant getting married in general or getting married to Yann, she didn't specify, but friends observe that marriage and the impulsive Lally were a bad mix.

Now she was looking for something to do, preferably in the field of journalism (she had worked briefly for *The Boston Globe* while she was married) and preferably in the family business. Even people who do not much like her—and there are plenty—give Lally her due as a woman who might have luxuriated in family money to the exclusion of all else. Instead, while luxuriating in family money, she began to carve out a career as a writer and editor of magazine articles and books. She edited the book *Thomas Jefferson: The Man, His World, His Influence* for publisher George Weidenfeld, who became her friend and later one of many men linked to her romantically. She also edited *America in 1876: The Way We Were.* She acutely wanted to be taken seriously as a professional, and she was, for the Jefferson book in particular.[2]

She watched, without much pleasure, as her younger brother Donny, happily married, former president (that is, editor) of *The Harvard Crimson* (also former editor of the *St. Albans News*), with real-life experience as a soldier and a policeman behind him, joined the *Post* as heir apparent and golden boy the very year of her divorce.

"Of course Lally resented the paper's being given to Don," says Jean Friendly[3]—especially since, it is said, Lally does not like him much and disdains his intellect. "And it was a mistake that Lally didn't have some big role in the paper, because Lally's bright as hell." Lally has reportedly told friends at least once that "were her father still alive, he would want her to be where Donny is now." She has described Phil as the person she cared for most in the world; after he died, she "thought it was the end."[4]

Lally must have known since she was old enough to understand such things that the paper was destined for her younger brother—not because he was better suited by temperament or training, but simply because he was the oldest male. When Kay was tossed into the fray, and family expectations might have been revised, that one survived, "because that's the way [Kay] decided it would be," says Mark Edmiston. "The oldest male would take over the company and [all the others were] told to find their own careers."[5]

Kay had chosen, Roswell Gilpatric explains, to have only one of her children involved in the paper. "If you have two or more children on the scene, you're going to have rancor, bitterness and so forth."[6] She wanted only one Graham learning the ropes. *Post* president Paul Ignatius recalls her "very strong belief that nepotism was the downfall of companies; [we] would often talk about the *Star*'s [having so many] problems in part because there was so damn much family there."[7]

That background is invariably ignored when men such as Mark Meagher dismiss Lally as "a totally spoiled rich little bitch" who is "enormously jealous of Don" and thinks that "the *Post* should have been given to her," even though "she didn't work there, she hasn't accomplished anything that would entitle her to it."[8] But if Lally had been launched on a carefully plotted training program that year of her divorce, when she was searching for a new role; if she had been groomed since childhood to run a newspaper in the capital of the Western world, would she have grown into a steady, serious, responsible woman?

What she grew into is, from many perspectives, not a very pretty picture. The image of Lally as mean, unpredictable, unmanageable has been magnified by the assiduous coverage given her by the New York and Washington media. No one was assigning profiles of Donny, because he seemed so colorless, so much the dutiful son. A 1990 profile by Henry Alford in *Spy* magazine was full of demeaning anecdotes—Lally "regally" informing *Newsweek* staffers, "My mother is *really mad* at you," or usurping the magazine's seat on a campaign plane, banishing the working correspondent to the back, where he could no longer watch exchanges between the candidate and his wife.[9] Andy Warhol described in his diaries Lally's reaction when Ronald Reagan, Jr., declined her request for an interview, explaining, "I don't do interviews—I'm only doing one . . . and it's for [Warhol's] *Interview* magazine." "How can you work for that homosexual publication?" Lally reportedly asked. "The two of us are more the same kind of person. I mean, I've got top family and *you've* got top family, and you're giving an exclusive to *that*?"[10]

Given Lally's desire to be taken seriously as a journalist, her mood was not sweetened when she discovered how much more likely her name and opinions were to appear in the gossip columns than in the news columns. Her views on Thomas Jefferson were not much sought, nor were her analyses of the latest foreign policy crisis—international affairs having become her passion. There was, however, plenty of interest in her public temper tantrums—such as the one at a Manhattan restaurant when she was forced to wait five minutes for a table[11]—and in the goings-on at one or another of her parties.

It was, for example, at one of Lally's dinners that the famous fistfight between Gore Vidal and Norman Mailer erupted. When Lally pleaded with her guests, who included Clay Felker, then editor of *Esquire,* John Kenneth Galbraith, Susan Sontag, and Jacqueline Onassis, to pull the writers apart, Felker ordered her, "Shut up. This fight is making your party."[12]

Lally vented her rage most often at her mother. "Kay is in many ways not really a very likable woman," says Nick von Hoffman, "but compared with Lally she's Mother Teresa."[13] What galled Lally was not so much not being given the *Post* to run—that was a battle lost before she even knew she could fight it—but being given no role whatsoever in the company. "I've been present at many a tense session between the mother and the daughter," Roswell Gilpatric says. "[Lally] felt that as the [oldest] child and the one who had been in journalism as a free-lance writer, she should have at least been on the board. She'd at least like to have a voice in its editorial policy."[14] According to Marietta Tree, Lally's "anger just reverberated for years around New York and Washington. She said, 'Well, at least you can give me *Newsweek.*' "[15]

Mark Edmiston, who refers to Lally as "the unguided missile," sees Kay as leery of her daughter, never certain what she will do next.

For that reason, perhaps, Kay allows Lally "to treat her like a child, tell her what she should do—'You're doing it the wrong way, Kay. You've got to do it this way.' " And, he marvels, "Kay takes it."[16]

Ed Kosner, who became Lally's friend, argues that "it's historical. Kay had a terrible relationship with her mother." Just as children of alcoholics become alcoholics and abused children become child abusers, "Kay had a much more difficult relationship with Lally than she had with [her sons]."[17]

The mother-daughter relationship was marked by high ups and very low downs. "Her mother gets perfectly furious with her, which is different from [getting hostile]," Marietta Tree explained. "She basically loves her, she really does, and they're constantly coming together. I think [Kay] is just very wary about her, about what she's going to do next."[18] Polly Kraft says, "When they're not fighting, they're very, very close."[19] One old friend of Kay's speculates that "whatever is going to bug Kay is going to attract Lally."[20]

Meanwhile, Lally's childish behavior became her trademark. "Lally is probably not ever going to grow up," June Bingham concludes. "You could not leave a newspaper to Lally. I would not leave a newspaper to her. I like her, but she's too volatile."[21] Polly Kraft agrees: "That's [how] Kay and Lally are so different. Kay is very methodical, and takes her responsibilities very seriously. She is responsible as a friend, she's responsible as a business associate, and she has a real sense of community. Lally's never had to have that, because she lives in New York and she's never had to run anything."[22]

In the early months of 1971, Fritz Beebe told Kay Graham that she could no longer defer a difficult decision: Should she allow her privately held, family-run company to go public by offering shares of its stock to outside investors? Beebe advised her that she really had no choice: Dow Jones had gone public eight years earlier, and since then so had Time Inc., Gannett, the New York Times Company, and Knight.

Among Beebe's most potent arguments was that going public was the only way to avoid enormous inheritance taxes. He warned Kay that if she were to die suddenly, those taxes might cause Donny to lose the paper. Phil had handed out so many stock options that the company was forced every year to spend millions to buy back shares of stock that its own employees had been given or allowed to buy.

The result was a cash drain and dangerous illiquidity. Beebe advised Kay there were only two ways out—either offer stock to the public, or sell the *Post*'s highly profitable Jacksonville, Florida, television station.[23]

The year before, Beebe had hired Mark Meagher as vice-president of finance and administration, with orders to build a corporate structure that would consolidate what were then basically three separately managed companies—the newspaper, the magazine, and some television and radio stations. His version of Kay's choices exactly matched Beebe's: "Either sell off some properties or go public."[24]

The plan was to offer 1.3 million shares of class B stock to raise $35.1 million. Arrangements for the offering were made by Lazard Frères.[25]

What decided it for Kay was the ingenious plan—public trading but private control—crafted by George Gillespie III, a partner at Cravath, Swaine who would become a director of the *Post* and Kay's personal counsel. The class B shares that would be traded to the public on the American Stock Exchange were virtually nonvoting; the class A, voting shares were held by Kay, who controlled more than fifty percent,* and her children. (The class A shareholders would have the right to elect the majority of the company's board of directors.) According to Gillespie's partner Roswell Gilpatric, this gave the Graham family "indefinite control," and it was in place before other media companies figured out how to "perpetuate the family control in spite of death or taxes."[26]

Still, Kay found the prospect of going public, losing her privacy, threatening—most immediately because her salary would be published, along with other details of the company's finances. "It was like letting strangers into the house," wrote David Halberstam, referring to the fact that going public meant bringing outsiders on the board of directors. (There had been outsiders before, but they had been trusted retainers and friends, such as Roswell Gilpatric and William P. Rogers, a former attorney general and future secretary of state, who was another of Kay's and the *Post*'s lawyers.) "She did not like the idea of having to go before the top Wall Street people and hustle her paper," Halberstam added. "The idea of asking all those rich men for money was appalling."[27]

---

*Today Kay owns 28.4 percent of the class A stock and has the right to vote enough of her children's shares to bring her interest to a controlling 50.1 percent.

*

Just before the Post Company's stock was to go on sale to the public on Tuesday, June 15, the paper once again found itself at odds with the Nixon administration. "Style" writer Judith Martin (lately known as "Miss Manners") had described Tricia Nixon, whose wedding was to be held at the White House on Saturday, June 12, as looking like a vanilla ice cream cone. The Nixons were so angry that press secretary Ron Ziegler summoned Eugene Patterson to the White House to tell him that he had better assign a different reporter, because Martin would not be issued a press pass. "Good," Patterson said, "then we won't cover Tricia's wedding." Patterson told Martin what had happened, and "the next thing I knew, every woman reporter covering the White House [had] heard about it, [and] called Judy up and said, 'You don't have to come, we'll be a pool and report to you.' And so [without sending a reporter], the *Post* had the best coverage of Tricia's wedding of any paper in the country."[28]

But it was not *The Washington Post* that next sparked the president's ire. On Sunday, June 13, alongside the photograph of the bride and her father on the front page of *The New York Times,* ran a four-column headline: "Vietnam Archive: Pentagon Study Traces 3 Decades of Growing U.S. Involvement."

Thus began the first installment of the top-secret documents that became known as the Pentagon Papers. This history and analysis of American involvement in Southeast Asia from 1944 to 1968 had been leaked to the *Times* three months earlier by Daniel Ellsberg, an analyst for the Defense Department and then for the Rand Corporation, a hawk on Vietnam who had helped write the papers and in the process become a critic of the war. Holed up in a Manhattan hotel for those three months, working in supposed secrecy, *Times* editors and reporters had prepared daily installments.

Ben Bradlee, whose single goal was to make the *Post* genuinely competitive with the arrogant "paper of record"—particularly on Washington stories—"was driven crazy by the *Times'* having this enormous and important material," Kay later recalled.[29] The substance of the Pentagon Papers was almost beside the point, maybe even boring, but the idea of being clobbered by *The New York Times* in his own backyard was more than Bradlee could bear. He would say that every word of it was written in his blood, but the humiliation, he recognized, was inevitable—a legacy of the era of Phil Graham and Al Friendly. The *Post's* kowtowing-to-the-establishment reputation lingered, and it must have occurred to Ellsberg that the *Times* was more likely than the *Post* to have the guts to publish.

It is said that the *Post* was caught completely by surprise. Not completely. The history had been ordered by none other than one of the war's major architects, Kay's friend and confidant Robert McNamara. Several days before the *Times* began publishing, McNamara himself told Phil Geyelin about the papers during a chat about the World Bank (of which McNamara had become president). "Have you heard about the thing the *Times* is doing?" Geyelin recalls McNamara asking. "They've got a whole lot of documents, and they're trying to reconstruct a history of the Vietnam war. I started all this." McNamara told Geyelin of his conviction that it would be "terribly important" that the record of policy-making be assembled in one place "so that future historians would know how the decisions were made," and most important, that the history be comprehensive, "because only then [would] people know what questions were never even raised and what warnings were never given." According to Geyelin, McNamara "turned it over [in 1967] to an assistant secretary of defense, who not much later was killed with his entire family in a plane crash. That's when it spun out of control and got into the hands of [Defense Department staffer and former Harvard professor Morton Halperin and others]. McNamara had lost interest, and so what emerged was not what he had in mind at all. I asked him if he [had] ever read the [papers], and he said, 'No. I couldn't bear to.'"

Geyelin briefed Murrey Marder, and there was a desperate but fruitless scramble.[30] The *Times* published installments that Sunday and for the next two days, before the Nixon administration's lawyers went to court and obtained a restraining order halting further publication. The ball was then in the *Post*'s court.

Two days later, on Thursday, June 17, the *Post*—along with the *St. Louis Post-Dispatch* and *The Boston Globe*—got its own set of the Pentagon Papers. The hero of the chase was *Post* national editor Ben Bagdikian, who deduced that Ellsberg was the source of the leak to the *Times* and then persuaded Eugene Patterson to send him to Boston, where Ellsberg then lived. "Bagdikian said we couldn't have the papers unless we committed to publish them," Patterson recalls. "I said, 'Well, we commit to publishing. Go get them.'" Patterson had no authority to make such a promise. On the return flight Bagdikian bought two seats, one for himself and one for the cartons containing some 4,400 sheets of paper.[31]

Bradlee told Bagdikian to take the cartons to Bradlee's George-town house so that the reporters and editors he chose—George Wilson, Murrey Marder, Chalmers Roberts, Don Oberdorfer, Phil Geyelin, Meg Greenfield, and Howard Simons—could sift through them and prepare the *Post*'s excerpts in privacy. Bradlee did not want the rest of the staff to know that the *Post* had the papers until the final authority—Kay Graham—gave permission, essentially, to break the law (the government's injunction against the *Times*) by publishing them. If the staff knew that the *Post* had them and the decision was no, Bradlee feared, there would be a newsroom rebellion. He asked Patterson "to stay at the paper and play like nothing was going on. About five minutes went by, and everybody began noticing who was missing. People would come by and wink. They knew."[32]

While Roberts and Oberdorfer went to work on the papers, Geyelin recalls, the rest of their group "sat around arguing with the lawyers."[33] Fritz Beebe was there with two young men from the *Post*'s New York firm, Rogers & Wells (as in Kay's friend William Rogers), joined by *Post* president Paul Ignatius.

The assembled reporters and editors were eager to go to press. Not so the *Post*'s lawyers and executives. Beebe warned that the paper would be breaking the law, and his speech was heavy with the expression "willfully and knowingly." He argued that the *Times* conceivably could have asserted that the government did not appear to care about the documents' classified status and thus that publishing them was neither a willful nor a knowing violation. But before the *Post* had to make a decision, Geyelin recounts, "the *Times* had already been enjoined, the government had gone to court and made its case. So Fritz was saying we were in even greater jeopardy than the *Times*."[34] Ignatius, who had, after all, been hired through the good offices of Robert McNamara, was also opposed to publishing.

The arguments against were compelling. The Post Company had gone public two days before. Its stock, offered to underwriters but not yet sold, might be hurt; also, a clause in the legal agreement for the sale of the stock stipulated that the sale could be canceled if a catastrophic event struck the company. An injunction halting distribution of the paper and a possible criminal indictment to follow could, legally, be construed as a "catastrophic event."[35]

Even the editorial people had to admit that Beebe's advice was precisely the sort any good lawyer would have given. "If you could come up with a felony conviction or even a charge of one, you're going to spook Wall Street and your stock issue is going to go to hell," admits Eugene Patterson. "Financial disaster stared the Post Company in the face."[36]

And then there was the future of the very lucrative television stations. Beebe stressed too that the company could be charged with a felony, and a felon cannot hold television licenses. As events proved, this fear was not exaggerated or paranoiac. Kay would later remember a "blood-chilling" message delivered to her via a *Post* reporter who met Nixon's deputy attorney general, Richard Kleindienst, socially: The Justice Department might begin a criminal prosecution, and no one under criminal indictment can own television stations.[37]

As Geyelin observes of Beebe's admonitions, "It was all very well for us journalists to say freedom of the press, First Amendment. Katharine had a whole lot of other things to worry about that didn't necessarily worry some of the working stiffs on the news side who said, 'Go with it.' "[38]

Kay Graham knew that for the first time in her eight years at the helm, she was the one who would have to make the decision. Production deadlines were fast approaching; the presses had already been held. If an excerpt was to run in the next morning's edition, Kay Graham had to say so immediately.

That evening she was hosting a retirement party at her house for Harry Gladstein, the paper's longtime circulation director, a valued employee considered one of the key players in building the *Post* into a successful business. Patterson stopped at Kay's house to pay his respects to Gladstein—and to talk to Kay. "I found Kay on the back porch, and told her, 'If we don't print, the immortal soul of *The Washington Post* is going to be in trouble.' And she said, 'Oh God, I know.' And so I left. I had no idea what her decision was going to be at that point."[39]

Kay's toast to Gladstein was interrupted by a phone call from Bradlee and Beebe. She excused herself from the group gathered on her lawn and took the call in her library.

"We were all sitting on the floor in [Ben's] dining room," Geyelin recalls. "Ben for a moment entertained the idea of letting the government know that we had the papers and giving it a day. I'm not sure that Ben was not being a devil's advocate. We were all trying to figure out some way to take Katharine off the horns of this god-awful dilemma. I remember Don Oberdorfer saying [about Ben's idea],

'That's the most chicken-shit argument I've ever heard in my life,' and Murrey Marder said, 'I don't think I could come to work for a newspaper that could withhold the news it had.' " Beebe signaled to Geyelin to get on the extension. Kay asked him what he thought. "There's more than one way to destroy a newspaper," he told her. "You can destroy it in the courts, but you can also destroy it by destroying the esprit de corps of the news staff."[40]

If Ben Bradlee did entertain the notion of waiting, he soon dropped it. "It was one of his better moments," says Marder.[41] The lore that has grown around Bradlee has him issuing Kay an ultimatum: "Mama, this looks like a motherfucker," he warned her, and then added that if the *Post* did not start running the story the next day, she could look for a new executive editor.[42]

When Beebe, who had been in Kay's corner since her first day at the *Post,* came on the phone and advised her not to publish, she was, she later recalled, shocked. But she soon recognized that if Beebe had said, "You can't do it, you're going to throw the company down the drain," she would have been trapped. But " 'I guess I wouldn't,' is how he put it. That made it possible. You felt there was a door there you could go through if you wanted."[43]

Her first instinct was that she needed more time. "Why can't we wait?" she wondered. "*The New York Times* waited three months."[44] But a delay, she knew, was impossible. It would soon be news— national news—that the *Post* had the papers but was too cowardly to publish. Not only that, *The Boston Globe* and the *St. Louis Post-Dispatch* were set to go. To be humiliated by two smaller papers was intolerable.

"Let's go. Let's publish," she said. With those words she pushed the *Post* up from where it had languished under her male relatives and their predecessors, as a second- and sometimes third-rate paper or worse, into the big leagues. Ben Bradlee would give his boss his highest praise: "She's got the nerve of a burglar," he said[45]—an observation often made about him.

Ignatius, Patterson, and Geyelin agree that not only did Beebe give her the opening to publish, but he would have been disappointed in her had she decided not to. "Beebe felt strongly," says Ignatius, "that if you were loyal to the tenets of good journalism, the financial reward would come as a concomitant. And I would think that, within that general gambit, [he] would think this was something a paper of the stature of the *Post* probably ought to do."[46] Geyelin agrees: "I'm sure he was proud of her, because it was a very gutsy, principled decision."[47]

Risking the store and publishing the Pentagon Papers is routinely cited as Katharine Graham's finest hour. Kay herself describes it as the "real crucible."[48] When she did not take Beebe's advice, Patterson says, "that was really where Kay did her growing up."[49]

She also showed that she was a journalist first. She recognized that her personal predilection, which would have been to protect Bob McNamara—no one, after all, was more tarnished by the details of those papers than he—was irrelevant.

The *Post* then had to prepare to go to court. Geyelin says that he and the others gathered at Bradlee's had argued "that everything in the Pentagon Papers more or less had been published in some form or another already. I sat up with Murrey Marder until five in the morning, going through the morgue [back issues of the *Post*] looking for evidence that this stuff had been published. We were due in court at eight."[50]

The next morning, an official from the Nixon administration called to demand that the *Post* cease publication of the papers. When it refused, the government went to work on obtaining a restraining order, as it had done against the *Times*. The *Post* published for two days before it too was enjoined. In the meantime, *The Boston Globe* and the *St. Louis Post-Dispatch* had started to publish and were similarly ordered to stop.

Not surprisingly, as soon as Kay gave the go-ahead, Geyelin recalls, she began to have second thoughts.[51] Was she sending her company on the road to financial ruin? Was she hurting her country, as her friend Henry Kissinger, who was enraged by the publication of the papers, contended, or putting lives at risk, or committing treason, as Nixon's men intimated? "Have you heard that Anatoly Dobrynin [the Soviet ambassador] is saying that there is nothing more for him to do in Washington, now that the *Post* has published all the country's secrets?" Kissinger scolded Kay. Dean Rusk charged that the documents would prove valuable to the Soviets and the North Vietnamese.[52] Solicitor General Erwin Griswold, former dean of Harvard Law School, who argued the government's case before the Supreme Court, warned that publication of the documents "will affect lives . . . the process of the termination of the war . . . the process of recovering prisoners of war."[53] Later, in a speech, Kay defended herself by saying that "only a few paragraphs in the forty-seven volumes of the Pentagon Papers were truly sensitive, and they were never considered for publication."*[54]

On June 30, the Supreme Court decided in favor of the newspapers, ruling against prior restraint. For a short time, at least, *The Washington Post* seemed on a par with *The New York Times.*

Ironically, the Pentagon Papers served as an indictment of the *Post* itself, which had so steadfastly supported the Johnson policy on Vietnam. The *Post* had blasted Wayne Morse and Ernest Gruening, for example, the two senators who voted against the Gulf of Tonkin resolution, editorializing: "There is no substance in Senator Morse's charge that the resolution amounts to a 'predated declaration of war.' " In fact, the Pentagon Papers confirmed that during the six months preceding the Gulf of Tonkin incident, American forces clandestinely attacked North Vietnam.[56]

Ben Bradlee ended up with even more power. In an apparent paradox—as one top *Post* editor puts it, "It was the only time on record when a major firm won a lawsuit and got fired"[57]—Kay transferred some of the Post Company legal business from William Rogers and his firm to Edward Bennett Williams (Bradlee's best friend and among those who had urged Kay to hire him) and his. In the heat of the arguments over whether to publish, Kay had called Williams in Chicago, where he was working an $80 million divorce suit. He advised her to ignore the stodgy advice of the New York lawyers, to stiffen her spine and publish.[58]

Speculation had it that Bradlee "pushed Bill Rogers out." It was beyond speculation that Bradlee ousted Eugene Patterson, who left the paper later in 1971. "It was not my best time in this business," Patterson says. "There was no place for me at the *Post.*"[59] Bradlee made sure of that, and later admitted that he appropriated the managing editor's province of determining the play given major stories. "Gene was born to run something. I wouldn't let him be managing editor. He ended up by doing the scut work."[60] As he departed, Patterson observed, "Bradlee needs a managing editor like a boar needs tits." Bradlee's retort was meaner: he was sorry to see the

---

*Some eighteen years afterward, in a remarkable opinion piece in, of all places, *The Washington Post,* Griswold admitted that the papers did not pose a serious security risk; that "the principal concern of the classifiers [was] not with national security, but rather with government embarrassment."[55]

Pulitzer Prize winner go because he was "the best Irish tenor we ever had here."[61]

All along, Bradlee had wanted his own man, Howard Simons—and he knew that it was just a matter of time before he got him. Bradlee had needed to fill the slot immediately, and he could sell Patterson to Kay more quickly than he could Simons. Patterson, a stopgap, was doomed to fail. "I think [Bradlee] was bent on choosing [someone] who would recognize that he and only he was the real power," says Morton Mintz. "When you bring in somebody from the outside who is a renowned figure in journalism, but you say, 'I want you to be my office boy,' that's not going to work. But when you take anyone from your own staff who owes his promotion to you, are you going to get the same level of independence? I don't think so."[62] (Patterson ended up at the St. Petersburg, Florida, *Times* as editor and president.)

It was reported at the time of Patterson's departure that he had been warned against accepting the job at the *Post* because it was a "snakepit." Patterson couches it in more gentlemanly terms: "It's a highly volatile workplace because you've got so much talent and ambition penned up in one room."[63]

Others describe it less benignly. Andrew Barnes, a *Post* reporter who left to accept Patterson's offer of a job at the St. Petersburg paper, explains that he was "kind of pissed" at Bradlee, Kay, and others at the *Post*. "They [took] an awful lot of bright people and then forced them to compete to get in the paper rather than somehow concert their actions and let them feel that they were part of something important."[64] George Reedy, while a professor of journalism at Marquette University, was asked by Bradlee to spend time in the *Post* newsroom, interviewing reporters and studying the causes of employee dissatisfaction. "One of the [things people told] me was that Ben would assign the same thing to three people on the theory that they'd all fight like hell to [outdo each other]."[65] Bill Greider, defending Bradlee's style, points out that the *Post* "had about two or three times more reporters than it needed to publish the paper every day, because Bradlee, with Mrs. Graham's money, hired them. That sets up a fundamental competition. And you either rise to that and try to write stories that get in the paper, or you sit back and say, 'It makes me uncomfortable, so I'm just going to do my chores and go home at night.' "[66]

The system Bradlee implemented and encouraged became known

as "creative tension" to devotees and "Bradlee's rat-fuck"[67] to detractors. And as Greider points out, it could not have existed "without some sort of implicit authorization from Mrs. Graham,"[68] whose father or even whose husband would not have tolerated such an atmosphere. "Although there were disagreements at the old *Post*," says Ben Gilbert, "you generally knew where you stood."[69]

The ugly, elitist side to Bradlee's star system was that it encouraged his personal favorites—almost always reporters on the national side—and rewarded them with the most prestigious assignments, sometimes even with a column. Those who in Bradlee's estimation were not stars—many of them with the experience, seasoning, and knowledge that the Ivy Leaguers and Rhodes scholars whom Bradlee favored would never acquire—guessed correctly that Bradlee barely scanned their stories. It was a vicious circle: Because they were not stars they got mundane beats, and because they had mundane beats Bradlee mostly ignored them.[70] Reporters who were shy by nature, who lacked the repartee that Bradlee so prized, found themselves overlooked. "He uses inattention as a management tool," Greider observed.[71]

George Reedy recalls his first day at the *Post* on Bradlee's assignment: "I looked out over that newsroom and I couldn't believe my eyes. I could hardly look across the thing. I said, 'For the love of God, Ben, who are those people at the other end of the room against that wall?' He said, 'George, I don't think I know a quarter of them.' On a newspaper it's very important that the editor know his people."[72]

Bradlee would say he was simply "shaking things up. If there's no tension, everybody's sitting around fat and happy."[73] But the mix of his sarcastic tongue and his low boredom point resulted in a superficiality in editorial tone and decision-making that would eventually get the *Post* in trouble. As David Halberstam reported, daily news conferences, theoretically a forum for testing and exchanging ideas, became contests to see who could get off the most clever line; reporters and editors vied with Bradlee, the all-time master of the one-liner.[74] "Many of the *Post*'s most successful editors and reporters," wrote one former reporter, Rudy Maxa, "are professional wise guys."[75]

The Pentagon Papers behind her, Kay was feeling her muscle. She again turned her attention from editorial to business; and like the child who has been bullied so often that, given the chance, she becomes the biggest bully of all, Kay Graham became a boss from hell. Rather than enshrine every syllable of advice that issued from her executives' lips, she began to belittle them.

Irrationally, she blamed the hapless Paul Ignatius for the new building, which indeed turned out to be remarkable only in its mediocrity and, worst of all, not even functional. "When you build a building that you outgrow in five years, that's not something you can forget," she said.[76] Kay "bad-mouthed" Ignatius, according to one witness,[77] and he was flabbergasted, particularly because he considered his relationship with Kay to be "very close. She was quite open with me and talked to me about things of quite a personal nature."[78]

Kay had hired Ignatius for one reason only—because Bob McNamara told her to. Had she asked others, she might have found, as Eugene Patterson did, that Paul Ignatius was a "prince of a guy, but he didn't know anything about the newspaper business. We just asked the impossible of Paul."[79] Frank Waldrop says that Ignatius was a "tough mug" who spoke to Kay in a patronizing way, "which is just what would cause her to reach for her stiletto."[80]

A veteran Washington newsman observes, "It was said about Kay Graham that you could hear her brass balls clank as she crossed the city room floor. Ignatius didn't hear them. That was the problem."[81]

Ignatius also had the misfortune to land at the *Post* as it was on its way to becoming what is now routinely dubbed a media empire, and he did not recognize that Kay truly wanted to lead the business side. That she did not have the confidence or knowledge to do so frustrated her, and made her increasingly vindictive and cruel. When she made derogatory remarks about "lady publishers," he did not hear what she was saying. Twenty years later, looking back on his two years at the *Post*, Ignatius shakes his head. "Beebe thought I was working for him, I thought I was working for him."[82]

Because Ignatius knew nothing about newspaper technology, he depended on the very people who irritated Kay; people, he claims, whom she "wanted to get rid of or undermine"—the production manager, for example, in whom she had lost confidence, concluding that he was moving too slowly on the installation of new systems that would allow the *Post*, like the *Los Angeles Times,* to publish zoned editions. It bothered Kay that her cross-country rival had a capacity that her paper lacked. She did not wish to hear about start-up problems, even though the production manager had, Ignatius argues, some legitimate excuses. "We were changing buildings while all this was going on. It [was] like rebuilding an airport at the same time you're landing airplanes."[83]

Kay wanted everything done right away; it would thus have been difficult to invent a man more irritating to her than the very prudent Ignatius, who, says Mark Meagher, engaged in "a huge amount of planning and talk."[84] While Ignatius credits Kay with an "intuitive feel" for the business side, he says "she didn't have an appreciation for the way organizations work and the need to have some kind of structure in order to get things done."[85]

There were also massive, unyielding labor problems that had accumulated over so many years ("swept under the rug," Ignatius says) that solving them in any orderly, rational way was impossible. Kay seemed to blame Ignatius—she said he was too soft—for problems that more fairly should have been laid at the feet of her own husband. The *Post* was still using technology invented after the Civil War and, at the unions' insistence, Ignatius explains, ignoring such post-1950 technology as offset printing and cold type. There was featherbedding galore and a preposterously wasteful practice called "reproduce," make-work that cost the Post Company millions.[86]

Kay did an about-face and decided to replace Ignatius with an industry insider. She realized, says one former top executive, that "you don't run a newspaper the way you'd run a war or run General Motors."[87] Instead of going for advice to an outsider such as McNamara, she went, in the fall of 1971, to three fellow newspaper publishers. Two of the three put at the top of their lists John Prescott, a high executive at Knight Newspapers, then running the business side of the Philadelphia *Inquirer* and *Daily News*.[88] Ignatius describes his replacement as "the real hotshot of Knight, the rising star."[89]

Prescott says that Kay was "presold" on him, but he was not on her. So indiscreet was she in disparaging Ignatius that Prescott had witnessed her routine and was reluctant to work for her. "She was really very tough on him," Prescott says. "She's an LBJ kind of person, either you're on her side or you're not, and if you fall out of favor, well . . ."

As much as she exaggerated Ignatius's deficiencies, so she inflated Prescott's potential. Because he knew the ins and outs of production and had had experience in Philadelphia and Detroit in resolving union stalemates—in the latter city he had steered a Knight paper through a 134-day strike—Prescott would be her man to take on the unions. He was known for being both tough and effective, someone who could "break the logjam," a "roll up your shirtsleeves" type.[90]

She also felt that Prescott, unlike Ignatius and Sweeterman, would encourage her to learn the business of newspaper publishing. As Prescott puts it, she thought, "I've got the right person in Prescott, and it'll be fun instead of a chore digging out and having to feel like a stranger at every meeting." She "looked forward with enthusiasm to tackling the nuts and bolts of the business. She's a very smart person, works hard, hours and hours, tremendous. She was prepared to spend a lot of time at it." But Prescott soon recognized that Kay's ignorance of labor relations was combined with impatience—a deadly mix: "You don't do things quickly, you have a history of twenty to thirty years of a certain kind of environment in labor relations. It takes some time to build credibility with unions and employees."[91]

While Kay was trying to figure out her role, Donny knew exactly what his should be. Exceedingly sensitive to how it looked for him to join the paper, he was determined to be a working newsman, not a spoiled scion. He followed the pattern he established when he arrived in Vietnam and pleaded with a fellow soldier who had been a Harvard classmate not to tell anyone who his mother was.[92] At the *Post,* he would work in nearly every department, often at entry-level positions; his self-imposed training program included writing and editing but also selling ads, driving a truck, trying to decipher the secrets of circulation, promotion, and production.[93] This was Donny's desire, despite his mother's more old-fashioned belief in the prerogatives of privilege.

Knowing that about the boss, some of Kay's editors could not restrain themselves from helping her son along. On the editorial side, his first job was as a metropolitan beat reporter. According to Eugene Patterson, Harry Rosenfeld, who had become metro editor the year before, "would constantly try to be of assistance to him, and Donny wouldn't give him the time of day. He would accept no favors, no special coaching or comment on his news stories. Instead of hanging out with the brass, he hung out with the guys, steered clear of anybody who wanted to butter him up."[94] (Donny came to appreciate and respect one of the assistant city editors, Leonard Downie, both for his knowledge of how the city worked and for his seeming disinterest in Donny's birthright.[95])

John Prescott, who choreographed parts of Donny's training program, was impressed. "I have a tremendous regard for him. [He's] a very hardworking guy, very sound and rational and different from his mother." Donny was "down there and learning the business and winning over the people." It was not an easy assignment, Prescott explains, because the *Post* already had "tremendous production problems and lateness problems"—the latter allegedly caused by the typographers' union's deliberate stalling of the presses.

Slowdowns were a particular problem for the *Post* because rather than run its own trucking department, it used independent distributors and dealers. "So," says Prescott, "at midnight a couple hundred ma-and-pa trucks pull up waiting to get their papers while the typographical union is deciding just how much longer this sub rosa wildcat activity would [go on] before they allowed us to get our paper out. This would cause tremendous financial problems for these independent dealers. Donny went around and tried to explain what was going on. After his circulation stint, I arranged for him [to] work as an assistant production manager. He was a model publisher's son."[96]

Although Donny had none of Phil's charisma, he did have his ability to make his employees, especially the lunch-bucket contingent, feel that he cared about them. He knew their names, he knew about their families and their problems, he hung around the pressmen, and he stayed after hours.

In this regard, Donny bore no resemblance to his mother. "A trip through the composing room with Katharine," recalls Prescott, "which she'd like to do once in a while, was the most Lady Bountiful kind of experience." She would glare at him if he greeted a worker.[97]

Kay's tastes ran much more toward world travel. In 1970 she had finally convinced Kermit Lansner, editor of *Newsweek* since 1969, to accompany her on one of what had become annual foreign treks—that year, her first visit to Israel. Lansner had mixed emotions about traveling with Kay, which he knew would be difficult at best and nerve-wracking at worst. "Oz [Elliott] would go on these trips and end up carrying her hatbox. Just the kind of thing you fell into because she's imperious and used to her ways and she gets all uptight. She can be a pain in the neck."[98]

Having declined previous invitations, Lansner made certain requests that likely caused Kay to raise an eyebrow, although she said nothing. He asked that the trip be "short and self-contained," and that he be allowed to take his wife along, because they planned to go to Europe afterward. Lansner understood that an invitation to his wife, or anyone's wife, was not a given; that the only woman whose presence Kay expected was Liz Hylton, who had been Phil's personal secretary and was now hers, and who served as planner, agent, lady's maid, and scapegoat when plans went awry.

The trip turned out better than he expected, Lansner recalls, although "I wouldn't say we had a ball." For Kay, it was just fine. In Israel she was a most important person: the publisher of the most powerful newspaper in the world—"in the sense," Lansner explains, "that Washington has such a say over Israel's destiny, in terms of money and everything else."

Lansner was "wonderfully entertained" by Moshe Dayan, Abba Eban, and others, who thus paid off old debts. "We had entertained these people in New York and Washington. Dayan threw a beautiful party for us in his backyard—all the generals [were] there." Dayan showed his guests his impressive collection of antiquities. "Isn't it against the law, General, to collect these things?" Lansner's wife asked. "So who's going to arrest me?" he replied.

Lansner says that Kay "had a crush on Dayan. He was a very attractive man. He had a feline quality to him. And the patch he used very effectively." With Lansner, Kay called on Prime Minister Golda Meir. "Clearly, I was the working journalist on this trip," Lansner says; it was obviously expected that he would write up the interview with Meir.[99] Kay also met with Egyptian president Gamal Abdel Nasser, on that occasion accompanied by *Newsweek*'s Cairo bureau chief.

About a year later Lansner was traveling again—without Kay, this time—to visit *Newsweek* bureaus in Japan and Hong Kong. While he was away, she decided to get rid of him.

The firing was strangely bland and, says Lansner, "totally unexpected. Kay decided she didn't want me around, and that was that." On his first day back, happy to hear that Kay was in her office at *Newsweek,* a jovial Lansner knocked on her door. "Let me tell you about my trip to Japan," he said. "First let me tell you something," Kay replied. "Yes, what is it?" "You're fired," she said.[100] According to Arnaud de Borchgrave, "Kermit was reeling. Just couldn't get over it. First he thought it was a joke, but that's the way she does it."[101]

There had been no warning of her dissatisfaction with him, Lansner insists, as does Lester Bernstein, who, as managing editor, was Lansner's number two. Bernstein explains that her lack of self-confidence accounted for this bizarre termination scene. "It has probably always been terribly difficult for her to fire somebody, and that's why, I suspect, more often than not it's done with the swiftness, the cruelty, of a decapitation."[102]

Lansner was most astonished because it was evident Kay liked him. He speculates that his fate was payback for his habit of keeping his distance. "My wife has said that I never courted Kay and she resented it."[103] Bernstein agrees that Kay had with Lansner "the most genuinely warm and agreeable personal relationship that [she] ever had with anyone at the magazine," but he argues that Lansner's failure to take Kay seriously contributed heavily to his downfall. In his mind, she remained the timid, deferential widow of 1963 who, Bernstein adds, "obviously wouldn't dare to suggest that she talk to you as if you were her boss. Kermit, for example, might change a cover at the last minute. Kay wouldn't have even known what the first cover was because he didn't pay that much attention [to her]."[104]

While Lansner was in Japan, Kay asked Oz Elliott to take back the job. He had not been a notable success on the business side as president of *Newsweek,* and he agreed to return to editorial. That disturbed Lester Bernstein, who saw it as a message that he would never be more than number two. "I was so shocked that I didn't start thinking until the next day, Why should Oz be coming back to do that job?" He went to see Kay, who admitted that he had not even been considered. "You're perfectly right," she told him. "You're entitled to be considered." By then, Bernstein recalls, Elliott's new position "had already been announced, so we went through a twenty-four-hour charade, an impulse on her part to placate me and to do what she thought was the right thing. Then, after the day was over, she recognized that it was not possible to do anything, and told me that."[105] (Bernstein went to work as a PR man for RCA.)

Jim Truitt, still keeping abreast of who was getting fired from *Newsweek* and the *Post*—he had most recently mocked Eugene Patterson on his departure—sent a note to Lansner: "It happens to everyone. Fuck you."[106]

For all the attention *The Washington Post* received over the Pentagon Papers, for all the attention Kay Graham received because of her rare status as a woman at the head of a major media company, she was hardly a household name. Outside of newspaper circles and the Beltway, she was still "Kay who?"

That all changed on Saturday morning, June 17, 1972, when Joseph Califano, Jr., then general counsel of the Democratic National Committee, called his friend Howard Simons, managing editor of the *Post,* to tell him that there had been a break-in at DNC headquarters at an office complex in Washington. The five masked men arrested in the early hours of that morning were carrying wiretapping equipment. As was his practice, Simons called Kay at Glen Welby to tell her what would be appearing in the next day's paper: the DNC break-in would be one of the stories.[107]

And so began the scandal that would topple a president and transform *The Washington Post,* Kay Graham, and Ben Bradlee into national celebrities: Watergate.

Bradlee, for one, did not deserve such top billing. Howard Simons, with help from editors Harry Rosenfeld and Barry Sussman, immediately took charge of the day-to-day coverage. Simons "led the charge," Bradlee himself would concede, but not until seventeen years later when interviewed by a *New York Times* reporter for Simons's obituary.[108] Bob Woodward, who became, with partner Carl Bernstein, one of the most famous reporters in America, characterized Simons as "the day-to-day agitator, the one who ran around the newsroom inspiring, shouting, directing, insisting that we not abandon our inquiry, whatever the level of denials or denunciation." It was Simons who gave the name "Deep Throat" to the background source so prized by Woodward and Bernstein.[109]

"Of course it was Howard's story, not Bradlee's," says Ben Gilbert. "Bradlee did not really become interested until it looked like it might topple Nixon, and then he got involved."[110] According to *Washingtonian* writer Barbara Matusow, Simons "thought Watergate *was* a story from the start. Ben Bradlee sat in his office doing crossword puzzles that summer when Rosenfeld and Sussman sweated out every comma with their star reporters. As far as most people in the newsroom were concerned, the Metro team was off on an ill-advised goose chase."*[111]

---

*Former *Post* reporter John Hanrahan recalls, "One day some guy walked in and handed me a bunch of memos from the special prosecutor's office. He didn't tell me what his name was, but it was clear he took out the trash at the Watergate special prosecutor's office. He said, 'If you want to, you can come every night to this loading dock'—public property—'and just take all this trash,' [which consisted of] drafts of memos on key issues. Then the [question] became, Do we go back and raid their trash every night? Great debate." Bradlee was out of town at the time; five or six editors met and phoned him. "As soon as Bradlee hung up with us he called [special prosecutor] Archibald Cox: 'Archie, I want you to know that somebody gave us these documents. I just want you to know, Arch, you've got a trash problem.' Again I thought, Yeah, the old-boy network is at work."[112]

Kay Graham was ultimately the person who counted most. If she had called Simons off the chase, he would not have been able to do a thing about it but quit. By encouraging and financing the Watergate investigation—and by agreeing that she would go to jail sooner than comply with a subpoena for her reporters' notes—she deserves top billing, as she did when she published the Pentagon Papers.

She allowed her reporters and editors to pursue Watergate even when the *Post* appeared to be alone in its conviction that Watergate was more than a third-rate burglary. As she recalled later, "We thought, If this is such a hell of a story, where is *The New York Times*? Hell, usually if you have a great scoop everyone else is over it like a wet blanket the next day. And here we were alone with this . . . cow mess walking down a street and nobody came near it. It was awful."[113]

When she was alone, especially in the middle of the night, she had grave doubts. Kissinger called to warn her that the *Post* was all wrong about Watergate. When Carl Bernstein called Nixon campaign counsel John Mitchell to read him something the *Post* would be running the next morning—a story that linked him, while attorney general, to control of a secret Republican fund to gather dirt on Democrats, the same fund that paid the Watergate burglars—Mitchell howled, "Katie Graham is gonna get her tit caught in a big fat wringer if that's published."[114]

She knew he meant that the reelected president (surely Nixon would win in a landslide) would see to it that she had trouble renewing federal licenses for her television stations. The tapes that Nixon was secretly making reveal his telling Robert Haldeman and John Dean, "The main thing is the *Post* is going to have damnable, damnable problems. . . . They have a television station. . . . Does that [federal broadcasting license] come up too? The point is, when does it come up? . . . The game has to be played awfully rough."[115]

On October 27, 1972, Nixon's special assistant Charles Colson, famous for concocting the enemies list of people to be hounded by government agencies, and for saying that he would run over his own grandmother if it would help get Nixon reelected,[116] wrote a short memo to White House staffer Pat O'Donnell: "Please check for me when any of the *Washington Post* television station licenses are up for renewal." At other times, Colson wished aloud that he could blow up the *Post* and told Bradlee that he would like to try him and his reporters as war criminals.[117]

Nixon's minions at one point challenged license renewals for the

Post Company's television stations in Miami and Jacksonville.[118] Kay watched her company's stock drop from $38 a share in December 1972 to $21 in May 1973, probably as a result of uncertainty over the effects of Nixon's fury with her newspaper.[119]

Barry Sussman, then special Watergate editor, recalls that those threats never filtered down to him. "What we were worried about was being right, we had to be right. My job was to go after the story." In an address years later, Kay would recall her profound relief in October 1972, when "Walter Cronkite took us national on the *CBS Evening News.* That same month we ran the two biggest stories on the interconnection of many of these events and showed that they led directly to the White House."[120]

It was only when one of the burglars, James McCord, implicated John Mitchell and Nixon's counsel John Dean, among others, that the case blew open—especially when Dean fingered Haldeman and Ehrlichman. And it was only then that the Pulitzer Prize board, overturning its jury's recommendation, gave its award for distinguished public service to *The Washington Post.*[121]

Ben Gilbert has said that under the regimes of Kay's father or husband, Watergate would have been just another fleeting story.[122] But at least one former top *Post* writer, in an attempt to downplay her courage in pursuing the story, has argued that had Nixon not spurned Kay's advances, her invitations to dine at her house as other presidents had done, "it's less likely that [reporting of Watergate] would have appeared in the *Post.* The *Post* might have listened if the administration had pulled its trump card, which is always CIA, national security, state secrets, 'Boys will get killed if you publish that.' "[123]

Richard Nixon promoted the image of Kay Graham as the spiteful, irrational, rejected woman. As investigation of Watergate ground on, he grew obsessed with policing members of his administration to be certain that no one was fraternizing with the enemy. In his book *Breach of Faith,* Theodore White describes the unexpected fall from grace of Peter Peterson, whom Nixon held in great esteem and named secretary of commerce in 1972. Peterson suddenly found his access to the president cut off and was then pushed out of the Cabinet and offered the job of "superambassador," to be based in Brussels. According to White, when Peterson explained that with five children he could not just up and leave, and asked if he could start his new position with several months' work mapping strategy in the

United States, John Ehrlichman replied, in effect, "Get out of Washington—now."

Peterson asked Charles Colson why, after his widely acknowledged superior service, the dismissal was so abrupt. "Without any unfriendliness," wrote White, "quite candidly, Colson explained: Peterson had been going to parties at the home of Katharine Graham. . . . Not only that, he had even spent a weekend at her country home."[124]

On October 16, 1972, *The Washington Post* moved into its new and undistinguished building at 1150 15th Street NW, the paper's sixth headquarters in its ninety-five-year history. Instead of costing upward of $50 million, as Pei's plan had projected, it cost $25 million; but it impressed no one, least of all Kay Graham, who was embarrassed and depressed at the prospect of presiding over such an ill-planned box.

Most memorable about the dedication ceremony was the presence, as guest of honor, of William Rogers, Nixon's secretary of state and formerly the *Post*'s lawyer. It was, Kay quipped in her welcoming speech, "like [having] Anwar Sadat . . . speak at a B'nai B'rith convention." Rogers responded by quoting Thomas Jefferson's remark that "newspapers are an evil from which there is no remedy."[125] It may be that Rogers was there because he had already lost the power struggle with national security advisor Henry Kissinger over who would control foreign policy (Nixon would name Kissinger secretary of state the next year), and he had nothing to lose in accepting his old friend's invitation.

Kay's newspaper was her life, and the men in her life were all, in one way or another, tied to her by the newspaper. Although nearly a decade had passed since Phil's suicide, Kay seldom talked about him, even to close friends. The pain she still felt from her public humiliation over Phil's philandering became obvious in her disapproval, even anger, at men in her employ who behaved likewise. One former *Post* writer describes her "fierce sense of identification with older wronged wives who were discarded by husbands running off with younger [women]."[126]

National editor Ben Bagdikian, who had secured the *Post*'s copy of the Pentagon Papers, was involved with a woman who not only was younger than he but also was a reporter on the *Post*—a double offense in Kay's eyes, because it reminded her of Phil's tie to *Newsweek* staffer Robin Webb. When, after he had asked his wife for a divorce, Bagdikian brought the woman to a party at Kay's house, Kay said in her best hauteur, "This is an invitation for Mr. and Mrs. Ben Bagdikian."[127] He later told Lynn Rosellini, "She gave me a long lecture about how I shouldn't do anything to hurt my [wife]. She said, 'I know what it's like.' "[128] (Bagdikian soon left the *Post*; colleagues cite unrelated reasons for his departure.)

Another casualty was a well-respected, highly placed editor. According to Phil Geyelin, the editor was "having an affair with someone on the 'Style' section," violating the company policy of "no fishing off the company dock."[129]

Pierre Salinger, journalist and press secretary to John Kennedy, had become very important to Kay. Having moved with his wife to Paris shortly after Robert Kennedy's assassination, Salinger became one of those people who arranged dinners for Kay—with men of the stature of prime minister and president—when she was in the French capital. But as important as he was to her, Kay ostracized him when he too chose to divorce his wife (who happened to be his third, but the only one Kay knew). She no longer asked him to choreograph her Paris social life.[130] (There were others in the city—such as correspondent Jim Hoagland—who played this role.)

In 1973, Ben Bradlee left his wife and children and their house in Georgetown, and soon set up housekeeping with Sally Quinn. As always, when it came to Bradlee, Kay made an exception. Ben Bagdikian lost his job over just such behavior, but not Ben Bradlee. "Ben is the only guy who could discard his wife, marry a reporter, and get away [with it]," says one former *Post* writer.[131]

The affair started when Quinn left the *Post* to become coanchor of *The CBS Morning News*—an appointment that network executives hoped would knock Barbara Walters from her dominance at NBC. A friend of Bradlee's recalls that it was about three in the afternoon when Sally went to his office to resign. "Well, what are you doing for the rest of the day?" Bradlee asked her.[132]

After Quinn flopped colossally at CBS—her extreme nervousness resulted in a bad case of acne; she made a ludicrously inappropriate comment after a wrenching report on child labor, griping that as a girl she had had to clean her own room—she landed a job at *The New York Times*. That was just fine with Kay. Phil Geyelin remembers a very emphatic Kay telling him, "She will not come back to this newspaper." But come back she did. The *Times* job lost its luster even before Quinn's first day, when an editor unceremoniously up-braided her, as if she were a naughty child, for free-lancing for the *Post* an attention-grabbing, outrageously frank profile of Alice Roosevelt Longworth at age ninety.

Bradlee engineered her return to "Style," even as Kay repeated that Quinn could not work there while he was executive editor. "Ben managed to turn the argument around," says Geyelin: " 'Look, she's working for the *Times* and I'm working for the *Post*. What the hell can we talk about? I can't tell her about the big story that I'm working on at the *Post,* and she can't tell me about the big story that they're working on at the *Times.* We can't talk shop.' And as has happened on so many occasions, Ben had an enormous ability to turn Kay around."[133]

Some *Post* staffers felt that Quinn, through Bradlee, had far too much power at the *Post*. Nancy Collins, a former "Style" writer, commented: "In spite of her live-in affair with the boss, Sally had stayed on in 'Style,' exercising her influence far beyond the feature pages and creating an enormous amount of free-floating resentment among reporters."[134]

David Halberstam wrote that Ben Bradlee's ability to have his affair and maintain his special relationship with Kay was a reflection of his "personal power." Kay had accepted the affair because "if Ben needed his Sally to be a good editor, as Grant had needed his liquor to be a good general, then so be it."[135]

Chapter 18

"THE QUEEN BEE"

Fritz Beebe, chairman of the Washington Post Company, died on May 1, 1973, of the intestinal cancer that had first appeared five years before and was thought to be cured. He might have led the *Post* for another decade or longer, giving Kay more time to find her footing.[1] As unsure of herself as she was, she had, predictably, taken to criticizing Beebe; not meanly as she would other executives, but still, to many in her employ her sniping seemed ungrateful. Fritz had not been adventurous enough, or sufficiently entrepreneurial.[2]

While he was alive, understandably, she did not take for herself the title and responsibilities of chairman. Once he died, she had no choice but to try to fill his shoes—that or send the message to those inside and outside her organization that she was essentially a figurehead. With Beebe's death, there was also no excuse to retain corporate headquarters in New York, a peculiarity from the Phil Graham era that allowed Beebe to oversee *Newsweek*.[3]

To no one's surprise, when the board of directors met eight days after his death, Kay was named CEO and chairman of the board of directors. At the same meeting, Larry Israel was elected company president and chief operating officer.

Five years before, Beebe had hired Israel, then president of the Westinghouse Broadcasting Station Group, to run the Post Company television stations. Some wondered how a man whose experience was in broadcasting would fare as president of a company whose major components were a newspaper and a magazine, but Kay was enthusiastic about Israel. According to John Prescott, who would remain president of the newspaper and who did not need anyone to tell him he had been passed over, she saw Israel as the next Fritz Beebe, but better.

Larry Israel would never become the next Fritz Beebe. Once Kay met Warren Buffett, a little-known investor from Omaha, chairman of a company called Berkshire, Hathaway, Israel did not stand a chance. Buffett would come closer than anyone to becoming the Ben Bradlee of the business side.

Buffett had asked Charles Peters, an acquaintance of Kay's, to make the introduction in 1971. (Peters's magazine, *The Washington Monthly,* had been saved the year before by a cash infusion from Buffett.) Buffett had a specific reason for wanting to meet her: he owned stock in *The New Yorker,* which, he believed, might be for sale, and he wanted to interest Kay in attempting a takeover, arguing that the *Post* would be the perfect owner for the magazine. Kay dismissed his suggestion.

In the spring and summer of 1973, Buffett started buying the Washington Post Company's B stock, which he recognized was selling at bargain prices. He saw that the *Post,* although not yet a monopoly, so dominated its market that it almost fit his description of a monopoly daily as an "unregulated tollbooth."[4] He calculated that the Post Company was worth between $400 and $500 million but that the market valued its stock at only $100 million. For $10.6 million he bought nine percent of the company.*[5]

Like most people at that time, Kay had never heard of Berkshire, Hathaway,[8] and she only vaguely remembered meeting Warren Buffett. She was, recalls Peter Derow, then a *Newsweek* senior vice-president, "very frightened" when she realized that some stranger, some hick from Nebraska, was buying large chunks of her company. Derow, Nicholas Katzenbach,† and others tried in vain to reassure Kay and remind her that because she and her family owned one hundred percent of the A stock, the voting stock, there was no way for Buffett, or anyone, to take over her company.[9]

She did not know how to respond to Buffett: whether, as she put

---

*Eleven years later, in a letter to Kay, he would exult that his investment was worth about $140 million.[6] Eventually his investment in the company would grow to more than a sixth of its B stock and would appreciate by some 2,000 percent.[7]

†Katzenbach, former attorney general and later general counsel of IBM, was a new member of the Post Company's board.

it, to "stiff-arm him or welcome him."[10] Having decided on the latter, she invited him to dine with her in Washington. Not only did he charm her, but he reassured her that his purchase was purely an investment, and that he would be happy to let Donny Graham vote all of his shares.[11] (He has given the proxy for his 17.5 percent stake in the B stock to Donny.[12])

Kay responded by taking Buffett at his word. She invited him to join her board (he did in 1974) and soon made him chairman of the finance committee.

"Kay was one of the first people on the East Coast who thought that Warren Buffett was a real smart guy," says Peter Derow.[13] When he was *Post* ombudsman, Richard Harwood would describe Buffett as "a sort of guru in the evolution of the corporate philosophy adopted by . . . Katharine Graham."[14]

The two developed a student-teacher relationship of the sort that so appealed to Kay. Her friend Polly Kraft places Buffett in the same category as Robert McNamara, as a man whom Kay "counts on" and trusts "completely."[15] "I've had two great professors," Kay told a *Washingtonian* writer. "One is Warren Buffett, and the other is experience."[16] Those who knew her history might have been surprised that Fritz Beebe's name did not follow, or even precede, Buffett's.

Post and *Newsweek* executives soon realized that no one had more influence on Kay than Warren Buffett. He talked to her daily, and she considered his judgment nonpareil.[17] Some of her executives found her profound reliance on Buffett irritating and irrational even as they recognized the high quality of his counsel. "You didn't know if you were persuading Kay or persuading Warren," said one executive. "It could be on anything, it could be on the color of the tapestry: 'Warren's here, let's ask him.' 'Oh Jesus, when did he become the expert?' "[18] Mark Edmiston was also troubled by Kay's habit of consulting Buffett on "very minor items."[19]

Kay's relationship with Buffett—the exclusivity, the extreme dependence—may account for her having what is generally regarded as a weak board of directors. Presumably, as she selects its members, she prefers it that way. Edmiston describes the board as "a bunch of famous names";[20] another former *Post* executive says, "These people were in there with the full knowledge that their [role] was to help shelter Katharine."[21] Derow characterizes the board as "weak, terrible," and explains: "As long as the family controlled the stock, the board was there to serve the family. The [board] served at her pleasure, she didn't serve at their pleasure." Derow wanted the board's concerns to extend beyond the estate of the Grahams. "I said to her, 'What we've got to do is get on some operating CEOs.' " But, Derow claims, because of her own lack of operating experience and her myriad insecurities, Kay was afraid to have them, afraid of looking stupid; she had "the sense that someone [might be] snickering [at her]."[22]

"I can't attract those people," she would insist to Derow, who would insist back, "Yes you can. They'll add value. You'll listen and learn."[23] Except when the teacher was Warren Buffett, she was disinclined to do either.

Serving on the Washington Post Company board carried a great deal of prestige, especially in the wake of Watergate. The board also had the reputation of being "fun"—pre-meeting dinners at Kay's house and post-meeting lunches with top editors and reporters in her dining room at *The Washington Post,* the latter inspired by board member Arjay Miller,* who wanted the "inside-Washington scoop" to take back with him to California.[24]

Kay was gracious at the meetings and meals but could be vicious behind the backs of her directors. According to one former executive, she started out trusting and respecting Richard Paget, the management consultant whom her father had charged with cutting annual losses to half a million dollars, but she soon turned on him: "The jerk's getting old. He won't do this, he won't do that." George Gillespie, the man who devised the two-tier stock system that she considered so brilliant, also came in for her scorn: "He never had to operate anything. What would he know?" "She could go around and knock off that whole board," says the executive. "She'd say, These are all jerks. What she was really saying was, I'm not a complete person, so I'm not going to let them be."[25]

When a full decade had passed since Phil Graham's death, she began to talk about him. To the surprise of some of her friends, she remembered him fondly.

Kay invited Phil Geyelin and Meg Greenfield for a weekend at Glen Welby. "She told me more graphically than I wanted to hear,"

*Miller is dean of Stanford's graduate school of business and a former president of Ford Motor Company.

Geyelin recalls, "what room she was sitting in [when] he was in the downstairs lavatory. She was able to talk about it in a composed way, but I couldn't figure out how she could go back to that house."[26] Polly Kraft remembers an evening at Glen Welby when Kay found letters that Phil had written to her. "She read them by the fire. They were so funny. It was Phil's black humor that was coming through, and she would laugh and [say], 'Didn't he have his own special take?' or 'Could you imagine anybody looking at life this way?' I don't think she ever alluded to the dark Phil." Kraft too did not have the sense that Kay found it painful to be at Glen Welby.[27]

Charles Peters marvels at the affection with which Kay remembers her husband. She talks about him, Peters says, "with incredible affection. I don't think I could have risen above those bad years, but clearly she has."[28]

Along with her nostalgia for Phil and their marriage came a renewed interest in men. For the most part, this took the form of what friends call "crushes," almost always, says Kermit Lansner, on "big, powerful figures": abroad, the dashing Moshe Dayan or former West German chancellor Willy Brandt;[29] at home, typically, Wasps in the Phil Graham or Ben Bradlee mold.

The fifty-six-year-old widow saw several obstacles in the path of marriage. The first was her uncertainty over whether a man would want her or her money.[30] Second, she worried that a certain kind of man might want her for her power, her contacts, the capacity of her media properties to shape opinion. Some men might even court her with an eye toward easing her into the background and taking over. She liked to joke—with more than a little bite—that when men began signaling their sexual availability, she would think to herself, "You'd really like to fuck a tycoon, wouldn't you?"

Then there was the fear that no man she would want would be able to accept a woman who came and went as she pleased, who traveled to world capitals accompanied by her male bureau chiefs and editors. In an interview by Jane Howard for *Ms.* magazine, Kay pondered, "Singleness is much more okay now than it used to be, isn't it? Besides, I lead such an odd life, always off somewhere, that I'm no bargain. I can't imagine anyone wanting to marry me."

With that, Howard concluded, "Gossip has it that since Watergate not one male guest has [woken] up anywhere in the Graham house on [R Street], much as some might like to, largely because such an overnight visit would be federally noted."[31]

Howard was wrong. Warren Buffett spent the night under Kay's roof[32] and, one friend speculates, under her covers. He was thirteen years her junior and married, but Kay could still think him a good match. He accepted and encouraged her position, power, and responsibilities. This "aw-shucks, rumple-suited Nebraskan"[33] had no desire to share Kay's limelight, not even a corner of it. A multimillionaire, soon a billionaire, he certainly did not need her money.*[34]

Richard Clurman—although he says he can't prove it—believes they had an affair that lasted "for years and years. [Kay] and Warren were an item. He, in a sense, led a double life. I would guess that everybody knew that they had a life together in Washington that was different from his life in Omaha," where he was known as a strait-laced husband and father of three.[36]

"I think she adores Warren," says Polly Kraft, "and I think she is much too realistic, practical, [and] self-effacing about herself with men to think that she could ever marry and hold on and not be finally enormously hurt by somebody thirteen years younger."[37]

One close friend says that Kay also had a "big crush" on Bob McNamara, that she "adored him."[38] But because he was married, and his wife was a member in good standing of the same Washington establishment that claimed Kay, she would never act on her desire any further than to continue to lean on him for advice and to savor his presence on the Post Company board.

Mostly, though, Kay relied on escorts—sometimes married men whose wives were elsewhere or did not care or were given no choice; sometimes men who were between wives—to take her through her demanding social life. John Kenneth Galbraith, who is married, was one. Nicholas von Hoffman, who was divorced, was another. "She used me as an escort a few times. When I say she used me, I was happy to be used, because otherwise I never would have gotten my nose into those precincts."[39]

"Those precincts" were extremely rarefied. By the spring of 1974, Kay Graham had become a larger-than-life role model, a national treasure revered for both her power and her courage.

After resigning the presidency, Nixon paid his nemesis the ultimate compliment when he said that he would have had more power as president of *The Washington Post* than he had as president of the

---

*By 1992, *Forbes* estimated his net worth at $4.4 billion.[35]

United States. "When Watergate was over," says Mel Elfin, "she had become the most powerful woman in America."[40] To George Reedy, she had become "the symbol of the Press. If Kay was at a party and she made some remark about politics, you could be sure that the president would have a note about it on his desk the next morning. She was regarded as a Washington institution, almost the way people would regard Queen Victoria in England."[41]

So it seemed all in a day's work when Robert Redford came calling on Kay Graham for a breakfast meeting on the veranda of her Georgetown house. According to Deborah Davis, who set the scene in her biography of Graham, Redford was seeking the publisher's cooperation in making a movie about how *The Washington Post* brought down a president. Joining Redford were Dustin Hoffman and their real-life counterparts, Bob Woodward and Carl Bernstein, whose just published book on Watergate, *All the President's Men*, would provide the basis for Redford's movie. Donny Graham, who had been promoted to assistant managing editor of sports and now sat on the Post Company board of directors, was also there. As Kay feared, the atmosphere was awkward. Her movie star guests were rendered nearly speechless in her presence. She tried to lighten things up with a story about Henry Kissinger taking her to the movies and being so preoccupied about being called a war criminal that after sitting through the entire movie he couldn't remember the plot.

Redford got down to business. According to Davis, he told Kay that "he would need photographs and measurements of the newsroom, her office, Ben Bradlee's office, in order to build accurate sets. . . . He would want to ship their trash to the Burbank studio; he and Hoffman would have to spend several weeks in the newsroom observing real reporters at work. He would want to feature the *Post* prominently, use real names, engage a major actress to play Mrs. Graham's part; Lauren Bacall was mentioned." It was a heady experience, and Katharine agreed to everything.[42]

As the years passed, it would be Kay Graham who would be credited—or discredited—for the toppling of Richard Nixon. Friends and colleagues say that she had the good sense and good taste not to gloat about her role in Nixon's downfall. After Nixon's resignation, she told Bob Woodward, "If I get one more [expletive] award, I'm going to get sick."[43] It was Ben Bradlee—it could never have been Kay Graham—who decorated a conference room with the original metal type from the *Post*'s "Nixon Resigns" headline.[44]

Newbold Noyes remembers that Kay seemed positively chastened, humbled during the breakthrough days of Watergate. The two were at an AP meeting in New York when, Noyes recalls, "somebody came in and told her that the smoking gun had turned up in the Nixon tapes. It was the real break that told them that not only had the *Post*'s effort on Watergate paid off, but they had come up with a total victory. The remarkable thing to me was her reaction: instead of [feeling] elation or pride, she was absolutely stunned. She turned white and said, 'My God, what have we done here? What's going to happen now?' I think she realized in a flash that the result of this was going to be the bringing down of a president and putting the whole political system in jeopardy. I was very impressed. I'm sure that in the newsroom people were dancing around the desks, but she just sort of clutched her brow and sat down."[45]

To Paul Ignatius, who had no reason to feel kindly toward Kay, "after Watergate there was a sobering realization of the enormous power of this paper in this city and the obligation to use that power wisely."[46] This is not to say that Kay did not savor that power, but in quieter moments she worried about a feeding frenzy, led by her own reporters, some of whom showed a mindless disrespect toward men in public life. This breakdown in authority troubled Kay Graham, who, after all, mixed in circles of just such men and was the daughter of the public servant par excellence and the widow of a man who aspired to the same.

Other matters occupied Kay in April 1974, when James Reston called to tell her he had heard that an outsider, a Texan, was angling to buy the *Washington Star* from the Kauffmann and Noyes families, who, having failed to stem the flow of red ink, were ready to sell.* Reston immediately called the CEO of Time Inc., Andrew Heiskell, to urge that his company buy the *Star* and thus save Washington and Kay Graham from Joe Allbritton, a Houston lawyer who owned hotels and a chain of funeral parlors and cemeteries, and held interests in banking, insurance, and stock brokerage. (Reston knew that Kay would prefer as competition a member of the club, which Allbritton, emphatically, was not.) Heiskell was interested. Five years

---

*Two years earlier the *Star*'s circulation perked up, but only temporarily, when it bought the assets of the weakest of the three remaining Washington dailies, the *Daily News,* which folded. For a time, the paper was known as the *Star-News.*

before, his company had looked at the *Star* but the Kauffmanns and Noyeses were not ready to sell.[47]

Time Inc. executives looked again and decided that while the broadcasting properties were attractive, the newspaper was a loser. That year, the *Star* had only 32.5 percent of Washington advertising linage. Featherbedding ran rampant.[48] So Allbritton did not have to compete to buy the *Star*. For $25 million he got a thirty-seven-percent controlling interest in the newspaper and broadcasting properties, which included Washington's Channel 7—WJLA, the ABC affiliate, which Allbritton named for himself—with an option to buy more. Forcing concessions from the unions, Allbritton slashed the payroll, instituted a four-day work week, laid off workers, and sent others into early retirement.[49]

While Kay imagined Time Inc. as a gentlemanly competitor that would have perked up the *Star* a bit without threatening the *Post,* she saw Allbritton as a ruthless tycoon who played by his own rules. According to Mark Meagher, she "was scared to death of Joe Allbritton. For some reason I could never figure out, [she] thought he was smarter than any of us, [that] he was going to be able to bring the *Star* back."[50] For a while, it looked as if he might. He brought in as editor James Bellows, then associate editor of the *Los Angeles Times,* formerly editor of the late *New York Herald Tribune.* Bellows was an irreverent, outspoken liberal who was determined to make the *Star* work, to give it "a tone and personality."[51]

Bellows had nothing but disdain for the old regime at the *Star,* whom he referred to as "coupon clippers." The *Star* was not arrogant like the *Post,* but it was, in his opinion, even worse—it was complacent.[52]

Kay fretted that Bellows was making the *Star* livelier, and he was. He brought in for short stints Jimmy Breslin, Larry King, and Willie Morris. He hired Diana McLellan to write "The Ear," a sometimes outrageous gossip column in which she picked mercilessly on the *Post,* which she called the "O.P.," as in "other paper." Ben Bradlee and Sally Quinn, dubbed the "Fun Couple," were other favorite targets. "Hey, Ben, this is what I've got to do to try to make this paper work," Bellows told an irritated Bradlee.*[53]

---

*That McLellan got under Bradlee's supposedly tough skin was obvious. According to a reporter for the *Post* who previously, and happily, worked for the *Star*: "Bellows once asked Bradlee for permission to reprint a column to which the *Post* had syndication rights. Bradlee said he would allow it on one condition: that ["The Ear"] make no mention of the Fun Couple

*

With Warren Buffett at her elbow, Kay was determined to make her company bigger and much more profitable. That year, 1974, the Post Company bought WTIC-TV in Hartford, Connecticut, and renamed it WFSB in honor of Fritz Beebe. Also that year Kay approved the decision to acquire the Trenton, New Jersey, *Times*, a stodgy afternoon daily that competed with the *Trentonian*—a feisty morning paper which, that very year, won a Pulitzer Prize and seemed on the upswing even though it had smaller circulation and advertising revenue than the *Times.* Kay's broadcasting expert, Larry Israel, was very much behind this acquisition, with Kay giving the final go-ahead.

Owned by the Kerney family for more than seventy years, the Trenton *Times* seemed as dated as its newsroom and production facilities. Nevertheless, the Washington Post Company paid the family's asking price of $16 million, only to learn later that the Kerneys would have sold for $12 million, especially because James Kerney, Jr., the son of the family patriarch, was impressed, in the wake of Watergate, by Kay Graham and her paper.[55]

Post president John Prescott, charged with being the liaison between the Trenton paper and its new owners and with making personnel decisions, recalls, "We decided to get [*Post* assistant managing editor] Dick Harwood to go up and be editor. The current publisher, part of the owning family, was not the right one to be running [the paper] but was a great figurehead."[56] Half of the reporters on staff when Harwood arrived eventually quit, were fired, or retired, and they were replaced by eager, young, often inexperienced reporters who saw the Trenton *Times* as a stepping-stone to the glamorous *Washington Post*. (*Post* editors too saw the *Times* as a kind of minor league.) The reporters Harwood attracted wanted to write big-league stories of the "holy shit" variety so coveted by Bradlee. Trenton readers wanted coverage of schools, zoning, goings-on in garden clubs and churches. Harwood would later admit, "You can't produce a *Washington Post* in a small town. You have to pay attention to chicken suppers. I brought to a small town a large-town mentality."[57]

While the *Post* spent millions to reequip the Trenton paper, its

for a month. Bellows made the deal, then posted the agreement on the newsroom bulletin board, to howls of laughter."[54]

advertising and circulation slid—Sears switched more than a million lines of advertising to the *Trentonian*—and a frustrated Kay Graham asked, "Who ever decided to buy this thing?" "You did, Kay," answered Larry Israel.[58]

To Kay, too many of the men she had placed in charge seemed to be doing too little and not doing it fast enough. John Prescott knew that his star was waning when, in 1973, Kay had bypassed him and chosen Larry Israel to be Post Company president and CEO. But Prescott thought he was doing a top-notch job in the arena he knew best—heading the newspaper. She had hired him to get tough with the unions, and he had done just that. One week before a fateful encounter with Kay, Prescott enjoyed "the greatest success we'd ever had"—the signing of an eight-year contract with the typographers' union.* He imagined that Kay would feel "very encouraged by management's achievement." She had a strange way of showing it.[59]

To celebrate the printers' ratification of the ground-breaking agreement, Prescott's colleagues planned a surprise party, complete with $1,400 worth of luggage for him. The day of the party he had another surprise: Kay called him to her office and, with Larry Israel at her side, told him, "We've got a lot of things to do in the company. We want to acquire more newspapers. There are lots of challenges out there that we need someone like you [to handle]." Then she mentioned Mark Meagher as the "kind of fellow who can run the nuts and bolts of the business now."

Prescott would be made president of the newspaper division, with a mandate to look for other newspapers, and responsibility for the Trenton *Times,* half a newsprint mill, and a newsprint storage facility in Alexandria, Virginia.[60] He swallowed his anger and his pride, and accepted what amounted to a demotion. As he explained later, he had emotional investments in people in the company and in projects that he had started and wanted to see completed.[61]

While Prescott had alleviated some labor problems, in 1973 he had let the pressmen—who had walked out in sympathy with the printers, whom *Post* executives had locked out—outsmart him, and that infuriated Kay Graham. She had endorsed Prescott's plan to use white-collar employees to run the presses, and to keep that fact from

---

*Prescott estimates that at the time of the agreement, the composing room was manned by 850 workers; it is down today to some 300.

the pressmen. When they arrived at the paper and gave Prescott, who was blocking the door with his body, their word that they had come to run the presses, he let them in and ushered out the scabs, who had webbed up the presses with newsprint. The pressmen immediately refused to run the presses until the printers were allowed back into the building. "I lied to you," the union leader told Prescott, who had no choice but to capitulate. Left unsaid was, "Just as you lied to me."[62]

Likewise, Prescott was making inroads on some management problems, but not fast enough for Kay. "She made up her mind that somehow or other it wasn't going to work with me," Prescott says, "because of this impatience. I wasn't the quick study, the quick comeback."[63]

In his opinion, Kay Graham simply did not have the stuff to oversee a company of that size and complexity. Before she could understand a management strategy it would have to be explained to her repeatedly. "If there were six people in a room," Prescott says, "five of us would walk out with some understanding." He also quickly saw that Kay, probably because of a "lack of confidence, could pay an awful lot of attention to the last person she talked to. She might sit next to somebody at an ANPA meeting and she'd have a new opinion." Ben Bradlee advised Prescott that to understand Kay one had to "find out whom she had dinner with [the night before]. Maybe that's what caused a new opinion, a new question, or a new angle."[64]

Prescott's demotion was not good for morale. Reporter Robert Kaiser later wrote, "To this day many *Post* executives don't know what Prescott did wrong."[65] Prescott believes that Kay offered him another position instead of simply firing him because if she had fired him, "an awful lot of key people [would have said], 'Hey, wait a minute. That's not fair. You're crazy to do that.' "[66]

Mark Meagher had promised Prescott to seek his counsel, had told him that he would play "a major role." Predictably, Meagher consulted his predecessor "less and less," and Prescott could no longer justify staying.*[67]

*

---

*Prescott went to Whitney Communications, which then, like the *Post,* owned one-third of the *International Herald Tribune.* As a director of that paper he would see Kay at board meetings, where their exchanges were "very perfunctory."[68]

Prescott's fear that Kay would disparage him as she had his predecessor turned out to be justified. "I know for an absolute fact that in
the first year or so after I left, that same stuff was going on about
me," Prescott says sadly.[69]

"People thought she was a little fickle," says Roswell Gilpatric.[70]
This is quite an understatement to those who knew her then. She
struck fear and frustration in the hearts of the most cocky, self-
assured men. To those who passed through and failed, she was
unpredictable, sometimes hysterical, mean, vindictive, and so indiscreet that she casually told the most humiliating stories behind an
executive's back and/or lambasted him in front of his peers.

Lester Bernstein attributes Kay's relentless dissatisfaction with her
top men not only to her "anxiety-ridden and insecure" nature but,
more important, to the unrealistically high standards she set for
herself. "She's a person of enormous determination. I don't think she
has any particular flair or special talent for running a communications company. She is obsessed with the notion that she dare not fail
the tradition behind her. She's always seeking new ideas to improve
what she has."[71] Whoever was in place, no matter how good, could
never satisfy her for the long term.

Because Kay's top executives and, consequently, her disgruntled
former executives were all men, there was a palpably sexist tone to
much of the criticism. She liked to "emasculate" men, it was said,
"cut off their balls." "To see Kay with a group of men is interesting,"
commented Bernard Nossiter, echoing an oft-stated observation that
Kay's sacking of powerful men was a form of displaced anger with
Phil. "She loves being the queen bee. And she loves to sting. There's
a very cruel, harsh side to Kay. Kay's revenge. Kay's eating on raw
meat to build herself up."[72]

To Nicholas Katzenbach, the high turnover was to Kay's credit
and, in any case, had nothing to do with her gender. "I think she was
probably right. Her judgment was that these were not the people to
run [the company]. My guess is that they began doing an awful lot
of things without consulting [her]. And she doesn't like that. She likes
to know what's going on." Eugene Patterson says that "Kay was in
a learning situation. At least she had the guts to try to find an
extraordinary performer."[73]

"They keep yelling at me for firing people," she once complained
to Mark Edmiston. "That's not right. They should yell at me for
hiring the wrong people in the first place."[74]

*

In 1974, Richard Snyder approached Kay Graham to gauge her interest in buying Simon & Schuster. She passed up the opportunity. Mark Meagher, then climbing the corporate ladder, considers his failure to persuade Kay to grab the offer one of two major mistakes he made during his decade-long tenure. According to him, she did not even give Snyder's proposal serious consideration, dismissing it as she had three years earlier dismissed Warren Buffett's suggestion that she contemplate a takeover of *The New Yorker.*

Snyder, now Simon & Schuster CEO, had chosen the Post Company because, according to Meagher, "he wanted to see Simon & Schuster go where he thought it would be friendly." Two years before, as Simon & Schuster's executive vice-president, Snyder had signed Woodward and Bernstein to write *All the President's Men.*

The asking price, says Meagher, in a voice that still betrays pain at the missed opportunity, was $17 million—just a million more than the Post Company paid that year for the struggling Trenton *Times.* Meagher, who had come to the company from McGraw-Hill, was ecstatic at the prospect of acquiring a book publisher; he loved the book business and recognized this as a once-in-a-lifetime opportunity.[75]

Meagher and Larry Israel arranged to introduce Katharine to the patriarch of the company—its first employee—Leon Shimkin, then sixty-seven, who had run Simon & Schuster as president and chairman of the board.[76] He had also cofounded the phenomenally successful Pocket Books and helped launch Golden Books.

The meeting, Meagher recounts with a shudder, "was a disaster, just a disaster. Katharine and Shimkin just did not like each other instantly, and we couldn't proceed from there. He [was] a crusty old guy and a real power, and well-known, and Katharine expects people to treat her regally."[77]

Richard Snyder recalls that it was as if Kay and Shimkin were on different planets. Kay was obviously repulsed by Shimkin, whom Snyder describes as not exactly vulgar but "a little uncouth"; Kay could never allow him "to sit at her table." Consequently, she could not do business with him. "It wasn't the deal she didn't like," Snyder explains, "it was the man."[78]

Meagher decided that circumstances were such—with his promotion, he was working two jobs—that he "just couldn't push it. We let it slide." He blames himself for not being more aggressive in making the case for the acquisition.[79]

Snyder found his buyer the next year—Gulf + Western, now

known as Paramount Communications. Paramount currently looks to Simon & Schuster, the largest book publisher in the world, with sales of $1.55 billion in 1991, for more than one-third of its revenue.[80]

The Kay Graham who emerged from this crucible of challenges showed no perceptible boost in self-confidence. She was a woman who still seemed uncomfortable in her shoes, and uncomfortable with her background—especially the Jewish half. She showed the sort of private-club anti-Semitism that flourished in the cave-dweller society that had sometimes rejected her father. Harvey Segal recalls mentioning to her, in the course of conversation, the name of Phil's psychiatrist, Leslie Farber. She referred to him as "our little Jewish dentist."[81]

Alan Finberg describes Kay as "in some ways almost prototypically Waspish, and with that Waspishness there does indeed come a strain of anti-Semitism. There was a time when she would sometimes call me Marty [confusing him with Post Company vice-president Martin Cohen] and, I assume, would sometimes call him Alan. 'Yeah, there's a couple of Jewish boys out there.' I don't think that was ever related to not advancing or promoting someone whose merits she recognized."[82]

Stephen Birmingham, whose book *Our Crowd* focuses on assimilated German Jews of the Eugene Meyer stripe, wrote an essay for *More* magazine excoriating Spiro Agnew for his attacks on the press, which Birmingham perceived as nakedly anti-Semitic. In the essay he described Kay Graham as the daughter of a Jewish publisher, implying that she could also be so categorized. He received a handwritten note from her, marked "not for publication," in which she protested that she did not think of herself, or identify herself, as a Jewish publisher. To Birmingham, she seemed to have missed the point.[83]

Edgar Siskin, the Yale graduate student and New Haven rabbi who had tried to help Kay's brother find his Jewish identity, also took it upon himself to hector Kay about her heritage as well as about her paper's stance on the Middle East. In a letter he reminded her that her father was a Jew and that her brother had sought his, Siskin's, spiritual counsel. He charged that "the *Post* has a pattern, if not a policy, on the Middle East which is pro-Arab and anti-Israel" and "to that extent it may reap the whirlwind of anti-Semitism." Kay's response, which the rabbi characterizes as "very curt" and "barely civil," was to dismiss his "lurking accusations of pro-Arab and anti-Semitic encouragement" and his reminder of her father's "distinguished Jewish heritage" as not constructive and "beside the point." Although Siskin feels her comments were not anti-Semitic, he does think they "indicated a relationship to Jews and Judaism which was not altogether friendly or positive."[84]

Others might say Kay showed a certain spunkiness in not being cowed. What gave Jews the right to lecture her about her responsibility to Jews and Israel any more than Lutherans had the right to lecture her about her responsibility to Lutherans and Germany?

In his letter, Rabbi Siskin had lamented having lost contact with Bill Meyer. Even Kay might have wished that the two had stayed in touch, that Bill had continued to seek guidance from the rabbi. For Bill Meyer had grown into a man who lost his way.

He had risen to be chairman of his department at Johns Hopkins, where he was a full professor of both medicine and psychiatry; he had an intelligent, attractive wife, lovely children, loads of money from inheritance and Post Company stock. He had insisted on carving out his own career and succeeded at it, refusing to recast himself in the image of his father or of his brother-in-law Phil.

Yet it was telling that after Phil's death, nobody, certainly not Agnes, suggested turning to Bill Meyer to hold things together for the family. One reason was that Bill, soft-spoken, shy, and humble, was so obviously unsuited to running a paper. Another was that he had crippling back problems, as well as even more debilitating problems with alcohol. It was said by friends that the first caused the second, but whatever the sequence, Bill, they say, was alcoholic and, some add, addicted to morphine and other drugs. For years, until his death, he wore an unsightly, unwieldy brace. "It was one goddamned medical disaster after another," says Bis.[85]

He also had emotional problems, which, friends say, originated in his childhood. "One sometimes feels that the genders were mixed up in that family," Joanna Steichen observes, "that he should have been one of the daughters."[86] "I think it was very hard for him," said Luvie Pearson, "because he should have been the heir apparent and Phil took over."[87]

In an attempt to overcome his addictions, Bill was hospitalized at Sheppard Pratt. Kay felt that the treatment did little for him.[88] To the surprise of no one who knew Bill and his wife, Mary, an epidemiologist, their marriage came apart.[89]

June Bingham, who calls Bill "a lost soul, but a brave one, gutsy," says that she is "sure he didn't like having people feel sorry for him, but there we were. He was suffering, his career had been spoiled by booze, and his marriage was gone."[90]

He moved from Baltimore to Washington, where he saw more of Kay, but they were not particularly close. Phil Geyelin, who came to know and like Bill, comments simply, "I don't know how supportive she was."[91] It is said that Kay, who so valued physical perfection, was embarrassed by him.[92] Still, in 1971, when her company went public, she gave her ailing brother a place on her board. He attended meetings religiously, saying little, contributing less, and wearing his onerously thick steel neck brace.[93] One executive would see him standing alone before or after a board meeting and would talk to him. "Kay did not take Bill under her wing." Her attitude toward him, the executive adds, was rather that "Bill didn't matter."[94]

Bill was delighted to answer medicine-related questions from reporters and editors, but he would wait to be asked. "When there was some news involving psychiatry," Ben Gilbert says, "we called him up. He was very helpful."[95] Karl Meyer, then writing obituaries for the *Post,* describes his first conversation with Bill—an exchange reminiscent of Kay Meyer's sheepishly handing her wedding announcement to the society editor: "I heard this hesitant voice. 'Hellllhelloo. My name is Dr. Eugene Meyer, Jr. Ahhhhh . . . one of my colleagues died here and I want to give you some notes.' He was so apologetic for bothering us."[96]

But he did have strong opinions—especially on politics. He was a staunch liberal and had contributed heavily to George McGovern. Meyer recalls discussions with Bill about Vietnam: "He was more on my side than on the paper's. He was much more critical of the war and Johnson and the paper than I was. We discussed the difficulties of saying anything to Kay about it."[97]

Bill Meyer died of cancer in 1982. Sir Isaiah Berlin remembers him, at the end, as "rather pathetic" but also as "a very nice man, gentle, serious."[98] The description is echoed by many, who implicitly marvel that the same family could produce two such different personalities.

Chapter 19

A PULITZER PRIZE
IN MANAGEMENT?

In July 1975, Kay Graham decided to fire *Newsweek* editor Osborn Elliott, who was then vacationing at his summer house in Connecticut. Upon returning home from the beach, he got a message that Kay had called from Washington.

"Kay's voice was tight when I reached her," he recounted in his memoirs. " 'They've done it to us again,' she said. 'We've got to talk.' 'Who's done what?' I asked. It was *Time,* with a cover story called 'Can Capitalism Survive?' which Kay thought *Newsweek* should have done. 'I've got to see you,' she said stiffly." Elliott had another week of vacation left and suggested that they meet when he got back. The end, he told his wife, was at hand.

The night before his "date" with Kay, he took managing editor Edward Kosner to dinner. "I gather Our Lady of the Potomac is upset," Elliott said to Kosner. "Whereupon Kosner revealed to me the degree of her dismay and the urgency of her desire to replace me."[1] Kay, in fact, had broached to Kosner the possibility of his replacing his boss three or four months before Elliott went on vacation. "If you ask me to be the editor," Kosner claims to have told her, "I'll be the editor, but I'm not going to participate in Oz's downfall."[2]

Kay had concluded that Elliott had lost his zest for the magazine, that, in his words, he had become "uninterested, selfish, self-centered, not committed anymore"[3]—a view that some of his closest colleagues shared. Lester Bernstein explains that he simply "got tired of doing it. He wasn't pursuing the job as intensely as he had."[4]

During their meeting, Elliott reminded Kay that when he had agreed to return from the business side to be editor, he promised to stay one year, which had stretched into three. He knew that she was about to fire him and he decided not to protest, but he also decided to let her have it: " 'To get this word from my Number Two, and not from you, is just not the way you do things. One thing I learned in the Navy is that there is such a thing as loyalty *down* as well as up.' Kay was bathed in remorse. She knew she had been wrong. She apologized for having said those things to Kosner. . . . Then we talked for a while about who the next editor should be. We agreed that Kosner was the best qualified. . . . A moment of silent embarrassment. And then I blurted out, good-naturedly: 'Kay, why don't you go fuck yourself?' Kay said: 'I would if I could.' Then suddenly—and this can best be described in pulp-fiction prose—I was in her arms. We kissed warmly and a bit tearily. Breaking off the mouth-to-mouth resuscitation, which was obviously too late to work, I said: 'Say, I'm beginning to enjoy this.' "*[5]

What really went wrong in this relationship is unclear to *Newsweek* insiders. Oz Elliott, a Brahmin and a charmer, should have been an exception to Kay's pattern of firing.[7] But Peter Derow places Elliott squarely in that group of men who "made the mistake of not thinking she was relevant."[8] Elliott notes in his memoirs that at his farewell party, after his firing, Kay "delivered a cozy speech, which she asked me to help her write."[9]

Newsweek was not the only part of Kay's empire that troubled her. In 1975, the *Post*'s earnings dropped sharply—for the first three quarters, net income fell twenty-eight percent from the same period the year before. The newspaper's profit margin slid from about fifteen percent in 1969 to nine percent in 1974.[10] Kay blamed the unions.

Early in 1972, she had told a group of security analysts: "Some costs resist [cutting] more stubbornly than others. The most frustrating kind are those imposed by archaic union practices that deprive the company of the savings we ought to achieve from modern technology. This is a problem we are determined to solve; we hope it can

---

*After an excerpt from Elliott's memoirs was published featuring that scene, Kay told Mark Edmiston, "It's not true. Never kissed him." She also denied having cried, but said nothing about the accuracy of the "go fuck yourself" exchange.[6]

be solved in an amicable, constructive spirit. In any event, we fully intend to deal with it."[11]

Winning a Pulitzer Prize in management—a goal she so frequently held aloft—meant bringing the unions to heel, ridding her operation of deliberate slowdowns, outrageous overstaffing, absurd amounts of overtime. Mark Meagher, then the *Post*'s general manager, confirmed that his goal—and hers—was to return the company to a fifteen-percent profit margin.[12]

That goal did not bode well for the unions. In a stunning example of bad timing, they chose the years 1974 to 1976 to strike.

In 1964, when Kay had been at the helm for just over a year, the Newspaper Guild, the union to which she had once so proudly belonged, threatened to strike. She came to believe that she had been browbeaten by federal mediators into accepting a contract that made her reporters, at $200 a week, the highest-paid in the country. The passage of a decade had not eased her bitterness at having caved in, at having been taken for a weak and foolish woman.

When the Newspaper Guild—a union that covered editorial staffers as well as workers in classified and display advertising—went on strike in the spring of 1974, Kay was ready. This was not, however, much of a test of her resolve. The Guild was more like a club than a hard-line union. The strike was disorganized and, according to former *Post* reporter and union activist John Hanrahan, "very misguided. There were no picket lines, and we didn't ask other unions to join us. Ben Bradlee and other editors covered the main stories and put in wire copy, and the paper looked exactly the same, a few more AP and UPI [stories]."[13]

The Guild described its action as "withholding excellence" (namely, bylines) and claimed that readers and advertisers were so distressed at the absence of those bylines that the Post Company lost $1 million in revenues. Company spokesmen countered that it had actually saved money during the strike because it did not have to pay some salaries. The *Star-News* gleefully reported its "random telephone survey of twenty-five *Post* subscribers on . . . the eighth day of the strike. Fourteen of the twenty-five said they noticed no difference in their paper"—a remarkable result, because the paper, which normally required some four hundred reporters, copy editors, and photographers, was being put out by about forty people.[14]

One of them was Kay, who described the two stories she wrote as "one cruddy, one rather fun."[15] Presumably, "cruddy" applied to the story that carried the unmemorable lead: "Homa Homayoun, the powerful, political and Pucci-dressed sister of the swinging Iranian Ambassador Ardeshir Zahedi, is one of seventeen women members of the Iranian Parliament."[16]

She also took classified ads. "You sound overqualified," one caller told her. "Either you know a lot about a Mercedes or you're Katharine Graham." "Right on both counts," she replied.[17]

Jane Howard reported that a picket sign leaned against a wall in Kay's office with the misspelled demand "Impeach Kathryn Graham." She obviously got a kick out of it. "I shouldn't imply that I *enjoyed* the strike," Kay said, "but it was such a together time."[18]

In explaining why they went on strike, reporters argued that it was they who had made the *Post* into the nationally renowned paper that broke Watergate, and won a Pulitzer and kudos from around the globe. Further, they deserved a bigger share of what they believed were the paper's spiraling profits.

But George Reedy, whom Ben Bradlee had asked to probe the dynamics of the newsroom to determine the causes of the strike, concluded that it had "practically nothing to do with wages and hours." He discerned a "snakepit creative-tension" atmosphere, but identified the crux of the complaint as the perception that Bradlee, preoccupied with his divorce and new affair, could not protect the editorial side from encroachment by the business side. Reedy recalls a phrase floating around: " 'If Kay only knew . . .' It reminded me of that saying in Russia, 'If the czar only knew . . .' The people on both the editorial and [the] business side saw Kay as a queen who could step in and straighten things out. But she was aloof, she did not know what was going on." (Reedy put his findings in a letter to Bradlee, which Bradlee never answered or even acknowledged.)[19] Any hopes of Kay's showing solidarity with the reporters were soon shattered, however. She was, Bernard Nossiter said, "absolutely tough as nails."[20]

As it turned out, the Newspaper Guild had done Kay a big favor by striking. Its disarray gave her an easy victory, and when the *Post* was hit the next year by a serious (that is, blue-collar) strike, she was raring to go. She told her shareholders that the Guild strike had been a turning point in her company's attitude toward labor relations: "To be very blunt about it, in past years this newspaper developed a reputation for avoiding a strike at almost any cost—and when we said last year that those days [were] gone forever I'm sure many people just didn't believe it." The decision had been made, she said, "to offer a fair contract and to stand by that offer—and be willing to take a strike, if necessary, to demonstrate our determination to keep our costs under reasonable control."[21]

With visions of that Pulitzer in management dancing in her head and after pep talks from her top executives, Kay Graham realized she could "take" a printers' and pressmen's strike; she could win the kind of respect from her fellow owner-publishers that the coup of Watergate would never bring. While automation had made it possible to produce a newspaper even if pressmen and printers and ad takers walked out, automation meant nothing unless the paper could be delivered. Because of its nonunion deliveries (a brilliant maneuver Phil Graham had devised, converting drivers from teamster employees to independent contractors*[22]), the *Post* was virtually strikeproof, and Kay knew it.

This former labor reporter and admirer of Harry Bridges had no real sympathy for the craft unions, as she felt that they, the printers especially, were cheating her with their lifetime job guarantees and ridiculously wasteful practices—the craft's sheer irrelevance in the face of such new technologies as offset printing that largely displaced the skilled printer. She had dumped Paul Ignatius and hired John Prescott in 1971 in large part because of Prescott's tough tactics in taming the unions. He in turn hired Larry Wallace, who had worked for him in Detroit and had a reputation as a union buster, to handle labor relations.[24]

Kay made the printers her first target. Relations were so bad that she screamed at Bill Greider in the middle of the newsroom, "Stop romanticizing those bastards!" after he wrote what he felt was an objective story on the brewing struggle between the *Post* and its printers. She was angry, Greider explains, because the printers "were doing occasional sabotage on the composing room floor, slowdowns and dumping type, which infuriated her."[25]

But she was handed the luxury of first taking on the smaller pressmen's union after the pressmen stupidly forced a confrontation. "They were the easiest ones to beat," says Mark Meagher, "because they were the easiest to replace. There were 680 printers at the *Post*. At that time there was a need for half of them. In the whole press-

---

*Bernard Nossiter described Phil's invention as "ingenious and horrifying. He saw that that's how you could ultimately stop the trade unions."[23]

men's union there might have been two hundred people full-time, and need for only half of that."[26]

Kay's victory over the pressmen was not Pulitzer material. She won the strike because Washington, unlike New York, is not a union town, and because her exquisitely educated reporters and editors identified about as closely with members of the pressmen's union as they did with members of the night cleaning crew. She won because of the nonunion delivery system and because of the pressmen's major tactical error.

At midnight on September 30, 1975, the pressmen's contract expired. At 4:35 a.m. on October 1, the pressmen stopped work and started to destroy the newspaper's nine presses and set them aflame. They disabled fire extinguishers, cut hoses, smashed gears and gauges, slashed wiring, and beat up the foreman, opening a deep gash on his forehead.

Mark Meagher had been sleeping in his office, awaiting the resumption of negotiations, to which the union had agreed, when he was awakened by the foreman, "holding a towel to his head, bleeding all over the place." Meagher phoned Kay at home. "I jumped into my car and drove downtown," she later recalled in a speech. "I rounded the corner to the *Post*'s building and confronted a surging mass of fire engines, police cars, television crews, and a thousand pickets. Leaving my car with the police at the corner, I walked down the middle of the street, crossed the picket line, and entered our building, which was deserted, smoke-filled, and had a foot of water on the press-room floor."[27]

Anticipating a strike and recognizing that it might be long and ugly, Post Company executives had hired the public relations firm of J. Walter Thompson. The smashed and smoldering presses made great television, and the story was improved upon when Post Company executives wildly exaggerated the amount of the damage. John Hanrahan terms the *Post*'s coverage of the rampage "incredibly distorted, shameful. They talked about millions of dollars as if the presses had been destroyed, wiped out. In fact, somebody on the foreign desk had called up the company that provided the replacement parts and found out [that the damage would require] $13,000 worth of replacement parts. They made it sound [as if] this group of barbarians had wrecked the pressroom."[28] Hanrahan recalls that "even when you gave [Guild members] information that the presses were not destroyed, they swallowed whole management's line."[29]

The Guild had not invited the pressmen to join its strike, but the pressmen pleaded for Guild support. They did not receive it. Scores of Guild members crossed the picket line, citing their aversion to violence and to bigotry (the pressmen's union had no women or black members—a fact, Hanrahan claims, about which concern was never expressed before; the *Post* then had one black editor). Hanrahan remains bitter that his colleagues turned it into "an us-and-them situation. We, the white-collar professionals in the newsroom, versus the blue-collar workers who [were] out to destroy this newspaper. One reporter got up at [a meeting] and referred to the pressmen as slack-jawed cretins."[30]

The violence proved to be the pressmen's fatal error. "Had they gone to their lockers and walked out," says John Prescott, "I don't think the *Post* would have been able to win. What really won it was Mark [Meagher's] being able to go down the next morning with some people from the Guild and say, 'Look what they left.' "[31]

The *Post* missed only one day of publication. On subsequent days, the editions were thin, nonunion products. But slowly the paper grew fatter with editorials and advertising. The Post Company adopted a take-it-or-leave-it negotiating style. At the time the pressmen began striking, the number of men on a press crew could run as high as twenty-one; the *Post*'s goal was to cut the crews to nine to thirteen. But during the strike, management discovered that as few as six men could run the presses. Eventually, Meagher recalls, "as we got more and more hard-nosed, our demands escalated. Toward the end we said, 'Look, guys, we're running the presses with six guys. There's just no way in hell that we're going to have a contract with you fellows that does anything but man the presses the way we want to do it.' "

Meagher and other executives worked themselves into such a frenzy of righteous indignation over what they charged was the planned trashing of the presses that bringing the union to its knees became as much a crusade as a business strategy. "It made 'scab' a term of endearment for me," Meagher says.[32] Ben Bradlee reportedly would greet picketers with his middle finger as he crossed their line each morning.[33]

But Kay alternated between elation and despair as she confronted a range of thorny problems. The most immediate was where to print the *Post*—the subject of a luncheon discussion at the F Street Club. Joining Kay were Arthur Ochs Sulzberger, publisher of *The New*

York Times; Clifton Daniel, Washington bureau chief of *The New York Times* (and Harry Truman's son-in-law); Joe Allbritton, publisher of the *Star;* and his editor, Jim Bellows. A few weeks before the strike, Kay had asked Allbritton if the *Star* would suspend publication in support of the *Post.* The answer was no, so she was there that afternoon to ask again. If the answer was still no, as she expected it would be, the next question to Allbritton would be whether the *Star* would print her paper until the presses were repaired.

No to both questions, still.

What Allbritton's answer might have been, had he not been accompanied by Bellows, is a matter of conjecture. He knew that if he accommodated Kay Graham, Bellows would quit. Bellows recalls telling Allbritton, "You certainly can't go along with Katharine Graham to make a united front against the pressmen. The chance of your saving this paper are very slim, but they're certainly zip if you don't take advantage of this to show what's in the *Star* [to people] who don't have that other paper for a while."[34] And Bellows knew that if the *Star* printed the *Post,* it would push its own pressmen to strike, because pressmen for both papers belonged to the same local.

Sulzberger insisted that he had not been dispatched to the F Street Club to press Kay Graham's case on Allbritton but rather to brief Allbritton, for his own good, on the New York newspaper strike of 1963, when the publishers—with the exception of Dorothy Schiff of the *New York Post*—had agreed that a strike against one would be considered a strike against all.[35] But Bellows had already briefed Allbritton on the real lesson of the 1963 strike: The only reason the *Post* had survived was that its publisher alone had refused to go along with the guys.* Don't be bamboozled, Bellows pleaded, by the "country club atmosphere among publishers."[36]

No one, in Bellows's opinion, was a member in higher standing of that club than Kay's friend Scotty Reston, who soon produced a column charging the *Star* with acting like a "fearful bystander." He warned—threatened, actually—that the *Post* now had no reason ever to enter into a joint printing agreement with the *Star,* an agreement that would have allowed the *Star* to cut its deficit and survive.[37]

When Reston's column hit Bellows's desk (the *Star* obtained it through the New York Times News Service), Bellows asked Jimmy

---

*Among the casualties in New York were the *Herald Tribune,* the *Mirror,* the *Journal-American,* the *World-Telegram,* and the *Sun.*

Breslin to respond. As Bellows recalls happily, he "just savaged Mr. Reston"; Bellows ran the columns side by side. Breslin dismissed Reston's argument as "a Washington gentleman's version of freedom of the press: Come along with us, you Allbritton, or we'll bury you." He also pointed out that Sulzberger "did not say the [New York] *Times* was suspending its Washington circulation . . . in sympathy with *The Washington Post.*" In fact, the *Times* boosted its shipment of Sunday papers.

Kay Graham's fury mounted. "Allbritton took quite a bit of heat from Mrs. Graham," recalls Bellows. It was one of Allbritton's "finer moments. He was willing to say, 'Okay, I'll stand up to them all.' "38

Having been spurned by Allbritton, *Post* executives made a deal with six small newspapers within a few hundred miles of Washington. Type was set in house by computer at the *Post;* photographs of the pages were picked up by helicopters, which landed on the roof of the *Post* building, and shuttled to the cooperating newspapers, whose identities were kept strictly secret. The newly printed papers were then trucked to the Washington area, where nonunion distributors picked them up.

Inside the *Post* building a warlike mentality prevailed—a sense of siege, excitement, danger, and camaraderie, managers eating and sleeping on the premises. The helicopter pick-up was referred to as "the airlift."39 "SWAT team" was the name Mark Meagher used for those in charge of the operation, who included commanding officer Donny Graham and second in command Roger Parkinson. Thirty-four years old, a Harvard MBA and a Green Beret in Vietnam, Parkinson organized the airlift and regularly served rooftop watch duty, binoculars poised to scan the skies. "Sort of like the Battle of Britain," said Kay, who found Parkinson so heroic that she once popped into his office unannounced just to hug him.40 Bill Meyer, liberal though he was, came down squarely on the family side and reported regularly to the *Post* to set headlines. "That was a great moment for him," recalls Alan Finberg. "He reveled in that."41

During the strike, Katharine came to be known as "the Iron Lady" for her coolheadedness (some called it coldness). She did not back down: not when a veteran pressman, despairing of ever working again, shot himself to death;42 not when demonstrators marched to her house holding candles flickering inside brown paper bags in tribute to the dead pressman, whose means of suicide resembled

Phil's; not when wives of pressmen stood vigil outside the gate of her Georgetown house pleading, "You live in luxury, your family will never have to do without," and "You're Jewish, you should know what oppression is." She didn't flinch when strikers burned her in effigy. She hardly winced when a striker strode back and forth across the entrance to the *Post* building carrying a sign that read "Phil Shot the Wrong Graham."

Mark Meagher, however, says Kay was so scared, so hysterical, that she needed constant bucking up: "I lived with a terrible sinking feeling that Katharine was going to back down."[43]

Her exaggerated assessment of Allbritton's abilities was, explains Meagher, "one of the things that made her argue long and hard about why we should settle."[44] When, in October, the initial month of the strike, the *Star* had its first profitable month in five years, Katharine was sure that Allbritton was going to take the lead forever.[45] "I was the one who had to sit alone with her," Meagher recounts, "and try to keep her resolve. There was great vacillation the first month." But he also remembers that "when it was clear that we could make it and do it, Jesus Christ, the backbone got real, real stiff."[46]

In December, with the strike into its third month, Kay refused to agree to neutral arbitration. She announced that her company would hire nonunion pressmen to replace the strikers. Several hundred eager applicants lined up outside the *Post* building, in spitting distance of the dispirited strikers.[47]

In a speech some fourteen years later, Kay coolly recalled that when the *Post* offered a final contract and the pressmen refused it, "we replaced the union."[48]

For liberals such as Joe Rauh, who loved Kay and liked to think that she was still a liberal, the strike was painful. He was among those who signed a full-page ad in the *Star* urging Kay to seek mediation or arbitration. Hubert Humphrey and George McGovern also signed, as did Adrian Fisher, who had been Phil's general counsel and labor negotiator. With victory hers for the taking, Kay could not be moved.

Nor could Donny. In February 1976, after the union was "effectively broken," some striking pressmen asked John Hanrahan, who knew Donny both professionally and personally, to plead with him to give them back their jobs. "I thought it was probably pretty hopeless, but I agreed to do it. [Donny] was friendly but very firm.

Under no circumstances would they come back to the *Post.*" Hanrahan persisted, telling Donny: "I see a growing gap between the people we're supposed to cover and ourselves. We purport to be able to go out and write about people living in poverty, and this to me shows we have no understanding or concern at all." Donny's response showed Hanrahan only that he missed the point: "Yeah," Donny said, "it's really amazing, since I've come [here] the education level of the people we're hiring is much greater. We're getting people with master's degrees."[49]

Kay Graham and her men accomplished what seemed the impossible and actually made money during October, November, and December—again, as during the Guild strike, because of lower payroll costs. Most satisfying to Kay, by November the *Star* was back in the red.[50]

The long-term savings for the Post Company were spectacular and helped turn the paper into the money machine it is today—its profits skyrocketing from $7 to $10 million in 1975 to $25 to $30 million in 1979–1980. Labor cuts would account for about one-third of the *Post*'s profit boom. (In 1976, for example, $1.2 million in overtime was eliminated and productivity jumped twenty percent.)[51]

After the one-two punch of the failure of the Guild and pressmen strikes, the unions at the paper would never be the same. "Unions have no strength today at the *Post,*" Mark Meagher asserts, and backs his boast with numbers. Before the pressmen's strike, in 1974, the *Post* had about 3,000 employees in Washington, 250 of whom were nonunion; after the strike, that labor base fell to about 2,400, some 800 of whom were nonunion.[52]

AFL-CIO president George Meany wondered publicly what Kay Graham would have done if the pressmen had accepted the *Post*'s final offer. Her answer to his question was widely reported: "Slit my throat."[53]

Meagher credits Donny—whose promotion to assistant general manager coincided with the start of the strike, and whose main duty consisted of seeing that the paper got out during the strike—as the one who showed great resolve. "Donny was magnificent. [He] would always say, 'We've got to go through with it.' "[54]

Others, such as Kermit Lansner, credit Meagher with winning the strike. He "probably did as much for that paper on the business side as anybody. [Kay and her top executives] were prepared to buckle. He was the steel that helped break that strike."[55]

Meagher modestly—and correctly—credits John Prescott, the man Kay fired for not being tough enough on unions: "He was the guy who planned it. All I did was carry some of it out, and [I] happened to be the lucky guy who sat there when [the strike] blew."[56]

Although Kay would vigorously deny it, that she set out to break the pressmen's union is an opinion not much in dispute. "The feeling was widespread," says former *Post* reporter Morton Mintz, "that she was out to bust all the unions and intended thereby to make her reputation as a great business leader in America."[57] When Phil ran the *Post* and was having his own problems with the unions, he listened eagerly to a proposal that the *Post* send managers to strikebreakers' school. He decided not to, largely because of Adrian Fisher, who pleaded, "This is not what this place is about."*[58] Kay decided the opposite—sending managers to what was dubbed "the school for scabs," in Oklahoma—which Bernard Nossiter later cited as evidence that she meant to break the union. "You don't train your executives at scab school to man printing presses unless you expect to publish during the strike. [Not only did] she show intent, she showed how it could be done."[61]

John Hanrahan observes, "A lot of people in the pressmen's union said it may have been her objective not to eliminate the union totally, but to put it in a position where it was so subservient that it was really more of a house union that didn't pose any real challenge." That was the fate, Hanrahan adds, of the Newspaper Guild, which he characterizes as a union of "compliant members" after its failed strike.[62]

What was certain was that Kay Graham had the largest of objectives in mind. "You can't afford to lose control of your organization," she commented in a speech. "Clearly, we had to pay whatever price was necessary to regain control."[63] She admitted that "the

---

*Phil used to argue with Nossiter and Erwin Knoll, both strong union men, that, in Nossiter's words, "there was no longer any role for a trade union in the modern corporation; that [it] was run by such enlightened executives like him that all the workers' potential needs would be recognized and catered to."[59] While Phil enjoyed the give-and-take of arguing about the value of unions and, both men say, never held their activism against them, Kay was different: she wanted the unions out of her life and certainly, says Knoll, didn't "enjoy that kind of adversarial relationship."[60]

strike enabled us to achieve in one blow what we had intended to do over a period of years. If we had started out with the intention to regain right away all the control we had given up over the years, we never could have succeeded."[64]

By breaking the union, one analyst said, "the *Post* had made a gift to all the newspapers in the land."[65] Labor lawyer Theodore Kheel agrees: "She gave a lot of encouragement to other publishers by her victory. She showed the unions could be beaten. Similar strategies were being developed by publishers in New York, particularly [of] *The New York Times,* with great success."[66] Kay, who throughout her career regretted her lack of formal business training, was delighted that her company's approach to emasculating the pressmen's union was one of the cases studied at Harvard Business School.[67]

She was the envy of her fellow publishers, at least one of whom could not bear the fact that a woman had done, so to speak, a man's job on the unions. Kay telephoned a prominent New York publisher whose paper was facing a strike. After speaking to her, he slammed down the phone. "I'm not gonna let that goddamned woman . . . be tougher than [I am]," he snarled at a lawyer who witnessed the call.

Nowhere was the weakness of the unions and the strength of the *Post*'s public relations machine more evident than in the lobby of the John F. Kennedy Center for the Performing Arts before the international premiere of the movie *All the President's Men* in 1976. The liberal establishment of politicians and media stars and moguls came out in droves and waded through a lobby where two hundred strikers picketed, singing, "Pressmen shall overcome."

The star of the show was Kay Graham. She loved the movie, and its portrayal of how her paper had brought down a president, even though she was nowhere to be seen in it. Executive producer and star Robert Redford had cut her character and all but one reference to her—John Mitchell's ugly threat, "Katie Graham is gonna get her tit caught in a big fat wringer if that's published"—when, in midproduction, she changed her mind about cooperating with the filmmaker and instructed her lawyers to stop Redford from finishing.[68]

Barely behind the scenes was the bitterness that surfaced between the Hollywood version of the reporters and the real things. "It's a battle of glamour," Sally Quinn gloated, "and the movie people have found out they're losing."[69] Then there were those at the *Post* who really hated the movie: Howard Simons, for example, who had been the guts behind the investigation, but who in Martin Balsam's portrayal came off as a timid soul who lobbied to get the young and green Woodward and Bernstein removed from the story, only to be overruled by the crusading Ben Bradlee. In fact, Simons had fought to keep "Woodstein" on when others, Bradlee included, argued for their removal or paid next to no attention.[70] Leonard Downie, who meticulously edited the paper's Watergate coverage, was portrayed as a bespectacled mope, a local yokel whose vision extended only as far as the "Metro" section, incapable of understanding the significance of Watergate.

What gnawed at Simons was his fear that, in the public's mind, the movie version of Watergate would overtake the reality. He was right. In a glowing *New York Times* profile of Bradlee, a reporter noted, "[Jason] Robards's portrayal of Mr. Bradlee as a hands-on editor involved in every twist and turn of the story is said to be an accurate one."*[71]

On December 1, 1976, when Donny was thirty-one, just about the age Phil was when his father-in-law gave him *The Washington Post,* Kay Graham gave her son Mark Meagher's old job as general manager and executive vice-president of the newspaper. She then promoted Meagher, whose star was obviously on the rise, to president of the newspaper division. Donny would continue to report to him.

The month before, having finally decided to sell the *New York Post,* Dorothy Schiff had her eye on Kay Graham as a buyer. Roswell Gilpatric, whose firm had been counsel to the Schiff family, explains that Schiff "ran out of resources to put into the *Post* and she wanted to combine with an enterprise [such as *The Washington Post*] that had liquidity and the cash flow that could keep [her paper] going." In Kay's view, the New York paper, with its hideous labor problems, was the least attractive of all the papers her company was considering. Kay had emerged as big business's heroine of the decade, and she was not about to take on the New York unions and fail.[73]

So Schiff sold the tabloid to Rupert Murdoch. The Australian was a recent acquaintance of Kay's, a man she felt she had to know, given his position as one of the world's most powerful publishers. She had

---

*At the *Post*'s memorial service for Simons, Bob Woodward said simply, "I'm sorry, Howie."[72]

invited him to her farm for a weekend, but she did not quite approve of him. Mark Edmiston explains that Kay had two problems with Murdoch: she considered him a "philistine," who "lowered the quality of newspapers" by publishing, in Britain, a tabloid featuring bare-breasted women, and she considered him "brash."[74] She would soon discover just how brash.

Kay had a new and intriguing friend—magazine wunderkind Clay Felker, creator, editor, publisher, and spirit behind the then bold and exuberant *New York* magazine.* Felker had an incomparable knack for anticipating the next trend, the most chic social ill, the most current source of angst afflicting the urban upwardly mobile. *New York,* a magazine that the hip and affluent—and those aspiring to be—felt they had to read, attracted a demographic slice that advertisers coveted. And Felker had a similar knack for spotting writing talent. If Ben Gilbert could not appreciate Tom Wolfe, Felker could, and Wolfe wrote for Felker, as did Jimmy Breslin, Gay Talese, Ken Auletta.

Eleven years Kay's junior and once married to actress Pamela Tiffin, Felker was the sort of risk-taker Kay admired, and he followed his instincts to what seemed invariable triumph. She invited both Murdoch and Felker for a weekend at Glen Welby, hoping that the former could be of service to the latter. According to Theodore Kheel, who served as *New York* magazine's lawyer, Felker talked far too much that weekend. "He was very frank with Murdoch, more than he ever should have been, in telling him about the property, his hopes, his aims, his expectations. That attracted Murdoch's interest."[75]

Felker's intention was to convince his new friend to help him regain control of the company that published *New York.* He had lost control in 1969, when he had taken the company public and thus been forced to dilute his equity. When it became apparent that Murdoch was looking to take over *New York,* as well as its sister publications *The Village Voice* and the recently launched *New West,* Felker proclaimed that he considered himself "raped" by Murdoch[76] and turned for rescue to Kay Graham.

Felker urged Kay to attempt a friendly takeover, leaving him in

*Felker had also worked for *Time, Life,* and *Esquire;* helped develop *Sports Illustrated;* and been *The Village Voice*'s editor and publisher. *New York* magazine had begun as the Sunday supplement to the *Herald Tribune,* with Felker as its editor. In 1967, after that paper and its successor, the *World Journal Tribune*—an unwieldy, short-lived merger of three failing New York dailies—folded, Felker and some backers bought the rights to the name *New York.*

352 POWER, PRIVILEGE, AND THE *POST*

charge.[77] Given Murdoch's straightforward admonition, "You and I could never work together," Felker knew that otherwise his days were numbered.[78] According to Edward Kosner, then editor of *Newsweek,* "Felker was desperate to stave off Murdoch, and Kay very much wanted to do it."[79]

It was said that Donny Graham also wanted to acquire *New York*—that of all the magazines the Washington Post Company considered, this was the most attractive[80]—but some claim that Kay's feelings for Felker were the impetus. "She went after *New York* because of Clay," says Mark Edmiston. "She threw everything into the ring to try to get *New York.* For Clay. She said those words, 'For Clay.' "[81]

In actuality, the properties were not financially robust, at least not with Felker at the helm, and Murdoch had surely reached this conclusion. Nobody doubted Felker's editorial genius, but the company's profit margin was anemic at 1.8 percent, downright pitiful when compared with the Post Company's ten to fifteen percent. *New York* was fat with advertising—in 1975, seventh in ad pages among U.S. consumer magazines—but some people charged that Felker was a poor manager and was spending the company into near unprofitability. One former *New York* executive described the company as "Felker's personal playpen."[82]

Kay had told Felker that she was reluctant to get into a "bidding war" with Murdoch, but that is exactly what happened.[83] Murdoch had the advantage because he dispassionately assessed Felker's strengths and weaknesses, and calculated how to acquire the magazine. Kay, on the other hand, approached Felker and the takeover with a teary emotionalism.

"Clay never realized there are simple ways to deal with a board of directors," Murdoch once said. "He could have had them to lunch twice a year with Teddy Kennedy or somebody. Instead, he made enemies of them one by one."[84] Felker's bitterest enemy was Carter Burden, Jr., who also held the biggest chunk of stock in the magazine's parent company. Burden had acquired his block in 1974 by selling *The Village Voice* to the New York Magazine Company for cash and stock.[85]

Murdoch promptly allied himself with Burden, then a New York City councilman (he was also a great-great-great-grandson of Cornelius Vanderbilt; heir to a California oil fortune; and ex-husband of Babe Paley's daughter and Bill Paley's stepdaughter Amanda). Burden hated Felker because, says Theodore Kheel, at a board meeting Felker had referred to Amanda Burden's rumored affair with Edward Kennedy.[86] (Presumably, Murdoch realized that Teddy Kennedy would not be an appropriate guest for a board meeting.)

In friendlier days, Felker and Burden had signed an agreement giving Felker the right to bid on the publications should Burden decide to sell. They also had a shareholders' agreement that required them to vote together, so as to protect Felker's position of control—unless the company was consistently losing money, in which case Burden would be free to vote his shares as he wished. Depending on the method of accounting used, it could then have been argued that the company was profitable or that it was not. *New York* was making money, as was *The Village Voice;* but *New West,* founded earlier in 1976, was, like most start-ups, losing plenty and draining the parent company. Burden chose to interpret the figures as a loss and argued that therefore his shareholders' agreement with Felker was null and void. (Felker and Burden would end up in litigation on this point.)

For advice Kay went not to Larry Israel, who opposed the acquisition—he feared that the purchase would diminish the Post Company's earnings and that the strong-willed Felker would prove impossible to control—but to Warren Buffett and her friend Felix Rohatyn, one of New York's premier specialists in the art of the takeover.

Reaction in *New York*'s editorial offices to Kay's angling for control was mixed, but it was jubilant compared with the reaction to the news that Rupert Murdoch was also bidding. Threats of a mass editorial walkout should Murdoch emerge victorious were already in the air. "It's funny," one editorial staffer said, "people who didn't like Kay Graham are suddenly looking on her as the . . . savior."[87]

Kay was desperate to succeed, but things looked bad. Rohatyn had delivered the Post Company's check for some $3.2 million—$7.50 a share for Burden's stock—to Burden's lawyer, Peter Tufo; he refused to accept it. "Burden was so furious at Felker he would not consider anyone allied with him," Kay said later.

On December 31, 1976, Murdoch formally took control of the *New York Post,* and the same day, Murdoch and Kay Graham went to the mat over *New York.*[88] With her in *Newsweek*'s executive suite were Rohatyn, Felker, and *Newsweek* executives Peter Derow and Kenneth Auchincloss. Gail Sheehy, later Felker's wife, described the scene, as they waited for Burden—who was skiing in Sun Valley,

Idaho, and supposedly could not be reached—or his lawyer to call
and accept the offer or at least negotiate. "The humiliation level in
the room rises considerably. . . . Katharine Graham, queen mother
of one of the most highly respected publishing organizations in the
world, has been waiting for two days for the phone to ring. It doesn't.
Carter Burden is treating her like a jilted dance-hall dolly. . . . At
eight p.m. Katharine Graham takes the phone with its last feeble
connection to Peter Tufo and . . . implores, 'What is it you really
want? Should I fly out to see Carter? I'll do anything.' 'Kay, don't,'
Felix [Rohatyn] whispers. 'It's demeaning to you. The whole thing is
obscene. At least keep your dignity.' 'Is there anything humanly
possible?' Katharine Graham pleads."[89] In sheer frustration Rohatyn screamed at Tufo, "Get that yo-yo off the slopes!"[90]

Rohatyn may have thought flying to Sun Valley would be demeaning, but Murdoch did just that; and with an offer of $8.25 a share,
he closed the deal. "Kay thought that her 'position' would assure
that Carter Burden would respond to her and answer her phone
calls," explains Derow, who in the final forty-eight hours tried to
breathe life into the deal.[91] When time ran out, Kay was disconso-
late—"almost tearful," says Mel Elfin.[92] It undoubtedly occurred to
her that Phil Graham would somehow have found a way to make
this deal, moving fast and charming Burden on the slopes, if necessary. As a final indignity, on that very day Edward Kosner was eight
days away from closing an issue of *Newsweek* that featured Murdoch
as its cover story; now it would have to include his acquisition of *New
York*.[93]

Kay Graham and Clay Felker would not be joined in business—or
romance, although the *Newsweek* rumor mill had them as a couple.
Polly Kraft, who, with her husband, introduced Kay to Felker,
giggles at the thought of a serious affair between the two. "I think
Clay adored Kay. I think she found him wonderful fun, and I don't
think she took him seriously for a minute. Kay has a real sense of
what's appropriate for herself."[94]

Kay Graham embarrassed Larry Israel by ignoring his warnings
not to attempt to buy *New York* magazine, but the Post Company
president still had reason to feel good. By the end of 1976, the value
of the Jacksonville and Hartford television stations had doubled.
Newsweek's performance had sagged in 1974 and 1975 but had
perked up in 1976—which, despite the pressmen's strike, was a year
of record earnings.

In 1977, the numbers would continue to look good. The profit margin jumped to sixteen percent, from nine percent in 1974. Even the Trenton *Times* was doing better, showing a net profit before taxes—thanks in part to Mark Meagher, who had installed a tough new publisher, "really ruthless," Meagher says. On the editorial side, Richard Harwood was recalled to *The Washington Post,* replaced as editor by a veteran *Times* employee who had lived in Trenton most of his life.[95]

But Kay was not satisfied, and the target of her dissatisfaction was Larry Israel. It was at the time of his ascent that Kay became infatuated—in both a business and a personal sense—with Warren Buffett, reducing to nil Israel's chances of succeeding. He felt that Kay had shoved him aside in favor of Buffett; as in the case of the *New York* acquisition, she ignored his advice while treating Buffett's as gospel.

Other executives blame Kay's management style for Israel's problems. Mark Meagher says that Israel "couldn't cope with [her] making a decision twelve times and changing it twelve times."[96] In Peter Derow's assessment, "Larry pulled his hair out. He showed his frustration. You can't do that. There were times when he'd say [to her] in front of others, 'Kay, I'll explain this once again to you. Maybe you didn't understand it the first time.' You could see his teeth tighten up." And, Derow adds, "Larry was fifty-five at the time. How much can you adapt your behavior?"[97]

"The Washington Post Company has announced the resignation of its president, Larry H. Israel, effective February 1 [1977]," was the extent of the explanation offered to *Post* readers. Kay would say no more. She was becoming increasingly irritable about charges that her executive suite had a revolving door. She was described as "livid" when *Post* ombudsman Charles Seib criticized the paper's "bare-bones coverage" of the resignation and complained that readers of *The New York Times* were told more than readers of the *Post.* "If people say I murder and use arsenic I still won't comment," she replied.[98]

Paul Ignatius says Israel left "feeling very bitter."[99] The bitterness, presumably, was sweetened by an exit fee of $650,000, plus a retirement benefit of about $20,000 annually. Morton Mintz published that information in *Fruits of Your Labor,* the annual bulletin he started in desperation because "when [Kay] killed off the pressmen's union, a lot of us felt she was trying to kill all the unions." The bulletin was a "way of fighting back."[100]

Kay had once called Mintz "the thorn in all of our sides": at *Post* luncheons he would interrogate heads of multinational corporations and other guests instead of maintaining the superficial conversation Kay wanted. Now she could call him a dagger: by examining the Post Company's filings with the Securities and Exchange Commission as well as its messages to shareholders, Mintz was able to describe in embarrassing detail what he saw as the enormous salaries, bonuses, and stock options that Kay lavished on her top men, specifically the "so-called incentive compensation plan for professionals and executives. Professionals, I think, meant Ben Bradlee. It certainly didn't mean us." What exercised Mintz the most, however, was the increasingly extravagant golden parachutes that Kay used to rid herself of unwanted executives—as if to cushion the blow and make them go quietly away.[101]

Then, the same year that Israel left the paper, Kay decided the editorial page under Phil Geyelin was passionless, dull, too "gelatinous," with too much of an "on the one hand . . . but on the other" approach.[102] Meg Greenfield, who had become her close friend, would, Kay was certain, bring intensity back to the page.

But Geyelin was close to Ben Bradlee—"Phil's the closest thing to a godfather you'll ever have," Bradlee once told his son Dominic.[103] Still, Kay called him in.

"She and I had a heart-to-heart," Geyelin remembers, "a fairly rough conversation. She said that I was washed up and tired. We'd been through the Pentagon Papers and Watergate, and she asked me if I'd like to go to London." Shades of Bob Estabrook and Al Friendly. "I really wouldn't," Geyelin replied. "Look, the [editorial] page has deteriorated," she persisted. "You may be right. I'll put it back," he promised. That would not be an easy task because, as he says, "I didn't think it was any different [from what] it had been." They ended the discussion with his vowing to prove to her that she was wrong.

Nothing more was said. Geyelin speculates that Kay asked herself, "Why fight this? Because when Donny takes over there's a perfectly legitimate and easy way to do it." In any event, she was uncharacteristically patient, probably recognizing that Bradlee did not want to see his friend ousted.

The next year, 1978, an association of graduates of women's colleges gave Geyelin an award in recognition of his editorship of the editorial page. He photocopied the citation and sent it to Kay with the postscript, "Two thousand women's college graduates can't all be wrong." She delivered her written response in person: she stuffed her note of congratulations in his pocket and said, "This woman's college graduate agrees, it's greatly improved." And then followed a scene that Geyelin calls "almost identical" to the one Oz Elliott described in his memoirs, in which he and Kay fell into each other's arms, kissed, and shed some tears. But Kay did not fire Geyelin—she told him that "everything was fine."[104]

Everything was not fine. She knew it, and Geyelin should have known it. He relaxed and fell back into his old expectations.

In November 1977, Mark Meagher had officially become president and chief operating officer of the Washington Post Company. By early spring, 1978, the Trenton *Times* having returned a small cash dividend and provided enough incentive for Kay to buy other papers, Meagher was busily acquiring. For $25 million, the company bought *The Herald,* in Everett, Washington, twenty-five miles north of Seattle.[105]

Next, Meagher tried to purchase the *Morning-News* and *Evening Journal* in Wilmington, Delaware; the Du Pont Corporation had put up both papers for sale. To him, this was a no-lose proposition: the papers were a monopoly and ad rates could be set at whatever level would reap a tidy profit for the owner.

The competition for this gold mine was Gannett. Kay thought the papers were worth $40 million but was authorized by her directors to go as high as $60 million. She decided to bid $55 million, later explaining, "We expected when Gannett got involved that they would be the high bidder, [as was] their usual practice. We thought that they'd bid $57 or $58 million and it would be negotiable at that point."

Once again, Kay Graham believed too fervently in her paper's prestige. As Howard Bray wrote: "She and her executives anticipated that Du Pont would give preference to their company's publishing distinction, in the wake of Watergate, in choosing among close bidders. But Du Pont, to the [Post Company's] surprise, speedily accepted Gannett's offer of $60 million. 'We called it wrong,' Kay Graham admitted. Asked why she bid $5 million less than the amount her board had sanctioned, she said, 'Five million dollars is a lot of money.' Apparently, Du Pont thought so, too."[106]

*

In her own front yard, Joe Allbritton was still making Kay Graham nervous. There were signs of change at the *Washington Star* that she did not know how to interpret, and as usual, she took them as impending disaster. Jim Bellows had recently quit as editor; he "left when Allbritton was putting a squeeze on the paper, trying to tighten it so he could put it up for sale."[107]

In March 1978, precisely when Kay and company were proffering their misguided $55 million bid for the Wilmington papers, Allbritton was in the process of selling the *Star* to Time Inc. for a mere $20 million—$5 million less than the Post Company paid for the paper in Washington state.* Kay was petrified. Allbritton was bad enough, but Time Inc. was a behemoth that made her company seem puny by comparison.

The sale would attract worldwide attention because the companies would become instantly symmetrical—each owning a paper in the nation's capital and each owning a newsweekly. The *Post* was, of course, bigger, richer, more powerful than the *Star,* but *Time* was richer and more powerful than *Newsweek.* Kay, who so feared looking foolish, did not relish being placed in such a provocatively competitive position.

Time Inc. funneled $60 million to the *Star,* but still, as far as the newspaper was concerned, a calmer, more confident owner than Kay would have realized that there was very little to worry about. For openers, Time Inc. was a magazine company with little experience in newspapers. Second, it had bought the newspaper for the wrong reasons. At first, editor in chief Hedley Donovan said, "you would think a large, growing, and very affluent metropolitan center could support two papers, and particularly, as the *Star* was perceived as being somewhat more conservative than the *Post,* it was, at the price we paid, a not unreasonable gamble." But the real reason, he admitted, was that "Jim Shepley, then president of Time, and I had both been Washington reporters. And the idea of Time having a newspaper presence in Washington had a lot of sentimental appeal."[108]

Then there was the fact that the *Star* was an afternoon paper; although some were doing well, since the early 1960s, ten afternoon dailies in metropolitan areas had folded. And by the most awful of coincidences, on the very day that Time Inc. announced its intention

---

*Although the newspaper had proven a loser for Allbritton, the radio and television stations that had been part of the deal he made in 1974 left him with a profit of more than $150 million.

to buy the *Star,* Marshall Field V announced his intention to shut down his family's distinguished 102-year-old afternoon paper, the *Chicago Daily News.*[109]

The *Star* was losing plenty of money—about a million dollars a month.* In addition, Donovan seemed to have chosen just the wrong editor—a man who downplayed the strengths of the paper, such as the strong local coverage that made it an attractive alternative to the *Post.* In June 1978, Donovan tapped Murray Gart, assistant managing editor of *Time* and chief of the Time-Life News Service, to replace Sidney Epstein, who had held the title of editor since Bellows's departure. Washington reporters Michael Kilian and Arnold Sawislak wrote that Gart "immediately transformed [the *Star*] into a miniature, cheapo version" of *The New York Times.*[111]

Murray Gart was known, however, for very aggressive coverage of the Washington party scene. But the event *Star* reporters would have loved to cover was one they could not get near—the October 20, 1978, wedding of Sally Quinn and Ben Bradlee. Not only did Kay forgive Bradlee his infidelities, but along with Art Buchwald and Edward Bennett Williams, she was a witness at the wedding—so exclusive an affair that the only guests were the three witnesses.[112]

Phil Graham was dead and Ben Gilbert departed, but social engineering was alive and well at the *Post.* In 1978, his first elected term having expired, Walter Washington was running for reelection as mayor. The key was the Democratic primary, whose winner would be a shoo-in in the general election. The venerable Washington was pitted against city council chairman Sterling Tucker and Marion Barry, Jr., who had only recently shed his dashiki and his activities as a street organizer to win election to the city council.

The *Post* severed its long and close tie to Mayor Washington and, by pushing Marion Barry's candidacy in seven separate editorials, saw to it that Barry won.

Walter Washington was shocked and hurt. He had had a mutually admiring relationship not only with Agnes Meyer but also with Kay. According to his friend and former aide Ben Gilbert, Washington

---

*Star circulation stood at 329,000 daily and 316,000 Sunday, versus 562,000 and 801,000, respectively, for the *Post.* The *Post*'s share of total advertising was 71.9 percent, the *Star*'s was 28.1 percent. The editorial budgets and staffs were likewise uneven—$20 million and 490 people at the *Post,* and $8.6 million and 225 people at the *Star.*[110]

speculates that Kay thought he had sided with the pressmen (in fact, he had stayed neutral), and so turned on him.

Gilbert denounces the *Post*'s editorial campaign on behalf of Marion Barry for having gone "way beyond the normal journalistic restraints. It was day after day, and it was a mean campaign, primarily on the editorial page, but also to a certain extent on the news pages. One day there was a story [with] three gross errors about what Washington had done. I said, 'Let me call Ben Bradlee and point out the factual errors, not argue the merits of the point, but just point out the factual errors.' And Walter said, 'There's no use. You will get three more stories, all of which will be negative.' I did call Bradlee. He said he would look into it, and if it was the way I said, they would run a correction. What they ran was three more dirty stories."[113]

That the *Post* elected Marion Barry was beyond dispute. Phil Geyelin recalls that Barry was "running third then, a bad third. He had a lot of the black vote, and the honky [newspaper's endorsement] was something he needed." Barry's thirst for editorial endorsements, Geyelin claims, was insatiable. "[He] called me up three days before the election, when we'd already written six editorials, and he said he wanted just one more. I was always writing one more. In fact we did write one more, for Sunday, before the election. I think he's uncomfortable to this day that he owes everything to *The Washington Post*."*[114]

It was the first of these editorials that sparked the only "bad exchange" Geyelin ever had with Kay. "We had to start laying out our case for [Barry] in August"—the month that Kay traditionally spends in Martha's Vineyard. Geyelin claims he phoned her to let her know the editorial was coming. "She wasn't there, but I knew she had no problem with what we were doing."

The next morning, Kay received a call from a prominent Washingtonian, an avid backer of Walter Washington, Geyelin suspects, who

---

*Marion Barry soon proved a disappointment to Kay Graham and her editors. But the paper continued to support him in subsequent elections, including his run in 1986, when the *Post* gave him a lukewarm endorsement. For its steadfast support, the paper took much criticism, especially from *The Washington Monthly;* a reporter from the magazine pointed out that the *Post* not only installed Barry in the first place but "kept supporting [him] and suppressing bad news about him long after his last shred of promise had disintegrated."[115] By the late 1980s, with charges flying about drug use, philandering, and a scandal-a-day administration, the *Post* turned on Barry as vigorously as it had once supported him. It went so far, in fact, that not only Barry but *Washingtonian* magazine accused it of staging a vendetta to bring him down.[116] In February 1990, the *Post* called on him to resign.

screamed, "What the hell are you doing?" Kay had to confess that she had not read the editorial: her editorial-page editor had not sent it to her or read it to her over the phone. She felt humiliated. "That was just the kind of spot I never wanted to put her in," Geyelin says. "And I probably should have held the editorial for a day."

When Kay contacted Geyelin, she was incensed. She "insisted I hadn't called, but I had." Geyelin stresses that she wasn't unhappy about the substance of the editorial. "She was unhappy about the process. I breached the no-surprise rule." Geyelin had taken her too much for granted, had acted as if she did not matter.[117]

In 1979, soon after Donny took over as publisher, Geyelin went to see him. "How do you feel about the editorial page?" he asked. "Well, I like some parts of it," Donny replied. "I don't like others." Hardly a ringing endorsement.

There was some evidence that Bradlee thought Geyelin had become lazy and, even worse, had lost his edge. But that did not mean Bradlee wanted to see his friend replaced. "Watch your ass, buddy," Bradlee warned him. "Don't you understand she wants your job?" "She," of course, was Meg Greenfield, Geyelin's deputy, who in 1978 had won a Pulitzer for editorial writing. (Geyelin won his in 1970.) "I don't believe you," Geyelin told Bradlee. Geyelin regarded Greenfield as "a very, very close friend. In the salad days, the mid-seventies, she was probably as close to me as anybody. I didn't even need to finish my sentences with her. We came to think the same way."[118]

Yet Geyelin didn't consider that Kay and Greenfield had developed a closeness that was unmatched by any of Kay's other friendships, except that with Polly Wisner (now Fritchey, after her marriage to Agnes's friend columnist Clayton Fritchey). In some ways this friendship was even more important, because Greenfield could bolster Kay when she felt insecure professionally as well as personally.

Greenfield was Kay's speechwriter, teacher, briefer, worldwide traveling companion. When Kay gave a dinner party, she was almost always there. An editor who knows them both well points out that "the two people who were really close to her were a kind of a mother figure and a Phil figure. Meg has the confidence that Kay lacks. She's tough the way that Agnes [Meyer] was tough. Ben [Bradlee] has all the glamour."[119]

As Kay had planned, it was Donny who eventually dismissed

Geyelin and replaced him with Greenfield. Few doubted that Kay's hand was behind the decision, but Donny was not merely doing his mother's bidding. Geyelin believes that Donny, who did not reveal his political views, wanted a change. "I've been told that he felt we were too liberal."[120]

Donny showed himself to be at least his mother's equal in the clumsiness with which he handled Geyelin's removal. After Donny informed Geyelin, they agreed that the official announcement would be delayed for two weeks. Geyelin was chairman of the music committee of the annual Gridiron show, then in rehearsals, and felt that news of his dismissal would be painfully awkward. During a Saturday dress rehearsal, Geyelin remembers, he was paged by Donny, who told him that "the *Star* had the story and had to [print] it the next morning. And I said, 'Look, I can't deal with that right now. If you feel you have to, go with it.' For a guy like Ben [Bradlee], the idea of the *Star*'s beating the *Post* on a story about the *Post* was unacceptable, so by the time I got back to the office, Don had already notified every member of the staff of the editorial page. I would have liked to talk to my own people. I would [have liked] to be asked for a comment—the usual way those things are done—but it was done in a big hurry, and both Don and Ben said afterward [that] it couldn't possibly have been done worse."

Geyelin accepted Donny's invitation to write a column but not his offer of an office. "I didn't want to be put into some cubbyhole someplace just to be in the building." He went instead as a fellow to the Johns Hopkins School of Advanced International Studies.

Geyelin claims to have no regrets about hiring Greenfield. "I hired Meg because I thought you should hire a deputy who could replace you. [There are] two kinds of deputies, one who's no threat and no help, and one who is a lot of help and maybe a threat. Personally, I'd rather have someone who's a lot of help."[121]

That same year, Kay Graham decided that *Newsweek* needed a new editor. She wanted Edward Kosner out, but she wanted someone else to tell him.

"She didn't even fire me," Kosner says in a tone that still betrays shock and indignation. "Peter Derow fired me. He led me in to her. He did the actual firing. I didn't have the heart to get into a discussion with her. I just said, 'Okay, we'll make a settlement.' "[122] Derow recalls that Kay simply wouldn't fire Kosner herself. "You do it," she ordered him.[123]

"I should have known," says Kosner, "that my demise was coming, but I didn't."[124] The firing came as a surprise to almost everyone, with the exception, of course, of Derow and of Lester Bernstein, who had hired Kosner in 1963. Before ordering Kosner fired, Kay had offered the job to Bernstein, who was still at RCA—where he had gone in disillusionment when Kay fired Kermit Lansner and did not offer Bernstein, then *Newsweek*'s managing editor, the top job. "She had lined up Lester before she bagged me," Kosner says mordantly, "even as she lined me up before she bagged Oz [Elliott]."[125] (And even as she lined up Elliott before she "bagged" Lansner.) Bernstein took the job. "You couldn't very well regard yourself as a red-blooded American and not take that job when it was offered to you," he explains.[126] Before leaving the building, Kosner insisted that he be allowed to tell his staff—an opportunity denied Phil Geyelin.

Two reasons are generally given for Kosner's undoing: The first was that he made *Newsweek* too jazzy, too pop. "They ripped up the magazine," says Thelma McMahon. "We went from a Victorian, straitlaced magazine to something that was very avant-garde."[127] Kay Graham was heard to complain that Kosner, especially in his choice of covers, had made the magazine "frivolous."[128] (In that regard, Kosner may have been ahead of his time; as Bernstein puts it, he anticipated what newsmagazine editors "evidently now feel the marketplace imposes on them."[129])

The second reason, according to someone who talked to Kay shortly before the ouster, was that "Kosner had run the magazine increasingly as a one-man operation, failing to encourage input from those below him."[130] One colleague comments: "Ed is brilliant. But Ed is also as neurotic as hell. Ed needed to prove to everybody that he was the smartest guy in the world. It was so discouraging for anyone. [He] puts people down, always puts people down. Never encourages, never says thank you. He'd get crazy, scream at people. People were afraid, and an organization that's afraid doesn't produce."[131]

Still, Kosner was obviously smart, energetic, and in his instincts for what would appeal to the public, a match for Clay Felker. If Kay Graham had told Kosner of her concerns, he might have taken them to heart. But she did not want him to change, she just wanted him out.

What irritated her most was not tone or morale, but Kosner himself—how he looked, how he talked, how he acted. "She couldn't stand him," says a former Post Company executive. "He was a status

seeker, a social climber. It offended Kay. Either you have it or you
don't, and he doesn't, so don't climb."[132] (For that reason, perhaps,
she never invited Kosner on any of her grand tours.)

In the spring of 1978, Kay Graham enjoyed a glowing tribute in
a *Vassar Quarterly* profile by her old college friend Betty Frank.
Depicted as "the toughest publisher in business," Kay couldn't have
asked for better press. In 1977, *U.S. News & World Report* conducted
a poll of business and political leaders, and Kay was voted the "top
leader and shaper of national life" among women.

In 1976, when Joe Allbritton still owned the *Washington Star,* he
directed Jim Bellows to assign a reporter to an in-depth profile of
Katharine Graham. Bellows chose a talented young features writer
named Lynn Rosellini, who had come to the *Star* the year before
from *Newsday*'s Washington bureau.[133] "It was something that none
of us wanted to do," Rosellini recalls. "I thought, You can't win on
a story like that when you're the other newspaper. If you write
something nice, people are going to say, 'You're just sucking up to
the other publisher,' and if you write something that's tough, then it
sounds like it's sour grapes and you're just out to get her."[134] But
Allbritton, who was vitally interested in the piece and in fact served
as a source for gossip and anecdotes about his rival, insisted; and
Rosellini got to work.

Kay Graham initially refused to cooperate, but she later agreed to
two interviews. Many others who depended on her for current or
future jobs or favors would not talk. One editor who did talk remembers meeting Rosellini "in a lot of dark bars."[135]

In the meantime, Rosellini was trying to back out of the assignment. Allbritton wanted it so much, however, that she kept at it. She
began to work on the profile full-time in June, and completed what
was designed as a five-part series in October. She was delighted with
the finished product; it was very tough on Kay Graham but, she
thought, fair and entertaining. She had tapped myriad sources, including one of Kay's sisters and her daughter. Rosellini was eager to
see it in print.[136]

Then rumors started that Joe Allbritton had decided to delay or
even kill the series. His own employees—Bellows, columnist Mary
McGrory, editorial-page editor Edwin Yoder—tried to persuade
Allbritton to change his mind.[137] So worried was he that the profile
would somehow be released anyway that he demanded a promise in

writing. The document said that "while he owned the paper, I wouldn't run the series without his specific permission," recalls Bellows. Managing editor Sidney Epstein had to sign it too.[138]

Bellows has no idea why Allbritton was so spooked by the profile. Rosellini feels that although his staff did not know it, Allbritton had decided to sell the *Star* and "didn't want to do anything that might ruffle the waters."

Suddenly Allbritton, who had been so available to Rosellini, would not return her phone calls. "I was really upset," she remembers. It was "the only time I've ever cried in the newsroom."

Then Allbritton sold to Time Inc., and according to Rosellini, the *Star*'s new editor, Murray Gart, "discovered this series about Mrs. Graham. He thought it was good and also thought this was a way to let people know: Time Inc. is in town now and we've taken over this paper, and we're going to make ourselves known here, and what better way than to run this series."[139]

So, for five days, starting on November 13, 1978, the Kay Graham profile ran—not in any way toned down from the original ordered by Allbritton. With all the subtlety of a British tabloid, the paper sported a different front-page teaser each day. One heralded Katharine Graham as "an imperious bitch." "She's both 'Katharine the Great' and 'Katharine the Terrible,' " read another, which noted that the descriptions were compliments from one of Kay's "closest friends." The sides of *Star* delivery trucks were plastered with excerpts from some of the more insulting material.

A news story about the series encapsulating the ugliest of the anecdotes went out over the Chicago Tribune News Service to scores of newspapers, including *The Miami Herald,* where Phil Graham's family could see it. The *Los Angeles Herald Examiner,* where Bellows went as editor after leaving the *Star,* ran the syndicated series. To add insult to injury, the series received good reviews from people Kay thought should have known better, including William Safire; in his *New York Times* column, he noted that it was "no hatchet job; well-researched, sometimes surprisingly revealing, often admiring, sympathetic and evenhanded."[140]

It is not known whether the *Star* sold many more copies in those five days, but what is known is that for a glorious, if brief, time, it seemed as if the *Star* and the *Post* were true rivals. A week after the series ended, the *Post*'s ombudsman, Charles Seib, a former managing editor of the *Star,* wrote that Rosellini took "dead aim at the jugular. . . . If there was any doubt that Time Inc. . . . plans to give the dominant *Post* . . . a run for its money, the series removed it. It served as both a bid for Washington's attention and a declaration of war."[141]

For Kay, who, in Bellows's words, "would be angry if two sentences were written about her," the articles were pure torture.[142] "Anguish, it was anguish," observes Peter Derow.[143] Kay's mood was not boosted by the fact that anyone who knew her, including her friends, knew that Rosellini had gotten her remarkably right. "I thought it described the real Kay," says Richard Clurman.[144]

Rosellini had written that during the interviews Kay was "no-nonsense tough one minute—and unexpectedly vulnerable the next. After the first interview, the powerful woman pleaded: 'Protect me.' After the second, she said: 'Pray for me.' A day later, she telephoned to beg that a reporter not use certain quotes. 'My fate is in your hands,' she said. Pause. 'And when I read it, I'll come after you. But I'll only bring a .22.' "[145]

"Months later we talked," Rosellini recalls, "and she said she didn't go out of the house for days because she was so embarrassed, and what a horrible trauma it had been for her, and how mortifying."[146] "I saw her once in tears after that series appeared," says one *Newsweek* editor. "It was the first time that anybody had really ripped the scab off of those horrible months when she was flat on her back with TB, and Phil had the *tsatske,* as we called [Robin Webb]."[147]

Kay's friends rallied, including Polly Wisner Fritchey. But Polly was in a dreadful bind because Graham Wisner, her son, was about to get married—and the bride-to-be was Lynn Rosellini. Kay, who had been invited to the wedding, had to make the painful decision not to go.

When it appeared that Allbritton had consigned her series to permanent holdover, Rosellini considered resigning in protest. She did not, but when Time Inc. took over the *Star,* and before the decision was made to run her series, she obtained a year's leave of absence and signed a contract with Simon & Schuster to expand her profile into a biography.[148]

But then, again, something strange happened. "Before I got the contract," Rosellini recounts, "I went back to some of my sources and sounded them out about the possibility of a book. People were very encouraging. Armed with that knowledge, I set out on this book [project], but then to my amazement I discovered that when I would call them back to set up appointments, [these sources] would suddenly not be in, or gosh, they 'just left the country.' It was an unnerving experience. Finally people began admitting that they'd called Mrs. Graham, and basically the feeling was that they shouldn't talk. I'm putting it nicely. They were just scared to death."[149]

Kay Graham then wrote to Simon & Schuster chief Richard Snyder asking that the publisher not proceed with the book. But Snyder wasn't impressed. "That just made him mad," says Rosellini. "That made [him] all the more stubborn about going ahead with it."[150]

It was Rosellini who backed down. Taking on Kay Graham seemed bound to end in frustration and failure.

So Kay won, temporarily. She stopped one book. But there was another, which was then wending its way, inexorably, to the marketplace.

Chapter 20

ALL THE PUBLISHER'S PROBLEMS

Twenty-five years had passed since Kay Graham had encouraged her friend Sidney Hyman to write her father's biography. When Hyman was dropped from the project and Merlo Pusey stepped in, that was fine too: Pusey was her employee and the book was authorized; the family had control over the content.

Kay had strictly discouraged other biographies of herself or her family—even when the hopeful writer was someone who knew the Meyer and Graham families well, and was unlikely, by dint of experience and professional standing, to produce a one-dimensional attack. She was even closed to suggestions that she write her memoirs.[1]

Kay knew that a young woman named Deborah Davis had, for three years, been working on an unauthorized biography of her. Davis had written Kay requesting an interview, and Kay tried to discourage her in a friendly way: "I hope you will try to understand. I haven't the time or the inclination while I'm still working to enter into such a project. . . . I'm sorry not to be able to help since you are clearly investing a lot of time."[2]

Then, one Sunday in May 1976, Betty Beale led off her *Washington Star* gossip column with the item that "a book on the most powerful woman in America, Katharine Graham, is at last in the works. Feisty freelance reporter Deborah Davis . . . got 200 interviews here in two weeks with people who know [Graham]. . . . But [she] refused to see Deborah." Beale quoted Davis's agent, Lucianne Goldberg, as calling the writer "a bird-dog reporter [who] doesn't give up" and promising that the book would reveal "a secret romance of Mrs. Graham—a multimillionaire who fits into a father image."[3]

That was just the sort of hype Davis did not need. Graham put the word out to friends, family, and associates not to talk to the young writer.

Kay was enough of a journalist to know that the "200 interviews . . . in two weeks" were probably exaggerated by at least 190. In fact, according to an article by Michael Moore (later of *Roger and Me* fame), Davis admitted, "No one would talk to me. And I mean *no one*."[4] That did not stop Davis, but it changed the book's focus from strict biography to a mix of biography and an exposé of what Davis charged were Ben Bradlee's and Phil Graham's ties to the CIA.

Davis's publisher, Harcourt Brace Jovanovich, was setting the book up as a top nonfiction selection for the fall and positioning it as a best-seller.[5] When *Katharine the Great* arrived in the stores in November 1979, Kay Graham and Ben Bradlee were horrified.

"Ben was madder than I was," Kay recalled later, and he wrote to Davis's editor. According to Kay, Bradlee complained, "I'm mentioned on thirty-four pages and there are thirty-four errors. Like, I was supposed to have known [CIA director Richard] Helms when I was a child; I met him when I was forty. Demonstrable errors."[6]

Bradlee's letter, dated November 20, 1979, and accompanied by a list of thirty-nine inaccuracies, was more than angry—it was threatening. Although he probably had grounds to sue for libel, he wrote, he would not. "What I can do, however, is to brand you as completely irresponsible, to tell author friends to steer clear of you as though you had the plague, to brand Miss Davis as a fool, and to put your company in that special little group of publishers who don't give a shit for the truth."[7]

That Davis's young editor, Gene Stone, did not answer the letter is understandable: "I was quite scared—in fact very scared. I mean, here was *Ben Bradlee,* the hero of American journalism, and I was just this little dork."[8]

Had Bradlee written to William Jovanovich, the fifty-nine-year-old chairman of the publishing house, he would undoubtedly have received a prompt response. Not surprisingly, given their prominence, Kay knew Jovanovich. As she later recalled, "Billy Jovanovich is a friend of mine, and I said [to Ben], 'Why don't you send that letter to Bill, because I don't think he knows.' So Ben did. That's what tore." Jovanovich checked the book, found that Bradlee's charges were true and withdrew the publisher's name from it."[9]

"Billy" Jovanovich did more than that. He ordered the book recalled from stores and shredded—some 20,000 copies two months after the book's official publication date—and issued an edict to his employees: "You are to make sure that these books are not only disposed of but actually destroyed. After the books have been destroyed, give us a notarized statement to that effect."[10]

What followed was correspondence between Jovanovich and Kay dripping oleaginous goodwill.[11] When writers' groups accused Jovanovich of censorship, he claimed that he had lost "confidence in the author" after learning that the book was riddled with errors. And when those same groups charged Kay with censorship, her Pentagon Papers–inspired reputation as the fearless protector of the First Amendment suffered, and she responded to criticism by questioning both Davis's skills as a journalist and her mental health: "I had a woman write a biography of me who's . . . just nuts. I never saw her, never went near her, never had anything to do with her, told other people not to because I heard . . . she'd go in and have hysterics in front of people. . . . Then she published this total pack of—I mean, it was a figment of her imagination."[12]

Continuing in a hyperbolic tirade, Kay came close to accusing Davis of plagiarism: "She went down to the Library [of Congress], and the first eighty pages were straight from a biography of my father that was started but not finished. She used that. I thought it was so straight maybe she plagiarized, but she just mocked it up enough to not . . . Apparently somebody can do anything to you and you can't protect yourself, and if you say it's not true and prove it, then you're trying to censor it."[13]

The publisher reverted the rights to Davis, but by then the book was so discredited that she could not have paid a major house to publish it. If she was certifiable in any way, it was as a pariah. Writer friends, Davis claimed, "were afraid to incur the wrath of the *Post*. No one wanted to lose out on having their op-ed pieces printed, so I became a nonperson."[14] All subsidiary rights—a *New York* magazine excerpt, a Literary Guild featured alternate selection, publication in Britain, and interest from paperback houses—evaporated.[15]

Katharine the Great was out just long enough to receive an extraordinarily negative review: "The book and its tortured thesis are rubbish. . . . One can't help wondering whether the manuscript was even read by the publishers," wrote *Wall Street Journal* reporter David Ignatius, son of former *Post* president Paul Ignatius—which fact was not disclosed in the review. (There is no reason to think that Ignatius's son would be kind to the tool of his father's humiliation.

Still, David Ignatius did go to work for the *Post*—he is currently business editor—six years after the review appeared.)

The plunge from such high hopes to no hope at all for her first book left Davis dangerously depressed. Kay was lucky that when Davis finally roused herself in 1982 to sue her publisher for breach of contract, hours before Davis's lawyer was to depose Harcourt officials, they offered her a $100,000 settlement, which she promptly accepted.*

For Davis, the moral of the story was that, as A. J. Liebling put it, "freedom of the press is guaranteed only to those who own one." Her charge of suppression seemed justified. Kay Graham and especially Ben Bradlee did not want this book published, and they stopped it. As for the "demonstrable errors," what work of popular nonfiction is without them?

Had the allegations of CIA connections not so dominated *Katharine the Great,* Bradlee probably would more or less have ignored it, and Kay would have followed his lead. But these charges, which he called "bullshit and murderous," went to the heart of his career, and he knew he would be judged by the current standard of deep suspicion of the CIA rather than by the cold war standard, under which cooperation with the agency was considered the patriotic duty of all men of goodwill.[16]

Deborah Davis would later lament: "Rather than join the company of other prominent journalists who now freely say they worked with the CIA in the 1950s because times were different . . . Bradlee set about to discredit the book and ruin me as a writer."[17]

Davis claimed that his job as press attaché at the American embassy in Paris—Bradlee had left the *Post* for that job in 1951—was a CIA front. She asserted that he wrote propaganda aimed at persuading Europeans that Julius and Ethel Rosenberg were spies and deserved to be executed.[18]

Bradlee did not like that, certainly, but he liked even less her accusation that the CIA had used Bradlee and *The Washington Post* to bring down Richard Nixon. According to Davis, "Deep Throat" was Richard Ober, a Harvard classmate of Bradlee's who ostensibly

*In 1987, a second edition of *Katharine the Great,* published by National Press, a small house in Bethesda, Maryland, included a preface by Davis describing her battle with Jovanovich, Graham, and Bradlee. As Kay surely hoped, the book disappeared with barely a murmur. An updated, third edition was published in 1991 by Sheridan Square Press in New York.

was working for Henry Kissinger as a senior staff officer but actually was working for the CIA. Davis's scenario had the agency concluding that Nixon was insane, wanting him out of the White House, and thus concocting Watergate and using the *Post* to blow it into an offense so egregious that Nixon would be forced to resign. Bradlee flatly denied ever knowing Ober.[19]

People who would seem in a position to know say that they doubt Bradlee had ties to the CIA. "I have no information that Bradlee ever worked for the CIA," says Pierre Salinger. Arnaud de Borchgrave, who knew Bradlee when he was press attaché in Paris, gives a flat no, as does ex–CIA man Cord Meyer, Bradlee's former brother-in-law. Phil Geyelin readily admits that he himself worked for the CIA, "but Ben didn't."*[20]

Frank Waldrop is less definite, speculating that while Bradlee might have used the CIA to "get himself under way, get a leg up," he would not have let the agency use him more than he wanted to be, which was probably not much. "I don't think Ben's that susceptible."[22]

But Phil Graham's tie to the CIA—so cavalierly dismissed by his widow—is more plausible, given the times in which he operated. Kay was there, during the friendship with Frank Wisner, and that with CIA chief Allen Dulles; newsmen and CIA types mixed effortlessly at those Sunday suppers at her house. Her calling the alleged connection a "fantasy"[23] and dismissing the possibility out of hand is dishonest.

What is a matter of speculation is precisely how Phil Graham used his friends in the CIA or they him. Bob Estabrook says that Phil was in daily touch with people in the intelligence community and that he knew more about the Bay of Pigs, for example, than he would tell his own reporters.[24] "Phil was using [Wisner] as a source," Ben Gilbert believes. "[He] had no trouble finding out where the CIA was on particular issues when [he] needed to. I never thought that the relationship was more than a comfortable relationship between sources and the news gatherers."[25]

Deborah Davis cast a more sinister light by charging that Wisner "owned" reporters in the major media. "Over a period of months, at the Graham salon and other meeting places," she wrote, "Wisner

---

*Geyelin says that his stint with the CIA, which occurred long before he joined the *Post*, lasted all of eleven months. "I wasn't a spy for the CIA. I never got out of the first taxi zone."[21]

[and Phil] discussed which journalists were for sale and at what price." She claimed that Phil recommended target reporters and that Wisner, "knowing Phil's frustration at being unable to afford foreign correspondents for the *Post,* reciprocated by paying for *Post* reporters' trips, which was not the same, Phil believed, as the [CIA's] 'owning them.' " Davis even maintained that the CIA and its operatives helped Phil acquire the *Times-Herald* and WTOP-TV—presumably to make the *Post* safe not only for Donny but also for Wisner's covert operations.[26]

Davis may not have proved that Phil had any formal tie to the CIA, but there is little doubt that he created an atmosphere that allowed his top people to feel comfortable about cooperating. Bernard Nossiter recalled the days when a reporter who interviewed a Soviet diplomat had to file in triplicate, one copy for Al Friendly to forward to the CIA.[27] "I know that Al Friendly had some CIA involvement," says Erwin Knoll. "I know there was a pipeline to the CIA that provided occasional guidance on stories." He remembers what happened during the U-2 incident:* "I found myself riding in the elevator with Bob Estabrook, and I said to him, 'That's a hell of a story out of the Soviet Union today, isn't it?' And he said, 'Oh yeah, we've known about those flights for several years, but we were asked not to say anything.' Now that just astonished me, that the paper knew about things it was asked not to report on, and it complied with those wishes." After an American pilot flying for the resistance to President Sukarno in Indonesia was shot down, the *Post*'s foreign editor warned Knoll to be careful about reporting on the pilot, who, he said, was CIA. Knoll thinks the *Post* "was definitely on the team as far as fighting the cold war was concerned."[28]

Since the Davis debacle, Kay and Bradlee have done what they could to prevent outsiders from writing books about them or about the *Post.* John Hanrahan says that when Bradlee suspected him and Ben Bagdikian—both had written articles that dealt in part with the paper—of working on books about the *Post,* he dispatched his spies to investigate.[29]

*

*In 1960, a U-2 reconnaissance plane piloted by Francis Gary Powers was shot down by the Soviets. The State Department first denied and then admitted that Powers was on a spy mission; the Soviets found Powers guilty of espionage and sentenced him to ten years in prison. He admitted his guilt, explaining that he was "only following orders from the CIA." In 1962, he was traded for a Soviet spy who had been held in the United States.

There was nothing new or exciting anymore about being called the most powerful woman in America, if not the world. It had become one of those lazy, reflexive media judgments, the kind that moves from one clip file to another with no time out for reevaluation.

But when Jimmy Carter was elected president in 1976, Kay undoubtedly wondered whether there was any truth left in the label. With the *Post*'s endorsement of Carter over Gerald Ford—and with conventional wisdom casting Carter as a reaction to Nixon, and *The Washington Post* as far and away the single most important force in alerting the nation that it had reason to react—Kay Graham should have been on Jimmy Carter's A list of guests and confidants.

Howard Bray reported that soon after Carter took office he asked Kay if she wanted to be an ambassador. She said no. She had more influence than any ambassador could dream of having.[30] And with that, Carter, for all intents and purposes, stopped giving much thought to Kay Graham.

Kay resented the inattention. Eugene Patterson recalls "her frustration that [President Carter] didn't seem to understand the need to become part of the town." In 1978, when Patterson was president of the American Society of Newspaper Editors, Kay gave her former managing editor a dinner reception at her R Street home on the eve of ASNE's convention—a meeting that brought to Washington most of the nation's newspaper editors. "She invited all the big-hitters in ASNE to her house, including a big cross-section of the Washington establishment," Patterson remembers. "It was a real R Street special, the whole nine yards." Kay assumed that because Patterson, like Carter, is a native Georgian, the president and his top men would be out in full force. "In the midst of the furor in [Kay's] living room, she turned to me and said, 'Have you noticed that none of the White House people are here to honor one of their fellow Georgians? They just don't understand. They ought to be in here working this room.' That's a very astute Washington assessment of one of Carter's central problems. His people were not in there working that room."[31]

Relations between the president and the publisher were not sweetened when, late in 1979, Sally Quinn profiled Carter's national security advisor, Zbigniew Brzezinski, and implied that he had unzipped his fly in front of a female reporter from *People* magazine. An accompanying photograph seemed to confirm it. The reporter, Clare Crawford-Mason, vehemently denied that such a thing had occurred. Carter's counsel, Lloyd Cutler, demanded a full retraction, which the *Post* ran the next day, along with a tortured apology—

"The poses, shadows and backgrounds of the picture create an accidental double entendre." Bradlee reportedly insisted to his staffers that, whether or not Brzezinski actually exposed himself, he deserved the story.[32]

In December 1980, after Ronald Reagan had defeated Jimmy Carter but before his inauguration, the *Post*'s new gossip columnist, Diana McLellan, reported that the talk of the town was that the Carters had bugged Blair House, the official presidential guest house, in order to eavesdrop on the Reagans. (Thus, McLellan claimed, the Carters knew that Nancy wanted them out of the White House before the inauguration so that she could redecorate.) The bitter and demoralized Carters, in no mood for such shenanigans, demanded an apology and threatened to sue the *Post*. Ben Bradlee told a reporter for *The New York Times* that he would rather go bare-assed down Pennsylvania Avenue in a barrel than apologize to Carter. A grudging retraction was printed and an apology issued.[33]

So disenchanted was Kay with Jimmy Carter that as she thought back to 1976 and the *Post*'s endorsement of him, she belatedly changed her mind. In a casual conversation with Jim Cannon, who after leaving *Newsweek* had gone to work for Nelson Rockefeller and then for Gerald Ford in the White House, she admitted, "I think we made a mistake in supporting Jimmy Carter. . . . We were so unhappy about Nixon, I think that's why we went for Carter, but Ford . . . was a better president." Cannon said, "Katharine, I think that's wonderful. Why don't you write him a letter to that effect?" She responded, "I don't think I can do that, but why don't you tell him that's what I think." Cannon did, and Ford answered: "Well, it's pretty late to do that now."[34]

Even during the Carter years, an invitation to dine at Kay Graham's was still the most coveted in Washington—after an invitation to the White House.

Friends say she worried that if she let Donny take over, the enormous social power she enjoyed would evaporate. Although he had passed the age at which his father, who had had no newspaper experience, had received the paper from Eugene, Katharine had yet to turn it over to Donny, who had plenty. But, says Mark Edmiston, when Donny came to her and said, "Mom, it's time. I'm ready to take over the newspaper,"[35] she reluctantly relinquished the publisher's role.

On January 10, 1979, Kay Graham announced that she was giving up day-to-day management of the newspaper to allow Donny, then executive vice-president and general manager, to take over as publisher. But she retained her eighth-floor office, her role as chairman of the board and chief executive officer, the bulk of the voting stock (Donny has the second biggest chunk), and the real power. She would continue to oversee the business and editorial sides of the *Post, Newsweek,* and the television stations and would work closely with company president Mark Meagher on planning, evaluating possible acquisitions, and charting the company's future. "This will surely be a full-time job," she said.[36]

"Today, as in the rest of my life, my mother has given me everything but an easy act to follow," Donny told a gathering of *Post* employees.[37] Frank Waldrop recalls that privately Kay mused, "Publishers' sons are notorious dopes."[38] Publicly she said that her son had "one unique advantage in taking over the job. . . . He has had time to be trained for it."[39]

Donny's trainer, Mark Meagher, was astonished by his patience. Donny "never pushed, never tried to move his mother out of the way." Meagher, who was feeling the first rumblings of Kay's discontent, believed that Donny deserved his promotion and then some. "A lot of the good things at the *Post* can be attributed to Donny," who is "very focused, very bright, a student of the business." Meagher claims to have recognized early on differences between mother and son: "Donny knows what he wants to do. Katharine didn't know what she wanted to do. [She] was terribly self-conscious of her lack of experience." Meagher adds that Donny is unwaveringly loyal to his employees; Kay is loyal only when she feels like it.[40]

Kay and Donny seemed to get along well, although they maintained an oddly formal posture in business settings. When Donny talked about his mother to other Post Company executives, he always referred to her as "Mrs. Graham." During meetings, when he needed to get her attention, he called her, as did most everyone else, "Kay." "Never 'Mother,'" says Peter Derow, "oh, never." But Derow also describes "mutual warmth and trust" between mother and son; she was "supportive of him, didn't try to diminish him." While Donny would never put his arm around her shoulder as they left a room—"she'd think it was patronizing"—Kay might put her arm around his and say, "Donny, you're becoming a good publisher."[41]

After he became publisher, Donny continued his conspicuously subdued style. Some thought he feared expressing himself strongly because it might signal that the time belonged to him and, by implication, that his mother's time had passed. "Don does not express things forcefully," Nicholas Katzenbach says; but he is "very persuasive" in a quiet, organized way. "I've never seen him involved in a debate with anybody."[42] Mark Meagher describes the new publisher as working "in a shadow. I think he's afraid to go full steam with his own thoughts. I believe he has them. I'm not quite sure what they are."[43]

No one, asserts a former Post Company executive, knows "what Don is about"; he struggles with "the role that his mother has established, Washington society, and the fear that his father was crazy. It's a terrible burden to carry." The executive describes Donny as "very tense, very self-possessed, to the extent that he even looks like something could snap somewhere."[44] In the opinion of some, Donny, more than any of his siblings, exhibits Phil's high-strung quality: "He always looked to me as if he were struggling to keep himself from blowing apart. I've always assumed that he is haunted by the question of whether this disease will seize him the way it seized his father," explains Nicholas von Hoffman.[45] One editor says that Donny "almost deliberately overdoes it" in his efforts to be solid, low-key; "he doesn't want to be like his father. I'm sure when your father kills himself you worry about yourself." Jay Lovinger, former editor of *The Washington Post Magazine,* observes that Donny "turns everything in on himself. We used to joke that if somebody came up to him and said, 'You fucking, cocksucking idiot,' he would say, 'Well, that's a very interesting point you make, but have you ever considered this way of looking at it?' "[46]

Donny's eyes are frequently mentioned as a window into a psyche somehow out of kilter: "those unsmiling eyes," von Hoffman describes them, "which I find so incongruous when he smiles—smiling features and dead eyes."[47] Milton Viorst, who lives next door to Donny, says he always looks "a little spacy," as if "there's nobody home behind the eyes."[48]

Von Hoffman credits Donny's wife, Mary, with being "the keel that kept that boat reasonably afloat."[49] The family lives in an unassuming, comfortable-looking Victorian frame house in Cleveland Park, close to a Metro stop; Donny travels to work each day by subway. (Before the subway was built, he took the bus.) So while his mother is chauffeured to work, Donny, in a suit fit for a mid-level civil servant, joins the straphangers. His wife explains that he rides the subway because by doing so he "finds out a few things about who's buying papers and what's going on."[50]

That this seemingly commendable habit irritates some people shows how difficult Donny's position is. Joe Laitin, who would run into him on the Metro, finds it "a little pretentious" because Donny, "with all his money and position, could come to work in a chauffeured car the way his mama does." He likens the habit to Donny's "trips through the newsroom: [he's] trying to show he's one of the boys, but he ain't one of the boys. When you can afford to live better and you deliberately don't, I have mixed feelings about that. It's the opposite of conspicuous consumption."[51]

Donny is, after all, a very rich man who grew up in a home with servants and a mother who cooked only on Sundays—the cook's day off. Perhaps it was the inescapable knowledge of that wealth that gave him a detached quality. Mark Edmiston sees Donny as typical of those with inherited wealth, always asking, "Why [are these people] being nice to me? They obviously want something. Not because of me."[52]

His sister, Lally, has similar insecurities, but she expresses them very differently.

During her marriage, Lally Weymouth was a rather traditional drawing room liberal. A writer for *Vogue* magazine described Lally and Yann in 1970, the year before their divorce, as belonging to "the new young breed that thinks the way to tackle ghetto problems is to wade in and help."[53] By the late 1970s, Lally had turned radically left, falling under the tutelage of her then boyfriend, Marxist writer Alexander Cockburn. At the time of Donny's investiture as publisher, Lally was in what Edward Kosner calls "her Palestinian phase, very left-wing days. Her politics certainly made it impossible for her to be given responsibility for the paper."[54] As a radical she cut a wide swath and left much laughter in her wake. "It was enough to make you shudder," says Nicholas von Hoffman. "She was so ignorant, and so foolish that you could not take her seriously. When she would say something you agreed with, you were embarrassed by the reasons she gave for saying it—enough to reconsider your own position."[55]

Lally became irresistible to writers covering the Manhattan party scene. "On one typical night," wrote *Spy*'s Henry Alford, "sitting in a stretch limousine outside a Broadway theater, Weymouth became enraged at her chauffeur for not moving hastily enough and screamed for *someone* to make this *idiot* fucking *drive.* Finally, her boyfriend the socialist firebrand was obliged to get out of the back-seat, . . . go the driver's window and ask the servant nicely if he would drive, please. When gossip hound and conscience-of-the-left Liz Smith saw a picture in *Women's Wear Daily* of the two lovebirds together at a party, she felt it necessary to scribble off a note to Cockburn: 'Your father [once Washington correspondent for the London *Times* and contributor to *The Daily Worker*] would turn over in his grave to see you in black tie going to a party at the Bill Paleys'.' "[56]

Next Lally was linked romantically with Edward Said, a professor of English and comparative literature at Columbia University, a Palestinian activist, and a member of the Palestine National Council. She had no hesitation about denouncing the family newspaper as a vehicle for Zionist propaganda.[57]

Speculation persisted over whether Lally's left-wing politics preceded or followed her choice of lovers—of which there were many. One former *Newsweek* editor recalls that Kay was worried about Lally's two young daughters, "because Lally had been in and out of every bed in New York and Washington."[58] Andy Warhol once noted in his diary that a friend had gone to a party at Lally's, "which was for lots of heavies, and I was complaining that I wasn't invited and [the friend] said, '*You* didn't sleep with her.' "[59]

Those who describe Lally as volatile often follow with the observation that she is very much like Phil: "mercurial, attractive, fascinating, brilliant" are adjectives that Roswell Gilpatric selects for both father and daughter.[60] Nicholas Katzenbach sees in Lally "her father's brilliance and energy."[61] "Lally adored her father," remarks Polly Kraft. "I think they have quite a few of the same mannerisms." When asked if Lally reminds her of Kay, Kraft responds, "No, not at all. Lally is much more like her father, much more hyperactive and nervous."[62]

But some of Phil's more ardent admirers argue that stressing the similarities between Lally and Phil does a grave disservice to Phil. A close family friend describes Lally as "a certifiable hysterical person" and contends that Phil was not at all that.[63] "When I see Lally, I don't see Phil," insists Arnaud de Borchgrave. "She's riddled with complexes and her mother's riddled with complexes. Phil didn't have any complexes at all. Kay's very uptight and Lally's very uptight."[64]

In fact, it is Lally and her mother, some say, who share an indelible family resemblance—beyond the obvious physical similarity. A former *Newsweek* executive describes Lally as "a whirling dervish . . . the arms, the legs, the mouth. It was Kay writ large, it was Kay out of control to be with Lally."[65] Kermit Lansner says, "Lally has a good deal of her mother's disagreeableness in her."[66]

Unlike their sister, William and Stephen Graham have kept low profiles, are not controversial, and do not seem to mind being out of the line of succession. Billy, it is said, did not want to play a role in the family company but wanted to establish himself in his own profession and on his own turf. Trained as a lawyer and formerly associated with Edward Bennett Williams's firm, he lives in Los Angeles and runs an investment partnership that includes some family money. He is, says Peter Derow, the most easygoing of the children. "He's terrific, a guy you want to put your feet up on the sofa and just relax with"[67]—different, in other words, from Donny.

Billy is twice divorced, mostly recently from Caroline Graham, West Coast editor of *Vanity Fair*. His first wife was artist and poet Jorie Pepper, daughter of Beverly Pepper and Bill Pepper, formerly *Newsweek*'s Rome bureau chief. The Peppers were close to Phil; they squired him and Robin around Rome during Phil's last fling through Europe.[68] The marriage of the Peppers' daughter to her son was not easy for Kay, who associated Bill and Beverly with Phil's crash and who did not like Beverly. She "exuded confidence," says Mel Elfin, "just blew out every other woman in the room."[69]

While Derow and others insist that Billy did not resent not being in the company, and in fact defied his mother's hopes that he would help run it, one editor raises the possibility that "Billy and Lally [might somehow form] a legal alliance and upset the present arrangements," under which, as he puts it, "Donny inherits the earth." (Control of the company would fall to him alone should Kay die suddenly.) A person who knows them well recalls hearing that, as adolescents, Lally and Billy "ganged up on Donald because he was so square." Were they to ally themselves again, it would be "a repeat of what they did as adolescents."[70]

Stephen Graham, who, friends say, inherited Phil's wit, is a theatrical producer in New York—one of the original investors in *Annie*. He has recently been reported to have grown "frustrated over his lack of financial success" and, having earned a master's degree in creative writing, has started course work toward a Ph.D. in comparative literature.[71] He had the roughest going as an adolescent. "Stevie was a real problem for Katharine," says Mark Meagher. He took part in a "big drug-and-booze scene. I can remember a couple of times Donny dashing to New York to provide some care."[72] One former editor calls Stephen "a creature of the sixties."[73] A close family friend claims that Stephen "had a lot of trouble, not with Phil's disease but with drugs." He adds that Stephen is clean now, that his drug use is history.[74]

Like Lally, Stephen makes a few sad appearances in Andy War-hol's diaries, as a "nutty" kid hanging out at Studio 54 with *Rolling Stone* publisher Jann Wenner and his wife, Jane, and, with her, taking Quaaludes.[75] Today, Stephen owns a piece of *Spy,* the magazine that takes such pleasure in ridiculing his sister. He recently married illustrator Cathy Barancik, daughter of a Chicago architect.

"Do you know the word *naches*?" asks June Bingham. "I don't think Kay has had *naches* from her children. From Donny and [his wife] Mary, yes . . . otherwise not much."[76] Mel Elfin recalls a *Newsweek* luncheon at the 1976 Republican National Convention in Kansas City: "The Ford children [were there], one girl and three boys, who were so protective of their father, and so warm and effusive. After it was over, Kay, who has one girl and three boys, said, 'Aren't they wonderful, aren't they wonderful?'"[77]

Lester Bernstein had known Kay Graham since 1963, the year he joined *Newsweek* and she took over the company. He knew how achingly insecure she was, and he was determined not to repeat the mistakes of his predecessors. Attention must be paid, he reminded himself, and so he thought of her, for example, when Barbara Walters invited him to a small dinner for Fidel Castro, then in New York for a meeting of the United Nations General Assembly. Walters had invited various media editors, but not Kay Graham. Ben Bradlee was on the guest list, but he was taking Sally Quinn. So Bernstein asked Kay to come as his guest. She said yes, and was, Bernstein recalls, "enormously grateful."

From the start, Bernstein "tried to keep her informed whenever there was anything that she might be embarrassed [about] by not knowing. I tried to keep her in mind at all times."[78] He seemed off to a good start when, in 1980, he fired Arnaud de Borchgrave. Kay had wanted to get rid of him in 1963 but was stymied by her own inexperience and lack of confidence, and by Oz Elliott's refusal to do the deed. For some reason—behavior that seems out of character, given Kay's lack of hesitancy about firing men—she had just let de Borchgrave be, exiling him to Europe, and, in his words, he "traveled around the world for the next seventeen years until they finally got around to firing me."[79]

Bernstein summoned him to New York and, with no niceties, as de Borchgrave recalls, told him, " 'You are fired.' Just like that, after thirty years. And I said, 'On what grounds, if I may be so bold as to inquire?' And he said, 'On the grounds of disloyalty.' " De Borchgrave had complained to Peter Derow that *Newsweek* editors had killed his story that was critical of the Soviet invasion of Afghanistan.[80] "I felt that he had been insubordinate, and I had other reasons as well," explains Bernstein. "I didn't like his whole performance. I thought he was a correspondent with an ax to grind, and I couldn't believe what he was saying."[81]

Still, de Borchgrave maintains that Bernstein no more made the decision to fire him than Peter Derow made the decision to fire Edward Kosner. "Kay wanted me fired," he says, "because she had to focus her hostility on someone over what had happened [between Phil and Robin]."[82]

Larry Collins, a good friend of de Borchgrave's, and the man who, in fact, albeit innocently, brought Robin and Phil together, says de Borchgrave was done in by his colleagues, not by Katharine Graham. Arnaud was "very arrogant, and he can be arrogant particularly to his lessers"—who, of course, eventually became his "betters." According to Collins, "There were a couple of guys at the top of the masthead, now Arnaud's bosses, on whose sensibilities he had trodden when they were young, and they just never forgot it. When they had the chance to put a knife between his shoulder blades, they did." Collins also points out that not only did Arnaud lead a glamorous life abroad, where he preferred to live anyway, but his career "soared" when Kay was running the magazine.[83] As *Newsweek*'s senior interviewer, he always got a byline and he became a celebrity.

Lester Bernstein insists that Kay "leaned over backward for Arnaud, in an effort to avoid appearing vindictive." He remembers that when he informed Kay of his intention to fire de Borchgrave, "she started to make noises, as if she wanted to discuss [whether we should] really do it. I said, 'Kay I'm not consulting you about this, I'm informing you that it's done.' "[84]

Kay thought that Bernstein's firing of de Borchgrave took enormous courage, and as much as admitted that she would not have done it. Why not? Probably because she feared that once no longer in her employ, de Borchgrave, of all people, would not pause a moment before disgorging every unsavory, humiliating detail of Phil's relations with his wife and his girlfriend.

She was right. De Borchgrave has done that precisely. But she has found a way to pay him back. To his colossal annoyance, she treats him as if he were beneath her notice, so insignificant that she has no interest in his history, especially where it intersects with Phil and Robin's. One day in the early 1970s, when they were together in Kay's office, de Borchgrave said, " 'I think we should clear the air.' 'About what?' she said. 'About [your thinking] that I was responsible for Robin Webb.' 'What on earth are you talking about?' 'That was the reason you wanted me fired, I assume—because you thought I had something to do with the whole Robin Webb episode.' 'I can't understand what you're talking about.' 'Well, you did ask Oz to fire me.' 'Of course not. What on earth gave you that idea?' "[85] In a recent profile of Kay, Meryl Gordon reported that she was "furious" when she found herself seated next to de Borchgrave at a dinner given by Joint Chiefs of Staff chairman Colin Powell. "Somebody didn't do their homework," she complained to Ben Bradlee the next day. De Borchgrave took advantage of his proximity to try again to engage Kay in a conversation about Robin Webb. According to Gordon, Kay tried repeatedly to change the subject, finally saying, "in her most steely tone, 'Arnaud, I don't know what you're talking about.' "[86]

Chapter 21

KAY GRAHAM
GETS "FIRED"

In 1979, Mark Meagher had the second biggest regret of his career at the Washington Post Company. (His first was not buying Simon & Schuster.) Joel Chaseman, who took over running the Post Company's broadcasting operation from Larry Israel, wanted to beat Ted Turner on the air with an all-news cable network. Meagher and Chaseman had lined up Warner Communications to do the marketing and distribution and to provide a start-up audience of some three million. "Joel and I could have done it, but I couldn't get the board's support. [Warren] Buffett was opposed to it, and if Buffett's opposed to it, that's it. You get your final hearing, but it's obvious that Katharine isn't hearing."[1]

Katharine increasingly relied on Buffett and rebuffed the man whom she, after all, had chosen as her president. By early 1980, Meagher, who had watched Larry Israel fall from grace, knew he was headed in the same direction. If Edward Kosner did not look like the man she wanted to head her magazine, then Meagher certainly did not look like the man she wanted to head her entire company. "Kay's a snob," says Kermit Lansner, "and she was uneasy with Mark." He is, in Lansner's words, "originally an accountant."[2] There was no St. Albans or Phillips Exeter or Harvard College or even Harvard Business School on his résumé. She saw Meagher, explains one former Post Company executive, as a clerk. Take his ideas seriously? She could not see past his clothes, which ran to brown shirts and white ties. "It would kill her," the same executive recalls. "She hated it when she had to introduce this guy as president of the Washington

Post Company. It offended her. Once that bell goes off, don't bring me the greatest idea in the world, because I can't stand looking at the shirts."[3]

More than ten years later, Meagher still insists that he quit.* "I just can't get over it. That was all I wanted all my life. I loved the challenge, the intrigue. I loved being the CEO and thought I was a terrific one." His bitterness seems unrelieved by the passage of a decade. "I never felt pushed out by Don," he says. "I felt discarded by Katharine."[5]

During Meagher's first full year on the job, 1978, the company had its best year ever, boasting a twenty-eight-percent return on equity—tenth in that category among Fortune 500 companies.[6] On the other hand, at the time of his dismissal, the company's profits were dragging: earnings would drop from $80 million in 1979 to less than $66 million in 1980. Still, Meagher saw himself as a wronged man, and he spouts a litany of complaints longer and more detailed than that of the other presidents Kay fired. He recalls that Buffett would "ascribe some things to Katharine that I never could see. He used to think that she had tremendous integrity, and I used to gag at the word 'integrity' because I thought she certainly lacked integrity—in the sense of being able to empathize with people, understand other people, think of them as [individuals] whose feelings should be considered, even if they weren't at the level that she was. Katharine scorns people."

Meagher is just getting wound up: "To work for Katharine is to eat a ton of shit, a lot, a lot, a lot, because the myth is so unreal. She's not a decisive woman, she's not a woman of steel. She's so flexible that the shape doesn't take any substance until a lot of forces put it together. There's no way to go, to make a decision, yes or no. Do you know what that puts executives through? It just tears them apart." He also complains bitterly about Kay's tendency to listen to the last

*"People say I was fired, and I was not. I could have stayed for the other two years [of a five-year contract]. I was asked to finish out the contract." Not so, says Mark Edmiston: "Kay announced early in the year that that was it, he was gone. He was fired but not told to leave. You had these very unusual [scenes] where you were sitting in a budget meeting with a guy who had been fired. You knew he was not going to be around." Meagher's contract specified that at the end of three years either party could effect an exit. If Kay wanted out, she had to pay him off. If Meagher wanted out, he walked away with nothing. He describes the million-dollar-plus payout on the two years remaining on his contract as a sort of consolation prize from Kay. Meagher claims that she told him, "Look, there's no reason for you to go out of here on your own when so many people have been fired and gotten huge payoffs."[4]

person she talks to. "You can go and have discussions about things, then an [Edward Bennett] Williams or a Warren Buffett says something and it's all upside down again."*[7]

Another executive who fell into Kay's disfavor describes himself as worn down by her penchant for listening to whoever her latest smart man happened to be. He recalls her telling him that John Kenneth Galbraith had deemed *Newsweek* irrelevant. "Jesus Christ," he says, "it may not be relevant to a near Nobel Prize–winning economist, but it is relevant to twelve million Americans." This same executive found it especially exhausting to try to explain the logic of his position to Kay when she lacked shared experience. She would then talk to someone else, and "generally not understand or communicate the full position. You were defending your position from someone who heard only part of it."[9]

The men who worked for her—and granted that many of them were Kay Graham castoffs—have little respect for her abilities as a businesswoman. "*Business Week* once voted her one of the seven best managers of the year," says Kermit Lansner. "Everybody roared with laughter, but it sort of gives you an insight into American business."[10] A former *Newsweek* executive recalls that when *Fortune* ran a piece naming her one of the five outstanding female executives in the country: "We [fell] down laughing."[11] Because she did not come up through the ranks, Nicholas Katzenbach explains, she needed someone to take care of the financial end of things and "the nuts and bolts. Usually the chairman is somebody who has done all those things. That's not true of Kay."[12]

Some blame Kay's natural pessimism for her deficiencies as a business leader. "She doesn't know how to rejoice," says a former Post Company executive, "doesn't know how to look at the good [news]."[13] The corollary is her inclination to see the worst in people. Mark Edmiston calls her a "consensus builder," but not in the positive sense. "She'll come up to you and say, 'I think that person's an idiot, what do you think?' Given her position in Washington, most people would say, 'I don't think that person's very good, Kay.' After a while she says, 'Everybody thinks that person's not very good,' and so [the person has] to go."[14]

---

*Recognizing that Kay could turn "180 degrees on people," Lester Bernstein asked Ben Bradlee—as John Prescott had before him—"What do you do about the problem that Kay always listens to the last person she spoke to?" "Be the last person she spoke to," Bradlee replied.[8]

Mark Meagher says, "I never felt she brought anything to the party. And there's an enormous amount of catering that has to go on to create an atmosphere in which the leader is the hero. That's why I say that Katharine Graham is a myth. I saw too much of it."[15]

Others can be equally unforgiving, yet gentler in their conclusions. Peter Derow asserts that Kay is not "a typical CEO. If she had to work her way through any hierarchy and become a CEO, [she] would never have made it." But that, he adds, is a plus and a minus. She brings to the job "a kind of nonbureaucratic inspiration."[16] Similarly, Mark Edmiston describes Kay as "intuitive." He has seen her "operate in a couple of situations where her judgments, even though not particularly well informed—she hasn't read the documents— have been quite good."[17] Larry Kramer agrees that Kay performed best when she followed her instincts. "When she was put in the position of having to make the decision and make it fast, she made it best." She followed her instincts on the Pentagon Papers and Watergate, and "those were the two greatest decisions in the company's history, probably."[18]

Meagher misses something extremely important that Kay brought to the table. She never lost sight of the fact that she headed a company with a newspaper as its heart and reporters as its lifeblood; that she was selling information, not widgets. She never lost her reverence for journalists, and in a way, she shared the typical editorial disdain for the "bean counters" who run newspapers. Edmiston recalls that during a meeting of *Post* and *Newsweek* journalists with officials from a foreign government, she rebuked him for asking a question. "She pointed out to me that after all I'm not a journalist and I should shut up. She really thinks there's something magic that happens to you when you have a press card." And because she had this feel for print journalism, she allowed her eye to stray from the bottom line, which to her was "important but not critical."[19]

She also brought to the table what Lester Bernstein calls her "fierce determination to succeed." It is particularly impressive, he argues, because she lacks the talents that would make her shine in this role. "I don't think she's a very good CEO. She certainly doesn't pretend to be an editor."[20]

Derow looks beyond Kay's deficiencies to her extraordinary determination. "If my father had been Phil Graham, could my mother have stepped in and done what Kay did? That answer is no. She didn't ask for the job. She's done really well. Perfect? No, not perfect,

[but] better than most who would have been put into it the way she was."[21]

Having said all that, however, Peter Derow could not work for Kay Graham. He left the Post Company in June 1981 and returned to CBS to run that company's magazine division and build the publishing group he knew was beyond his reach at the *Post*.

It is often said—although he denies it—that Derow, when chairman and president of *Newsweek*, fired Kay Graham. "He gave her the kind of speech the boss would give someone whom he was firing," says Lester Bernstein, "the speech about her inadequacies and what was wrong with working for her."[22] "He told her off," says Mark Edmiston. "He told her what a terrible manager she was, and really laid all of his frustrations out on her . . . possibly unfairly."[23]

"I'm not that kind of person," Derow insists. "I don't burn bridges. What's the point?"[24]

The fact remains, however, that Kay Graham wanted the ambitious, handsome, Harvard-educated Derow to replace Mark Meagher. She offered him that opportunity and he flat-out refused.

Kay was crushed. For her it was the type of rejection she had not suffered since the heydays of Phil and Agnes. "She was hurt," Derow recalls. "She said to me, 'This is because I'm not Tom Wyman. I didn't work my way through Polaroid, [Green] Giant, and Pillsbury. You want to grow. You want to work for someone like that. You don't want to work for me.' "

Derow maintains, "I didn't say, 'You don't know your ass from third base, and I'm getting out of here.' I really loved the woman. We were pals. I would help her out of binds that she would find her way into." His leaving and rejecting the job as president of the Washington Post Company—"any ambitious able-bodied American would take it," Derow says—brought others to conclude about him: "You found her unacceptable. You're the guy who fired Kay Graham."[25]

Edmiston says that Kay offered Derow "the world to try to keep him."[26] She even offered to let him run the Post Company from New York, where his family was settled and wanted to remain. But Derow would not be swayed. "We had some basic disagreements about the way the company was run."[27]

The biggest was whether the company, through acquisitions, would become a major media player, as was Derow's desire, or whether, as he puts it, "it wanted to remain a metropolitan, essentially monopoly newspaper with a focus on Washington, and an excitement about Washington but not about becoming a serious media company." Derow got impatient as he watched others grow into what he envisioned for the Post Company: Capital Cities and "what it has done with ESPN and ABC," he offers as an example; or the Times Mirror Company, which, he says, has turned from a family-dominated company to the serious media company that owns *Newsday,* among other papers; or the New York Times Company, which has "migrated effectively from a single product to a multi-product company to a multidimensional organization"; or Gannett, which launched *USA Today* and has been buying every paper in sight. Although the Post Company had successfully entered the cable business, it waited until 1984, lagging behind other companies, Time Inc., for example, which plunged into the cable market in the 1970s. The Post Company could have done all this, Derow contends. "I wanted to see it grow. And [the company's] notion was, Don't push the envelope. I think [the notion] was Kay's, and frankly I think it was also Don's."[28]

Phil Graham, on his tremendous acquisitive kick, was the kind of chief executive who might have appealed to Derow, and no one knew that better than Kay. Phil had embraced the concept of synergy long before it became fashionable.

Derow took his frustrations to Dick Paget, the board member who had known Kay the businesswoman as long as anyone. Paget tried to persuade Kay of Derow's vision that the Post Company could be "one of the great companies in the world" and that "organizations either grow or die." Derow claims that instead of listening Kay would "denigrate" Paget.

At the end of the day, Derow says, he would ask himself: "Was I put on this earth to do this job?"[29]

Having decided that he wasn't, he focused on helping Kay find his successor; it was time that the Post Company retain a professional search firm and that Kay force herself to define the president's job. That was difficult for her, and, says Mark Edmiston, "She never really got around to the job description."[30] But she did agree to the headhunter, so long as Derow did the initial interviewing. "I found myself in the curious position of interviewing my potential boss because I'd always been helpful," he recalls. "I'd ask questions that she'd have a hard time answering: What about the budgeting process? What about the strategic-planning process?"[31]

Those who passed muster with Derow and the headhunter were granted an audience with Kay. The next step, at Kay's request, was a meeting with Robert McNamara or George Gillespie or Richard Paget. "She didn't trust her capacity to make a decision," one executive explains.[32]

Kay's off-with-his-head reputation was not the only reason why finding the right successor to Mark Meagher was difficult. Most candidates knew, the executive claims, that she was a boss bound to generate endless frustration.[33]

Kay Graham is said to hate Peter Derow so much for humiliating her that the mere mention of his name sends her into a rage. Mark Edmiston explains that Kay was genuinely fond of Derow and felt "betrayed" by him. "It's much too much to say that she treated him like a son, but there was something about that. Peter is only a few years older than Don, and he had worked in the company since the middle 1960s."[34]

When Derow left, not only was Kay saddled with finding a new president of the company, she also had to find a new chairman and president of *Newsweek*. Edmiston, who had then been at the magazine for eight years, first as international circulation director, then running the international and later the U.S. edition, got the nod. He explains that when "Peter left, I was the only candidate for the job. She had to appoint me, but didn't really know me that well."[35]

Derow never interviewed the man who became president of the Post Company in September 1981. Richard Simmons came there having lost the race to move up from president to chairman of Dun & Bradstreet. Morton Mintz claimed in *Fruits of Your Labor* that Simmons was paid "more than a quarter of a million dollars just for agreeing to come," as part of a $1.2 million compensation/benefit package. (Mintz compared that with the settlement for Mark Meagher, who, Mintz said, received $1.8 million—which includes more than a half-million paid up front for surrendering his stock options—"for going away.")[36]

Simmons's knowledge of the media world was so scant that when he took the job he was unaware that the Post Company owned *Newsweek*.[37] He was a portfolio manager; a man whose goal was to push up the stock price by making his managers boost their margins and cut their costs,[38] a man who could have sold toothpaste as easily as newspapers. Simmons was not impressed with the bottom-line performance of the company and vowed to turn things around.

"Consistency in earnings growth was not something the Post Company was known for in the early 1980s," he said dryly.[39]

The ink had barely dried on Simmons's employment contract when he decreed death for the Trenton *Times* and also for *Inside Sports,* the company's struggling monthly which had debuted in April 1980.

The Trenton *Times* had last turned a profit in 1978. By 1980, when Larry Kramer, a former *Post* reporter who became the *Times'* executive editor, arrived, Kay was very nervous—so much so that in meetings she called the paper her Vietnam. It was losing advertising, losing market share, and, says Kramer, "losing money in a big way."

But under Kramer things seemed to improve. Barely thirty years old and, since college, never editor of anything, Kramer had been born and brought up in Hackensack and was thus supposedly free of the Washington stigma. He started as metropolitan editor and was quickly promoted to managing and then executive editor. The "ruthless" publisher whom Meagher had installed left to work for Hearst. The new publisher was Ed Padilla, a regular guy who had come up through the ranks of the news business; he had once been a pressman for *The Miami Herald.* He and Kramer converted the paper to morning publication. "Things were really starting to turn around," says Kramer.

But Simmons had made the Trenton *Times* balance sheets his first order of business, and he was not so pleased. Kramer and Padilla were summoned to New York in the fall of 1981. Awaiting them at the *Newsweek* building were Simmons, Kay, and general counsel Alan Finberg. "I was the only person at the table who believed we should keep it," said Kramer. He argued that the *Times* was a wonderful training camp for the *Post,* perpetuating the "minor league" notion, and that the market was going to revive.

He remembers Kay as "very pleasant, very interested in hearing what I had to say. She didn't speak up that much." The next day Simmons called Kramer back to New York for a one-on-one. Kramer thought he "didn't have a snowball's chance in hell"—and he was right.

The Post Company sold the paper for less than it had bought it for. The buyers included Joe Allbritton; this harsh reality did not give much pleasure to Kay—or to Kramer, who says he knew "they would savage the staff and do terrible things to the paper, which they did." (Allbritton later sold to Newhouse.) As Kramer had predicted, the Trenton economy did improve, "from a struggling market to a high-end market, and the Trenton *Times* is doing very well now."[40]

Kramer returned to the *Post* to work on what Kay called "new ventures," including what then seemed to constitute the Post Company's idea of expansion—a national weekly edition of the paper, which, for someone like Derow, would have ranked on the excitement scale somewhere around an employee newsletter. The idea had been around since Eugene Meyer's time[41] and came to the fore again as the company renewed its decision not to follow *The New York Times* on a quest for national circulation.

Simmons next turned his attention to *Inside Sports*. Its editor, John Walsh, formerly of *Rolling Stone* and "Style," says that at the start Kay had been quite enthusiastic, "greatly supportive." She relished the idea of taking on Time Inc. in the sports magazine realm, breaking the dominance of *Sports Illustrated*.

Walsh and others argued desperately that with more time the magazine would prosper. He claims the company had committed to a five-year plan, and "all the ad salespeople from *Sports Illustrated* said, 'Holy God, we were really afraid of you guys, you were about to turn the corner.' " (Jay Lovinger, then an editor at the magazine, argues that *Inside Sports* would have broken even the next year—"it already had lost most of the money it was going to lose"—and that, given the current popularity of sports television, radio, and books, "it doesn't take a genius to know it would be doing pretty well now.")[42]

Peter Derow, with his vision of a bustling synergistic magazine empire, had been *Inside Sports'* biggest backer.[43] He alone might have had the clout to buy more time. When he left the Post Company, the magazine was doomed. He blames the economy—"interest rates hit an all-time high"—and Kay: "Kay would be asked about it by reporters, and [would] say, 'Great editor, John Walsh is terrific, but we're losing millions.' And then the word would be out; 'Kay Graham says we're losing millions.' Not, 'We expect losses for the first four [or] five years. *Sports Illustrated* took x number of years. We anticipated it. I have total confidence that this is going to succeed.' This is, again, a chief executive talking about an investment. You also recognize that the echoes [of what you say] are going to go through many, many communities—the editorial community, the advertising community, the salespeople."[44]

Simmons had the numbers and did not want to hear about potential. *Inside Sports* had lost $12 million during its start-up period, four times what it was forecast to lose in the first year.[45] Kay Graham would attribute the decline in the company's first-quarter earnings to the drain of *Inside Sports,* then just a year old.

Simmons summoned Walsh and the magazine's publisher, Dan Capell, to a meeting in Kay's office in the *Newsweek* building. She and Donny were there, but this was obviously the new president's meeting. "About two minutes into the conversation," Walsh recalls, "Simmons said, 'I have a certain reputation on Wall Street for being ruthless, and I rather enjoy it. You boys have some big problems. You have to do something radical, because if this continues to go the way it's going—' and then he [moved] his hand as if he [were] chopping off his own head or slitting his own throat, he just gave the signal that he was going to terminate it."

During the meeting, held the day before Walsh's wedding, Kay was "very quiet. She didn't say anything. She just watched [Simmons]. And they all came up and shook hands with me, [for] my wedding. I have ever since questioned the diplomacy and timing of the meeting. For Kay was otherwise impeccable in matters of etiquette."

There was one more meeting—"just a final plea in October," the month the Trenton *Times* was sold. "We were called in and told that that was it," Walsh remembers. Simmons, "true to his reputation, was ruthless. He was going to dry up all the red ink, and Kay would say, 'Now, run it by me one more time why you think this should go on,' and then I would give her my rationale, and then she would listen. But it was clear that she had ceded the power to Simmons. She tried, [yet] I don't think she understood [what] the investment's gestation period would be."

Walsh expected nothing more from Simmons or, for that matter, from Kay, but he did expect more from Donny, a sports lover who had taken a special interest in *Inside Sports.* "He had told me earlier in Washington, 'Now, if there's any problem with anything, you be sure to call me.' [When] I called him and said, 'There are some problems,' he just turned a cold shoulder to it, as if he hadn't had the previous conversation with me. He said, 'Oh God, we'll just have to get through it.' I sensed the corporate pressure on Donny. I don't think that personally he would have endorsed the chain of events."[46] *Inside Sports* had cost the Grahams more than $20 million.*[47]

Not surprisingly, Walsh calls Simmons's decision to pull the plug

---

*They sold the magazine to a group in Seattle, who, Walsh says, "were in way over their heads." The magazine ultimately folded in November 1982.

a dark day for the *Post*. "He ensured that the Post [Company] would be well-heeled and that the stock would go up, and it has gone up. The company has lost the zeal for real media entrepreneurship, [and its] editorial-entrepreneurial sense. The company once had a vigorous reputation for being entrepreneurial, from Watergate coverage to Osborne Elliott's years at *Newsweek*. That's what [is] lost."[48]

Hedley Donovan admits that Time Inc. executives enjoyed watching Kay and company squirm as their sports magazine failed. But that same year Time Inc. faced its own failure: the *Washington Star* published its last edition on August 7, 1981, and with it went 129 years of continuous publication, $85 million of Time Inc.'s money, and Donovan's dreams of building the paper into a true competitor to the *Post*.*

Despite its many pious pronouncements about the importance of competing newspapers in a democracy, the *Post* battered the *Star* into surrender. Donovan readily admitted to having made a mistake that no serious player in a two-newspaper market should ever make: "The *Post* increased its advertising rates by seventy percent, and we naively thought, 'Oh, here's a little break for us. We'll hold our rates where they are and pick up some of the *Post* advertising.' Well, it was exactly the opposite. Advertisers figured they couldn't afford not to be in the *Post,* so they cut down on their advertising in the *Star*." Mark Meagher says that the *Post*'s exploitation of this seeming inconsistency ensured the *Star*'s death.[50] Donovan was angry enough to consider going to the Justice Department and alleging "predatory pricing, a deliberate effort to drive us out of business."† He soon thought better of it, but he did go to the Justice Department to make a last-gasp plea to save the *Star* by means of a Joint Operating Agreement with the *Post*. The Newspaper Preservation Act of 1970 allowed two competing papers to save money by combining their production, circulation, and advertising departments while maintaining separate editorial staffs—if the failing paper could make its

---

*Time Inc. had savored precious few victories in Washington in the three years that it owned the sinking *Star*. The most magnificent came in May 1979, when Time bought twenty percent of Universal Press Syndicate, distributor of Garry Trudeau's *Doonesbury,* pulled the strip from the *Post,* handed it to the *Star,* and publicized the hell out of the move.[49]

†Sidney Epstein, then executive editor of the *Star,* charges that *Post* advertising salesmen were "threatening department stores: 'The *Star* is going out of business, and if you take any business away from us, wait until we're the only paper in town.' "[51]

case that it would go under unless it drastically reduced its costs. By 1981, the law had saved papers in a number of cities.[52]

In his book on the death of afternoon dailies, Peter Benjaminson wrote that Time Inc. executives were so encouraged by the concern that Kay and Donny and Ben Bradlee had regularly expressed at the prospect of Washington's becoming a one-newspaper city that they had come to believe that a JOA would be accepted. He quoted from a *Post* editorial published when Joe Allbritton was negotiating to buy the *Star*: "We believe in a freely competitive press. And that's precisely why we also believe the nation's capital needs at least two competing newspapers."[53]

According to Donovan, the Justice Department "would not have objected to our making such an agreement." The *Star* offered to stop its Saturday and Sunday editions and to commit to afternoon publication, thus leaving the *Post* free of weekend and morning competition. But Kay, conferring with Donny and Warren Buffett, rejected those terms. She would go along only if Time Inc. would guarantee the *Post* a profit margin consistent with that enjoyed by a paper in a monopoly position. If actual earnings were higher, the *Star* would share them; if they were lower, the *Star* would be required to reimburse the *Post* for the difference.[54]

After the closing was formally announced, Kay sent "Dear Murray [Gart]"—the editor who had unleashed the Rosellini series that Allbritton had kept buried—a handwritten note on pale blue paper: "My heart is broken for you." "The demise of the *Star* is dreadful for Washington and for anyone who loves newspapers," wrote Donny.[55]

The *Star*'s death represented a financial boon for the *Post*. Until the next year, with the appearance of *The Washington Times*—which, at its best, has never had more than a small fraction of the *Post*'s circulation and advertising—the *Post* enjoyed a monopoly. It also enjoyed a big boost to its circulation, with, on one day alone, new subscriptions peaking at 7,000. By the end of 1981, daily circulation had climbed by twenty-three percent and Sunday circulation by seventeen percent.[56]

There was not much gloating in the newsroom over the death rattles of the *Star,* for also in 1981, the paper that won the Pulitzer Prize for unraveling Watergate won another Pulitzer and was forced to give it back. Robert Christopher, administrator of the prizes (and a former *Newsweek* editor), said that had the *Post* not voluntarily returned the prize, it would have been the first paper in history to be stripped of it.[57]

The shocking story of an eight-year-old heroin addict, headlined "Jimmy's World," was published on September 28, 1980. Its author was a twenty-six-year-old reporter named Janet Cooke who had supposedly watched the pseudonymous "Jimmy" being shot up with heroin by his mother's boyfriend. The story caused an uproar, with public outrage so stirred that Mayor Marion Barry ordered police to find the boy. When they could not, Barry denounced the story as a fake. *Post* editors spurned demands that Cooke tell city officials where to find Jimmy. Although some in the *Post* newsroom suspected deceit, her editors not only stuck by her but submitted her article to the Pulitzer judges.

Eugene Patterson was the only member of that year's Pulitzer board who would not cast his vote for Cooke. "I remember [former *Post* editorial writer] Roger Wilkins swept the day by saying, 'Within ten blocks of this room where we're sitting at Columbia University, that kind of thing [drug use by children] is going on.' So everybody assumed Roger knew." But to Patterson, "it didn't smell right, and that's why I wondered why somebody at the *Post* didn't sniff it."[58]

The "somebody" was the metropolitan editor, who as a reporter had been in part responsible for winning the *Post* its Pulitzer for Watergate—Bob Woodward. "It's the editor's fault," Patterson contends. "You've got to have a system that will reveal something phony before you print it."[59] But the buck had to stop at Bradlee's desk. He, after all, set the tone, and the tone was one that promoted the "holy shit" story over all else and was almost contemptuous of the average reader.[60]

Bradlee simply refused to take responsibility for the fiasco. At an American Society of Newspaper Editors convention soon after, Patterson remembers, "most of the questions turned to Bradlee," who "played hard-nosed," refused to apologize, and in the way of explanation offered only: "How do you defend yourself against a pathological liar?"[61]

Woodward paid for his mistake. Until then, he had been Bradlee's heir apparent, and Donny quietly let him know that he was off that track. He sent Woodward back to reporting and put Leonard Downie, who was decidedly "second echelon," into position to replace Bradlee.[62] Bradlee seemed to be living up to his description as the "Teflon editor." Mark Edmiston recalls that the *Newsweek* crowd used to marvel, "No one could have survived the Janet Cooke mess. Only Ben could survive that." But Bradlee also paid. No longer free to choose his successor, he was stuck with the unsophisticated, public school–educated Downie.[63]

Kay Graham was not happy. Janet Cooke was never to be heard from again, but her mess could not be swept away. She was headline news in papers, magazines, and broadcasts around the world. The timing could not have been worse. Kay was chairman and president that year of the American Newspaper Publishers Association, and when she spoke at the group's annual convention in Chicago in May 1981, she had to address the topic of the fraudulent story instead of waxing nostalgic over Watergate or the Pentagon Papers.[64] During her speech to stockholders at their 1981 annual meeting, members of Accuracy In Media would not give Kay Graham a break. They called for Bradlee's and Woodward's resignations. Kay answered that the two were "first-rate people" and that "the company doesn't intend to ask for their resignation." One stockholder demanded that the salaries of all editors involved, including Bradlee, be cut by one-third and that the *Post* reimburse the D.C. government for $2 million in extra manpower consumed in the search for "Jimmy." Reed Irvine, AIM chairman and a relentless critic of Kay and the *Post,* blasted the paper for not accepting an AIM ad that demanded that its editors reveal the name of "Deep Throat" in order to prove that he too was not a fabrication.[65]

Lester Bernstein, who on taking the job as *Newsweek*'s editor in 1979 had vowed "to keep [Kay] in mind at all times," had never lapsed. He thought he was doing everything right, so he was shocked when the invitations went out for Kay's Reagan dinner, to be held a month before his 1981 inauguration, and he did not receive one— although others at *Newsweek,* such as Peter Derow, still chairman, and Mel Elfin, Washington bureau chief, did. "I was so outraged that I picked up the phone and called [Kay] and demanded to know why I had not been invited. She very crossly [said] that it was her party and she was inviting her friends, and if she didn't want me to come, that was her decision because it was a social occasion. I wasn't thinking of this in terms of a social occasion. This was business. I let her know that I was miffed and she let me know that she didn't care, and it also gave me a pretty good idea of where I stood."

Nothing more was ever said about it, although they saw each other regularly afterward. Bernstein knew he was in trouble when Kay started to ask him if he had yet identified a successor. He was saddened and startled—although it is hard to understand why—but told her that, yes, he had in mind two possibilities, Richard Smith and Michael Ruby, both of whom he was "bringing along" so that either would be ready when his contract expired in three years.*

Then Bernstein began reading in the gossip columns that Kay was talking to this one or that one about becoming editor of *Newsweek*. The name of Harold Evans, former editor of the London *Sunday Times*, was one that came up. Bernstein recalls that when he asked Kay about the rumors, "she would usually volunteer that there was nothing to them."[66]

Peter Derow understands exactly how the rumors started. "She would say to Harold Evans, 'If you were the editor, what would you do?' It's a small town. [Later] Harold says, 'I just had lunch with Kay Graham. She's [asking] me if I were the editor, what would I do?' Bernstein says, 'Jesus Christ, what's going on here?' It would never occur to her that that would absolutely undermine [people]. She'd never say to a Harold Evans, 'I think *Newsweek* is terrific. What do you think?' Kay would go out and say, 'I think things are terrible. Don't you agree?' The word gets out." Had Kay had to work her way up, Derow argues, she would not have behaved so insensitively and counterproductively.[67]

That Lester Bernstein had hoped he could save his job was understandable. In April 1982, he won two National Magazine Awards— one for general excellence and one for a single topic. On the business side there was much embarrassment, Bernstein says, because traditionally magazines that were finalists for the coveted awards (*Newsweek* was a finalist that year in three categories) bought ads touting their achievement. That year, *Newsweek* salesmen stopped promoting, and even mentioning, the awards, because "they were afraid people would say, 'Why is your editor leaving?' "[68]

In any case, winning National Magazine Awards left Kay feeling worried and vaguely dissatisfied. What would the magazine do for an encore? ("If you said to her, 'We just won the National Magazine

---

*Richard Smith is the current editor in chief and president of *Newsweek,* and Michael Ruby, with his wife, Merrill McLoughlin, is coeditor of *U.S. News & World Report.* Bernstein, who was fifty-nine when he left an RCA corporate vice-presidency to return to *Newsweek,* was given a six-year contract with the expectation that he would work until age sixty-five.

Award,' " Peter Derow explains, "she'd say, 'Yeah, but our coverage from Cairo stinks.' "[69]) She made up her mind that Bernstein, then past sixty, was too old to improve. If *Newsweek* had been too "pop" under Ed Kosner, she considered it too serious and intellectual under his successor. "She kept asking me, 'Shouldn't we be putting out a magazine for the eighties?' " says Bernstein. "I think she regarded me as an interim custodian. She felt that there was no more time to be wasted, and she wanted to get in the real guy."[70]

It also irritated her that Bernstein lived in the suburbs. "You have to live in the city to do this job," she would harangue Derow, who considered her irrational on the subject. "He's out there, so he can't be doing the job."[71] Mark Edmiston finds it a curiously old-fashioned, *Front Page* view: "When the fire breaks out in the tenement, you've got to be a few blocks away." But at the heart of it, he says, is the fact that Kay lost respect for Bernstein because he did not stand up to her. "She was beating up on [him] and he'd cringe rather than try to come back at her."[72]

It was out of character, but when she told Bernstein that he was finished she did not have his successor lined up. Mel Elfin claims that she sounded him out about the job but he refused it; he had by then built a life in Washington.[73] Others say she was in no hurry to replace Bernstein with yet another member of the same cast of characters.

This time she made Bradlee her partner on the search committee. But it was her son Billy who urged his mother to meet William Broyles, the superstar editor of *Texas Monthly* and then *California* (the renamed version of *New West,* once edited by Kay's friend Clay Felker). She was very impressed. Bernstein believes that Broyles was the object of one of her famous crushes. "I'm not suggesting for a moment that there was hanky-panky of any kind, but I think she had a crush on him."[74]

Worried about how the dizzying changing of the guard appeared to those inside the industry and out, Kay decided to involve still others in making the final call on Broyles. She asked him to fly to Washington, and was delighted that Bradlee loved him. Elfin also pronounced him just right.

Reaching a new height of insensitivity, Kay asked her jilted editor to take her intended to lunch. Bernstein doesn't see this request as especially cruel. "She knew very well that she had this awful reputation about beheading editors, and she wanted it to look as if in the ripeness of time I had decided that it was time to move out. And she felt that if I met this guy I would be taken with him just as she was."

Nonetheless, Kay put Bernstein in the peculiar position of approving his own replacement. He declined to do so. Instead he told her that it was "folly to put a weekly newsmagazine in the hands of someone who had never worked at a high level at a newsmagazine, because it [was] a very complex animal and you had to have demonstrated skills for working at it. It wasn't enough to come in and think big thoughts." Bernstein has no doubt that Kay dismissed his concerns "out of hand," understandably considering them self-serving.

A "should we hire Broyles?" meeting followed. Kay was so frightened of making a mistake, of again choosing the wrong man, that she literally put the matter to a vote—"This is going to be either a home run or a strikeout," Donny said[75]—and the vote was five to zero for hiring. Still, according to Elfin, Kay ordered everything short of an FBI background check. Broyles garnered consistent raves, Elfin recalls—but "there was still some little thing about how hard he was willing to work, laid-back California style."[76]

Kay asked Broyles to meet her in San Francisco for dinner and offered him the job. "It took me about a third of a second to say yes," Broyles remembered. Her expectations were sky-high. "She had the notion that Bill Broyles would be some kind of miracle worker," says Lester Bernstein.[77]

Kay had more on her agenda than hiring a top-notch *Newsweek* editor. With encouragement from Ben Bradlee, she also wanted to send a message: No more old-boy network. Broyles, a native-born Texan, was the outsider brought in to shake things up, the cowboy who was going to saunter into town to show all these used-up New Yorkers how to do it. (That he had a degree from Oxford, along with a Bronze Star for service with the Marines in Vietnam, made him all the more attractive.) Finally, Kay had an editor who had nothing to do with Phil.[78] She would no longer have to abide his men and their behind-her-back smirks, their habit of humoring her; their tendency to accept eagerly her dinner-table gossip from "Henry" or some other high-level source but let her know that issues of real substance were best left to her editors.

That Bradlee was so vocally delighted with Broyles annoyed the magazine's old guard, who wondered why the executive editor of *The Washington Post* should have any role in the selection of the editor of *Newsweek*. "I was always shocked when I [talked] to Ben about it," says Kermit Lansner. "He'd say, 'Washington is gonna really take control of this. We're not gonna have you bastards up in New York run it your own way.' We're all old good friends, and I was surprised at the intensity of this idiotic position." In Bradlee's mind, says Lansner, "Broyles was Washington's triumph over New York."[79]

If Bradlee saw Broyles as a tough guy from the West who would shake the magazine to its self-satisfied rafters, Thelma McMahon saw him as "carrying a soft saddle and a soft voice, a nice man but . . ." Any resemblance between the new editor and a cowboy seemed limited to Broyles's Gary Cooperish, man-of-few-words style. Culture shock set in. It took the *Newsweek* veterans, who were nothing if not good talkers, time to adjust.

McMahon was asked to arrange a dinner to welcome Broyles to the Washington bureau. "It was the worst party I ever threw at *Newsweek*. My husband said, 'And that's going to be the editor of *Newsweek*?' There was this totally quiet man who didn't have a thing to offer, and by the same token he almost stifled anyone saying anything to him." She recalls that "he never got excited."[80]

But then, at Mark Edmiston's suggestion, Kay had bestowed on Broyles the new title of editor in chief, a revised role that did not seem to require much shouting. Maynard Parker, once *Newsweek*'s chief correspondent in Vietnam, was promoted to editor, the nuts-and-bolts, day-to-day manager who actually put the magazine out.

Edmiston had for some time been mulling over changes that he thought newsmagazines had to make. They had to be more features-oriented, he concluded, less focused on hard news that was already old when the magazine reached subscribers.[81] Broyles's assignment was to broaden the magazine, to hire people from different backgrounds, to think about the future and formulate a five-year plan. Kay believed, says Ed Kosner, that the editor was "too preoccupied with changing semicolons when [he] should have been going to Germany and seeing Willy Brandt."[82]

Until then, says Lester Bernstein, the editor had "a very hands-on job. [He] actively supervised all the editors in the chain below and read every last word that went into the magazine."[83] Kosner did not see how the top editor, at least at the beginning, could do it any other way. He took Broyles to lunch and offered some advice: "Agree with her, tell her you'll do it, but for six months put your ass in the chair and learn how a newsmagazine works, [or] it will go on without you. You will not be able to influence its activities."[84]

It is said that on his first day at *Newsweek,* Broyles made his first big mistake. As Richard Clurman heard it, he announced that he "intended to preside at the magazine, not edit it. He wanted to take a long view, which the editor of a newsmagazine doesn't do."[85]

It had been arranged that Bernstein's and Broyles's tenures would overlap. "For a couple of weeks we had a very civilized passing of the torch," Bernstein recalls. "Broyles sat behind me watching me work for at least one week. When it was over he said, 'It had not been my intention to operate this way, but I can see I'm really going to have to do what you're doing, for six months anyway, so I can make some sense of it, take hold.' I later learned he never even tried it for a week."[86]

For *Newsweek*'s fiftieth birthday, in 1983, Kay Graham threw an enormous black-tie party at Lincoln Center in New York, designed to culminate in a slide show and a parade of famous names paying tribute to her and her magazine. Had Truman Capote planned it, he would have known better, but it was orchestrated by Kay with the help of professional party planners.

One top *Newsweek* editor remembers that Art Buchwald, whom Kay had long depended on to lighten up various occasions, was among several people who warned her that the event was destined to be unforgettably dull. "It was going to wind up as a talkfest, and there would be six people left in the auditorium when it was all finished."[87]

Not even Art Buchwald could save this party. In fact, the best line of the evening belonged to Henry Grunwald, who succeeded Hedley Donovan as editor in chief of *Time.* Donovan recounted that when Grunwald finally got his chance to speak, at about 1:15 a.m., "he said that his distinction on the program was that he was the only editor in the room who had been neither hired nor fired by our hostess, Kay Graham."[88]

So petrified was Kay about speaking to this gathering of celebrities from around the world that she read her entire speech from index cards. The party was, on almost every level, a graceless affair. Kay or one of her planners had concocted the idea of A and B guest lists. Thelma McMahon, who had worked for *Newsweek* for more than thirty years, rated only the B list. "There was an A list of the glittering people of this world," she recalls, "and then there was the B list. They were differentiated all the way down the line." The A list got the sit-down dinner; the B list, also in formal attire, got to wander around in a humiliating exile.[89]

The guest list was tricky. So many people had left the magazine under bitter circumstances, but Kay recognized that this was *Newsweek*'s party and she had to invite them. She did draw the line at Arnaud de Borchgrave and relented only after Oz Elliott threatened that he would not serve as her emcee unless de Borchgrave were invited. (De Borchgrave later described Kay's performance as "unbelievably unpoised"; her talk was "banal and obvious," and she had to "look at a cue card for the word 'welcome.' "[90]) The seating plan was even trickier, especially in the wake of Lally, whom Mark Edmiston remembers rushing in the day before the party to make Kay rearrange the seating.[91]

The event was so mobbed, so badly planned, that Mel Elfin, who had come up from Washington with his wife, could not get in at all: someone had forgotten to leave their tickets at the door. Approaching the entrance with Avery Fisher and Alexander Haig, both of whom were admitted upon showing their A list tickets, *Newsweek*'s longtime Washington bureau chief was turned away. "It was very embarrassing for me, so my wife and I spent the night at the Waldorf bar."

It was just as well, Elfin sighs. "Everybody came back holding their heads. I didn't want to see her afterward." He describes Kay as "humiliated [after the party]. She wanted to hide."[92]

But for Kay the party had one saving grace. She was able to seat *Newsweek*'s former president, Peter Derow, next to the kitchen.[93]

Perhaps the most important of the links left to Phil was lost that year with the suicide of Al Friendly. It was only a matter of time before throat cancer would have killed him—he had already lost his larynx to the disease—and he chose to put himself and his family out of the misery of useless suffering.

"At the very end of his life, a day or two before he killed himself," Jean Friendly recalls, "Kay asked him to help her write a speech to give [for] Russ Wiggins's eightieth birthday. She was going up to Maine [where Wiggins lives], and [later] I found what Alfred had tried to write for her. That killed him as much as anything. He couldn't put his words together. He had been such a graceful writer. He just couldn't organize his thoughts."[94]

Chapter 22

THE HITLER HOAX AND OTHER PROBLEMS

Kay Graham's peers, if pressed, would have to admit that Janet Cooke could have happened to any of them. They all shared the presumption that reporters do not make up their copy. But nobody who pretended to a reporter's natural skepticism, not to mention common sense and even a modest knowledge of World War II history, could imagine falling for the bogus Hitler diaries—diaries, it would turn out, that were sloppily forged by a petty German thief.

In the spring of 1983, Maynard Parker, the man who was running *Newsweek* while William Broyles engaged in the loftier pursuit of planning, was tipped off by the editor of the German picture weekly *Stern* that sixty-two volumes of diaries supposedly written by Adolf Hitler had been discovered and publication rights were available. Parker, envisioning the story of the century, was intrigued, and he and Mark Edmiston rushed to Zurich, where the diaries were being kept under the tightest security. "We were ushered into a bank," Edmiston recalls, "and guards with Uzis—I think for show more than anything else—go into this room and bring out these dusty copybooks written in a classic German, which they pointed out to us was taught in the schools in the 1890s, when Hitler would have been learning how to write. And there were sketches of Eva Braun, hand-signed, which looked pretty good to me, I didn't know." The Germans specifically forbade them from copying any of the pages. Still, Edmiston, who does not know German, admits, "I sort of bought the whole story. You had to have been there to have gotten really caught up in it . . . battered tin box, copybooks covered with dust."

Kay retained her initial skepticism. "From day one, [she] very much insisted that we have a handwriting expert and a historian evaluate them."[1]

The provenance of the diaries strained credibility: As Berlin fell in 1945, the sixty-two volumes supposedly were sent out of the city on a plane, which crashed near Dresden. The boxes containing the diaries were then buried, and they stayed buried until they were found some forty years later. Kay called friends in the CIA—former deputy director Bobby Ray Inman, for example—to ask whether this could actually have happened, whether a plane could have left Berlin on that particular day. The answer, Edmiston remembers, was, "Yes, one or two light planes landed right on the street outside [Hitler's] bunker, and yes, they did get out." No one would say, "It could not have happened."[2]

Kay, however, clung to the suspicion that the diaries were counterfeits and the belief that *Newsweek* should not publish them. But her editors were divided, and she lacked confidence in her convictions. She convened another meeting and put the matter to a vote. Richard Smith, then executive editor and a strong voice on the no side, argued that there were too many questions. Maynard Parker, who outranked him, argued passionately for throwing caution to the wind and making a "last-minute deal" with the Germans. Bill Broyles, Edmiston says, didn't participate. He "let the conversation happen around him."[3]

Parker carried the day, and a telephone bid of $3 million for the American rights was made. Edmiston was dispatched to Hamburg to sign the contract.

At the invitation of the Germans, who hoped to spark a bidding war, Rupert Murdoch had joined the race, eager to publish the diaries in his papers *The Australian, News of the World,* and the *New York Post.* Edmiston called him and suggested that they work together. "Why should the Germans screw us?" he told Murdoch. "We'll screw the Germans." Murdoch agreed, chartered a jet, and he and the *Newsweek* contingent took off for Hamburg. His arriving with Murdoch, Edmiston says, "shocked the Germans." During the twelve-hour meeting the sellers continued to insist that there was no time for serious verification.

Murdoch and a newly suspicious Edmiston, who was "furious with [the Germans] for the way they acted," broke off negotiations. "I went home and Murdoch went home," Edmiston recounts, "and

Murdoch turned around and then negotiated a deal by telephone."[4] Murdoch thus inadvertently saved *Newsweek* from spending millions for the rights to phony diaries. But the editors still moved ahead on their cover story, which reported on the finding, on its significance— the diaries would, some said, rehabilitate Hitler by showing that he knew nothing of the Holocaust—and which featured diary excerpts obtained during the failed negotiations. (Broyles did make one important contribution to the hodgepodge by insisting that the unwieldy subtitle include the question "Are They Genuine?" above "How They Could Rewrite History.")

"We were the laughingstock," says Thelma McMahon. In the last paragraph of the story, the *Newsweek* writer claimed that the discovery of the diaries was important in itself and that "Jews will have to face their fears again," and concluded that "it doesn't really matter in the end" whether the diaries were genuine or not. Other journalists, including *New York Times* editorial writers, ripped into an assertion so ridiculous on its face. Meanwhile, *Newsweek* was the butt of television jokes such as Mark Russell's: "I knew those diaries were phony the minute I saw them written on Holiday Inn stationery."[5]

Kay realized, of course, that her cast-off editors must be splitting their sides laughing at her pain, and assuring everyone that under their editorial leadership such a fiasco would not have occurred. "I could almost guarantee that that story never would have been in the magazine under the editorship of anyone up to Mr. Broyles," says Lester Bernstein.[6]

Then there was the sniping from Washington. Bradlee could not really partake in it, because he had so vigorously lobbied for Broyles. Kay's own Washington bureau chief, Mel Elfin, blamed what he called the "unmitigated horror" on the fact that "it was all held tightly in in New York. That's why it got as far as it did. We were frozen out. After it was over I said, 'Hey, I could have gotten to the FBI, we could have tested the paper.' Franchise was riding on that thing."[7]

A shakeup at *Newsweek* followed, but not the tornado that some expected. As Lester Bernstein observed, Kay could "hardly have blown a gasket, given that she was present at the creation."[8]

Broyles had slipped, in her estimation, from wunderkind to incompetent. It infuriated her that while nineteen people struggled to make a decision, Broyles abstained. "He was the top editor," says Edmiston. "It was his decision. That meeting [about whether to publish the diaries] should never have been held, as far as she was concerned."[9]

But Kay had been impatient with Broyles almost from the start. Once, when a major story broke over a weekend and he was at his house on Long Island, he issued directives over the telephone, unwilling to sacrifice his family life. And the only story that seemed to engage him was Vietnam. Thelma McMahon recalls that when the Vietnam Veterans Memorial was dedicated in Washington, he spent three days with *Newsweek*'s chief photographer "just reliving the war."*[10]

Officially, Broyles quit. Edmiston says that Richard Simmons, who had been pushing Kay to "get Broyles straightened out," called a meeting at which he and Kay were going to tell him "what he had to do to do his job better." Broyles was not interested in finding out. "Thank you very much for your advice," he said, "but I'm probably not the right person for this job. So why don't we just call it a day."[11]

The fault, Edmiston charges, lay with Kay, not Broyles. "She changed the rules on him in the middle of the game." She hired him for one job. Then she "basically expected him to do a different job" (namely, that of the traditional, hands-on editor). Broyles also faced even more than the usual backstabbing. The old *Newsweek* staff did not want him to survive.[12] "In their heart of hearts," Mel Elfin agrees, they hoped he would fail, "because he's an outsider."[13]

Since Kermit Lansner's ouster in 1972, Broyles was the fifth editor of *Newsweek* to go. On the very day that Broyles "quit," Richard Clurman and Osborn Elliott were lunching at the Century Club. Lansner joined them, and then in came Lester Bernstein, who was followed by Edward Kosner. The five were sitting and talking when up the stairs came Broyles. "Wait a minute," said Elliott, "this is not the most exclusive club in New York." The five former editors all joked about their experiences and "tried to figure out Kay Graham," Clurman recalls.[14] "Kay must have loved ex-editors of *Newsweek*," Bernstein cracked, "because she made so many of them."[15]

The other career that, at the time, seemed irreparably damaged was Maynard Parker's. As Broyles's number two, he certainly would

---

*Broyles would later find his niche in co-creating *China Beach,* the critically acclaimed (but since canceled) television series about the Vietnam war.

have been the successor had he not led Kay and her company into the Hitler-diary hoax. The opposite of Broyles, Parker is a hands-on, high-energy type, daring, the quintessential newsman and foreign correspondent, and a resident of Manhattan to boot.

No one would have been surprised if Kay Graham had ordered Edmiston to give Parker forty-five minutes to exit the building, especially because she was said always to have found him too naked in his desire to get ahead. Instead, she pleaded with him to stay and offered him a raise. She feared that, embarrassed by his "constant bridesmaid's" role, he would bolt and leave no one on staff who knew how to get the magazine out. Richard Smith was then too far down the masthead. But Smith, who lived in Hoboken, New Jersey, and who worked for Maynard, "moved up by a substantial amount" in Kay's estimation, says Edmiston.[16] She would not forget his caution as compared with Parker's push to buy the diaries.

In 1984, Kay named Smith editor in chief, with Parker under him as editor. Smith was the important man and quickly became, except for Meg Greenfield, the most constant of her traveling companions. "Certainly Rick Smith has been to hell and back with her," says Thelma McMahon.[17] For a long time, Smith's wife lived abroad, and thus he had the freedom to go where and when Kay wanted.

Kay eventually forgave him for living in Hoboken, which happens to be minutes by subway from the *Newsweek* building, although "as far as Kay's concerned," says Mark Edmiston, "New Jersey's a place you fly over between Washington and New York."[18] Smith also became Kay's *Newsweek* soulmate, which boded ill for Mark Edmiston. "She deals with only one person at a time," he explains.

Conventional wisdom has it that since putting Smith and Simmons in place, Kay has renounced her off-with-his-head ways. Both men would enjoy the long tenures that a Bernstein or a Meagher would have loved. The biggest change, says Kermit Lansner, is in Kay herself, and Smith "is really the beneficiary of a certain common sense that has overtaken her. The joke was on us in a way, but it became an embarrassment to her. You can't have picked so badly that five people in a row in the course of ten years were bounced."[19]

Kay, pushing seventy, was concerned about how history—publishing history at least—would view her. She did not, says Edmiston, want the reputation of the "arrogant queen who would dismiss people at a whim." Ed Kosner sees a geriatric maturation finally setting in: "As the years went on, she realized that it's a long-haul business and every week isn't the decisive moment." She came to accept that the business is cyclical, that if *Time* beat *Newsweek* one week, *Newsweek* might beat *Time* the next.[20]

Then again, she liked what Smith was doing for her magazine and what Simmons was doing for her bottom line. Smith and his editors, who talked a lot about "reinventing" *Newsweek,* moved it from the newsmagazine tradition of group-speak made famous by *Time,* to something more interpretative, with longer, forcefully argued and signed articles.[21] From a business perspective, the Post Company would perform spectacularly, in large part because Simmons did not insist on loading it with overpriced media properties.

In 1984, after twenty-two years at the *Post,* managing editor Howard Simons left to head the Nieman Foundation at Harvard. Although he was not fired, he recognized that he had no choice but to leave: Donny Graham wanted Leonard Downie in the managing editor's slot as a way station to the top. (At sixty-three, Bradlee was quickly approaching retirement age.)

Simons was bitter. He told a colleague that the real reason he wouldn't become executive editor was that he was Jewish.[22] Mel Elfin says that in Kay's eyes, Simons had other deficiencies. He didn't live in Georgetown, "he wasn't social," and he made her uncomfortable.[23] "A smart-ass," Mark Meagher calls him, "sarcastic, irreverent." While Bradlee is all those things and more, at least he could make Kay laugh.*[24]

Kay would certainly not have selected Simons to replace Bradlee, but neither would she have picked Downie, with whom she is said to have no "personal chemistry."[26] (Kay's choice would probably have been Jim Hoagland, a well-traveled former foreign correspondent, foreign editor, then assistant managing editor for foreign news, who often planned Kay's trips abroad and shepherded her through them. When he did not get the nod, he eventually returned to Paris as chief foreign correspondent.) But the message was that Donny would soon be running things and must be allowed to choose his own man.

---

*At Simons's memorial service five years later, Kay Graham delivered a eulogy that surprised Barry Sussman. "She paid Howard a real tribute. At one point she went back to old memos he had written urging her to do certain things with the paper. All of her remarks had to do with Howard's having more foresight than most anybody around. Howard felt that Kay didn't care for him at all. She had to have [had] some real feeling for him—maybe she didn't want him to be the boss, but [her talk] was moving and heartfelt."[25]

If given the option, Bradlee himself might have tapped Bill Greider, who, when he saw that it was not Bradlee's decision and that Donny Graham was set on Downie, left the *Post*. Bradlee was also especially fond of Shelby Coffey III; a former editor of "Style," and a favorite of Sally Quinn's, he was, until Downie's appointment was announced, often referred to as Bradlee's protégé. Coffey left in 1985 for *U.S. News & World Report* and later landed at the *Los Angeles Times* as executive editor. The joke around the *Post* was that in July 1984, when Downie's appointment to managing editor was announced, "you could hear the sound of briefcases snapping shut."[27]

Few in Kay's employ had been of greater service to her than Mel Elfin, that year celebrating his twentieth anniversary as *Newsweek*'s Washington bureau chief. Since the occasion, two decades before, when he had written a speech for her that drew laughter and applause from the audience and praise—albeit faint—from her mother, he had continued not only to heed her calls for help but to anticipate when she would need it. Some would say that Elfin was self-serving, but he understood Kay's insecurities and knew better than anyone but Ben Bradlee how to calm them.

The two developed a routine. "You'd know the signal," says Elfin.[28] "Melsie, I've got to speak to the newspaper editors . . . and I need five pages," Thelma McMahon recalls Kay almost purring; she was never demanding or imperious. She would not hesitate to call him at home, and as Elfin's wife told McMahon, whatever he was doing would be put aside to tend to the needs of Kay Graham.[29] "The story I always heard," says one former *Post* editor, "is [that] he's the one who protected her all those years."[30]

Elfin apparently hadn't a clue—she did not stop asking him for help with her speeches—that as early as 1979, Kay had begun to contemplate replacing him. Lester Bernstein says that when he became editor that year, "one of the first things I did was to save his job. She expressed great unhappiness with Elfin, felt he had stayed too long, and she wanted to get rid of him. I defended him. I felt that he did a good job and he was useful, and so he stayed."[*][31]

By all accounts, it was Richard Smith who wanted Elfin out. Elfin

---

[*]Bernstein still nurses a grudge against Elfin for not sharing with him, in 1982, the information that Kay was about to replace him with Bill Broyles.[32]

thinks he knows why: "Rick was happy to get rid of me. I was a rival for her affections. I was able to exert more power than some of the other bureau chiefs. I had established an independent barony to protect the people who worked for me." Smith's goal, Elfin charges, was to replace him with "somebody who did not have that sort of barony and who would therefore be subservient."[33]

Kay was open to suggestions from Smith that it was time for a change in the position that, after all, had once belonged to Bradlee. The appointment that year of a new bureau chief at *Time* helped Smith immeasurably in getting Kay to see things his way. *Time*'s new man was Strobe Talbott (Nelson Strobridge Talbott III), Hotchkiss, Yale, Rhodes scholar at Oxford, a world-renowned scholar and historian of international affairs, author of two books on arms control, fluent in Russian, translator of Khrushchev's memoirs—"Tyrone Power with brains," a *Washingtonian* writer called him. Not even Elfin's mother would have called Mel that.

The fact that Elfin was a very good bureau chief got lost in the backstabbing. He was, says Thelma McMahon, "very hands-on. He knew everything, [from what] I was doing on the office checkbook to what the reporters were doing at the State Department." He did not do much writing himself, but "he brought out the best in everyone,"[34] building one of the best print bureaus in the capital, filled with talent that he spotted and nurtured.

By announcing that he was burned out (he had been hospitalized in 1984 with an illness related to stress and high blood pressure) and that in a year or so he wanted to make some changes, Elfin inadvertently made it easy for Kay and Smith. What he really wanted was to be offered inducements to stay, such as a column and perhaps fewer administrative responsibilities.

"New York [that is, Rick Smith] took that thought and ran with it," says Thelma McMahon. "New York convinced Mrs. G. that it was a good idea to ease him out. [And] once that worm turned, there was no turning back, no saying, 'Hey, guys, I was just joking.' " The man Bill Greider called "the ultimate survivor" could see that he had played the wrong card. Did he have any candidates for succession, Elfin soon found himself being asked.[35]

Not on his list was the man who got the job, Morton Kondracke, formerly executive editor of *The New Republic* and a regular on *The McLaughlin Group,* who had been suggested to Kay by Meg Greenfield. Kay and Smith were looking for a person who could and would write, and Kondracke seemed perfect. In fact, they had to talk him out of his demand for a regular column and persuade him to settle instead for a promise that he could substitute whenever *Newsweek* columnists George Will or Meg Greenfield went on vacation.[36]

Kondracke did not last long. The next year he was back at *The New Republic.* "I'm not here to be a leader of men," he was heard to say at a bureau meeting. "I was hired to be an individual star reporter." The bureau, says one person who worked there, dissipated into "twenty free-lancers who came in to use the typewriter."[37] Kondracke's first commitment was to *The McLaughlin Group,* which was taped on Friday afternoon, a crucial time at the newsmagazine. In the face of a breaking story, says Thelma McMahon, "he taped"; he was, in her words, "a disaster."

Warehoused in the position of "senior editor," assigned to redesign the computer system, Elfin did nothing, according to McMahon. "He was pushed aside, [it was] just awful. It was a waste." His two-decade relationship with Kay "cooled very quickly. He became a nonperson." Kondracke never asked for his advice. At parties Elfin and Kay studiously avoided making eye contact; McMahon finds this "very sad, because they had a lot to give each other."[38]

In 1986, Elfin left *Newsweek* to be "editor of special reports" at *U.S. News & World Report.* When he made his decision to leave, Kay was on a trip to the Far East. "Mel, you must call Mrs. Graham," McMahon urged him. He tried to reach her but could not; he never tried again, and she never called him.[39] For the next two years, he says, he got from her "the deep-freeze treatment."[40]

During the Reagan years, Katharine Graham and Nancy Reagan saw each other often; they stuck to their determination not to let *Post* reporters come between them. It was hard sometimes, for example when Sally Quinn so relentlessly ridiculed Nancy. But Kay's advice, Nancy wrote in her memoirs, *My Turn,* helped her put these attacks in perspective. The articles, Kay told her, were "written by younger women who were caught up in the feminist movement. 'They just couldn't identify with you,' [Kay] said. 'You represented everything they were rebelling against.' "[41]

Nancy happily accepted Kay's invitations, whether to lunch at Meg Greenfield's or to stay at Kay's house on Martha's Vineyard,*

---

*In her memoirs, Nancy described her visit as a simple beach weekend, but it was star-studded even by Vineyard-in-August standards. Among the lunch and dinner guests were Mike Wal-

where Nancy took a "heaven[ly]" walk on the beach with Kay and Rick Smith. When the Iran-contra scandal surfaced, Nancy found two shoulders to cry on—Meg's and Kay's. "It was a dark and hurtful time," the First Lady confessed. "My pals called me often with encouragement: Kay Graham, Meg Greenfield, George Will and Dick Helms."[43] All this in the face of Ben Bradlee, who, Nancy complained, "had recently called the Iran-Contra affair 'the most fun I've had since Watergate.' "[44]

Kay's alliances with the likes of Nancy Reagan have brought the predictable charge that she arranges special treatment in the pages of the *Post* for her friends. In the case of Mrs. Reagan, the charge seems false, although the suggestion that there was something not quite right about the relationship endures. In his slashing review of *My Turn*, R. W. Apple, Jr., then chief Washington correspondent for *The New York Times,* noted that "Mrs. Reagan denies that she fomented a campaign against [Reagan chief of staff Donald] Regan in the press, but it is hard to give total credence to that when she speaks repeatedly of her telephone conversations at that time with those she calls her 'pals,' including . . . Katharine Graham and Meg Greenfield."[45]

And charges persist that Kay is quietly helpful to friends who live at levels of influence somewhere beneath the White House—although not all that far beneath. Former "Style" gossip columnist Nancy Collins claims that her editor, Shelby Coffey, warned her, "You can write about everybody in town, except Mrs. Graham's friends." New at her job and thinking that Coffey was joking, Collins reported that two of Kay's friends, former ambassador to Denmark and to the Philippines William McCormick Blair, Jr., and his socialite wife had kept their swimming pool heated during the energy crisis. Ambassador Blair called Kay to complain, and she was "not amused. Though the source, as [Coffey] was chagrined to learn, was a prominent *Post* reporter, he was forced to dutifully direct me to run a correction. The Blairs swore they had, in the name of patriotism, cooled it."[46]

Joe Laitin compares Kay Graham with Saddam Hussein—in the sense that people act in certain ways not because of anything she says but because of who she is. "I can't cite you a single case of cause and

lace, Walter Cronkite, Ruth Gordon, Garson Kanin, Beverly Sills, Jacqueline Onassis, Cyrus Vance, Robert McNamara, Edward Bennett Williams, William Styron, Warren Buffett, and of course, Meg Greenfield.[42]

effect," he admits, "where she said, 'Do this,' and it was done. She doesn't have to." He uses as an example what happened with Sondra Gotlieb—"a great favorite of Kay's, and Meg's too"—wife of Canada's ambassador to Washington, and for a time a columnist for the *Post.* (Gotlieb's column, "Letter from Washington," consisted of reports to an apocryphal friend describing the tribal rites of Washington society and featuring such characters as Popsie Tribble, socialite; Lionel Portant, "world-famous columnist and media star"; and Baron Spitte, "the dusty diplomat.")

In real life, just before an official dinner in honor of Canadian prime minister Brian Mulroney, Gotlieb slapped her social secretary so hard that her earring went flying, in view of a reporter; apparently, the secretary had not informed her that Deputy Treasury Secretary Richard Darman would not be attending. The slap, said to have been heard around the world, earned eight-column banner headlines in Canada and a place on page three of *The New York Times.* But it was not heard in the next morning's *Washington Post,* either in the news section or in "Style." Kay, Meg Greenfield, and Ben Bradlee were all guests at the embassy dinner, as was reporter Liz Becker, who wrote the story that finally made it into "Style" a few days later.[47]

More recently, Tai Collins, a former Miss Virginia who claimed to have had an affair with Virginia senator Charles Robb, son-in-law of Lady Bird Johnson, charged that editors at the *Post,* on orders of Kay Graham, killed a story about the alleged affair after a phone call to Kay from the former First Lady. Appearing on the CNN show *Larry King Live* to promote her nude pictorial in *Playboy,* Collins explained that she spent months being interviewed by two *Post* reporters in 1990 but that no story ran in the paper until April 1991, when, with Senator Robb calling attention to the charges in trying to discredit them, the allegations became front-page news in papers around the country. Leonard Downie insisted that *Post* editors decided the previous December not to run the story because it "did not meet our standards." As distasteful as she must have found it to publicize the scandal, Kay Graham felt she had to respond. She told *Post* media writer Howard Kurtz that Collins's charge was "a total, hundred-percent lie . . . total fiction. I have never killed a story in my life—never once in twenty-eight years, never."[48]

She probably has not. But there is always the point, made by Joe Laitin, that Kay is the five-hundred-pound gorilla and it is wise simply to avoid provoking her. That's a more difficult charge to prove, and in her decades of leadership no one has. Increasingly, though, she has been charged with using her power to affect other major media. In *The Nation,* Robert Sherrill asserts, but again does not prove, that Kay called CBS chief Laurence Tisch (the two had become friendly through Warren Buffett) to kill a *60 Minutes* piece on *Silent Coup,* a book on Watergate whose authors try to discredit Woodward and Bernstein's reporting.[49]

The Washington Post and its owner—once, in the public mind at least, the quintessential liberal newspaper and publisher—had become increasingly conservative; this was evident in Kay's decision to take her paper public and the resulting new accountability to stockholders. Warren Buffett, although a Democrat, is also thought to have nudged Kay to the right.[50] Kay, Greenfield, and Bradlee view politics more theoretically than practically; they are not activists in the way Agnes Meyer and Phil Graham were.*

Kay's friend Marietta Tree placed her "right of center," adding that Kay would identify herself not as a Republican but rather as an independent.[52] The editorial page put out by Meg Greenfield, a registered independent who has become known as a neoconservative, is thought to reflect Kay's politics accurately. "Meg is me," Kay has said. "She thinks the way I do."[53]

Kay was in the audience when Richard Nixon addressed the American Newspaper Publishers Association in April 1986. He received an extremely warm reception, complete with a standing ovation and an affectionate laugh when he answered a question about what lesson Watergate held—"Just destroy all the tapes." Nixon biographer Stephen Ambrose reports that "the camera clicks reached a crescendo when he shook hands with Katharine Graham . . . and shared a friendly laugh with her. Graham was so impressed that she ordered her editor to put a smiling picture of Nixon on the cover of . . . *Newsweek* with a headline reading, 'He's Back: The Rehabilitation of Richard Nixon.' "†[54]

---

*For example, the *Post* editorially opposed the 1985 D.C. rent control referendum, but none of the three voted. Likewise, all three failed to vote in the 1985 and 1987 school board elections, despite editorials calling for reform of the D.C. public schools.[51]

†The six-page cover story and three-page interview, entitled "The Sage of Saddle River" (Nixon then lived in Saddle River, New Jersey), gave the former president his best platform yet to make his excuses, resurrect his reputation, and appear to Americans as a wise man commenting and advising on national and international affairs.[55] Nixon later wrote an op-ed column for *The Washington Post* analyzing the situation in the Soviet Union.

While Nancy Reagan and Richard Nixon were finding Kay to be so hospitable, Joe Rauh sensed the building of a barrier between him and his old friend. The source of the coolness was her paper's endorsement of the confirmation of Edwin Meese as attorney general of the United States. Rauh submitted an op-ed piece opposing the endorsement to Meg Greenfield, who first called him to say it was offensive and would hurt Kay's feelings—"Al Friendly and Alan Barth are rolling over in their graves," he had written—and then took him to lunch to try to talk him out of it.

It surprised Rauh that not only did his piece not run but neither did a single letter to the editor on the subject.[56] Morton Mintz was also surprised, and outraged, by the pro-Meese editorial and by the fact that no letters of disagreement appeared in response—with the exception of an op-ed column by Senator John Glenn. Mintz was puzzled too at Joe Rauh's treatment and at the fact that the editorial appeared at the bottom of the page: "If *The Washington Post* is going to endorse Ed Meese, why not do it proudly and openly at the top of the page? Why is it down at the bottom?"

Mintz suspects that Kay may have wanted something from Meese, who, before becoming attorney general, was Ronald Reagan's White House counsel. She may have been hoping for help from the White House in defeating legislation that would have lifted a restriction prohibiting the seven regional Bell companies from competing directly with newspapers.* Mintz admits that he lacks "the kind of evidence you take into court. It ain't evidence, but my viscera told me, That explains it."[58]

Meg Greenfield invited Rauh to a meeting with the full editorial board of the *Post*. Donny Graham also attended. Kay did not. "That was a very interesting session," said Rauh. "It was the first time I realized that the paper was going to be more conservative under Don. We argued, we disagreed on affirmative action. They called it reverse discrimination. But the center of [the meeting was the *Post*'s] not printing my op-ed piece. We had a couple of hours' talk, and then we were starting to repeat ourselves. I broke up the meeting."

---

*The Baby Bells were lobbying Congress for legislation that would permit them to own information services by which, via fiber optic lines, they could offer consumers everything from news flashes to classified. It would have been difficult to find a newspaper publisher who did not strenuously oppose the legislation; these information services would, after all, threaten the classifieds—a newspaper's lifeblood. Kay Graham, then ANPA president, actively lobbied against it.[57]

Rauh walked with a pronounced limp, and Donny saw him to a taxi. "Mr. Rauh," he said, "you have to remember one thing: This is not the liberal paper that you remember."*[59]

Donny is considered more conservative, certainly more than his father was—"by a long shot" says Robert Nathan[61]—and even more than his mother. By most accounts, however, he is not dictatorial or heavy-handed. Greenfield went to him to say that she and her editorial-page staff had decided to come out against the confirmation of Judge Robert Bork to the Supreme Court. She asked for his approval. According to Joe Laitin, who was told this by Greenfield, "Donny said he disagreed with the staff, but [also] said, 'if you feel that way about it, don't worry about my feelings, go ahead and do it.' " Barry Sussman, who went to work for the *Post* in 1965, credits Donny with opening to blacks not only the newsroom but also other departments of the paper, such as advertising. "If you went into the *Post* before Donny, there were very few blacks. Now blacks are everywhere. I'm personally persuaded that Don said, 'This is going to be done.' "[62]

Donny has been seen as hopelessly anti-union by the likes of Morton Mintz and Bernard Nossiter. Mintz cites Donny's acrimonious relations with the Newspaper Guild, which worked for long stretches without a contract. Donny signed a five-year contract with the Guild, but it included a no-strike pledge, the first ever in the Guild's history at the *Post*. The strained relationship has, says Laitin, changed the way in which Donny relates to his newsroom employees. "[He] used to like to come to the newsroom, make the rounds, knew everyone by name. [But he] no longer does that, because he was upset with the Guild negotiations and can't stand the hostility."[63]

Donny had other problems on his mind—the most embarrassing of which may have been his sister, Lally. She had moved from her far-left politics to the far right, and once more had become an object of derision. By the late 1980s, *Spy* had taken to calling her "right-

---

*Rauh stopped writing for the *Post*. "I had several turndowns after this from Meg. I finally wrote her a letter saying, 'It [isn't] cost-efficient to write things for you. If you want anything, why don't you call me up.' " He sent Kay a copy of his letter to Greenfield but received no response from either woman.

When Rauh died in 1992, the *Post* ran a front-page obituary and an editorial praising him as a "giant force" in "American public life and laws."[60]

wing boytoy Lally Weymouth," and again wondered "which came first, the conservative beliefs or the conservative men."[64]

Although they both denied it, Lally was alleged to have had an affair with her mother's friend and employee George Will. "That was obviously during her [right-wing] period," Marietta Tree explained.[65] *Washingtonian* reported that Will, then married to his first wife, found the contents of his study, including his furniture, piled in front of his Chevy Chase house with a note demanding, 'Take it somewhere else, buster.' "[66] There was also an alleged affair with writer R. Emmett Tyrrell, Jr., whose syndicated column has appeared in the *Post* and whose far-right views make George Will seem moderate.*

Her political transformation aside, Lally was a working journalist, and sometimes quite a good one. She was writing for *The New York Times Magazine, Esquire,* and *New York,* where she was listed as a contributing editor and became a friend of publisher Ed Kosner, who volunteers that he "really helped Lally's career a lot" and that Kay was "really, really grateful" to her former employee for giving Lally work. Kosner assigned Lally such plums as covering the trial of Madeira headmistress Jean Harris and the tribulations of Claus von Bülow.

But Lally's heart was with the columns that she wrote on international affairs for the Los Angeles Times Syndicate. It helped that she was Kay Graham's daughter when she tried to land interviews with very important men, and she was getting an increasing number of those—including one in 1982 with PLO chairman Yasir Arafat and one in 1985 with German chancellor Helmut Kohl, who was known for not giving interviews. Still, she had become, in her own right, says Kosner, "an extremely intrepid reporter." He praises her for her hard work and for going "to places [where] I wouldn't even think of going—Pakistan, Somalia." She carried off the sorts of interviews, he points out, that Arnaud de Borchgrave had made famous in *Newsweek.*[68]

Kay's loathing for de Borchgrave continued unabated. While Joe Laitin was ombudsman, he wrote weekly internal memos pinpointing what he considered problems in the organization, such matters as

---

*Tyrrell has called leaders of NOW "hags" and has written that feminists have "lived their whole lives in canvas underwear, burdened by a splitting headache, halitosis, body odor." He placed President Jimmy Carter's knowledge of history as "somewhere between that of the washroom attendant at '21' and [that of] a modestly educated welfare queen," and praised colonialism as a means of both civilizing and industrializing Africa.[67]

ethical lapses, sloppy and slanted reporting, and more. They were sent to a very select group of top editors and executives. To Laitin's dismay, he discovered that de Borchgrave, then editor in chief at the *Washington Times,* was receiving those incriminating, probing memos. While talking to Kay about this leak, Laitin allowed that de Borchgrave "must have a lot of class, because never once, but never once, did anything from our memos get into the *Times.*" She looked at him with a frozen face and said, "I wouldn't describe him that way."[69]

"Arnaud delights in making Kay uncomfortable," says Kermit Lansner, who recalls that de Borchgrave "once had a little bit of stock and would come to [Post Company shareholder] meetings and ask embarrassing questions."[70] But it was not until six years after his dismissal that de Borchgrave hatched a worthy plan to embarrass Kay Graham.

Lally's skills as an interviewer gave de Borchgrave at the right-wing *Times*—the upstart daily owned by members of the Reverend Sun Myung Moon's Unification Church, more derisively known as "Moonies"—a brilliant idea. In the fall of 1986, Lally left the Los Angeles Times Syndicate, which, she complained, was not pushing her increasingly conservative worldview into enough newspapers.[71] De Borchgrave, informed by a "mutual friend" in New York that Lally was interested in working for his paper, invited her to Washington for Sunday lunch at the Jockey Club. (Nothing was said of the meal they had shared more than twenty years earlier at the Carlyle in New York, when Phil introduced Lally to Robin Webb.)

De Borchgrave did not choose the Jockey Club because he wanted privacy. He knew that they would be seen, and he took enormous pleasure in imagining Jockey Club regulars dashing to tell Kay that they had seen her daughter with the hated de Borchgrave.

"I only want to work with you, report to you," Lally told de Borchgrave, "because otherwise my stories may get buried, and you understand immediately how important a foreign story is. I want to go all over the world." "That's all very expensive," de Borchgrave replied, but he suggested they "go back to the office to discuss it." They went into minute detail about Lally's "mandate." "If something is worked out," de Borchgrave told her, "you could become the Oriana Fallaci of the right. With the kinds of stories and interviews you'll get, your work would demand display—probably most of the time at the top of page one."[72] He promised her she would write the big-splash exclusives for his paper that he used to write for her mother's magazine.

Lally seemed ready to sign but told de Borchgrave that she had to tell her mother. He offered her his car, his driver, and a warning: "I don't think your mother is going to take kindly to this. She will find ways of blocking [it]." "Don't worry," Lally replied, "I can handle Mother."[73]

Lally was supposed to be on the five-o'clock shuttle to New York. When de Borchgrave learned that his car was parked in Kay's driveway well into the night, he knew he was in trouble. When he didn't hear from Lally the next day or the day after that, he feared defeat. Through his New York friend, he learned that "Kay had thrown a temper tantrum."[74]

Lally returned to New York unsure of what to do. Her mother, on the other hand, had grown so alarmed by the notion of Lally's working not only for Arnaud but for the repugnant "Moonie" *Times* that she and Donny decided to ask Lally to work at the *Post*. Kay's long-held concerns about nepotism crumbled in the face of de Borchgrave. Donny flew to New York to make Lally the offer of writing occasional op-ed pieces, sweetened with the assurance that, when Ben Bradlee retired, the paper would become more conservative.[75]

Lally still did not know what to do. She sought advice from friends George Will, Rupert Murdoch, Sir James Goldsmith, Norman Podhoretz. De Borchgrave's offer was much more attractive than her mother's because, for openers, Lally feared that her work would get killed before it could see print at the *Post*.[76]

When, three or four days after their lunch, Arnaud called Lally and she didn't call back, he concluded that "something was terribly amiss." On finally reaching her, he announced, "I'm taking you to Paris." He explained that he had an appointment to interview French prime minister Jacques Chirac and that she could share the questioning and the byline. "Oh, I'm just looking at my diary," she replied. "I can't. I've got a dinner that night." He suggested that she take the Concorde. "No, I have another dinner," she replied.[77]

Apparently, Lally's hesitation in grabbing her mother's first offer panicked Kay, and she made a better one: Lally would be made the *Post*'s roving correspondent and would appear twenty-six times a year in the "Outlook" section. *Washington Times* managing editor Wes Pruden, who was involved in the negotiations with Lally, claims that Kay promised Lally that Bradlee "would be told, not asked, to make sure there was no funny business about relegating Lally's stories to the back pages with the truss ads."[78]

It was often said that Lally deliberately extorted a place for herself on the *Post* by threatening to work for de Borchgrave. Ed Kosner strenuously disagrees: "Arnaud wanted to torture them, but from Lally's standpoint, I think her strongest motivation was an appropriate outlet for her work. It was really important to be in Washington. Who cares about an interview with Jonas Savimbi except the Beltway foreign-policy crowd. It worked as a lever, but I don't think it was a self-conscious strategy."[79]

Was de Borchgrave recruiting Lally only for the pleasure of annoying Kay? "I thought it would be a hell of a coup to have Lally," he explains ("the most embarrassing defection since Joseph Stalin's daughter left the Soviet Union," one Washington reporter wrote). As an afterthought, almost, de Borchgrave adds that he wanted Lally also because "I thought she was damned good." He admired her pieces on Afghanistan and Pakistan, and recognized her "good connections with intelligence and with that whole *mujaheddin* gang."[80]

With the power of the *Post* and her mother behind her, Lally's genuine talent was quickly lost in the resentment and contempt she provoked. She became a pesky irritant to *Post* and *Newsweek* correspondents, who felt they could not compete with her when she set her mind to wangling an interview from a particular head of state. She continued to demand first-class travel arrangements—and pronto—and to threaten to tattle to her mother when she felt insufficiently deferred to.

Nicholas von Hoffman calls Lally a "bizarre lightweight" and suggests that "they should have let her go [to *The Washington Times*]. I think she's truly undistinguished. If she had not been born under the circumstances that she was, she'd be making her living in an insurance company office pounding a computer."[81] To Joe Laitin, "her stuff seemed no better, no worse than anybody else's. I thought it would have been much more interesting if she'd gone and worked for the *Times,* but to buy her out that way, and the fact that she accepted . . ."[82]

Her berth in the family company did not moderate her outrageous and impulsive behavior. Writer Stephen Birmingham met Lally for the first time when she sat on his right at the New York Public Library's Literary Lions dinner. Having known him for under an hour, and with her mother seated across the table, Lally confided to

him, "You're the man of my dreams." Birmingham says he was
terrified. "She wrote me a letter telling me I was charming, fascinating." At their second meeting, she suggested—facetiously, he
hoped—that they get married. Knowing her family's history, he was
taken aback when he later heard Lally say, in frustration when
something did not go her way, "I'm so angry I'm going to commit
suicide."[83]

When Kay decided to fire Mark Edmiston in 1986, she had Richard Simmons do it. Edmiston says that his dismissal did not surprise
him and that it had nothing to do with his role in the Hitler-diary
disaster. "I was a thorn under Dick Simmons's saddle for a long
time. It was just a matter of time before he was able to convince her
that I should be dumped."

His last conversation with Kay was curiously detached. "I said,
'Look, sorry it didn't work out, doesn't surprise me a whole lot, and
I wish you all the best.' And she was very good, saying, 'I'm sorry it
worked out this way.' She said good luck and I said good luck, and
[it] was finished." There was no discussion of the terms of his dismissal or the reasons for it, and he did not try to get his job back. "I
walked out. I never spoke directly to her again. She never made any
attempt to talk to me."[84]

Edmiston was the last of the men Kay Graham fired. She seemed
finally to have found the right men and was eager to settle down to
enjoy her position.

Chapter 23

HANGING ON,
TO HER POWER
AND INSECURITIES

On June 16, 1987, Kay Graham turned seventy, and used the occasion to announce that she had no intention of retiring. While no one expected that she would give up her position as chairman of the board, this birthday seemed the logical, graceful time to anoint Donny as CEO.

When it did not happen, even those closest to her hesitated to guess when it would. "When will he take over?" asked Marietta Tree. "It's like, When will Elizabeth II step down? She'll give Donny more and more administrative responsibility, but she'll hold on to it until she dies, and why shouldn't she?"[1] Peter Derow predicted that she would stay "essentially forever, because what's the next best thing? Where is there to go?"[2]

She had, for the most part, given Donny the *Post* to run, but she kept her hand in *Newsweek*. That was just fine with Donny, whose first love was the *Post* and who took no more interest in the magazine than he did in the company's television stations, even the newly acquired cable stations. Far from being impatient to take over as CEO, says Nicholas Katzenbach, he was "very satisfied, too satisfied, too involved in the *Post* and not sufficiently involved in the rest of the group."[3] At board meetings, when division heads presented their reports to the directors, Donny would behave as if he were one of the former. "He never acted as a director in my presence," says Mark Edmiston. "He didn't question my report or in any way take that role. This is not a guy who is the CEO of a company and could move over and be the CEO of another company." He was happy tending to the paper and spending evenings with his family. "Don would rather go out and see the Safeway vice-president of advertising," Edmiston adds, "than mix with the powers that be.[4]

There are some who thought Donny carried his dislike of the public role too far. "Sometimes Don really should do some of the things Kay does very well," says Katzenbach. "She uses her social position very skillfully for the interests of the whole corporation. Don doesn't like that, and that's going to be a problem. Don will get out of things by saying he can't get a baby-sitter. Well, good God, he could afford to solve that problem."[5]

Within the *Post* itself, Donny consistently showed his preference for local news over national, bucking complaints that in his zeal to emphasize the former he was making the paper dull. To those who longed to see the *Post* a national paper like *The New York Times* he offered no hope. His vision extended only so far as Maryland and Virginia. Larry Kramer recalls "times when [Donny] would come downstairs when I was metro editor, and he would sit in my office, and without using any cheat-sheet, he would reel off the names of just about everybody on my staff and ask how they were doing individually. I had over a hundred people on my staff. I sometimes felt that I was in the job he really wanted. He loved local news."[6]

Kay Graham did not worry much about Donny's lack of enthusiasm for running her company. She enjoyed good health, a profitable company, a stable group of executives and editors—finally—and a son who was a bit square and narrow for her taste but who would take over when she chose. In the meantime, she was having fun.

She understood perfectly that the many honors and appointments that came her way came because she ran the company. She was happy to serve on the boards of universities (she was the first woman trustee of the University of Chicago) and journalism organizations (she was the first woman elected to the board of the Associated Press). In 1985, a survey of editors and reporters from newspapers across the country found her to be the most influential woman in America. (Astronaut Sally Ride took second, and Supreme Court justice Sandra Day O'Connor and Nancy Reagan tied for third.)[7] She was happy to be in a class by herself as the only woman CEO of a Fortune 500 company, happy to have become almost generic— "How many Katharine Grahams can you come up with?" an executive recruiter complained to a reporter for *The New York Times Magazine* about the scarcity of women suitable for major corporate boards.[8]

And she was delighted when Willy Brandt asked her to help him explore relationships between industrialized and underdeveloped nations, delighted to travel to Eastern Europe with investment banker Peter Peterson and David Rockefeller and other prominent men—"little groups of eminent people going to talk to prime ministers," as Kermit Lansner describes them.[9]

Kay moved in an orbit beyond the standard Washington and New York bigwigs. Marietta Tree recounted that after she invited Kay to a dinner "for one of her great friends, Arthur Schlesinger, her secretary called and said, 'Kay's very sorry she can't come, but she's got to do something about [Lee] Iacocca's birthday.' I thought, 'How times have changed.' "[10] At a state dinner for Italian prime minister Giulio Andreotti, Arnaud de Borchgrave watched enviously as the assembled heavyweights cultivated Kay to the exclusion of de Borchgrave himself. "One guy [I'd] been close to for a long time [was] national security advisor Brent Scowcroft. Whom was he hovering over? Kay Graham—that's where the real power [was]."[11]

Of course she attended Malcolm Forbes's seventieth-birthday bash at his Tangier palace overlooking the Mediterranean, along with everyone else who mattered, just as, the next year, she attended his funeral, where she was ushered to a front pew to join Mrs. Douglas MacArthur, Elizabeth Taylor, Richard Nixon, Lee Iacocca, and Blaine Trump.[12]

On June 30, 1987, Kay's children threw her a seventieth-birthday party that provided flesh-and-blood evidence of their mother's standing. Six hundred guests paid homage at a black-tie dinner held in a cavernous federal auditorium festooned with giant bouquets, sixty-foot curtains draping the building's soaring columns.[13] In *The New York Times,* Maureen Dowd called it "by far the largest and most impressive party in the capital since President Reagan's second inaugural."[14] Reagan himself paid Kay an almost unprecedented tribute by staying the whole evening, rather than the customary fifteen minutes. After the fish course he led Kay to the dance floor for a spin to the music conducted by society bandleader Peter Duchin.

Lally, who hatched the idea for the party and organized it—Donny served as emcee—had gone to Henry Kissinger for his suggestions on whom to invite. He was heavy on world leaders. "Heads started rolling on my mother's bedroom floor," Lally would later recall, as Kay insisted that only friends be invited. Friends indeed.

A cast of luminaries helped Kay celebrate: At dinner, she sat between the president and Secretary of State George Shultz. Also in attendance were justices of the Supreme Court, senators, ambassadors from several countries, network anchors, nearly every member of Reagan's Cabinet, the heads of Sony, IBM, Ford, General Motors, General Electric, Dow Jones. Among the others were Oscar de la Renta, who had designed the black-and-white polka-dotted gown Kay wore that evening, Malcolm Forbes, Rupert Murdoch, Otis Chandler, William Paley, Punch Sulzberger, Barbara Walters, Ted Koppel, H. Ross Perot, Warren Buffett, Helmut Kohl, former British prime minister James Callaghan, Israeli prime minister Yitzhak Rabin, I. M. Pei, Jack Valenti, Clare Boothe Luce, Brooke Astor, Ethel Kennedy, and Gordon Getty.

As usual, Art Buchwald was asked to make a toast. He brought down the house when he observed: "There's one word that brings us all together here tonight, and that word is 'fear.' " In his toast, Henry Kissinger paid sentimental tribute to his friendship with Kay Graham, calling it "one of the most important events of my life."[15] Meg Greenfield, George Will, and Mike Wallace also made toasts. The windup spot belonged to President Reagan, who took his wineglass with him to the podium and, after praising Kay, rasped, in a fine Humphrey Bogart imitation, "Here's looking at you, kid."[16]

Although the most celebrated figures in the national and international media were there to wish her well, Kay preferred that the working press not cover her own words of appreciation that evening. Perhaps the memory of her appalling performance at *Newsweek*'s fiftieth-anniversary party was too fresh.

Kay's decision to make the party off-limits to the press was criticized as "déclassé" by *Post* ombudsman Joe Laitin.[17] Given the scathing coverage of Washington parties in "Style," it was also considered hypocritical. Not even the guest list was released. Her top reporters and editors were invited guests—Bob Woodward, for example, but not Carl Bernstein*—but those who had to cover the event as the news it was were stuck interviewing limousine drivers, caterers, florists, and arriving luminaries. They pounced on Malcolm Forbes, who came via helicopter bearing a bottle of Château Lafite-Rothschild from 1916. "I chose one . . . that was laid down the

---

*Nora Ephron, his ex-wife, was invited, as was Margaret Jay, his former lover, who accompanied her father, James Callaghan.

same year she was," he commented. "Like Kay Graham, it's beyond price."[18]

The New York Times devoted half a page to two stories on the party. When Ben Bradlee noticed his rival, executive editor Max Frankel, making frequent runs outside to feed information to *Times* reporter Maureen Dowd, Bradlee followed suit, leaving the dinner or sending others to deliver dispatches to *Post* reporters.

Even that party, an unabashed tribute largely planned and executed by Lally, made Kay anxious. No matter how often she entertained, how well, or how coveted the invitations to her parties, she was always noticeably nervous. "Here's a woman who had everyone in Washington in her home," says Thelma McMahon, "and it was like day one for each event—her tables wouldn't be right, or everything wouldn't be perfect."[19]

Newsweek parties at presidential nominating conventions were most nerve-wracking for Kay because there was competition for the most important guests. Mel Elfin remembers that before one luncheon at a Republican convention, she said, "Nobody's going to come. Why are we doing this?" She ordered her people to the telephone to call "their contacts who had turned it down, the big names, pleading with them to come."[20] The lunch was called for twelve noon, and precisely at noon the first guest, Nelson Rockefeller, arrived. Kay's transformation from raving boss to gracious hostess was astonishing.

She left nothing to chance or spontaneity. Hers, says Lester Bernstein, were "well-managed parties."[21] She agonized over her guest lists. If the president of a university was on the list, then the *Post*'s education editor had to be. That he would attend was a given. No excuses or regrets were tolerated. This was work, and his role was to keep the conversation going, relevant, provocative—to a point—and current.

Andrew Barnes recalls receiving what was really more a summons than an invitation when he was education editor at the *Post*. "Very much like being a servant," he says. His orders were clear: he was to "appropriately question and further the conversation with the invited guest."[22] Certain unwritten rules applied. "You were never supposed to talk to other staffers," says Mel Elfin, "you were always supposed to talk to the guests. [She would] grab me by the arm: 'you, you go over and talk to him.' "[23]

Just as Kay acted as if every party were her first, so she acted as if every speech were her first. She continued to shake as she spoke, and even before the most congenial and admiring of audiences. And if a live audience frightened Kay Graham, television cameras were a nightmare. Richard Clurman mentions the paradox that this woman, routinely called the most powerful in the world, "is someone who falls to pieces in front of your face when she has to appear on a television program."[24]

Then there were the trips abroad, which, no matter how often she traveled, continued to make her almost as nervous as they made her designated companions. "People who traveled internationally with her tended to wind up on the floor," says a former *Newsweek* editor, who claims relief at not having been among the chosen. "Everything had to go right, everything. If anything went wrong, God help the person involved."[25]

Kay reportedly still suffered from memories of a gaffe she had committed in Japan in 1965 during an audience with Emperor Hirohito: "Mrs. Graham, it's wonderful to have you here," the Emperor told her. "Is this your first trip to Japan?" "Yes, it is," she replied, and then, gesturing to her companion, Osborn Elliott, she added, "Mr. Elliott has been to Japan many times, and of course, Mr. Elliott was here during the war."

Subsequently, says a former *Newsweek* employee, she would become "petrified" before interviews with foreign officials. "I can't do it," she would moan. "I hope I don't do the Emperor of Japan again." If she sometimes took her frustration out on her companions, she was toughest on herself. "She agonized," recalls the man. "She couldn't sleep. [She] stayed up all night worrying about the image [she] gave to the Emperor of Japan."[26]

In 1986, Mark Edmiston escorted Kay on a tour of Asia, assiduously arranging every detail, even renting an extra hotel room in South Korea and stocking it with twelve locals whose job it was to see that the cars for Kay and her entourage arrived on time. A *Post* reporter fell asleep at a banquet in Korea and, even worse, asked dumb questions when he was awake. As punishment, he was made London bureau chief.[27]

Kay's expectations of her employees were so high because she recognized her own dearth of knowledge about foreign affairs. Worse yet, she knew that others recognized it. "To be blunt about it," says Murrey Marder, "none of us was very impressed with Kay's knowledge. She just did not know that much about world affairs."[28] A former editor observes that "if you get into a discussion with the lady about anything serious, it's not going to last very long, because she's out of her depth immediately." He claims that prior to an interview with West German chancellor Helmut Kohl, she was seen in the lobby of a Bonn hotel being briefed by Meg Greenfield, Jim Hoagland, and a former Reagan administration official on "unbelievably elementary" points of German affairs.[29]

Part of the problem was that Kay found it difficult to bone up by reading. "I think [she] absorbed a lot of her information orally, in conversation," says Karl Meyer. "I don't think she was a reader of books."[30] Consequently, she demanded intensive briefings, which *Newsweek* editors delivered via color-coded briefing books. "Make it simple," one magazine executive advised Maynard Parker. "Going to Singapore, blue; going to Manila, orange; get the orange folders out, take the blue ones back, never read the wrong folder. Here are all the clips, here are the key issues, here are the people you're going to meet, boom, boom, boom."[31]

But if she became frightened, the executive explains, she instantly forgot all she had learned. "Her lack of self-confidence deep down made it more difficult for her to learn." It should have become easier with each trip, but it did not. Kay seemed unable to apply and adapt what she had learned about one country's coup or civil war or stagnant economy or parliamentary system to another's. It was as if she were starting from scratch each time, as if she had no background.

The person who worked the hardest and bore the brunt of Kay's anxieties was Liz Hylton, whom Peter Derow describes as Kay's "secretary, assistant, unpacker, packer."*[32] Liz is, by all accounts, a remarkably sweet-tempered person—"an absolute saint," says Thelma McMahon.[34] Liz did not hold grudges, she was not vindictive, she was understanding. She was, in other words, a good target for Kay to strike at in fear and frustration.

Mark Edmiston remembers the stop in South Korea during the Asia tour: "We had a breakfast at seven with the foreign minister. And we all arrived. At seven the foreign minister [was there]. We all greeted him. No Katharine; seven-ten, still no Katharine. Not typi-

---

*"Liz was always left behind [at the airport] with the baggage," recalls Mel Elfin. "I would find there were fifteen pieces of luggage, and there was poor Liz."[33]

cal, so I called her room. No answer. My first thought was she'd been kidnapped. I thought, 'Oh, my God. Not on my watch, please.' We sent people all around the hotel. Finally, at about seven twenty-five she just kind of strolled in and was shocked to find the foreign minister there. She thought [the breakfast was at] seven-thirty. I heard from one of my people who worked up in the suite [that later] she practically chased poor Liz Hylton around the room."[35]

One editor describes Liz as "married to Kay. If some man came along and wanted to marry Liz, Kay would offer this guy hundreds of thousands to get out of town."[36]

Bob Estabrook recalls Kay's mother descending upon London expecting the grand treatment. "She was obviously accustomed to having things go her way, and when she commanded the Savoy, it behaved."[37] For Kay, no matter how many years and how many trips, the Savoy would never quite completely behave.

Still, those who accompanied Kay recognized that for a CEO who owns the company, she did much more than she had to. As Mark Edmiston says, "She works hard at doing the job. She is not as quick as the best, by any means. But as a corporate CEO, she works a lot harder than [most]."[38]

And in her depth of knowledge, she is not so unlike other journalists. "We're all quick studies in a journalistic sense," says Kermit Lansner. He gives Kay her due as "a very intelligent woman" and argues that she is no different from Punch Sulzberger today or William Randolph Hearst or Henry Luce in the past: they all traveled with editors and prompters and briefers.[39] Even Murrey Marder argues that tales of Kay's ignorance on foreign affairs are overdone: "compared to what?"[40]

To her credit, when interviewing presidents and prime ministers, she never tried to hog the limelight or to tack her byline on someone else's work. When she did get the byline, it was almost always because her position brought her opportunities that would not otherwise have come her way. When Mikhail Gorbachev came to Washington in 1987, for example, she accepted an invitation to interview him at the Soviet embassy; and in 1979, she agreed to interview the deposed Shah of Iran in Cairo shortly after he had had surgery to remove his cancerous spleen.

Back at the *Post,* she was humble and self-deprecating. When she had administration officials and other VIPs in for lunch she would, says Murrey Marder, "mostly listen." Her innocence of the details of some issues could assist the experienced journalists in the room. "Sometimes it helps to have somebody ask an unsophisticated question."[41]

And it is to Kay's credit that she strove to prove and improve herself. When they visited South Korea, Mark Edmiston recalls, they "did everything, including go into the tunnels. Kay was there, down in the ground underneath the DMZ. She wanted to do everything."[42]

Neither the world nor the Post Company's bottom line would have suffered if Kay Graham had stayed home, or if she had traveled but been unable to distinguish the foreign minister of one African country from the prime minister of another. She could have received foreign dignitaries as they passed through Washington instead of seeking out these people on their turf—each time with her notebook and her reputation in hand.

She never stopped pushing herself. A person with a sweeter temper and a stronger self-image might have pushed herself without requiring those around her to suffer, but it is still more remarkable that Kay would not rest on her family fortune and the Pentagon Papers and Watergate laurels.

Although this one might dismiss her as not as smart, certainly not as educated, as her mother; and that one might dismiss her as not nearly as knowledgeable about world affairs as her husband, Kay never stopped trying to match Agnes and Phil. And that is what makes Kay Graham Kay Graham; what distinguishes her from scores of rich widows who make a show of running their husbands' businesses while they devote themselves to good works and pleasant lunches.

Eugene Patterson calls Kay multifaceted: "She can be very cruel as well as very sensitive and kind. She's got it all. She instantly regrets any unkindness that she commits. Her face is like a schoolgirl's sometimes."*[43]

Jean Friendly cannot forget how Kay unceremoniously shoved Al Friendly aside. And yet she also cannot forget that after Kay was notified of Al's suicide, "she must have stayed up most of the night. She wrote me a letter that [was] incredible, it was so wonderful, and

---

*At lunch once with Patterson and Bradlee, Kay joked about LBJ's secretary of state, Dean Rusk, a man with no family money, accepting a teaching post at a public school. "And now he's going to the University of Georgia, for God's sake." She was flushed with embarrassment when she realized that Patterson was a Georgia graduate.[44]

she was here the next morning to see me. [She] had a wonderful celebration of his life at the *Post,* where a lot of people spoke, and it was exactly what he would have wanted. Kay was fabulous."[45]

Lester Bernstein is more bitter than most on the subject of Kay Graham, and yet he says that "she's capable of the really compassionate gesture." When his son, a schizophrenic, committed suicide, Bernstein was working at RCA, having left *Newsweek* and not intending to return. "I got this wonderfully compassionate letter from her written out of her own experience with Phil, and I was bowled over by it. There was no reason for her to do it. I was a figure of the past. It must have been a painful thing for her to have done."[46]

Even Morton Mintz, whom William Greider describes as "the incarnation of the 'Last Angry Man,' " left the *Post* with a warm feeling for Kay. In the spring of 1988, Mintz wrote a note to Ben Bradlee reminding him that eighteen years had passed since Mintz's last merit raise, that he was making $44 less a week than the average white male reporter—despite much praise by Bradlee, among others, and many awards. Bradlee's reply, Mintz says, was "so goddamned nasty that that was what snapped it. I said, 'I'm getting out of this place.' "

Having pummeled Kay for ten years in *Fruits of Your Labor,* Mintz was surprised to see her at his retirement party. She had not been scheduled to speak, but after everyone else had spoken—including Bradlee, who heaped high praise on Mintz—and Mintz was on his way to the microphone, Kay gestured to him and asked if he would mind her saying a few words. "She made a very gracious little impromptu talk," Mintz recounts, in which she observed that he was one of the few people who had been at the *Post* so long that he spanned her husband's tenure, her own, and her son's. "It was genuinely warm," Mintz says, still sounding astonished two years later.

Mintz also gives Kay Graham her due as a publisher. Revealing the chicanery of the rich and powerful was often key in stories Mintz reported. "In a way I was going after her people, and I think she put up with it a hell of a lot better than a lot of publishers would."[47]

Eugene Patterson remembers conversations with Kay about this or that upcoming Washington party in which she started "sounding like the quintessential snob, but she [was] capable of making very touching gestures." Around the same time that Mintz was retiring, a few of Patterson's friends, recognizing that he was approaching the end of his newspaper career, decided to throw a party for him in Washington. They took over the dining room at the National Press Club and invited some 250 of his friends. The hosts asked him whom from the *Post* they should invite, and Patterson gave them a list of names that did not include Kay Graham's. "I did not want to bother Kay. This was a provincial party. This was not a Washington party." About a week before the event, Kay's secretary called his: " 'Mrs. Graham has not received her invitation to Mr. Patterson's party yet, and she knows it must have gotten lost in the mail. Could you please send her another one?' She showed up [at the party], and sat there. It was a plebeian evening by her entertainment standards. These were just working stiffs. She fit right in and made me feel like a million bucks."[48]

For old friends, Kay offered kind words and concrete help. She did all she could to secure medical help for Edward Prichard, who, at the end of his life, was diabetic and blind. She was determined, says his widow, Lucy, "to get him to Baltimore to see if something more could be done." Nothing could. Kay attended a dinner friends of his gave in his honor in Kentucky shortly before he died.[49]

When Joseph Kraft died in 1986, Kay was at Polly's side within hours. She delivered a eulogy at his funeral, and she opened her house for a reception immediately after. Polly recalls warnings from friends in New York: " 'Washington is a cold and dreadful town, and it's going to be tough, and you're going to be alone.' I wasn't at all, and one of the reasons I wasn't was Kay. People can say how difficult she is, and she can be moody and all of the things people will tell you, very tough and rough and men. But for me she has always been extraordinarily human."[50]

"Unpredictable" may be a better word to describe Kay than "moody." She can turn from friendly to dismissive without warning or apparent reason, even with good friends. "When I see her now," says Richard Clurman, "it can be as if she's seeing a stranger, or her arms can be around me. Which of the two emotions I will be exposed to is totally unpredictable."[51] According to one former editor, "Something will strike her in the middle of a conversation, and the temperature will go from near boiling to something cryogenic. That's her style."[52]

Joe Laitin had known Kay before he went to work at the *Post,* because during stints as a PR man he had accompanied Cabinet members to her luncheons. He is still not certain why Kay turned on him. "The first year I was there, this woman fell all over me, and I must say I was flattered." His first day on the job, she came to his office and told him how "delighted" she was that he was the new ombudsman. " 'Oh, look,' " she said, suddenly getting up, " 'I'm expecting a call from Italy. Would you mind too much coming up to my office and talking to me, because I don't want to miss this call.' I spent an hour and a half, she sat in a chair with her leg over the arm, real tomboy. I saw a side of her that I had never seen before. She talked like a truck driver. I was taken aback a little. I several times made a gesture to rise, but she wanted to talk. 'Look, now Joe, I hope that anytime you want to see me, you'll feel free to come up here.'

"Every time I ran into her, in the hallway, at receptions, she'd seek me out, she'd introduce me as though she was proud. I was practically walking on holy water, and then *whammy.*" It was obvious that she had "soured" on him, but he could not figure out why. He guesses that somebody on the *Post* who thought she was putting him on too much of a pedestal had "poisoned" her against him; it might have been somebody such as Bob Woodward, whom Laitin had criticized in his popular internal memos. Or it could have been something more obvious and simple—Kay's wealth, for instance. "I have found very often that very wealthy, insulated people can turn you off like that," Laitin says, snapping his fingers.

When he went to pay his "last respects" to Kay, "she was pretty frosty to me. She opened the conversation by saying, 'I understand that you've developed a scratchy relationship with a lot of the editors and reporters on the fifth floor.' I said, 'Well, if I didn't, I don't think I would be doing the job that I assume *Post* management brought me in to do.' We went on this way, and I was really disheartened at this kind of a farewell." The tone of the conversation did not improve. "You've been here two years," she said to him. "What do you think the *Post* needs most?" "Competition," Laitin answered, and that sparked what he describes as "a fifteen-minute lecture on the virtues of monopoly." She argued that because the *Post* was effectively the only place to put advertising, "we [got] more money, which we [could] then put back in the paper."

That day, it seemed to Laitin as if every topic of conversation was the wrong one. For a long time thereafter, he would never be the right topic of conversation for Kay Graham.

At a luncheon a few months after Laitin left the *Post,* he sat next to former CIA chief Richard Helms, who told him that he had had lunch with Kay the week before and mentioned how much he missed Laitin's Sunday column. "I wish somebody had told me that was the wrong thing to say to Kay Graham," Helms noted.

Later a thaw began, but it was never complete. Laitin saw Kay at a cocktail reception preceding a banquet for the president of South Korea. He decided to "bite the bullet and go right up to her." She was "not uncordial, a little bit snappish. She didn't ask what I was doing or whether I was making a living." After Kay was presented with a journalism award, she gave a short talk and took questions from the audience. Laitin recalls that "someone asked her about the [job of] ombudsman, and she said, 'Well, there's a former ombudsman of the *Post* sitting right in the front row, why don't you ask him?' I took that as a signal that all was forgiven, whatever I was guilty of."[53]

Laitin notes how surprised he was by Kay's swinging her leg over the arm of the chair and talking like a truck driver; he was obviously charmed by this behavior. Indeed, Kay's employees and friends found these unexpected spurts of earthiness enormously appealing.

The day after *Newsweek*'s fiftieth-anniversary party, a reception was held for staffers who had helped as ushers and in other such roles. Edmiston asked Kay to thank them personally, and she did, with unforgettable candor. "I had to go to the bathroom before I went onstage," she confessed to the group of workers about the evening before. "I was afraid I was going to pee in my pants."[54]

Kay Graham employed a handsome young man to organize meetings for *Newsweek*. No one knew better than he how handsome he was, and as he did the advance work for these meetings, many of them in warm climates, he liked to strut about in very short shorts. Kay attended one sales meeting at which he was sporting a particularly skimpy pair. "I was really proud of myself," she told Mark Edmiston over breakfast the next day. "I walked in yesterday, and there was that goddamned [guy] in little tiny short pants and he had his feet up on the table like this"—she was wearing a dress, but she showed Edmiston anyway—"and I walked right over to him and said, 'I can see your balls, put your feet down.' I'm so proud of myself. It really bothers me that he does that, and I walked over and told him that."[55]

Chapter 24

LETTING GO

Kay had begun to spend more and more time at her house on Martha's Vineyard, and next to none at Glen Welby, which she happily sold to Donny. The Virginia farm, with its memories of her strangled marriage and Phil's suicide, thus passed to the next generation. She had bought the house on the Vineyard—in the town of West Tisbury, on 183 acres commanding an ocean view and a secluded beach—in the early 1970s, and it was hers alone. Neither Phil nor Agnes had ever stirred the sand or dominated the conversation or diminished Kay there.

In that house, Kay is the star, and on an island full of media stars—more summer celebrities on the East Coast than anywhere outside the Hamptons—she is as awesome as any of them. Walter Cronkite has a house there, as do Mike Wallace and Art Buchwald and James Reston, who co-owns the summertime semiweekly *Vineyard Gazette.* Also in August and weekend residence are Jacqueline Onassis and Robert McNamara and scores of others who can be found in Georgetown or on Manhattan's Upper East Side when they are not pretending to get away from it all by going to the Vineyard.

Another neighbor is Robert Bernstein, former chairman and president of Random House, who finally, after summers of trying, in 1989 persuaded Kay to sign a contract to write her memoirs for Alfred A. Knopf, a division of Random House.*[1] (Knopf had also published Merlo Pusey's biography of her father.)

---

*Two weeks later, Bernstein was deposed by the owner of Random House, S. I. "Si" Newhouse, Jr. In April 1992, with Kay's memoirs not yet scheduled for publication, her editor, Elisabeth Sifton, resigned from Knopf.

Writing one's memoirs, wrapping things up and acknowledging that life is approaching its close, is seldom easy. And for Kay it was especially hard. Not only was there the pain of trying to come to terms with the ruin of her childhood and her marriage, but her lack of assurance made her fear that she could not do it, that her memoirs would be banal, boring. Unlike a speech, which was fleeting, a book sat on the shelf to be looked at, and perhaps laughed at, for years to come.

Except for her letters of condolence, when her feelings and sometimes her regrets ran so strong that she could get them on paper, Kay had never distinguished herself as a writer. Yet her image was tied to crusading journalism. While she was known never to write first drafts of speeches or articles, for the woman who had become the nation's most admired and prominent publisher a ghostwriter was out of the question.

So she approached this project in a way that those in the writing business found highly peculiar. She quietly lined up a speechwriter and a vice-president for research from the Washington Post Company, along with a young man whose position might be best described as "technician," to gather material, organize it, and write the first draft of the book. She then began the arduous process—as if she were the biographer of someone else—of interviewing people who knew her well, who knew Phil, who knew her parents. It was as if she were not confident of getting the facts of her own life right, as if she did not trust her memory or her interpretation, or her insights.

She had to struggle to sort out and describe her relationship with her mother, and also to guard against Phil Graham's taking over her book as he had her life. Charles Peters recalls recent lunches with Kay in which they "chewed over" anecdotes from her life, most of which featured Phil in the starring role.[2]

Lester Bernstein cannot get over how peculiar he finds Kay's interviewing others about herself: "What it does in a funny way is recapitulate the way she has lived her career, constantly leaning on other people, so that now she apparently needs other people even to tell her about her [own] life."[3]

Bernstein was among several of Kay's fired employees whom she asked, with no evident embarrassment, to sit for interviews. Liz Hylton called Mark Meagher: "Mrs. Graham wants you to do a favor for her." Meagher replied, "I'll think about it," and now says, "I'm still thinking about it."[4]

Several people who know Kay well, all of whom have been interviewed or have been asked for an interview, question whether she will complete the book. Mark Meagher says that it "may be too painful for her to publish when she gets it finished."[5] One old and close friend who has been interviewed doubts that the memoirs will appear. "I think Kay is slipping. Her memory is not what it was. The more I saw her, the more I talked to her, I had a feeling that probably it [was] too late."[6] June Bingham had a similar sense about her old friend when Kay came to interview her: "I think her memory is coming and going." A former editor of *The Washington Post Magazine* recalls a dinner with Kay in the mid-1980s: "All of a sudden she would seem to be on another planet." She appeared to be "looking for something or somebody, and [not aware] you were there anymore."[7]

As early as 1985, Kay told Mark Edmiston that she had hired someone who was "collecting notes" for her memoirs, but that she would not publish them while she was in a position of power.[8] Her signing with Knopf, as well as the front-page story about it in "Style," was a hint, certainly, that she had moved a step closer to letting Donny take the position for which he had been slated since childhood. He was then forty-four. Anyone who knew Kay in 1963, when she was thrust into Phil's role, would have bet that Donny would not have had to wait that long.

There were hints aplenty, however, that for all his self-effacing ways, Donny was going to be a tough leader. He was methodically maneuvering his people into place: people whose loyalties were to him, whose personalities suited him, who made him feel comfortable and confident. Ben Bradlee, who could not help but compare the son with the father, was not one of them. Since the day in 1984 when Donny promoted his choice, Leonard Downie, to managing editor en route to executive editor, Donny had started to declaw Ben Bradlee.

Donny asked Joe Laitin to assess objectively a contretemps involving a *Post* story that had angered a White House staffer and Bradlee's insistence that the paper not accede to the man's demand for an apology. Laitin agreed with Bradlee that no apology should be made. Donny then asked Laitin to call the White House aide and explain the decision. Laitin was reluctant but felt he had no choice. He told Bradlee what he was about to do, and Bradlee became furious, Laitin recalls. "That guy's just off the radar screen," he said.

"I don't think you should call him. That matter is settled and done with." Laitin agreed to wait until Bradlee tried again to persuade Donny that no call should be made. Two hours later Bradlee returned, looking defeated. "Well, I tried," he said, "go ahead and do your thing." That Donny Graham had overruled Bradlee after he had gone in to see him, Laitin concludes, "told me an awful lot." Laitin could see that Bradlee was "toothless. He really had no power."

Laitin also remembers Bradlee's anger when, long before he had expressed an intention of retiring anytime soon, Leonard Downie told a *Wall Street Journal* reporter that Donny had tapped him as Bradlee's successor.[9] For Bradlee, being shoved into an editor emeritus role was enormously embarrassing, even degrading.

The atmosphere and expectations took their toll. For some time, the big stories that used to get Bradlee's juices going were slipping by him. The quintessential insider seemed somehow out of the loop. *Post* media critic Howard Kurtz later reported that during the Persian Gulf war "it was clear that the editor's baton had been passed. Downie served as field commander, overseeing the deployment of reporters. . . . Bradlee . . . played the role of retired general."[10] On one story that turned into a front-page shocker, with lurid tales about a congressional aide, suicide, homosexuality, and sexual harassment, Bradlee was not even consulted. Downie later explained that he had forgotten to tell Bradlee about it before he went home.[11]

With the ascendancy of Donny and Downie, it grew more acceptable to criticize Bradlee. It became almost a cliché to describe Bradlee as superficial, all one-liners, all style, while the substance was handled by the likes of Howard Simons, who wouldn't attract a second look, much less a cult of idolators. Nods of understanding greeted the complaint by one editor who emerged from a meeting griping that Bradlee had the attention span of a gnat.[12]

It became fashionable to observe that the hated *Washington Times* covered local news better than the *Post* did, and did it with one-tenth the staff. Joe Laitin points out that the *Post*'s "Metro" staff numbered 155—more than the entire staffs of many respectable dailies— and Frank Waldrop suggests, "If they fired every second man it would improve the paper."[13]

Others lamented that for too long, local reporting was seen as something to transcend; that Bradlee was constantly trying to scoop *The New York Times* rather than put out the best paper he could for readers in the District, Maryland, and Virginia. "If it wasn't political scandal or politics on the national level," says John Hanrahan, "Bradlee was pretty much not interested in it." Some regretted that the subjects Morton Mintz paid attention to so bored Bradlee that a reporter of Mintz's quality was derided rather than nurtured. "What are you writing this crap for?" Bradlee asked one man who covered agriculture.[14]

It was left to the old guys to remember that Bradlee could be an inspirational leader who could pull more out of reporters and editors than any editor anywhere else. "Ben isn't an intellectual, he is superficial," says Kermit Lansner. "But he's one hell of a good newspaperman."[15]

Lansner remembers seeing Bradlee the day he turned sixty-eight. What was he going to do? Lansner asked him. "First he goes through this long routine: 'I've got a letter on Donny's desk. It's a letter saying, "I resign. Anytime you want it, just sign it and I resign." ' But really he's saying, 'You'll have to carry me out. You'll have to fire me.' "[16]

That was something Kay Graham would never do, and she, after all, was still in charge, still hanging on.

When she said a few years before that she believed in mandatory retirement for everyone except owners,[17] she might have added, "And Ben Bradlee." Some said that she was not eager for Bradlee to go because once he did, the pressure would increase on her to give up the CEO position to Donny. Kay and Bradlee were so strongly linked that it was hard to imagine her staying on beyond him, or vice versa. "Once Watergate consummated everybody's relations," says Kermit Lansner, "they were together for the ages." The *Post* would have had to become third-rate, Lansner comments, before Kay would have forced Bradlee's retirement.[18]

While it was reported that Kay had even taken to disparaging him occasionally—"Ben hasn't had an original idea in twenty years," she is alleged to have said—that was irrelevant. Ben Bradlee was an icon. The Post Company's corporate image was tangled in his image. Nicholas von Hoffman calls him "a major corporate asset," as Walter Cronkite was to CBS. Getting rid of Bradlee would have been like trying "to fire the Statue of Liberty."[19]

In mid-March 1991, Kay Graham refuted Marietta Tree and Peter Derow and Arnaud de Borchgrave, who had begun saying that she was "going to be like Queen Victoria, going to die on the job." She announced that she was stepping down as CEO.

She was passing the title and responsibilities of CEO of the corporation to Donny, putting under his purview the television stations, the cable stations, *Newsweek,* the Everett *Herald,* and other properties. In addition, Donny would retain his cherished role as publisher of *The Washington Post.* (She would remain chairman of the board of directors.)

She was giving Donny something more—letting him choose his own team. And so Richard Simmons's retirement as president and chief operating officer of the corporation was announced at the same time as Kay's retirement. Donny would be president. The title of chief operating officer as well as the newly created title of executive vice-president went to Donny's pick, Alan Spoon, the thirty-nine-year-old president of *Newsweek;* he had worked in marketing and finance at the *Post,* in the supervision of the Post Company's television stations, and elsewhere throughout the company.

"I really owe a lot to Dick Simmons," Kay said as she credited him with making the company a "much better managed and more profitable enterprise."[20] Simmons reciprocated, in a way: "We're the odd couple, but we've had a hell of a run," he told a *New York Times* reporter.[21] His numbers were spectacular. Wall Street analysts commended him for avoiding the 1980s rush to overpay for media properties. One analyst called Simmons's tenure "one of the best ten years that anybody has seen in any company in any stock." In 1981, when Simmons joined the company, its stock was trading at $27 a share. Ten years later it was trading at $245 a share.[22]

Simmons, fifty-six, was not Kay's exact chronological contemporary, but they had been together so long—at least by Post Company standards—that he was seen as the most important player on her business team. He would remain both a director of the company and president of the *International Herald Tribune,* but would retire to teaching at Queens College in New York and the University of Richmond business school.

Kay's *Newsweek* team stayed together, but with some changes. Rick Smith retained the title of editor in chief and succeeded Spoon as president, thus, for the first time, breaching that iron newsmagazine rule of separation of church and state. Maynard Parker, of Hitler-diary fame, kept his title as editor and took over day-to-day control of the magazine. Mark Edmiston had said that because of the diary fiasco, "as long as Kay was around, Maynard would never be editor of *Newsweek*."[23] But now Donny was calling the shots.

Kay was careful to say, and say again, that she would not be looking over Donny's shoulder. But she also insisted that she did not plan to retire to tennis and travel.[24] She expected to be at the office every day—there were those memoirs to write—but she vowed not to interfere with her son and his men. "Don and Alan are well prepared by talent, training, and experience to lead the company into the twenty-first century," she reiterated.[25] She said nothing about the other key member of the team, Leonard Downie.

Once Kay announced her departure, that Bradlee's announcement would follow turned from speculation to inevitability. It came, finally, in June 1991, a month after Kay formally passed the torch to Donny. And just as CBS would never really let Cronkite go, neither would the Post Company let Bradlee go. He would become a vice-president of the newspaper and a director of the company, and he too would write his memoirs. Leonard Downie was named the new executive editor, and Robert Kaiser was promoted from deputy managing editor to managing editor.

On the day Bradlee was to make his announcement, in the lower left-hand corner of the *Post*'s front page was a story slugged "ozone"—a ruse to keep the news from leaking until later that day. It was also an inside joke, among those who knew that few subjects made Bradlee's eyes glaze over more quickly than the depletion of the ozone layer. Under the new regime, in-depth stories about science, the environment, and business would be more than inside jokes.

After Bradlee, the person on the *Post* most closely identified with Kay Graham was Meg Greenfield—also the person considered most likely the next to go. Although it is true that Donny had just become publisher when Phil Geyelin was deposed and Greenfield anointed, it was clear that she had been Kay's choice. And while Greenfield is known for ruling her page with an iron hand, she is also known for being extremely deferential to, almost frightened of, Donny.[26] Just after Kay announced her retirement, *Washingtonian* reported that Greenfield bought a house near Puget Sound. "Another sign of a retirement?" the magazine asked, and noted that then foreign editor David Ignatius—Paul's son—"covet[ed]" her job.[27]

As for the new regime, Donny Graham and Leonard Downie had been allies from the start of Donny's career on the *Post*. Both men had an interest in local and suburban news, and a love for the *Post* rather than an awe for the corporation. Both were family men, private men, men who despite their vastly dissimilar backgrounds (Downie is the son of a milkman) would always feel uncomfortable in political and social Washington. Likewise, the older generation of newsmen would never feel comfortable with Downie—or Donny for that matter. "I'm not very happy about his putting Mr. Downie in there," says Harvey Segal. "[He] struck me as a very colorless kid from Ohio."[28] Joe Laitin calls him "bloodless, a tough goody-two-shoes. He'll always come in under budget, the paper will always go to press on time, he'll always have six inches on one side and six inches on the other."[29]

About the paper the two men produce, William Greider says, "It fits Don's character, and Downie's too." He points out that nobody plays the role of "house crank" any longer, as he did in the 1970s, when he was encouraged to "write eccentric things, go off in odd directions. There's no Morton Mintz. It's a blander, more moderated place."[30] Another former staffer terms it "boring. Downie's only larger picture is not to make trouble. The *Post* has become a dull, gray place under him." And about Downie's boss, one former editor observes, "If Ben Bradlee is the Humphrey Bogart of journalism, Don Graham is the Wally Cox."[31]

In a sense, Kay Graham was born in 1963, when she was forced into the fray. For everything else that can be said of her, she conquered that challenge.

Today, she is one of the wealthiest women in the world, worth some $490 million; at her retirement, she was one of only two female heads of Fortune 500 companies. Her empire, besides the *Post* and *Newsweek,* encompasses the Everett *Herald;* the Washington Post Writers Group; a fifty-percent interest in the Los Angeles Times/ Washington Post News Service; a fifty-percent ownership of the *International Herald Tribune;* twenty-six percent of Cowles Media, which includes the Minneapolis *Star Tribune;* a twenty-percent interest in the *National Journal;* one-third of a Virginia newsprint mill; four television stations and fifty-three cable television systems; the Stanley H. Kaplan Education Center, a chain of schools at which students are tutored for college admissions tests; Legi-Slate, a service which tracks actions of Congress and federal regulatory agencies; part ownership of American Personal Communications, which is developing a tiny wireless phone; eighty percent of the Gaithersburg Gazette Company, publisher of eleven weekly papers; and fifteen percent of ACTV, a producer of interactive television.

During the 1980s, profits in several sectors of her company were spectacular—a profit margin of thirty-nine percent in the middle of the decade for the television stations, for example—but profits at the *Post,* which contributes about half of the company's profits and sales, gave new meaning to Warren Buffett's assertion that a monopoly newspaper is like an "unregulated tollbooth." The *Post* enjoyed profits four times higher than the national average for newspapers.

Kay Graham is not only one of the country's wealthiest women, but also one of its most powerful *people.* As is said to the point of cliché, whoever controls the means of communication has the power. Via *The Washington Post* and *Newsweek,* the correspondents from Kay's company cover the world. A survey of members of Congress showed that eighty-two percent read *The Washington Post* each day (compared with sixty-seven percent for *The New York Times* and thirty-one for *The Wall Street Journal*); so do the president, justices of the Supreme Court, and virtually every member of the Washington bureaus of newspapers from across the country and around the world. When *The Washington Post* takes an editorial position, hundreds of editorial-page editors follow suit. "The power is to set the agenda," Kay Graham once said. "What we print and what we don't print matter a lot." Her *International Herald Tribune* brings *Post* editorials and stories to the world's business and governing elite (at least one in four readers is on the board of directors of a major corporation).[32] Her Los Angeles Times/Washington Post syndicate dispatches *Post* stories to some four hundred dailies nationwide.

"She didn't know from nothing," says Betty Frank.[33] And yet somehow she chose the right people—Ben Bradlee on the editorial side and, ultimately, Richard Simmons on the business side—and turned what at Phil's death was a small and somewhat parochial family business into a behemoth.

It is true that Phil took the critical step—persuading his father-in-law in 1954 to buy the *Times-Herald*—that started the Post Company on its way to become the money machine it is today. Had Phil not made that move, the *Post* might not even exist, and had it survived, it likely would not have spawned a thriving communications company.

But it was Kay who made the company a financial success. Phil was always interested in power more than in profit, in politics more than in the bottom line. To Phil, says George Reedy, "a newspaper was just something that was useful as a political instrument, a social instrument, persuading people that they ought to do this or do that."[34] Kay's concern was never that. She was obsessed with making the company successful. She never had the political savvy or ambitions Phil had. She was haunted by the fear of not doing the job right. If the *Post* were not passed on to the next generation, it would be her fault.

Peter Derow and others could criticize Kay for not being bold enough in acquiring other media properties, but somehow—no matter who was actually making the decisions; in the end, she approved them all—the right decisions were made, especially in the 1980s, when other media companies paid too much, expanded too quickly, and suffered the consequences. While her competitors were acquiring big-city dailies that turned out to be shaky, Kay Graham was acquiring cellular phone systems, and then quickly selling them for a hefty profit. In a thorough examination of Kay's business performance, Larry van Dyne wrote that "sometimes the best decision in business is a decision *not* to make a deal." He supported that with an assessment made by another publisher: "Over the past twenty years she has made virtually all the key business decisions right." The proof, says van Dyne, is in the stock. Warren Buffett bought his shares in the Post Company in 1973 for $10.6 million. In 1991 those shares were worth $325 million.[35]

But what Kay Graham could be proudest of was that along with her financial success she achieved editorial quality. The mist of nostalgia about Phil Graham obscures the fact that, for all his brilliance, all his energy, all his nerve, he published what William Greider calls a "political-hack paper."[36] Frank Waldrop reduces Phil to "transition figure"; the *Post* "came to life under Katharine."[37] Kay brought it off by swallowing her fears and insecurities long enough to put Bradlee in charge. Whatever the arguments that the *Post* is overrated, under Bradlee it became a great American newspaper.

James Reston observes that Kay "has done a job Phil couldn't have done. He was too political, too hot. She brought balance that, brilliant as he was, he couldn't have."[38] Reston had earlier called Kay's role "one of the greatest achievements of journalism in this country."

The argument might be made that the *Post* has coasted for too long on its Pentagon Papers and Watergate fame, but the fact remains that in those two cases Kay made the right decisions—decisions that she knew could cost her her company. For that reason Bernard Nossiter, who had no trouble seeing Kay's shortcomings, called her "a great figure in American journalism. She risked the whole store twice on great issues of free press." To him, she was "considerably more than a businesswoman." It was a "brilliant, marvelous vision she had, not being cowed by the Johnson administration's security boys and [John] Mitchell's bully boys."[39] Kermit Lansner echoes that "under her tenure the two stories of our time were allowed to proceed. She did not stop them. However scared she was, however terrified, it doesn't matter. She did it."[40]

Frank Waldrop credits Kay with having "something very few people have: the capacity to be underestimated. It's a priceless gift. Phil was overestimated."[41] It is touching that Kay is not one who believes that Phil was overestimated. On the day in 1979 when she made Donny publisher, she paid tribute to his father for "infusing [the *Post*] with quality, energy, drive, momentum, local strength, and national impact, and—last but not least—his own characteristics: irreverence, healthy skepticism, and gaiety."[42]

Katharine Graham got out of the business at just the right moment—a time of gloominess over the economy, of plunging circulation and advertising, of threatened competition for classifieds from the Baby Bells. Richard Simmons called 1990 "a simply dreadful year." Advertising, he explained, "fell off a cliff." Kay admitted that it was "the first year in ten that we failed to meet our financial objectives." She correctly predicted that 1991 would be no better. In fact, it was worse.[43] Net income at the Washington Post Company dropped fifty-nine percent.*[44]

It is Donny Graham, not Kay, who will face some very tough business decisions which will, inevitably, have an impact on the editorial side. He took over when the only thing more dismal than the economy were the demographics facing the newspaper industry, with circulation headed nowhere but down.

Profits at *Newsweek* also were down in 1991. Operating income declined sixty-six percent from the year before.[45] What, if anything, to do about *Newsweek* will be one of the problems that Donny

---

*Things rebounded in 1992, when second-quarter earnings rose twenty-two percent over the same quarter in 1991; but advertising volume at the *Post* declined by 3.8 percent.

Graham will face. *Newsweek*'s own columnist Robert Samuelson has described newsmagazines as dinosaurs, struggling to compete with such nationally distributed newspapers as *USA Today* and *The Wall Street Journal*; with the increasing number and success of smaller "niche" magazines aimed at specific readers; with television news; with newspapers themselves, which increasingly resemble newsmagazines in their emphasis on features, on interpretation, on boxed sidebars. "The real value of newsmagazines?" says Mark Edmiston. "I'm not sure what it is. One could argue that there isn't any reason for them to be around."[46]

That Kay Graham was on the brink of selling *Newsweek* has been rumored for years. Just as unfailingly, she has denounced the reports as "one big lie from start to finish."[47] In fact, when she gave the *Post* over to Donny, she seemed increasingly focused on the magazine. She was, says Alan Finberg, "one of the proudest protectors of *Newsweek*. The question always comes up: You're a publicly owned company, don't you owe it to your stockholders to sell it? And she says consistently, 'No. It performs a very valuable service to this country. And I think we should continue to own it, improve it, do what we can for it.' "[48]

Those who understood Kay knew that she would never sell *Newsweek* because its international edition opened so many doors. It was on the strength of *Newsweek,* not that of the *Post,* that she obtained interviews with world leaders. She would not even let Richard Simmons terminate the Latin American edition of *Newsweek,* which was not profitable.[49]

On most business issues she deferred to Simmons, but never on the matter of *Newsweek.* "He would love to sell *Newsweek,*" says Edmiston. "He told me, 'I would sell this tomorrow if Kay would let me.' It's an underperformer by his way of operating. The *Post* has a twenty-percent [profit] margin, the television stations a forty-percent margin, *Newsweek* a ten- or twelve-percent margin. [A manager like Simmons] sells the underperforming asset, takes the cash, and reemploys it in something else. That's how I know Kay does care about it very much."[50]

The people at the magazine fear that Donny will not take the same approach. "Don could sell *Newsweek,*" says one former executive, who imagines him reasoning, "I really do want this to be a smaller company. I don't want to worry about this thing, it's not my cup of tea."[51]

Although Mark Edmiston acknowledges that Donny does not feel about *Newsweek* the way Kay does, he argues that Donny will hang on to it; that, as with Kay, his feelings for it are mingled in his feelings for Phil. Just as in business meetings Donny calls his mother "Mrs. Graham" or "Kay," he speaks of his father as "Phil." "The only time I ever heard him refer to his father as 'Dad,' " Edmiston observes, "was in [saying], 'My dad bought *Newsweek.*' "[52]

By the time Kay Graham retired, her children were long grown up, her brother and one sister dead, and the likelihood that she would marry again next to nil.

She continued to find her talented and "sparkling" older sister Bis somewhat daunting. On Bis's seventy-fifth birthday, Kay made a speech, Bis recalls, "about how she always envied me and my sophistication."[53] But the two grew closer by inclination and necessity. They were the surviving children who handled the details of Agnes's estate, the disposition of her art collection. The other sister, Ruth, remained apart. "Ruth was always on the sidelines," says Joanna Steichen.[54] But for Kay the most fulfilling family relationships were with her grandchildren. In those, especially with Lally's daughters, she shone.

In her relationships with men the questions remained: Did they want her or her money? Wouldn't the sort of man whom she would find appealing also be the sort who would want to take over her company?

And as Polly Kraft reflects, "What could a man give to Kay that she can't really get on her own? She said to me, not long ago, 'I might have married . . . but oh, Polly, to share a toothbrush or a bathroom with somebody at my age.' "[55]

The one man Kay might have married—had he asked her—was Robert McNamara. He had been very eligible since 1981, when his wife, Margaret, died. Like Kay, he had homes in Washington and on Martha's Vineyard; he was a year older than she; and he was the man on whom, after Warren Buffett, she relied most for business advice. He had spent more than two decades trying to redeem himself for his role in Vietnam, including thirteen years heading the World Bank. She knew that he did not want to run the Washington Post Company.

She also knew that he was attracted to Washington socialite Joan Braden. Despite her marriage to Tom Braden, she had carried on a very public affair with McNamara, becoming his frequent traveling and dinner partner. Not surprisingly, Polly Kraft reports, the two women dislike one another.[56]

Kay was jealous of Joan Braden, one top editor says; Kay "was the woman scorned." When she heard that Braden was going on a safari with McNamara, she is alleged to have said, "I hope it pours."[57] Braden also felt jealous of Kay, or so she claims in her "intimate memoir," *Just Enough Rope.* She opens the chapter "A Special Friend" by asking, "Am I keeping Robert McNamara from getting married?"—and admitting that she does not know the answer.[58]

In 1984, "Style" ran a long series on Robert McNamara that explored his relationship with Joan Braden. True to her hands-off-the-editorial-side policy, Kay did not try to interfere. She told Larry van Dyne, "That's the sort of thing they layer away from me, and it's something I *want* layered away from me."[59]

Kay's relationship with Warren Buffett became a business and personal friendship, although Buffett is separated—literally if not in the legal sense—from his wife.* Kay and Donny became part of a very exclusive, high-powered network around Buffett that includes such honchos as former ambassador and magazine publisher Walter Annenberg, American Express CEO James Robinson III, Microsoft chairman William Gates, all of whom look to Buffett as something of a guru.[61]

Buffett remains a major shareholder of the Washington Post Company (thirteen percent) and a close financial advisor—both business and personal—to Kay and Donny.[62] It was Buffett who, in 1985, advised Kay to make the biggest acquisition of her company's history. The Post Company paid $350 million for fifty-three cable systems owned by Capital Cities Communications. Federal regulations required that company, then trying to acquire ABC, to unload the cable systems because ABC had stations in some of the same markets as Capital Cities. The deal helped Kay—in 1991, operating income from her noncable television stations was down twenty-nine percent, while operating income from her cable stations was up twenty percent—and it also helped Buffett. He had become a major shareholder (seventeen percent) of Capital Cities, and the $350 million helped the

*Buffett continues to have an unconventional relationship with his wife, Susan, whom he reportedly sees about once a month. According to a recent profile in *The New York Times Magazine,* Susan lives in San Francisco, while Buffett lives in Omaha with Astrid Menks, "his companion and housekeeper."[60]

company finance its merger with ABC.[63] Shortly after the ABC deal was consummated, Buffett became a member of the Capital Cities/ ABC board and so had to leave the Post Company's board; serving on both would have been a conflict. But his ties to it remain.[64]

Kay has sometimes claimed not to like the phrase that seems welded to her name—"the most powerful woman." As she once told Betty Frank, "That makes me feel like a lady weightlifter."[65] More recently, she snapped, "That's a sexist remark and I really dislike it." But she has also joked about it. Shirley Povich told this story about Kay and his daughter, Lynn, then a *Newsweek* editor. They were on a beach in Barbados before a *Newsweek* meeting, and Lynn "happened to be on a part of the beach where the sun wasn't shining. Kay came along and said, 'Lynn, why don't you come to my end of the beach, and maybe the sun will come out.' And as soon as they reached Kay's sector of the beach, here it comes—the sun. Whereupon . . . Kay said, 'This is why they call me the most powerful woman in Washington.' "[66]

George Bush had courted her, and it appeared that his successor, Bill Clinton, whom her paper had endorsed, would do likewise. She was among the group invited to Pamela Harriman's dinner for Bill Clinton shortly after the election, and two and a half weeks later Kay threw her own dinner for him at her Georgetown home. Yet Kay would never have the public visibility to match her power. She has been too remote a figure, seldom seen on the streets of Georgetown or downtown Washington or Manhattan in such everyday pursuits as hailing a taxi or picking up a carton of milk. When editors at *Washingtonian* recently asked twenty people in Washington and twenty in New York City to identify photographs of famous people from both cities, Katharine Graham came in last, recognized by only ten percent each of Washingtonians and New Yorkers. "Almost no one on the street recognized Katharine Graham," according to the magazine. "She was identified as Marilyn Quayle, Jean Harris, Marjorie Merriweather Post, Letitia Baldrige, and the Queen of Morocco."[67]

When Katharine Graham's memoirs are ready, the media will come calling on one of their own. There will surely be an interview in *The New York Times,* a chat with her friend Mike Wallace on *60 Minutes,* or perhaps with Barbara Walters at ABC. *Today* and *Good*

Morning America will vie for the chance to interview her. "Style" will play the story very large.

Equally certain is that en route to those interviews, this woman who struggled and anguished and won will be as nervous, as unsure of herself and her worth and her place in the world, as she was on that day in 1963 when she trembled her way into Phil's office, positive that she could never take his place.

Many people reminded her, deliberately or inadvertently, that, in fact, she never did quite take his place; she did not need to be reminded. Others told her that when it came to transforming the family business into a powerhouse, neither could Phil have filled her shoes. She would never really believe that. Nor would she believe that Eugene Meyer could not have done the job his daughter did.

But even she could have no doubt that Agnes Meyer could never have pulled it off. And from that realization, Kay Graham surely derives no end of pleasure.

NOTES

In the notes that follow, an asterisk preceding a name or names indicates an interview with the author. These abbreviations are used throughout:

AP	Associated Press
BAAAS	*Bulletin,* American Academy of Arts and Sciences
CT	*Chicago Tribune*
MH	*The Miami Herald*
NYT	*The New York Times*
NYTM	*The New York Times Magazine*
SEP	*The Saturday Evening Post*
UPI	United Press International
WDN	*Washington Daily News*
WP	*The Washington Post*
WPESN	*The Washington Post E-Streeters News*
WPM	*The Washington Post Magazine*
WS	*Washington Star*
WSJ	*The Wall Street Journal*
WSN	*Washington Star-News*

Chapter One
FROM A LONG LINE
OF RABBIS AND MINISTERS

1. Richard and Clara Winston, *Letters of Thomas Mann, 1889–1955* (Berkeley and Los Angeles: University of California Press, 1970), p. 325.

2. Deborah Davis, *Katharine the Great: Katharine Graham and The Washington Post* (Bethesda, MD: National Press, 1987), p. 13.

3. Sidney Hyman, "Seven Presidents Sought His Aid in War & Economic Emergencies," *WP*, July 18, 1959.

4. Merlo J. Pusey, *Eugene Meyer* (New York: Knopf, 1974), pp. 7–8.

5. Davis, *Katharine the Great*, p. 14.

6. Marquis W. Childs, "Squire of Washington," *SEP*, June 5, 1943; Davis, *Katharine the Great*, p. 15.

7. Pusey, *Eugene Meyer*, p. 9.

8. Ibid.

9. Davis, *Katharine the Great*, p. 15.

10. Pusey, *Eugene Meyer*, pp. 9–10.

11. *Sidney Hyman.

12. Davis, *Katharine the Great*, p. 16.

13. Ibid.

14. Pusey, *Eugene Meyer*, pp. 8–9.

15. Hyman, "Seven Presidents."

16. Ibid.

17. *Morris Siegel.

18. Pusey, *Eugene Meyer*, p. 10.

19. Ibid., pp. 16–17.

20. Ibid., p. 17; *Elizabeth Meyer Lorentz.

21. Davis, *Katharine the Great*, pp. 21–22.

22. Liam Lenihan, "A Glimpse of Eugene Meyer," unidentified magazine, June 24, 1939.

23. *Sidney Hyman.

24. Ibid.

25. Davis, *Katharine the Great*, pp. 23–24; Tom Kelly, *The Imperial Post* (New York: Morrow, 1983), p. 16.

26. Davis, *Katharine the Great*, p. 24.

27. Hyman, "Seven Presidents."

28. Ibid.

29. Pusey, *Eugene Meyer*, p. 78.

30. Hyman, "Seven Presidents."

31. Ibid.; Lenihan, "Glimpse"; David Halberstam, *The Powers That Be* (New York: Dell, 1980), p. 253.

32. Davis, *Katharine the Great*, p. 26.

33. Hyman, "Seven Presidents."

34. Ibid.

35. Davis, *Katharine the Great*, pp. 26–27.

36. *Sidney Hyman.

37. *June Bingham.

38. Pusey, *Eugene Meyer*, p. 75; Agnes E. Meyer, *Out of These Roots: The Autobiography of An American Woman* (Boston: Little, Brown, 1953), p. 6.

39. *Joanna Steichen; Meyer, *Out of These Roots*, pp. 15–16.

40. Ibid., p. 11.

41. Ibid., p. 41.

42. Davis, *Katharine the Great*, p. 34; Lenihan, "Glimpse"; Elsie Carper, Agnes Meyer obituary, *WP*, September 2, 1970; Katharine Graham, "Learning by Doing," *BAAAS*, 42 (May 1989).

43. Meyer, *Out of These Roots*, pp. 65–66.

44. Ibid., p. 65.

45. Ibid., p. 67.

46. Ibid.

47. Ibid., p. 101.

48. Pusey, *Eugene Meyer*, p. 75.

49. *Elizabeth Meyer Lorentz.

50. Davis, *Katharine the Great*, p. 36.

51. Elsie Carper, "Her Greatest Crusade Has Been for Schools," *WP*, June 15, 1958.

52. Meyer, *Out of These Roots*, pp. 84, 81, 83, 85.

53. *June Bingham.

54. *Joanna Steichen.

55. Meyer, *Out of These Roots*, p. 95.

56. Pusey, *Eugene Meyer*, p. 77.

57. Ibid.

58. Meyer, *Out of These Roots*, p. 97.

59. *Sidney Hyman.

60. Pusey, *Eugene Meyer,*
pp. 77–78.
61. *Sidney Hyman.
62. Pusey, *Eugene Meyer,*
pp. 78–79.
63. Ibid., p. 81.
64. *Sidney Hyman, Joanna
Steichen.
65. Meyer, *Out of These Roots,*
p. 102.
66. Ibid., p. 156.
67. Pusey, *Eugene Meyer,* p. 103.
68. Meyer, *Out of These Roots,*
p. 103.
69. Carper, "Her Greatest
Crusade."
70. Pusey, *Eugene Meyer,*
pp. 98–99.
71. Ibid.
72. Meyer, *Out of These Roots,* p. 98.
73. *Joanna Steichen.
74. *Joanna Steichen, Elizabeth
Meyer Lorentz.
75. Kelly, *Imperial Post,* p. 30.
76. Ibid., p. 51.
77. Meyer, *Out of These Roots,*
p. 108.
78. Kelly, *Imperial Post,* p. 51.
79. Pusey, *Eugene Meyer,* p. 112.
80. *Sir Isaiah Berlin.
81. Meyer, *Out of These Roots,*
p. 76.
82. Ibid., p. 104.
83. Pusey, *Eugene Meyer,* p. 104.
84. Ibid., p. 105.
85. Ibid., pp. 105–106.
86. Ibid., p. 108.
87. Ibid., p. 104.
88. Ibid., p. 106.
89. Ibid., pp. 107–108.
90. Ibid., p. 109.
91. Meyer, *Out of These Roots,*
p. 106.
92. *Harvey Segal.
93. Ibid.
94. Alfred Friendly, "Butch," *WP,*
June 5, 1983.

95. Hedley Donovan, *Right Places,
Right Times* (New York: Holt, 1989),
p. 72.
96. Meyer, *Out of These Roots,*
p. 107.
97. *Elizabeth Meyer Lorentz.
98. Pusey, *Eugene Meyer,* p. 110.
99. *Joanna Steichen.
100. Ibid.; Pusey, *Eugene Meyer,*
pp. 111–112.
101. Hyman, "Seven Presidents."

Chapter Two
ROUGH BEGINNINGS:
MR.—AND MRS.—MEYER
GO TO WASHINGTON

1. *Elizabeth Meyer Lorentz.
2. Ibid.
3. Sarah Booth Conroy, "Life Was
a Happy Whirl," *WDN,* September 2,
1970.
4. Merlo J. Pusey, *Eugene Meyer*
(New York: Knopf, 1974),
pp. 136–137.
5. Ibid., pp. 138–139.
6. Deborah Davis, *Katharine the
Great: Katharine Graham and The
Washington Post* (Bethesda, MD:
National Press, 1987), p. 44.
7. Sidney Hyman, "Seven
Presidents Sought His Aid in War &
Economic Emergencies," *WP,* July
18, 1959.
8. Davis, *Katharine the Great,*
p. 48.
9. Howard Bray, *The Pillars of the
Post* (New York: Norton, 1980), p. 5.
10. John Hammond, *On Record*
(New York: Ridge/Summit, 1977),
p. 33.
11. *Harold Taylor.
12. Marquis W. Childs, "Squire of
Washington," *SEP,* June 5, 1943.
13. Pusey, *Eugene Meyer,* p. 112.
14. *Harold Taylor.

15. Pusey, *Eugene Meyer,* p. 111; *Marietta Tree.

16. *Elizabeth Meyer Lorentz.

17. *Joanna Steichen.

18. Pusey, *Eugene Meyer,* p. 195.

19. Hyman, "Seven Presidents"; Childs, "Squire"; Liam Lenihan, "A Glimpse of Eugene Meyer," unidentified magazine, June 24, 1939.

20. Hyman, "Seven Presidents."

21. Pusey, *Eugene Meyer,* p. 242.

22. *Jean Friendly.

23. *Libby Rowe.

24. *Elizabeth Meyer Lorentz.

25. Pusey, *Eugene Meyer,* pp. 242–243.

26. Hyman, "Seven Presidents"; Childs, "Squire."

27. Elsie Carper, "Agnes E. Meyer: On Her 80th Birthday, Much to Do," *WP,* January 2, 1967.

28. Agnes E. Meyer, *Out of These Roots: The Autobiography of an American Woman* (Boston: Little, Brown, 1953), pp. 164–165.

29. *Jean Friendly.

30. *Source wishes to remain anonymous.

31. *Elizabeth Meyer Lorentz.

32. Meyer, *Out of These Roots,* pp. 166–167.

33. *Elizabeth Meyer Lorentz.

34. Meyer, *Out of These Roots,* p. 40.

35. Ibid., p. 105.

36. *Elizabeth Meyer Lorentz.

37. Doris Fleeson, "She Came Down from Her Ivory Tower," *St. Louis Post-Dispatch,* June 16, 1946.

38. *Elizabeth Meyer Lorentz.

39. *Libby Rowe.

40. Ibid.

41. Ibid.

42. Lynn Rosellini, "The Katharine Graham Story," *WS,* November 13–17, 1978 (five-part series).

43. *Elizabeth Meyer Lorentz.

44. Quoted in Liz Smith, *The Mother Book* (Garden City, NY: Doubleday, 1978), pp. 121–122.

45. Ibid.

46. *Source wishes to remain anonymous.

47. *Libby Rowe.

48. *Elizabeth Meyer Lorentz.

49. Pusey, *Eugene Meyer,* p. 195.

50. Rosellini, "Katharine Graham Story."

51. Pusey, *Eugene Meyer,* p. 196.

52. *Elizabeth Meyer Lorentz.

53. Ibid.

54. Ibid.

55. *Joanna Steichen.

56. Fleeson, "She Came Down."

57. Meyer, *Out of These Roots,* pp. 346, 352–353.

58. *Elizabeth Meyer Lorentz.

59. *Arthur Schlesinger, Jr., Elizabeth Meyer Lorentz.

60. Pusey, *Eugene Meyer,* p. 201.

61. Ibid., pp. 192, 203.

62. Unidentified newspaper article, May 2, 1929.

63. Pusey, *Eugene Meyer,* p. 243.

64. Jonathan Daniels, *Washington Quadrille* (Garden City, NY: Doubleday, 1968), p. 231.

65. Sanford D. Horwitt, *Let Them Call Me Rebel: Saul Alinsky—His Life and Legacy* (New York: Knopf, 1989), p. 194.

66. Meyer, *Out of These Roots,* pp. 82–83; Conroy, "Life Was"; Pusey, *Eugene Meyer,* p. 198.

67. Pusey, *Eugene Meyer,* p. 197.

68. Ibid., p. 200.

69. Ibid., p. 201.

70. Hyman, "Seven Presidents."

71. Lenihan, "Glimpse."

72. *Elizabeth Meyer Lorentz.

73. *Libby Rowe.

74. Letter to author from Allegra Maynard.

75. Rosellini, "Katharine Graham

Story"; *Jean Friendly; "E-Streeters Hear Katharine Graham," *WPESN,* November 5, 1990.

76. Pusey, *Eugene Meyer,* pp. 219, 224.

77. *Elizabeth Meyer Lorentz.

78. *Sidney Hyman.

79. Pusey, *Eugene Meyer,* pp. 219–220, 225.

80. Ibid., p. 222.

81. *Bernard Nossiter.

82. *Sidney Hyman; Hyman, "Seven Presidents."

83. *Robert Nathan, Bernard Nossiter, Hedley Donovan.

84. *WP,* November 1, 1945.

85. Ralph G. Martin, *Cissy: The Extraordinary Life of Eleanor Medill Patterson* (New York: Simon & Schuster, 1979), p. 328.

86. Pusey, *Eugene Meyer,* p. 241.

87. *Sidney Hyman.

88. Pusey, *Eugene Meyer,* p. 243.

89. *Frank Waldrop.

90. Tom Kelly, *The Imperial Post* (New York: Morrow, 1983), p. 67; Pusey, *Eugene Meyer,* p. 239.

91. *Eugene Patterson.

Chapter Three
EUGENE—AND HIS
DESCENDANTS—GET
A NEWSPAPER

1. Paul E. Healy, *Cissy: A Biography of Eleanor M. "Cissy" Patterson* (Garden City, NY: Doubleday, 1966), p. 3.

2. Ibid., p. 4.

3. Ralph G. Martin, *Cissy: The Extraordinary Life of Eleanor Medill Patterson* (New York: Simon & Schuster, 1979), p. 204.

4. Ibid., p. 329; Merlo J. Pusey, *Eugene Meyer* (New York: Knopf, 1974), p. 244.

5. Agnes Meyer's diary quoted in Pusey, *Eugene Meyer,* p. 244.

6. Pusey, *Eugene Meyer,* p. 245; Martin, *Cissy,* p. 330.

7. *Hope Ridings Miller.

8. Pusey, *Eugene Meyer,* p. 245.

9. Martin, *Cissy,* p. 330.

10. Pusey, *Eugene Meyer,* p. 246; Marquis W. Childs, "Squire of Washington," *SEP,* June 5, 1943.

11. Childs, "Squire."

12. Pusey, *Eugene Meyer,* p. 252.

13. Jonathan Daniels, *The Time Between the Wars* (Garden City, NY: Doubleday, 1966), p. 90.

14. Martin Walker, *Powers of the Press* (New York: Adama, 1982), p. 246.

15. Shirley Povich, "A Sporting Life," *WPM,* October 29, 1989.

16. Peter Perl, "Nation's Capital Held at Mercy of the Mob," *WPM,* July 16, 1989.

17. Quoted in Cleveland Amory, *Who Killed Society?* (New York: Pocket, 1962), p. 153.

18. Michael Teague, *Mrs. L: Conversations with Alice Roosevelt Longworth* (New York: Doubleday, 1981), p. 170; Alice Roosevelt Longworth, *Crowded Hours* (New York: Scribner's, 1933), p. 324.

19. Quoted in Amory, *Who Killed Society?,* p. 153.

20. *WPESN,* May 23, 1990.

21. Walker, *Powers of the Press,* p. 248.

22. *Frank Waldrop.

23. Erwin D. Canham, "The Story Behind an Editorial," *The Christian Science Monitor,* May 20, 1939.

24. Alfred Friendly, "Butch," *WP,* June 5, 1983.

25. *WPESN,* December 1988.

26. "Guest at Breakfast," *Time,* April 16, 1956.

27. Pusey, *Eugene Meyer,* p. 252.

28. David Halberstam, *The Powers That Be* (New York: Dell, 1980), p. 252.

29. *Frank Dennis; "E-Streeters Hear Katharine Graham," *WPESN,* November 5, 1990.

30. *Ben Gilbert.

31. *Elsie Carper.

32. "E-Streeters Hear."

33. *Bernard Nossiter.

34. *Hedley Donovan; Hedley Donovan, *Right Places, Right Times* (New York: Holt, 1989), p. 72.

35. Halberstam, *Powers That Be,* p. 259.

36. "Guest at Breakfast."

37. Donovan, *Right Places,* p. 73.

38. *Frank Waldrop.

39. *WPESN,* January 1990; "E-Streeters Hear."

40. Pusey, *Eugene Meyer,* p. 249.

41. Ibid., p. 250; Healy, *Cissy,* p. 254.

42. Pusey, *Eugene Meyer,* p. 250; Healy, *Cissy,* p. 253.

43. Pusey, *Eugene Meyer,* pp. 250–251; Martin, *Cissy,* p. 331; Healy, *Cissy,* p. 254.

44. Martin, *Cissy,* p. 331; Healy, *Cissy,* p. 255.

45. *Frank Waldrop.

46. *Hope Ridings Miller.

47. *Luvie Pearson.

48. Martin, *Cissy,* p. 332; *Luvie Pearson.

49. *Hope Ridings Miller.

50. *Hedley Donovan.

51. *Elsie Carper.

52. Friendly, "Butch."

53. *Hedley Donovan.

54. Donovan, *Right Places,* p. 72.

55. *Robert Estabrook.

56. *WPESN,* January 1990.

57. *Hedley Donovan; Donovan, *Right Places,* pp. 71–72.

58. Katharine Graham, "Learning by Doing," *BAAAS,* 42 (May 1989).

59. *WPESN,* December 1988.

60. Ibid.

61. *Hedley Donovan.

62. Donovan, *Right Places,* p. 80.

63. Chalmers M. Roberts, *In the Shadow of Power: The Story of The Washington Post* (Cabin John, MD: Seven Locks, 1989), p. 216.

64. *Frank Dennis.

65. Roberts, *In the Shadow,* p. 216.

66. *WPESN,* January 1990.

67. Canham, "Story Behind an Editorial."

68. *Ben Gilbert.

69. "E-Streeters Hear."

70. *Lucy Prichard; Pusey, *Eugene Meyer,* p. 365; "E-Streeters Hear."

Chapter Four
KATHARINE STARTS HER
EDUCATION

1. Merlo J. Pusey, *Eugene Meyer* (New York: Knopf, 1974), p. 364.

2. *Connie Ellis (telephone).

3. *Vivian Cadden.

4. Elizabeth Pope Frank, "Vassar's Most Powerful Alumna: Katharine Meyer Graham, '38," *Vassar Quarterly,* Spring 1978; *Connie Ellis (telephone).

5. *Vivian Cadden.

6. *Jane Beyer.

7. *Elizabeth Frank, Jane Beyer.

8. *Vivian Cadden.

9. *Elizabeth Frank.

10. *Harold Taylor.

11. *Elizabeth Frank.

12. *Elizabeth Meyer Lorentz.

13. *Jane Beyer.

14. *Elizabeth Frank, Vivian Cadden; Elaine Kendall, *Peculiar Institutions* (New York: Putnam, 1975), p. 169.

15. Deborah Davis, *Katharine the Great: Katharine Graham and The Washington Post* (Bethesda, MD: National Press, 1987), p. 53.

16. *Connie Ellis (telephone),
Elizabeth Frank.

17. *Jane Beyer.

18. Ibid.

19. Ibid.

20. *Elizabeth Frank.

21. *Jane Beyer.

22. Ibid.

23. *Vivian Cadden.

24. *Jane Beyer.

25. Lynn Rosellini, "The Katharine
Graham Story," *WS,* November
13–17, 1978 (five-part series).

26. *Jane Beyer.

27. Ibid.

28. *Nancy Wechsler.

29. *Elizabeth Frank.

30. Frank, "Vassar's Most
Powerful."

31. *Vivian Cadden.

32. *Jane Beyer.

33. *Richard Clurman.

34. *Vivian Cadden.

35. Edward T. Folliard, "Meyer the
Journalist Built Post on Public
Service," *WP,* July 18, 1959; Pusey,
Eugene Meyer, p. 272.

36. *Elizabeth Meyer Lorentz.

37. Pat Munroe and Caryl Rivers,
"Kay Graham Talks About Her Job
at the Helm of Washington Post,"
Editor & Publisher, May 2, 1964.

38. *Roswell Gilpatric.

39. *June Bingham.

40. *Rabbi Edgar Siskin.

41. Ibid.; letter to the author from
Rabbi Siskin.

42. *Elizabeth Frank.

43. Frank, "Vassar's Most
Powerful."

44. Liam Lenihan, "A Glimpse of
Eugene Meyer," unidentified
magazine, June 24, 1939.

45. *Elizabeth Meyer Lorentz.

46. Pusey, *Eugene Meyer,* p. 332.

47. AP, "Capital Publisher's
Daughter Tired but Gay As Debut
Nears," January 3, 1937.

48. Pusey, *Eugene Meyer,* p. 331.

49. *Source wishes to remain
anonymous.

50. *Sidney Hyman.

51. *Joanna Steichen, Harold
Taylor.

52. Paul E. Healy, *Cissy: A
Biography of Eleanor M. "Cissy"
Patterson* (Garden City, NY:
Doubleday, 1966), pp. 145, 111.

53. *Sidney Epstein.

54. Healy, *Cissy,* pp. 365, 376–378.

55. Alice Albright Hoge, *Cissy
Patterson* (New York: Random
House, 1966), p. 162; Gwen Morgan
and Arthur Veysey, *Poor Little Rich
Boy: The Life and Times of Col.
Robert R. McCormick*
(Carpentersville, IL: Crossroads,
1985), p. 351.

56. Hoge, *Cissy Patterson,*
pp. 162–163; Ralph G. Martin, *Cissy:
The Extraordinary Life of Eleanor
Medill Patterson* (New York: Simon
& Schuster, 1979), p. 378; Healy,
Cissy, p. 145; Frank C. Waldrop,
McCormick of Chicago (Englewood
Cliffs, NJ: Prentice-Hall, 1966), p. 250.

57. Herbert Mitgang, "A Woman
Remembered for Her Words and
Life," *NYT,* August 8, 1990.

58. Peter Kurth, *American
Cassandra* (Boston: Little, Brown,
1990), p. 255.

59. *Hedley Donovan.

60. *Roswell Gilpatric.

61. Pusey, *Eugene Meyer,* p. 335.

62. Tom Kelly, *The Imperial Post*
(New York: Morrow, 1983),
pp. 69–70.

63. Agnes E. Meyer, *Out of These
Roots: The Autobiography of an
American Woman* (Boston: Little,
Brown, 1953), p. 184.

64. Chalmers M. Roberts, *In the
Shadow of Power: The Story of The
Washington Post* (Cabin John, MD:
Seven Locks, 1989), p. 366.

Chapter Five
KATHARINE PREPARES
FOR THE *POST*

1. *Lucy Prichard.
2. *Harold Taylor, June Bingham, Sidney Hyman, Elizabeth Frank.
3. *Jane Beyer.
4. Harry S. Ashmore, *Unseasonable Truths: The Life of Robert Maynard Hutchins* (Boston: Little, Brown, 1989), p. 129.
5. Ibid., pp. 129–132; *George Reedy.
6. *Elizabeth Frank.
7. "E-Streeters Hear Katharine Graham," *WPESN,* November 5, 1990.
8. *Sidney Hyman.
9. *George Reedy.
10. Deborah Davis, *Katharine the Great: Katharine Graham and The Washington Post* (Bethesda, MD: National Press, 1987), pp. 66–67.
11. *Sidney Hyman, Drexel Sprecher.
12. *George Reedy.
13. *Sidney Hyman.
14. Ibid.
15. Ibid.
16. *George Reedy.
17. Lynn Rosellini, "The Katharine Graham Story," *WS,* November 13–17, 1978 (five-part series); Sanford D. Horwitt, *Let Them Call Me Rebel: Saul Alinsky—His Life and Legacy* (New York: Knopf, 1989), p. 124.
18. *Sidney Hyman.
19. Elizabeth Pope Frank, "Vassar's Most Powerful Alumna: Katharine Meyer Graham, '38," *Vassar Quarterly,* Spring 1978.
20. *Sidney Hyman.
21. *June Bingham.
22. *Sidney Hyman.
23. Rosellini, "Katharine Graham Story."

24. Chalmers M. Roberts, *In the Shadow of Power: The Story of The Washington Post* (Cabin John, MD: Seven Locks, 1989), p. 366.
25. Merlo J. Pusey, *Eugene Meyer* (New York: Knopf, 1974), p. 333.
26. Roberts, *In the Shadow,* p. 367.
27. *Elizabeth Meyer Lorentz.
28. Rosellini, "Katharine Graham Story."
29. Ibid.
30. Roberts, *In the Shadow,* p. 367.
31. Pusey, *Eugene Meyer,* p. 333.
32. Gwen Morgan and Arthur Veysey, *Poor Little Rich Boy: The Life and Times of Col. Robert R. McCormick* (Carpentersville, IL: Crossroads, 1985), p. 250; Alice Albright Hoge, *Cissy Patterson* (New York: Random House, 1966), p. 165; Paul E. Healy, *Cissy: A Biography of Eleanor M. "Cissy" Patterson* (Garden City, NY: Doubleday, 1966), p. 149.
33. Pusey, *Eugene Meyer,* p. 288.
34. Quoted in Roberts, *In the Shadow,* p. 367.
35. Larry van Dyne, "The Bottom Line on Katharine Graham," *Washingtonian,* December 1985.
36. Pusey, *Eugene Meyer,* p. 199.
37. Ibid., p. 336.
38. *Sidney Hyman.
39. Richard and Clara Winston, *Letters of Thomas Mann, 1889–1955* (Berkeley and Los Angeles: University of California Press, 1970), p. 226.
40. Ibid., p. xxxii.
41. Hermann Kesten, ed., *Thomas Mann Diaries 1918–1939* (New York: Abrams, 1982), p. 301; Winston, *Letters of Mann,* p. 295.
42. *John Oakes.
43. *Sidney Hyman.
44. *Source wishes to remain anonymous.
45. Kesten, *Mann Diaries,* p. 301.

46. *Elizabeth Meyer Lorentz.

47. Agnes E. Meyer, *Out of These Roots: The Autobiography of an American Woman* (Boston: Little, Brown, 1953), p. 175; *Elizabeth Meyer Lorentz.

48. "E-Streeters Hear."

49. *June Bingham.

50. *Morris Siegel.

51. Hedley Donovan, *Right Places, Right Times* (New York: Holt, 1989), p. 77.

52. *John Oakes.

53. *Theodore Kheel.

54. *Elizabeth Meyer Lorentz.

55. Pusey, *Eugene Meyer,* p. 330.

56. AP, "Capital Publisher's Daughter Tired but Gay As Debut Nears," January 3, 1937.

57. Pusey, *Eugene Meyer,* p. 331; *Elizabeth Meyer Lorentz.

Chapter Six
THE MOST OUTSTANDING MAN OF HIS GENERATION

1. *John Oakes.

2. *Sidney Hyman.

3. *Marietta Tree.

4. "Guest at Breakfast," *Time,* April 16, 1956; Chalmers M. Roberts, *In the Shadow of Power: The Story of The Washington Post* (Cabin John, MD: Seven Locks, 1989), p. 256.

5. "Ex–State Senator Graham, Pioneer Cattleman, Dies," *MH,* March 16, 1964.

6. William A. Graham, "The Pennsuco Sugar Experiment," *Tequesta,* 11 (1951).

7. *John Stembler.

8. Graham, "Pennsuco."

9. "Guest at Breakfast."

10. *Frank Waldrop.

11. *John Stembler.

12. Nancy Beth Jackson, "The Growing Empire of a Farmer's Sons," *Tropic,* March 1, 1970.

13. *George Smathers. Sources for the biographical material on Ernest Graham: Graham, "Pennsuco"; "Graham Gains Strong Support over State," *Miami Daily News,* April 29, 1944; Dave Schultz, "Bob Graham Works Hard to Shed His Rich-Kid Image," *Miami News,* August 30, 1978; "Our Sunday Portrait," *Miami News,* July 1, 1962; Roberts, *In the Shadow,* p. 256; David Halberstam, *The Powers That Be* (New York: Dell, 1980), pp. 233–234; unidentified obituary of Phil Graham, March 14, 1964; *John Stembler; "Guest at Breakfast"; Deborah Davis, *Katharine the Great: Katharine Graham and The Washington Post* (Bethesda, MD: National Press, 1987), pp. 87–88; M. W. Anderson, "Ernest Graham's Seedlings Flourished," *Update,* 9, no. 3 (August 1982); Robert Hooker, "Bob Graham," *Floridian,* July 2, 1972; Charles Whited, "Newsman Graham, Ex-Miamian, Kills Self with Shotgun," *MH,* August 4, 1963; Jack Roberts, "Graham Caught His Political Bug as a Boy," *Miami News,* November 8, 1978.

14. *George Smathers; Davis, *Katharine the Great,* p. 88; Halberstam, *Powers That Be,* p. 234; Jackson, "Growing Empire."

15. *George Smathers.

16. *John Stembler.

17. *George Smathers.

18. "Guest at Breakfast."

19. *George Smathers.

20. *John Stembler.

21. *George Smathers.

22. *Sources wish to remain anonymous.

23. *John Stembler.

24. Claude Denson Pepper with Hays Gorey, *Pepper: Eyewitness to a

Century (New York: Harcourt Brace Jovanovich, 1987), p. 27.

25. *John Stembler.

26. Pepper with Gorey, *Pepper,* p. 27; *John Stembler.

27. *Philip Elman.

28. Davis, *Katharine the Great,* p. 79.

29. *Philip Elman.

30. Felix Frankfurter papers, Harvard Law School Library, Cambridge, MA.

31. *Nathan Halpern.

32. *Theodore Tannenwald, Jr.

33. *Nathan Halpern.

34. Felix Frankfurter, letter to the editor, *WP,* August 20, 1963.

35. Halberstam, *Powers That Be,* p. 226.

36. *Bennett Boskey.

37. *Lucy Prichard.

38. *Theodore Tannenwald, Jr.

39. *Ben Gilbert.

40. *Lucy Prichard.

41. Frankfurter papers, Harvard.

42. *Nathan Halpern.

43. *Theodore Tannenwald, Jr.

44. Ibid.

45. Quoted in Davis, *Katharine the Great,* p. 79.

46. Ronald Steel, *Walter Lippmann and the American Century* (Boston: Atlantic/Little, Brown, 1980), pp. 120–123; Merlo J. Pusey, *Eugene Meyer* (New York: Knopf, 1974), p. 142.

47. *John Oakes.

48. Ibid.

49. Ibid.

50. *Harvey Segal.

51. *John Oakes.

52. Roberts, *In the Shadow,* p. 257.

53. *John Oakes.

54. Ibid.

55. Pusey, *Eugene Meyer,* p. 333.

56. Ibid., p. 261; *Elizabeth Meyer Lorentz.

57. Halberstam, *Powers That Be,* pp. 234–235.

58. Robert (Bob) Graham, quoted in Hooker, "Bob Graham."

59. *Sources wish to remain anonymous.

60. *Hope Ridings Miller.

61. *Sidney Hyman.

62. *Alan Finberg.

Chapter Seven
KAY TAKES VERY EARLY RETIREMENT

1. Chalmers M. Roberts, *In the Shadow of Power: The Story of The Washington Post* (Cabin John, MD: Seven Locks, 1989), p. 368.

2. Merlo J. Pusey, *Eugene Meyer* (New York: Knopf, 1974), p. 334.

3. *Elizabeth Meyer Lorentz.

4. Roberts, *In the Shadow,* p. 368.

5. Ibid.

6. *Joseph Rauh.

7. *Philip Elman.

8. *Joseph Rauh.

9. "Guest at Breakfast," *Time,* April 16, 1956.

10. David Halberstam, *The Powers That Be* (New York: Dell, 1980), pp. 246–247.

11. Roberts, *In the Shadow,* p. 231.

12. *Robert Estabrook.

13. Roberts, *In the Shadow,* p. 231.

14. Alice Albright Hoge, *Cissy Patterson* (New York: Random House, 1966), p. 195.

15. *Robert Nathan.

16. James F. Simon, *The Antagonists* (New York: Simon & Schuster, 1989), p. 135.

17. *Joseph Rauh.

18. *Nancy Wechsler.

19. *Libby Rowe.

20. Lynn Rosellini, "The Katharine Graham Story," *WS,* November 13–17, 1978 (five-part series); *June Bingham, Nancy Wechsler.

21. *Libby Rowe.

22. Rosellini, "Katharine Graham Story."

23. *Joseph Rauh.

24. *Elizabeth Frank.

25. *Newbold Noyes.

26. *Luvie Pearson.

27. *Rabbi Edgar Siskin.

28. John Hammond, *On Record* (New York: Ridge/Summit, 1977), pp. 33, 35.

29. *Elizabeth Meyer Lorentz.

30. Quoted in Deborah Davis, *Katharine the Great: Katharine Graham and The Washington Post* (Bethesda, MD: National Press, 1987), p. 104.

31. Ibid., p. 103.

32. *Joanna Steichen.

33. Felix Frankfurter papers, Harvard Law School Library, Cambridge, MA.

34. Pusey, *Eugene Meyer*, p. 332.

35. Ibid., p. 340.

36. *Sir Isaiah Berlin.

37. *Sidney Hyman.

38. *Bernard Nossiter.

39. Pusey, *Eugene Meyer*, p. 340.

40. Katharine Graham, "Learning by Doing," *BAAAS*, 42 (May 1989).

41. *Ben Gilbert.

42. Tom Kelly, *The Imperial Post* (New York: Morrow, 1983), p. 95.

43. *Frank Dennis.

44. Quoted in Edward T. Folliard, "Meyer the Journalist Built Post on Public Service," *WP*, July 18, 1959.

45. Quoted ibid.

46. *Hedley Donovan.

47. *Joseph Rauh.

48. Pusey, *Eugene Meyer*, p. 341.

49. Elizabeth Pope Frank, "Vassar's Most Powerful Alumna: Katharine Meyer Graham, '38," *Vassar Quarterly*, Spring 1978.

50. "E-Streeters Hear Katharine Graham," *WPESN*, November 5, 1990.

51. Richard and Clara Winston, *Letters of Thomas Mann, 1889–1955* (Berkeley and Los Angeles: University of California Press, 1970), pp. 299–300.

52. Ibid. p. 306.

53. Ibid., pp. 319–320.

54. *June Bingham.

55. Winston, *Letters of Mann*, p. 300.

56. *Elizabeth Meyer Lorentz; Winston, *Letters of Mann*, p. 286.

57. Hermann Kesten, ed., *Thomas Mann Diaries 1918–1939* (New York: Abrams, 1982), p. 301.

58. *June Bingham.

59. Jane Howard, "Katharine Graham: The Power That Didn't Corrupt," *Ms.*, October 1974.

60. *Roswell Gilpatric.

61. *Joanna Steichen.

62. *Harold Taylor.

63. *June Bingham.

64. *Source wishes to remain anonymous.

65. *Frank Dennis.

66. Alfred Friendly, "Butch," *WP*, June 5, 1983.

67. *Frank Dennis.

68. Liam Lenihan, "A Glimpse of Eugene Meyer," unidentified magazine, June 24, 1939.

69. Ibid.

70. Marquis W. Childs, "Squire of Washington," *SEP*, June 5, 1943.

71. Ibid.

72. Pusey, *Eugene Meyer*, p. 309.

73. "Graham Gains Strong Support over State," *Miami Daily News*, April 29, 1944.

74. Frankfurter papers, Harvard.

75. William Grimes, "Pare Lorentz, 86, a Film Director on Socially Conscious Matters," *NYT*, March 5, 1992.

76. *Harold Taylor.

77. *Joanna Steichen.

78. *Sidney Hyman.

79. "Guest at Breakfast," *Time,* April 16, 1956.

80. Davis, *Katharine the Great,* p. 95.

81. Roberts, *In the Shadow,* p. 331.

82. Ibid., p. 242.

83. *WPESN,* December 1988.

84. *June Bingham.

85. *Source wishes to remain anonymous.

86. *June Bingham.

87. *Robert Estabrook.

88. "E-Streeters Hear."

89. Pusey, *Eugene Meyer,* pp. 346–347.

90. Roberts, *In the Shadow,* p. 258.

91. "Farewell Luncheon Given Meyer by Employees of *Post,*" *WP,* June 15, 1946.

92. Pusey, *Eugene Meyer,* p. 351.

93. Roberts, *In the Shadow,* p. 258.

94. Pusey, *Eugene Meyer,* p. 352.

95. Ibid., p. 353.

96. Ibid., p. 354.

97. Alfred Friendly, "Meyer Resigns as President of World Bank," *WP,* December 5, 1946.

98. Pusey, *Eugene Meyer,* pp. 358–359.

99. *Paul Ignatius.

100. Davis, *Katharine the Great,* pp. 114–115; Diana McLellan, "Inside Georgetown," *Washingtonian,* May 1989.

101. Davis, *Katharine the Great,* pp. 114–115.

102. *Bernard Nossiter.

103. *Luvie Pearson.

104. Friendly, "Butch."

105. Davis, *Katharine the Great,* pp. 117–118.

106. *Morris Siegel.

107. *Murrey Marder.

108. *Albert Manola.

109. *Robert Estabrook.

Chapter Eight
PHIL AND AGNES JOCKEY
FOR POSITION

1. *Hope Ridings Miller.

2. Doris Fleeson, "She Came Down from Her Ivory Tower," *St. Louis Post-Dispatch,* June 16, 1946.

3. Peter Kurth, *American Cassandra* (Boston: Little, Brown, 1990), p. 328.

4. Elsie Carper, "Her Greatest Crusade Has Been for Schools," *WP,* June 15, 1958.

5. Fleeson, "She Came Down."

6. Katharine Graham, "Learning by Doing," *BAAAS,* 42 (May 1989).

7. *Ben Gilbert.

8. *Source wishes to remain anonymous.

9. *Ben Gilbert.

10. *Elsie Carper.

11. "Mrs. Meyer Makes School Fund Plea," *WP,* May 30, 1947.

12. *Elsie Carper.

13. Elsie Carper, Agnes Meyer obituary, *WP,* September 2, 1970.

14. Carper, "Her Greatest Crusade."

15. Fleeson, "She Came Down."

16. Carper, Agnes Meyer obituary.

17. *Elsie Carper.

18. Quoted in Elsie Carper, "Agnes E. Meyer: On Her 80th Birthday, Much to Do," *WP,* January 2, 1967.

19. Carper, Agnes Meyer obituary; *Ben Gilbert.

20. Agnes E. Meyer, *Out of These Roots: The Autobiography of an American Woman* (Boston: Little, Brown, 1953), p. 121.

21. Tom Kelly, *The Imperial Post* (New York: Morrow, 1983), p. 95.

22. Sanford D. Horwitt, *Let Them Call Me Rebel: Saul Alinsky—His Life and Legacy* (New York: Knopf, 1989), p. 179.

23. Ibid., p. 178.

24. Ibid., p. 194.

25. Meyer, *Out of These Roots,* p. 251.

26. *Nicholas von Hoffman.

27. Ibid.

28. Horwitt, *Let Them Call,* p. 195.

29. Kelly, *Imperial Post,* p. 112.

30. Meyer, *Out of These Roots,* pp. 293–295.

31. Joseph P. Lash, *Eleanor: The Years Alone* (New York: Norton, 1972), p. 163.

32. Charles A. Fecher, ed., *The Diary of H. L. Mencken* (New York: Knopf, 1989), pp. 457–458.

33. *Harvey Segal.

34. Ibid.

35. *Jean Friendly.

36. *Morris Siegel.

37. *Elsie Carper.

38. Merlo J. Pusey, *Eugene Meyer* (New York: Knopf, 1974), p. 365.

39. Deborah Davis, *Katharine the Great: Katharine Graham and The Washington Post* (Bethesda, MD: National Press, 1987), p. 114.

40. *Elsie Carper.

41. *Roswell Gilpatric.

42. *Elizabeth Meyer Lorentz.

43. *Bernard Nossiter.

44. Paul E. Healy, *Cissy: A Biography of Eleanor M. "Cissy" Patterson* (Garden City, NY: Doubleday, 1966), p. 402.

45. Ibid., p. 392.

46. Pusey, *Eugene Meyer,* p. 366.

47. Healy, *Cissy,* p. 401.

48. Gwen Morgan and Arthur Veysey, *Poor Little Rich Boy: The Life and Times of Col. Robert R. McCormick* (Carpentersville, IL: Crossroads, 1985), p. 407.

49. Pusey, *Eugene Meyer,* p. 367.

50. Ibid., pp. 368–369.

51. Frank C. Waldrop, *McCormick of Chicago* (Englewood Cliffs, NJ: Prentice-Hall, 1966), pp. 182, 275.

52. Ralph G. Martin, *Cissy: The Extraordinary Life of Eleanor Medill Patterson* (New York: Simon & Schuster, 1979), p. 474.

53. *Frank Waldrop.

54. "Guest at Breakfast," *Time,* April 16, 1956.

55. Ibid.

56. *Ben Gilbert.

57. *Joseph Rauh.

58. *Hedley Donovan.

59. *Sir Isaiah Berlin.

60. Pat Munroe and Caryl Rivers, "Kay Graham Talks About Her Job at the Helm of Washington Post," *Editor & Publisher,* May 2, 1964.

61. "Philip Graham Buys Estate in Fauquier," *WS,* January 11, 1951; "Treasury Official Buys Graham Farm," unidentified newspaper, February 18, 1966; Barbara Matusow, "Citizen Don," *Washingtonian,* August 1992.

62. *Jean Friendly.

63. Horwitt, *Let Them Call,* pp. 242–243.

64. Felix Frankfurter papers, Harvard Law School Library, Cambridge, MA.

65. *Robert Estabrook; Frankfurter papers, Harvard.

66. *Sir Isaiah Berlin.

67. Chalmers M. Roberts, *In the Shadow of Power: The Story of The Washington Post* (Cabin John, MD: Seven Locks, 1989), p. 300.

68. *Murrey Marder.

69. *Bernard Nossiter.

70. Pusey, *Eugene Meyer,* p. 300.

71. Kelly, *Imperial Post,* p. 9.

72. Pusey, *Eugene Meyer,* p. 376; Roberts, *In the Shadow,* p. 30.

73. Roberts, *In the Shadow,* p. 301; Kelly, *Imperial Post,* p. 116.

74. David Halberstam, *The Powers That Be* (New York: Dell, 1980), p. 273.

75. Roberts, *In the Shadow,* p. 303.
76. *Erwin Knoll.
77. Pusey, *Eugene Meyer,* p. 378.
78. Howard Bray, *The Pillars of the Post* (New York: Norton, 1980), p. 10.
79. Roberts, *In the Shadow,* p. 302.
80. *Robert Estabrook.
81. "Publisher Says McCarthy Makes Goebbels Amateur," unidentified newspaper, May 19, 1953.
82. AP, "McCarthy Seeks Cost of Post Service for 'Typical' Papers," *WS,* August 23, 1953; "Philip L. Graham of Post Kills Self with Shotgun," *WS,* August 4, 1963.
83. "The Slugger," *Time,* March 2, 1953.
84. *Karl Meyer.
85. *Murrey Marder.
86. *Joseph Rauh.
87. Halberstam, *Powers That Be,* pp. 272–273; Bray, *Pillars,* p. 107.
88. Halberstam, *Powers That Be,* p. 262.
89. *Erwin Knoll.
90. Halberstam, *Powers That Be,* p. 270.
91. *Robert Estabrook.
92. *Erwin Knoll.
93. "Guest at Breakfast"; various AP reports.
94. "Guest at Breakfast."
95. *Ben Gilbert.
96. Kelly, *Imperial Post,* p. 106; Bray, *Pillars,* pp. 161–162.
97. Quoted in Bray, *Pillars,* pp. 167–168; quoted in Kelly, *Imperial Post,* p. 103.
98. Kelly, *Imperial Post,* p. 94.
99. *Ben Gilbert.
100. Kelly, *Imperial Post,* p. 138; *Ben Gilbert; Howard Kurtz, "Bradlee Retiring as Editor of the Post," *WP,* June 21, 1991; Peter J. Boyer, "The Bradlee Mystique," *Vanity Fair,* September 1991.

101. Kelly, *Imperial Post,* pp. 105–106.
102. *Ben Gilbert.
103. Halberstam, *Powers That Be,* p. 228.
104. Ibid.
105. Bray, *Pillars,* p. 66.
106. *Eugene Patterson.
107. Boyer, "Bradlee Mystique."
108. Kelly, *Imperial Post,* pp. 103–105.
109. *Ben Gilbert; Bray, *Pillars,* pp. 166–167.
110. *Robert Estabrook.
111. James Reston, *Deadline* (New York: Random House, 1991), p. 199.
112. Ordway Tead, "Portrait of an American Woman," *WP,* October 18, 1953.
113. Davis, *Katharine the Great,* p. 120.
114. *Sidney Hyman.
115. Ibid.
116. Davis, *Katharine the Great,* pp. 119–120.
117. *Sidney Hyman.
118. Quoted in Davis, *Katharine the Great,* p. 121.

Chapter Nine
ELATION AND DECLINE

1. *Frank Waldrop.
2. Merlo J. Pusey, *Eugene Meyer* (New York: Knopf, 1974), pp. 381–382.
3. *Frank Waldrop.
4. Ibid.
5. Frank C. Waldrop, *McCormick of Chicago* (Englewood Cliffs, NJ: Prentice-Hall, 1966), pp. 249–259; Pusey, *Eugene Meyer,* p. 320.
6. Waldrop, *McCormick,* p. 279.
7. J. Y. Smith, "Post Advertising Executive W. Frank Gatewood Dies," *WP,* May 3, 1990.
8. Gwen Morgan and Arthur

Veysey, *Poor Little Rich Boy: The Life and Times of Col. Robert R. McCormick* (Carpentersville, IL: Crossroads, 1985), p. 430.

9. *George Reedy.

10. Pusey, *Eugene Meyer,* p. 382.

11. *Fred Holborn.

12. Pusey, *Eugene Meyer,* p. 383.

13. Morgan and Veysey, *Poor Little Rich Boy,* p. 430.

14. Ibid.

15. Pusey, *Eugene Meyer,* p. 384.

16. David Halberstam, *The Powers That Be* (New York: Dell, 1980), p. 423.

17. Pusey, *Eugene Meyer,* p. 385.

18. Tom Kelly, *The Imperial Post* (New York: Morrow, 1983), p. 118.

19. Quoted in Pusey, *Eugene Meyer,* p. 342.

20. "The Press—Publishers—A Discontented Man," *Time,* August 19, 1963; "Guest at Breakfast," *Time,* April 16, 1956.

21. *Bernard Nossiter, Hedley Donovan.

22. *Newbold Noyes.

23. Deborah Davis, *Katharine the Great: Katharine Graham and The Washington Post* (Bethesda, MD: National Press, 1987), p. 125.

24. *WPESN,* December 1988.

25. *Bernard Nossiter.

26. *Elizabeth Meyer Lorentz.

27. Jack Roberts, "Graham Caught His Political Bug as a Boy," *Miami News,* November 8, 1978.

28. "Guest at Breakfast."

29. *Morris Siegel.

30. Nancy Beth Jackson, "The Growing Empire of a Farmer's Sons," *Tropic,* March 1, 1970.

31. Pusey, *Eugene Meyer,* p. 338.

32. Michael Moore, "After the Shredding Party: Kay Graham, the CIA, and the Writer Who Wouldn't Go Away," *Regardies,* September 1987.

33. *Robert Estabrook.

34. *Sir Isaiah Berlin.

35. Pusey, *Eugene Meyer,* p. 394.

36. Halberstam, *Powers That Be,* p. 530.

37. *Frank Waldrop.

38. *Philip Elman.

39. *George Smathers.

40. Sally Bedell Smith, *In All His Glory: The Life of William S. Paley: The Legendary Tycoon and His Brilliant Circle* (New York: Simon & Schuster/Touchstone, 1991), p. 333.

41. Halberstam, *Powers That Be,* p. 224.

42. *Jean Friendly.

43. "Guest at Breakfast."

44. *Lester Bernstein.

45. Ibid., *James Cannon.

46. "Guest at Breakfast."

47. *Jean Friendly.

48. William L. Shirer, *The Rise and Fall of the Third Reich* (New York: Fawcett Crest, 1962), pp. 19, 207, 278.

49. *Bernard Nossiter.

50. Ibid.

51. *Libby Rowe.

52. *Jean Friendly.

53. Davis, *Katharine the Great,* p. 195.

54. Chalmers M. Roberts, *In the Shadow of Power: The Story of The Washington Post* (Cabin John, MD: Seven Locks, 1989), p. 369.

55. *Jean Friendly.

56. Ibid., *Morris Siegel.

57. *Morris Siegel, Myra MacPherson.

58. Lynn Rosellini, "The Katharine Graham Story," *WS,* November 13–17, 1978 (five-part series).

59. *Marietta Tree.

60. *Luvie Pearson.

61. Roberts, *In the Shadow,* p. 369.

62. Kelly, *Imperial Post,* p. 129.

63. Roberts, *In the Shadow,* pp. 368–369.

64. Davis, *Katharine the Great,* p. 126.

65. Roberts, *In the Shadow,* p. 369.

66. *Bernard Nossiter.

67. *Erwin Knoll.

68. *Sidney Hyman.

69. Larry van Dyne, "The Bottom Line on Katharine Graham," *Washingtonian,* December 1985.

70. Halberstam, *Powers That Be,* p. 430.

71. *Richard Clurman.

72. *Source wishes to remain anonymous.

73. Van Dyne, "Bottom Line."

74. Rosellini, "Katharine Graham Story."

75. Roberts, *In the Shadow,* p. 369.

76. Felix Frankfurter papers, Harvard Law School Library, Cambridge, MA.

77. *Joanna Steichen.

78. Ibid.

79. Doris Fleeson, "She Came Down from Her Ivory Tower," *St. Louis Post-Dispatch,* June 16, 1946.

80. Porter McKeever, *Adlai Stevenson: His Life and Legacy* (New York: Morrow, 1989), p. 331.

81. *Marietta Tree.

82. *Sidney Hyman; source wishes to remain anonymous.

83. *Marietta Tree.

84. *Karl Meyer.

85. *Robert Estabrook.

86. *George Reedy.

87. *Robert Estabrook.

88. *Erwin Knoll.

89. *Arnaud de Borchgrave.

90. *George Smathers.

91. *Libby Rowe.

92. *George Reedy.

93. William E. Leuchtenburg, "A Visit with LBJ," *American Heritage,* May/June 1990.

94. *Philip Geyelin.

95. *Joseph Rauh.

96. Ibid.

97. Kelly, *Imperial Post,* p. 122.

98. James Reston, *Deadline* (New York: Random House, 1991), p. 342.

99. *Robert Estabrook.

100. *Source wishes to remain anonymous.

101. "Guest at Breakfast."

102. *Robert Estabrook.

103. *Newbold Noyes.

104. *Nathan Halpern.

105. *George Reedy.

106. Roberts, *In the Shadow,* p. 331.

107. *Jean Friendly.

108. Jane Howard, "Katharine Graham: The Power That Didn't Corrupt," *Ms.,* October 1974.

109. *Robert Estabrook.

110. *Erwin Knoll.

111. *Joseph Rauh.

112. *Newbold Noyes.

113. *Frank Dennis.

114. *Source wishes to remain anonymous.

115. *Karl Meyer.

116. *Murrey Marder.

117. *Karl Meyer.

118. *Milton Viorst.

119. *Frank Waldrop.

120. *Frank Dennis; "Guest at Breakfast."

121. *Karl Meyer.

122. Smith, "Post Advertising Executive Gatewood Dies."

123. Halberstam, *Powers That Be,* pp. 425–426.

124. *Erwin Knoll.

125. *Murrey Marder.

126. Ibid.

127. Ibid.

128. *Milton Viorst.

129. *Elizabeth Meyer Lorentz.

130. *Sidney Hyman.

131. *Bernard Nossiter.

132. Pusey, *Eugene Meyer,* p. 395.

133. Ibid., p. 393.

134. Ibid.

135. *Sidney Hyman.

136. *Elizabeth Meyer Lorentz.

137. Davis, *Katharine the Great,* p. 183; *Elizabeth Meyer Lorentz.

138. Davis, *Katharine the Great,* pp. 152–153.

139. *Sidney Hyman.

140. "AFL-CIO Honors Work of Agnes Meyer," *WP,* November 18, 1960.

141. "Mrs. Meyer Honored by University," *WP,* November 6, 1965.

142. *Joanna Steichen.

143. *Karl Meyer.

144. *Sidney Hyman.

145. Davis, *Katharine the Great,* pp. 153–154.

146. *Bernard Nossiter.

147. Nathan Miller, *Spying for America* (New York: Paragon, 1989), p. 244n.

148. *Karl Meyer, Frank Waldrop.

149. *Harvey Segal.

150. Arthur M. Schlesinger, Jr., *A Thousand Days* (Boston: Houghton Mifflin, 1965), p. 119.

Chapter Ten
THE KENNEDY YEARS

1. Robert Hooker, "Bob Graham," *Floridian,* July 2, 1972; Joe Swickard, "Bob Graham Tells of Life as Philip's Kid Brother," *Miami News,* December 6, 1978.

2. *Marietta Tree.

3. *Robert Estabrook.

4. Theodore H. White, *The Making of the President, 1964* (New York: Signet, 1966), p. 483.

5. Doris Kearns Goodwin, *Lyndon Johnson and the American Dream* (New York: Harper & Row, 1976), p. 208.

6. White, *Making of the President, 1964,* p. 485.

7. James Reston, *Deadline* (New York: Random House, 1991), p. 342.

8. *Hedley Donovan.

9. Taylor Branch, *Parting the Waters* (New York: Touchstone, 1989), p. 319.

10. White, *Making of the President, 1964,* p. 490.

11. Arthur M. Schlesinger, Jr., *A Thousand Days* (Boston: Houghton Mifflin, 1965), p. 56.

12. Thomas C. Reeves, *A Question of Character: A Life of John F. Kennedy* (New York: Free Press, 1991), p. 177.

13. *Joseph Rauh.

14. *Robert Nathan.

15. *Joseph Rauh.

16. *Hope Ridings Miller.

17. Reeves, *Question of Character,* p. 179.

18. "Restless Publisher: Philip Leslie Graham," *NYT,* March 10, 1961.

19. *Sidney Hyman.

20. *Bernard Nossiter.

21. Osborn Elliott, *The World of Oz* (New York: Viking, 1980), p. 3.

22. *Morris Siegel.

23. *Ben Gilbert.

24. David Halberstam, *The Powers That Be* (New York: Dell, 1980), p. 512.

25. Howard Bray, *The Pillars of the Post* (New York: Norton, 1980), p. 26.

26. "*Newsweek*'s News," *Time,* March 17, 1961.

27. Elliott, *World of Oz,* pp. 4–7.

28. "*Newsweek*'s News."

29. Elliott, *World of Oz,* p. 6.

30. Bray, *Pillars,* p. 63.

31. *Kermit Lansner.

32. Halberstam, *Powers That Be,* p. 511.

33. Ibid.; Bray, *Pillars,* p. 26; Tom Kelly, *The Imperial Post* (New York: Morrow, 1983), p. 125.

34. Elliott, *World of Oz,* pp. 6–8.

35. Ibid., p. 6.

36. Halberstam, *Powers That Be,* p. 513.

37. Elliott, *World of Oz,* p. 52.

38. Halberstam, *Powers That Be,* p. 526; Benjamin C. Bradlee, *Conversations with Kennedy* (New York: Norton, 1984), p. 187.

39. "Restless Publisher."

40. Elliott, *World of Oz,* pp. 9, 14.

41. *James Cannon.

42. *Thelma McMahon.

43. Ibid.

44. Ibid.

45. *Ben Gilbert.

46. Martin Walker, *Powers of the Press* (New York: Adama, 1982), p. 241.

47. *Kermit Lansner.

48. *Arnaud de Borchgrave.

49. *James Cannon, Arnaud de Borchgrave, Kermit Lansner, Cord Meyer, Jean Friendly, Harvey Segal, Thelma McMahon.

50. *Cord Meyer.

51. *Harvey Segal, Thelma McMahon, Jean Friendly.

52. Elliott, *World of Oz,* p. 10; "Restless Publisher."

53. "Guest at Breakfast," *Time,* April 16, 1956.

54. *Ben Gilbert.

55. *Libby Rowe.

56. *Kermit Lansner.

57. *Roswell Gilpatric.

58. Chalmers M. Roberts, *In the Shadow of Power: The Story of The Washington Post* (Cabin John, MD: Seven Locks, 1989), p. 349.

59. *Pierre Salinger.

60. Ibid.

61. Theodore C. Sorenson, *Kennedy* (New York: Harper & Row Perennial, 1988), pp. 252, 271.

62. Schlesinger, *Thousand Days,* p. 134.

63. Ibid., p. 135.

64. *C. Douglas Dillon.

65. *Philip Elman.

66. Deborah Davis, *Katharine the Great: Katharine Graham and The Washington Post* (Bethesda, MD: National Press, 1987), p. 159.

67. *Ben Gilbert.

68. *Karl Meyer.

69. *Joseph Rauh.

70. Halberstam, *Powers That Be,* p. 524.

71. *Robert Estabrook.

72. Ibid.

73. *Pierre Salinger.

74. Ibid.

75. Rudy Maxa, "The Book on Bradlee," *Washingtonian,* May 1987.

76. Peter J. Boyer, "The Bradlee Mystique," *Vanity Fair,* September 1991.

77. Halberstam, *Powers That Be,* p. 527.

78. Boyer, "Bradlee Mystique."

79. *Pierre Salinger.

80. *Thelma McMahon.

81. Quoted in Tom Kelly, *The Imperial Post* (New York: Morrow, 1983), pp. 212–213.

82. *Karl Meyer.

83. *Kermit Lansner.

84. *James Cannon.

85. David E. Rosenbaum, "An Editor Who Left His Mark in Capital," *NYT,* June 22, 1991.

86. *Nicholas Katzenbach.

87. *James Cannon.

88. *Roswell Gilpatric.

89. *Sidney Hyman.

90. *Harold Taylor.

91. Davis, *Katharine the Great,* p. 121.

92. *Sidney Hyman.

93. *Arthur Schlesinger, Jr.

94. *Luvie Pearson.

95. *Harold Taylor.

96. *Arnaud de Borchgrave.

97. *Joanna Steichen.
98. *Luvie Pearson.

Chapter Eleven
BREAKUP AND BREAKDOWN

1. Ronald Steel, *Walter Lippmann and the American Century* (Boston: Atlantic/Little, Brown, 1980), p. 539; Osborn Elliott, *The World of Oz* (New York: Viking, 1980), pp. 14–15; David Halberstam, *The Powers That Be* (New York: Dell, 1980), p. 515.
2. *James Cannon.
3. Elliott, *World of Oz,* pp. 16–17.
4. *Richard Clurman.
5. *Larry Collins.
6. *Arnaud de Borchgrave.
7. Ibid.
8. Ibid.
9. *Larry Collins.
10. *Arnaud de Borchgrave.
11. *Larry Collins.
12. *James Cannon.
13. *Larry Collins.
14. *Arnaud de Borchgrave.
15. *Kermit Lansner.
16. *Mel Elfin.
17. *Source wishes to remain anonymous.
18. *Arnaud de Borchgrave.
19. *Arthur Schlesinger, Jr.
20. *Jean Friendly.
21. Herbert S. Parmet, *JFK* (New York: Dial, 1983), p. 306; Ron Rosenbaum, "The Mysterious Murder of JFK's Mistress," in *Travels with Dr. Death* (New York: Penguin, 1991), p. 131; "Mary Meyer's Diary," *Washingtonian,* October 1990.
22. *Frank Waldrop.
23. "Mary Meyer's Diary."
24. *Cord Meyer.
25. *James Cannon.
26. *Arthur Schlesinger, Jr.
27. *Theodore Kheel.
28. *Nancy Wechsler.
29. *Larry Collins.
30. *Kermit Lansner.
31. Halberstam, *Powers That Be,* p. 514.
32. *Erwin Knoll.
33. Ibid.
34. *James Cannon.
35. Ibid.
36. *Clark Clifford; Halberstam, *Powers That Be,* p. 528.
37. Ibid., p. 529.
38. *Hedley Donovan.
39. Halberstam, *Powers That Be,* p. 529.
40. Ibid.
41. *Robert Estabrook.
42. *Karl Meyer.
43. *Mel Elfin.
44. Halberstam, *Powers That Be,* p. 531.
45. *Harvey Segal.
46. *Philip Geyelin.
47. *Robert Estabrook.
48. Lynn Rosellini, "The Katharine Graham Story," *WS,* November 13–17, 1978 (five-part series); *Philip Geyelin.
49. "Guest at Breakfast," *Time,* April 16, 1956.
50. *Sir Isaiah Berlin.
51. *Jean Friendly, Joseph Rauh.
52. *Harvey Segal.
53. *Alan Finberg.
54. *Karl Meyer.
55. *Erwin Knoll.
56. *Robert Estabrook.
57. *Jean Friendly.
58. *Arnaud de Borchgrave.
59. *Kermit Lansner.
60. *Jean Friendly.
61. *Arnaud de Borchgrave.
62. *Jean Friendly.
63. *Kermit Lansner.
64. *George Reedy.
65. *Erwin Knoll.
66. *Arnaud de Borchgrave.

67. *June Bingham.
68. *Source wishes to remain anonymous.
69. *Kermit Lansner.
70. Ibid.
71. *Arnaud de Borchgrave.
72. Rosellini, "Katharine Graham Story."
73. Ibid.
74. *Marietta Tree.
75. *June Bingham.
76. Halberstam, *Powers That Be,* pp. 534–535.
77. *Joanna Steichen.
78. Rosellini, "Katharine Graham Story."
79. *Marietta Tree.
80. *Joseph Rauh.
81. Liz Smith, *The Mother Book* (Garden City, NY: Doubleday, 1978), p. 122.
82. *Source wishes to remain anonymous.
83. *Kermit Lansner.
84. *Harvey Segal.
85. *Elizabeth Meyer Lorentz.

Chapter Twelve
PHIL FALLS

1. "Philip L. Graham Dies; Victim of Long Illness Takes Own Life at 48," *WP,* August 4, 1963; *Clark Clifford.
2. *Theodore Kheel; "His Vision Now Reality, a Union Leader Retires," *NYT,* June 15, 1990.
3. *Theodore Kheel.
4. Richard Kluger, *The Paper* (New York: Knopf, 1986), p. 654.
5. *Bertram Powers.
6. *Larry Collins, Kermit Lansner.
7. *Bertram Powers.
8. *Theodore Kheel.
9. *Bertram Powers.
10. Ibid.
11. Kluger, *Paper,* p. 654.
12. *Theodore Kheel.
13. Ibid.
14. Howard Bray, *The Pillars of the Post* (New York: Norton, 1980), p. 226.
15. *Bertram Powers.
16. *Jean Friendly; David Halberstam, *The Powers That Be* (New York: Dell, 1980), p. 529; Chalmers M. Roberts, *In the Shadow of Power: The Story of The Washington Post* (Cabin John, MD: Seven Locks, 1989), p. 362.
17. *Lester Bernstein.
18. *Bertram Powers.
19. *Sir Isaiah Berlin.
20. *Robert Estabrook.
21. *Larry Collins.
22. Ibid.
23. *Arnaud de Borchgrave.
24. *Robert Manning.
25. Roberts, *In the Shadow,* p. 361.
26. Tom Kelly, *The Imperial Post* (New York: Morrow, 1983), p. 125.
27. Osborn Elliott, *The World of Oz* (New York: Viking, 1980), p. 22.
28. *Marietta Tree.
29. *Joseph Rauh.
30. *Newbold Noyes.
31. James Reston, *Deadline* (New York: Random House, 1991), pp. 342–343.
32. Halberstam, *Powers That Be,* pp. 531–532.
33. *Richard Clurman.
34. *Marietta Tree.
35. *Jean Friendly.
36. *Arnaud de Borchgrave.
37. *James Bellows.
38. Halberstam, *Powers That Be,* p. 535.
39. *Arnaud de Borchgrave.
40. *Elizabeth Frank, Jean Friendly.
41. *Newbold Noyes.
42. Deborah Davis, *Katharine the Great: Katharine Graham and The*

Washington Post (Bethesda, MD: National Press, 1987), p. 165.

43. *Jean Friendly.

44. *Arnaud de Borchgrave, Jean Friendly; Davis, *Katharine the Great*, pp. 165–166; Halberstam, *Powers That Be*, p. 535.

45. *Arnaud de Borchgrave.

46. Ibid.

47. *Joanna Steichen.

48. *Source wishes to remain anonymous.

49. *Jean Friendly.

50. Meryl Gordon, "Oh Kay!" *Mirabella*, June 1991.

51. *Larry Collins.

52. Letter to author from Robin Webb.

53. *Luvie Pearson.

54. Elliott, *World of Oz*, p. 23.

55. *Jean Friendly.

56. Ibid.

57. *Joseph Rauh.

58. *Jean Friendly.

59. "Philip L. Graham of Post Kills Self with Shotgun," *WS*, August 4, 1963; "Philip L. Graham Dies; Victim of Long Illness Takes Own Life at 48," *WP*, August 4, 1963; Charles Whited, "Newsman Graham, Ex-Miamian, Kills Self with Shotgun," *MH*, August 4, 1963; "A Discontented Man," *Time*, August 19, 1963.

60. "Philip L. Graham of Post Kills Self."

61. *Joseph Rauh.

62. *Morris Siegel.

63. *Elizabeth Meyer Lorentz.

64. *June Bingham.

65. Sandra G. Boodman, "The Mystery of Chestnut Lodge," *WPM*, October 8, 1989.

66. *Frank Waldrop.

67. *June Bingham.

68. *Richard Clurman.

69. *Jean Friendly.

70. Theodore H. White, *The Making of the President, 1964* (New York: Signet, 1966), p. 482.

Chapter Thirteen
KAY RISES

1. *Jean Friendly.

2. Ibid.

3. *Luvie Pearson; "Philip L. Graham of Post Kills Self with Shotgun," *WS*, August 4, 1963.

4. *Karl Meyer.

5. "Philip L. Graham," *WP*, August 4, 1963.

6. Felix Frankfurter, letter to the editor, *WP*, August 20, 1963.

7. *Harvey Segal.

8. Herbert Block, "Legacy," *WP*, August 6, 1963.

9. "Philip L. Graham, 1915–1963," *Newsweek*, August 12, 1963.

10. "A Discontented Man," *Time*, August 19, 1963.

11. Quoted in Osborn Elliott, *The World of Oz* (New York: Viking, 1980), pp. 26–27.

12. *Harvey Segal.

13. Eulogies quoted in "Philip L. Graham of Post Kills Self"; "Memorial for Graham on Tuesday," *WP*, August 5, 1963.

14. *Joseph Rauh.

15. William F. Buckley, Jr., "The Cause Is Woman," *MH*, August 11, 1963.

16. M. W. Anderson, "Ernest Graham's Seedlings Flourished," *Update*, 9, no. 3 (August 1982); "Ex–State Senator Graham, Pioneer Cattleman, Dies," *MH*, March 16, 1964.

17. *Arnaud de Borchgrave.

18. *George Reedy.

19. *Joseph Rauh.

20. *Karl Meyer.

21. "Philip L. Graham Dies; Victim

of Long Illness Takes Own Life at 48," *WP,* August 4, 1963; "Memorial for Graham."

22. Larry van Dyne, "The Bottom Line on Katharine Graham," *Washingtonian,* December 1985.

23. *Richard Clurman.

24. Elizabeth Pope Frank, "Vassar's Most Powerful Alumna: Katharine Meyer Graham, '38," *Vassar Quarterly,* Spring 1978; Jane Howard, "Katharine Graham: The Power That Didn't Corrupt," *Ms.,* October 1974.

25. "A Discontented Man."

26. *Ben Gilbert.

27. Ibid.

28. *Elizabeth Meyer Lorentz.

29. Howard Bray, *The Pillars of the Post* (New York: Norton, 1980), p. 59.

30. Ibid., p. 198.

31. Chalmers M. Roberts, *In the Shadow of Power: The Story of The Washington Post* (Cabin John, MD: Seven Locks, 1989), p. 363.

32. *Richard Clurman.

33. *James Cannon.

34. Elliott, *World of Oz,* p. 25.

35. Van Dyne, "Bottom Line."

36. Howard, "Katharine Graham."

37. *Jean Friendly.

38. Lynn Rosellini, "The Katharine Graham Story," *WS,* November 13–17, 1978 (five-part series).

39. *Joanna Steichen.

40. *Sir Isaiah Berlin, C. Douglas Dillon, George Ball.

41. *Roswell Gilpatric.

42. *Karl Meyer.

43. *Frank Waldrop, Kermit Lansner.

44. *Philip Geyelin.

45. Katharine Graham, "Learning by Doing," *BAAAS,* 42 (May 1989).

46. Ibid.

47. Rosellini, "Katharine Graham Story."

48. Bray, *Pillars,* p. 59.

49. Rosellini, "Katharine Graham Story."

50. Ibid.

51. Van Dyne, "Bottom Line."

52. *Karl Meyer.

53. *Philip Geyelin.

54. Rosellini, "Katharine Graham Story."

55. *Elizabeth Meyer Lorentz.

56. Rosellini, "Katharine Graham Story."

57. *Alan Finberg.

58. *Frank Waldrop.

59. Rosellini, "Katharine Graham Story"; van Dyne, "Bottom Line."

60. Bray, *Pillars,* p. 59.

61. *Mel Elfin.

62. *James Cannon.

63. *Arnaud de Borchgrave.

64. *Karl Meyer.

65. *Peter Derow.

66. Fred Kaplan, "Facing the Test," *CT,* June 2, 1991 (reprinted from *The Boston Globe*).

67. *Philip Geyelin.

68. *Polly Kraft.

69. Elliott, *World of Oz,* p. 39.

70. *Kermit Lansner.

71. Arthur M. Schlesinger, Jr., *A Thousand Days* (Boston: Houghton Mifflin, 1965), pp. 1025–1026.

72. *Source wishes to remain anonymous.

73. *Arnaud de Borchgrave.

74. Ibid.

75. Letter to author from John Stembler.

76. Charles Whited, "Newsman Graham, Ex-Miamian, Kills Self with Shotgun," *MH,* August 4, 1963.

77. Robert Hooker, "Bob Graham," *Floridian,* July 2, 1972; *George Smathers.

78. *George Smathers.

79. *Ben Gilbert.

80. Deborah Davis, *Katharine the*

Great: Katharine Graham and The Washington Post (Bethesda, MD: National Press, 1987), p. 201.

81. *Ben Gilbert.

82. Bray, *Pillars,* p. 36; Tom Kelly, *The Imperial Post* (New York: Morrow, 1983), p. 131.

83. Kelly, ibid.; Roberts, *In the Shadow,* p. 372.

84. Bray, *Pillars,* pp. 36–37.

85. Deborah Davis, *Katharine the Great,* p. 209; unidentified newspaper article, August 29, 1964.

86. Roberts, *In the Shadow,* p. 372.

87. Davis, *Katharine the Great,* p. 210.

88. David Halberstam, *The Powers That Be* (New York: Dell, 1980), p. 738.

89. Bray, *Pillars,* p. 52.

90. "E-Streeters Hear Katharine Graham," *WPESN,* November 5, 1990.

91. *Frank Waldrop.

92. Pat Munroe and Caryl Rivers, "Kay Graham Talks About Her Job at the Helm of Washington Post," *Editor & Publisher,* May 2, 1964.

93. *Frank Waldrop.

94. *Elsie Carper; "E-Streeters Hear."

95. *Joanna Steichen.

96. *Clark Clifford.

97. Unidentified newspaper article, October 30, 1965; *James Bellows, Mel Elfin.

98. Meryl Gordon, "Oh Kay!" *Mirabella,* June 1991.

99. *Harvey Segal.

100. *James Cannon.

101. *Karl Meyer.

102. Rosellini, "Katharine Graham Story."

103. *Jean Friendly.

104. *Source wishes to remain anonymous.

105. Howard, "Katharine Graham."

106. Rosellini, "Katharine Graham Story."

107. Felix Frankfurter papers, Harvard Law School Library, Cambridge, MA.

108. Davis, *Katharine the Great,* p. 218; *source wishes to remain anonymous.

109. Kelly, *Imperial Post,* p. 132.

110. Halberstam, *Powers That Be,* p. 738.

111. Bray, *Pillars,* p. 35.

112. *Source wishes to remain anonymous.

113. *Harvey Segal.

114. *Karl Meyer.

115. Elliott, *World of Oz,* pp. 91–92.

116. Bray, *Pillars,* p. 35.

117. Halberstam, *Powers That Be,* p. 739.

118. Bray, *Pillars,* p. 35.

119. *Murrey Marder.

120. Elsie Carper, Agnes Meyer obituary, *WP,* September 2, 1970.

121. Ibid.

122. *Ben Gilbert.

123. *Joanna Steichen.

124. Ibid.

125. Halberstam, *Powers That Be,* p. 721.

126. *Mel Elfin.

127. *Karl Meyer.

128. Ibid.

Chapter Fourteen
KAY AND BEN

1. Quoted in James Reston, *Deadline* (New York: Random House, 1991), p. 343.

2. Gay Talese, *The Kingdom and the Power* (New York: Bantam, 1970), pp. 413–415.

3. Reston, *Deadline,* pp. 341–344.

4. Ibid.

5. Talese, *Kingdom,* pp. 413–415.
6. *Robert Manning.
7. *Richard Clurman.
8. *Erwin Knoll.
9. *Bernard Nossiter.
10. Howard Kurtz, "Bradlee Retiring as Editor of the Post," *WP,* June 21, 1991.
11. *Robert Estabrook.
12. *Robert Manning.
13. *Bernard Nossiter.
14. *Ben Gilbert.
15. Peter J. Boyer, "The Bradlee Mystique," *Vanity Fair,* September 1991.
16. *Richard Clurman.
17. *Jean Friendly.
18. Letter to author from Pat Munroe.
19. *Source wishes to remain anonymous.
20. *Jean Friendly.
21. *Robert Estabrook.
22. *Jean Friendly.
23. *Robert Estabrook.
24. Kurtz, "Bradlee Retiring."
25. David Halberstam, *The Powers That Be* (New York: Dell, 1980), p. 756.
26. Boyer, "Bradlee Mystique."
27. Diana West, "Ben and Sally: The Final Days," *M Inc.,* June 1991.
28. *Columbia Journalism Review,* July/August 1991.
29. Kurtz, "Bradlee Retiring."
30. Jane Howard, "Katharine Graham: The Power That Didn't Corrupt," *Ms.,* October 1974.
31. Lynn Rosellini, "The Katharine Graham Story," *WS,* November 13–17, 1978 (five-part series); *Lawrence Kramer.
32. Ibid.
33. *Mel Elfin.
34. *Source wishes to remain anonymous.
35. *Mark Edmiston.

36. J. J. Hunsecker, "Naked City," *Spy,* May 1990.
37. *Lawrence Kramer.
38. *Bernard Nossiter.
39. *Eugene Patterson.
40. *Peter Derow.
41. *Mark Edmiston.
42. *Edward Kosner.
43. *Karl Meyer.
44. Boyer, "Bradlee Mystique."
45. *Ben Gilbert.
46. Halberstam, *Powers That Be,* p. 817.
47. Ibid., p. 748.
48. *William Greider.
49. Boyer, "Bradlee Mystique."
50. *Polly Kraft.
51. *Philip Geyelin.
52. *Richard Clurman.
53. Tom Kelly, *The Imperial Post* (New York: Morrow, 1983), p. 163.
54. Rosellini, "Katharine Graham Story."
55. Chalmers M. Roberts, *In the Shadow of Power: The Story of The Washington Post* (Cabin John, MD: Seven Locks, 1989), p. 383.
56. *Richard Clurman, Polly Kraft.
57. Gerald Clarke, *Capote* (New York: Ballantine, 1988), p. 373.
58. *Richard Clurman, Polly Kraft.
59. Clarke, *Capote,* pp. 376–377.
60. *Karl Meyer.
61. Rosellini, "Katharine Graham Story."
62. *Harvey Segal; Clarke, *Capote,* photo insert caption.
63. *Philip Geyelin; Henry Alford, "Mom Always Liked Him Best," *Spy,* June 1990; Barbara Matusow, "Citizen Don," *Washingtonian,* August 1992.
64. Barbara Matusow, "He's Not Bradlee," *Washingtonian,* July 1988.
65. Howard Bray, *The Pillars of the Post* (New York: Norton, 1980), pp. 40–45.

66. Ibid., p. 54; *Extra,* January/February 1990.
67. Karl E. Meyer, "Newspaper Columnists: Literature by the Inch," *The New York Times Book Review,* March 18, 1990.
68. *Robert Estabrook.
69. *Karl Meyer.
70. *Philip Geyelin.
71. *Frank Waldrop.
72. *Philip Geyelin.
73. Bray, *Pillars,* p. 38.
74. Halberstam, *Powers That Be,* p. 809; Roberts, *In the Shadow,* p. 392.
75. *Philip Geyelin.
76. Ellis Cose, *The Press* (New York: Morrow, 1989), pp. 42–43.
77. *Ben Gilbert.
78. Ibid.
79. Bray, *Pillars,* p. 168; Kelly, *Imperial Post,* p. 135.
80. Boyer, "Bradlee Mystique"; Bray, *Pillars,* p. 168.
81. Kelly, *Imperial Post,* p. 135.
82. Halberstam, *Powers That Be,* p. 756.
83. Rosellini, "Katharine Graham Story."
84. *Roswell Gilpatric.
85. *Clark Clifford, George Reedy.
86. *Frank Waldrop.
87. *William Greider.
88. Bray, *Pillars,* pp. 37–38.
89. Halberstam, *Powers That Be,* p. 808; Kelly, *Imperial Post,* p. 142; Bray, *Pillars,* p. 38; Roberts, *In the Shadow,* p. 392.
90. Halberstam, *Powers That Be,* p. 739.
91. *Extra,* January/February 1990.
92. Deborah Davis, *Katharine the Great: Katharine Graham and The Washington Post* (Bethesda, MD: National Press, 1987), p. 211.
93. *Philip Geyelin.
94. *Eugene Patterson.
95. Ibid.
96. Ibid.
97. *Nicholas von Hoffman.
98. *Ben Gilbert.
99. *Nicholas von Hoffman.
100. *Ben Gilbert.
101. Bray, *Pillars,* p. 166.
102. *Ben Gilbert.
103. *Meet the Press* (NBC), transcript, August 4, 1968.
104. *Mel Elfin.
105. Larry van Dyne, "The Bottom Line on Katharine Graham," *Washingtonian,* December 1985.
106. Quoted in Michael Moore, "After the Shredding Party: Kay Graham, the CIA, and the Writer Who Wouldn't Go Away," *Regardies,* September 1987.
107. *Joanna Steichen.
108. *Harvey Segal.
109. *Joanna Steichen, Jean Friendly.
110. *Paul Ignatius.
111. Ibid.
112. Elsie Carper, Agnes Meyer obituary, *WP,* September 2, 1970.
113. Van Dyne, "Bottom Line."
114. Alford, "Mom Always."
115. Rosellini, "Katharine Graham Story."
116. Matusow, "Citizen Don."
117. *Eugene Patterson.
118. Susan Watters, "The New Mrs. Graham," *W,* May 13–20, 1991.

Chapter Fifteen
THE *POST* GETS "STYLE"

1. Chalmers M. Roberts, *In the Shadow of Power: The Story of The Washington Post* (Cabin John, MD: Seven Locks, 1989), p. 400.
2. *Eugene Patterson.
3. Ibid.
4. Richard Lee, "Style Unzipped," *Washingtonian,* July 1989.
5. Ibid.
6. Ibid.; Tom Kelly, *The Imperial*

Post (New York: Morrow, 1983), pp. 158, 235.

7. Lee, "Style Unzipped."

8. *Eugene Patterson.

9. Rudy Maxa, "The Book on Bradlee," *Washingtonian,* May 1987.

10. Lee, "Style Unzipped."

11. Peter J. Boyer, "The Bradlee Mystique," *Vanity Fair,* September 1991.

12. *Philip Geyelin.

13. *Arnaud de Borchgrave, Jay Lovinger.

14. *Joseph Laitin.

15. *Nicholas von Hoffman.

16. *Harvey Segal.

17. Meryl Gordon, "Oh Kay!" *Mirabella,* June 1991.

18. *Frank Waldrop.

19. *Mel Elfin, source wishes to remain anonymous.

20. *Nicholas von Hoffman.

21. *Harvey Segal.

22. *Kermit Lansner.

23. *Mel Elfin.

24. Ibid.

25. *Thelma McMahon.

26. *Nicholas von Hoffman.

27. *Eugene Patterson, Kermit Lansner.

28. Ron Rosenbaum, "The Mysterious Murder of JFK's Mistress," in *Travels with Dr. Death* (New York: Penguin, 1991), pp. 131–133.

29. David Halberstam, *The Powers That Be* (New York: Dell, 1980), p. 843.

30. *Eugene Patterson.

31. Conversation of May 5, 1971, quoted in *WP,* June 9, 1991.

32. Larry van Dyne, "The Bottom Line on Katharine Graham," *Washingtonian,* December 1985; Mary Anne Dolan, "Kay Graham: Love Affair with Capital," *WS,* March 16, 1975; Sally Quinn, "The Demise of the Washington Hostess," *WPM,* December 31, 1987.

33. *Eugene Patterson.

34. Osborn Elliott, *The World of Oz* (New York: Viking, 1980), p. 157.

35. *Mel Elfin.

36. "Publisher Sees New Repression," unidentified newspaper, May 23, 1970.

37. UPI, November 1972.

38. *William Greider.

39. Dolan, "Kay Graham: Love Affair."

40. Lynn Rosellini, "The Katharine Graham Story," *WS,* November 13–17, 1978 (five-part series).

41. *Eugene Patterson.

42. *Arnaud de Borchgrave.

43. *Kermit Lansner.

44. *Lester Bernstein.

45. Van Dyne, "Bottom Line."

46. *Edward Kosner.

47. *Philip Geyelin.

48. *Ben Gilbert.

49. *Harvey Segal.

50. *Ben Gilbert, Philip Geyelin.

51. *Philip Geyelin.

52. Ibid.

53. *Mel Elfin.

54. *William Greider.

55. Ibid.

56. Boyer, "Bradlee Mystique"; Walter Isaacson, *Kissinger: A Biography* (New York: Simon & Schuster, 1992), p. 583.

57. *Harvey Segal.

58. Letter to author from George Wilson.

59. Howard Kurtz, "Bradlee Retiring as Editor of the Post," *WP,* June 21, 1991.

60. Ibid.; Boyer, "Bradlee Mystique."

61. *Paul Ignatius.

Chapter Sixteen
FREE AT LAST

1. *Mark Meagher.

2. *Polly Kraft.

3. *Philip Geyelin.

4. *Mark Meagher.

5. Ibid.

6. David Halberstam, *The Powers That Be* (New York: Dell, 1980), p. 748.

7. *Ben Gilbert.

8. Ibid.

9. *Source wishes to remain anonymous.

10. *Ben Gilbert.

11. *John Prescott.

12. *Paul Ignatius.

13. *Ben Gilbert.

14. *Kermit Lansner.

15. *Paul Ignatius.

16. Larry van Dyne, "The Bottom Line on Katharine Graham," *Washingtonian,* December 1985.

17. *Paul Ignatius.

18. Van Dyne, "Bottom Line."

19. *Paul Ignatius.

20. *Eugene Patterson, Philip Geyelin.

21. *Eugene Patterson.

22. *Philip Geyelin.

23. *Philip Geyelin, Eugene Patterson.

24. Ibid.

25. Quoted in van Dyne, "Bottom Line."

26. Osborn Elliott, *The World of Oz* (New York: Viking, 1980), p. 144.

27. Ibid., p. 146.

28. Janet Chusmir, "Katharine Graham's Spoiled and You'd Better Believe It," *MH,* March 24, 1970.

29. Elizabeth Drew, "Barbara Bush at Wellesley: A Lesson," *WP,* May 8, 1990.

30. Elliott, *World of Oz,* p. 142.

31. *Kermit Lansner.

32. *Eugene Patterson.

33. *Lucy Prichard.

34. Chusmir, "Katharine Graham's Spoiled."

35. *Mark Edmiston.

36. *Joseph Laitin.

37. *Lester Bernstein.

38. *Mark Edmiston.

39. *Myra MacPherson.

40. Elizabeth Pope Frank, "Vassar's Most Powerful Alumna: Katharine Meyer Graham, '38," *Vassar Quarterly,* Spring 1978; Chalmers M. Roberts, *In the Shadow of Power: The Story of The Washington Post* (Cabin John, MD: Seven Locks, 1989), p. 149.

41. *Mel Elfin, Katharine Graham (for author's *Alice Roosevelt Longworth*); Jane Howard, "Katharine Graham: The Power That Didn't Corrupt," *Ms.,* October 1974.

42. Nancy Beckham, "Right On, Gridiron," *WS,* February 18, 1972; van Dyne, "Bottom Line"; Howard, "Katharine Graham"; "Gridiron Bid Is Rejected by Chisholm," unidentified newspaper, February 20, 1972.

43. *Robert Manning.

44. *Polly Kraft.

45. *Hedley Donovan.

46. Hedrick Smith, *The Power Game* (New York: Ballantine, 1989), pp. 102–103.

47. Joy Billington, "Kudos for Agnes," *WS,* February 26, 1971.

48. *Eugene Patterson.

49. AP, "Mrs. Meyer Denounces Birth-Control Hypocrisy," January 19, 1956.

50. *Roswell Gilpatric.

51. *Mel Elfin.

52. Sarah Booth Conroy, "Life Was a Happy Whirl," *WDN,* September 2, 1970.

53. *Marietta Tree.

54. *Roswell Gilpatric.

55. *Philip Geyelin.

56. *Eugene Patterson.

57. "Agnes E. Meyer, Noted Author, Widow of Post Publisher, Dies," *WP,* September 2, 1970.

58. *Elizabeth Meyer Lorentz.

59. Peter Osnos, "350 Attend

Service for Mrs. Meyer," *WP,*
September 5, 1970.

60. *Eugene Patterson.
61. *Nicholas von Hoffman.
62. *June Bingham.
63. *Roswell Gilpatric.
64. *Eleni Sakes Epstein; van Dyne,
"Bottom Line."
65. Robin Adams Sloan, *WSN,*
August 10, 1973.

Chapter Seventeen
KAY PASSES THE TEST

1. Henry Alford, "Mom Always
Liked Him Best," *Spy,* June 1990.
2. *Alice Arlen (for author's *Alice
Roosevelt Longworth*).
3. *Jean Friendly.
4. Alford, "Mom Always."
5. *Mark Edmiston.
6. *Roswell Gilpatric.
7. *Paul Ignatius.
8. *Mark Meagher.
9. Alford, "Mom Always."
10. Pat Hackett, ed., *The Andy
Warhol Diaries* (New York: Warner,
1989), p. 329.
11. Alford, "Mom Always."
12. Ibid.; Lloyd Grove, "Feud for
Thought: After 8 Years, Mailer and
Vidal Face Off Once Again," *WP,*
November 18, 1985.
13. *Nicholas von Hoffman.
14. *Roswell Gilpatric.
15. *Marietta Tree.
16. *Mark Edmiston.
17. *Edward Kosner.
18. *Marietta Tree.
19. *Polly Kraft.
20. *Source wishes to remain
anonymous.
21. *June Bingham.
22. *Polly Kraft.
23. Larry van Dyne, "The Bottom
Line on Katharine Graham,"
Washingtonian, December 1985.

24. *Mark Meagher.
25. Van Dyne, "Bottom Line."
26. *Roswell Gilpatric.
27. David Halberstam, *The Powers
That Be* (New York: Dell, 1980),
p. 811.
28. *Eugene Patterson.
29. Alex S. Jones, "Cool or
Collegial, Katharine Graham Reflects
on Her Past and Image," *NYT,* July
1, 1987.
30. *Philip Geyelin.
31. *Paul Ignatius.
32. *Eugene Patterson.
33. *Philip Geyelin.
34. Ibid., *Paul Ignatius.
35. Katharine Graham, "Learning
by Doing," *BAAAS,* 42 (May 1989).
36. *Eugene Patterson.
37. Graham, "Learning."
38. *Philip Geyelin.
39. *Eugene Patterson.
40. *Philip Geyelin.
41. *Murrey Marder.
42. Tom Matthews, "The Bradlee
Treatment," *Newsweek,* July 1, 1991.
43. Van Dyne, "Bottom Line."
44. Fred Kaplan, "Facing the
Test," *CT,* June 2, 1991 (reprinted
from *The Boston Globe*).
45. *Frank Waldrop.
46. *Paul Ignatius.
47. *Philip Geyelin.
48. Jones, "Cool or Collegial."
49. *Eugene Patterson.
50. *Philip Geyelin.
51. Ibid.
52. Richard Nixon, *The Memoirs of
Richard Nixon* (New York: Grosset &
Dunlap, 1978), p. 509.
53. Erwin N. Griswold, *Ould Fields,
New Corne* (St. Paul, MN: West,
1992), pp. 300–301.
54. Graham, "Learning."
55. Erwin N. Griswold, "Secrets
Not Worth Keeping," *WP,* February
15, 1989.

56. Howard Bray, *The Pillars of the Post* (New York: Norton, 1980), p. 37.

57. *Source wishes to remain anonymous.

58. *Philip Geyelin, Morton Mintz; Rudy Maxa, "The Book on Bradlee," *Washingtonian,* May 1987; van Dyne, "Bottom Line."

59. *Eugene Patterson.

60. Bray, *Pillars,* p. 79.

61. Ibid., pp. 78–79; *Eugene Patterson.

62. *Morton Mintz.

63. *Eugene Patterson.

64. *Andrew Barnes.

65. *George Reedy.

66. *William Greider.

67. *Joseph Laitin.

68. *William Greider.

69. *Ben Gilbert.

70. Barbara Matusow, "He's Not Bradlee," *Washingtonian,* July 1988.

71. Maxa, "Book on Bradlee."

72. *George Reedy.

73. Howard Kurtz, "Bradlee Retiring as Editor of the Post," *WP,* June 21, 1991.

74. Halberstam, *Powers That Be,* p. 754.

75. Maxa, "Book on Bradlee."

76. Elizabeth Pope Frank, "Vassar's Most Powerful Alumna: Katharine Meyer Graham, '38," *Vassar Quarterly,* Spring 1978.

77. *John Prescott.

78. *Paul Ignatius.

79. *Eugene Patterson.

80. *Frank Waldrop.

81. *Source wishes to remain anonymous.

82. *Paul Ignatius.

83. Ibid.

84. *Mark Meagher.

85. *Paul Ignatius.

86. Ibid.

87. *John Prescott.

88. Ibid.

89. *Paul Ignatius.

90. *John Prescott.

91. Ibid.

92. Matusow, "He's Not Bradlee."

93. Lynn Rosellini, "The Katharine Graham Story," *WS,* November 13–17, 1978 (five-part series); van Dyne, "Bottom Line."

94. *Eugene Patterson.

95. Matusow, "He's Not Bradlee."

96. *John Prescott.

97. Ibid.

98. *Kermit Lansner.

99. Ibid.

100. Ibid.

101. Ibid., *Arnaud de Borchgrave.

102. *Lester Bernstein.

103. *Kermit Lansner.

104. *Lester Bernstein.

105. Ibid.

106. *Kermit Lansner.

107. Van Dyne, "Bottom Line."

108. Alex S. Jones, "Howard Simons, a Former Editor at Washington Post, Is Dead at 60," *NYT,* June 14, 1989.

109. Noel Epstein, "Howard Simons, Ex–Managing Editor of Post and Nieman Curator, Dies," *WP,* June 14, 1989.

110. *Ben Gilbert.

111. Matusow, "He's Not Bradlee."

112. *John Hanrahan.

113. Lawrence Leamer, *Playing for Keeps in Washington* (New York: Dial, 1977), p. 39.

114. Van Dyne, "Bottom Line."

115. Bray, *Pillars,* pp. 132–133.

116. Eleanora W. Schoenebaum, *Profiles of an Era: The Nixon–Ford Years* (New York: Harcourt Brace Jovanovich, 1980), p. 138.

117. Bruce Oudes, ed., *From: The President: Richard Nixon's Secret Files* (New York: Harper & Row, 1989), pp. 557, 429.

118. Bray, *Pillars,* pp. 133–134.

119. Ibid., p. 132.

120. *Barry Sussman; Graham, "Learning."

121. Douglas Bates, *The Pulitzer Prize: The Inside Story of America's Most Prestigious Award* (New York: Birch Lane, 1991), p. 118.

122. *Ben Gilbert.

123. *Source wishes to remain anonymous.

124. Theodore H. White, *Breach of Faith—The Fall of Richard Nixon* (New York: Atheneum, 1975), p. 177.

125. "Post Dedicates New Building," *WSN,* October 17, 1972.

126. *Source wishes to remain anonymous.

127. *Mel Elfin.

128. Rosellini, "Katharine Graham Story."

129. *Philip Geyelin, Karl Meyer.

130. *Pierre Salinger.

131. *Source wishes to remain anonymous.

132. Ibid.

133. *Philip Geyelin.

134. Nancy Collins, *Hard to Get* (New York: Random House, 1990), pp. 140–141.

135. Halberstam, *Powers That Be,* p. 817.

Chapter Eighteen
"THE QUEEN BEE"

1. *Kermit Lansner, Paul Ignatius; Larry van Dyne, "The Bottom Line on Katharine Graham," *Washingtonian,* December 1985.

2. *Peter Derow.

3. *Mark Meagher.

4. John Morton, "Buffett No Longer Bullish on Newspapers," *Washington Journalism Review,* June 1991.

5. L. J. Davis, "Buffett Takes Stock," *NYTM,* April 1, 1990.

6. Van Dyne, "Bottom Line."

7. *Extra,* January/February 1990.

8. *Nicholas Katzenbach.

9. *Peter Derow, Nicholas Katzenbach, Mark Edmiston.

10. Van Dyne, "Bottom Line."

11. *Nicholas Katzenbach.

12. *Morton Mintz.

13. *Peter Derow.

14. Richard Harwood, "From the Top II," *WP,* April 14, 1991.

15. *Polly Kraft.

16. Van Dyne, "Bottom Line."

17. *Nicholas Katzenbach, Peter Derow.

18. *Source wishes to remain anonymous.

19. *Mark Edmiston.

20. Ibid.

21. *Source wishes to remain anonymous.

22. *Peter Derow.

23. Ibid.

24. *Nicholas Katzenbach.

25. *Source wishes to remain anonymous.

26. *Philip Geyelin.

27. *Polly Kraft.

28. *Charles Peters.

29. *Kermit Lansner.

30. *Source wishes to remain anonymous.

31. Jane Howard, "Katharine Graham: The Power That Didn't Corrupt," *Ms.,* October 1974.

32. Howard Bray, *The Pillars of the Post* (New York: Norton, 1980), p. 197.

33. *Peter Derow.

34. Davis, "Buffett Takes Stock."

35. *Forbes,* July 20, 1992.

36. *Richard Clurman.

37. *Polly Kraft.

38. *Source wishes to remain anonymous.

39. *Nicholas von Hoffman.

40. *Mel Elfin.

41. *George Reedy.

42. Deborah Davis, *Katharine the Great: Katharine Graham and The Washington Post* (Bethesda, MD: National Press, 1987), pp. 8–10.

43. Fred Kaplan, "Facing the Test," *CT*, June 2, 1991 (reprinted from *The Boston Globe*).

44. Howard Kurtz, "Bradlee Retiring as Editor of the Post," *WP*, June 21, 1991.

45. *Newbold Noyes.

46. *Paul Ignatius.

47. Curtis Prendergast with Geoffrey Colvin, *The World of Time Inc.* (New York: Atheneum, 1986), p. 512.

48. Ibid., pp. 513–514.

49. Ibid., pp. 514–515; Howard Kurtz, "A Star Is Mourned," *WP*, August 6, 1991.

50. *Mark Meagher.

51. *James Bellows.

52. Bray, *Pillars*, p. 60; *James Bellows.

53. Ibid.

54. Kurtz, "Star Is Mourned."

55. Bray, *Pillars*, pp. 199–200.

56. *John Prescott.

57. Bray, *Pillars*, p. 205.

58. Ibid., p. 203.

59. *John Prescott.

60. Ibid.; Bray, *Pillars*, p. 249.

61. *John Prescott.

62. Bray, *Pillars*, pp. 237–241; *John Hanrahan.

63. *John Prescott.

64. Ibid.

65. Quoted in Bray, *Pillars*, p. 250.

66. *John Prescott.

67. Ibid.

68. Ibid.

69. Ibid.

70. *Roswell Gilpatric.

71. *Lester Bernstein.

72. *Bernard Nossiter.

73. *Nicholas Katzenbach, Eugene Patterson.

74. *Mark Edmiston.

75. *Mark Meagher.

76. Bennett Cerf, *At Random* (New York: Random House, 1977), p. 195.

77. *Mark Meagher.

78. *Richard Snyder.

79. *Mark Meagher.

80. Ibid.; Edwin McDowell, "Is Simon & Schuster Mellowing?" *NYT*, October 29, 1990; Roger Cohen, "Profits—Dick Snyder's Ugly Word," *NYT*, June 30, 1991.

81. *Harvey Segal.

82. *Alan Finberg.

83. *Stephen Birmingham.

84. *Rabbi Edgar Siskin; letter to Katharine Graham from Siskin, May 1, 1981; letter to Siskin from Graham, May 15, 1981.

85. *Jean Friendly, Philip Geyelin, Joanna Steichen, Alan Finberg, Elizabeth Frank, June Bingham, Peter Derow, Elizabeth Meyer Lorentz.

86. *Joanna Steichen.

87. *Luvie Pearson.

88. *Philip Geyelin.

89. *Joanna Steichen, Jean Friendly.

90. *June Bingham.

91. *Philip Geyelin.

92. *Source wishes to remain anonymous.

93. *Paul Ignatius; source wishes to remain anonymous.

94. *Source wishes to remain anonymous.

95. *Ben Gilbert.

96. *Karl Meyer.

97. *Nicholas Katzenbach, Karl Meyer, Joseph Rauh.

98. *Sir Isaiah Berlin.

Chapter Nineteen
A PULITZER PRIZE
IN MANAGEMENT?

1. Osborn Elliott, *The World of Oz* (New York: Viking, 1980), pp. 215–217.

2. *Edward Kosner.

3. Elliott, *World of Oz,* pp. 216–217.

4. *Lester Bernstein.

5. Elliott, *World of Oz,* pp. 215–217.

6. *Mark Edmiston.

7. *Richard Clurman.

8. *Peter Derow.

9. Elliott, *World of Oz,* p. 240.

10. *WS,* January 5, 1976.

11. Larry van Dyne, "The Bottom Line on Katharine Graham," *Washingtonian,* December 1985.

12. *Mark Meagher.

13. *John Hanrahan.

14. Michael Satchell, "About That Other Paper," *WSN,* April 13, 1974.

15. Jane Howard, "Katharine Graham: The Power That Didn't Corrupt," *Ms.,* October 1974.

16. Satchell, "About That Other Paper."

17. Howard, "Katharine Graham."

18. Ibid.

19. *George Reedy.

20. *Bernard Nossiter.

21. *Alan Finberg; unidentified newspaper article.

22. *Theodore Kheel.

23. *Bernard Nossiter.

24. *Morton Mintz.

25. *William Greider.

26. *Mark Meagher.

27. Ibid.; Katharine Graham, "Learning by Doing," *BAAAS,* 42 (May 1989).

28. *John Hanrahan.

29. Ibid.

30. Ibid.

31. *John Prescott.

32. *Mark Meagher.

33. Howard Kurtz, "Bradlee Retiring as Editor of the Post," *WP,* June 21, 1991.

34. *James Bellows.

35. Howard Bray, *The Pillars of the Post* (New York: Norton, 1980), pp. 265–266.

36. *James Bellows.

37. Bray, *Pillars,* p. 266.

38. *James Bellows.

39. Van Dyne, "Bottom Line."

40. Bray, *Pillars,* p. 270.

41. *Alan Finberg.

42. "Pressmen March on Graham's Home," unidentified newspaper, March 17, 1976.

43. *Mark Meagher.

44. Ibid.

45. Curtis Prendergast with Geoffrey Colvin, *The World of Time Inc.* (New York: Atheneum, 1986), p. 515.

46. *Mark Meagher.

47. Van Dyne, "Bottom Line."

48. Graham, "Learning."

49. *John Hanrahan.

50. Prendergast with Colvin, *World of Time,* p. 515.

51. *Mark Meagher.

52. Ibid.

53. *Joseph Rauh; Bray, *Pillars,* p. 278.

54. *Mark Meagher.

55. *Kermit Lansner.

56. *Mark Meagher.

57. *Morton Mintz.

58. Ibid.

59. *Bernard Nossiter.

60. Ibid.; *Erwin Knoll.

61. *Bernard Nossiter.

62. *John Hanrahan.

63. Graham, "Learning"; John Hanrahan.

64. Graham, "Learning."

65. Tom Kelly, *The Imperial Post* (New York: Morrow, 1983), pp. 206–207.

66. *Theodore Kheel.

67. Van Dyne, "Bottom Line"; *Mark Meagher.

68. Deborah Davis, *Katharine the Great: Katharine Graham and The*

Washington Post (Bethesda, MD: National Press, 1987), p. 10.

69. Richard Lee, "Style Unzipped," *Washingtonian,* July 1989.

70. Noel Epstein, "Howard Simons, Ex–Managing Editor of Post and Nieman Curator, Dies," *WP,* June 14, 1989.

71. David E. Rosenbaum, "An Editor Who Left His Mark in Capital," *NYT,* June 22, 1991.

72. *CT,* June 28, 1989.

73. *Roswell Gilpatric.

74. *Mark Edmiston.

75. *Theodore Kheel.

76. Jerome Tuccille, *Rupert Murdoch* (New York: Fine, 1989), p. 59.

77. *Theodore Kheel.

78. Quoted in Tuccille, *Rupert Murdoch,* p. 59.

79. *Edward Kosner.

80. Van Dyne, "Bottom Line."

81. *Mel Elfin, Lester Bernstein, Mark Edmiston, Robert Manning.

82. John Holusha, "Bidding War Between Graham, Murdoch?" *WS,* December 31, 1976.

83. Van Dyne, "Bottom Line."

84. William H. Taft, *Encyclopedia of Twentieth-Century Journalists* (New York: Garland, 1986), p. 112.

85. *Theodore Kheel; Holusha, "Bidding War."

86. *Theodore Kheel.

87. Holusha, "Bidding War."

88. Ibid.

89. Quoted in Bray, *Pillars,* p. 218.

90. Quoted in Tuccille, *Rupert Murdoch,* p. 61.

91. *Peter Derow.

92. *Mel Elfin.

93. *Edward Kosner.

94. *Polly Kraft.

95. *Mark Meagher; Bray, *Pillars,* p. 205.

96. *Mark Meagher.

97. *Peter Derow.

98. Quoted in Bray, *Pillars,* pp. 219, 285.

99. *Paul Ignatius.

100. *Morton Mintz.

101. Ibid.

102. Chalmers M. Roberts, *In the Shadow of Power: The Story of The Washington Post* (Cabin John, MD: Seven Locks, 1989), p. 490.

103. *Philip Geyelin.

104. Ibid.

105. Bray, *Pillars,* p. 206.

106. Ibid., pp. 205–206.

107. *James Bellows.

108. *Hedley Donovan.

109. Prendergast with Colvin, *World of Time,* p. 517.

110. Ibid., pp. 520, 524.

111. Michael Kilian and Arnold Sawislak, *Who Runs Washington?* (New York: St. Martin's, 1982), p. 206.

112. Rudy Maxa, "The Book on Bradlee," *Washingtonian,* May 1987; Diana West, "Ben and Sally: The Final Days," *M Inc.,* June 1991.

113. *Ben Gilbert.

114. *Philip Geyelin.

115. Scott Shuger, "Post Paternalism or Black Blackmail?" *The Washington Monthly,* February 1990.

116. "Who Speaks for Washington?" and Barbara Matusow, "Marion Barry Under Fire," *Washingtonian,* April 1989.

117. *Philip Geyelin.

118. Ibid.

119. *Source wishes to remain anonymous.

120. *Philip Geyelin.

121. Ibid.

122. *Edward Kosner.

123. *Peter Derow.

124. *Edward Kosner.

125. Ibid.

126. *Lester Bernstein.

127. *John Walsh, Thelma McMahon.

128. "Newsweek Editor Fired; Ex-Staffer Named to Job," unidentified newspaper, June 26, 1979.

129. *Lester Bernstein.

130. "Newsweek Editor Fired."

131. *Source wishes to remain anonymous.

132. Ibid.

133. Richard G. Zimmerman, "Allbritton Kills Series on Graham," *Washington Journalism Review,* September/October 1978.

134. *Lynn Rosellini.

135. *Source wishes to remain anonymous.

136. *Lynn Rosellini.

137. Zimmerman, "Allbritton Kills Series."

138. *James Bellows.

139. *Lynn Rosellini.

140. William Safire, "Here's to Media Wars," *NYT,* November 27, 1978.

141. Charles B. Seib, "A Bid for Washington's Attention," *WP,* November 24, 1978.

142. *James Bellows.

143. *Peter Derow.

144. *Richard Clurman.

145. Lynn Rosellini, "The Katharine Graham Story," *WS,* November 13–17, 1978 (five-part series).

146. *Lynn Rosellini.

147. *Source wishes to remain anonymous.

148. *Lynn Rosellini; Zimmerman, "Allbritton Kills Series."

149. *Lynn Rosellini.

150. Ibid., *Richard Snyder.

Chapter Twenty
ALL THE PUBLISHER'S PROBLEMS

1. *Bernard Nossiter.

2. Michael Moore, "After the Shredding Party: Kay Graham, the CIA, and the Writer Who Wouldn't Go Away," *Regardies,* September 1987.

3. Betty Beale, "Book on Katharine Graham Is at Last in the Works," *WS,* May 16, 1976.

4. Moore, "After the Shredding Party."

5. Ibid.

6. *Katharine Graham (for author's *Alice Roosevelt Longworth*).

7. Moore, "After the Shredding Party."

8. Ibid.

9. *Katharine Graham (for author's *Alice Roosevelt Longworth*).

10. Moore, "After the Shredding Party."

11. Deborah Davis, *Katharine the Great: Katharine Graham and The Washington Post* (Bethesda, MD: National Press, 1987), p. x; Davis, *Katharine the Great,* 3rd ed. (New York: Sheridan Square Press, 1991), pp. xix–xx; Moore, "After the Shredding Party."

12. *Katharine Graham (for author's *Alice Roosevelt Longworth*).

13. Ibid.

14. Moore, "After the Shredding Party."

15. Ibid.

16. Davis, *Katharine the Great* (1987), p. xi.

17. Davis, *Katharine the Great* (1991), p. xii.

18. Davis, *Katharine the Great* (1987), p. xii.

19. Ibid., pp. 230, 278.

20. *Pierre Salinger, Arnaud de Borchgrave, Cord Meyer, Philip Geyelin, Bernard Nossiter.

21. *Philip Geyelin.

22. *Frank Waldrop.

23. Davis, *Katharine the Great* (1987), p. viii.

24. *Robert Estabrook.

25. *Ben Gilbert.

26. Quoted in Moore, "After the Shredding Party"; Davis, *Katharine the Great* (1987), p. ix.

27. *Bernard Nossiter.

28. *Erwin Knoll.

29. *John Hanrahan.

30. Howard Bray, *The Pillars of the Post* (New York: Norton, 1980), p. 87.

31. *Eugene Patterson.

32. Richard Lee, "Style Unzipped," *Washingtonian,* July 1989; Diana West, "Ben and Sally: The Final Days," *M Inc.,* June 1991.

33. Michael Kilian and Arnold Sawislak, *Who Runs Washington?* (New York: St. Martin's, 1982), p. 177.

34. *James Cannon.

35. *Mark Edmiston.

36. William H. Jones, "Donald Graham Takes Post Stewardship," *WP,* January 11, 1979.

37. Ibid.

38. *Frank Waldrop.

39. Jones, "Donald Graham Takes Post Stewardship."

40. *Mark Meagher.

41. *Peter Derow, Mark Edmiston.

42. *Nicholas Katzenbach.

43. *Mark Meagher.

44. *Source wishes to remain anonymous; Jay Lovinger.

45. *Nicholas von Hoffman.

46. *Source wishes to remain anonymous.

47. *Nicholas von Hoffman.

48. *Milton Viorst.

49. *Nicholas von Hoffman.

50. Susan Watters, "The New Mrs. Graham," *W,* May 13–20, 1991.

51. *Joseph Laitin.

52. *Mark Edmiston.

53. *Vogue,* June 1970.

54. *Edward Kosner.

55. *Nicholas von Hoffman.

56. Henry Alford, "Mom Always Liked Him Best," *Spy,* June 1990.

57. Ibid.

58. *Source wishes to remain anonymous.

59. Pat Hackett, ed., *The Andy Warhol Diaries* (New York: Warner, 1989), p. 44.

60. *Roswell Gilpatric.

61. *Nicholas Katzenbach.

62. *Polly Kraft.

63. *Source wishes to remain anonymous.

64. *Arnaud de Borchgrave.

65. *Source wishes to remain anonymous.

66. *Kermit Lansner.

67. *Peter Derow.

68. *Larry Collins.

69. *Mel Elfin.

70. *Source wishes to remain anonymous.

71. Barbara Matusow, "Citizen Don," *Washingtonian,* August 1992.

72. *Mark Meagher.

73. *Source wishes to remain anonymous.

74. *Source wishes to remain anonymous.

75. Hackett, *Warhol Diaries,* pp. 112, 123.

76. *June Bingham.

77. *Mel Elfin.

78. *Lester Bernstein.

79. *Arnaud de Borchgrave.

80. Ibid.

81. *Lester Bernstein.

82. *Arnaud de Borchgrave.

83. *Larry Collins.

84. *Lester Bernstein.

85. *Arnaud de Borchgrave.

86. Meryl Gordon, "Oh Kay!" *Mirabella,* June 1991.

Chapter Twenty-one
KAY GRAHAM GETS "FIRED"

1. *Mark Meagher.

2. *Kermit Lansner.

3. *Source wishes to remain anonymous.

4. *Mark Meagher, Kermit Lansner, Peter Derow, Mark Edmiston.

5. *Mark Meagher.

6. Rudolph A. Pyatt, Jr., "Katharine Graham: Is Her Pay Too High?" *WS*, May 10, 1979.

7. *Mark Meagher.

8. *Lester Bernstein.

9. *Source wishes to remain anonymous.

10. *Kermit Lansner.

11. *Source wishes to remain anonymous.

12. *Nicholas Katzenbach.

13. *Source wishes to remain anonymous.

14. *Mark Edmiston.

15. *Mark Meagher.

16. *Peter Derow.

17. *Mark Edmiston.

18. *Lawrence Kramer.

19. *Mark Edmiston.

20. *Lester Bernstein.

21. *Peter Derow.

22. *Lester Bernstein.

23. *Mark Edmiston.

24. *Peter Derow.

25. Ibid.

26. *Mark Edmiston.

27. *Peter Derow.

28. Ibid.

29. Ibid.

30. *Mark Edmiston.

31. *Peter Derow.

32. *Source wishes to remain anonymous.

33. Ibid.

34. *Mark Edmiston.

35. Ibid.

36. *Morton Mintz.

37. *Mark Edmiston.

38. Larry van Dyne, "The Bottom Line on Katharine Graham," *Washingtonian*, December 1985.

39. Ellis Cose, *The Press* (New York: Morrow, 1989), p. 87.

40. *Lawrence Kramer.

41. Pat Munroe and Caryl Rivers, "Kay Graham Talks About Her Job at the Helm of Washington Post," *Editor & Publisher*, May 2, 1964.

42. *John Walsh, Jay Lovinger.

43. Ibid.

44. *Peter Derow.

45. *Mark Edmiston.

46. *John Walsh.

47. John Sansing, ed., "Capital Comment," *Washingtonian*, December 1988.

48. *John Walsh.

49. Curtis Prendergast with Geoffrey Colvin, *The World of Time Inc.* (New York: Atheneum, 1986), p. 258; *WP*, October 1989.

50. *Hedley Donovan, Mark Meagher.

51. *Sidney Epstein.

52. *Hedley Donovan; Prendergast with Colvin, *World of Time,* p. 532; Peter Benjaminson, *Death in the Afternoon* (Kansas City, MO: Andrews, McMeel & Parker, 1984), p. 119.

53. Benjaminson, *Death,* pp. 120–121.

54. *Hedley Donovan; Prendergast with Colvin, *World of Time,* p. 532; Benjaminson, *Death,* pp. 121–122.

55. Benjaminson, *Death,* p. 122.

56. Van Dyne, "Bottom Line."

57. Douglas Bates, *The Pulitzer Prize: The Inside Story of America's Most Prestigious Award* (New York: Birch Lane, 1991), p. 6.

58. *Eugene Patterson.

59. Ibid.

60. *Joseph Laitin.

61. *Eugene Patterson.

62. *Joseph Laitin.

63. *Mark Edmiston; Rudy Maxa, "The Book on Bradlee," *Washingtonian*, May 1987.

64. UPI, "Katharine Graham Warns Publishers Not to Panic," *WS,* May 4, 1981.

65. Pyatt, "Katharine Graham: Is Her Pay?"

66. *Lester Bernstein.

67. *Peter Derow.

68. *Lester Bernstein.

69. *Peter Derow.

70. *Lester Bernstein.

71. *Peter Derow.

72. *Mark Edmiston.

73. *Mel Elfin.

74. *Lester Bernstein.

75. *Mark Edmiston.

76. *Mel Elfin.

77. William H. Taft, "William Broyles," *Encyclopedia of Twentieth-Century Journalists* (New York: Garland, 1986); *Lester Bernstein.

78. *Edward Kosner, Kermit Lansner.

79. *Kermit Lansner.

80. *Thelma McMahon.

81. *Mark Edmiston.

82. *Edward Kosner.

83. *Lester Bernstein.

84. *Edward Kosner.

85. *Richard Clurman.

86. *Lester Bernstein.

87. *Source wishes to remain anonymous.

88. *Hedley Donovan.

89. *Thelma McMahon.

90. *Arnaud de Borchgrave.

91. *Mark Edmiston.

92. *Mel Elfin.

93. *Mark Edmiston.

94. *Jean Friendly.

Chapter Twenty-two
THE HITLER HOAX AND OTHER PROBLEMS

1. *Mark Edmiston.

2. Ibid.

3. Ibid.

4. Ibid.

5. *Thelma McMahon; "Hitler's Secret Diaries: Are They Genuine? How They Could Rewrite History," *Newsweek,* May 2, 1983; Charles Hamilton, *The Hitler Diaries* (Lexington: University Press of Kentucky, 1991), pp. 180–181.

6. *Lester Bernstein.

7. *Mel Elfin.

8. *Lester Bernstein.

9. *Mark Edmiston.

10. *Thelma McMahon.

11. *Mark Edmiston.

12. Ibid.

13. *Mel Elfin.

14. *Richard Clurman.

15. *Lester Bernstein.

16. *Mark Edmiston, Mel Elfin.

17. *Thelma McMahon.

18. *Mark Edmiston.

19. *Kermit Lansner.

20. *Mark Edmiston, Edward Kosner.

21. Edwin Diamond, "Next, 'U.S. Timeweek,' " *New York,* December 5, 1988.

22. *Source wishes to remain anonymous.

23. *Mel Elfin.

24. *Mark Meagher.

25. *Barry Sussman.

26. *Morton Mintz.

27. Barbara Matusow, "He's Not Bradlee," *Washingtonian,* July 1988.

28. *Mel Elfin.

29. *Thelma McMahon.

30. *William Greider.

31. *Lester Bernstein.

32. Ibid.

33. *Mel Elfin.

34. *Thelma McMahon.

35. Ibid.

36. Richard Lee, "The *Time–Newsweek* War," *Washingtonian,* July 1985.

37. *Source wishes to remain anonymous.

38. *Thelma McMahon.

39. Ibid.

40. *Mel Elfin.

41. Nancy Reagan with William Novak, *My Turn* (New York: Random House, 1989), pp. 34, 36.

42. Ibid., pp. 281–284; Larry van Dyne, "The Bottom Line on Katharine Graham," *Washingtonian,* December 1985.

43. Reagan with Novak, *My Turn,* p. 320.

44. Ibid., p. 325.

45. R. W. Apple, Jr., "Nancy Reagan's Revenge Is to Tell Her Versions of the Stories," *NYT,* November 1, 1989.

46. Nancy Collins, *Hard to Get* (New York: Random House, 1990), pp. 145–146.

47. *Joseph Laitin.

48. Howard Kurtz, "Media Notes," *WP,* September 7, 1991.

49. Robert Sherrill, "Bob & Al's Bogus Journey," *The Nation,* October 7, 1991.

50. *Extra,* January/February 1990.

51. Drew Lindsay, "Reporter," *Washingtonian,* December 1990.

52. *Marietta Tree.

53. *Eugene Patterson.

54. Stephen E. Ambrose, *Nixon: Ruin and Recovery 1973–1990* (New York: Simon & Schuster, 1991), pp. 560–561.

55. Ibid.

56. *Joseph Rauh.

57. *Morton Mintz; Edmund L. Andrews, " 'Baby Bells,' Newspapers in a Brawl," *NYT,* November 11, 1991.

58. *Morton Mintz.

59. *Joseph Rauh.

60. Ibid.; "Joseph L. Rauh, Jr.," *WP,* September 5, 1992.

61. *Robert Nathan.

62. *Joseph Laitin, Barry Sussman.

63. *Morton Mintz, Bernard Nossiter, Joseph Laitin.

64. *Spy,* September 1989; Henry Alford, "Mom Always Liked Him Best," *Spy,* June 1990.

65. *Marietta Tree.

66. Quoted in Alford, "Mom Always."

67. Jim Spencer, "Liberal Doses of the Right Stuff," *CT,* December 10, 1984.

68. *Edward Kosner.

69. *Joseph Laitin.

70. *Kermit Lansner.

71. Wes Pruden, "Inside the Beltway," *Washington Times,* November 18, 1986.

72. Ibid.

73. *Arnaud de Borchgrave.

74. Pruden, "Inside the Beltway."

75. Ibid.

76. Ibid.

77. *Arnaud de Borchgrave.

78. Pruden, "Inside the Beltway."

79. *Edward Kosner.

80. *Arnaud de Borchgrave.

81. *Nicholas von Hoffman.

82. *Joseph Laitin.

83. *Stephen Birmingham.

84. *Mark Edmiston.

Chapter Twenty-three
HANGING ON, TO HER POWER AND INSECURITIES

1. *Marietta Tree.

2. *Peter Derow.

3. *Nicholas Katzenbach.

4. *Mark Edmiston.

5. *Nicholas Katzenbach.

6. *Lawrence Kramer.

7. "The Most Influential Women," *WP,* December 11, 1985.

8. *NYTM,* April 1, 1990.

9. *Kermit Lansner.

10. *Marietta Tree.

11. *Arnaud de Borchgrave.

12. Bob Colacello, "In Memoriam," *Vanity Fair,* May 1990.

13. Victoria Dawson and Mike McIntyre, "Feting a 70th Edition," *WP,* July 1, 1987.

14. Maureen Dowd, "Birthday Party for Washington Post Chief Attracts 'All the Big Names,' " *NYT,* July 1, 1987.

15. Dawson and McIntyre, "Feting a 70th."

16. Ibid.

17. *Joseph Laitin.

18. Dowd, "Birthday Party."

19. *Thelma McMahon.

20. *Mel Elfin.

21. *Lester Bernstein.

22. *Andrew Barnes.

23. *Mel Elfin.

24. *Richard Clurman.

25. *Source wishes to remain anonymous.

26. *Source wishes to remain anonymous.

27. *Source wishes to remain anonymous.

28. *Murrey Marder.

29. *Source wishes to remain anonymous.

30. *Karl Meyer.

31. *Source wishes to remain anonymous.

32. Ibid.

33. *Mel Elfin.

34. *Thelma McMahon.

35. *Mark Edmiston.

36. *Source wishes to remain anonymous.

37. *Robert Estabrook.

38. *Mark Edmiston.

39. *Kermit Lansner.

40. *Murrey Marder.

41. Ibid.

42. *Mark Edmiston.

43. *Eugene Patterson.

44. Ibid.

45. *Jean Friendly.

46. *Lester Bernstein.

47. *Morton Mintz.

48. *Eugene Patterson.

49. *Lucy Prichard.

50. *Polly Kraft.

51. *Richard Clurman.

52. *Source wishes to remain anonymous.

53. *Joseph Laitin.

54. *Mark Edmiston.

55. Ibid.

Chapter Twenty-four
LETTING GO

1. Jacqueline Trescott, "Knopf Signs Katharine Graham," *WP,* October 16, 1989.

2. *Charles Peters.

3. *Lester Bernstein.

4. *Mark Meagher.

5. Ibid.

6. *Source wishes to remain anonymous.

7. *June Bingham, Jay Lovinger.

8. *Mark Edmiston.

9. *Joseph Laitin.

10. Howard Kurtz, "Bradlee Retiring as Editor of the Post," *WP,* June 21, 1991.

11. Barbara Matusow, "He's Not Bradlee," *Washingtonian,* July 1988.

12. *Steve Mendelson, Joseph Laitin.

13. *Joseph Laitin, Frank Waldrop.

14. *John Hanrahan.

15. *Kermit Lansner.

16. Ibid.

17. *Andrew Barnes.

18. *Kermit Lansner.

19. *Nicholas von Hoffman.

20. David A. Vise, "Post Executive Sees Industry Challenges Ahead," *WP,* May 10, 1991.

21. Alex A. Jones, "Donald

Graham to Succeed Mother at Washington Post," *NYT,* March 15, 1991.

22. Frank Swoboda and Howard Kurtz, "Donald Graham Is Named Post Co. President, CEO," *WP,* March 15, 1991.

23. *Mark Edmiston.

24. Meryl Gordon, "Oh Kay!" *Mirabella,* June 1991.

25. Swoboda and Kurtz, "Donald Graham Is Named."

26. *Steve Mendelson.

27. *Washingtonian,* April 1991.

28. *Harvey Segal.

29. *Joseph Laitin.

30. *William Greider.

31. *Steve Mendelson, Jay Lovinger.

32. Martin Walker, *Powers of the Press* (New York: Adama, 1982), pp. 241–261; Howard Bray, *The Pillars of the Post* (New York: Norton, 1980), p. 2.

33. *Elizabeth Frank.

34. *George Reedy.

35. Larry van Dyne, "The Bottom Line on Katharine Graham," *Washingtonian,* December 1985.

36. *William Greider.

37. *Frank Waldrop.

38. *James Reston (telephone).

39. *Bernard Nossiter.

40. *Kermit Lansner.

41. *Frank Waldrop.

42. William H. Jones, "Donald Graham Takes Post Stewardship," *WP,* January 11, 1979.

43. Susan Watters, "The New Mrs. Graham," *W,* May 13–20, 1991.

44. "Post Co.'s Earnings Off 59% in Year," *WP,* February 5, 1992.

45. Ibid.

46. Robert J. Samuelson, "The Time Inc. Fight Is Not About Journalism," *WP,* June 28, 1989; *Mark Edmiston.

47. Edwin Diamond, "Next, 'U.S. Timeweek,' " *New York,* January 13, 1989.

48. *Alan Finberg.

49. *Mark Edmiston.

50. Ibid.

51. *Source wishes to remain anonymous.

52. *Mark Edmiston.

53. *Elizabeth Meyer Lorentz.

54. *Joanna Steichen.

55. *Polly Kraft.

56. Ibid.

57. *Source wishes to remain anonymous.

58. Joan Braden, *Just Enough Rope* (New York: Villard, 1989), p. 235.

59. Van Dyne, "Bottom Line."

60. L. J. Davis, "Buffett Takes Stock," *NYTM,* April 1, 1990; Ron Suskind, "Legend Revisited: Warren Buffett Aura as Folksy . . . Masks Tough Polished Man," *WSJ,* November 8, 1991.

61. Davis, "Buffett Takes Stock."

62. *Charles Peters.

63. Suskind, "Legend"; "Post Co.'s Earnings."

64. *Nicholas Katzenbach.

65. Elizabeth Pope Frank, "Vassar's Most Powerful Alumna: Katharine Meyer Graham, '38," *Vassar Quarterly,* Spring 1978.

66. "E-Streeters Hear Katharine Graham," *WPESN,* November 5, 1990.

67. "DC–NY: Who's More Honest? Smarter?" *Washingtonian,* July 1989.

INDEX